SAME TIME . . .
SAME STATION

SAME TIME . . . SAME STATION

An A–Z Guide to Radio
from Jack Benny to Howard Stern

Ron Lackmann

Facts On File, Inc.

AN INFOBASE HOLDINGS COMPANY

Same Time . . . Same Station: An A–Z Guide to Radio from Jack Benny to Howard Stern

Facts On File, Inc.
11 Penn Plaza
New York, NY 10001

Library of Congress Cataloging-in-Publication Data

Lackmann, Ronald W.
Same time, same station: an a–z guide to radio from Jack Benny to Howard Stern / Ron Lackmann.
p. cm.
Includes bibliographical references and index.
ISBN 0-8160-2862-1 (alk. paper)
1. Radio programs—United States—Encyclopedias.   2. Radio
programs—Canada—Encyclopedias.   3. Radio broadcasters—United
States—Encyclopedias.   4. Radio broadcasters—Canada—
Encyclopedias.   I. Title.
PN1991.3.U6L32   1996
791.44′75′0973—dc20   96-5662

Facts On File books are available at special discounts when purchased in
bulk quantities for businesses, associations, institutions, or sales
promotions. Please call our Special Sales Department in New York at
212/967-8800 or 800/322-8755.

Jacket design by Steve Brower

This book is printed on acid-free paper.

Printed in the United States of America

VB VC 10 9 8 7 6 5 4 3 2 1

*For my dear friends
James C. English,
Barbara Gelman,
and Sandra Brett
who care.*

Contents

Foreword

Let's hear it for the encyclopedists, compilers, etymologists, bibliographers, lexicographers, fact-finders, and almanackers of the world. They were and are, every last one, hunters, anglers, spelunkers, sifters, and miners who obviously loved what they were doing or they wouldn't have taken the pains. Starchy Noah Webster, frowning Samuel Johnson, acerbic Henry Mencken, and gentlemanly Eric Partridge all had a passion for words, and it shows in their dictionaries. Wits and poets, essayists and novelists, artists and scientists have also worn the insignia, among them Irving Wallace (*People's Almanac*), John Ciardi (*A Browser's Dictionary*), Norris and McWhirter (*Illustrated Encyclopedia of Facts*), Retsner and Wechsler (*Encyclopedia of Graffiti*), Maurice B. Strauss (*Familiar Medical Questions*), and also Bergen Evans, Michael Jackman, Frank Magill, Harry Haun, Paul Dickson, Joseph T. Shipley, Edmund F. Penney, Lillian Feinsilver, and so on—and now Ron Lackmann, with his *Same Time . . . Same Station: An A–Z Guide to Radio from Jack Benny to Howard Stern.*

Mr. Lackmann enters a field, radio, that was previously plowed by historians in several books—including John Dunning's *Tune In Yesterday,* a landmark work (now out of print)—but he has broadened his time span from the 1920s to the present and, at the same time, has narrowed his range to cover North American *network* radio, thus eliminating independent and foreign programs. Even though he wisely irised down from the whole globe to the northern half of the Western Hemisphere, his encyclopedia still contains an impressive number of pages.

As an old frequenter, consumer, and beneficiary of reference libraries, I can testify that there can never be too many volumes for an elusive quarry. So I cordially welcome Mr. Lackmann to the stacks and hope there will be a large *ad hoc* committee of well-wishers to greet his research and to make use of it.

—Norman Corwin

Introduction

My fascination with radio began when I was eight years old: I fell in love with a voice I heard over the airwaves, a most wonderful and unusual voice. The actress to whom it belonged had what seemed a very exotic-sounding name: "Masaydees Macaimbridge!" Because I had only heard the name, I didn't know it was actually spelled M-E-R-C-E-D-E-S M-C-C-A-M-B-R-I-D-G-E, but I was entranced by that name and fascinated with its owner's deep, rich, throaty, totally unique voice.

"Masaydees" was a regular on the DICK TRACY adventure series, which I listened to faithfully at the end of my school day. I also heard "Masaydees" when I came home from school for lunch on BIG SISTER, a soap-opera series that my mother always listened to middays, and on such memorable prime-time radio programs as INNER SANCTUM MYSTERIES and ABIE'S IRISH ROSE. I even got to see "Masaydees" in the flesh, so to speak, when my mother took my sister, Joyce, and me to see a live broadcast of the *Abie's Irish Rose* program at New York's Radio City in 1943.

Spinning the dial to hear more of "Masaydees's" magic voice, I discovered, and learned to appreciate, the many other wonders that radio had to offer: Myriad mystery, crime, adventure, comedy, music, and quiz programs—an entire world of sound-oriented life experiences—were mine simply by tuning them in.

Years passed, and the business of getting on with things and then the all-encompassing activities of college life made me forget about the joys of radio. Before I knew it, television had insidiously replaced radio as America's favorite home-entertainment medium. By the time I was graduated from college, there was no comedy or drama nor much of anything other than recorded music and news programs on radio. The older I became, the more I remembered radio, and the more I longed to relive those "thrilling days of yesteryear" when, in the privacy of my own room or around the big console radio in the living room, I listened to the radio with Mom, Dad, and Joyce.

In the fall of 1990, when a dreadful new season of television programming had begun, I decided to recall to mind some of radio's magic by compiling a list of important personalities and programs from radio's golden days. In the back of my mind, I must have known that a book was formulating; if it were to materialize, however, it would be a simple listing of the names of prominent radio people and the programs on which they had been heard.

When I finally accepted the fact that I wanted to write a *reference work* on radio, I knew that a great deal more information would have to be included if this book was to be of any real value to anyone but me. It would have to include brief biographies of the most prominent figures (performers, writers, directors, sound-effects technicians, inventors, innovators) and provide synopses, cast lists, theme songs, sponsors, histories, and air times of radio programs. General information about the major networks (including National Public Radio and the Canadian Broadcasting Corporation) would also be necessary. My simple, personal list of radio celebrities and shows burgeoned into research material covering all aspects of North American radio from the 1920s to the present.

Almost as soon as I began my research, I found that my considerable tape collection of vintage radio programs, my entertainment library, and my personal recollection of what radio had been like and had become would be insufficient if my book was to include as much detailed, accurate information as I felt it should contain. Names of many radio performers and contributors as well as of numerous programs had never officially been recorded anywhere because radio was thought to be "a totally disposable" medium, unworthy of being taken seriously by anyone, especially by many of the people who were an active part of it and would have preferred work on the stage or in films.

Dates were especially difficult to substantiate and/or confirm. Former radio contributors were not always very reliable sources of factual information; either they remembered only what they wanted to remember—when they were born and which shows they had worked on—or what they *wished* had happened. Except for the most prominent performers, whose careers had been previously documented, the birth and/or death dates of many of radio's active participants had either never been recorded or were known only to actors' union officials—they refused to release "such personal information" for publication. Radio fan magazines of the time and the few available reference books on radio, such as Buxton and Owen's *Big Broadcast* and John Dunning's *Tune In Yesterday*, did not always supply accurate dates of programs and correct spellings of names. I and previous authors found the same discrepancies and inaccuracies.

Because I wanted my facts, especially the dates, to be as correct as possible, careful decisions were made. Researchers', collectors', and catalogists' lists that were compiled by vintage-radio-program enthusiasts proved to be the most reliable sources of information. It was easier to confirm facts concerning current radio programs and personalities because publicists and performers were eager to promote these projects and, therefore, themselves.

A major source of information and fact confirmation was Danny Goodwin, a native of Lincoln, Maine, who had been collecting radio-related facts for many years. Although he was born in 1954 when television had already replaced radio as America's favorite home-entertainment medium, he developed a keen interest in vintage radio programs because of his mother's fond memories of old radio commercials. When Danny was a child, Mrs. Goodwin would tell him of the foghorn on the Lifebuoy soap commercial that belched "Beeeee oooooh!" (B. O. for "Body Odor"), would repeat many of the other familiar radio slogans, and would sing many of the jingles she had heard. Mrs. Goodwin's reminiscences led Danny to research sponsors of past radio programs as well as the times those programs were on the air, general cast lists, and so forth. He compiled his lists and placed them in binders. Danny's research material was invaluable to me as a cross-reference for the facts I had assembled from various books, magazines, and collectors' listings.

Another source of information was the amazing memory of a good friend and fellow vintage radio-show collector, David Davies. David's mind is a virtual storehouse of entertainment trivia. He was, for instance, able to identify Hopalong Cassidy's horse as Topper, a name that sixteen entertainment reference works in my personal library and numerous volumes in various libraries (including those in the New York Public Library's prestigious entertainment-oriented reference room at Lincoln Center) failed to reveal. David's wife, Barbara, is a radio-memorabilia dealer whose company, Treasure Hunters, supplied me with many books and magazines used in preparing this book. She and David can certainly be called valuable contributors to this project.

In addition, information supplied by Jay Hickerson, founder of the Friends of Old Time Radio, and by my friend and fellow collector Charles Stumpf (a radio nostalgia buff who supplied me with countless dates and made his vast photograph collection available to me) added immeasurably to this work.

I am also indebted to my friends radio actresses Miriam WOLFE and Peg LYNCH; the kindness of performers Alice REINHEART, Betty WINKLER, Florence WILLIAMS, Vivian DELLA CHIESA, Nancy Coleman, Arnold STANG, William N. ROBSON, Gwen DAVIES, Louise FLETCHER, Louise ERICKSON, Ralph Bell, Bill ZUCKERT, Fran CARLON, Robert DRYDEN, Frank NELSON, Jean COLBERT, Laurette FILLBRANDT, Arthur ANDERSON, Gil-

bert Mack, George Ansbro, Adele RONSON; collectors John M. Eccles, Jr., Robert Matthews, David Price, Martin Tytun, SHADOW expert Anthony Tolin, LONE RANGER expert Karl Rommel, SUSPENSE expert Don Ramlow, archivist and records manager Fr. Denis Sennett, S.A., of the Graymoor Friars of Atonement at Garrison, New York, Howard Mandelbaum of Photofest in New York; the Gasman brothers; sound-effects technician Ray Erlenborn; and longtime CBS employee Ann Nelson for their generous assistance, information, photographs, and remembrances. I would also like to acknowledge the wonderful research work done by Master Sam Brett, who spent many hours in various libraries tracking down hard-to-find dates. Also extremely helpful were the Library of Congress, the Museum of Television and Radio in New York City, the New York Public Library at Lincoln Center, the Scranton Public Library, the Canadian Broadcasting Corporation, National Public Radio, WOR in New York, and *The Illustrated Press, Radio Digest,* and *Hello Again* vintage-radio-program newsletters. Special thanks are in order to Helen Petronas, who first suggested the idea of a radio encyclopedia to Facts On File.

Criteria for Inclusion

The personalities, programs, and general categories chronicled in this encyclopedia were selected because of their recognized and well-publicized importance to the broadcasting industry, their popularity with the public when they were on the air, or the unique and/or significant impression—either performance related or historical—that made them noteworthy. Fan magazines of the time and consultations with many collectors, authors, and cataloguers were also extremely important when deciding the programs and personalities that would have individual entries in this book. Regrettably, space limitations forbade separate entries for everyone associated with radio. Many of these are cited in the appendix, Additional Radio Personalities. In addition, entries for radio shows list known performers, writers, producers, directors, and other relevant personnel; these names can easily be found in the Index. Except in the case of a show that had such a cultural impact that it had to be named, only shows that were aired for more than one season are included in the text.

A Note About the Book's Format

Dates   Birth and death dates of show-business personalities vary considerably from source to source. When a decision had to be made, I went with the most reliable source and, as a rule of thumb, the earliest date I located because many actors invariably "choose" the younger age. Dates in doubt have been preceded by a letter *c* for "circa." An asterisk indicates that no definitive dates could be found for a birth date, death date, air time, or air date. The notation *d* is used if a personality has most certainly died but his or her actual date of death remains unknown.

Actual Show Titles Because sponsors changed and performers' popularity increased, program titles changed. My criteria for deciding which program title for a show to list was to select the title that eventually became best known or longest lasting. I always chose in favor of the title that the majority of listeners and, in several cases, radio fan magazines of the time used to identify the show. The birth names of performers are indicated only if they differed from the performers' professional names. These birth names are in parenthesis and precede the birth and death dates.

Alphabetical Order I have followed the word-by-word alphabetizing system (*The Barry Wood Show* comes before Lionel Barrymore). The only idiosyncrasies are that *Mc* follows *Ma* and that articles such as *a* and *the* are placed after the major name of the title (e.g., *Adventures of Sam Spade, The*).

Sponsor Identifications Every available means at my disposal was used to identify the names of as many sponsors of vintage radio shows as possible. In addition to listening to thousands of hours of old radio shows, I also reviewed hundreds of old radio fan magazines, looking at advertisements that often listed the names of programs that a product was sponsoring on radio. I also depended upon the expertise of the aforementioned Danny Goodwin in this area.

Program Identifications Names of radio programs are italicized, but names of individual episodes of these shows are placed in quotes in order to make the distinction between the two clear to the reader. Films, books, magazines, and newspapers are italicized. Television programs, however, are in quotation marks.

Air Times Most of the air-time entries recorded in this book are Eastern Standard Time be-

cause they were mainly obtained from East Coast magazine and newspaper radio-program schedules.

Theme Music A series' theme music was listed only for entries that used well-known popular or classical music as their musical signatures. Many shows used theme music written especially for their particular series. If a theme song is not listed with the show entry, it is because it could not be identified other than as—say—"The Theme from Box 13." This would be meaningless; because readers could not hear the music itself, they would be unable to associate it with the show as "The Theme from Box 13."

Producers The producers of network programs were seldom identified when the program's credits were given unless they had some sort of a financial stake in the production or had originated the idea for the show. This was rare as far as network offerings were concerned: networks usually assigned staff members as producers of their various programs, and a show's producer could change weekly, according to the network's needs.

Syndicated Shows The names of directors, writers, and sometimes even performers of syndicated, recorded shows that were sold to individual radio stations around the country were usually not given. This information has become lost, in most cases, in the hidden-away files of numerous independent companies that in most instances are no longer in business. I hesitated to state who some of the performers might be for fear of being wrong, even when I thought I had identified a familiar voice.

Concerning "Uncredited" Radio Personalities Where the phrase "were (was) uncredited" is used, no written record could be found of a show's director, writers, or, sometimes, performers. When listening to a tape of such a program to learn the missing information, I found its personnel uncredited at the beginning or the end of the program.

Here then is the result of all my memory probing and information gathering, *Same Time . . . Same Station: An A–Z Guide to Radio from Jack Benny to Howard Stern.*

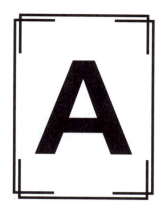

A

A AND P GYPSIES, THE

1924–1926	Local New York City station WEAF		9 PM
1926–1927	NBC Red	Mon.	9 PM
1927–1931	NBC Red	Mon.	8:30 PM
1931–1932	NBC Red	Mon.	9 PM
	NBC Blue	Thurs.	10 PM
1932–1936	NBC Red	Mon.	9 PM

The A and P Gypsies, in reality Harry Horlick and his Orchestra, became one of radio's earliest major musical attractions. First aired in 1924, sponsored by the A&P food company, this half-hour show was carried on six stations, an unprecedented number for that time. Tenor Frank PARKER was the orchestra's chief vocalist; Ed Thorgenson, Phil Carlin, and Milton CROSS did the announcing. The show's theme music, "Two Guitars," became the number-one hit in America. In the New York City area, WEAF became one of America's most listened-to radio stations while *The A and P Gypsies* was on the air. From 1926, *The A and P Gypsies* was networked across the country by NBC.

ABBOTT AND COSTELLO (ABBOTT, WILLIAM "BUD": 1895–1974; COSTELLO, LOUIS "LOU" FRANCIS CRISTILLO: 1906–1959)

Radio, TV, and film comedians Abbott and Costello were the country's most popular comedy team throughout the 1940s and 1950s. Tall, slick Bud Abbott, who was born in Asbury Park, New Jersey, into a show business family, was the team's straight man. His short and pudgy partner, Lou Costello, was born in Patterson, New Jersey. Abbott's character was fast-talking, sharp, and something of a con man, while Costello's persona was childlike, lovable, and a bit dim-witted.

The team first worked together in vaudeville in 1932 and subsequently made their radio debut on *The* KATE SMITH SHOW in 1940. They appeared regularly on Smith's program until they began their own series, *The* ABBOTT AND COSTELLO SHOW, in 1942. The team's immensely popular "Who's on First?" baseball sketch, which they had performed on *The Smith Show,* became a staple classic routine for them.

Abbott and Costello made their motion picture debut in *One Night in the Tropics* (1940); their other commercially successful films included *Abbott and Costello Meet Frankenstein* (1948), *Abbott and Costello Meet the Invisible Man* (1951), and *Abbott and Costello Meet the Mummy* (1955). In the 1950s, Abbott and Costello became guest stars on television's "The Colgate Comedy Hour" and in the mid-1950s had their own half-hour situation-comedy series, "The Abbott and Costello Show." In 1957, the team amicably agreed to go their separate ways. Costello died shortly after the team parted.

ABBOTT AND COSTELLO SHOW, THE

1940 (Summer)	NBC	Wed.	9 PM
1942–1947	NBC	Thurs.	10 PM
1947–1948	ABC	Wed.	9 PM
1948–1949	ABC	Thurs.	8 PM

Part situation-comedy and part variety format, *The Abbott and Costello Show* was a relatively long-running hit on radio. Besides Bud Abbott and Lou Costello's usual double-talk routines, which they had perfected in vaudeville, the half-hour program featured singers Marilyn Maxwell and Connie Haines, the comic talents of screen tough girl Irish Adrian and comedian Sid Fields, and the formidable voice versatility of actor Mel BLANC. Will Osbourne and Skinnay Ennis led the orchestra at different times, and Ken NILES was the show's announcer. *The Abbott and Costello Show*'s talented staff of writers included Pat Costello, Martin Ragaway, Ed Forman, Don Prindle, Ed Cherokee, Len Stern, and Paul Conlan. The program's theme music was a swing version of the popular C-A-M-E-L-S jingle, Camel cigarettes being the show's sponsor.

ABBOTT MYSTERIES

| 1945–1946 | Mutual | Sun. | 6 and later 5:30 PM |
| 1947 (Summer) | Mutual | Sun. | 5:30 PM |

The Abbotts were similar to the celebrated crime-solvers Nick and Nora Charles (the major characters in the *Thin Man* film series that began in 1934 and on the popular radio program *The ADVENTURES OF THE THIN MAN*). Like Nick and Nora, Pat and Jean Abbott were a husband-and-wife team who had a talent for stumbling upon and solving mysteries.

Based on the best-selling Frances Crane novels, *The Abbott Mysteries* had a relatively short tenure on radio compared with *The Thin Man*, lasting only two seasons. Jean Abbott was played by Alice REINHEART and then by Julie STEVENS. Pat Abbott was played by Les TREMAYNE and then by Charles "Chuck" Webster. Regular cast members were Luis VAN ROOTEN, Sidney Slon, and Jean Ellyn. Frank Gallop was the program's announcer. Frances Crane wrote many scripts for the series. Carlo DEANGELO directed the show, which was sponsored by Camel cigarettes.

ABE BURROWS SHOW, THE

| 1947–1948 | CBS | Sat. | 7:30 PM |
| 1949 (Summer) | CBS | Mon. | 9:30 PM |

It wasn't often that a radio writer became the star of an evening comedy-variety program, but Abe Burrows, who wrote scripts for such shows as DUFFY'S TAVERN and SKY KING, and co-authored the book for the Broadway musical *Guys and Dolls*, managed to do just that. Burrows, who had a wonderful wit, later made numerous best-selling comedy recordings and starred on his own evening radio series in the late 1940s. Sponsored by Listerine mouthwash, the half-hour program remained on the air for one year. In the 1950s, Burrows became a major television personality and was a frequent game-show panelist.

ABIE'S IRISH ROSE

| 1942–1944 | NBC | Sat. | 8 PM |

For two years, *Abie's Irish Rose* was one of the most successful half-hour situation-comedy series on radio.

Even though the show had a large listening audience, it was canceled by NBC because of protests by groups that found its broad stereotyping of Jewish and Irish people offensive.

The show was based on a 1921 long-running Broadway play by Ann Nichols, who also wrote scripts for the radio series.

Like the play, the series centered around a young Jewish man named Abie Levy (played at different times by Richard Bond, Sidney Smith, Richard Coogan, and Clayton "Bud" COLLYER) and his Irish-Catholic bride, Rose Murphy (played by Betty WINKLER, Mercedes MCCAMBRIDGE, Julie STEVENS, and Marion Shockley). Major attractions of the program included the couple's feuding fathers, Solomon Levy (played by Alfred White, Charlie Cantor, and finally by Alan Reed, aka Teddy Bergman) and Patrick Murphy (played by Walter KINSELLA), and their comical neighbors, the Cohens (played by Yiddish theater stars Menasha SKULNIK and Anna Appel). Regular supporting players were Carl Eastman as David Lerner, Bill ADAMS as Father Whelan, Ann Thomas as Miss Casey (Abie's secretary), Fred Sullivan as Dr. Mueller, Charme Allen as Mrs. Mueller, Florence FREEMAN as Mrs. Brown, Amanda RANDOLPH as the maid Lillie, and child impersonator Dolores Gillen as Abie and Rose's twins.

The program's announcers were Howard Petrie and Richard Stark. The show's theme music was "My Wild Irish Rose." Joe Rines and "Rip" Van Runkle directed the program, and Morton Friedman wrote the series' scripts. Sponsors were Special Drene shampoo, Drene, and Ivory soap flakes.

ACE, GOODMAN, AND JANE (GOODMAN ESCHOKOWITZ: 1899–1982; JANE EPSTEIN: 1900–1974)

Goodman Ace was one of radio's most talented comedy writers and performers. Born in Kansas City, Missouri, Ace had an urbane style and a sophisticated wit that popularized programs such as *The BIG SHOW*, *The DANNY KAYE SHOW*, and *EASY ACES*. On *Easy Aces*, Ace played the ever-exasperated husband; Jane, his addlepated wife, was played by Ace's real-life wife, Jane Epstein. Goodman and Jane Ace met while attending high school in Kansas City and were married shortly after graduating. Ace worked as a drama critic and a newspaper columnist for twelve years before he entered radio as a writer. He teamed up with Jane on *Easy Aces* in 1929; the program eventually became a network show in 1932, after being aired on various local stations. Ace, later a prized television writer, worked for Sid Caesar and several other top TV performers.

ACUFF, ROY (1903–1992)

A country-western performer and one of the longtime stars of the popular GRAND OLE OPRY, Roy Acuff was born in Maynardsville, Tennessee. He excelled in all sports while in high school and decided to pursue a professional athletics career.

A serious case of sunstroke forced him to drop out of athletic competitions and turn down offers from professional baseball scouts for future placement in the minor leagues. This led to a nervous breakdown. While recuperating, Acuff practiced playing his fiddle, worked on his father's farm, and even preached at the local Baptist church.

In 1932, he joined a medicine-show tour as a musician and singer, and in 1938 promoter Joseph J. L. Frank persuaded WSM radio to schedule Acuff for an appearance on the *Opry*. Acuff and his band, the Smoky Mountain Boys, were an immediate success on the program and spotlighted the show every week thereafter for more than thirty years.

Some of Acuff's popular song hits included "The Wabash Cannonball," "The Great Speckled Bird," and "The Precious Jewel." In 1962, Acuff was inducted into the Country Music Hall of Fame.

ADAMS, MASON (1919–   )

Born in New York City, actor Mason Adams is well known to TV viewers as Lou Grant's editor-boss, Charlie Hume, on the "Lou Grant" TV show. Adams, who holds a master's degree in theater from the University of Wisconsin, was a popular juvenile and leading man on radio throughout the 1940s and 1950s in PEPPER YOUNG'S FAMILY (in which he played Pepper), BIG TOWN, GASOLINE ALLEY, GANGBUSTERS, GRAND CENTRAL STATION, *The Molle* MYSTERY THEATER, INNER SANCTUM MYSTERIES, and many others. Currently Adams is a frequent guest star on many television shows and has also appeared in several feature films. Adams's voice is also frequently heard on TV commercials, most notably for Smuckers jellies and jams, Kix cereal, and Cadbury chocolate.

ADAMS, WILLIAM "BILL" (1887–1972)

One of radio's busiest character actors, Bill Adams was born in Tiffin, Ohio. He attended Heidelberg College in Tiffin, where he studied prelaw but decided he wanted to become a professional singer. He transferred to the College of Music in Cincinnati. In 1912, Adams obtained his first acting job with the Edward Sothern-Julia Marlowe Shakespeare Company and subsequently appeared in such plays as *Peter Ibbetson* (1917) with John Barrymore and in Arthur Hopkin's production of *Hamlet* (1918). He then directed Barrymore in a London production of *Hamlet* in 1920.

Adams began to act on radio in 1927 and soon became one of that medium's most sought-after performers. He was Uncle Henry on *The* COLLIER HOUR program and was regularly heard on PEPPER YOUNG'S FAMILY, *The* STORY OF MARY MARLIN, BIG TOWN, LIGHT OF THE WORLD, CAVALCADE OF AMERICA, *The* MARCH OF TIME, ABIE'S IRISH ROSE, *The* ADVENTURES OF MR. MEEK, *The* GIBSON FAMILY, ROSEMARY and YOUR FAMILY AND MINE. His deep, resonant, grandfatherly voice is perhaps best remembered as Uncle Bill on the long-running children's fairy-tale series LET'S PRETEND. Adams was spokesman for the show's sponsor, Cream of Wheat cereal, and narrated each week's story. He remained with the show until it left the airwaves in 1954. The actor retired from acting in the early 1960s.

ADVENTURES OF ARCHIE ANDREWS, THE

1945–1949	NBC	Sat.	10:30 AM
1949–1950	NBC	Sat.	7:30 PM
1950–1951	NBC	Sat.	11 AM
1951–1953	NBC	Sat.	10 AM

"Yes, here is the youngster millions of readers of Archie Andrews comics know so well, brought to you by Swift and Company. Archie Andrews and his gang," said the announcer who opened the half-hour *Adventures of Archie Andrews* radio program. Bob Montana's popular teenage comic book hero, Archie Andrews, and his pals Jughead, Betty, and Veronica, were heard on the NBC radio network on Saturday mornings for several years. The show was a favorite among young listeners throughout the United States. Charles Mullen, Jack GRIMES, and Burt Boyer played Archie at various times, but it is actor Bob HASTINGS who is best remembered in the role and played the part for six years. Harlan "Hal" Stone, Jr., and then Cameron Andrews played Jughead; Doris Grundy, Joy Geffin, and Rosemary RICE played Betty; Gloria Mann and then Vivian SMOLEN played Veronica. Also heard on the series were Paul Gordon, Vivian Block, Vivien Hayworth, Art Kohl, Reese Taylor, Grace Keddy, Alice Yourman, Peggy Allenby, Maurice Franklin, Arthur Maitland, Bill Griffis, and others. Kenneth BANGHART, Dick Dudley, and Bob Shaerer announced the program. Written for radio by John L. Goldwater, the series was directed by Kenneth MACGREGOR, Floyd Holm, and Herbert M. Moss. For most of the years the show was on the air, it was sponsored by Swift meat products.

ADVENTURES OF BABE RUTH, THE (AKA HERE'S TO BABE RUTH; THE SINCLAIR RUTH PROGRAM; THE BABE RUTH BASEBALL QUIZ)

1934–1935	NBC Blue	Mon., Wed., Fri.	8:45 PM
1936	Mutual	Tues.	(Time *)

1937	CBS	Wed.–Fri.	10:30 PM
1937–1943	(Off the air)		
1943–1944	NBC	Sat.	10:45 PM

"Play ball! Play ball with Babe Ruth! Play ball with the Navy! The United States Navy brings you *The Adventures of Babe Ruth*," the series' announcer said at the beginning of each 15-minute, and later half-hour, program. Although he was only actually heard on the program briefly in 1937 when he delivered the sports news every Wednesay through Friday on CBS, baseball legend Babe Ruth was the major character. This series related incidents that had occurred during "the Bambino's" long and distinguished career. Jackson BECK was the show's announcer at one time, and the stories were narrated by a fictional sports reporter named Steve Martin. At one time sponsored by the U.S. Navy, the show was written by Peter Freeman, produced by Woody Close, and directed by Ronald Davis. Its theme music was "Take Me Out to the Ballgame."

ADVENTURES OF BULLDOG DRUMMOND, THE

1941–1943	Mutual	Sun.	6:30 PM
1943–1944	Mutual	Sun.	8:30 PM
1944–1945	(Off the air)		
1945–1946	Mutual	Mon.	8 PM
1946–1947	Mutual	Fri.	9:30 PM
1947–1953	(Off the air)		
1953–1954	Mutual	Sun.	6 PM

"Out of the fog . . . out of the night . . . and into his American adventures . . . comes . . . Bulldog Drummond!" the announcer stated at the beginning of this mystery-adventure series. British actors George COULOURIS and then Sir Cedric Hardwicke, and American actors Santos ORTEGA and Ned WEVER played Drummond, an urbane, sophisticated British private detective; Wever played the role the longest. Everett SLOANE, Luis VAN ROOTEN, and Rod Henrickson played Denny, Drummond's valet. Agnes MOOREHEAD, Mercedes MCCAMBRIDGE, Paul Stewart, and Ray COLLINS were often featured in various supporting roles on this series. Ted Brown and Henry MORGAN announced the series. Himan BROWN was the program's producer and frequent director. Jay Bennett wrote the program for several seasons. The show was sponsored by Tums antacid and Dodge automobiles.

ADVENTURES OF CHARLIE CHAN, THE

1932–1933	NBC Blue	Fri.	7:30 PM
1933–1937	(Off the air)		
1937–1938	Mutual	Mon.–Fri.	5:15 PM
1938–1944	(Off the air)		
1944–1945	NBC Blue	Thurs.	7:30 PM
1945–1947	(Off the air)		
1947–1948	Mutual	Mon.	8:30 PM

Asian Hawaiian private detective Charlie Chan, with his "number-one son" at his side, solved numerous crimes over the years this adventure series was heard on the radio. The 15-minute daily, finally half-hour weekly, radio program like the popular film series was based on the successful Charlie Chan mysteries by Erle Derr Biggers.

At different times, Walter Connolly, Ed BEGLEY, and Santos ORTEGA starred as the sleuth who quoted ancient Chinese proverbs. Leon JANNEY and Rodney Jacobs played his number-one son. At one time, Dorian St. George was the program's announcer.

The *Charlie Chan* radio series, which was often accused of being racist by various civil-rights groups, was produced and directed by Alfred Bester and Chick Vincent during its earliest years. Alfred Bester, John Cole, Judith Bublick, and Janet Erthein wrote its scripts; and Esso oil and gasoline, Lifebuoy soap, Rinso cleanser, and Feen-A-Mint breath mints sponsored the series.

ADVENTURES OF DICK TRACY, THE

1935–1937	Mutual	Mon.–Fri.	5:45 PM
1937–1939	NBC Red	Mon.–Fri.	5 PM
1939–1943	(Off the air)		
1943–1945	ABC Blue	Mon.–Fri.	5:15 PM
1945–1946	ABC	Mon.–Fri.	5:15 PM
1946–1947	ABC	Mon.–Fri.	4:45 PM
1947–1948	ABC	Mon.–Fri.	5 PM

The five-days-a-week 15-minute-a-day *Adventures of Dick Tracy* series, based on the famous comic-strip detective created by Chester Gould, debuted in the mid-1930s and remained on the air until the late 1940s. A typical *Dick Tracy* adventure pitted the celebrated detective against such archvillains as Flattop, The Mole, and Scarface. Tracy's familiar two-way wrist radio figured prominently in his solving many of his cases. Most of Gould's other comic-strip characters—Tracy's girlfriend Tess Trueheart, his partner Sam, B. O. Plenty, Junior, Pat Patton, Vitamin Flintheart, Gravel Gertie, and Snowflake—were also on hand.

Ned WEVER, Matt CROWLEY and Barry Thomson played Tracy, and Helen Lewis played Tess. Andy Donnelly and Jackie KELK were featured as Junior. Also heard were Walter KINSELLA, Lawson Zerbe, Howard Smith, Beatrice Pons, Mercedes MCCAMBRIDGE, Gil Mack, John Griggs, Craig McDonnell, James Van Dyk, and Ralph Bell. Don Gardiner, George Gunn, Dan SEYMOUR, and Ed HERLIHY announced.

The series was directed by Mitchell Grayson and Charles Powers and written by Sidney Slon, Irwin Shaw, John Wray, and others. It was sponsored by Quaker puffed wheat and puffed rice breakfast cereals.

ADVENTURES OF ELLERY QUEEN, THE

1939–1940	CBS	Sun.	10 PM	
1940–1941	CBS	Sun.	7:30 PM	
1941–1942	(Off the air)			
1942–1944	NBC Red	Sat.	7:30 PM	
1944–1947	CBS	Wed.	7:30 PM	
1947	NBC	Sun.	6:30 PM	
1947–1948	ABC	Thurs.	7:30 PM	

Private detective Ellery Queen, his police inspector–father, and his assistant, Nicki, were creations of novelists Frederic Dannay and Manfred Bennington Lee. Actors Hugh MARLOWE, Howard Culver, Lawrence Dobkin, Carlton YOUNG, and Sidney Smith played Ellery Queen on this half-hour series at different times. William "Bill" Smith and Santos ORTEGA were heard as Police Inspector Queen, Ellery's father. As an amateur detective and mystery writer, Ellery Queen spent most episodes assisting his father in solving difficult cases. Marion Shockley, Barbara Terrell, Virginia GREGG, Charlotte Keane, and Gertrude Warner each played Nikki. Howard Smith, Ted De-Corsia, and Ed Latimer played Sergeant Velie. Roger Krupp, Ernest CHAPPELL, Paul Masterson, and Bert PARKS announced; Phil Cohen, William P. Rousseau, Robert S. Steele, and Gregory Zachery directed the series at different times. Gulf oil, Bromo Seltzer antacid, Anacin pain reliever, and Kolynos toothpaste each sponsored the series.

ADVENTURES OF MAISIE, THE

1945–1947	CBS	Fri.	10:30 PM	
1947–1948	(Off the air)			
1948–1949	(Syndicated series. Various stations and times)			
1951–1952	Mutual	Fri.	8 PM	

At the beginning of each half-hour *Maisie* show, listeners heard the sound of high heels clicking down the street; then a man would say, "Hi-ya, Babe! Say, how about a lit . . ." The sound of a slap would interrupt the man, and then actress Ann SOTHERN would say, "Does that answer your question, Buddy?" Maisie Revere, the tough showgirl with a heart of gold, was a character introduced to the public in a series of MGM films such as *Maisie* (1939), *Maisie Gets Her Man* (1942), *Maisie Goes to Reno* (1944). Maisie had a talent for stumbling upon murders among her adventures, usually on the high seas as she traveled from one exotic port to another. From sipping drinks in mysterious cafés in Istanbul to fighting thieves who had taken over her ship, Maisie followed the winds of adventure the world over. The program, first heard on radio in 1945, was retired from the airwaves in 1947 but was brought back by popular demand two years later for an additional three years. Among Sothern's supporting cast were Elliott LEWIS as Maisie's boyfriend Bill, and John Brown, Wally Maher, Norman Field, Donald WOODS, and Lurene TUTTLE. The program was directed by Cal Kuhl and William Rousseau and written by Art Phillips. Ken NILES was the program's announcer. Eversharp-Shick razors sponsored the series.

ADVENTURES OF FRANK MERRIWELL, THE

1934	NBC Red	Mon., Wed., Fri.	5:30 PM
1934–1946	(Off the air)		
1946–1949	NBC	Sat.	10 AM

"An echo of the past," the announcer began at the opening of *The Adventures of Frank Merriwell*: "An exciting past . . . a romantic past. The era of the horse and carriage . . . gaslit streets . . . and free-for-all football games. The era of one of the most beloved heroes in American fiction . . . Frank Merriwell." A typical *Frank Merriwell* adventure had Frank travel cross-country in a hot-air balloon as he tracked down a dangerous spy.

This half-hour series, first heard on radio in 1934, was based on the novels of Gilbert Patten (pen name, Burt L. Standish). Actor Lawson Zerbe played Frank Merriwell; Jean Gillespie, and then Elaine Rost, played Inza Burrage; Hal Studer played Bart Hodge; and Patricia Hosley played Elsie Bellwood in the 1940s.

Harlow WILCOX was the show's first announcer, and Ed King and Fred Weihe directed the original series. Scripts were written by Bill Welch and Ruth and Gilbert Brann. Dr. West's toothpaste was one of the show's sponsors.

ADVENTURES OF MR. AND MRS. NORTH, THE

1942–1946	NBC	Wed.	8 PM	
1946–1947	(Off the air)			
1947–1954	CBS	Tues.	8:30 PM	
1954–1955	CBS	Mon.–Fri.	9:30 PM	

Joseph CURTIN and Alice FROST are best remembered in the title roles on the *Mr. and Mrs. North* mystery-adventure series, where they played the parts the longest (1943–1954). For the 1954–1955 radio season, the television stars of "Mr. and Mrs. North," Barbara Britton and Richard Denning, took over as Pam and Jerry in an unsuccessful attempt to attract television viewers to the radio show.

The program was an audience favorite not only because the scripts were well written and well acted, but also because they were full of humor. A typical *Mr. and Mrs. North* story had Pam leading her publisher husband, Jerry, on what seemed like a scatter-brained, wild-goose chase, as they tracked down a criminal (they seemed to have a talent for attracting the criminal element). Pam's deductions were, of course, totally logical, and the police always ended up apprehending the sought-after murderer or thief based on her tips.

With Frost and Curtin on the show were Betty Jane Tyler as Pam's niece, Susan; Walter KINSELLA as Sergeant Mullins; and Mandel KRAMER as Mahatma McGoin. Staats COTSWORTH, Frank LOVEJOY, and Francis DeSales played the North's police detective friend, Bill Weigand. The announcers on the Frost-Curtin series were Joseph King, Charles STARK, and Ben GRAUER, while Art Ballinger announced the Britton-Denning version. The half-hour weekly Frost-Curtin version was produced and directed by John Loveton, and written by Hector Chevigny, Michael Morris, Jerome Epstein, Louis Vittes, and Robert Sloane. Britton–Denning's director and writers were uncredited. The show's theme was "The Way You Look Tonight." Woodbury soap, Jergens lotion, Halo shampoo, Colgate tooth powder, Cashmere Bouquet soap, and Palmolive soap sponsored the series.

ADVENTURES OF MONSIEUR HERCULE POIROT, THE

1945–1947	Mutual-Syndicated	Thurs.	8:30 PM
		Sun.	9 PM

Mystery writer Agatha Christie's elegant Belgian detective Hercule Poirot, the major character on this half-hour radio series, was played by character actor Harold Huber. Also heard at various times in supporting roles were Cathy LEWIS, Joseph KEARNS, Hans CONRIED, and Alan REED. The series was directed by Carl Eastman.

ADVENTURES OF NERO WOLFE, THE

1943	NBC Blue	Mon.	8:30 PM
1943–1944	(Off the air)		
1944	NBC Blue	Fri.	7 PM
1944–1945	(Off the air)		
1945–1946	Mutual	Sun.	(Time *)
1946–1950	(Off the air)		
1950–1951	NBC	Fri.	8 PM

An orchid-loving gourmand and private detective, Nero Wolfe was a mystery-novel character created by Rex Stout in 1934. The fat PI usually conducted his investigations in the comfort of his lovely town house; his young assistant, Archie, did the necessary legwork.

Wolfe had several radio incarnations and later a television series, "The Adventures of Nero Wolfe," starring William Conrad. On radio, however, Wolfe was played by Santos ORTEGA and then by motion-picture actors Francis X. Bushman and Sydney Greenstreet. Louis Vittes played Archie on the first radio series. Also heard were Louis VAN ROOTEN, Elliott LEWIS, Gerald MOHR, Harry Bartell, Herb Ellis,

and Lawrence Dobkin. Don Stanley was the announcer, Johnny Green was the musical director, and Williams Shave Cream, Jergens lotion, and Plymouth automobiles were among its sponsors.

ADVENTURES OF OZZIE AND HARRIET, THE

1944–1945	CBS	Sun.	6 PM
1945–1948	CBS	Fri.	9:30 PM
1948–1949	NBC	Sun.	6:30 PM
1949	CBS	Sun.	6:30 PM
1949–1953	ABC	Fri.	9 PM

On this comedy program, which became a television show in 1952, Ozzie NELSON and Harriet HILLIARD played themselves. Their sons were first played by Tommy Bernard, Joel Davis, and Henry Blair and then by the couple's real-life sons, David and Ricky. John Brown played the Nelson's neighbor and friend, Thorney; Lurene TUTTLE, Harriet's mother; Janet WALDO, Emmy Lou; Bea BENADERET, both Gloria, the maid, and Mrs. Wallington; and Francis "Dink" Trout, Roger Waddington. The basic humor on *The Ozzie and Harriet Show* evolved from typical marital situations, including raising two teenage sons. On one program, for example, Ozzie had forgotten to bring home meat for the supper Harriet was preparing; the family ended up going out to eat at a very expensive restaurant. The sons, who were children when the show was first aired, grew up to be teenage heartthrobs. Vocalists on the program were the King Sisters (Donna, Alice, Yvonne, and Louise).

Dave Elton and sometimes Ted Bliss produced and directed. Writers included Ozzie Nelson, Jack Douglas, John P. Medbury, Sherwood Schwartz, John L. Greene, Ben Gershman, Rupert Pray, Sol Saks, Bill Davenport, Frank Fox, Bill Manhoff, Paul West, Selma Diamond, Hal Kanter, Don Nelson, Dick Bensfield, and Perry Grant. Billy May's Orchestra provided the music when Nelson's acting chores became more important than his bandleading. Verne Smith was the program's announcer. Sponsors included International Silver and Heinz foods.

ADVENTURES OF PHILIP MARLOWE, THE

1947 (summer)	CBS	Sun.	8:30 PM
1949–1951	CBS	Sat.	8:30 PM
			10 PM

This series began in 1947 as a summer replacement starring film actor Van Heflin as private detective Philip Marlowe. Two years later, Gerald MOHR took over the role of the hard-boiled, tough-talking shamus, Philip Marlowe, when it became a regular, half-hour weekly program. Marlowe was created by mystery writer Raymond Chandler in his novel *The Big Sleep* (1939) and appeared in several subsequent

Chandler novels including *Farewell My Lovely* (1940) and *Playback* (1958).

Other actors heard on this series included Vivi Janis, Byron Kane, Berry Kroeger, Laurette FILLBRANDT, Jack Kruschen, Harry Bartell, John Dehner, Jay Novello, Paul Frees, Jeanne Bates, Larry Dobkin, Irene Tedrow and Ed BEGLEY. Roy Rowen announced the series, Norman Macdonnell produced and directed, and scripts were written by Robert Mitchell, Gene Levitt, and Kathleen Heidt among others. Original music was composed by Richard Aurant and conducted by Wilber Hatch. Wrigley's chewing gums sponsored the show.

ADVENTURES OF RED RYDER, THE

1942–1949   (Syndicated series. Various stations and times)

"From out of the West comes America's famous fighting cowboy ... Red Ryder!" this 15-minute weekday series began. Produced for children and young teens, *Red Ryder* was an adventure program in which the Western hero and his young Indian friend, Little Beaver, tracked down outlaws. During its radio run, Carlton KaDell, Reed Hadley, and Brooke Temple played Red Ryder; Tommy Cook and Henry Blair played Little Beaver. The series was produced, written, and directed by Paul Franklin and was based on a comic strip that was both created in 1940 and drawn by Fred Harman.

ADVENTURES OF SAM SPADE, DETECTIVE, THE

1946	ABC	Fri.	8 PM
1946–1949	CBS	Sun.	8 PM
1949–1950	NBC	Sun.	8 PM
1950–1951	NBC	Fri.	8 PM

Mystery writer Dashiel Hammett's hard-boiled private detective, Sam Spade, a character he first introduced in 1930 in his novel *The Maltese Falcon*, became the hero of a weekly radio mystery-adventure series in 1946. Spade had previously been played in film adaptations of *The Maltese Falcon* by actors Ricardo Cortez in 1930 and Humphrey BOGART in 1941. Howard DUFF became a star through the radio role.

Sam's weekly "capers" (as his cases were called) were dictated to his faithful-if-flighty secretary, Effine Perrine; their humorous slant became the prototype for many mystery-adventure series. Episodes had such intriguing titles as "The Dry-Martini Caper," "The Love-Letter Caper," "The Apple-Eve Caper," and "The Bluebeard Caper." Not long after the program debuted, many Americans knew that Sam's private-detective license number was 137596 and that he ended each weeks' dictation to Effie with "Period.

End of report," as she gushed her sympathy and/or admiration for her adored boss. Actress Lurene TUTTLE played Effie during the series' entire run. Duff left the show in 1949 after a contract dispute with CBS. The show played for an additional two years with actor Steve Dunn filling Spade's gumshoes, but the public, used to hearing Duff in the role, lost interest in the program, and when the 1951 season ended, the show was retired from the airwaves with its lowest ratings.

Several actors claimed that *Sam Spade* was one of their favorite programs to work on because the scripts were always "very well written" and the atmosphere in the studio was "always such great fun." Regular supporting players included Hans CONRIED, Joan BANKS, June Havoc, Mary Jane CROFT, Betty Lou GERSON, Lois Kibbee, Alan REED, Joseph KEARNS, Jeanette NOLAN, Cathy LEWIS, and Bea BENADERET.

The series was directed by master radio director William SPIER. *The Adventures of Sam Spade, Detective* was written by Gil Doud and Bob Tallman. The music on the show, which certainly added to the series' effectiveness, was orchestrated and conducted by Lud GLUSKIN. Dick Joy was the program's announcer. Wildroot Cream Oil hair dressing was the show's sponsor. Its commercial jingle—"Use Wildroot Cream Oil, Charlie; it keeps your hair in trim"—became well-known countrywide.

ADVENTURES OF SHERLOCK HOLMES, THE

1930–1931	NBC Red	Mon.	10 PM
1931–1932	NBC Red	Wed.	9 PM
	NBC Blue	Thurs.	9:30 PM
1932–1933	NBC Blue	Wed.	9 PM
1933–1934	NBC Blue	Mon.	10:30 PM
1934–1935	NBC Blue	Sun.	9:45 PM
1935–1936	(Off the air)		
1936	Mutual	Sat.	10:30 PM
1936–1939	(Off the air)		
1939–1940	NBC Blue	Mon.	8:30 PM
	Mutual	Wed.	8:30 PM
1940–1941	NBC Blue	Sun.	8:30 PM
1941–1942	NBC Blue	Sun.	10:30 PM
1942–1943	(Off the air)		
1943–1946	Mutual	Fri.	8:30 PM
		Mon.	8:30 PM
1946–1947	ABC	Sat.	9:30 PM
1947–1949	Mutual	Sat.	8:30 PM
1949–1950	ABC	Wed.	8:30 PM
1950–1955	(Off the air)		
1955–1956	NBC	Sun.	9 PM
1960s	(Syndicated NPR series originally heard in England over the BBC network)		

Sir Arthur Conan Doyle's celebrated English detective Sherlock Holmes, a master sleuth who lived on Baker Street in London, was the major character on several different radio series over a period of more than thirty years. Holmes was introduced in Doyle's novel *A Study in Scarlet,* which was published in 1887.

Among the actors to play Holmes on radio were William Gillette—who also played the part for many years in a popular stage version—and Richard Gordon, Clive Brooks, Ben Wright, Louis Hector, Basil RATHBONE, Tom Conway, Ben Wright, and John Stanley. All had their own idea about how the character should be played, but Basil Rathbone's interpretation, which he recreated in many films, is certainly the most memorable.

In the 1970s, the British Broadcasting Corporation *Sherlock Holmes* radio series was heard in the United States on NPR stations. Sir John Gielgud played Holmes; Sir Ralph Richardson, Watson. Leigh Lowell, Nigel Bruce, George Stelden, Eric Snowden, Alfred Shirley, and Ian Martin played Holmes's faithful friend and companion in crime-solving, Dr. Watson, on the various other versions. As in Doyle's stories, Watson narrated the tales on radio. As Holmes's archenemy, Professor Moriarty, from time to time were Orson WELLES, Louis Hector, and Ian Martin. Agnes MOOREHEAD, Harry Neville, Lucille WALL, Junius Matthews, Louis Hector, William Shelley, Ben Wright, and Harry Bartell played supporting roles.

Unquestionably, the public's favorite Holmes and Watson were Basil Rathbone and Nigel Bruce, the actors who played the characters in fourteen films in the 1930s and 1940s. In the Rathbone–Bruce version, actor Harry Bartell interviewed Watson before, during, and after the story. The Rathbone radio series and the BBC *Sherlock Holmes* series can still be heard in syndication on various local radio stations throughout the United States and Canada.

At one time, the radio series was produced by actress Edna Best and directed by Basil Loughrane; Joseph Bell, who also interviewed Holmes and always suggested that they have a cup of George Washington coffee (the program's sponsor at the time) together, Tam McKnight, and Glenhall Taylor. Many adaptations of Doyle's stories and many original scripts were written by Edith Meiser, Bruce Taylor, Dennis Green, Anthony Boucher, Howard Merrill, and Max Erlich. Theme music for the show was Gilbert and Sullivan's "March of the Ancestors." Announcers for the various *Sherlock Holmes* series included John Conte, Joseph Bell, Knox Manning, Harry Bartel, Herb Allen, and Cy Harrice. In addition to George Washington coffee, sponsors included Household Finance insurance, Bromo Seltzer antacid, Petri wines, Kreml shampoo, and Kreml hair tonic, the Selma Company, and Trimont clothing.

British actor Jeremy Brett has been the most recent performer to play Holmes. This television series was

produced by the BBC and is telecast in the United States by the Public Broadcasting Corporation on its "Mystery" series.

ADVENTURES OF SUPERMAN, THE

1938	(Brief radio run on NBC)		
1938–1940	(Off the air)		
1940–1943	Mutual	Mon.–Fri.	5:30 PM
1943–1944	Mutual	Mon.–Fri.	5:45 PM
1944–1948	Mutual	Mon.–Fri.	5:15 PM
1948–1949	Mutual	Mon.–Fri.	5:30 PM
1949–1950	Mutual	Mon.–Fri.	5 PM
1950–1951	ABC	Mon., Wed.	5:30 PM
1951	ABC	Tues., Thurs.	5:30 PM

"It's a bird! It's a plane! It's *Superman!*" listeners learned at the beginning of this weekday-afternoon children's adventure program. The famous comic-book character created by Jerry Siegel and Joe Shuster for *Action* comics arrived on radio and the newsstands the same year—1938. The 15-minute weekday show was not immediately successful as was the comic book; it was withdrawn from the airwaves after less than a year. In 1940, the Mutual network tried the series again, this time successfully in a five-day-a-week format.

The now extremely familiar plot has the man from the planet Krypton, who is "faster than a speeding bullet (and) more powerful than a locomotive," disguised as mild-mannered *Daily Planet* reporter, Clark Kent. Superman and his co-workers—reporter Lois Lane, editor Perry White, and copyboy (later photographer) Jimmy Olson fought the forces of evil in Gotham City. They often had the help of superhero friends Batman and Robin.

Canceled after two years on the air, the public brought the program back that same year through a letter-writing campaign. In 1950, the show moved to ABC, where it remained until it was retired in 1951.

Clayton "Bud" COLLYER played Superman for most of the show's radio years, but he was replaced by Michael Fitzmaurice when it became a half-hour series in 1950. Joan Alexander played Lois Lane; Julian Noa, Perry White; Jackie KELK, Jimmy Olson. Batman was played by Stacy Harris, Gary MERRILL, and Matt Crowley; Batman's "ward," Robin, was played by Ronald LISS. Frequently heard in supporting roles were Mandel KRAMER, George Petrie, Robert DRYDEN, and Guy Sorel. Jackson Beck, George Lowther, and Frank Knight were the program's narrators-announcers.

The series was produced by Robert and Jessica Maxwell and George Lowther. It was directed, at different times, by Allen DuCovny and Mitchell Grayson and was written by B. P. Freeman. Kellogg's Pep and Kellogg's Rice Crispies cereals sponsored the series.

ADVENTURES OF THE THIN MAN, THE

1941–1942	NBC Red	Wed.	8 PM
1942–1943	CBS	Wed.	8 PM
1943–1944	CBS	Sun.	10:30 PM
1944–1945	CBS	Fri.	8:30 PM
1945–1946	CBS	Sun.	7 PM
1946–1947	CBS	Fri.	8:30 PM
1947–1948	(Off the air)		
1948	NBC	Tues.	9 PM
1948–1949	Mutual	Thurs.	10 PM
1949–1950	(Off the air)		
1950	ABC	Fri.	9 PM

The popular *Thin Man* mystery films starred William Powell and Myrna Loy as Nick and Nora Charles. The half-hour radio series arrived in 1941 with Les DAMON and Claudia MORGAN playing the celebrated detective and his supersleuth wife. The radio characters were familiar to anyone who knew their movie counterparts; Nick was the detective, but Nora usually solved the cases. The couple were urbane and sophisticated city dwellers, and the radio program, like the

Claudia Morgan and Les Damon as Nick and Nora Charles on *The Adventures of the Thin Man* (NBC)

film series, featured Nora's purringly sexy voice and Nick's responsive reactions, with a balanced blend of comedy and adventure.

Playing Nick at different times were Les TREMAYNE (when Damon entered the military during World War II), David GOTHARD, and Joseph CURTIN. Curtin is perhaps the best-remembered Nick Charles on radio, having played the part for the longest period of time. Parker FENNELLY was often heard as Ebenezer Williams, sheriff of Crabtree County, where the Charleses had a summer home. Announcers on the program were Ron Rawson and Ed HERLIHY. Himan BROWN produced and directed the series. Writers included Milton Lewis, Eugene Wang, Robert Newman, and Louis Vittes. The show's sponsors were Post Toasties cereal, Pabst Blue Ribbon beer, Heinz catsup, Sanka instant coffee, and Woodbury facial soap.

AFFAIRS OF DR. GENTRY, THE

1957–1959	NBC	Mon.–Fri.	2:45 PM

In the 1930s and 1940s, Madeleine Carroll appeared in such notable films as *The Thirty-Nine Steps* (1935) and *My Favorite Blonde* (1942). By the 1950s, however, her motion-picture career was on the wane. She began to concentrate on radio acting and became the star of a 15-minute, Monday-through-Friday daytime drama series called *The Affairs of Dr. Gentry*. Sustained by NBC, the story told of an unmarried, young doctor (Carroll) who worked in a big-city hospital. "In everyone's life, there are moments of great happiness . . . moments of deep sorrow," Carroll said at the beginning of each program. "There is doubt and deceit. But there is also hope, faith, and the courage to go on. I am Ann Gentry. Mine is such a story." Cal Kuhl directed the series.

AGAINST THE STORM

1939–1940	NBC Red	Mon.–Fri.	5:15 PM
1940–1941	NBC Red	Mon.–Fri.	11:30 AM
1941–1942	NBC Red	Mon.–Fri.	3 PM
1942–1949	(Off the air)		
1949–1950	Mutual	Mon.–Fri.	11:30 AM
1951–1952	ABC	Mon.–Fri.	10:45 AM

"Against the storm, keep thy head bowed, for the greatest storm the world has ever known came to an end one sunny morning" opened the "inspirational" 15-minute NBC daytime drama series *Against the Storm*, heard five days a week for twelve years.

The leading characters, Christy and Paul Cameron, were played by Gertrude Warner and then Claudia MORGAN and by Arnold MOSS, and then Alexander SCOURBY. Alan Devitt played the senior Mr. Cameron. Supporting roles were played by Roger DeKoven,

Sarah Burton, Florence Malone, James Monks, Walter Vaughn, William "Bill" Quinn, Charlotte Holland, Lawson Zerbe, Ethel Owen, Elliott Reid, Chester STRATTON, Joan Tompkins, Joan Alexander, Rex Ingram, Grant Richards, Sam Wanamaker, Ian Martin, baby impersonator Dolores Gillan, and Lenore Kingston.

Nelson CASE, Richard Stark, and Ralph EDWARDS announced the show at various times. Axel GRUENBERG directed, and Sandra Michael wrote the series. The program's familiar theme songs were "The Song of Bernadette" and "Ich Liebe Dich" (I Love You). Sponsors included Ivory flakes, Ivory soap, and Philip Morris cigarettes.

AIR ADVENTURES OF JIMMY ALLEN, THE

1933–1936	(Syndicated series. Various stations and times)
1936–1942	(Off the air)
1942	(Syndicated series. Various stations and times)

One of radio's earliest 15-minute, five-days-a-week children's adventure serials, *The Air Adventures of Jimmy Allen* originally starred Murray McLean as Jimmy Allen, a sixteen-year-old messenger and pilot-in-training at a Kansas City airport who became involved in numerous exciting, cliff-hanging air adventures. One of the series' best-remembered sequences was the great international air race, which included an exciting blind-luck landing by Jimmy in China, as well as a delayed parachute jump. In 1943, after being off the air for many years, the program made a brief comeback as a summer-replacement series. For both of its radio runs, the series was a syndicated program and was heard on hundreds of local stations around the country, mostly on Mutual network outlets, and it was sponsored by various local advertisers.

AL PEARCE AND HIS GANG (AKA WATCH THE FORDS GO BY)

1933–1935	(*)		
1935–1937	NBC Blue	Fri.	9 PM
1935–1937	CBS	Tues.	9 PM
1937–1938	NBC Red	Mon.	8 PM
1938–1940	CBS	Wed.	8 PM
1940–1942	CBS	Fri.	7:30 PM
1942–1943	(Off the air)		
1943–1944	NBC Blue	Sun.	4 PM
1944–1945	NBC Blue	Mon.–Fri.	3 PM
1945–1946	ABC	Mon–Fri.	3 PM

Several of radio's favorite comic characters were first heard on the half-hour *Al Pearce and His Gang*. Regular characters included Mr. Kitzel, played by Artie AUERBACH, who later became a popular character on *The* JACK BENNY SHOW; Lizzie Tish, played by Bill Comstock; the Laughing Lady, played by Kitty O' Neill;

Yahbut, played by Jennison Parker; and as "the human chatterbox," Arlene Harris, who did nonstop telephone monologues. Pearce himself introduced such comic creations as Elmer Blurt and Eb to the listening public, and they became popular characters with fans. Featured on the program at various times were singer Marie Green and her Merry Men, Elvia ALLMAN, and Alan REED.

At one point, the show was called *Watch the Fords Go By*, with the Ford Motor Company as its sponsor. Pepsodent, Grape Nuts, Dole pineapple juice, Camel cigarettes, and Dr. Pepper soda also sponsored the program.

Ken ROBERTS, Bill GOODWIN, and Wendell NILES each served as announcer. Sound effects—car crashes, doors slamming, and a variety of whistles and horns—heard on this program were executed expertly by technician Ray Erlenborn and others. The orchestra was conducted by Carl Hoff, then by Harry SOSNICK, and Larry Marsh. The program was written by Arthur Hargrove, Don Prindle, Roz Rogers, and Jennison Parker. Its theme songs were "Bojangles of Harlem" and "Ain't She Sweet?"

ALAN YOUNG SHOW, THE

1944	NBC	Wed.	9 PM
1944–1946	ABC	Tues.	8:30 PM
1946–1947	NBC	Fri.	8:30 PM
1947–1948	(Off the air)		
1948–1949	NBC	Tues.	8:30 PM

Comedian Alan Young, later star of the popular "Mr. Ed" TV series, had his own half-hour weekly comedy series on ABC in the late 1940s. He played a shy and retiring young man who worked in a grocery store. Charlie CANTOR, Louise ERICKSON, Jean Gillespie, Ed BEGLEY, and Ruth Perrott gave Alan expert comic support on the program, but it was actor and comedian Jim BACKUS who stole the show as the funny, rich snob Hubert Updike. James "Jimmy" WALLINGTON, Larry Elliott, and Michael Roy were the show's announcers, and Eddie Pola was its director. The show was written by Jay Sommers, Norman Paul, Dave Schwartz, and Sam Packard. Ipana toothpaste, Sal Hepatica, and Tums antacids sponsored the program.

ALDRICH FAMILY, THE

1939	NBC Red	Sun.	7 PM
1939–1940	NBC Blue	Tues.	8 PM
1940–1944	NBC Red	Thurs.	8:30 PM
1944–1946	CBS	Fri.	8 PM
1946–1952	NBC	Thurs.	8 PM
1952–1953	NBC	Sun.	7:30 PM

The Aldrich Family originated from a hit Broadway stage comedy, *What a Life* (1937), which was about a

(From left) Jackie Kelk (Homer) and Ezra Stone (Henry) are seen during an *Aldrich Family* broadcast. (NBC)

typical, middle-class, small-town American teenager named Henry Aldrich. The character was first heard on radio in 1938 as a featured ten-minute sketch on *The* RUDY VALLEE SHOW. It proved so popular among Vallee's large listening audience that *The Aldrich Family* sketches became a regular feature on *The* KATE SMITH HOUR program and eventually its own half-hour weekly series. Ezra STONE played the part of Henry Aldrich on Broadway and on radio and is the best-remembered actor to play the part. When Stone was unavailable, either Norman Tokar, Raymond Ives, Dickie Jones, or Bobby Ellis played Henry. Henry Aldrich was always getting into all sorts of teen trouble, but most of his problems usually concerned hopeful encounters with members of the opposite sex. Jackie KELK played Henry's pal, Homer: Clyde Fillmore, House JAMESON, and, for a short time, Tom Shirley played Henry's long-suffering father: Lea Penman, Mary Mason, Katherine Raht, Alice Yourman, and Regina Wallace played his mother. Ethel Wilson played Henry's Aunt Harriet.

Other actors who appeared on the series at various times included Betty Field, Jone Allison, Charita

Bauer, Mary Rolfe, Mary Shipp (as Henry's sister, Mary), and Ed BEGLEY, Bernard Lenrow, Ken Christy, Jean Gillespie, Arthur Vinton, Eddie BRACKEN, Agnes MOOREHEAD, Harlan Stone, Dick Van Patten, Patricia RYAN, and Ward Wilson. Announcers on the show included Dwight WEIST, Andre BARUCH, Dan SEYMOUR, Ralph Paul, George Byron, and Harry VON ZELL.

This half-hour series was on the air continuously for seventeen years, but amazingly the Henry Aldrich character never grew one year older. General Foods was the show's longtime sponsor. *The Aldrich Family* was directed and/or produced over the years by Bob Welsh, Sam Fuller, Edwin Duerr, Joseph Scibetta, Lester Vail, Day Tuttle, and George McGarrett. The series' writers included Norman Tokar, Ed Jurist, Frank Tarloff, Clifford Goldsmith, Phil Sharp, Sam Taylor, and Pat and Ed Joudry. The show's theme music was "This Is It."

ALEC TEMPLETON SHOW, THE

1939	NBC Red	Tues.	9:30 PM
1939–1940	NBC Red	Mon.	9:30 PM
1940–1941	NBC Red	Fri.	7:30 PM
1941–1943	(Off the air)		
1943	NBC Blue	Mon., Wed., Fri.	10:30 PM

Blind pianist Alec Templeton was one of radio's most successful pop musicians in the early 1940s. His half-hour program was heard and enjoyed by millions of listeners each week. Appearing with Templeton on his program were singer Edna O'Neill and Billy Mills and His Orchestra. Fort Pearson was the show's announcer. Templeton's sponsors included Johnson wax, Alka Seltzer antacid, and Dubonnet wine.

ALEY, ALBERT (1919–1986)

Actor-writer-producer Albert Aley was born in New York City. A beautiful child whose parents were of Dutch and Spanish extraction, Aley became a model when he was five years old and attended the Professional Children's School in New York. The school principal, impressed with Aley's talents and good looks, introduced him to Nila MACK, director of CBS's successful children's program LET'S PRETEND. He became a member of the show's regular cast in 1929 and remained with it until the early 1950s. When Mack went on vacation in 1938, Aley directed a *Let's Pretend* episode, and CBS billed him as "radio's youngest director." As a young actor, Aley was also heard on such radio programs as *The* AMERICAN SCHOOL OF THE AIR, STELLA DALLAS, and *Sunday Mornings at Aunt Susan's*. The same year he directed the *Let's Pretend* show, Aley also wrote a script for the FIRST NIGHTER series and was then called "radio's youngest writer" by radio fan magazines. In 1942, Aley began to write scripts for such programs as *Superstition,* HOP HARRI-GAN, and DON WINSLOW OF THE NAVY.

In 1952, Aley decided to concentrate on writing and became the executive producer and chief writer of *The* TOM CORBETT, SPACE CADET series, which he also produced for television. The show was one of television's earliest children's show successes. Aley continued to write television scripts for such TV series as "Cheyenne" (1958), "Have Gun, Will Travel" (1957), "The Rifleman" (1958), and "Laramie" (1959). He wrote the screenplay for Walt Disney's *The Ugly Dachshund* (1966) and became the head writer and producer of the "Cimarron Strip" (1962) and "Ironsides" (1966) series. Aley also produced the popular "Paper Chase" (1970) programs. He retired in the early 1980s.

ALIAS JIMMY VALENTINE

| 1937–1938 | NBC | Tues. | 9:30 PM |
| 1938–1939 | NBC | Mon. | 7 PM |

It wasn't often that a criminal became the hero on a radio series, but that is exactly what happened when NBC presented the half-hour *Alias Jimmy Valentine* series. Valentine, a reformed safecracker, was the creation of short-story writer O. Henry ("The Retrieved Reformation"). In 1909, Paul Armstrong adapted the story into the popular stage play, *Alias Jimmy Valentine.* On the radio series, Valentine, whose real name was Lee Randall (thus the "Alias" in the title), used his safecracking abilties and former criminal contacts to aid the forces of law and order. The role of Valentine was played by Bert LYTELL and then by James MEIGHAN. Dick Joy announced the show. Doris Halman was one of the show's major writers. Edgeworth pipe tobacco and Dr. Lyon's toothpaste sponsored the series. Frank and Anne Hummert produced it for radio.

ALL THINGS CONSIDERED

| 1971–present | NPR | Mon.–Fri. | 6 PM |

NATIONAL PUBLIC RADIO's early evening news magazine program set new standards for broadcast journalism when it first went on the air more than twenty years ago. Today, it continues to be one of the finest in-depth news programs on radio. This one-hour offering has been hosted by Susan Stamberg, Noah Adams, and several others and airs detailed features such as interviews with political, social, and show-business celebrities, and on-the-spot reports from international locales and news reports by such regular NPR news staffers as Robert Siegel, Deborah Amos, Neal Conan, Scott Simon, Deborah Wang, Lou Carpenter, Andrew Dietrich, Eileen Weiss, and Nina Tottenberg. During the Gulf War challenge in 1991, NPR provided around-the-clock live coverage and twenty-four-hour newscasts. MORNING EDITION and *All Things Considered* extended into the late evening to bring all the news of this confrontation. As the need for national dialogue grew, NPR brought an afternoon call-in program to the airwaves to meet the challenge.

ALLEN, BARBARA JO ("VERA VAGUE": 1904–1974)

An accomplished dramatic actress heard on such radio programs as ONE MAN'S FAMILY, DEATH VALLEY DAYS, I LOVE A MYSTERY, and HAWTHORNE HOUSE, Barbara Jo Allen was born in New York City and attended the University of California and the Sorbonne in Paris. Allen first introduced the down-to-earth, comically man-hungry Vera Vague character on the *Matinee* series in 1939 and later brought her to such comedy shows as *The* BOB HOPE SHOW, *The* JIMMY DURANTE SHOW, AL PEARCE AND HIS GANG, and *The* EDGAR BERGEN–CHARLIE MCCARTHY SHOW. The actress also appeared in numerous films including *Melody Ranch* (1940), *Larceny, Inc.* (1942), *Rosie the Riveter* (1944), and *The Opposite Sex* (1956). The actress retired from show business in the mid-1960s.

ALLEN, FRED (JOHN F. SULLIVAN: 1894–1956)

With his nasal, flat-sounding voice and his droll, intelligent wit, comedian Fred Allen (who claimed he took his professional name from "a Revolutionary War figure who wasn't using it") was one of radio's biggest stars.

Allen was born and raised in Sommerville, Massachusetts. As a young man, he worked in the Boston Public Library, where he said he developed a love of literature and "read everything" he "could get his hands on." He also became an expert juggler and began to perform professionally on the vaudeville stage. Fred told a few jokes as he juggled, and audiences responded with laughter. As a vaudeville headliner, he found success on Broadway in *The Passing Parade* (1915), *The Little Show* (1929), and *Three's a Crowd* (1930), and later became a radio star.

Allen was as good a writer as he was a performer, and he wrote most of his own material. His first radio appearance was on a program called *The Linit Bath Club Review,* which was followed by several other programs that did not bear his name until, finally, he starred on *The* FRED ALLEN SHOW. Fred was the first comedian to appeal to his listeners' imaginations through sound effects, spoofs of current news items, and outrageous and satirical situations rather than through the typical vaudeville routines (little more than plays on words) relied upon by so many other radio comedians. Because of Allen's genius, the sound of radio comedy changed for the better.

Fred Allen (CBS)

In addition to his work on radio, Allen also appeared in several motion pictures, such as *Thanks a Million* (1935), *It's in the Bag* (1945), *We're Not Married* (1952), and *Full House* (1953). Shortly before he died, Allen was seen on TV on "The All Star Review" (1953), was a regular panelist on "What's My Line?" (1951), and hosted "Judge for Yourself" (1953).

ALLEN, GRACIE

See BURNS AND ALLEN.

ALLEN, MEL (MELVIN ALLEN ISRAEL: 1913–   )

Born in Birmingham, Alabama, announcer-sportscaster Mel Allen attended the University of Alabama and then Columbia University law school. He became a broadcaster for the University of Alabama's radio station after he graduated. Mel made his network broadcasting debut in 1935 on a show called *Liberty News Flashes*.

In 1936, CBS hired him as a staff announcer, and he went on to become one of radio's busiest announcers and then sportscasters. As an announcer, Allen introduced such programs as the THIS DAY IS OURS, HER HONOR, NANCY JAMES, *One Hundred Men and a Girl*, VIC AND SADE, and TRUTH OR CONSEQUENCES. Well known to sports fans as "The Voice of the Yank-

ees," Allen did the play-by-play for the New York Yankees baseball team on CBS for many years and was one of the major sportscasters of the annual World Series. Allen was also the on-the-spot sportscaster at the Kentucky Derby races and for the Giants football team.

ALLISON, FRAN (1908–1989)

Although she had a substantial radio career, Fran Allison was best known as the actress who talked to hand puppets Kukla and Ollie on NBC–TV's popular "Kukla, Fran, and Ollie" show in the late 1940s and early 1950s. But for more than thirty years, she played the humorous gossip, Aunt Fanny, a lady who had a story for every occasion and whose theme song was "She's Only a Bird in a Gilded Cage" on Don McNeill's BREAKFAST CLUB radio program.

Allison, who was born in Waterloo, Iowa, became an actress after teaching school for a few years. She played the role of Clara on CLARA, LU, AND EM, which is said to have been one of radio's first daytime drama series. She also costarred with Forrest Lewis on the MEET THE MEEKS radio series. Allison retired from show business after leaving the "Kukla, Fran, and Ollie Show" in the late 1950s.

ALLMAN, ELVIA (ELVIA A. PYLE: 1904–1992)

Actress-comedienne Elvia Allman, whose gushingly loud voice was heard on numerous radio shows throughout the 1930s, 1940s, and 1950s, was born in Concord, North Carolina. She debuted as a radio actress in 1930 on WHJ in Los Angeles on the *Uncle John's Children's Hour* program.

Allman specialized in playing aggressive, overbearing characters and was a regular on such programs as BLONDIE (as Cora Dithers), *The* BOB HOPE SHOW, *The* JACK BENNY SHOW, *The* JIMMY DURANTE SHOW, BURNS AND ALLEN, FIBBER MCGEE AND MOLLY, ABBOTT AND COSTELLO, *Town Hall Tonight, The* EDGAR BERGEN-CHARLIE MCCARTHY SHOW, CINNAMON BEAR, and AL PEARCE AND HIS GANG. She also appeared in many Hollywood films of that era and was often featured on such television situation-comedy and variety shows as "I Love Lucy" (1951) and "The Jack Benny Show" (1952).

AMANDA OF HONEYMOON HILL

1940–1941	NBC Blue	Mon.–Fri.	3:15 PM
1941–1943	CBS	Mon.–Fri.	10:30 AM
1943–1945	CBS	Mon.–Fri.	11 AM

Frank and Anne HUMMERT, the producers, writers, and sometime directors of many of radio's most popular programs, were responsible for the 15-minute, five-days-a-week daytime drama series *Amanda of Honey-*

moon Hill. The show debuted in 1940 and became a very successful addition to NBC's ever-increasing list of daytime serial offerings.

The show's opening best described the program's basic premise. *"Amanda of Honeymoon Hill,"* the announcer began, "the story of love and marriage in America's romantic South. The story of Amanda and Edward Leighton, *Amanda of Honeymoon Hill* is laid in a world few Americans know."

Joy Hathaway played Amanda, the poor girl who married a rich young Southern boy; Boyd Crawford, George Lambert, and Staats COTSWORTH were heard, at various times, as her rich husband, Edward. Jackie KELK, Evie Juster, Juano Hernandez, Roger DeKoven, Helen Shields, Ruth Yorke, Alice REINHEART, Muriel Stark, Jack MacBryde, John Brown, Cecil Roy, Rod Hendrickson, Joy Meredith, Reese Taylor, Linda Watkins, Florence Malone, and many other actors had ongoing roles on this series at one time or another. Frank Gallop, Hugh Conover, John Paul King, and Howard Clancy each announced the show. The series was directed by Ernest Rocca, Stephen Goss, and Arnold Michaels and was written by Elizabeth Todd. At one time, the show's theme music was "Jeannie with the Light Brown Hair." Cal-Aspirin, Haley's MO, Phillips Milk of Magnesia antacids and toothpaste, and Ironized yeast tablets sponsored the series.

AMAZING MR. MALONE, THE (AKA MURDER AND MR. MALONE)

1947–1948	ABC	Sat.	9:30 PM
1948–1949	ABC	Sat.	8:30 PM
1949–1950	ABC	Wed.	8 PM
1950–1951	ABC	Fri.	9 PM

This half-hour ABC mystery-adventure series featured a private detective named Malone, who was a master crime solver, played in turns by Eugene Raymond, Frank LOVEJOY, and George Petrie. The program, which was sustained by ABC, was directed by Bill Rousseau and written by Gene Wang.

AMECHE, DON (DOMINIC FELIX AMICI: 1908–1993)

Singer, actor, and radio-program host Don Ameche was born in Kenosha, Wisconsin, to parents of Spanish-German-Italian-Scottish-Irish descent. Ameche originally studied law in college but turned to theater and made his stage debut as an actor in 1930.

In Chicago, he appeared on the FIRST NIGHTER program. Subsequently, he became the star of many popular network radio shows, including *The* DON AMECHE SHOW, *The* EDGAR BERGEN–CHARLIE MCCARTHY SHOW, *The* CHASE AND SANBORN HOUR (again with Bergen), GRAND HOTEL, JACK ARMSTRONG, ALL AMERICAN BOY, *The* JIMMY DURANTE SHOW, *The* NATIONAL HOME AND FARM HOUR, and *The Old Gold Show,* on which the Bickersons sketches were introduced.

An Adam-and-Eve sketch written by Arch Obler, performed by Ameche and screen siren Mae West on a *Chase and Sanborn Hour* in the late 1930s was considered very risqué, mainly because of West's very obvious sexual innuendos. Thereafter, all radio programs were carefully censored.

In addition to his radio performances, Ameche became a major motion-picture star in the late 1930s and appeared in such classic films as *The Story of Alexander Graham Bell* (1939), *Alexander's Ragtime Band* (1938), and *Heaven Can Wait* (1943). On Broadway, Ameche starred in the Cole Porter musical comedy *Silk Stockings.*

In 1986, Ameche won the Academy Award as Best Supporting Actor for his performance in Ron Howard's film *Cocoon.* Ameche continued to work in films and on TV until shortly before he died.

See also BICKERSONS, *The.*

AMECHE, JIM (JAMES AMICI: 1915–1983)

Like his brother Don, Jim Ameche was born in Kenosha, Wisconsin, and had a very active career as a radio performer. Jim played the title role on the popular JACK ARMSTRONG, ALL AMERICAN BOY children's daytime adventure serial for several years and was also prominently featured on such programs as *Attorney at Law,* BIG SISTER, GRAND CENTRAL STATION, ARMSTRONG OF THE SBI, *Hollywood Playhouse,* HERE'S TO ROMANCE, *Win Your Lady, The* LUX RADIO THEATER, *The* TEXACO STAR THEATER, and SILVER EAGLE. Ameche continued to work as a radio and TV announcer until illness forced him to retire in the late 1970s.

AMERICAN ALBUM OF FAMILIAR MUSIC, THE

1931–1932	NBC Red	Sun.	9:15 PM
1932–1933	NBC Red	Sun.	9 PM
1933–1942	NBC Red	Sun.	9:30 PM
1942–1950	NBC	Sun.	9:30 PM
1950–1951	ABC	Sun.	9:30 PM

For twenty years, *The American Album of Familiar Music* was one of the most popular classical and semiclassical music programs on radio. This one-hour NBC network show featured such music celebrities as tenors Frank MUNN and Donald Dane, sopranos Evelyn McGregor, Jean Dickenson ("The Nightingale of the Airwaves"), Elizabeth Lennox, the Buckingham Choir, Bertrand Hirsch, Daniel Liebenfeld, pianists Arden and Arden, and Gustave Haenschen's Orchestra. The program was produced by Frank and Anne HUMMERT.

The format of the show presented various songs introduced simply by mellow-voiced announcers such as Andre BARUCH, Roger Krupp, and Howard Clancy. The fact that this program had little, if any, commentary made it unique and undoubtedly added to its appeal to music lovers.

The series was directed for many years by James Haupt and written by various NBC and ABC staff writers. Bayer aspirin sponsored the show. "Dream Serenade" was the program's theme music.

AMERICAN BROADCASTING COMPANY (ABC)

The American Broadcasting Company's history actually began when the Radio Corporation of America's NATIONAL BROADCASTING COMPANY (NBC) found itself with an excess of affiliated stations in the same cities. The Federal Communications Commission claimed that the Radio Corporation of America was operating a monopoly and forced it to relinquish one of the networks. The Radio Corporation of America had two NBC networks, Red and Blue. NBC retained the Red network as its sole radio broadcasting outlet.

In 1943, Edward J. Noble, owner of the Life Savers candy company, bought NBC's Blue network and one year later renamed it the American Broadcasting Company (ABC). Noble was determined to make his new Red network a "quality" group of stations. For many years, Noble refused to allow daytime serial drama programs on his network, convinced that they catered to overly romantic and sentimental tastes.

In 1949, under a consent decree in a U.S. antitrust suit, the government sought to separate motion-picture companies from theater ownership, and Paramount Theaters was divorced from Paramount Pictures. In 1953, Paramount Theaters merged with the American Broadcasting Company.

AMERICAN FORUM OF THE AIR (AKA MUTUAL FORUM HOUR)

1935–1937	Mutual	(Times varied)	
1937–1943	Mutual	Sun.	7 PM
1943–1949	Mutual	Tues.	(*)
1949–1956	NBC	Sun.	(*)

Originally called *The Mutual Forum Hour*, this half-hour Mutual network discussion program was created, hosted, and moderated by Theodore Granik and produced and directed for many years by Larry Dorn. The program was one of the most effective political shows on the air, and the discussions quite often became very heated. Celebrated political commentators and observers such as Donald Nelson, Leon Henderson, Rear Admiral Land, Francis Biddle, Dorothy Thompson, and William Allen White were frequent guests. Mr. Granik's skillful and diplomatic moderation always brought the show back on target, even when the discussions resulted in some vicious name calling. Granik often stated that his sole purpose in presenting *The American Forum of the Air* was "to promote free speech." For a time, the series was sponsored by the American Truckers Association.

AMERICAN MELODY HOUR

1941–1942	NBC Blue	Wed.	10 PM
1942–1947	CBS	Tues.	7:30 PM
1947–1948	CBS	Wed.	8 PM

One of the most popular classical and semiclassical music programs on the air in the 1940s, *The American Melody Hour* featured singers such as Vivian DELLA CHIESA, Conrad Thibault, Frank *Munn*, Jane PICKENS, who performed selections by such composers as Handel, Mozart, Gershwin, and Léhar. Frank Black led the program's orchestra. Andre BARUCH, among others, introduced the music heard on the program. The series was sponsored for many years by Bayer aspirin.

AMERICAN PUBLIC RADIO

American Public Radio, which was formed in 1983, is a competitor of NATIONAL PUBLIC RADIO. The service offers features that can be heard for twenty-four hours a day. It is available to local public radio stations that do not subscribe to National Public Radio programs offered at the same times. American Public Radio provides national and international news coverage, music programs such as *Music Through the Night*, and even rebroadcasts of programs that had originally been heard on the CANADIAN BROADCASTING CORPORATION (CBC) or on the British Broadcasting Corporation (BBC).

AMERICAN SCHOOL OF THE AIR, THE

| 1930–1948 | CBS | Tues., Thurs. | 2:30 PM, 9:15 AM, 5 PM |

CBS staff announcer Robert Trout was the longtime host of this daily program, which was "required listening" for many American schoolchildren in the 1930s, 1940s, and 1950s. Dramatizations of important historical events, adaptations of works of literature, and contemporary news happenings were regularly featured on this sustained program. The touring Hamilton family—played by Gene Leonard and Betty GARDE as Mr. and Mrs. Hamilton, and James Monks, Ruth Russell, Walter TETLEY, and Albert ALEY as the Hamilton children—gave daily geography lessons as they "traveled" around the world.

A regular one-hour feature on CBS for almost eighteen years, the series won many awards from educational and governmental agencies. Educator Dr. Lyman Brysson and actors Ray COLLINS, Jack "Jackie" Jordan, Miriam WOLFE, Gwen DAVIES, Mitzi Gould, Parker FENNELLY, Chester STRATTON, and others made regular appearances on the program. *The American School of the Air* had a long list of directors over the years. This list includes Earle McGill, Leon Levine, Albert Ward, Marx Loeb, Brewster Morgan, Howard Barnes, Oliver Daniel, Richard Sanville, Kirby Hawkes, Robert L. Hudson, and John Dietz. The show was written by Howard Rodman, Edward Mabley, and Harry Granich.

AMERICA'S TOWN MEETING OF THE AIR

1935–1940	NBC Blue	Thurs.	9:30 PM
1940–1942	NBC Blue	Thurs.	9 PM
1942–1945	NBC Blue	Thurs.	8:30 PM
1945–1947	ABC	Thurs.	8:30 PM
1947–1949	ABC	Tues.	8:30 PM
1949–1954	ABC	Tues.	9 PM
1954–1956	ABC	Sun.	8 PM

Topics of national importance were discussed on this one-hour weekly audience-participation/news program. Guest panelists would answer questions asked by people in a studio audience. George V. Denney, Jr., moderated this show, which originated from Town Hall in New York City. Announcers for the series included Ed HERLIHY, Gene Kirby, and George Gunn. The program was directed by Wylie Adams, Richard Ritter, and Leonard Blair. *Reader's Digest* magazine was the program's longtime sponsor.

AMOS AND ANDY

1929–1930	NBC Blue	Mon.–Fri.	7 PM
1930–1932	NBC Blue	Mon.–Sat	7 PM
1932–1936	NBC Blue	Mon.–Fri	7 PM
1936–1938	NBC Red	Mon.–Fri	7 PM
1938–1943	CBS	Mon.–Fri	7 PM
1943–1945	NBC	Fri.	10 PM
1945–1948	NBC	Tues.	9 PM
1948–1954	CBS	Sun.	7:30 PM
1954–1960	(Various times and stations)		

Celebrated Irish playwright George Bernard Shaw once remarked, "There are only three things I'll never forget about America: the Rocky Mountains, Niagara Falls, and Amos and Andy on the radio." One of radio's all-time favorite programs, *Amos and Andy* was originally known as *Sam and Henry* when it went on the air in 1926. Its title was changed to *Amos and Andy* in 1928, when the show's stars changed stations. *Amos and Andy* remained on the air for thirty-four more years, making it the longest-running series in radio history. In 1931, *Amos and Andy* was so popular that it had a regular listening audience of more than 40 million people—a record for that time.

Set in New York City's Harlem, Amos and Andy owned the "Fresh Air Taxi Company," so called because they had only one very dilapidated, roofless taxicab. The main characters on the half-hour series were two African-American men, although the actors who played the parts, Freeman GOSDEN and Charles CORRELL, were white. One of the most popular characters on the show (the central character when the program was seen on television) was Amos and Andy's smooth-talking friend, George "Kingfish" Stevens, who had a million "get-rich-quick" schemes. This part was played by Charles Correll, who also played Amos on the program. Regular cast members, many of whom *were* black actors, included Elinor Harriott as Ruby Taylor; Harriette WIDMER and Amanda RANDOLPH as Madam Queen; Terry Howard as Arabella; Lou Lubin as Shorty, the barber; Ernestine Wade, who played such characters as Sapphire Stevens, Sarah "Needlenose" Fletcher, and Mrs. Henry Van Porter; Eddie Green as Stonewall, the lawyer (who was known as Calhoun the lawyer on the TV series); and Madaline Lee as the duo's secretary Miss Blue, whom Andy always signaled by calling, "Buzz me, Miss Blue!"

In 1951, a television version of *Amos and Andy*, produced by Gosden and Correll, was launched on CBS. Even though the TV series featured an all-black cast (Tim Moore as Kingfish, Alvin Childress as Andy, and Spencer Williams as Amos) and was extremely popular with the public, it was canceled in 1953 amid a storm of protest by civil-rights groups that claimed the program fostered "unflattering racial stereotyping." In spite of this setback, the *Amos and Andy* radio program remained on the air, with Gosden and Correll continuing to play the leads until 1960.

The executive producers of the *Amos and Andy* radio programs were Bob Connolly and Bill Moser, and the series was directed by Glenn Middleton and Andrew Love. Writers included Gosden and Correll, Bob Connolly, Bill Moser, Octavius Roy Cohen, Bob Fisher, Robert J. Ross, Bob Moss, Arthur Slander, Paul Franklin, Harvey Helm, and Shirley Ilo. Bill HAY was the show's longtime announcer; Del SHARBUTT, Olan SOULE, and Harlow WILCOX subsequently announced the series. *Amos and Andy's* familiar theme songs were "The Perfect Song" and "Angel's Serenade." Sponsors of *Amos and Andy* over the years included Rexall drugs, Ironized yeast tablets, Pepsodent toothpaste, Campbell's soups, Rinso cleanser, Vimms vitamins, Lifebuoy soap, Swan soap, and Chrysler automobiles.

ANDERSON, ARTHUR (1922–   )

Born on Staten Island in New York City, Arthur Anderson was one of radio's busiest juvenile performers in the late 1930s. He regularly played on Orson WELLES'S MERCURY THEATER ON THE AIR program, most notably starring as Jim in Welles's adaptation of *Treasure Island* on that program.

The cast of *Amos and Andy*—(from left) Lou Lubin, Madaline Lee, Charles Correll (Amos), Ruby Dandridge, Freeman Gosden (Andy), and Eddie Green—during a broadcast. The Jubalaires singing quartet are seen behind the actors. (NBC)

Anderson, who first acted at the Children's Theater on Staten Island, was heard on many other dramatic anthology programs and on other series as well. A longtime regular on Nila MACK's celebrated LET'S PRE-TEND children's program, he also performed frequently on shows such as the HELEN HAYES THEATER and *Tony and Gus* (his first radio acting job in 1935)

and was also a supporting player in the 1970s on the RADIO PLAYHOUSE series *The Little Things In Life*.

Anderson continues to appear on radio and TV commercials: he was heard as the voice of Lucky the Leprechaun in the Lucky Charms candy commercials for twenty-nine years. He can be seen in such films as *The Group* (1966), *Death Dream* (1972), and *Green*

Card (1990). Off-Broadway, Anderson was featured in *The Fantasticks* (1960) and on Broadway in *1776* (1970). Finally, he is the author of a book about his time on *Let's Pretend* that was published in 1994.

ANDERSON, EDDIE "ROCHESTER" (1906–1977)

One of the reasons for the immense popularity of *The* JACK BENNY SHOW on radio was its wonderful cast of supporting players. Without question, the program's favorite was Jack's black valet, Rochester, played by actor Eddie Anderson. Born in Oakland, California, Anderson became a professional actor at fourteen years of age and appeared on the Pantages vaudeville circuit.

He had a gruff, gravelly voice that was the result of a childhood illness, and it proved to be a blessing in disguise as far as his performing career was concerned. His unusual voice made his unique, wonderful comic timing and such predictable remarks as his sarcastic "Ok, Boss" and his "Oh! Oh!! Ohhhh!!!!!"—usually said with a growing understanding of something he heard—one of the show's best assets.

In addition to his work on Benny's show, Anderson appeared in several films including *Gone with the Wind* (1939), *Buck Benny Rides Again* (1940), *Cabin in the Sky* (1943), and *It's a Mad, Mad, Mad, Mad World* (1963).

Eddie "Rochester" Anderson of *The Jack Benny Show* (CBS)

He was also a regular cast member on Jack Benny's TV series.

ANDRE KOSTELANETZ (AKA THE CHESTERFIELD PROGRAM; TUNE UP TIME; THE PAUSE THAT REFRESHES)

1931	CBS	Sun.	5:30 PM
1931–1932	CBS	Wed.	10:15 PM
1931–1933	CBS	Sun.	8:15 PM
1933–1934	CBS	Mon., Thurs	9:15 PM
1934–1935	CBS	Mon., Wed., Sat.	9 PM
1935–1936	CBS	Wed., Sat.	9 PM
1936–1938	CBS	Wed.	9 PM
1938–1939	(Off the air)		
1939–1940	CBS	Mon.	8 PM
1940–1944	CBS	Sun.	4:30 PM
1944–1945	(Off the air)		
1945–1946	CBS	Thurs.	9 PM
1946–1947	(Off the air)		
1947–1949	CBS	Sun.	6:30 PM

This program featured music conductor Andre KOSTELANETZ, who also starred on several other popular classical and semiclassical music programs heard on the CBS network over the years. Humorist Robert Benchley and musicologist Deems TAYLOR hosted the series. Among the musical celebrities who guest-starred on this hour-long series were singers Albert Spaulding, Lawrence Tibbett, Lily Pons, and Nino Martini. David Ross was the program's announcer. The series was sponsored by Chesterfield cigarettes, Ethyl fuel oil, Coca-Cola, and Chrysler automobiles.

ANDREWS SISTERS, THE (PATTY: 1920–   ; MAXENE: 1918–   ; LAVERNE: 1915–1967)

Born in Minneapolis, Minnesota, the swing-singing trio had a Greek and Norwegian background and as children were great admirers of the singing BOSWELL sisters. The girls auditioned for Larry Rich's touring "Kiddie Show" in 1936 when the show was playing in Minneapolis; their close, three-part harmonies impressed him. When they were asked to join the show, their professional singing career was launched. A hit recording of an old Yiddish song, "Bei Mir Bist du Shoen" in 1940 catapulted the sisters into overnight stardom; soon they were featured on numerous radio programs as well as in such films as *Buck Privates* (1941), *In the Navy* (1941), and *The Road to Rio* (1947). Numerous hit recordings—among them "Apple Blossom Time," "The Beer Barrel Polka," and "Rum and Coca Cola"—followed.

The sisters starred on radio on the ANDREWS SISTERS' EIGHT-TO-THE-BAR RANCH, as well as on the CLUB FIFTEEN program for several seasons. They were frequent guest stars on *The* BING CROSBY–KRAFT MUSIC HALL, *The* BOB HOPE SHOW, *The* FRED ALLEN SHOW, COMMAND PERFORMANCE, MAIL CALL, *The* TEXACO THE-

ATER, and many other programs. The Andrews Sisters provided the singing voices for characters in the Walt Disney feature-length cartoon films *Make Mine Music* (1946) and *Melody Time* (1948). Laverne died in 1967, but Patty and Maxene starred in the Broadway show *Over Here* in the 1970s. Patty and Maxene continue to make personal appearances, although not together.

ANDREWS SISTERS' EIGHT-TO-THE-BAR RANCH, THE (AKA THE ANDREWS SISTERS SHOW; N–K MUSICAL SHOW)

1944–1945	NBC Blue	Sun.	4:30 PM
1945–1946	CBS	Wed.	10:30 PM

When *The Andrews Sisters' Eight-to-the-Bar Ranch,* a half-hour show, was first aired in 1945, the ANDREWS SISTERS—Patty, Maxene, and Laverne—ran a fictional dude ranch out West. Movie veteran character-actor George "Gabby" Hayes offered a bit of comic relief, and a somewhat feeble story line was sandwiched in between the sisters' singing. Before the end of the first season, the Western setting was abandoned and the girls obtained a new costar, singer Curt Massey. Thereafter, the sisters and Massey simply sang, and all attempts at a story line vanished. Andre BARUCH and Marvin MILLER were the show's announcers, and guest stars on the program included such show-business luminaries as Bing CROSBY, Ethel MERMAN, Hoagy Carmichael, Gene AUSTIN, Al PEARCE, and ABBOTT AND COSTELLO.

The orchestra was conducted by Vic Schoen, and the girls' theme music was "Apple Blossom Time," one of their hit records. Manny Mannheim and Stanley Davis directed the series, which was produced by Lou Levy. *The Andrews Sisters' Show* was written by Cottonseed Clark, Stanley Davis, Elon Parker, and

The Andrews Sisters: (from left) Maxene, Patty, and Laverne (Paramount)

Joe Errens. Nash-Kelvinator sponsored the program's second season.

ANNOUNCERS

In addition to acting as spokesmen for various sponsors' products and reading the opening and closing of programs, many announcers, during the "Golden Age of Radio" (the 1930s and 1940s), became featured performers on the shows they were announcing and achieved stardom in their own right. Announcers often became inextricably identified with a particular show or performer: Don WILSON, for example, was known for his work on *The* JACK BENNY SHOW; Harry VON ZELL for the BURNS AND ALLEN *Show;* Harlow WILCOX for his appearances on FIBBER MCGEE AND MOLLY; Peter DONALD for acting and announcing on *The* FRED ALLEN SHOW; Milton CROSS for his METROPOLITAN OPERA BROADCASTS; Andre BARUCH for YOUR HIT PARADE; and Bill HAY for heralding AMOS AND ANDY. Announcer Ed HERLIHY became particularly well known for being the spokesman for Kraft foods, as was Frank Knight as announcer on the *Longine's Symphonette* program. Other announcers' names were familiar to radio listeners at that time because of the impressive number of programs they were associated with: George Ansbro, Ralph EDWARDS (who became the host and star of the popular TRUTH AND CONSEQUENCES program), Mel ALLEN, Bert PARKS (later of Miss America fame), Bill GOODWIN, Hugh James, Verne Smith, Jimmy WALLINGTON, Ford BOND, Tom Carr, and many others.

ANSWER MAN, THE

1937–1956	Mutual	Mon.–Fri.	(Times varied)

Albert Mitchell was "the Answer Man" and Don Cope the host of this 15-minute, early-evening information program. This syndicated show was heard on WOR in New York City and on other stations around the country. A wide variety of questions sent in by listeners were read by Cope and answered by Mitchell. The program was very successful and had a large following the entire decade it was on the air. The show was written by Bruce Chapman.

ANTHONY, JOHN J. (LESTER KROLL, 1898–1970)

Advice-giver John J. Anthony was born in New York City. After attending school in Europe, Anthony became interested in the "inequalities of the marital laws in this nation, as compared to Europe" and opened a center called the Marital Relations Institute. A local radio series that originated in New York City in 1930 was an immediate success and eventually led to a syndicated series of programs. In 1937, Anthony hosted *The* GOODWILL HOUR, on which he answered questions from listeners about their various personal problems, gave advice, and lectured about many other subjects. Anthony's famous lines, "No names, please" and "What is your problem, madam?" became much quoted throughout the nation. His book, *Marriage and Family Problems,* became a best-seller in the 1940s. The celebrated advice-giver continued to broadcast on local radio station WOR in New York City until shortly before his death.

ANTONINI, ALFREDO (1901–1983)

CBS musical conductor Alfredo Antonini was a versatile musician and a world-famous authority of folk, modern, operatic, and symphonic music. Born in Milan, Italy, Antonini won a scholarship to the Royal Conservatory of Music and assisted Arturo Toscanini at La Scala before moving to New York and joining the CBS music staff. At CBS, Antonini led the Pan American Orchestra, which was featured on numerous concert broadcasts and on the *Yours for a Song* program.

ARCHER, JOHN (RALPH BOWMAN: 1915–   )

Oceola, Nebraska-born John Archer is known on radio for being one of the actors who played "The SHADOW" (also known as Lamont Cranston). It was during the years 1944 and 1945 that he had the role. Archer was also regularly heard on *The* FBI IN PEACE AND WAR series, in which he played Field Agent Shephard, and the QUICK AS A FLASH quiz program. Archer was also one of Hollywood's most reliable actors, playing supporting and leading roles in many motion pictures including *Guadalcanal Diary* (1945) and *Colorado Territory* (1949). The actor was also featured in several stage shows around the country and appeared on television series such as "Gunsmoke" (1957) and "Perry Mason" (1957–1960).

ARCHIE ANDREWS, THE ADVENTURES OF

See ADVENTURES OF ARCHIE ANDREWS, *The.*

ARDEN, EVE (EUNICE QUEDENS: 1912–1990)

Hollywood film comedienne Eve Arden was known for droll wisecracks and sophisticated style. Equally popular on radio, TV and in films, she was most famous as English teacher Connie Brooks on OUR MISS BROOKS.

Arden, who was a Broadway Ziegfeld showgirl before becoming a film actress, was born in Mill Valley, California. The actress was prominently featured on such radio shows as *The* SEALTEST VILLAGE STORE, *The* KEN MURRAY SHOW, and *The* DANNY KAYE SHOW. She also played major supporting roles in numerous films including *Stage Door* (1937), *Mildred*

Eve Arden was English teacher Connie Brooks on *Our Miss Brooks.* (CBS)

Pierce (1945), *Anatomy of a Murder* (1959), *The Dark at the Top of the Stairs* (1962), and *Grease* (1978).

Arden starred in a television version of "Our Miss Brooks" (1953), "The Eve Arden Show" (1957–1958), and "The Mothers-in-Law" (1967–1969).

ARLIN, HAROLD W. (1895–1986)

Harold W. Arlin is reported to have been radio's first "actual" announcer. It is said that, while a staff member at KDKA in Pittsburgh (where he was born) in the early 1920s, Arlin was the first person to announce a feature as it was about to go on the air. The practice thereafter became commonplace.

Arlin was also one of the first broadcasters to give an on-the-air, play-by-play account of a football game—a game between the universities of West Virginia and Pittsburgh in the late 1920s—and the first announcer to introduce such world-famous celebrities as American William Jennings Bryant, Englishman David Lloyd George, and French Field Marshal Foch to radio listeners. Arlin remained active for many years, continuing his announcing at a small Pittsburgh radio station.

ARMED FORCES RADIO SERVICE

The Armed Forces Radio Service, which is presently called the Armed Forces Radio and Television Service, marked its fiftieth anniversary in 1992. Started by the United States Army during World War II, it was a means of boosting the morale of American troops who were stationed at various military installations around the world. The service broadcasted recorded American radio programs that had already been heard by the general public in the States. Special variety-comedy shows such as COMMAND PERFORMANCE, MAIL CALL, and JUBILEE featured major stage and screen stars including Bob HOPE, Bing CROSBY, Betty Grable, Bette Davis, Ginny SIMMS, and Dinah SHORE. These stars worked gratis for the privilege of entertaining the U. S. armed forces and aiding the war effort.

Well after World War II ended, the service continued to broadcast prerecorded shows, but in the early 1960s emphasis began to shift to disc-jockey shows airing popular music of the day. During the Vietnam War, offbeat army disc-jockey Adrian Cronauer, whose wartime broadcasting experiences in the late 1960s and early 1970s were portrayed by Robin Williams in the film *Good Morning, Vietnam,* was the type of radio personality most U.S. servicemen heard.

ARMSTRONG, EDWIN H. (1890–1954)

Modern electronics and certainly modern radio and television owe a large debt of gratitude to inventor Edwin H. Armstrong. Armstrong's basic circuit designs laid the foundation for the entire broadcasting industry. Born in New York City, he was the son of deeply religious, middle-class Presbyterian parents. At the age of fourteen, he read about Guglielmo MARCONI's exploits and became fascinated with how the inventor had sent the first wireless message across the Atlantic Ocean. Armstrong set out to follow Marconi's footsteps.

While attending college, he invented the regenerative circuit, which was the first amplifying receiver and the first reliable continuous sound-wave transmitter. In 1918, while serving in the U. S. Army Signal Corps during World War I, Armstrong developed the "super-heterodyne circuit." This was a highly selective means of receiving, converting, and greatly amplifying very weak, high-frequency electronic waves. This concept is the basis of all modern radio and television sound reception.

In 1933, Armstrong invented the wide-band frequency modulation, which is the foundation for basically static-free FM radio transmitting. During World War II, Armstrong turned to military research, mainly to escape the numerous patent suits involving his FM systems. In 1954, with most of his wealth gone due to countless court battles and feeling a lack of appreciation for his contributions to broadcasting, the brilliant inventor committed suicide.

ARMSTRONG THEATER OF TODAY, THE

1941–1954   CBS   Sat.   12 PM

This durable half-hour daytime dramatic anthology series was heard on Saturdays at noon. The program featured such major stars of film and stage as Humphrey BOGART, Bette Davis, Anita Louise, and Jane Wyman. Its radio plays were suitable for audiences of all ages. Elizabeth Reller and then Julie Conway were heard as "the Armstrong Quaker girl," who delivered the commercials on the program. They also acted as the show's hostesses and narrated the story of the week. Bob Sherry and George Byron were the program's announcers. The series, which presented original scripts by freelance writers, was produced by Ira Avery and directed by Ken Webb and Al Ward.

ARNOLD, EDWARD (GUNTHER SCHNEIDER: 1890–1956)

Edward Arnold was born in New York City and became a professional actor at the age of fifteen. A well-known character actor, he appeared in numerous movies from the 1930s to the 1950s, including *Diamond Jim* (1935), *Mr. Smith Goes to Washington* (1939), and *Johnny Eager* (1941). Arnold's voice was also familiar to radio listeners as the star of the MR. PRESIDENT series, on which he played many presidents of the United States. He was also heard on the *Good News,* CHASE AND SANBORN HOUR, LUX RADIO THEATER and SCREEN GUILD PLAYERS radio programs. Radio listeners enjoyed recalling the visual image of the smooth-talking, bulky star whose jovial laugh was not always to be trusted.

ARNOLD GRIMM'S DAUGHTER

1937–1938	CBS	Mon.–Fri.	1:30 PM
1938–1940	NBC Red	Mon.–Fri.	2:15 PM
1940–1942	NBC Red	Mon.–Fri.	2:45 PM

A middle-aged widower named Arnold Grimm, who owned a small general store, his daughter, Constance, and his grandchildren Gladys and Tom were the central characters on this 15-minute, Monday-through-Friday daytime drama series. Don Merrified played the kindly, gentle and loving Arnold; Betty Lou GERSON and then Luise Barclay played his daughter, Constance. James Andelin and then Frank Behrens played Tom, and Bonita Kay played Gladys. Also heard on this series were Cliff Soubier, Frank Dane, Fred Sullivan, Sidney Ellstrom, Louise Fitch, Herb Nelson, Sarajane Wells, John HODIAK, Jeanne Dixon, Robert Ellis, Margaretta Shanna, Mary Patton, Bill Bouchey, Jeanne Juvelier, Leo Curley, Ethel Wilson, Judith Lowry, Josephine Gilbert, Carl Kroenke, Gladys Heen, and Ed Prentiss. Margaret Sangster wrote the scripts for the series. Harlow WILCOX, Pierre Andre, Roger Krupp, and Verne Smith were the program's announcers; Gold Medal flour and Softasilk cake flour were the show's sponsors.

ARQUETTE, CLIFF (1907–1974)

Born in Ohio, actor Cliff Arquette began his show business career as a vaudeville performer while in his teens. Shortly thereafter, Arquette began to work on radio. In the 1940s, while broadcasting in Los Angeles, Arquette is reported to have set the record for the number of radio shows one actor was heard on in a single day (thirteen). His most famous radio role was that of the Old Timer on FIBBER MCGEE AND MOLLY, but he is also well remembered for performances on *The* DICK HAYMES SHOW, GLAMOUR MANOR, LUM AND ABNER, MYRT AND MARGE, POINT SUBLIME, and WELCOME VALLEY. As Charlie Weaver, a character he had originally developed for the "Dennis Day" TV show, Arquette became one of the most popular guests on Jack Parr's "Tonight Show" on television. He was also a regular panelist on the "Hollywood Squares" TV show until shortly before his death.

ARTHUR GODFREY TIME (AKA THE ARTHUR GODFREY DIGEST; AKA THE ARTHUR GODFREY SHOW)

1945–1946	CBS	Mon.–Fri.	9:15 AM
1946–1948	CBS	Mon.–Fri.	9:15 & 11 AM
1948–1949	CBS	Mon.–Fri.	10:30 AM
1949–1950	CBS	Mon.–Fri.	10:15 AM
1950–1958	CBS	Mon.–Fri.	10 AM
1958–1960	CBS	Mon.–Fri.	9:05 AM
1960–1964	CBS	Mon.–Fri.	10:05 AM
1964–1972	CBS	Mon.–Fri.	10 AM
Evening Shows:			
1950–1951	CBS	Sat.	9:30 PM
1950–1954	(Off the air)		
1954–1955	CBS	Fri.	8:30 PM
1955–1956	CBS	Fri.	8 PM

After he became a celebrity for his touching description of President Franklin D. Roosevelt's funeral in 1944, Arthur GODFREY hosted the popular hour-and-one-half-long talk/variety series *Arthur Godfrey Time,* which became a most listened-to program. In the 1950s, Godfrey brought his music-variety program, "Arthur Godfrey and His Friends," to television. Soon he was one of the most famous and best-loved personalities in show business.

Godfrey's casual, down-to-earth conversations with program regulars—vocalists Janette Davis, Bill Lawrence, the Mariners quartet, Richard Hayes, Ethel Ennis, and Luann Simms; Hawaiian singer Haleloke; tenor Frank PARKER; soprano Marion Marlowe; the Chordettes, Carmel Quinn, and the McGuire Sisters; and orchestra leader Archie Bleyer—were always

Arthur Godfrey was the host and star of CBS radio's *Arthur Godfrey Time* and *Arthur Godfrey's Talent Scouts.* (CBS-TV)

frothy and funny, although sometimes caustic and cruel. His on-the-air firing of singer Julius LaRosa, whose "lack of humility" offended Godfrey, made newspaper headlines across the United States. But it was Godfrey's occasional singing as he accompanied himself on his ukelele and his humorous, if critical, commercial messages that endeared him to his listeners.

Tony Marvin was Godfrey's longtime announcer, and Frank Dodge the show's director. The long list of products advertised on the *Arthur Godfrey Time* program prove that the sponsors certainly didn't mind his kidding, as long as he continued to sell their products as well as he did. Those sponsors included Lipton tea, Scotch tape, Ban deodorant, Vitalis hair dressing, Bufferin pain reliever, Chesterfield cigarettes, Hebrew National meats, Saran Wrap, Snow Crop orange juice, Pillsbury flour, Rinso cleanser, Minute Rice, Frigidaire refrigerators, Lanolin Plus shampoo, Mountain Valley's foods, Lipton main dishes, Pepto Bismol antacid, Glass Wax window cleaner, Listerine mouthwash, Wildroot Cream Oil hair dressing, Kleenex tissues, Easy Washer-Dryer, Lux liquid soap, Columbia TV, Sta-Flo, Instant Chase and Sanborn coffee, Chrysler-Plymouth automobiles, Lipton soups, Unguentine ointment, Gold Seal wood cream, Star Kist tuna fish, Pepsodent toothpaste, Nabisco cookies, Ban deodorant, Ipana toothpaste, Accent flavor enhancer, Schick razors, and Hershey's chocolate. Godfrey's theme music "Seems Like Old Times" was composed by Carmen Lombardo and John Jacob Loeb. The song, which opened and closed the show, became a standard as a result of this exposure.

ARTHUR GODFREY'S SUNDIAL SHOW, THE

1937–1938	CBS	Mon., Wed., Fri.	9 PM
	Mutual	Wed.	7:45 PM
1938–1940	CBS	Mon.–Fri.	6:30 AM
1940	Mutual	Mon.–Fri.	9 AM

Arthur GODFREY's first program of any significance was an early-morning show called *Arthur Godfrey's Sundial*. It caught on with the public in CBS's 6:30 AM time slot in the late 1930s and was therefore the first program many people heard when they woke up in the morning. On the program, Godfrey read the news of the day and articles of interest from the daily newspapers, and he occasionally interviewed a visitor to his studio. Godfrey's sponsors, often the butt of his jokes, included Musterrole back-rubbing cream, Barbasol shaving cream, Pepsi Cola, Force toasted wheat-flakes cereal, Gulf oil, Minit Rub ointment, Bond's clothing stores, and Alka Seltzer antacid.

ARTHUR GODFREY'S TALENT SCOUTS

1946–1947	CBS	Tues.	9 PM
1947–1956	CBS	Mon.	8:30 PM

The *Arthur Godfrey's Talent Scouts* program began each show with the following theme song, sung to the tune of "Sing a Song of Sixpence":

Here comes Arthur GODFREY, your *Talent Scouts* MC,
Brought to you by Lipton, the brisk Lipton tea.
You know it's Lipton tea when its B-R-I-S-K.
You know its Arthur Godfrey when you hear him play . . .

The orchestra then lead into "Seems Like Old Times," Godfrey's theme song. This talent competition show gave many entertainers their first big break at performing for a national audience. Ordinary people acquainted with or related to the entertainers acted as their "talent scouts" and introduced them to Godfrey, who in turn introduced them to his radio—and later television—audience. On the show, the performers competed for show-business bookings. A studio-audience applause meter determined the weekly winner of each program.

Arthur Godfrey was the program's host and brought his same casual, sometimes caustic, presence—so effective on his popular *Arthur Godfrey Time*—to this show. George Bryan and Tony Marvin were the show's announcers. Peggy Marshall and the Holidays sang the show's opening and closing theme. However, unlike the popular *Original Amateur Hour* talent program, the performers heard on the show were not necessarily amateurs; indeed, they were usually professionals, such as comedian Lenny Bruce and aspiring actress-model Ann-Margret, who were looking for national exposure. The series was produced by Jack Carney and Irving Mansfield and directed by Carney. Sponsors included Lipton tea, Lipton soup, and Toni home permanent.

ARTS TONIGHT, THE

1988–present	CBC Stereo (FM)	Mon.–Fri.	7 PM
	CBS Radio (AM)	Mon.–Fri.	10 PM

The three-hour *Arts Tonight* is heard on both AM and FM networks of the CANADIAN BROADCASTING CORPORATION. The series, hosted by Shelagh Rogers and Peter Tiefenbach, presents reviews of the latest books, movies, and theater and examines such controversial issues as censorship and book banning, the politics of arts funding, culture and identity, and artistic freedom. The program also offers an overview of current world events and highlights of the arts world. Anne Gibson is the executive producer both of the *Arts Tonight* and its weekend edition, *Arts Week*.

AS IT HAPPENS

1968–present	CBS	Mon.–Fri.	6:30 PM

This major current-affairs news feature from the CANADIAN BROADCASTING CORPORATION is heard in the United States on NATIONAL PUBLIC RADIO stations. The series, which presents in-depth coverage of national Canadian as well as international news stories, is heard weeknights from 6:30 until 8 PM. The program features hosts Michael Enright and Alan Maitland, who introduce listeners to the central figures of the day as well as to individuals whose stories might otherwise not be told. Whether the topics covered are political, social, or environmental, the series brings insight, humor, and emotion to the day's news. *As It Happens* is also carried on 48 stations affiliated with AMERICAN PUBLIC RADIO.

ASK-IT BASKET

1938–1939	CBS	Wed.	7:30 PM
1939–1941	CBS	Thurs.	8 PM

On this half-hour quiz program, four contestants selected from the studio audience answered questions about everything from "What was Lincoln's wife's maiden name?" to "Who is the current Secretary of State?" The questions, picked at random out of an "ask-it basket," if answered correctly could win contestants points, and the contestant who had the most points at the end of the show won $25. Second- and third-place contestants won $10 and $5. Jim McWilliams and Ed East were the program's hosts, and Del SHARBUTT was the show's announcer. Colgate dental cream sponsored the program the entire time it was on the air.

AUERBACH, ARTIE (1903–1957)

New York City–born Artie Auerbach is perhaps best remembered as Mr. Kitzel, the "pickle in the middle with the mustard on top" street vendor who was a character on The JACK BENNY and AL PEARCE AND HIS GANG programs. In addition to his Mr. Kitzel character, Auerbach, who was educated at New York University and worked as a reporter for the New York Daily News newspaper before becoming an actor, also had diverse roles on Defective Detectives (playing all of the characters on that show), The GOLDBERGS, HOUSE OF GLASS, Real Folks, Tony and Gus, The Wonder Show, Calling All Stars, The PHIL BAKER SHOW, The EDDIE CANTOR SHOW, The Mark Hellinger's Revue, and The ED SULLIVAN SHOW.

AUNT JEMIMA

1929–1930	CBS	Thurs.	9 PM
1930–1931	(Off the air)		
1931–1932	CBS	Tues., Wed., Thurs.	2 PM
1932–1933	CBS	Tues., Thurs.	2 PM
1933–1937	(Off the air)		
1937–1938	NBC Blue	Tues., Sat.	9:45 PM
1938–1943	(Off the air)		
1943–1944	CBS	Sat.	8:25 PM
1944–1952	(Off the air)		
1952–1953	CBS	Mon.–Fri.	3:45 PM

First a situation-comedy series and then various five-minute promotional spots for Aunt Jemima pancake mix, the Aunt Jemima radio program starred African-American actresses Amanda RANDOLPH and Tess Gardell, and Caucasian actress Harriette WIDMER (who specialized in playing African-American-dialect roles), as the fictitious black cook who narrated each story. When a series, the half-hour Aunt Jemima show was directed by Palmer Clark and written by Mason Ancker. Marvin MILLER was the program's announcer.

AUNT JENNY'S REAL LIFE STORIES

1936–1946	CBS	Mon.–Fri.	11:45 AM
1946–1954	CBS	Mon.–Fri.	12:15 PM
1954–1956	CBS	Mon.–Fri.	2:45 PM

This CBS series had a somewhat different format from other daytime serials on the air. Each week a complete story was presented in five episodes that were each 15 minutes long. The stories were narrated by a soft-spoken, motherly-sounding woman named Aunt Jenny, a character played by Edith Spencer and then Agnes Young. Both actresses also acted as the spokeswomen for the program's sponsor, Spry shortening, and later for Lux soap. The weekly stories heard on this program were generally directed toward the ladies of the house and usually centered around a domestic or romantic problem of some sort.

Dan SEYMOUR was Aunt Jenny's announcer, and animal imitator Henry Boyd was Aunt Jenny's whistling canary. Regular performers on the show included actors Ed JEROME, Ruth Yorke, Adelaide Klein, Nancy Kelly, Peggy Allenby, Sidney Ellstrom, Maurice Franklin, Vera Allen, Franc Hale, Margot Stevenson, Virginia Dwyer, Toni Darnay, Helen Shields, Alfred Ryder, and Eddie O'Brien.

During the twenty years the show was on the air, it was directed by Thomas F. Vietor, Bill Sweets, Robert S. Steele, Tony Wilson, John Loveton, and Ralph Berkley. Writers included Doris Halman, David Davidson, and Ruth Adams Knight. Aunt Jenny's theme music was "Those Endearing Young Charms."

AUNT MARY

1942–1944	NBC	Mon.–Fri.	9:15 AM
1944–1947	Mutual	(Syndicated series. Various times and stations)	

Aunt Mary was a daytime drama series produced and heard mainly on the West Coast for 15 minutes Monday through Friday. It took place in a fictional locale called Willow Road Farm. The title character was another of radio's many elderly ladies who had a talent for becoming involved—because of her generous, motherly nature—in other people's lives. Regulars on the series were actress Jane Morgan (best known as the landlady Miss Davis on the OUR MISS BROOKS radio and TV show) as Aunt Mary; and Irene Tedrow, Jack Edwards, Fred Howard, Jane Webb, Josephine Gilbert, Jay Novello, Marvin MILLER, Ken Peters, Tom Collins, Betty Lou GERSON, Pat McGeehan, and others. Aunt Mary was directed by George Fogle. The series was written by Gil Faust, Virginia Thacker, and Lee and Virginia Crosby. Marvin MILLER and Vincent Pelletier were the show's announcers. Numerous local companies sponsored the program.

AUNT SAMMY'S RADIO RECIPES

1926–1944	(Syndicated series. Various times and stations)

The United States Bureau of Home Economics produced this syndicated series, which featured a fictional character, Aunt Sammy, the wife of Uncle Sam. On this 15-minute program, Aunt Sammy, played by numerous actresses over the years, gave recipes and offered housekeeping tips in a lighthearted manner. Other characters included crusty old Uncle Ebenezer; six-year-old nephew Billy; her nosy but warmhearted next-door neighbor; her car Nettie; her cousin Susan, the menu specialist; and fussy eaters Pinicky Florine and Percy Wallington Waffle. The show's director and writers were uncredited.

AUSTIN, GENE (1901–1972)

Singer Gene Austin was born in Gainesville, Texas, and grew up in Los Angeles, California. One of radio's most popular performers throughout the 1920s and 1930s, Austin was the regular vocalist on *The* JOE PENNER SHOW and made frequent guest appearances on most of the music-variety shows on the air. His recording of the song "My Blue Heaven" sold more than 7 million copies—a record number of records for the time—and became the first Gold record ever awarded to a singer. His other hits included "Five Foot Two," "Romance," "That Lonesome Road," and "Sleepy Time Gal." Altogether, his recordings, many of which he wrote as well as sang, sold more than 87 million copies. At the height of his popularity, the singer appeared in several motion pictures, including *Sadie McKee* (1934). Austin's popularity came to an abrupt end in the late 1940s, and it was rumored that he had retired because of a problem with alcohol abuse. Except for a memorable guest appearance on *The* ANDREWS SISTERS SHOW in 1945, his radio appearances in the late 1940s and thereafter were infrequent.

AUTHOR MEETS CRITIC

1946–1947	Mutual	Wed.	10:30 PM
1947–1948	NBC	Sun.	4:30 PM
1948	NBC	Sun.	5 PM
1949–1950	ABC	Thurs.	10 PM
1950–1951	ABC	Sun.	11:30 AM

One of the few literary discussion programs on radio, the half-hour weekly *Author Meets Critic* was originally a production of a local New York City station, WOR, until it became a network program in 1946. During the first half of the show, two critics argued the pros and cons of an author's work. During the second half of the show, the author was given a chance to enter the discussion and either defend his or her work or acknowledge the praise. Authors who were guests on this series included Leon Uris, Kathleen Winsor, Anita Loos, and Isaac Asimov. Barry Gray and John K. M. McCaffrey were the show's hosts. The series was produced and directed by Martin Stone.

AUTHOR'S STUDIO.

See RADIO PLAYHOUSE.

Gene Autry—here with his horse, Champion—was heard on radio each week on *Melody Ranch*. (Republic Pictures)

AUTRY, GENE (ORVION AUTRY: 1907–   )

Singing cowboy star Gene Autry, the son of a rancher, was born in Tioga, Texas. He worked for a while as a cowboy and then began his singing career. He debuted on radio station KVOO in Tulsa, Oklahoma, in 1929 and then performed on WLS in Chicago for several years. Autry first received national attention as one of the featured singers on *The* GRAND OLE OPRY radio program in the early 1930s. He went on to become one of the most popular Hollywood cowboy stars and appeared in many films throughout the 1930s and 1940s, including *Boots and Saddles* (1932), *Melody Ranch* (1940), and *The Big Sombrero* (1949). He had a long-running radio show, MELODY RANCH, and guest-starred on most major radio variety programs.

Autry had best-selling hit recordings of "Here Comes Santa Claus," "Here Comes Peter Cottontail," and "Rudolph, the Red-Nosed Reindeer." But his radio and motion-picture work were suspended for three years during World War II while he served in the U. S. Air Force.

A millionaire many times over because of wise business investments made during his show-business career, Autry owns several radio and television stations, the Continental Hotel in Los Angeles, the Mark Hopkins Hotel in San Francisco, the California Angels baseball team, and a TV–motion-picture production company.

AVE MARIA HOUR, THE

1935–1969	(Syndicated series. Various stations and times)

In 1935, a friend of Fr. Anselm di Pasca, SA, a Graymoor Friar of Atonement, convinced officials at WOR, a local New York City station, that his idea to dramatize the lives of the saints—instead of presenting the usual prayer-and-sermon religious broadcast—would appeal to the general public. WOR enthusiastically endorsed the idea and produced the program, *The Ave Maria Hour*. WOR produced twelve broadcasts, and then another local station, WMCA, took over the production.

The broadcasts themselves originated from a studio at St. Christopher's Inn, at Graymoor in Garrison, New York, and were performed by professional actors. Recordings of these programs were made, duplicates were sent to other stations, and the series became a syndicated feature around the country.

The early shows consistently followed a temporal sequence; variety was obtained by the use of flashbacks or by the reminiscences of the narrator or the central character of each story. Listeners soon indicated that they preferred to hear an entire biography rather than a single incident from a particular saint's life. Mob scenes and loud shouting were avoided, and gentle organ music was used for musical bridges. During its years on the air, one of the program's most listened-to presentations was a forty-four-part series on the life of Christ.

The programs were produced and directed by Carlo DEANGELO. Richard Janover announced the show and became its producer as well as director when deAngelo died. In 1940, the program received the Knights of Columbus's First Annual Award for Meritorious Service in religious education. In 1952–53 and 1957–58, the series won first place and an honorary mention, respectively, from the American Exhibition of Educational Radio and Television Programs of Ohio State University and, in 1959, a Gold Bell Award. Hundreds of writers wrote scripts for *The Ave Maria Hour*, which, by 1959, was heard on over 750 stations, 400 of them on ARMED FORCES RADIO SERVICE. (See also RELIGIOUS PROGRAMS.)

B

BABE RUTH, THE ADVENTURES OF

See ADVENTURES OF BABE RUTH, THE.

BABY ROSE MARIE (ROSE MARIE MAZETTA: 1923–)

Years before she was well known as comedy writer Sally Rogers on "The Dick Van Dyke" TV series, for which she earned three Emmy nominations, New Jersey-born Rose Marie was a child singing star on radio. Billed as Baby Rose Marie in the early 1930s, the talented entertainer was as famous on the airwaves as movie moppet Shirley Temple. Only three years old when she made her radio debut on station WPG in Atlantic City with the song "What Can I Say After I Say I'm Sorry,"—for which she won a children's beauty-talent contest—she was called "a talent with an exceptional voice and delivery" by the show-business periodical *Variety*.

In 1930, she had her own popular 15-minute program, *The Baby Rose Marie Show,* on NBC's Blue network and she became a frequent guest star on most of the popular music-variety programs of the time, including *The* FLEISCHMANN HOUR and *The* TEXACO FIRE CHIEF. She can be seen in the W. C. Fields film *International House* (1933). Although her radio career ended in 1935, she was a nightclub favorite, singing such novelty tunes as "I Wish I Could Sing Like Durante." After six years on "The Dick Van Dyke" television show, Rose Marie continued to make television appearances ("The Doris Day Show" and "Hollywood Squares").

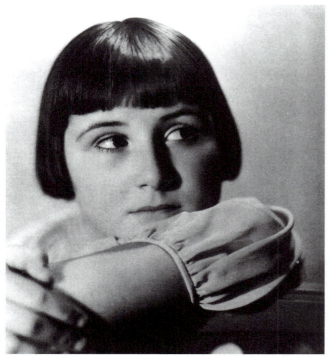

Baby Rose Marie (NBC)

BABY SNOOKS SHOW, THE

1944–1946	CBS	Sun.	6:30 PM
1944–1946	CBS	Fri.	8 PM
1946–1951	NBC	Tues.	8:30 PM

Comedienne Fanny BRICE first introduced her Baby Snooks character to radio audiences on the ZIEGFELD FOLLIES OF THE AIR program in the early 1930s. Her *Baby Snooks* sketches became regular features on the *Good News* musical-variety show in 1937; they subsequently became the main attraction on the MAXWELL HOUSE COFFEE TIME program in 1940. In 1944, Brice's

Fanny Brice as Baby Snooks (NBC)

Each week the show's theme music, "Ah, Sweet Mystery of Life," alerted listeners to the fact that they were about to hear the 15-minute, five-days-a-week *Bachelor's Children* daytime serial. A favorite program of daytime drama devotees during the 1930s and 1940s, this series was critically acclaimed as well. The leading characters were Dr. Bob Graham (played by Hugh STUDEBAKER and then Art Kohl) and his wife Ruth (played by Marjorie Hannan and then Laurette FILLBRANDT). The Grahams were a typical, middle-class American family who lived in a small town and dealt with life's domestic and social problems. What distinguished this series was that it was the first show to feature dialogue that was natural and made listeners believe that what they were hearing was actually happening. Because of this, *Bachelor's Children* won many awards, including *Movie-Radio Guide* magazine's "Best daytime serial on radio" in 1941. The program also received an award from The Inter-American Affairs Committee as "the most representative script on the way of life of an average American family."

Supporting actors on the series included Olan SOULE, Dora Johnson, Jane WEBB, Lenore Kingston, Frank Dane, Charles Flynn, Patricia Dunlap, Virginia "Ginger" Jones, Olga Rosenova, John HODIAK, Janice Gilbert, Helen Van Tuyl, David GOTHARD, Alice Hill, Mary Patton, Marie Nelson, Arthur PETERSON, Peg Hillias, Nelson OLMSTEAD, Sundra Love, Marjorie Hannan, Raymond Edward JOHNSON, and Ruth Bailey. Don Gordon and Russ Young were the program's announcers. J. P. Roche, Burr Lee, and Lloyd Meriwell directed the series. Sponsors included Old Dutch cleanser, Palmolive-Peet soap, Colgate toothpaste, and Wonder bread.

half-hour program became known as *The Baby Snooks Show*. Snooks's long-suffering "Daddy" was originally played by film actor Frank MORGAN, then by radio actor Alan REED, and finally, for most of the years the program was on the air, by actor Hanley STAFFORD, who is best remembered for the role. Lalive Brownell and Arlene HARRIS played Snook's mother; child impersonator Lenore Ledoux played her baby brother, Robespierre. Ken ROBERTS and Harlow WILCOX announced the program at various times. The *Baby Snooks Show* was directed by Walter Bunker, Ted Bliss, and Roy Rowen and written by Everett Freeman, Jess Oppenheimer, Bill Danch, and Jerry Seelen. *Baby Snooks* was sponsored by Maxwell House coffee, Post cereals, Sanka coffee, La France bleach, Spic-n-Span floor cleanser, Tums antacid, and Jell-O puddings. The program's theme song was "Rock-A-Bye Baby."

BACHELOR'S CHILDREN

1935–1936	Mutual	Mon.–Fri.	10:15 AM
1936–1940	CBS and	Mon.–Fri.	9:45 AM
	Mutual	Mon.–Fri.	10:15 AM
			11:30 AM
1940–1941	NBC Red	Mon.–Fri.	10:30 AM
1941–1942	NBC Red	Mon.–Fri.	10:15 AM
1942–1946	CBS	Mon.–Fri.	10:45 AM

BACKSTAGE WIFE

See MARY NOBLE, BACKSTAGE WIFE.

BACKUS, JIM (1913–1989)

Well known to viewers as Mr. Howell on the "Gilligan's Island" TV series (1964–1967), comedian-actor Jim Backus began his long career in radio comedy. He was born in Cleveland, Ohio, and attended the American Academy of Dramatic Arts in New York City. Backus became one of the stars of the "I Married Joan" (1952–1959) TV series, costarring comedienne Joan DAVIS. A regular performer on *The ALAN YOUNG SHOW*, Backus played the hilarious, ultrasnobbish Hubert Updike, a character not unlike his Mr. Howell characterization. He was also heard regularly on *The DANNY KAYE SHOW*, *The EDGAR BERGEN–CHARLIE MCCARTHY SHOW*, *The MEL BLANC SHOW*, and on the SOCIETY GIRL series. Backus's voice is, however, most familiar to people as that of the nearsighted Mr. McGoo of animated cartoon fame.

In addition to his radio and TV appearances, Backus also acted in numerous feature films, including *Man of a Thousand Faces* (1957) and *The Wheeler Dealers* (1963), and was the voice of several other popular films and TV cartoon characters such as *Pete's Dragon* (1977), "Yes, Virginia, There Is a Santa Claus" (1974), and "Gilligan's Planet" (1973–1974).

BAER, PARLEY (1914–   )

Character actor Parley Baer was born in Salt Lake City, Utah, and is perhaps best known to radio fans as Chester Wesley Proudfoot, Marshall Matt Dillon's deputy on the GUNSMOKE radio series. Baer, certainly one of the medium's most active performers, was heard on more than 10,000 radio broadcasts during the 1930s and 1940s. In addition to *Gunsmoke*, he was prominently featured on such shows as *The* COUNT OF MONTE CRISTO, *The* ADVENTURES OF PHILIP MARLOWE, *The* CBS RADIO WORKSHOP, ESCAPE, SUSPENSE, *The* FIRST NIGHTER, *Granby's Acres*, *Honest Harold*, THOSE WEBSTERS, and YOURS TRULY, JOHNNY DOLLAR.

Television audiences saw Baer as a regular cast member on such shows as "The Ozzie and Harriet Show" (1952) "The Andy Griffith Show" (1960, playing the mayor of Mayberry), and "The Double Life of Henry Phyfe" (1966). In recent years, he has appeared on the daytime TV drama series "The Young and the Restless" (1993). Baer acted in numerous films such as *Gypsy* (1962), *The Calloways* (1965), and *Dr. Detroit* (1968). TV viewers recognize Parley Baer's voice as that of the elderly Keebler elf on the Keebler cookie commercials. Baer has also served as ringmaster with several circuses.

BAILEY, BOB (1913–1983)

Prior to entering show business, California-born actor Bob Bailey worked as a sideshow barker, a salesman, a theater usher, a plumber's assistant, a policeman, a drummer, and a professional badminton player. In the 1940s, he became an active leading man on many radio programs, playing title roles in the LET GEORGE DO IT mystery series and YOURS TRULY, JOHNNY DOLLAR. Bailey appeared often on such popular programs as HOLLY SLOANE, MORTIMER GOOCH, THAT BREWSTER BOY, and TODAY'S CHILDREN. A 20th Century-Fox film contract player in the earliest years of his acting career, Bailey appeared in several Hollywood films, including *Guest in the House* (1944), before becoming active on radio. Bailey retired from show business in the early 1960s.

BAILEY, MILDRED

See MILDRED BAILEY SHOW, *The*

BAKER, ART (ARTHUR SHANK: 1898–1966)

Announcer-commentator-actor-host Art Baker's first major job on radio was as an announcer for Forest Lawn Memorial Park. Born in New York City, Baker, who had been a machine gunnery instructor during World War I and also worked as a choir director, an oil-burner salesman, a gravel hauler, and a car parker before entering radio, hosted such programs as *Hollywood in Person*, *Pull Over Hollywood*, *Never Too Old*, *The* GROUCH CLUB, *Hedda Hopper's Hollywood*, *The* BOB HOPE SHOW, and PEOPLE ARE FUNNY. On TV, Baker hosted "You Asked for It" in the early 1950s, which was seen on ABC-TV.

BAKER, BONNIE "WEE" (EVELYN NELSON: 1917–1990)

Singer Bonnie Baker was born in Orange, Texas, a suburb of Houston. Bonnie's sweet, youthful-sounding voice made her a popular vocalist on many radio programs in the late 1930s into the 1940s. Billed as "Wee" Bonnie Baker because of her diminutive size, she was a regular on YOUR HIT PARADE and frequently guest-starred on variety, music, and comedy programs such as *The* AMERICAN ALBUM OF FAMILIAR MUSIC and *The* CHAMBER MUSIC SOCIETY OF LOWER BASIN STREET. Bonnie had several hit recordings, the most notable being her rendition of "Oh, Johnny," which became a major hit and thereafter her signature song. She retired in the early 1950s.

BAKER, KENNY (1912–1985)

One of radio's major singing stars, tenor Kenny Baker was born in Monrovia, California, studied music as a child, and made his radio debut on a local station in Long Beach, California, in 1930. Baker was subsequently heard on many network shows in the late 1930s and early 1940s, including *The Pabst Blue Ribbon*

Kenny Baker (NBC)

Town Show, The FRED ALLEN SHOW, *The* JACK BENNY SHOW, *The* TEXACO FIRE CHIEF SHOW, and *The* TEXACO STAR THEATER. As a result of his radio success, Baker was signed to play leading roles in such films as *King of Burlesque* (1936), *The Mikado* (1939), and *52nd Street* (1939). The singer made his Broadway stage debut in the 1943 musical comedy *One Touch of Venus*. He gradually retired from show business in the late 1940s. Baker's theme song was "The Wandering Minstrel" by Gilbert and Sullivan.

BAKER, PHIL (1896–1963)

Quiz-show host and accordionist-turned-comedian, Phil Baker was a native of Philadelphia, Pennsylvania. The veteran vaudevillian played in the Ben Bernie Orchestra and was a regular performer on the FRED ALLEN SHOW before becoming the star of his own weekly comedy-variety program, *The* PHIL BAKER SHOW (aka *The Armour Show*) in 1943. Other shows featuring Baker included TAKE IT OR LEAVE IT and *Honolulu Bound*. Noted for his rapid-fire delivery and topical sense of humor, Baker was one of radio's most popular performers from 1933 until 1940, when he took a sabbatical from broadcasting. In 1943, Phil returned to radio as quizmaster-star of *Take It Or Leave It*. He became as popular as a quiz-show host as he was as a comedian. In addition to his work on radio, in

Phil Baker (NBC)

Baker also appeared in several films, including *The Goldwyn Follies* (1938), *The Gang's All Here* (1943), and *Take It Or Leave It* (1944).

BALL, LUCILLE (1910–1989)

Lucille Ball was called the most beloved comedienne in television history ("I Love Lucy," "Here's Lucy," and other shows) as well as a fine actress in films such as *Room Service* (1938), *The Dark Corner* (1946), and *Sorrowful Jones* (1947), and a Broadway musical comedy, *Wildcat* (1960). However, she was also an important radio star in the 1940s and 1950s.

Born in Jamestown, New York, Ball studied drama in New York and then went to California to try film acting. She worked on radio in the 1930s and was a regular guest panelist on *Leave It to the Girls* in the late 1940s. Her popular situation-comedy series MY FAVORITE HUSBAND featured her TV "Here's Lucy" costar, Gale Gordon. This series was the forerunner of her successful "I Love Lucy" TV series. I LOVE LUCY was also heard on radio for less than a year, without the success of the TV show.

Ball was also a frequent guest star on SUSPENSE, *The* SCREEN GUILD PLAYERS, *The* LUX RADIO THEATER, and other dramatic anthology radio shows, as well as many comedy and variety programs such as *The* JACK BENNY SHOW and DUFFY'S TAVERN.

BAND REMOTE BROADCASTS

Throughout the 1930s and 1940s, late-night supper clubs, which featured big-band music and were mainly located in big city hotels, flourished. Capitalizing on this craze, the four major networks, CBS, NBC, ABC, and Mutual, broadcasted the music of bands playing in these clubs for late-night listeners, after the 11 PM news had been presented. Latin American music, swing, jazz, and even waltz music could be heard on these remote broadcasts. A typical opening announcement was: "From the Palm Room of the Hotel Pierre in glamorous downtown New York City, NBC presents the music of Wayne KING, the Waltz King, for your listening and dancing pleasure."

Big-band leaders of the era and their vocalists included Xavier Cugat and the vocals of Lina Romay; Les Brown and vocalist Doris Day; Sammy KAYE's, Benny Goodman's, Gene Krupa's, and Tommy and Jimmy Dorsey's bands; pianist Carmen Cavallaro; pop singer Russ COLUMBO; Blue Barron's orchestra; Louis Prima's, Bob Chester's, Teddy Powell's, and Charlie Barnett's bands; Bob Crosby and the Bobcats; Meyer Davis's orchestra; pianist Eddie Duchin; Shep Fields's band; Glen Gray and his Casa Loma Orchestra, Red Nichols's Orchestra; Jack Teagarten's group; the Three Sons (Al Nevins, guitar; Morty Nevins, accordion; Art Dunn, electric organ); and Guy LOMBARDO and His

Royal Canadians. Lombardo's annual New Year's Eve broadcasts were considered essential listening across the country, especially for the orchestra's rendition of "Auld Lang Syne."

BANGHART, KENNETH (1910–1980)

Newscaster Kenneth Banghart was born in Newark, New Jersey, but grew up in New York City. In 1942, he took a leave from his Cook Travel Agency executive post to announce for NBC's local Washington station and was so well received that he remained with NBC for the next several decades. In addition to his nightly news-anchorman assignment on NBC radio and later on television, Banghart managed to find time to work as a radio-program panelist and an occasional regional-theater actor.

BANKHEAD, TALLULAH (1902–1968)

Deep voiced, ultrasophisticated, and outrageously "campy" stage and screen actress Tallulah Bankhead was born in Huntsville, Alabama, the daughter of a U. S. senator. Bankhead at fifteen won a movie fan-magazine competition and a trip to New York. After several years of playing minor roles on Broadway, she achieved stardom in such celebrated plays as Lillian Hellman's *The Little Foxes* (1939) and Thornton Wilder's *The Skin of Our Teeth* (1942).

Bankhead won the New York Film Critics Award as Best Actress in Alfred Hitchcock's *Lifeboat* (1944); in *A Royal Scandal* (1945), she quite effectively played the excessive Queen Catherine the Great of Russia. In the early 1950s, she hosted NBC radio's 90-minute variety program, *The* BIG SHOW. Bankhead guest-starred on such radio shows as *The* SCREEN GUILD PLAYERS, *Time to Smile*, *The* RALEIGH ROOM, *The* FRED ALLEN SHOW, *The* SCREEN DIRECTOR'S PLAYHOUSE, *The* LUX RADIO THEATER, and *The* THEATER GUILD ON THE AIR. The actress was also frequently heard during World War II on ARMED FORCES RADIO SERVICE shows, COMMAND PERFORMANCE and MAIL CALL. Bankhead continued acting until illness forced her to retire. Her last film appearance was in *Die! Die! My Darling!* (1965).

BANKS, JOAN (AKA JOAN LOVEJOY: 1918–)

Born in New York City, Joan Banks began to use husband Frank LOVEJOY's surname midway through her radio acting career. Banks, known for her pleasant and charming feminine voice, was regularly heard on such varied programs as YOUNG DR. MALONE, VALIANT LADY, THIS IS YOUR FBI, PORTIA FACES LIFE, MY FRIEND IRMA (substituting for Cathy LEWIS in the leading role of Jane), HOUSE IN THE COUNTRY, GANGBUSTERS, *The* FALCON, SUSPENSE, and *The* ADVENTURES OF SAM SPADE, DETECTIVE. She also played the title role on the

Joan Banks (RKO)

EDITOR'S DAUGHTER series. Banks also worked as an actress dubbing foreign films.

BARBER, RED (WALTER LANIER BARBER: 1908–1992)

Sportscaster Red Barber, well known to sports fans as "The Ole Redhead," was a World Series commentator whose broadcasts brought baseball into millions of American homes. Born in Mississippi and never losing his pronounced Southern drawl, he began his broadcasting career in 1930 while attending the University of Florida, substituting for one of his professors on a local farm-hour program. In 1934, he was hired by WLW in Cincinnati, Ohio, to live-broadcast the Cincinnati Reds' baseball games. In 1939, his sportscasting attracted the attention of NBC network officials, and he became a member of their sports staff, continuing to broadcast games and sports news on NBC for the next thirty years. Barber also wrote a sports column that was syndicated in hundreds of newspapers all around the United States. Until his death in 1992, Barber commented on the current sports scene on NATIONAL PUBLIC RADIO'S MORNING EDITION every Friday. "The Ole Redhead" was elected to the Baseball Hall of Fame for his sportscasting achievements.

BARLOW, HOWARD (1892–1972)

For seventeen years, distinguished conductor Howard Barlow was a music director for the NBC network and led the orchestra on *The* VOICE OF FIRESTONE. Born in Urbana, Illinois, he moved from NBC to ABC in the 1940s when the NBC Blue network was sold. He continued to conduct the orchestra on *The Voice of Firestone* until it left the air. Barlow was also music conductor on such shows as *The* HARVEST OF STARS, SATURDAY NIGHT SERENADE, and *The Old Curiosity Shop,* as well as such dramatic programs as *The* MARCH OF TIME and *The Story Hour with Mary and Bob.*

BARRY CRAIG, CONFIDENTIAL INVESTIGATOR

1951–1952	NBC	Wed.	10 PM
1952–1953	NBC	Sun.	10 PM
1953–1954	NBC	Tues.	8:30 PM
1954–1955	NBC	Sun.	8:30 PM

Motion-picture actor William Gargan starred as private detective Barry Craig on this half-hour mystery-adventure series that featured John Gibson as Craig's friend and confidant. Craig was a hard-boiled, tough-talking PI who took on any case, from finding a lost relative to helping the police department solve a murder. Regularly heard in the show's supporting cast were Joseph KEARNS, Betty Lou GERSON, Lurene TUTTLE, Mitzi Gould, and others. Jaime DEL VALLE directed the show, which was written by various freelance writers. Sponsors of the program included Tums and Bromo Seltzer antacids.

BARRY WOOD SHOW, THE (AKA JOHNNY PRESENTS)

1936–1937	NBC Red	Wed.	7:45 PM
1937–1938	CBS	Wed., Thurs.	6:45 PM
1938–1939	CBS	Sun.	10:45 PM
1939–1943	(Off the air)		
1943–1945	NBC	Sat.	10 PM
1945–1946	NBC	Tues.	8 PM

Bandleader Barry Wood had a successful music program on the air for more than ten years. The half-hour program featured popular songs of the day as well as standard hits of the past and featured singers Ruth Carhart, Margaret Whiting, and Patsy Kline, at various times. Barry Wood's shows were sponsored by Drene and Special Drene shampoo, Palmolive soap, and Philip Morris cigarettes. When Philip Morris sponsored the show, its theme song was "On the Trail" from Grofé's *Grand Canyon Suite.*

BARRYMORE, LIONEL (LIONEL BLYTHE: 1878–1954)

A celebrated leading man and character actor on the stage at the turn of the century, in silent and sound films, and then on radio, Lionel Barrymore was a member of the famous Drew–Barrymore theatrical family whose members included Lionel's brother John and sister Ethel. Born in Philadelphia, Pennsylvania,

Barrymore appeared on Broadway in *Sag Harbor* (1900), *The Jest* (1919), and *The Claw* (1921), and in such films as *Friends* (1909), *The Yellow Streak* (1915), *Sadie Thompson* (1928), *Grand Hotel* (1932), *It's a Wonderful Life* (1946), and *Key Largo* (1948). His most memorable film characterization, however, was in MGM's Dr. Kildfare series in which he played the cantankerous Dr. Gillespie.

On radio, Barrymore starred as the lovable but equally cantankerous MAYOR OF THE TOWN. He was also prominently featured on *The* LUX RADIO THEATER, *Silver Theater,* and *Family Theater.* He is most famous, however, for his annual performance as Scrooge in the radio adaptation of Charles Dickens's *A Christmas Carol,* which he first performed on *The* CAMPBELL PLAYHOUSE in 1939 and continued to perform for many years after on various anthology series. In the 1940s, he starred in a half-hour syndicated radio series produced by MGM, DR. KILDARE.

BARTON FAMILY, THE (AKA THE STORY OF BOB BARTON AND THOSE BARTONS)

1939–1940	NBC Blue	Mon.–Fri.	5:30 PM
1940–1941	NBC Blue	Mon.–Fri.	5:15 PM
1941–1942	NBC	Mon.–Fri.	11 AM

The ever-growing list of daytime serial dramas in the late 1930s included the 15-minute, five-days-a-week *Barton Family* series. About an American family living in a typical Middle Western town, the series lasted for only three years. Its audience indentified with the father, who had a white-collar job; the mother, who stayed at home and cleaned and cooked for her family; and their average two-child household.

The series starred Dick Holland as the Barton's teenage son, Bud, who became the show's most popular character, and Kathryn Card as Grandma Barton, a character also popular with listeners, and featured Cliff Soubier, Henry Hunter, Art Kohl, Rosemary Garbell, Donald Kraatz, Ed Prentiss, Bill BOUCHEY, Arthur PETERSON, Fern Persons, Ian Keith, Bob Jellison, and Jane WEBB. It was directed by Frank Papp and written by Harlan Ware. Duz laundry detergent sponsored the series.

BARUCH, ANDRE (1902–1991)

Andre Baruch was one of radio's busiest and most respected announcers. Born in Paris, France, Baruch grew up in New York City. He developed a rich, cultivated sound that made him a sought-after spokesman for such products as Lucky Strike cigarettes and Palmolive soap, as well as host of many radio shows from the 1930s to the 1950s. Baruch was the original announcer for YOUR HIT PARADE and also announced such successful radio programs as *The* SHADOW, MYRT

AND MARGE, *The* KATE SMITH SHOW, JUST PLAIN BILL, SECOND HUSBAND, *The* ALDRICH FAMILY, and MY SON AND I. He hosted *Waltz Time* and AMERICAN ALBUM OF FAMILIAR MUSIC. Until his death, he remained active on radio as a disc jockey and talk-show host in the Los Angeles area. On these shows, he worked with his wife, Bea Wain, former vocalist on the *Your Hit Parade* program when Baruch was its announcer.

BASIC BLACK

1983–present	CBC	Sat.	10:05 PM

Canadian humorist Arthur Black hosts this Saturday evening show on the CANADIAN BROADCASTING CORPORATION network. The one-hour program is a friendly mix of interviews, editorials, comedy segments, audience phone-in comments, and pop music. It also features people who have such unusual occupations and pastimes as flower breeding and collecting safety pins as well as old radio shows. The program, according to the CBC, "takes a quirky look at people, things, and events that are often taken for granted."

BATTLE OF THE SEXES

1938–1941	NBC Red	Tues.	9 PM
1941–1943	NBC	Tues	9 PM

On this half-hour quiz program, two-to-four-member teams of men and women competed against each other as they attempted to answer various gender-specific questions, such as "Is a woman's place in the home?" or "Do women have a better sense of direction than men?" The winning team received gender-specific prizes: men might typically receive fishing rods, while women typically received toasters or irons. Frank CRUMMIT and Julia SANDERSON, former Broadway musical-comedy stars, and then J. C. Flippen and Walter O'KEEFE were the show's hosts. Ben GRAUER and Jack Costello announced the series, and R. A. Porter directed it. Molle shaving cream and Energine vitamin supplement were the program's sponsors.

BAUKHAGE, HILMAR ROBERT (1889–1976)

News commentator Hilmar Baukhage was the commentator on the *Baukhage Talking* program. He was born in La Salle, Illinois, and was educated at the University of Chicago. After years as a writer for the U.S. News Service, Baukhage became one of the most listened-to news commentators on the air in the 1930s. He was considered by many people in broadcasting to be the originator of the casual, down-to-earth news-reporting style that became so popular on the airwaves and is still being used by many newscasters. Baukhage was heard on all four major networks at one time or another—CBS, NBC, ABC, and Mutual. He retired from broadcasting in the late 1960s.

BEASLEY, IRENE

See GRAND SLAM.

BEAT THE BAND

1940–1941	NBC Red	Sun.	6:30 PM
1941–1943	(Off the air)		
1943–1944	NBC	Wed.	8:30 PM

At different times, "The Incomparable" HILDEGARDE and then Perry COMO and Garry MOORE were the stars of this lively, weekly half-hour musical quiz show that was one of radio's most popular programs in the 1940s. Marvel Maxwell and Marilyn Thorne were featured vocalists.

The format of this program was simple. Listeners mailed in questions about a particular song, and the show's band tried to guess the song and then play it. If the listener managed to stump the band, he or she won $50 and two cartons of Raleigh cigarettes (the show's sponsor).

Marvin MILLER and Fort Pearson were the show's announcers, and the music directors were Harry SOSNICK, Elmo Turner, Country Washington, and Ted WEEMS. The series was written by Hobart Donovan and directed by Jack Simpson and David Owen. After Raleigh cigarettes relinquished sponsorship, General Mills's Kix cereal took over. The show's theme song was "Out of the Night."

BEATRICE FAIRFAX SHOW, THE

1936	CBS	Fri.	10:15 PM
1936–1937	(Off the air)		
1937–1938	Mutual	Tues., Fri.	2:45 PM

Advice-to-the-lovelorn newspaper columnist and author Beatrice Fairfax brought her particular brand of entertainment to the airwaves in the late 1930s in a 15-minute telephone call-in and letter-answering format. *The Beatrice Fairfax Show* was sponsored by General Foods Silver Dust flour.

BEATTY, MORGAN (1903–1975)

NBC radio and television newscaster Morgan Beatty became nationally known when he covered the Mississippi flood for the Associated Press in 1927. Beatty began his reporting career for a local newspaper when he was a high school student in Little Rock, Arkansas. In 1941, Beatty joined NBC's news staff as a military analyst and in 1946 became the editor-in-chief and major commentator on the news-roundup program. This was a post he maintained until his retirement in the mid-seventies. Beatty died only a few months after he retired.

BECK, JACKSON (1912–   )

Actor-announcer Jackson Beck is one of television's and radio's most familiar commercial voiceover an-

Jackson Beck as the *Cisco Kid* (WXYZ)

nouncers. The deep-voiced announcer for Little Caesar pizza, Kellogg's frosted flakes, and other products, Beck, whose father was silent-film actor Max Beck, was born in New York City and began his career on radio in the mid-1930s. He played the title roles on the CISCO KID and PHILO VANCE and was announcer and narrator of the SUPERMAN adventure serial. He was also heard on *The* WITCH'S TALE, DIMENSION X, *The* FBI IN PEACE AND WAR, *The* MYSTERIOUS TRAVELER, BIG SISTER, *Brady Kaye (playing Brady)*, *By Popular Demand*, LIFE CAN BE BEAUTIFUL, THIS DAY IS OURS, *The* SHADOW, BELIEVE IT OR NOT, EASY ACES, *The* LIFE OF MARY SOTHERN, SOCIETY GIRL, HOP HARRIGAN, *On Broadway, Doc Reardon's Daughters*, GRAND CENTRAL STATION, *The* MAN I MARRIED, *The* MAN BEHIND THE GUN, MYRT AND MARGE, QUICK AS A FLASH, MYSTERY THEATER, *The* MARCH OF TIME, and MARK TRAIL.

In addition to his announcing and acting assignments, Beck is an active member of the American Federation of Radio and Television Artists and is on its National Board of Directors. He was awarded the organization's George Heller Memorial Gold Card for his work on its behalf.

Beck was the speaking voice of numerous cartoon characters, most notably Bluto in the Max Fleischer "Popeye" cartoon series and several characters in the Noveltoons cartoons. He was also heard in the "King Leonardo and His Short Subjects" (1960–1963) and the "Tennessee Tuxedo and His Tales" (1963–1966) cartoons.

BEEMER, BRACE (1902–1965)

Well remembered as the actor who played the part of radio's *The* LONE RANGER for thirteen years—longer than any other actor in any medium—actor Brace Beemer was born in Mt. Carmel, Illinois. His rich baritone voice proved perfect for the role of the Lone Ranger when actor Earle Graser, who had been playing the part, died in an automobile accident in 1941. Beemer also played Sergeant Preston of the Northwest Mounted Police on CHALLENGE OF THE YUKON.

Noted for taking his assignment very seriously, the actor would dress in his Lone Ranger costume, complete with mask and usually with his horse, Silver, and visit orphanages, schools, and nursing homes without compensation or publicity. He did so to "raise the spirits of less-fortunate Americans." Interestingly, because he looked the part of the Ranger even when others played the role, Beemer made all of the personal appearances for station WXYZ before he began to play the role. He believed that his personal life should be conducted in a manner that reflected the values of the moral character he was portraying. The actor continued to make public appearances as the Lone Ranger until shortly before his death in Oxford, Michigan, at the age of sixty-three.

BEGLEY, ED (1901–1970)

Character actor Ed Begley, born in Hartford, Connecticut, was equally adept in films (*Twelve Angry Men* (1957), on television ("St. Elsewhere"), onstage (as Willy Loman in Arthur Miller's *Death of a Salesman* [1948]), or on radio: *The* ALAN YOUNG SHOW, BIG SISTER, *The* FAT MAN (as Sergeant O'Hara), JOYCE JORDAN, GIRL INTERN, LIFE CAN BE BEAUTIFUL, MYRT AND MARGE, *The* MYSTERIOUS TRAVELER, OFFICIAL DETECTIVE, RICHARD DIAMOND, P.I. (as Police Lt. Levenson), STELLA DALLAS, *The* INNER SANCTUM MYSTERIES, GANGBUSTERS, and *The* FBI IN PEACE AND WAR.

The actor tended to play flustered, self-important men who always seemed to have something to hide.

In addition to his Academy Award–winning role as Best Supporting Actor in *Sweet Bird of Youth* (1962), he appeared in such films as *Boomerang* (1947), *Patterns of Power* (1956), and *Firecreek* (1967). Begley was featured on many TV dramatic anthology series, such as "Studio One" and "Playhouse 90."

BEHIND THE MIKE

1931–1932	CBS	Mon.	9:15 PM
1932–1940	(Off the air)		
1940–1942	NBC Blue	Sun.	4:30 PM

This 15-minute and then half-hour series gave listeners a behind-the-scenes look at radio broadcasts using a news-documentary style. Typical topics covered on the series were soap-opera "script doctors," stories about such radio celebrities as Arthur GODFREY, radio show "bloopers," and the creation of sound effects. Graham MCNAMEE was the show's host and program guide, and Harry VON ZELL was its announcer. The director and writers of this series are unknown. Frostilla lotion sponsored the series.

BELIEVE IT OR NOT (AKA BAKER'S BROADCAST; ROMANCE; RHYTHM AND RIPLEY)

1930–1931	NBC Red	Mon.	7:30 PM
1931–1932	NBC Blue	Wed., Fri.	7:45 PM
1932–1934	(Off the air)		
1934–1935	NBC Blue	Sat.	10 PM
1936–1937	NBC Blue	Sun.	7:30 PM
1937–1938	NBC Red	Sat.	8 PM
1938–1939	NBC Red	Tues.	10 PM
1939–1940	CBS	Fri.	10:30 PM
1940–1941	CBS	Fri.	10 PM
1941–1942	NBC Blue	Sat.	10 PM
1942–1943	(Off the air)		
1943–1944	Mutual	Mon.–Fri.	9:15 PM
1944–1945	(Off the air)		
1945–1946	CBS	Thurs.	10:30 PM
1946–1947	(Off the air)		
1947–1948	NBC	Mon.–Fri.	1:45 PM

Robert RIPLEY's long-running radio program was based on his syndicated newspaper-cartoon feature, *Believe It Or Not.* This series reported strange occurrences, odd circumstances, and introduced to the public unusual personalities from all over the world, such as Gertrude Ederle, who swam the English Channel; Siamese twins; or a woman who could break glass by hitting a high C while singing. Presented in a 15-minute news-program format, the show occasionally used dramatizations of the events being reported.

Robert Ripley starred as program host. Actually, he seemed to be more interested in explaining how things happened than why; for example, Ripley focused on Gertrude Ederle's training schedule rather than on why she chose to swim the English Channel. On the show, Ripley also offered news scoops, and was the first reporter to break the "Wrong Way Corrigan" story, which was about a man who flew an airplane the wrong way from New York to Ireland, instead of from New York to California as planned.

B. A. Rolfe's orchestra, a quartet called The Men About Town (Jack Parker, Will Donaldson, Harry "Scrappy" Lambert, and Phil Duey), bandleader Ozzie NELSON and his vocalist Harriet HILLIARD, and actors Carl Eastman, Barbara Lee, Ethel Everett, and Peg Murray were featured on the program at various times. Announcers for the series included Bill Griffis, Greg Abbott, Clayton "Bud" COLLYER, Ted Jewett, and Don HANCOCK. David Davidson wrote the program for several seasons. Sponsoring the show were Colonial Beacon oil, Esso oil, Fleischmann's yeast, Huskies dog food, Post bran flakes, Royal Crown Cola, and Pall Mall cigarettes. The show's theme music was "March Moderne."

BELL TELEPHONE HOUR, THE (AKA THE TELEPHONE HOUR)

1940–1941	NBC Red	Mon.	8 PM
1941–1942	NBC Red	Mon.	9 PM
1942–1958	NBC	Mon.	9 PM

Donald VOORHEES and his fifty-seven-piece Bell Telephone Company Orchestra were the popular attractions on this long-running program of classical and semiclassical music that also featured guest artists from the concert and opera stages. The show was part of NBC's "Monday Night of Music" format for many years, other programs being *The* VOICE OF FIRESTONE and *The* RAILROAD HOUR.

Announcing the one-hour show over the years were Floyd Mack, Dick Joy, and Tom Shirley. At one time, actor Raymond Edward JOHNSON was heard as the voice of Alexander Graham Bell on the program, and the renowned stage actor Walter Hampden acted as the show's narrator on a 75th anniversary special presented by the Bell company. Some of the celebrated musical artists who made regular appearances on this program included violinist Jascha Heifetz; basso Ezio Pinza; baritone Nelson EDDY; contralto Marion Anderson, sopranos Grace Moore, Bidù Sayão, Lily Pons, and Helen Traubel; tenor James MELTON; pianists Jose Iturbi and Robert Casadesus; Ken Christie's Mixed Chorus; and singers Lucille Cummings and Francis White.

The series was directed for many years by Walter McCall and written by Norman Rosten and Mort Lewis. The show's sponsor was the Bell Telephone Company. The *Telephone Hour*'s theme song was "The Bell Waltz."

BEN BERNIE SHOW, THE (AKA BEN BERNIE AND ALL HIS LADS)

1931–1932	CBS	Tues.	9 PM
1932–1936	NBC Red	Tues.	9 PM
1936–1937	NBC Blue	Tues.	9 PM
1937–1938	CBS	Thurs.	10 PM
1938–1940	CBS	Sun.	5:30 PM
1940–1941	NBC Blue	Tues.	8 PM
1941–1942	(Off the air)		
1942–1943	CBS	Mon.–Fri.	5:45 PM

Orchestra leader Ben BERNIE had a popular-music/variety program on the air throughout the 1930s and into the 1940s featuring popular songs and comedy sketches. Vocalists on the show at different times were "Little" Jackie Heller, Mary Small, Jane PICKENS, Frank Prince, The Bailey Sisters (Sue and Jane), Dinah SHORE, Buddy CLARK, Gracie Barrie, and Dick Stabile. Comedians Fuzzy Knight, Bill Hillpot, Lew Lahr, "Scrappy" Lambert, as well as actress Agnes MOOREHEAD also appeared. Bernie's memorable closing statement on the program was: "And now the time has come to lend an ear. Au revoir. Pleasant dreams. Think of us when requesting your themes." Bob Brown, Harlow Wilcox, and Harry VON ZELL were the show's announcers. *The Ben Bernie Show* was written by Al Miller, Parke Levy, Gary Stevens, and Alan Lipscott. William Rousseau directed the series in the 1940s. Pabst Blue Ribbon beer, U.S. Rubber, American Aluminum Can Company, Half-and-Half powdered milk, Bromo Seltzer antacid, and Wrigley's gum sponsored the show.

BENADERET, BEA (1906–1968)

New York City–born actress Bea Benaderet's acting versatility allowed her to appear on a wide variety of radio programs from comedy to drama. As a child, she studied voice and piano and hoped to become a concert artist. She gained national fame as one of the funny telephone operators, Gertrude Gearshift, who dated Jack Benny on the JACK BENNY SHOW. Benaderet made her radio debut on station KGO and then worked at KFRC as a singer, announcer, writer, and producer. Later, she became one of radio's busiest actresses and was featured regularly on SUSPENSE and SAM SPADE, DETECTIVE. She also played Mrs. Anderson on the DAY IN THE LIFE OF DENNIS DAY series, Mrs. Carstairs on the FIBBER MCGEE AND MOLLY SHOW, Eve Goodwin on *The* GREAT GILDERSLEEVE, Wanda Werewulf on GLAMOUR MANOR, Amber Lipscott on MY FRIEND IRMA, Gloria the maid on OZZIE AND HARRIET, and several roles on the MEL BLANC SHOW. In the late 1930s and 1940s, Benaderet also played numerous supporting roles on *The* LUX RADIO THEATER.

In spite of her impressive list of radio credits, Bea Benaderet is probably best known for her TV role as the boardinghouse owner Kate Bradley, mother of two daughters, on "Petticoat Junction" and as George and Gracie's next-door neighbor Blanche Morton, on the "Burns and Allen" TV show. Benaderet was also the voice of Betty Rubble on "The Flintstones" TV cartoon series. Benaderet died while "Petticoat Junction" was still on the air.

BENDIX, WILLIAM (1906–1964)

Brooklyn-born actor William Bendix, who usually played gruff guys with a heart of gold, gained unexpected film stardom from his performance in the film *The Glass Key* (1942), which starred Alan Ladd and Veronica Lake. Bendix made his acting debut at the age of thirty in a Broadway production of *The Time of Your Life* and went on to appear in many films after *The Glass Key,* including *The Hairy Ape* (1944), *Lifeboat* (1943), *The Blue Dahlia* (1945), *The Time of Your Life* (1948), *Detective Story* (1951), and *Law of the Lawless* (1963). Bendix became a radio star when he replaced actor Lionel Stander as Chester A. Riley on *The* LIFE OF RILEY. He played this role on radio for more than six years and made a successful transition from radio to television with the show in 1953. Bendix's other radio performances included numerous guest-starring appearances on the LUX RADIO THEATER and other dramatic anthology programs.

BENNY GOODMAN'S SWING SCHOOL

1936–1937	CBS	Tues.	10 PM
1937–1938	CBS	Tues.	9:30 PM

Originally part of the 60-minute *Camel Caravan* show, *Benny Goodman's Swing School* became a separate half-hour series after one year and remained on the air for one season, 1937–1938. Master clarinet player and bandleader Goodman was the host of this program, which featured his swing band and announcers Dan SEYMOUR and Bill GOODWIN. Popular songs of the day were presented on this show, which frequently featured various singing stars as guests. Camel cigarettes and Prince Albert tobacco sponsored the series.

BENNY, JACK (BENJAMIN KUBELSKY: 1894–1974)

One of radio's most popular and talented comedians, Jack Benny was born in Chicago but grew up in Waukegan, Illinois, where his father, Meyer Kubelsky, had a store. At seventeen, Benny tried performing, somewhat unsuccessfully, in vaudeville and then enlisted in the U.S. Navy "to see the world." After discharge, he returned to vaudeville, first as a violinist and then as a comedian because no one could take his violin playing seriously. Benny's first radio appearance was in the late 1920s, but it was on Ed Sullivan's popular variety show in 1931 that he received national exposure and attention. He was so well received by the program's listeners that the next year he had a radio show of his own. He remained on the air until 1953, never missing a single season.

Like Fred ALLEN, Jack Benny was one of the first comedians to recognize the fact that performing on the radio was very different from performing onstage. Like Allen, Benny used sound—and even silence—to get laughs. The radio character Benny developed over the years was so convincing that some people attributed the stinginess of his radio character to the comedian himself, even though he was known as one of the most generous performers in the business. On his radio show, Benny is well remembered for his on-the-air banter with real-life wife, Mary LIVINGSTONE, his valet Eddie "Rochester" ANDERSON, his bandleader, and various tenors who were heard on the show. His program is also remembered for such outrageous running gags as Benny's keeping a pet polar bear, Carmichael, in his basement to guard his safe and therefore his money; his terrible violin playing; his baby-blue eyes; the fact that he wore a toupee; his ancient Maxwell automobile; and his dates with two telephone operators from Brooklyn.

His radio characterization became so well established in listeners' minds that when on one of his shows a mugger held a gun to his head and said, "Your money or you life," some of his radio audience began to titter. Supposedly stingy Benny paused for a long time, and more laughter followed. When the mugger repeated his line and Benny finally broke his silence to say, "I'm thinking ... I'm thinking," the studio audience—and presumably millions of listeners at home—laughed for another full minute-and-a-half.

In addition to his long and successful career on radio and TV, Benny also starred in numerous motion pictures, such as *Charley's Aunt* (1941), *George Washington Slept Here* (1942), *To Be or Not to Be* (1942), *The Horn Blows at Midnight* (1945), and *It's a Mad, Mad, Mad, Mad World* (1963). When Jack Benny died, *The New York Times* wrote: "He was adored by the public, and even the most sophisticated critics appreciated him as an outstanding comedian."

See also JACK BENNY SHOW, *The*.

BERCH, JACK

See JACK BERCH SHOW, *The*.

BERG, GERTRUDE (1899–1966)

Nationally known as the quintessential Jewish mother, Molly Goldberg (on her hit radio and TV series, *The* GOLDBERGS), writer-actress Gertrude Berg was a multitalented woman. Born in New York City, Berg wrote as well as starred in all of the thousands of *Goldbergs* episodes from 1927, when the show first aired on radio, until it moved to television from 1945 to 1953.

Berg began to write and act as a young woman at her father's Catskill resort hotel, where she often performed for guests. After finishing her schooling in New York City, she wrote plays for the Jewish Art Theater. In addition to her very successful *Goldbergs* program on radio, Berg also wrote and starred in the less-than-well-received HOUSE OF GLASS and KATE HOPKINS, ANGEL OF MERCY radio programs.

On *The Goldbergs,* the actress-writer became well known for such Molly Goldberg sayings as "Is anybody?" (when asking if anyone was home) and "Yoo hoo, Mrs. Kramer!" (when she was leaning out of her apartment window and calling to her next-door neighbor). Berg brought her Molly Goldberg character to Broadway in the hit play "Molly and Me" (1948) and also had a success in *A Majority of One* (1959). In 1955, Berg wrote *The Molly Goldberg Cookbook.*

BERGEN, EDGAR (1903–1978)

Ventriloquist Edgar Bergen, the talented son of Norwegian immigrants, was born on a farm in Decatur, Michigan. After attending Northwestern University, Bergen decided to pursue a career in show business. With his wooden dummies, Charlie McCarthy and Mortimer Snerd, Bergen became a vaudeville headliner and in 1936 a popular radio personality on the CHASE AND SANBORN *Hour* comedy-variety show, also starring Don AMECHE. A few years later, the show became known as the EDGAR BERGEN–CHARLIE MCCARTHY SHOW—Bergen and his dummies had by that time become household names. In fact, the Charlie McCarthy character was unquestionably the major reason for Bergen's phenomenal success on radio. Listeners absolutely adored the dummy, who actually seemed to be a real person: he was a bad little playboy who sported a tuxedo, a top hat, and a monocle. Charlie smoked cigarettes, was an outrageous flirt, and could match wits with such guest stars as W. C. Fields (with whom he had an ongoing "feud"). Bergen's other popular dummy character Mortimer Snerd, on the other hand, was Charlie's exact opposite: a country bumpkin with naive ways and slow-wittedness. It was, of course, the creative genius of actor-ventriloquist Edgar Bergen that made all of this great comedy happen.

In addition to starring on radio's *The Chase and Sanborn Hour* and *The Edgar Bergen–Charlie McCarthy Show,* Bergen was also active in motion pictures and was seen in films such as *Letters of Introduction* (1938), *Here We Go Again* (1942), and *I Remember Mama* (1947).

BERGMAN, TEDDY

See REED, ALAN.

BERLE, MILTON (MENDEL BERLINGER: 1908–)

A native New Yorker, comedian Milton Berle began his long, brilliant career in the entertainment industry at the age of ten in silent films. He performed on the vaudeville circuit and appeared regularly on radio many years before his success on TV. *The* MILTON BERLE SHOW first aired on radio in 1944 and contained some of the wild slapstick humor that became the trademark of his TV show—but it was not successful.

Berle was subsequently heard on the *Three Ring Time* and *Let Yourself Go* radio shows, both of which were even less successful than his first one. Berle continued to perform on radio in a 1947 revival of *The Milton Berle Show* and in STOP ME IF YOU'VE HEARD THIS ONE after making his way into American homes as "Uncle Miltie" on TV's immensely popular "Milton Berle Show," which ran from 1948 to 1956. He also occasionally appeared in films (*Always Leave Them Laughing* [1949] and *It's a Mad, Mad, Mad, Mad World* [1963]). A living legend for his durability and self-mocking talents at "joke thievery," Berle was honored in December 1993 as one of the first inductees into the Comedy Hall of Fame.

BERNIE, BEN (BERNARD ANCELOWITZ: 1891–1943)

Orchestra leader Ben Bernie was born in Bayonne, New Jersey, to Russian-Jewish immigrant parents. As a child, Bernie studied violin and at sixteen attended New York University, where he majored in engineering. Finding himself short of cash, he left school to work as a violin salesman. In 1920, Bernie formed a band and began to play in various motion-picture and vaudeville theaters. After a triumphant engagement at London's famed Kit Kat Club, Bernie and his band returned to the United States and began a long and illustrious career on radio in 1923. Bernie and his band starred on *The Pabst Blue Ribbon Malt Program* and *The* BEN BERNIE SHOW. Bernie died at the height of his radio career.

BETTY AND BOB

1932–1933	NBC Blue	Mon.–Fri.	3 PM
1933–1936	NBC Blue	Mon.–Fri.	4 PM
1935–1936	NBC Blue	Mon.–Fri.	4 PM
1936–1938	CBS	Mon.–Fri.	1 PM
1938–1940	NBC Red	Mon.–Fri.	2 PM
1940–1941	NBC Red	Mon.–Fri.	1:45 PM

One of radio's earliest daytime serial dramas was NBC's 15-minute *Betty and Bob*, which originated in Chicago. The series was about a young married couple, Betty and Bob Drake, and their friends and family, including an ever-present domineering, interfering mother-in-law. The stories were interesting enough to keep audiences involved five days a week for more than nine years. Six actresses played the part of Betty: Elizabeth Reller originated the role, followed by Beatrice Churchill, Alice Hill, Arlene FRANCIS, Edith Davis, and Mercedes MCCAMBRIDGE. Don AMECHE was the first Bob, followed by Les TREMAYNE, Onslow Stevens, Spencer Bentley, Carl Frank, J. Anthony Hughes, and Van Heflin. Ned WEVER, Francis X. Bushman, Louise Fitch, Art Kohl, Dora Johnson, Forrest

Lewis, Rita Ascott, Herb Nelson, Frank Dane, Bill BOUCHEY, Dorothy Shideler, Jim Goss, Olga Rosenova, Donna Reade, Edith Davis, Eloise Kummer, Eleanor Dowling, Loretta Poynton, Frank Pacelli, Don Briggs, Ethel Owen, Peggy Wall, and Henry Saxe were among the many actors who had supporting roles on the series. Pierre Andre and Verne Smith were among the show's announcers. David Owen directed the series in the 1940s, when the program was at the height of its popularity. The show's writers included Leonard Berovici and Edwin Morse. Sponsors of the show included Wheaties cereal, Gold Medal flour, and Bisquick. The show's theme music was "Salût d'Amour."

BETTY CROCKER SHOW, THE (AKA BETTY CROCKER MAGAZINE OF THE AIR)

1926–1927	NBC Red	Mon., Wed., Fri.	10:40 AM
1927–1928	NBC Red	Tues., Thurs.	11 AM
1928–1929	NBC Red	Wed.	11 AM
1929–1930	NBC Red	Tues., Thurs.	10:45 AM
1930–1931	NBC Red	Tues., Thurs.	10:30 AM
1931–1936	NBC Red	Wed., Fri.	10:45 AM
1936–1938	CBS	Wed., Fri.	1:15 AM
1938–1940	NBC Red	Wed., Fri.	2:45 AM
1940–1941	CBS	Wed., Fri.	9:45 AM
1941–1945	NBC	Fri.	2:45 AM
1945–1946	NBC Blue	Fri.	10:30 AM
1946–1951	ABC	Mon.–Fri.	10:30 AM
1951–1952	ABC	Mon.–Fri.	4 PM
1952–1953	ABC	Mon.–Fri.	2:30 PM

On this 15-minute program, actresses Zella Lane and Rita Ascott, among others, played the role of Betty Crocker, a fictional homemaker-cook invented by the Betty Crocker baking company to be their product's spokeswoman. On the program, Crocker gave her listeners recipes and information about food and nutrition as well as other household tips, such as how to take care of silverware and sew a button on a shirt. Win ELLIOTT and Pierre Andre were the show's announcers. *The Betty Crocker Show* was on the air for more than twenty-seven years and was sponsored by Betty Crocker cake mixes, Gold Medal flour, and Softasilk cake flour.

BETWEEN THE BOOKENDS

1935–1936	CBS	Mon.–Fri.	1:45 PM
1936–1937	CBS	Mon., Tues., Wed., Fri.	4 PM
1937–1938	Mutual	Mon.–Fri.	2:15 PM
1938–1940	NBC Blue	Mon.–Fri.	3:45 PM
1940–1941	NBC Blue	Mon.–Fri.	1:15 PM
1941–1942	NBC Blue	Mon.–Fri.	2:15 PM
1942–1943	NBC Blue	Mon.–Fri.	3:30 PM
1943–1944	NBC Blue	Mon.–Fri.	3:45 PM
1944–1945	NBC Blue	Mon., Tues., Wed., Fri.	8 PM

1945–1948	ABC	Mon.–Fri.	11:45 AM
1948–1949	ABC	Mon.–Fri.	11:30 AM
1949–1951	ABC	Mon.–Fri.	4:45 PM
1951–1956	ABC	Mon.–Fri.	1:15 PM

This long-running 15-minute one-man show was on the air for more than twenty years and starred master raconteur Ted MALONE, who had a warm, intimate manner of speaking that made listeners feel as if he were talking just to them. As organist Rosa Rio supplied a suitable musical background, Malone read his poetry and that of others and recounted personal incidents or observations that were usually amusing and always uplifting. Sponsors included Hinds honey and almond cream and Westinghouse electric products. Malone wrote the original material heard on the show. His theme music was "Auld Lang Syne."

BEULAH

| 1945–1953 | CBS | Mon.–Fri. | 7 PM |
| 1953–1954 | CBS | Mon.–Fri. | 7:15 PM |

The half-hour and then 15-minute, five-days-a-week *Beulah* situation-comedy series was one of radio's most successful "spin-off" programs. An African-American maid, Beulah was originally a character on the FIBBER MCGEE AND MOLLY show; the character became so popular among listeners that she was given a weekly show of her own in the mid-1940s. The first performer to play the part of Beulah was a white man named Marlin HURT. It was Hurt who originated some of Beulah's most quoted and audience-pleasing one-liners, such as, "Love dat man!" and "Somebody bawl for Beulah?" which were repeated by listeners all across America. When Hurt died of a heart attack at the height of his popularity in 1947, Academy Award-winning African-American actress Hattie MCDANIEL and then Lillian RANDOLPH and Louise Beavers played the role. Other well-known actors who were regularly heard on this series included Butterfly McQueen, Vivien and Ruby DANDRIDGE, Amanda RANDOLPH, Nicodemus Stewart, and Jester Hairson. Hugh STUDEBAKER and Jess Kirkpatrick played Beulah's boss, Mr. Henderson. Mary Jane CROFT, and then Lois Corbett, played Mrs. Henderson. Henry Blair played the Hendersons' son, Donnie. Originally, Marlin Hurt doubled as, and then Ernest Whitman played, Beulah's boyfriend, Bill Jackson. John Brown was also frequently featured in the supporting cast. The series was directed by Helen Mack, Tom McKnight, Jack Hurdle, and Steve Harris and written by Charles Stewart, Phil Leslie, Hal Kanter, Sol Stewart, Seeman Jacobs, Sol Schwartz, and Sol Sacks. The *Beulah* show was sponsored by Tums antacid and Proctor and Gamble products, Dreft cleanser, Postum drink, and

Hugh Studebaker and Mary Jane Croft during a broadcast of *Beulah*. (CBS)

Post Toasties breakfast cereal. Hank Weaver, Ken NILES, Marvin MILLER, and Johnny Jacobs were the show's announcers.

BICKERSONS, THE

1946–1947	NBC	Sun.	10 PM
1947–1948	CBS	Wed.	8 PM
1948–1951	(Off the air)		
1951	CBS	Tues.	9:30 PM

The Bickersons was originally a short comedy sketch that was heard on the CHASE AND SANBORN HOUR program. Don AMECHE and singer Frances LANGFORD, who were both regulars on that show, played the parts of a constantly bickering husband and wife, John and Blanche Bickerson. The forever-bickering couple became so popular among listeners that Ameche and Langford (later replaced by film actress Marsha Hunt) were given a half-hour weekly situation-comedy series, *The Bickersons*, in 1946. Actor-comedian Danny Thomas also appeared regularly on the series as John's brother, Amos. The show's announcers were Toby Reed and John Holbrook. The *Bickersons* was created by writer Phil Rapp, who wrote many Bickerson scripts. Sponsors included Drene shampoo, Dreft flour, and Old Gold cigarettes.

BIG JON AND SPARKIE

| 1948–1958 | (Syndicated series. Various stations and times) |

First heard on a local radio station in Cincinnati and then syndicated throughout the country, this children's adventure series starred Jon Arthur, who played all of the major roles on the show, including Big John, Sparkie, Mayor Plumpfront, and Ukey Betcha,

Episodes centered around Sparkie, a young boy, who would typically help to catch a thief, make a telephone out of two tin cans and string, or race in a soap-box derby. In 1950, the show was heard on the ABC network for one hour each weekday, Monday through Friday. Toward the end of its radio run, the show was reduced to 15-minutes each weekday, and its title was changed to *The Further Adventures of Big Jon and Sparkie.* William J. Mahoney was heard as a character named Gil Hooley, who led the show's marching band. Mahoney also served as the program's technical director. In addition to being the show's star, Jon Arthur was also its producer. The series was written by Donald Kortekamp. *Big Jon and Sparkie's* theme music was "The Teddy Bear's Picnic."

BIG SHOW, THE

| 1950–1953 | NBC | Sun. | 6 PM |

The glamorous, unpredictable, and often outrageous stage and screen star Tallulah BANKHEAD became a major radio personality when she hosted NBC's 90-minute comedy-variety show *The Big Show.* Each week, the deep-voiced Miss Bankhead greeted an impressive number of big-name film, stage, and radio stars on the show. She and her guests sang, acted in skits, told jokes, and promoted their latest projects. The first show, heard on December 17, 1950, featured such prominent guest stars as the comedy team of Martin and Lewis, actress Deborah Kerr, musician Louis Armstrong, and comedian Bob HOPE. Later guest stars included Bing CROSBY, FIBBER MCGEE AND MOLLY, Jack BENNY, Fred ALLEN, Groucho MARX, Jack CARSON, Lauritz Melchior, Ed GARDNER, Jimmy DURANTE, Danny Thomas, Mindy Carson, Jose Ferrer, Ethel MERMAN, Paul Lukas, Frankie Laine, Joan DAVIS, Herb Shriner, and George JESSEL. The show's music director was composer-conductor Meredith WILLSON, whose weekly greeting, "Good evening, Miss Bankhead, sir," made audiences squeal with delight. Tallulah ended each program singing "May the Good Lord Bless and Keep You." Although *The Big Show* was produced in the early 1950s to try to lure audiences away from television, it ultimately could not compete with TV's predominance, and the show departed the airwaves after three seasons. Ed HERLIHY was the show's announcer. *The Big Show's* chief writer and director was Goodman ACE. Sponsors included Anacin pain relievers, Chesterfield cigarettes, and Reynolds aluminum.

BIG SISTER

1936–1941	CBS	Mon.–Fri.	11:30 AM
1941–1946	CBS	Mon.–Fri.	12:15 PM
1946–1953	CBS	Mon.–Fri.	1 PM

Big Sister was first aired on CBS in 1936 and centered on the domestic affairs of a character named Sue Evans Miller and her relationship with her big sister, Ruth Evans.

Ruth had numerous domestic problems on the show, such as the death of her husband and her subsequent remarriage, but she always came to the rescue of her younger sister (who had husband trouble of her own) whenever possible. Actresses Alice FROST, Nancy Marshall, Marjorie Anderson, Mercedes MCCAMBRIDGE, and Grace MATTHEWS played "Big Sister" Ruth; Haila Stoddard, Dorothy McGuire, Peggy Conklin and Fran CARLON played "Little Sister" Sue. Also heard in featured roles were Vera Allen, Agnes MOOREHEAD, Alan REED, William "Bill" JOHNSTONE, Ruth Chatterton, ZaSu Pitts, Diana Barrymore, Michael O'DAY, Chester STRATTON, Helene Dumas, Ned WEVER, Louise Fitch, Barbara Lee, Linda Carlton, Charles Webster, Elspeth ERIC, Eric Dressler, Santos ORTEGA, Martin GABEL, Paul MCGRATH, Staats COTSWORTH, Ed BEGLEY, Charlotte Holland, Ann SHEPHARD, Ian Martin, Arnold MOSS, Susan Douglas, Jim Ameche, Jr. (Jim Ameche's son), Joe JULIAN, Barry Kroeger, Horace Braham, Harold Vermilyea, Alexander Kirkland, Patsy Campbell, Adelaide Klein, Anne BURR, Ralph Bell, Richard WIDMARK, Mason ADAMS, Teri Keane, and Everett SLOANE. The program's announcers were Fred Uttal, Jim AMECHE, Hugh MARLOWE, and Nelson CASE. Wilson Tuttle, Mitchell Grayson, and Thomas F. Victor directed the series in the 1930s and early 1940s. The series was written by Julian Funt, Carl Bixby, Robert Newman, and Bill Sweets. *Big Sister's* theme music was "Valse Bluette." Sponsors included Rinso cleanser, Lifebuoy soap, Lipton soup, Ivory soap, Spic and Span floor cleanser, Dreft detergent, and Joy dishwashing liquid.

BIG STORY, THE

| 1947–1951 | NBC | Wed. | 10 PM |
| 1951–1954 | NBC | Wed. | 9:30 PM |

Robert Sloane narrated this half-hour NBC series, which consisted of news-story adaptations from newspapers throughout the country. Each story dramatized won a $500 Pall Mall award for the reporter who wrote the original. At the end of each program, the reporter was introduced to the listening audience. Regular performers on this series included Robert DRYDEN, William J. Smith, Bill Quinn, Bernard Grant, Betty GARDE, Alice FROST, and Craig McDonnell. Cy Harrice and Ernest CHAPPELL were the program's announcers. Harry Ingram and Thomas F. Vieler, Jr., directed the series. The show was written by Gail and Harry Ingram. In addition to Pall Mall cigarettes, Lucky Strike cigarettes also sponsored the program.

The program's theme music was Richard Strauss's *Ein Heldenleben*.

BIG TOWN

1937–1940	CBS	Tues.	8 PM
1940–1941	CBS	Wed.	8 PM
1941–1942	CBS	Wed.	7:30 PM
1942–1948	CBS	Tues.	8 PM
1948–1951	NBC	Tues.	10 PM
1951–1952	CBS	Wed.	8 PM

"The freedom of the press is a flaming sword. Use it justly, hold it high, guard it well," the half-hour weekly *Big Town* series began. *The Illustrated Press*, a fictional big-city newspaper, was the headquarters for two crime solvers, editor Steve Wilson and star reporter Lorelei Kilbourne. When the show debuted in the late 1930s, film stars Edward G. Robinson and Claire Trevor played Wilson and Kilbourne. Walter GREAZA and Ona Munson also played the parts, but Edward PAWLEY and Fran CARLON are best remembered in the roles and played them the longest. Other actors regularly heard on the series included Ed Mac-Donald, Gale GORDON, Kate McComb, Dwight WEIST, Ted DeCorsia, Robert DRYDEN, Betty WINKLER, Lawson Zerbe, Bill ADAMS, Michael O'DAY (as the newsboy who hawked *The Illustrated Press* at the beginning of

Edward Pawley and Fran Carlon played *Big Town's* Steve Wilson and Lorelei Kilbourne. (NBC)

each show), Harlan Stone, Harry Haines, George Petrie, Mason ADAMS, Thelma Ritter, and Paula Winslow. The show's announcers were Ken NILES, John Conte, and Dwight WEIST. *Big Town* was created by Jerry McGill, who wrote and directed many of the episodes. Over the years, Richard Uhl, Joseph Bell, Crane Wilbur, and William N. ROBSON also directed. John Gart was the show's organist, and Leith Stevens was the music director. Rinso, Ironized yeast tablets, Bayer aspirin, Rinso cleanser, and Lifebuoy soap were the show's sponsors. "Tell the Story" was the show's theme music.

BILLIE BURKE SHOW, THE
See *GAY MRS. FEATHERSTONE, The*.

BILLY AND BETTY

1939–1940	NBC Red, CBS	Mon.–Fri.	5:15 PM

James "Jimmy" McCallion and Audrey Egan starred as Billy and Betty on this 15-minute, Monday-through-Friday children's serial about two youngsters who constantly seemed to be stumbling into dangerous situations, such as becoming mixed up in a spy network. In the supporting cast were Charles CANTOR, Paul Stewart, Selena Royle, Charles Dingle, and Van Heflin. The show's directors and writers were uncredited. Corn Kix cereal was the show's sponsor.

BING CROSBY SHOW, THE (AKA THE WOODBURY PROGRAM; PHILCO RADIO TIME)

1931–1932	CBS	Mon.–Fri.	7:15 PM
1932–1933	CBS	Wed., Sat.	9 PM
1933–1934	CBS	Mon.	8:30 PM
1934–1935	CBS	Tues.	9 PM
1946–1949	ABC	Wed.	10 PM
1949–1952	CBS	Wed.	9:30 PM
1952–1953	CBS	Thurs.	9:30 PM
1953–1954	CBS	Sun.	8 PM
1954–1955	CBS	Mon.–Fri.	9:15 PM
1955–1956	CBS	Mon.–Fri.	7:30 PM

Singer Bing CROSBY starred on his own radio show as early as 1931, but he became one of radio's biggest stars while on *The KRAFT MUSIC HALL* program. Prior to appearing on the show, Bing starred on the half-hour *The Bing Crosby-Woodbury Show*, which featured the BOSWELL SISTERS, The Mills Brothers, Georgie Stoll and his Orchestra, and announcer Ken NILES. Because his sponsor, Kraft foods, refused to allow him to record his shows, Bing left *The Kraft Music Hall* show in 1946 and became the star of *The Bing Crosby-Philco Radio Time* show, which featured his backup singers, the Rhythmaires, and an orchestra led by John Scott Trotter. The show remained on the air well after most big-name stars had deserted radio for television.

Crosby's longtime announcers were Ken NILES, Ken CARPENTER, and Glenn Riggs. His guest stars included Judy GARLAND (who was practically a regular on the show), Bob HOPE, the ANDREWS SISTERS, Tallulah BANKHEAD, Nat King Cole, Al JOLSON, Marlene Dietrich, Humphrey BOGART and Lauren Bacall, Henry Fonda, Ethel MERMAN, and guitarist Les Paul and his wife, Mary Ford. Crosby's producer for many years was Bill Murrow, and his longtime director was Murdo McKenzie. Sponsors of *The Bing Crosby Show* included Woodbury facial soap ("for the skin you love to touch"), Philco radios and phonographs, Chesterfield cigarettes, and the General Electric Company. Crosby's most familiar theme music was "When the Blue of the Night Meets the Gold of the Day," a song he had made famous in an early film, *The King of Jazz* (1930).

BLANC, MEL (1908–1989)

Mel Blanc was born in San Francisco, California, grew up in Portland, Oregon, and became one of the most talented and versatile performers who ever stood in front of a microphone. Although most famous as the voice of such celebrated Warner Brothers' cartoon characters as Bugs Bunny, Porky Pig, Daffy Duck,

Mel Blanc (NBC)

Speedy Gonzales, Sylvester, and Pepe Le Pew, Blanc also performed regularly on many popular radio programs from the mid-1930s through the 1950s. On *The* JACK BENNY SHOW, he played everything from the conductor who announced that the train was approaching "Anaheim, Azusa and Coooo . . . (pause) . . . camonga" to Benny's ancient, wheezing Maxwell automobile and his long-suffering violin teacher Professor LeBlanc.

Blanc's first major radio show was *Cobwebs and Nuts* on KEX in Los Angeles in 1934. Besides *The Jack Benny Show*, Blanc was regularly featured on *The* JUDY CANOVA SHOW (as Pedro and Roscoe Wortle), the BURNS AND ALLEN SHOW (as the Happy Postman), and MAJOR HOOPLE (as Mr. Twiggs). Unfortunately, Blanc was less successful as the star of his own radio program, *The Mel Blanc Show*. The series lasted for a brief year-and-a-half, despite Blanc's formidable talents. Blanc did TV and film cartoon-character voices until shortly before he died.

BLIND DATE

1943	NBC	Thurs.	8 PM
1943–1945	NBC Blue	Mon.	8:30 PM
1945–1946	NBC	Fri.	8 PM

Long before TV's *Dating Game* began to make love connections between couples, radio offered a similar service on a half-hour program called *Blind Date*. Contestants were chosen beforehand by the show's writers, who would arrange for an ideal blind date. After the blind took place, the couple would come back and report on it. Arlene FRANCIS was the show's hostess and one of its chief writers. *Blind Date* was directed by Tom Wallace. Sponsors of the program were Maxwell House coffee, Lysol disinfectant, and Hinds Honey and Almond face cream.

BLOCH, RAY (1903–1982)

One of radio's most sought-after music directors and conductors, Ray Bloch was born in Alsace-Lorraine, Germany, and first worked on American radio in 1930. Bloch led the orchestra on such varied programs as *The* MILTON BERLE SHOW, *The* PHILIP MORRIS PLAYHOUSE, QUICK AS A FLASH, JOHNNY PRESENTS, *Pick and Pat*, *Model Minstrels*, TAKE IT OR LEAVE IT, WHAT'S MY NAME? *Sing It Again*, *Songs for Sale*, and *The* GAY NINETIES REVUE.

See also ORCHESTRA LEADERS.

BLONDIE

1939–1943	CBS	Mon.	7:30 PM
1943–1944	CBS	Sun	7:30 PM
1944–1945	CBS	Sun.	8 PM

The stars of *Blondie*, Penny Singleton and Arthur Lake (Columbia Pictures)

1945–1948	CBS	Sun.	7:30 PM
1948–1949	NBC	Wed.	8 PM
1949–1950	ABC	Thurs.	8 PM

Artist Chic Young's popular comic strip *Blondie* became a half-hour situation-comedy series on radio in 1939 when CBS brought Young's characters to the airwaves. The program opener—"Uh ... Uh ... Uh ... UH! Don't touch that dial! It's time for ..." followed by Arthur LAKE's Dagwood wail, "Blonnnn ... die!"—became famous. Lake played Dagwood for the series' entire radio run. Penny SINGLETON, who played Blondie in the film series with Lake (two films a year for ten years from 1942 to 1952), was the first radio Blondie, succeeded by Alice White, Patricia Van Cleeve, and film star Ann Rutherford. Hanley STAFFORD and Elvia ALLMAN portrayed Dagwood's boss and his wife, Mr. and Mrs. Dithers; Frank NELSON, the Bumstead's next-door neighbor, Woodley; Lenore Ledoux, Baby Dumpling; Larry Sims, Jeffrey Silver, Dix Davis, and Tommy Cook, the older Baby Dumpling, named Alexander; and Marlene Ames, Joan Rae, and Norma Jean Nilsson played Cookie Bumstead. Also heard in regular roles were Veola Vonn, Lurene TUTTLE, and Arthur Q. BRYANT. Bill GOODWIN, Ken NILES, and Howard Petrie were the show's announcers. The series was produced and directed by Don Bernard (Bill Moore and Joe Donohue also directed), and written by Johnny Greene. Super Suds detergent, Camel cigarettes, Prince Albert smoking tobacco, Ford motors, and Colgate toothpaste sponsored the show.

BOB AND RAY (ELLIOTT, BOB: 1923–   ; GOULDING, RAY: 1922–1990)

At local radio station WHDH in Boston in the late 1940s, Bob and Ray first performed their later-to-be-famous skits on an early-morning talk-and-music program. Bob was the show's host, and Ray its announcer. Their satires of current well-known radio shows and their amusing commentaries became the talk of Boston, and in 1953 NBC executives offered them a network show of their own. Bon and Ray always ended their shows with "Write if you get work," and "Hang by your thumbs." Bob and Ray appeared in a two-man stage production, *The Two of Us* (1970), which eventually had a long, successful run on Broadway as well as at various regional theaters and colleges throughout the United States. In the 1970s, Bob and Ray returned to WOR in New York, but stage and television appearances required much of their time.

In addition to their stage show, the team guest-starred on several television variety shows, including "The Colgate Comedy Hour" (1952) and "The Ed Sullivan Show" (1955), and had their own "Bob and Ray Show" (1953). The team's voices also became familiar to millions as Burt and Ernie Piel on Piel's beer commercials. Ray's ill health forced them to retire

Bob Elliott and Ray Goulding (NBC)

their act. He died of a heart attack in 1990, but Bob continues to make public appearances on TV talk shows and as a guest speaker at college seminars and radio retrospectives.

BOB AND RAY SHOW, THE

| 1953–1954 | NBC | Sat. | 8 PM |
| 1955–1956 | Mutual | Mon.–Fri. | 5 PM |

Bob ELLIOTT and Ray GOULDING had such excellent on-the-air rapport as staff announcers at a local radio station in Boston that they were offered a national network show. NBC signed the team to a long-term contract, and before long theirs became one of radio's most frequently listened-to early-morning programs. Bob and Ray developed such memorable characters and sketches as Wally Ballou, "radio's highly regarded and totally inept" remote-broadcast reporter who always began his reports in the middle of a sentence because he had forgotten to turn on his microphone; Mary McGoon, the oddball talk-show hostess who was a combination of Mary Margaret MCBRIDE and Julia Child; "Mary Backstayge, Noble Wife," a soap-opera sketch that spoofed the MARY NOBLE, BACKSTAGE WIFE daytime radio series; "The Transatlantic Bridge"; "Robin Hood of Sherman Forest"; "Mr. District Defender"; "Tales Well Calculated to Keep you in Anxiety"; and "One Feller's Family," a parody of the long-running, popular radio series, ONE MAN'S FAMILY. Bob and Ray were on the air in various time slots on several local stations in Boston and New York and were heard on NATIONAL PUBLIC RADIO stations after the demise of their network show.

BOB BECKER TALKS ABOUT DOGS (AKA DOG HEROES)

1934–1935	NBC Blue	Sun.	2:15 PM
1935–1936	NBC Blue	Sun.	5:45 PM
1936–1937	(Off the air)		
1937–1938	NBC Blue	Sun.	4:45 PM
1938–1939	NBC Red	Sun.	3:45 PM
1939–1940	NBC Red	Sun.	5:15 PM
1940–1941	NBC Red	Sun.	3:45 PM
1941–1942	NBC Red	Sun.	3 PM

Bob Becker hosted this program all about the family dog. On the program, listeners were given tips on how to feed, take care of, train, and groom family pets. Appropriately, the show was sponsored by Red Heart dog food and was popular enough to remain on the air for eight continuous years. Becker wrote, directed, and produced his own shows.

BOB BURNS SHOW, THE (AKA THE ARKANSAS TRAVELER)

1941–1942	CBS	Thurs.	8:30 PM
1942–1943	NBC	Wed.	9 PM
1943–1946	NBC	Thurs.	7:30 PM
1946–1947	NBC	Sun.	6:30 PM

Bob BURNS's homespun country humor made him a regular guest star on many comedy-variety programs. Regularly featured on his own half-hour weekly *Bob Burns Show* were actors Shirley Ross, Ann Thomas, Edna May Oliver, "Bowery Boy" Leo Gorcey, and Jim BACKUS (who gave Bob comic support in sketches), and singers Ginny SIMMS and the Suitcase Six. The show was directed by Joe Thompson and Andrew Love, and written by R. E. Duke Atterbury, Victor McLeod, and Glenn Watson. Sponsors included Campbell soup, Lifebuoy soap, Rinso cleanser, Kolynos toothpaste and tooth powder, Hill's cold tablets, and BiSoDol mints. Burns's theme song was, quite appropriately, "The Arkansas Traveler."

BOB CROSBY SHOW, THE (AKA THE CAMEL CARAVAN)

1935–1936	NBC	Fri.	8:15 PM
1939–1941	CBS	Tues.	9:30 PM
	NBC	Sat.	10 PM
	Mutual	Fri.	10:30 PM
	NBC	Thurs.	9 PM
	NBC Blue	Thurs.	7:30 PM
1941–1943	(Off the air)		
1943–1945	NBC	Sun.	10:30 PM
1946	CBS	Tues.	10 PM & 9:30 PM
1946–1949	(Off the air)		
1949–1950	NBC	Sun.	10:30 PM

Bing CROSBY's younger brother, singer/orchestra leader Bob, had his own successful music-variety radio show for several years. The 15-minute and the half-hour show, which at one time also featured actor Les TREMAYNE as its cohost, presented music and comedy until the early 1940s, when Bob enlisted in the military. Peggy Lee was Crosby's female vocalist for several seasons. Most of its time the show was directed by Bob Brewster. It was written by Carroll Carroll and David Gregory. Camel cigarettes sponsored the program, which, for a time, was also sustained by CBS.

BOB HAWK SHOW, THE (AKA THANKS TO THE YANKS)

1942–1943	CBS	Sat.	7:30 PM
1943–1945	CBS	Mon.	7:30 PM
1945–1947	CBS	Mon.	7:30 PM
1947–1948	NBC	Thurs.	10 PM
1948–1951	CBS	Mon.	10:30 PM
1951–1953	CBS	Mon.	10 PM

Called *Thanks to the Yanks* from 1942 until 1945, the half-hour *Bob Hawk Show* featured comedian-host Bob HAWK as its master of ceremonies. A quiz program, contestants selected from the studio audience were interviewed briefly and usually humorously by Hawk and asked five questions. The answers always began sequentially with letters that eventually spelled C-A-M-E-L—the show's sponsor, Camel cigarettes. If the contestant answered all five questions correctly, he or she was asked a "Lemac" (Camel spelled backward) question. If all of the questions were answered correctly, the contestant won a cash prize of $25 for spelling Camel and Lemac and $250 for a special jackpot answer. The show's announcers were Charles STARK and Dennis James. When George Washington pipe tobacco became the show's sponsor, the format changed somewhat: George and Egroeg became the operative "special" words. Kenneth MacGregor directed the series.

BOB HOPE SHOW, THE (AKA THE PEPSODENT SHOW STARRING BOB HOPE)

1934–1938	(*)		
1938–1941	NBC Red	Tues.	10 PM
1941–1948	NBC	Tues.	10 PM
1948–1952	NBC	Tues.	9 PM
1952–1953	NBC	Wed.	10 PM
1953–1954	NBC	Fri.	8:30 PM
1954–1955	NBC	Thurs.	8:30 PM

Comedian Bob Hope had one of radio's longest-running and most popular comedy-variety programs. The

Bob Hope and his sidekick, Jerry Colonna, on *The Bob Hope Show* (NBC)

entertainer made his radio debut on *The* RUDY VALLEE SHOW in the early 1930s and proved so popular among listeners that he was offered a radio show of his own in 1934. On his half-hour radio shows, which aired for twenty-one years, Hope featured such audience-pleasing characters as bushy-mustachiod comedian Jerry COLONNA, the man-hungry Vera Vague (actress Barbara Jo ALLEN), two equally man-hungry, gushingly brash ladies named Brenda and Cobina (actresses Blanche Stewart and Elvia ALLMAN), guest stars Judy GARLAND, the ANDREWS SISTERS, Dorothy LAMOUR, Henry Fonda, Jane Wyman, and Bing CROSBY, and as regular vocalists Peggy Lee, Margaret Whiting, Six Hits and a Miss, Rosemary Clooney, Frances LANGFORD, Marilyn Maxwell, and Doris Day. Comedian Frank Fontaine played the nasal-voiced and somewhat simple John L. C. Sivoney, a character who later became popular on "The Jackie Gleason Television Show." Trudy Irwin was Miriam, the Pepsodent toothpaste girl who neglected Irium. Jack KIRKWOOD, Patricia Wilder, Claire Hazel, and Irene RYAN were regularly featured in the cast.

During World War II, many of Hope's shows were broadcast from various military installations both in the United States and abroad.

Wendell NILES, Art BAKER, Larry Keating, Bill GOODWIN, Charles Buck, and Hy Averback were Hope's announcers over the years. Al GOODMAN, Red Nichols, Skinnay ENNIS, and Les Brown led the orchestra at different times. Hope's longtime producer was Bill Lawrence; the show was directed variously by Bob Stephenson, Tom Sawyer, Norman Morrell, and Al Capstaff. His talented staff of writers included Milt Josefsberg, Mel Shavelson, Sherwood Schwartz, Jack Douglas, Norman Sullivan, Dave Murray, Fred Williams, and Reni DuPlessi. Hope's theme song was "Thanks for the Memory." In addition to Pepsodent toothpaste, sponsors were Swan soap, Rayve cream shampoo, Lux soap, Spry shortening, General Foods products, the American Dairy Association, and Camel cigarettes.

BOBBY BENSON'S ADVENTURES (AKA BOBBY BENSON AND THE B-BAR-B-RANCH)

1932–1936, 1949–1955	(Syndicated series. Various stations and times)

One of radio's earliest and most popular 15-minute, five-days-a-week children's adventure serials, *Bobby Benson's Adventures* thrilled young listeners every Monday through Friday. Bobby and his Western pals Polly Armstead, Windy Wales, Harka the Indian, Tex Mason et al. became as familiar to youngsters who listened regularly as their own friends and relatives. Ivan Curry, Clive Rice, and Billy HALOP played Bobby over the years, and Florence HALOP was heard as Polly. Don Knotts played Windy; Craig McDonnell was Harka the Indian and "Irish"; and Herb Rice, Neil O'Malley, Charles Irving, Al HODGE, and Tex Ritter played Tex. Also heard on the show regularly were Eddie Wragge and Lorraine Pankow. Andre BARUCH, Carl Warren, Bob Emerick, and Carl Caruso were the show's announcers at different times. Created by Herbert C. Rose, *Bobby Benson's Adventures* was directed by Bob Novack and written by Jim Sheehan. H. O. Oats cereal and Kraft cheese were the show's sponsors.

BOGART, HUMPHREY (1899–1957)

Born in New York City, actor Humphrey Bogart was the son of commercial artist Maude Humphrey and was her original baby model for the Gerber baby food label. Bogart's long and distinguished film career included such classics as *The Maltese Falcon* (1941), *Casablanca* (1942), and *African Queen* (1951), for which he won an Academy Award as Best Actor.

Bogart produced, narrated, and starred on a syndicated radio series in the late 1940s called HUMPHREY BOGART PRESENTS. With wife Lauren Bacall as his co-star, he also starred in a syndicated radio adventure series called BOLD VENTURE in the early 1950s. The actor, who "loved working on radio because people didn't have to look at my ugly puss," was also a popular guest star on the dramatic anthology programs LUX RADIO THEATER and the SCREEN ACTOR'S GUILD as well as on comedy and variety programs, notably *The* JACK BENNY SHOW and *The* BING CROSBY SHOW. In the mid-1940s, Bogart was heard on a CBS summer-replacement series that featured William Shakespeare's plays adapted for radio.

BOND, FORD (1904–1962)

Ford Bond was born in Louisville, Kentucky, and became one of radio's most popular announcers. His deep, resonant voice graced diverse genres including daytime serials (MARY NOBLE BACKSTAGE WIFE, DAVID HARUM, and STELLA DALLAS), musical programs (CITIES SERVICE CONCERTS and MANHATTAN MERRY-GO-ROUND), and the situation-comedy series EASY ACES. For many years, Bond was a staff announcer at NBC, where he introduced such shows as *The* COLLIER'S HOUR, *The* KRAFT MUSIC HALL, BELIEVE IT OR NOT, JUST PLAIN BILL, ALIAS JIMMY VALENTINE, ORPHANS OF DIVORCE, STELLA DALLAS, and YOUR FAMILY AND MINE.

BOOTH, SHIRLEY (THELMA BOOTH FORD: 1907–1992)

Dramatic actress, comedienne, and musical-comedy performer Shirley Booth played Hazel the maid on the popular "Hazel" TV series and was the original Miss Duffy on the DUFFY'S TAVERN radio series. Booth, a native New Yorker, used her regional accent to advantage playing a New York working girl on *Hogan's Daughter*, situation-comedy radio series, and was also a regular on *The* EDDIE BRACKEN SHOW, *The* THEATER GUILD ON THE AIR, and *The* FRED ALLEN SHOW as Dottie Mahoney. She starred in the Broadway musicals *A Tree Grows in Brooklyn* (1951) and *By the Beautiful Sea* (1954) and the plays *My Sister Eileen* (1940), *The Matchmaker* (1954), and *Come Back, Little Sheba* (1950); Booth won the Best Actress Academy Award in 1952 for her film performance in *Come Back, Little Sheba*. Booth retired from show business because of ill health shortly after her "Hazel" series left the air.

BORDONI, IRENE (1894–1953)

Known as the "Coty Playgirl" because her show was sponsored by Coty cosmetics, Corsican-born singer Irene Bordoni was one of U.S. radio's earliest singing stars: in the late 1920s, Bordoni was heard on *The Coty Program* and *The RKO Hour* and guest-starred on many variety-musical programs throughout the late 1920s and early 1930s. Bordoni sang "saucy" songs such as "It's a Lovely Day Tomorrow" and "Let's Do It" in vaudeville and Broadway shows such as *Paris* (1928), *Great Lady* (1937), and *Louisiana Purchase* (1940). Bordoni also starred in the film versions of *Paris* (1929) and *Louisiana Purchase* (1941), as well as *The Show of Shows* (1929). She gradually retired from show business in the 1940s.

BOSTON BLACKIE

1944	NBC	Fri.	10 PM
1945–1946	NBC Blue	Thurs.	7:30 PM
1946–1947	ABC	Tues.	7:30 PM
1947–1950	(Syndicated series. Various stations and times)		

"Boston Blackie! Enemy of those who make him an enemy, friend of those who have no friends," began radio's *Boston Blackie* detective series. The Boston Blackie character, who was a witty and sophisticated but tough, street-wise city dweller, was first seen in films in the early 1940s (*Boston Blackie Goes to Hollywood*, 1942), but in the mid-1940s, Blackie made a successful transition to radio. Blackie, his girlfriend and co-crime solver Mary, and his friendly antagonist Police Inspector Faraday solved many mysteries during the half-dozen years this half-hour, weekly series was on the air. Chester Morris, who had played the title role in the film series, was radio's original Blackie, but Richard KOLLMAR, who played the part the longest, is best remembered in the role. Lesley Woods and Jan MINER played Mary; Maurice TARPLIN, Richard Lane, and Frank Orth played Inspector Faraday.

Tony Barrett was Shorty, Blackie's friend and informant. Larry Elliott, Ken ROBERTS, and Harlow WILCOX announced the show. *Boston Blackie* was produced and directed for radio by Jeanne K. Harrison and written by Kenneth Lyons and Ralph Rosenberg. Sponsors included Rinso cleanser, Lifebuoy soap, Champagne Valvet beer, and R and H beer.

BOSWELL SISTERS, THE (CONNEE: 1908–1976; VET: 1911–1988; MARTHA: 1906–1958)

The singing, New Orleans–born Boswell Sisters were major pop-music attractions on such radio programs as MUSIC THAT SATISFIES and *The* BING CROSBY SHOW. The trio, real-life sisters, also appeared as guests on most major music-variety shows in the early 1930s; they had previously appeared on the vaudeville stage for years, singing songs such as "Dream," and "Smoke Dreams."

In 1935, Connee Boswell became a soloist when her sisters retired from show business. She regularly sang on Crosby's KRAFT MUSIC HALL and *The* BING CROSBY SHOW, was featured on *Good News, The* KEN MURRAY SHOW, *The* CAMEL CARAVAN, and had a short-lived show of her own, *The Connee Boswell Show*. In the 1950s, Boswell also frequently guest-starred on such TV variety shows as "The Colgate Comedy Hour" and "The Toast of the Town." The singer's list of hit recordings include renditions of the best-selling "I Cover the Waterfront," "Stormy Weather," and "They Can't Take That Away from Me." In films, Connee Boswell appeared with Jack Benny in *Artists and Models* (1937) and *High Society* (1956).

BOUCHEY, BILL (1907–1977)

A popular leading man on radio in the 1930s and 1940s, Bill Bouchey was born in Claire, Michigan. He played the title role on the children's adventure serial *Captain Midnight*, as well as various husbands and boyfriends on several major daytime serials, including ARNOLD GRIMM'S DAUGHTER, *The* BARTON FAMILY, *The Happy Gilmans*, WOMAN IN WHITE, MARY NOBLE, BACKSTAGE WIFE, *The* FIRST NIGHTER, BETTY AND BOB, *The* GUIDING LIGHT, *The* RIGHT TO HAPPINESS, *The* ROMANCE OF HELEN TRENT, KETTY KEENE, and ONE MAN'S FAMILY.

BOWES, MAJOR EDWARD (1874–1946)

The longtime host of *The* ORIGINAL AMATEUR HOUR, "Major" Edward Bowes was born in San Francisco, California, of Irish-American parentage. As a young man, Bowes was a successful realtor, which led to his becoming a theatrical producer in New York City. In 1918, Bowes built the Capitol Theater, which became the first theater to be used for broadcasting radio programs. In the 1920s, the Major hosted a radio program called *Family*, and in 1935 launched his *Origi-*nal Amateur Hour* series. Bowes earned his "Major" title while serving as a specialist with the Officer's Reserve Corps assigned to the Adjutant General's Office during World War I.

BRACKEN, EDDIE

See EDDIE BRACKEN SHOW, *The*.

BRADLEY, TRUMAN (1906–1974)

Announcer-commentator-actor Truman Bradley's dulcet voice was associated for many years with the popular SUSPENSE mystery series. Born in Sheldon, Missouri, Bradley was also the major product spokesman and/or announcer on such diverse shows as JACK ARMSTRONG, THE ALL AMERICAN BOY, a children's adventure serial; *The* RED SKELTON SHOW, a comedy series; and *The* STORY OF MARY MARLIN, a daytime serial drama; as well as *The Swift Revue, Ford Sunday Evening, News in Review,* and BURNS AND ALLEN. He worked as a TV announcer until shortly before his death.

BREAK THE BANK

1945–1946	Mutual	Sat.	9:30 PM
1946–1949	ABC	Fri.	9 PM
1949–1950	NBC	Wed.	9 PM
1950–1951	NBC	Mon.–Fri.	11 AM
1951–1953	ABC	Mon.–Fri.	11:30 AM
1953–1955	NBC	Mon.–Fri.	10:45 AM
	Mutual	Mon.–Fri.	12 PM

A top-rated half-hour quiz program for more than ten years, BREAK THE BANK was originally a Mutual network offering on which contestants could win money as long as they answered questions correctly. People who phoned in to answer questions could win from $100 to as much as $23,000 in merchandise by identifying songs played on the program. Others chosen from the studio audience got a chance to name the tune if the caller couldn't identify it.

Featured as hosts were John Reed KING and then Johnny Olsen, Bert PARKS, and Clayton "Bud" COLLYER. Bob Shepherd announced the program. Jack Rubin directed the show, which was written by Joseph Kane, Walt Framer, and Jack Rubin. The show's orchestra was under the direction of Peter Van Steeden. Ipana toothpaste, Trushay deodorant, Dodge automobiles, Philip Morris cigarettes, Vitalis hair dressing, Mum deodorant, Vicks Vaporub, and Alka Seltzer antacid were the program's sponsors. The show's theme music was "We're in the Money."

BREAKFAST CLUB, THE (AKA THE PEPPER POT)

1933–1938	NBC Blue	Mon.–Sat.	9 AM
1938–1940	NBC Blue	Mon.–Sat.	9:05 AM

| 1940–1945 | NBC Blue | Mon.–Sat. | 9 AM |
| 1945–1968 | ABC | Mon.–Fri. | 9 AM |

Called *The Pepper Pot* when it first went on the air, *The Breakfast Club* became the show's official title when Don MCNEILL became its host a few months after its debut. Playing for thirty-five consecutive years, this program was the longest-running early-morning show on radio on NBC and then on ABC. Featured on the program with McNeill were Fran ALLISON, who played country gossip Aunt Fanny; Sam Cowling as Sam Cowling ("Fact and Fiction from Sam's Almanac"); and in the show's early years, Jim and Marian JORDAN, Bill THOMPSON, Russell Pratt, and Gale Page. Performers heard on the program included the Morin Sisters, Johnny Johnston, Peggy Lee, Jack Owens, Franklyn Ferguson, and the Ranch Boys, the Three Romeos, The Vagabonds, Johnny Desmond, and Janette Davis.

The show frequently featured recipe contests. A listener's winning recipe was published by one of the sponsors, and the person who sent it in received $500.

Announcers on the program over the years included Charles Irving, Ken Nordine, Durwood Kirby, Fred Kasper, Bob Brown, Don Dowd, and Bob Murphy. Clark Dennis, who also announced, was a popular tenor on the program. Cliff Patterson was the show's longtime director. The program's sponsors included Kellogg's breakfast cereal, Philco radios and phonographs, Toni home permanent, Swift meats, O'Cedar mops, White Rain shampoo, and Bayer aspirin. *The Breakfast Club*'s final broadcast was heard on September 19, 1968; guests included Fran Allison and Burr Tillstrom of TV's "Kukla, Fran, and Ollie."

BREAKFAST IN HOLLYWOOD (AKA TOM BRENEMAN'S HOLLYWOOD)

| 1941–1945 | NBC Blue | Mon.–Fri. | 11 AM |
| 1945–1949 | ABC | Mon.–Fri. | 11 AM |

ABC's one-hour *Breakfast in Hollywood* was an early-morning, five-days-a-week series that was similar in format to *The Breakfast Club.* Tom BRENEMAN and then Garry MOORE and Jack McElroy hosted the show, Breneman being its longest-lasting and best-remembered host. Breneman and Don McNeill of *The Breakfast Club* show had one of radio's most famous, yet totally fictitious, on-the-air feuds for several years; the hosts of these shows regularly hurled exaggerated insults at each other.

A popular special feature was to give the oldest lady in the studio audience an orchid, jewelry, and $500 worth of merchandise. Listeners sent letters nominating a "good neighbor of the week." The neighbor chosen was also given an orchid and merchandise.

John Nelson and Carl Webster Pierce were the program's announcers. *Breakfast in Hollywood* was di-

rected by Jessie Butcher, John Masterson, John Nelson, Claire Weidenaar, and Carl Webster Pierce and produced by Charles Harrell and Ralph Hunter. The show's chief writers were Vince Colvig and Jack Turner. Ivory soap flakes, Kellogg's Pep and Kellogg's variety-pack breakfast cereals sponsored the series.

BRENEMAN, TOM (1902–1948)

Master of ceremonies, commentator, and host Tom Breneman was born in Waynesboro, Pennsylvania, and was first heard on the airwaves in 1927 on WFWB in Hollywood, California. He hosted such programs as *The Dream Singer, My Secret Ambition, Night Editor, Good Morning Neighbor, Spelling Beeliner, Yourself in Action,* and the *National Lead Quiz Program,* none of which were on the air very long, and the very successful BREAKFAST IN HOLLYWOOD program. Breneman died in an automobile accident at the height of his broadcasting career.

BRICE, FANNY (FANNIE BORACH: 1891–1951)

A major Broadway and vaudeville stage star and one of producer Florenz Ziegfeld's most popular performers, New York City–born singer-comedienne Fannie Brice made her first major radio appearance on *The* ZIEGFELD FOLLIES OF THE AIR. She sang some of the songs she made famous in *The Ziegfeld Follies* on Broadway, such as "My Man," "Second-Hand Rose," and "Whoops, I'm an Indian Too." She also recreated several of the wonderful stage characters she had introduced in the *Follies.* It was on the *Ziegfeld Follies of the Air* that Brice introduced her famous BABY SNOOKS character to the radio-listening public. Snooks was a noisy brat who constantly asked her parents "Why?" and generally drove them crazy with her childish high jinks.

In 1940, Brice became a regular on the MAXWELL HOUSE COFFEE HOUR, playing her Snooks character with movie character-actor Frank Morgan as her long-suffering "Daddy." In 1944, Brice's program became known as *The* BABY SNOOKS SHOW and remained on the air with that title until 1951. Except for occasional cameo appearances in films, Brice confined her performing to radio during the last years of her career. The stage musical *Funny Girl* (1964), the subsequent *Funny Girl* film (1968), and then *Funny Lady* (1976), which starred Barbra Streisand, depicted incidents from Brice's life.

BRIDE AND GROOM

1945–1946	NBC Blue	Mon.–Fri.	2:30 PM
1946–1949	ABC	Mon.–Fri.	2:30 PM
1949–1950	ABC	Mon.–Fri.	3 PM

For the five years this half-hour, Monday-through-Friday program was on the air, it was one of radio's most popular audience-participation shows. Each weekday, different engaged couples, chosen from letters that were sent to the show's producers, appeared on the program. They were interviewed on the air before they were married, and then returned on a later broadcast to report what their wedding and honeymoon had been like. The couples could win a second honeymoon and $1,000 worth of merchandise if the audience judged them their favorite couple of the day. Interviews were conducted by John Nelson, and the couple's answers were spontaneous and unrehearsed. The listening audience never knew what the young lovers would say, which always added to the fun.

Jack McElroy was the program's announcer. *Bride and Groom* was directed by John Nelson, Johny Reddy, Edward Feldman, and John Masterson. Sponsors of the program included Dr. Lyon's toothpaste, Double Danderine shampoo, Energine vitamins, Phillip's Milk of Magnesia antacid, Mulsified Coconut Oil shampoo, Bayer aspirin, and Fletcher's Castoria upset-stomach medication. The show's theme music was "Here Comes the Bride."

BRIGHT HORIZON

1941–1946	CBS	Mon.–Fri.	11:30 AM

One of the few radio spin-off series to gain a respectable audience of its own was the 15-minute, Monday-through-Friday *Bright Horizon* daytime drama series. Michael West, originally heard on BIG SISTER, became so popular that network officials decided the character should be featured on a show of his own. Joe JULIAN and then Richard KOLLMAR played Michael; Joan Alexander and Sammie Hill played Michael's wife, Carol. In regular supporting roles were Alice FROST, Ronald LISS, Vera Allen, Alice Goodkin, Sidney Slon, Rennee Terry, Lesley Woods, Lon CLARK, Jack GRIMES, Stefan Schnabel, Irene Hubbard, Audrey Totter, Frank LOVEJOY, Will Geer, and Santos ORTEGA. This show was one of the few programs on radio to feature a female announcer, Marjorie Anderson. *Bright Horizon* was directed by Henry Hull, Jr., and Day Tuttle and written by John M. Young, Stuart Hawkins, and Kathleen Norris. Swan soap and Vimms vitamins sponsored the series.

BRIGHTER DAY, THE

1948–1949	NBC	Mon.–Fri.	10:45 AM
1949–1952	CBS	Mon.–Fri.	2:45 PM
1952–1953	NBC	Mon.–Fri.	2:45 PM
	(and also heard on)		
	CBS	Mon.–Fri.	9:45 AM
1953–1955	CBS	Mon.–Fri.	2:45 PM
1955–1956	CBS	Mon.–Fri.	2:15 PM

The fictitious town of Three Rivers was the setting of this 15-minute daytime drama series, one of the last

soap operas to debut on radio before network dramatic programming all but ceased to exist. The Dennis family—Liz, Richard, Althea, Barbara, and Grayling—were the central characters on the show. Margaret Draper and then Grace MATTHEWS played Liz, the widowed mother of three children; William "Bill" Smith played her father-in-law, Poppa Dennis; Jay Meredith, Joan Alexander, Brooke Byron, Jayne Heller, Patricia Hosley, Bob Pollock, Mary K. Wells, Lorna Lynn, and Billy Redfield played Liz's children; and John LARKIN, Jeanette Dowling, Charlotte MANSON, Paul MACGRATH, Hal Holbrook, and Joe DeSantis played featured roles on the series. Bill Rogers, Ron Rawson and Len Sterling were the program's announcers. *The Brighter Day* was directed by Red Corday, Ed Wolfe, and Arthur Hanna. Orin Tovrov wrote the series for years, and it was produced by David Lesan. Sponsors included Dreft flour, Ivory soap flakes, Blue Cheer detergent, Swans Down cake mix, and Hazel Bishop lipstick.

BROADWAY IS MY BEAT

1949	CBS	Sun.	5:30 PM
		Thurs.	8 PM
1950	CBS	Fri.	9:30 PM
		Mon.	8:30 PM
1951	CBS	Sun.	9 PM
1952	CBS	Mon., Sat.	9:30 PM
1953	CBS	Wed., Fri.	9:30 PM
1954	CBS	Sun.	6:30 PM

One of the last major detective shows to debut on network radio, the half-hour *Broadway Is My Beat* series starred actor Larry Thor in the leading role of New York City homicide detective Danny Glover. Charles Calvin and Jack Kruschen were regulars on the program. This fast-paced, well-written and well-acted series frequently featured veteran radio performers Betty Lou GERSON, Hans CONRIED, Earle Ross, Florence Lake, Irene Tedrow, and Joseph KEARNS in the supporting cast. Bill Anders and George Walsh announced the program. The series was produced and directed by Elliott LEWIS. It was sponsored by Wrigley gum and Lux Toilet soap. The program's theme music was "I'll Take Manhattan."

BROADWAY VARIETIES (AKA BROADWAY MELODIES)

1935–1936	CBS	Wed.	8:30 PM
1936	CBS	Fri.	8:30 PM
1936–1937	CBS	Fri.	8 PM

Victor Arden led the orchestra on this musical-variety program that featured songs from Broadway musical comedies and light-opera stage productions. Heard on this half-hour program were Oscar Shaw, Carmella Ponselle, Helen Morgan, and Elisbeth Lennox. The series, which was on the air for two years, was sponsored by BiSoDol antacid.

BROKENSHIRE, NORMAN (1898–1965)

Host-moderator-announcer Norman Brokenshire was born in Murcheson, Canada. He had a sophisticated, diction-perfect voice and was called "Sir Silken Speech" by his peers in the industry. His vocal delivery added distinction and prestige to any radio program he hosted.

Brokenshire, who was first heard on radio on WJZ in New York City, covered the inauguration of presidents Calvin Coolidge and Herbert Hoover, was the announcer on *The* ORIGINAL AMATEUR HOUR, MUSIC THAT SATISFIES, *The* THEATER GUILD ON THE AIR, and, for a time, the *Uncle Don* children's program. He was also the first master of ceremonies of the Miss America Contest in 1927 and broadcast the first horse race to be heard over the airwaves. Brokenshire usually greeted his listeners by saying "How do you do, ladies and gentlemen, how *do* you do?" In the 1950s, he hosted "The Better Home Show" on television. He retired from show business shortly after the show left the air.

BROWN, HIMAN (1910–   )

Producer-director Himan Brown was the creative genius behind such popular radio programs as the IN-NER SANCTUM MYSTERIES, BULLDOG DRUMMOND, *The* THIN MAN, TERRY AND THE PIRATES, GRAND CENTRAL STATION, DICK TRACY, YOUR FAMILY AND MINE, HILDA HOPE, M.D., CITY DESK, *The* GUMPS and JOYCE JORDAN, GIRL INTERN. Brown, who was born in Brooklyn, New York, began his radio career when, as a teenager, he sold Gertrude Berg's *The Rise of the* GOLDBERGS series to NBC. In the early 1930s, he produced and directed what he claims was "the first daytime serial drama series ever heard on radio," MARIE, THE LITTLE FRENCH PRINCESS. In 1974, Brown made a valiant attempt to bring radio drama back to the airwaves with a series of one-hour daily mystery dramas, produced at CBS, called *The* CBS MYSTERY THEATER. The series was syndicated and featured on various local stations around the country. It remained on the air on a regular basis until 1977.

BRYANT, ARTHUR Q. (1899–1959)

Born in Brooklyn, New York, actor Arthur Q. Bryant's voice became familiar to millions as that of Elmer Fudd in countless cartoons until Mel Blanc assumed the voice. A very popular radio actor, Bryant began his show-business career as tenor in a barbershop quartet and was heard on radio as early as 1929. He played the title role on the MAJOR HOOPLE situation-comedy series and Fibber McGee's friendly enemy,

Doc Gamble, on the FIBBER MCGEE AND MOLLY SHOW. Bryant was also a regular on *The* GROUCH CLUB, *The* HALLS OF IVY, *The* BILLIE BURKE SHOW, BLONDIE, *The* FITCH BANDWAGON, *Forever Ernest*, *The* LUX RADIO THE-ATER, and *The* GREAT GILDERSLEEVE.

BUCK ROGERS IN THE 25TH CENTURY

1932–1933	CBS	Mon.–Fri.	7:15 PM
1933–1935	CBS	Mon.–Thurs.	6 PM
1935–1936	CBS	Mon.–Fri.	6 PM
1936–1937	(Off the air)		
1937–1940	CBS	Mon., Wed., Fri.	6 PM
1940–1946	(Off the air)		
1946–1947	Mutual	Mon.–Fri.	4:45 PM

Science-fiction fans had a 15-minute weekday dose of exciting adventure when the children's serial *Buck Rogers in the 25th Century* was on the air. Based on a comic strip created by John D. Dille, drawn by Dick Calkins, and written by Phil Nowlan, *Buck Rogers in the 25th Century* told of a spacecraft pilot's explorations in outer space. It was one of the first shows on radio to offer premiums such as rings, badges, and games to kids who sent in a box top from the sponsor's product and usually "one thin dime." Matt CROWLEY, Curtis Arnall, Carl FRANK, and John LARKIN played Buck at different times; Adele RONSON and Vilma Vass played Buck's girlfriend and fellow space traveler, Wilma Deering. Others on this series included Elaine Melchoir as arch-villainess Ardala Valmar; Dan Ocro as the notorious Killer Kane; Ronald LISS; Walter TETLEY; Junius Matthews; Walter Vaughn; Jack Rosleigh; Arthur Vinton; William Shelley; Edgar Stehli; Everett SLOANE; Paul Stewart; Walter GREAZA; Frank READICK; and Dwight WEIST. Fred Utal, Paul DOUGLAS, Kenneth Williams, and John Johnstone (who was producer and director for many years) were the announcers. The series was written by Joe A. Cross, Albert Miller, and Dick Calkins. *Buck Rogers in the 25th Century* was sponsored by Kellogg's breakfast cereal, Cocomalt chocolate-drink mix, Cream of Wheat hot cereal, Popsicle ice-cream bars, and the General Foods Company.

BULLDOG DRUMMOND, THE ADVENTURES OF

See ADVENTURES OF BULLDOG DRUMMOND, *The*.

BUNCE, ALAN (1900–1965)

Born in Westfield, New Jersey, actor Alan Bunce is well remembered for playing Albert Arbuckle opposite Peg LYNCH on the ETHEL AND ALBERT program. Bunce's natural style of acting on this show—with the support of Lynch's formidable talents as a writer and leading lady—actually made people feel as if they were eavesdropping on actual conversations between a husband and wife. In addition to *Ethel and Albert*, Bunce, who made his radio debut in 1933, was also heard on HOME OF THE BRAVE, *Hello Peggy*, DAVID HARUM, DOC BARCLAY'S DAUGHTERS, JOHN'S OTHER WIFE, PEPPER YOUNG'S FAMILY, YOUNG DR. MALONE, *The* COUPLE NEXT DOOR (also written and costarring Peg Lynch), and YOUNG WIDDER BROWN. Bunce repeated his Albert role on television with Lynch when *Ethel and Albert* became a regular feature on "The Kate Smith Show" and then a series in the mid to late 1950s.

BURKE, BILLIE

See GAY MRS. FEATHERSTONE, *The*

BURNS, BOB (1893–1956)

Bob Burns, "the Arkansas Traveler," was born in Van Buren, Arkansas. After studying to be an engineer, he became a vaudeville performer and then brought his dry, homespun wit to radio. He became a comedic favorite of listeners on *The* KRAFT MUSIC HALL when it starred Bing Crosby and on *The* RUDY VALLEE SHOW. Because of these appearances, Burns was given a

comedy-variety series of his own in 1941, *The* BOB BURNS SHOW. The comedian became almost as famous for playing an instrument called the "bazooka"—a crude musical instrument made of pipes and a funnel—as he was for his homespun Arkansas humor. Burns's film appearances included *The Big Broadcast of 1937* and *The Arkansas Traveler* (1938).

BURNS AND ALLEN (BURNS, GEORGE NE NATHAN BIRNBAUM: 1896–   ; ALLEN, GRACIE: 1904–1964)

George Burns was born on New York City's Lower East Side; his wife and partner, Gracie Allen, was born in San Francisco, California. Burns began his performing career as a vaudeville comedian, but he was not very successful until he teamed up with Gracie Allen, whom he married in 1926. In the couple's original vaudeville act, Gracie was the straight man and George was the comedian; in time, however, the team realized that Gracie's high-pitched voice, ditsy, addlepated questions, and illogical statements and malapropisms got more laughs than George's jokes, so they switched roles. They soon became vaudeville headliners.

In 1932, radio beckoned and Burns and Allen were offered a half-hour radio show of their own on CBS.

Bob Burns, who was called "the Arkansas Traveler" (NBC)

George Burns and Gracie Allen during a *Burns and Allen* show (CBS)

One of radio's earliest and most successful publicity stunts originally began on one of the BURNS AND ALLEN SHOW broadcasts: Gracie's brother supposedly disappeared, and the comedienne subsequently turned up on various popular radio programs of the time looking for him. This stunt increased the duo's popularity so much that they were rivaled on radio only by AMOS AND ANDY. In 1940, a similar publicity stunt occurred when Gracie announced that she was going to run for president of the United States on a fictitious "surprise ticket"; once again she turned up on every major comedy program of the time, campaigning for all she was worth.

Burns and Allen appeared in several films, including *The Big Broadcast* (1937), *College Swing* (1938), and *Damsel in Distress* (1937). The radio show remained on the air until 1950, when the couple decided to devote most of their time to television. After Gracie's death in 1964, George once again became a solo act and in 1975 replaced the late Jack Benny in the film *The Sunshine Boys*. Burns won an Academy Award as Best Supporting Actor. Other films followed—*Oh, God* (1977), *Sergeant Pepper's Lonely Hearts Club Band* (1978), and *Just You and Me* (1979). As he approaches his one-hundredth birthday, Burns remains something of a grand old man of comedy, continuing to guest-star on television specials, perform live, and appear in television commercials. In December 1993 he was among the first inductees into the Comedy Hall of Fame.

BURNS AND ALLEN SHOW, THE (AKA THE NEW SWAN SHOW AND MAXWELL HOUSE COFFEE TIME)

1935–1936	CBS	Wed.	9:30 PM
1936–1937	CBS	Wed.	8:30 PM
1937–1938	NBC Red	Mon.	8 PM
1938–1939	CBS	Fri.	8:30 PM
1939–1940	CBS	Wed.	7:30 PM
1940–1941	NBC Red	Mon.	7:30 PM
1941–1944	CBS	Tues.	9 PM
1944–1945	CBS	Mon.	8:30 PM
1945–1946	NBC	Thurs.	8 PM
1946–1949	NBC	Thurs.	8:30 PM
1949–1950	CBS	Wed.	10 PM

The husband-and-wife comedy team of George BURNS and Gracie ALLEN brought their successful vaudeville stage routines to radio in the mid-1930s. In addition to the talented Burns and Allen themselves, many other comical characters helped make the *Burns and Allen Radio Show* a long-running audience favorite, including Mel BLANC as the Happy Postman; Elvia ALLMAN as Tootsie Stagwell; Margaret Brayton as Mrs. Billingsley; Sara Berner as Muriel; and Clarence Nash as the Burns' pet duck, Herman. Other regulars were Richard CRENNA, Gale GORDON, and Hans CONRIED;

and vocalists Milton Watson, Tony Martin, Jimmy Cash, and Dick Foran. Ted HUSING, Harry VON ZELL, James "Jimmy" WALLINGTON, Toby Reed, Truman BRADLEY, Dick Joy, and Bill GOODWIN were the announcers. The show's orchestra was led by Jacques Renard, Ray NOBLE, Paul WHITEMAN and Meredith WILLSON, who also had running roles playing themselves. *The Burns and Allen Show* was directed by Ralph Levy, Al Kaye, Ed GARDNER, Bill Moore, and Joe Donohue. The program's writers included Paul Henning, Keith Fowler, Harmon J. Alexander, Henry Garson, Aaron J. Ruben, Helen Gould Harvey, Hal Black, and John P. Medbury. Robert Burns cigars, White Owl cigars, Campbell's soups, Grape Nuts cereal, Chesterfield cigarettes, Vimms vitamins, Jell-O pudding, Am-i-dent toothpaste, Hinds food products, Hormel meats, Swan soap, and Maxwell House coffee were *Burns and Allen*'s sponsors. *Burns and Allen*'s theme music was "Love Nest."

BURR, ANNE (1920–)

Actress Anne Burr had a throaty but attractive voice that became familiar to millions of radio listeners throughout the 1940s and 1950s. She was born in Boston, Massachusetts, and attended private schools in the United States and England until she was in her teens, when she attended Sweet Briar College in Virginia. Burr began to pursue a career as an actress in 1939. Her first major stage appearance was in a production of *Brief Moment*, presented by the Farragut Players in Rye, New Hampshire. Burr made her Broadway debut in the critically acclaimed play *Native Son* (1941). She subsequently appeared in *Dark Eyes* (1943) and *The Hasty Heart* (1944), replacing Mercedes MCCAMBRIDGE, who had originally been hired to play her role but was fired prior to the play's opening. Ironically, McCambridge later replaced Burr as leading lady on Fletcher MARKLE's weekly STUDIO ONE dramatic anthology radio series in 1947. In addition to *Studio One*, Burr was also heard regularly on MARY NOBLE, BACKSTAGE WIFE, (as the notorious Regina Rawlings), BIG SISTER, WHEN A GIRL MARRIES, WENDY WARREN, and frequently on the THEATER GUILD ON THE AIR series.

In the early 1950s, Burr became one of daytime TV's busiest leading ladies. She was seen on "As the World Turns" from 1956 until 1959, "The Greatest Gift" (1954), and "Way of the World" (1955). She was also featured on such prime-time TV programs as "Studio One" and "The Philco Playhouse" in the 1950s. After leaving her long-running role on "As the World Turns" in 1959, Burr retired from show business.

BURROWS, ABE

See ABE BURROWS SHOW, *The*.

BUSTER BROWN GANG
See SMILIN' ED AND HIS BUSTER BROWN GANG

BY KATHLEEN NORRIS

1939–1940	CBS	Mon.–Fri.	5 PM
1940–1941	CBS	Mon.–Fri.	10 AM
	& NBC	Mon.–Fri.	19:15 AM

On this series, the stories of best-selling romance novelist and short-story writer Kathleen Norris were adapted for radio in serialized versions. The programs, usually about romantic entanglements and domestic problems, featured Ethel Everett as Miss Norris, who narrated the stories. Appearing regularly on the 15-minute, Monday-through-Friday program were Helen Shields, James MEIGHAN, Chester STRATTON, Mildred Baker, Jay Meredith, Marion Barney, Mary Patton, Joan BANKS, Anne Teeman, House JAMESON, Arline Blackburn, Mary Cecil, Santos ORTEGA, Lawson Zerbe, Florence Malone, Betty GARDE, Effie Palmer, Nancy Sheridan, and Irene Hubbard. Dwight WEIST was the show's announcer. The series was produced by Phillips H. LORD and May Bolhower and directed by Jay Hanna and Lloyd Griffin. Wheaties cereal and various General Mills products sponsored the series.

CALL THE POLICE

1947	NBC	Tues.	9 PM
1947–1948	(Off the air)		
1948	NBC	Tues.	9:30 PM
1948–1949	(Off the air)		
1949	CBS	Sun.	7:30 PM

Joe JULIAN and then George Petrie played the major character of Police Detective Bill Grant on the half-hour weekly *Call the Police* crime series. Amzie Strickland and then Joan Tompkins played Grant's girlfriend. The program's opening stated, "Between you and evil, outside the law, stands a policeman in your community. He gives up his safety so you can be safe and sometimes . . . he gives up his life to protect yours." The stories on this series usually centered around events that took place in a typical big-city police station and involved such things as apprehending gang members and solving urban thefts and murders. A summer replacement for AMOS AND ANDY, and then for FIBBER MCGEE AND MOLLY, the show attracted a large and faithful listening audience of its own and was heard for three consecutive summers. John Cole produced and directed the stories heard on the show. Hugh James and Jay Simms were the program's announcers. Sponsors included Rinso cleanser, Lifebuoy soap, and Johnson's wax.

CALLING ALL CARS

1933–1940	CBS	Tues.	7 PM
		Sat.	6 PM

Calling All Cars was a half-hour radio series that utilized the Los Angeles Police Department's crime files as a major source of inspiration and information. A typical story of this police-adventure series in-volved staking out a gang of jewel thieves who had been stealing precious gems from a Los Angeles jewelry store, or the investigation of a string of similiar but apparently unconnected murders. Robert DRYDEN, Jackson BECK, and William ZUCKERT were often featured in the cast. Numerous freelance writers wrote scripts for the series. Frank Lindsley announced the show, and Robert Hixson was its director. Rio Grande Oil sponsored the series.

CALLING ALL DETECTIVES

1945–1950	(Syndicated show. Various stations and times)

Each week, listeners could receive prizes by solving mysteries they heard on the syndicated half-hour *Calling All Detectives* series. A narrator called "Robin" read each week's story and announced the prize winners. Everything ranging from murder to missing household objects were subjects on the show. Vincent Pelletier was the narrator Robin, and Frank LOVEJOY and Owen Jordan played the running roles of Neil Fowler and Toby on the series.

CAMEL CARAVAN (AKA THE BOB HAWK QUIZ SHOW; COMEDY CARAVAN)

1933–1943	NBC Red	Sat.	10 PM

During the ten years this program was on the air, it changed formats several times and starred at one time or another Bob CROSBY, Jimmy DURANTE, and Garry MOORE. Other performers who appeared on the series included Freddie Rich's orchestra, vocalist Connie Haines, humorist Herb Shriner, and Jack CARSON. Rotund, moon-faced movie comedian Jack Oakie hosted a segment called "Jack Oakie's College," which was part of the show when it was called *The Camel Caravan*. When Durante and Moore were in charge of the proceedings, singer Georgia Gibbs was a regular vocalist on the show. Bob HAWK hosted the series when it became a quiz show, and Camel cigarettes sponsored it. Harry Halcomb and Howard Petrie announced the series, which was written at different times by Jay Somers, Stanley Davis, Leo Solomon, Sid Reznivk, Jack Robinson, and Sid Zelinka.

CAMPBELL PLAYHOUSE.

See MERCURY THEATER OF THE AIR, THE,

CAMPBELL SOUP PROGRAM, THE

See JACK CARSON SHOW, *The*.

CAN YOU TOP THIS

1940–1941	Mutual	Mon.	9:30 PM
1941–1942	Mutual	Tues.	8:30 PM
1942–1947	NBC	Sat.	9:30 PM
1947–1948	NBC	Fri.	8:30 PM
1948–1949	Mutual	Wed.	8 PM
1949–1951	ABC	Tues.	8 PM
1951–1953	(Off the air)		
1953–1954	NBC	Mon.–Fri.	10:15 PM

A panel of comedians—"Senator" Ed Ford, Harry Hershfield, and Joe Laurie, Jr.—put their improvisational joke-telling skills to the test as they matched wits with listeners who sent in jokes that were told on the air by actor-comedian Peter DONALD. The panelists then told their jokes. The studio audience judged which joke was the funniest as their applause was recorded on a "laugh/applause meter." Ward Wildon was the show's host and moderator. Running features were Senator Ford's amusing characters Dopey Dilldock, Mrs. Fafoofnick, and Ditsy Bomwortle; Laurie's slightly "dim" way of telling a joke; and Harry Hershfield's rapid-fire delivery. Charles STARK was the program's announcer. Alan Dingwall, Jay Clark, and Roger Bower were the show's directors at different times. Sponsors were Kirkman's soap flakes, Kirkman's soap, Colgate dental cream, Palmolive shave cream, Lustre Cream shampoo, Ford automobiles, and Mars candy.

CANADIAN BROADCASTING CORPORATION (CBC):

Modern broadcasting in Canada, as in the United States, dates from the early 1920s, even though as early as 1919 Marconi station XWA (later CFCF) had started experimental broadcasts in Canada. The experiments were followed by the establishment of several commercial stations that began to spring up all over Canada. These stations were owned by small radio clubs, large corporations, church groups, universities, and—in one case—by a provincial government (Manitoba), as well as by the Canadian National Railways. By 1929, more than 75 Canadian stations—broadcasting in French as well as English—had been licensed. A regular network service was, however, gradually being developed by Canadian National Radio, connecting its own stations in Ottawa, Mancton, and Vancouver with about a dozen private stations that it leased across the country. The Canadian National schedules over the years offered an impressive variety of programming in both French and English, including light music and live symphony and opera broadcasts, talks, school broadcasts, and hockey and other sports programs. Historical and classical dramas with Tyrone Guthrie, who was imported from England as a producer-director, were also heard.

Only a half-dozen frequencies were exclusively Canadian, and because only Canadian National did much Canadian programming, it was easier for most of the stations around the country to use recorded music or to broadcast popular programs produced in the United States. In the early 1930s, the Canadian Radio League, determined to keep Canadian radio free from commercialism, set about to rally support for public ownership of all radio stations and for public-service endorsement by the Air Commission. Even though there was strong opposition to public ownership—especially by the Canadian Pacific Railway, private broadcasters, a number of newspapers, radio manufacturers, and indirectly from U. S. radio interests—these groups had little support among the general public. The constitutional issue of federal versus provincial control of broadcasting was especially debated in Quebec province.

In May 1932, the Canadian Broadcasting Act was passed, which authorized the appointment of a body to be known as the Canadian Radio Broadcasting Commission (CRBC). A number of CNR-produced programs, including the first Empire Christmas broadcast, were carried that winter under CRBC auspices. It wasn't until April 1933 that the Commission functioned formally and began to acquire stations and a broadcasting staff of its own to broadcast for one hour a day. Gradually, that service was increased, and by the end of 1933, the CRBC owned or leased five stations plus the Halifax studios that had been opened by CRBC in 1930 and had time reserved for its programs on a number of private English- and French-language stations across the country. It was broadcasting about 48 hours a week—30 hours on regional networks and 18 hours nationally. It offered ambitious and largely Canadian programming in two languages, its studios and transmitters were modernized, and some new facilities were set up, including a short-wave-receiving station to relay programs from Britain.

A new broadcasting act, based on the recommendation of a Parliamentary committee, was passed in 1936 that nationalized radio broadcasting in Canada. In 1938, the Canadian Broadcasing Corporation, which was established by the government, took over and centralized Canadian broadcasting. Leonard W. Brockingham, K.C., of Winnipeg was appointed chairman of the Board of Governors. By 1937 and 1938, the list of regular CBC productions included symphonic, chamber, and choral music performed by existing groups; original plays and adaptations of classic novels as well as serial dramas—a particular favorite of the French service; talks, discussions, and university debates; Canadian-press news bulletins; religious programs; variety programs like *The Happy Gang;* dance music; hockey games; children's programs; and, continuing from the CRBC, the NORTHERN MESSENGER broadcasts.

Although World War II put an end to major new construction projects, the war also took the CBC very actively overseas and hastened the development of some important services at home. The CBC news service, for example, was established in 1941. Until then, most of the CBC's news bulletins had been prepared by the Canadian press. By the end of 1941, more than 21 percent of the CBC schedule was devoted to news.

In the years after the war, the CBC renewed some of its most urgent capital projects and program development continued, with some notable successes: in 1947, the comedy team of Wayne and Shuster joined CBC radio, and *CBC Wednesday Night* introduced a program concept that was new to North America—a full evening of ambitious adult programming. Some of the CBC's most popular programs in the 1940s and 1950s were *Just Mary Stories, Maggie Muggins,* and *Jackie and the Kid* by W. O. Mitchell, Andrew Allen's *Stage Secrets, GE Show Time, The Ford Theater* (which was produced by CBS in the United States in the late 1940s); and *The Happy Gang* variety show.

To this day, the CBC has continued its innovations, uncommercial broadcasting advances, and original programming on its two networks—Radio, which is the CBC's equivilent of AM broadcasts in the United States, and Stereo, the equivilent of FM.

See also CBC NEWS, CBC SPECIALS, CBC SPORTS, and CBC STAGE.

CANDID MICROPHONE

1947–1948	ABC	Thurs.	8 PM
1948–1950	(Off the air)		
1950	CBS	Tues.	9:30 PM

Allen Funt was the host and Don Hollenbeck was the narrator of this half-hour program, the radio forerunner of the long-running "Candid Camera" television series. A hidden microphone eavesdropped on people in various humorous situations. When one of the people being overheard or interviewed said something the network considered too colorful for the airwaves, a lady's voice would softly say "Censored" and the program would continue. Ken ROBERTS announced the radio series as well as the early TV program, and Philip Morris cigarettes sponsored the show. The program's director was Joseph Graham.

CANOVA, JUDY (1916–1983)

Country-western comedienne and country singer Judy (Juliette) Canova was born in Jacksonville, Florida. She originally wanted to be an opera singer and received voice training at The Cincinnati Conservatory of Music. Her radio debut was *The* RUDY VALLEE SHOW singing country songs, and she was also featured on *The* ZIEGFELD FOLLIES OF THE AIR program in the mid-1930s.

For many years, she had a popular radio situation-comedy series, *The* JUDY CANOVA SHOW. The program

Judy Canova (CBS)

showcased Canova's vocal and comic talents to full advantage throughout the 1940s and 1950s. Canova's rendition of the song "Go to Sleepy, Little Baby," which she sang at the end of each *Judy Canova Show*, became one of her trademarks. In addition to her work on radio, Canova starred on Broadway (*Ziegfeld Follies of 1939*), appeared in films (*Singing in the Corn* [1946] and *Carolina Canonball* [1955]), and guest-starred on television shows such as "The Colgate Comedy Hour" (1953) and "The Ed Sullivan Show" (1954).

Canova was particularly noted for taking popular country and hit-parade songs of the day, such as "Night and Day" and "Dancing on the Ceiling," and singing them in a comic country style. The performer continued her show-business career well into the 1970s, singing and clowning at various state fairs and in concerts.

CANTOR, CHARLIE (1898–1966)

Whether he was playing a comic or serious role, performer Charlie Cantor's acting always convinced. He was born in Russia but grew up in Worcester, Massachusetts, and attended New York University before entering show business as a black-face vaudeville singer. He was first heard on radio in 1937 and was subsequently featured on *The* KATE SMITH HOUR, FRED ALLEN's *Town Hall Tonight, The Kitchen Cavalcade, Brenda Curtis,* TERRY AND THE PIRATES, *Spy Secrets, The Adventures of* MR. MEEK, *The Amazing Mr. Smith, Flash Gordon, The* PHILIP MORRIS PLAYHOUSE, DICK TRACY, BILLY AND BETTY, and *The* EDDIE CANTOR SHOW. Cantor's most famous radio characterization was the dim-witted Clifton Finnegan on the DUFFY'S TAVERN show. He is also well remembered as characters named Zero on *The* ALAN YOUNG SHOW, Socrates Mulligan on *The* FRED ALLEN SHOW, and Uncle Buckley on *The* LIFE OF RILEY. Cantor retired from show business in the early 1960s.

CANTOR, EDDIE (ISIDORE ITZKOWITZ: 1892–1964)

A major star in vaudeville and on the Broadway stage in such shows as *The Ziegfeld Follies* (1917, 1918, 1919), comedian-singer Eddie Cantor was born on New York City's Lower East Side and had one of the most successful comedy-variety shows on radio throughout the 1930s and 1940s. Bug-eyed Cantor was discovered by comedian Gus Edwards while Cantor was working in a Coney Island saloon as a singing waiter. His accompanist at the saloon was Jimmy DURANTE. In 1912, Eddie joined Edwards's "Kid Kabaret" touring show, which also featured George JESSEL and many other talented youngsters who later became vaude-

Eddie "Banjo Eyes" Cantor (NBC)

ville headliners. In 1931, Cantor made his first appearance on the airwaves, and by the late 1930s he was a major radio star. Cantor's wife, Ida, and his five daughters were the objects of many of the jokes on his program, but they never actually appeared on any of his shows. In addition to his work on radio and the stage, Cantor also starred in such Hollywood films as *Kid Boots* (1930), *Whoopee* (1930), which featured his song "Making Whoopie," *Show Business* (1944), and *If You Knew Susie* (1948). In 1953, actor Keefe Brasselle played him in *The Eddie Cantor Story*, a film based on his life. Eddie wrote his autobiography, *Take My Life*, in 1957.

See EDDIE CANTOR SHOW, *The*.

CAPE COD MYSTERIES

1983–1986   (Syndicated series heard on various NPR stations)

"It's a foggy night on old Cape Cod . . . a perfect night for a mystery," the half-hour *Cape Cod Mysteries* radio series began. One of NATIONAL PUBLIC RADIO's most listened-to dramatic program offerings, this radio show was created and directed by Steven Oney. It offered listeners excellent mystery stories of a sophisticated, sensational, and contemporary nature, effectively acted and having superb sound effects and original music. The series is occasionally repeated on contemporary PBS stations.

CAPITOL FAMILY HOUR, THE

See PRUDENTIAL FAMILY HOUR, THE.

CAPTAIN MIDNIGHT

1939–1942	Mutual	Mon.–Fri.	5:45 PM
1942–1945	NBC Blue	Mon.–Fri.	5:45 PM
1945–1948	Mutual	Mon.–Fri.	5:30 PM
1948–1949	Mutual	Mon.–Fri.	5:15 PM

Captain Midnight was one of young radio listeners' favorite children's adventure serials in the 1940s. The show's superhero, Captain Midnight, was a pilot who flew his single-engine plane all around the world, solving mysteries and fighting criminals—during World War II, Axis enemy spies. The serial, developed for radio by World War I aviator-heroes Robert Butt and Wilfred Moore, was heard five times a week for 15 minutes a day. Ovaltine dropped its longtime sponsorship of the LITTLE ORPHAN ANNIE program to sponsor the more up-to-date, action-packed *Captain Midnight* series. Ovaltine was also one of the first shows to offer premiums for a dime and a product label, including Captain Midnight badges, rings, and decoders, which have since become collector's items.

Ed Prentiss, Bill BOUCHEY, and Paul Barnes played Captain Midnight; Angeline Orr and then Marilou Neumayer played his friend, Joyce Ryan. Also heard regularly were Bill Rose, Hugh STUDEBAKER, Tommy Coons, Maurice Copeland, Earl George, Jack Bivens, Boris Aplan, Rene Rodier, Sharon Granger, Sherman Marks, Olan SOULE, and Marvin MILLER. Pierre Andre, Tom Moore, and Don Gordon were the program's announcers. Kirby Hawkes, Alan Wallace, and Russell Young directed the series at different times. *Captain Midnight* was also sponsored by Skelly oil.

CAREER OF ALICE BLAIR, THE

1939–1949	(Syndicated series. Various stations and times)

This series began, "*The Career of Alice Blair:* the transcribed true-to-life story of a lovely girl fighting for fame and happiness . . . facing the problems, the heartaches, and the thrills on the ladder of success in the business world." Transcribed, 15-minute weekday serials were the exception rather than the rule, and in this sense *The Career of Alice Blair* was unique. Film and stage star Martha Scott and then Rosemary DE CAMP starred as Alice Blair. Heard on the series in supporting roles were Willard WATERMAN, Mary Jane CROFT, Betty Lou GERSON, Lurene TUTTLE, and Joseph KEARNS. The program was sponsored by Flit starch, Daggett and Ramsdell chain stores, and Mistol cough drops. The show's theme music was "Love, Work, and Dreams."

CAREFREE CARNIVAL

1933–1934	NBC Red	Sun.	2 PM
1934–1935	NBC Blue	Mon.	8:30 PM
1935–1936	(Off the air)		
1936	NBC Blue	Mon.	9:30 PM

This half-hour program presented music and comedy and featured Ray Tollinger and Gene Arnold as hosts. Regulars were orchestra leader Meredith WILLSON, a character named "Senator Fishface" (played by Elmore Vincent), and Ben Klassen, Myron Niesley, Nola Lee, Tommy Haines, Charlie Marshall, and comic Pinky Lee. The show was sponsored by Crazy Water softening crystals and Blue Jay corn plasters.

CAREY, MACDONALD (1913–1994)

Well known as patriarch Dr. Tom Horton on the popular daytime TV series "Days of Our Lives" from 1965 until 1994, actor Macdonald Carey also had a very active career on radio and in films. Born in Sioux City, Iowa, Carey attended the University of Wisconsin and the University of Iowa before pursuing a career in show business. As a radio actor, he was regularly heard on such series as ELLEN RANDOLPH, *The* FAMILY THEATER, *The* FIRST NIGHTER, JOHN'S OTHER WIFE, JUST PLAIN BILL, STELLA DALLAS, *The* WOMAN IN WHITE, *Young Hickory,* and *Jason and the Golden Fleece.* Filmgoers saw Carey in many motion pictures, including *Shadow of a Doubt* (1943); *Blue Denim* (1959); and *The Damned* (1962).

CARLON, FRAN (1913–1993)

Fran Carlon is well remembered by radio listeners of the 1940s and 1950s as star newspaper reporter Lorelei Kilbourne of *The Illustrated Press* on BIG TOWN. The actress was born in Indianapolis, Indiana, but grew up in Scranton, Pennsylvania. After studying at the Goodman Dramatic School, Carlon began her acting career in a touring production of *Uncle Tom's Cabin.* As a teenager, she appeared in such films as *White Parade* (1933), *Music in the Air* (1934), and several Ritz Brothers movies at 20th Century Fox.

Her first major radio program was TODAY'S CHILDREN, when she became an NBC contract actress in Chicago in the late 1930s. Carlon was regularly heard on such programs as *This Changing World, Attorney at Law,* MARY NOBLE, BACKSTAGE WIFE, *Judy and Jane, Joan and Kermit,* DAVID HARUM, YOUNG WIDDER BROWN, *Blackstone the Detective,* BARRY CRAIG, CONFIDENTIAL INVESTIGATOR, *The* CHICAGO THEATER OF THE AIR, GIRL ALONE, LORA LAWTON, MA PERKINS, OUR GAL SUNDAY, *The* STORY OF MARY MARLIN, KITTY KEENE, *The* FORD THEATER, MR. KEEN, TRACER OF LOST PERSONS, and JOYCE JORAN, GIRL INTERN. She was also featured on such television programs as "Big Story," "Robert Montgomery Presents," as Portia in "Portia Faces Life" (1954–1955), and on "As the World Turns" (1968–1975). Carlon acted in numerous commercials.

CARNATION CONTENTED HOUR

1931–1932	NBC Red	Mon.	8 PM
1932–1942	NBC Red	Mon.	10 PM
1942–1949	NBC	Mon.	10 PM
1949–1951	CBS	Sun.	10 PM

This long-running half-hour musical radio series, sponsored by Carnation Evaporated Milk, featured the orchestras of Percy Faith, Josef Pasternack, and Frank Black and such singers and musicians as Buddy CLARK, Jo STAFFORD, Reinhold Schmidt, Josephine Antoine, the Doring Sisters, Gladys Swarthout, Dinah SHORE, Tony Martin, the Continental Quartet, Herman Larsen, Robert Kessler, Earle Tanner, Bob Child, Opal Craven (the Lullaby Lady), and the Carnation Chorus. Vincent Fletcher, Bret MORRISON, and James "Jimmy" WALLINGTON were the program's announcers. Holland Engle was the series' director in the early 1940s. The show's theme music was, quite appropriately, "Contented," and orchestral music consisted of popular and semiclassical pieces of a romantic nature.

CARNEGIE, DALE
See HOW TO WIN FRIENDS AND INFLUENCE PEOPLE.

CARNEY, ART (1918–   )
Known to millions as Ed Norton on Jackie Gleason's "The Honeymooners" TV series, Art Carney was born in Mount Vernon, New York, and was a radio actor long before he stepped in front of a TV camera. A character actor, he was regularly heard on such programs as CASEY, CRIME PHOTOGRAPHER, GANGBUSTERS, The HENRY MORGAN SHOW, Joe and Ethel Turp, LAND OF THE LOST, LORENZO JONES, The MARCH OF TIME (as the voice of Franklin D. Roosevelt), and DIMENSION X. Carney's film appearances include The Yellow Rolls Royce (1965) and Harry and Tonto (1974), for which he won the Academy Award as Best Actor. He has also guest-starred in several made-for-TV films. On Broadway, Carney starred in such plays as The Odd Couple (as Felix Unger [1965]), The Rope Dancers (1960), and Take Her, She's Mine (1962).

CARNEY, DON (HOWARD RICE: 1896–1954)
Don Carney was the famous Uncle Don on WOR radio in New York for more than twenty-one years. Although UNCLE DON was only on national network radio program for one year—from 1938 until 1939—few people interested in radio have not heard one story or another about Uncle Don's show. In spite of his years of success as a children's show host, Carney was never able to live down a rumor concerning an accidental on-the-air statement he reportedly made: "Well, I guess that should hold the little bastards for a while." Hundreds claim they actually heard Carney make such a statement, but in reality this probably never happened. Today it is believed that the story began as a joke told on the air by a Baltimore, Maryland, disc jockey who had never even heard the Uncle Don program. Even so, Carney's career was never the same after that rumor spread throughout the country, and he never had another network show.

CAROL KENNEDY'S ROMANCE

1937–1938	CBS	Mon.–Fri.	11:15 AM

Originally a segment on the Heinz Magazine of the Air series, Carol Kennedy's Romance featured Gretchen Davidson as Carol, a young working girl searching for romance. Regular supporting roles were played by Mitzi Gould, Carlton YOUNG, Gene Morgan, Elliott Reid, and Ed JEROME. In spite of a formidable letter-writing campaign by fans who wanted to keep the program on the air, Carol Kennedy's Romance was canceled after one season. The 15-minute daytime series was sustained by the CBS network.

CARPENTER, KEN (1900–1984)
Long associated with singer Bing CROSBY, announcer Ken Carpenter was born in Avon, Illinois. He was Crosby's chief introducer and sponsor's product spokesman for many years on such programs as The KRAFT MUSIC HALL and The BING CROSBY SHOW. In addition, Carpenter announced The EDGAR BERGEN–CHARLIE MCCARTHY SHOW, Hollywood Mardi Gras, TRUTH OR CONSEQUENCES, and, for many years, Carlton E. MORSE's long-running ONE MAN'S FAMILY. He was also a commercial announcer and a narrator of film and TV documentaries.

CARRINGTON, ELAINE STERNE (1892–1958)
Elaine Carrington was one of radio's most respected writing talents. A native New Yorker, she was the creative force behind such popular daytime serials as PEPPER YOUNG'S FAMILY, ROSEMARY, Trouble House, and WHEN A GIRL MARRIES, as well as the prime-time half-hour DR. CHRISTIAN series. Carrington's unique ability to make listeners feel as if they were hearing actual conversations instead of radio plays made her shows immensely popular. Carrington created one series for television, "Follow Your Heart," which was aired from 1953 to 1954.

CARSON, JACK (1910–1963)

Beefy actor Jack Carson was born in Carmen, Manitoba, Canada. He was the host of The CAMEL CARAVAN program and guest-starred on many major radio programs throughout the 1940s and 1950s. In 1943, Carson starred on the weekly JACK CARSON SHOW, a variety comedy show. In addition to his radio and TV work, he appeared in motion pictures: *Destry Rides Again* (1941), *The Male Animal* (1944), *Mildred Pierce* (1945), and *A Star Is Born* (1954).

See SEALTEST VILLAGE STORE, The.

CARTERS OF ELM STREET, THE

1939–1940	NBC Red	Mon.–Fri.	12 PM
1940–1946	Mutual	Mon.–Fri.	12 PM

In 1939, *The Carters of Elm Street* joined CBS's ever-growing roster of 15-minute Monday-through-Friday daytime serial dramas. The series centered around the joys and sorrows of a typical middle-class, small-town American family, as did so many of the daytimes dramas at that time. Vic Smith and Virginia PAYNE, (who also played Ma on MA PERKINS) were heard as Mr. and Mrs. Carter, and Virginia "Ginger" Jones, Lesley Woods, Herb Nelson, Bill Rose, and Ann Russell played their offspring. Caucasian actress Harriette WIDMER, who frequently played African-Americans on radio programs, had a running role as Mattie Belle. Jack Brinkley and Pierre Andre were the program's announcers. Robert Wilson directed the series, and Mona Kent wrote it. Ovaltine chocolate-flavored health drink was the program's sponsor. The show's theme song was "My Heart at Thy Sweet Voice."

CASE, NELSON (1910–1976)

Before joining the staff of regular announcers at NBC in the 1930s, Nelson Case was a newspaper reporter, a singer, and a pianist. Originally from Long Beach, California, and known for his resonant, articulate voice, he was a regularly heard announcer on such programs as AGAINST THE STORM, *Charlie and Jennie*, MY TRUE STORY, *Sky Blazers*, LIFE CAN BE BEAUTIFUL, HILDA HOPE, MD, HOUR OF CHARM, *Youth vs. Age*, The FORD THEATER, LONE JOURNEY, and The STORY OF MARY MARLIN. He also announced for NBC television and TV commercials.

CASEY, CRIME PHOTOGRAPHER (AKA CASEY-PRESS PHOTOGRAPHER; CRIME PHOTOGRAPHER)

1945–1946	CBS	Mon.	10:30 PM
1946–1950	CBS	Thurs.	9:30 PM

"Casey," whose first name was never revealed, was the major crime photographer at the fictional *Morning Express* newspaper. With the help of reporter Ann Williams, he tracked down criminals and solved numerous crimes on this popular mystery-adventure series. Casey and Ann often enlisted the aid of their police-officer friend Captain Logan during each week's half-hour episode. In between assignments, crime investigators Casey and Ann went to their favorite tavern, "The Blue Note," and discussed their adventures with their bartender-friend Ethelbert. Matt CROWLEY and Staats COTSWORTH played Casey, with the latter playing the role longer; Alice REINHEART, Betty Furness, Jone Allison, Lesley Woods, and Jan MINER (best remembered in the role) played Ann at different times. Jackson BECK and Bernard Lenrow were heard as Captain Logan, and John GIBSON played Ethelbert. Supporting players included Robert DRYDEN, John Griggs, James Kreiger, Art CARNEY, Bryna Raeburn, Jack Hartley, and Miriam WOLFE. Bob Hite, Bill CULLEN, Ken ROBERTS, and Tony Marvin were the show's announcers, and John Dietz its longtime director. Alonzo Dean COLE, Gail and Harry Ingram, and others wrote scripts for the program. Archie Blyer conducted the orchestra. Sponsors included Anchor-Hocking glass, Toni home permanent, Toni creme shampoo, and Philip Morris cigarettes.

CAVALCADE OF AMERICA

1935–1938	CBS	Wed.	8 PM
1938–1939	CBS	Tues.	8:30 PM
1939–1940	NBC Red	Tues.	7:30 PM
1940–1941	NBC Red	Wed.	7:30 PM
1941–1949	NBC	Mon.	8 PM
1949–1953	NBC	Tues.	8 PM

Little-known incidents and people who were merely footnotes in American history were featured each week on the half-hour *Cavalcade of America* series. Popular Hollywood and Broadway stars such as Clark Gable, Glenn Ford, Charles Laughton, Lionel BARRYMORE, Dick POWELL, Tyrone Power, Edward G. Robinson, Lucille BALL, Claude Rains, Agnes MOOREHEAD, Jean Arthur, Joan Caulfield, Robert Young, Ethel Barrymore, Alfred Lunt and Lynn Fontanne, and Orson WELLES played leading roles on the program. The series was narrated by Thomas Chalmers. The supporting casts consisted of many of radio's busiest working actors, including John MCINTIRE, Jeanette NOLAN, William "Bill" JOHNSTONE, Bill ADAMS, Joseph COTTEN, Luis VAN ROOTEN, Ted DeCorsia, Sidney Ellstrom, Kate McComb, Frank READICK, Ed JEROME, Raymond Edward JOHNSON, Everett SLOANE, Paul Stewart, and Ray COLLINS. The series was directed by John Zoller, Paul Stewart, Homer Fickett, and Bill Sweets, who also wrote scripts for the series with Ruth Adams Knight. Clayton "Bud" COLLYER was the series' longtime announcer, and Cy Harrice also announced for a time. Donald VOORHEES conducted the program's orchestra. The chief historical consultant for the series was Dr. Frank Monaghan. Original organ music heard on the show was supplied by Rosa Rio. This series was sponsored by the duPont Company the entire time it was on the air. It was on this program that duPont first made the claim that its products provided "Better things for better living."

CBC RADIO NEWS

The CANADIAN BROADCASTING CORPORATION's Radio and Stereo networks offer news throughout the day, as reported by newscasters Dwight Wylie, Barbara Smith, Russ Germain, and others. *World Report* is presented at 6, 7, and 8 AM and is hosted by Wylie. The CBC news department employs more than 200 broadcast journalists, reporters, editors, writers, producers, and correspondents from across Canada and around the world. Regional, national, and international events are covered.

CBC SPECIALS

Over the years, the CANADIAN BROADCASTING CORPORATION has presented numerous special broadcasts of world events, including the abdication of Edward VIII and the coronation of King George in the 1930s; the coronation of Queen Elizabeth in the 1950s; the inauguration of Trans-Canada Airlines; the French-language Congress in Quebec; a Christmas service from Bethlehem; and the Canadian-born Dionne quintuplets' third birthday party in 1937.

CBC SPORTS

The CANADIAN BROADCASTING CORPORATION offers a wide variety of sports coverage on its network of Radio (AM) stations. *Morning Sports,* hosted by Brandon Connor, is heard weekdays and gives daily sports reports. *Afternoon Sports,* hosted by Rich Cluff, presents sports information that reflects changes seen in the sports world. *The Inside Track,* hosted by Mary Hynes, examines the impact of sports on the lives of Canadians through documentaries, interviews, sound montages, columns, literary readings, drama, and comedy. *Weekend Sports,* hosted by Dwight Smith and Dzintars Cers, provides detailed world coverage of sports.

CBC STAGE

1940s–present   (Various times)

Over the years, the CANADIAN BROADCASTING CORPORATION has produced several programs with the title *CBC Stage.* This program offers outstanding original radio dramas, as well as adaptations of classic plays and novels. The plays, often by Canadian writers, were acted by what *The New York Times* called "the

best repertory group in this hemisphere"—Christopher Plummer, Tudi Wiggins, and Miriam Wolfe were often featured. During its 1994 season, the CBC offered *Studio 94* and *Stereodrama* as part of *Arts Tonight* Mondays through Fridays on the stereo (FM) network at 9:45 PM. The CBC radio (AM) network presents *Between the Covers,* serialized radio adaptations of various novels, Mondays through Fridays at 10:15 PM. CBC's mystery project is heard on the network's *Brand X* series on Saturdays at 4:30 PM.

CBS IS THERE

See YOU ARE THERE.

CBS MYSTERY THEATER

1974–1977   (Syndicated series. Various stations and times)

Radio drama enjoyed a brief renaissance in the mid-1970s when Himan BROWN, who was responsible for such popular radio programs as INNER SANCTUM MYSTERIES, *The* THIN MAN, and BULLDOG DRUMMOND, produced and directed for the COLUMBIA BROADCASTING SYSTEM a daily hour-long dramatic mystery series called the *CBS Mystery Theater.* The plays (usually original and sometimes adapted from classic novels and short stories) presented on this series involved murder, supernatural events, and assorted psychological problems such as suicides, witch hunting, and social mayhem. This program, heard in the United States and Canada, was hosted by veteran stage, screen, and TV actor E. G. Marshall. Although they were generally well written and well produced, far too many commercials distracted audience interest from the stories being presented.

Brown assembled radio's most reliable acting talent, including Agnes MOOREHEAD, heard on the series' first program, Mercedes MCCAMBRIDGE, Elspeth ERIC, who wrote as well as acted, Robert DRYDEN, Arnold MOSS, Roger DeKoven, Rosemary RICE, Ian Martin, Virginia PAYNE, Mary Jane HIGBY, Vicki VOLA, Evie Juster, Claudia MORGAN, Mason ADAMS, Staats COTSWORTH, Hans CONRIED, Alexander SCOURBY, Court Benson, Teri Keane, Gil Mack, Richard CRENNA, Robert READICK, Mandel KRAMER, and Ralph Bell. The series, which suspended production in 1977, also featured actors best known in other media: Marion Seldes, Keir Dullea, Julie Harris, Mandy Patinkin, Kevin McCarthy, Michael Tolan, Fred Gwynne, and Kim Hunter.

Henry Slesar wrote many of the series' original dramas. The program tapes were rereleased for syndication in the 1980s but once again failed to attract the kind of audience needed to justify a local station's production costs. Eventually it disappeared from the airwaves, although rumors of a revival on NATIONAL PUBLIC RADIO have persisted.

CBS RADIO WORKSHOP (AKA THE COLUMBIA WORKSHOP)

1956–1957	CBS	Fri.	8:30 PM
		Sun.	4 PM

In the tradition of the experimental half-hour drama series The COLUMBIA WORKSHOP, CBS produced a weekly series of original radio plays by such celebrated writers as William Saroyan, Archibald MacLeish, Lord Dunsany, Irving Reis, Ambrose Bierce, Dorothy Parker, and Norman Corwin. Orson WELLES (who also acted on the series), William N. ROBSON, Max Wylie, Douglas Coultier, and Davidson Taylor directed many presentations. Featured actors included Charles Laughton and wife Elsa Lanchester, Martin GABEL, Fredric March, Charme Allen, Hester Sondergaard, Joseph JULIAN, Minerva PIOUS, Joan Alexander, Arnold MOSS, Ralph Bell, Ruth Gilbert, and House JAMESON. The diverse offerings included an adaptation of Aldous Huxley's Brave New World; original plays such as "Voice of a City," which presented the sounds of a typical large American metropolis; the first dramatization of Subways Are for Sleeping, later a Broadway musical; and The Oedipus Complex, Colloquy #4, The Joe Miller Joke Book, and Space Merchants, Parts One and Two. The series was sustained by CBS.

CENTRAL CITY

1938–1941	NBC Red	Mon.–Fri.	10 AM

This 15-minute, five-days-a-week adventure-mystery series was set in a large fictional American metropolis and starred Elspeth ERIC as Emily Olson and Van Heflin and then Myron MCCORMICK as Bob Shellenberger. They played crime reporters for an urban newspaper. Also featured were Tom Powers, Frank Wilcox, Geoffrey Bryant, and Eleanor Phillips in supporting roles. Central City was directed by Kenneth W. MACGREGOR and Himan BROWN, and written by Frank Dahm, Frank Gould, and Stuart Hawkins. Oxydol detergent sponsored the program.

CHALLENGE OF THE YUKON, THE (AKA SERGEANT PRESTON OF THE CANADIAN MOUNTED POLICE)

1938–1947	WXYZ	(Days and times varied)
1947–1950	ABC	(Days and times varied)
1950–1955	Mutual	(Days and times varied)

Sergeant Preston and his faithful dog, Yukon King, were the major characters on this daily children's adventure serial. Set in the Canadian Northwest, the show was created and written by Fran STRIKER, creator of The LONE RANGER series. Jay Michael, Paul Sutton, and Brace BEEMER (the LONE RANGER) each played Preston, and John Todd ("Tonto" on the Lone Ranger series) was heard as the Inspector. Regularly heard on the series were Harry Goldstein, Bill Saunders, Paul Hughes, Ernie Winstanley, Lee Allman, Rollon Parker, and others who were also featured on both The Lone Ranger and The GREEN HORNET. Announcers on the half-hour program included Bob Hite and Fred Foy. The program's theme music was "The Donna Diana Overture." During its earliest years, the series was directed by Al HODGE, who later became well known as Captain Video on TV. Sponsors varied according to locality.

Sergeant Preston and his faithful dog, Yukon King, were the major characters on this daily children's adventure serial. Set in the Canadian Northwest, the show was created and written by Fran STRIKER, creator of The LONE RANGER series. Jay Michael, Paul Sutton, and Brace BEEMER (the LONE RANGER) each played Preston, and John Todd ("Tonto" on the Lone Ranger series) was heard as the Inspector. Regularly on the series were Harry Goldstein, Bill Saunders, Paul Hughes, Ernie Winstanley, Lee Allman, Rollon Parker, and others who were also featured on both The Lone Ranger and The GREEN HORNET. Announcers on the half-hour program included Bob Hite and Fred Foy. The program's theme music was "The Donna Diana Overture." During its earliest years, the series was directed by Al HODGE, who later became well known as Captain Video on TV. Sponsors varied according to locality.

CHAMBER MUSIC SOCIETY OF LOWER BASIN STREET, THE

1940–1941	NBC Blue	Sun.	9:30 PM
1941–1942	NBC Blue	Wed.	9 PM
1943	NBC Blue	Mon.	10:30 PM
1943–1944	NBC Blue	Sun.	10 PM
1950	NBC	Sun.	10 PM
1952	NBC	Sat.	10:30 PM

Milton CROSS and then Gene Hamilton, playing a fictional character named "Dr. Gino," hosted this popular music-comedy series. The program at one time featured Jack McCarthy as a host called "Dr. Giacomo," as well as comic routines and readings by Zero Mostel, Ernest CHAPPELL, and Jimmy Blair. Created and written by Welbourn Kelley, the half-hour Chamber Music Society show was directed by Tom Bennett. Vocalists on the program included singers Diane Courtney, Dinah SHORE (in her radio network debut), Jane PICKENS, and Lena Horne and featured the orchestras of Paul LaValle, Henry Levine, and others. The show's theme song was "Basin Street."

CHANCE OF A LIFETIME

1949–1950	ABC	Sun.	9:30 PM
1950–1951	ABC	Tues.	8 PM
		Tues.	8:30 PM
		Sat.	7:30 PM

Veteran radio quizmaster John Reed KING was the host of this half-hour show, which gave contestants a chance to fulfill a lifetime wish, such as being reunited with a long-lost loved one or singing on the radio if they answered a series of general questions correctly. Don WILSON was the show's announcer. *Chance of a Lifetime* was directed by Charles T. Harrell and was heard on the ABC network of stations.

CHANDLER, JEFF (IRA GROSSEL: 1918–1961)

Actor Jeff Chandler was born in Brooklyn, New York, and had one of the richest baritone voices on radio. Chandler was perhaps best known to radio listeners as English teacher Connie Brooks's love interest, science teacher Mr. Boynton, on the OUR MISS BROOKS situation-comedy series. He was private eye Michael Shayne on the MICHAEL SHAYNE, DETECTIVE program and was also heard on HOLLYWOOD STAR TIME, *The* LUX RADIO THEATER, *The* SCREEN GUILD PLAYERS, and *Frontier Town,* called by contemporary periodicals the first adult Western on radio. Chandler became a major motion-picture star after he appeared in the film *Sword in the Desert* (1949). He starred in such films as *Broken Arrow* (1952), *The Sign of the Pagan* (1956), and *Return to Peyton Place* (1962). Chandler died from blood poisoning at the age of forty-three after an operation for a slipped disk.

CHANDU, THE MAGICIAN

1932–1950	(Syndicated series. Various stations and times)

Master magician Chandu was the disguise for secret-service agent Frank Chandler the major character on the syndicated half-hour mystery-adventure series, *Chandu, the Magician.* Chandler had supernatural powers, learned from a Hindu yogi, that enabled him to uncover crimes and thereby apprehend gangsters. The ABC series was the creation of Harry A. Earnshaw. Jason Robards, Sr., Gayne Whitman, Howard Hoffman, and Tom Collins played the Chandu-Chandler character at different times. Also heard on occasion were Bryna Raeburn, Cornelia Osgood, Audrey McGrath, Margaret MacDonald, Olan SOULE, Ian Martin, and Leon JANNEY. The last time this series was on the air, *Chandu, the Magician* was produced by Cyril Ambrister and directed by Blair Walliser. The scripts were written by Dam Dunn and Vera Oldham.

CHAPLAIN JIM

1942	NBC	Sun.	2 PM
1942–1945	Mutual	Sun.	2 PM
1946	Mutual	Sun.	10:30 AM

This ABC series dramatized the exciting and inspirational wartime experiences of various military service members during World War II. Acts of heroism, suffering, and love encounters were related by the show's narrator, Chaplain Jim of the U. S. Army. Actors John Lund and Don MACLAUGHLIN played the chaplain at different times on the series. The program's announcers were George Ansbro and Vinton Hayworth. *Chaplain Jim* was produced by Frank and Anne HUMMERT and directed by Richard Leonard and Martha Atwell. The show's theme was "Onward Christian Soldiers," played in a march tempo.

CHAPLIN, W. W. (1895–1978)

News reporter W. W. Chaplin, best known to his colleagues as "Bill," was born in New York City. He became a newspaperman after serving in the army during World War I and joined the Associated Press a few years after the war ended. Chaplin worked as a news reporter and commentator in the late 1920s. During World War II, Chaplin reported the news from the European, Asian, and African fronts as a war correspondent. After the war, he continued to give newscasts and wrote five books discussing world events.

CHAPPELL, ERNEST (1903–1983)

Born in Chicago, Illinois, Ernest Chappell was a well-known radio announcer and quiz-show host of *Are You a Genius?* BIG STORY, *The* CHAMBER MUSIC SOCIETY OF LOWER BASIN STREET, among other programs. He further proved himself to be a very capable and talented actor/announcer when he starred on the well-written QUIET PLEASE radio series, a weekly tale of suspense, science fiction, and mystery. Chappell carried the major burden of the show, with only occasional assistance from supporting actors.

CHARLIE CHAN, THE ADVENTURES OF

See ADVENTURES OF CHARLIE CHAN, THE.

CHARLOTTE GREENWOOD SHOW, THE

1994 (summer)	NBC	Tues.	10 PM
1944–46	ABC	Mon.	8:30 PM

Film and stage comedienne of the 1940s Charlotte Greenwood appeared in such films as *Oh, You Beautiful Doll!* and *Moon Over Miami* and on Broadway in *So Long Letty.* She was also the star of a weekly half-hour radio program, *The Charlotte Greenwood Show,* for two seasons. Although the talented Greenwood

Chase and Sanborn Hour stars: orchestra leader Ray Noble, singer Dale Evans, actor-M.C. Don Ameche, Charlie McCarthy, and ventriloquist Edgar Bergen (NBC)

certainly gave her listening audience plenty of laughs, with her expert comic delivery and great characters, they probably missed *not* seeing her kick up her famous long legs in one of her celebrated comic dance routines. Also appearing on the series in a wide variety of supporting roles were John Brown, Harry Bartell, and Will Wright. The series was produced and directed by Miss Greenwood's husband, Martin Broones.

CHASE AND SANBORN HOUR, THE (AKA *THE EDGAR BERGEN–CHARLIE McCARTHY SHOW*)

1928–1948	NBC Red	Sun.	8 PM
1937–1948	NBC Red	Sun.	8 PM

Don AMECHE, Maurice Chevalier, Eddie CANTOR, Jimmy DURANTE, Bert Lahr, and Edgar BERGEN and Charlie McCarthy starred on this one-hour comedy-variety program at various times. Nelson EDDY also hosted a summer *Chase and Sanborn* series. Featured on the Ameche–Bergen series were Ray Noble and his orchestra; singers Anita Gordon, Dale Evans, Donald Dixon, Wally Maher, and Carol Richards; comedian Eddie Mayhoff; the Stroud Twins; the King Sisters quartet; and comedians ABBOTT AND COSTELLO. Because of the tremendous success of the Bergen–McCarthy shows, the program's title was eventually

changed to the *Edgar Bergen–Charlie McCarthy Show*. Bill Baldwin, among others, announced the series, and True Boardman and George Faulkner wrote many of its scripts. For many years, the show was directed by Abbott K. Spencer. Chase and Sanborn coffee sponsored the show.

CHESTERFIELD SUPPER CLUB, THE

1944–1949	NBC	Mon.–Fri.	7 PM
1949–1950	NBC	Thurs.	10 PM

Appropriately, the songs "A Cigarette, Sweet Music, and You" and "Smoke Dreams" were the themes on the 15-minute *Chesterfield Supper Club* shows. An impressive number of singers and musicians starred on this show, which presented popular songs with little if any commentary. At one time or another, Perry COMO, Johnny Johnston, the Satisfiers, Don Cornell, Bill Lawrence, Kay Starr, Jo STAFFORD, Peggy Lee, Frankie Laine, the Fontane Sisters, the Pied Pipers, Fred WARING and His Pennsylvanians, and Mary Ashworth starred accompanied by the orchestras of Dave Barbour, Ted Steele, Tex Beneke, Sammy KAYE, Mitchell Ayres, Glenn Miller, Paul Weston, and Lloyd Schaefer. Announcers on *The Chesterfield Supper Club* included Paul DOUGLAS, Martin Block, Clark Dennis, and Tom Reddy. The show was produced by Bob

Moss and Eldridge Packham and directed by Ward Byron and Eldrige Packham. Chesterfield cigarettes sponsored the series.

CHICAGO THEATER OF THE AIR, THE

| 1941–1945 | Mutual | Sat. | 9 PM |

The Mutual network presented this "live" one-hour variety program that featured music, dramatic plays, and comedy skits. The show's host was Colonel Robert McCormick; soprano Marion Claire, tenors Robert McCormick and Attilo Baggiore, baritones Bruce Foote and Earl Willkie, and contralto Ruth Slater were regulars on the program. Guest artists on the show included James MELTON, Thomas L. Thomas, Jan Peerce, Allan JONES, Richard Tucker, and Robert Merrill. Actors in the dramatic sketches included Marvin MILLER, Olan SOULE, Laurette FILLBRANDT, Rita Ascot, Bob Jellison, Patricia Dunlap, Willard WATERMAN, Luise Barclay, Barbara LUDDY, Jane WEBB, Betty Lou GERSON, Alice Hill, Charles Penman, Donna Reade, Everett Clark, Rosemary Garbell, Bret MORRISON, Bob BAILEY, Les TREMAYNE, John LARKIN, Marilou Neumayer, Phil Lord, Fran CARLON, and many others. Announcers included John Weigle and Marvin MILLER. Created by William A. Bacher, *The Chicago Theater of the Air* was directed by Fritz Blocki, Joe Ainsley, Kenneth W. MACGREGOR, and Jack LaFrandre and sponsored by *The Chicago Tribune* for many years.

CHICK CARTER, BOY DETECTIVE

| 1943–1945 | Mutual | Mon.–Fri. | (Times varied) |

Youngsters had a crime-solving detective hero their own age when the 15-minute weekday *Chick Carter, Boy Detective* was on the air. Chick was "the adopted son" of longtime adult detective-show character Nick Carter and was played by actors Bill LIPTON and Leon JANNEY. Jean McCoy and then her sister Joanne played the part of Chick's girlfriend, Sue. Also heard on the show were Gil Mack as Tex, and Stefan Schnable and Bill Griffis in supporting roles. The program was directed by Fritz Blocki and written by Blocki and Nancy Webb.

See also NICK CARTER, MASTER DETECTIVE.

CHILDREN'S HOUR, THE (AKA HORN AND HARDART'S CHILDREN'S HOUR)

See COAST TO COAST ON A BUS.

CHILDREN'S RADIO THEATER

| 1980s | NPR | (Various times and stations) |

In the early 1980s, a one-hour program called *The Children's Radio Theater* was produced by NATIONAL PUBLIC RADIO and made available to NPR stations around the country. The series presented dramatized adaptations of such well-known children's stories as "Beauty and The Beast" and "Cabbage Soup" and even presented a thirteen-part radio version of the popular film STAR WARS, starring members of the movie's cast, Mark Hamill and Anthony Daniels. A second *Star Wars* series, based on *The Empire Strikes Back,* was also presented. One of the most interesting features of this series, which was produced by a Washington, D.C.–based company, was the presentation of scripts written for radio by children. Each year the "Henny Penny Playwriting Contest" awarded winners such prizes as books, games, and even cash. The scripts were presented as they were written by the children, without corrections or additions made by adults.

CHRISTMAS CAROL, A

See MERCURY THEATER, THE; and CAMPBELL PLAYHOUSE, THE.

CINNAMON BEAR, THE

| 1937–1955 | (Syndicated series. Various stations and times) |

Paddy O'Cinnamon, Judy and Jimmy Barton, Crazy Quilt Dragon, Wintergreen Witch, and Milissa were characters regularly heard on this early-morning children's series. Each year, Judy and Jimmy and their tiny teddy bear, Paddy O'Cinnamon, searched Maybeland looking for their Christmas treetop ornament, the Silver Star, which had been stolen by the Crazy Quilt Dragon. The search for the ornament was an annual event for youngsters around the country. During the rest of the year, various guest actors would take Judy and Jimmy on adventures of interest to children, such as a trip to an ice-cream factory or a search for a lost dog.

Joseph KEARNS was the voice of Crazy Quilt Dragon, Frank NELSON and Howard McNear were featured regularly on the program. The series was directed and written by Granville and Elizabeth Meisch.

CISCO KID, THE

1942–1943	Mutual	Fri.	8:30 PM
1943–1944	Mutual	Tues.	8 PM
		Fri.	8:30 PM
		Sat.	8:30 PM
		Wed.	9:30 PM
1944–1947	(Off the air)		
1947–1956	(Syndicated series. Various times and stations)		

"Here's adventure! Here's romance! Here's the famous Robin Hood of the West—*The Cisco Kid!*" this children's adventure serial began. The Cisco Kid, a crime-fighting vigilante, and his sidekick Pancho were the main characters on this half-hour syndicated series: Jackson BECK and Jack Mather were heard as Cisco; Louis Sorin, Harry Lang, and Mel BLANC played Pancho. Regularly heard in supporting roles was Marvin MILLER. *The Cisco Kid's* announcers were Marvin Miller and Rye Billsbury. The series was directed by Jock MacGregor, Jeanne K. Harrison, and Fred Levings at different times and written by John Sinn, Ralph Rosenberg, and Ken Lyons.

CITIES SERVICE CONCERTS (AKA HIGHWAYS IN MELODY)

1927–1935	NBC	Fri.	8 PM
1935–1941	NBC Red	Fri.	8 PM
1941–1944	NBC	Fri.	8 PM

Cities Service Concerts were dedicated to music and were heard in both half-hour and one-hour formats. Lucille Manners and Jessica DRAGONETTE, two of radio's most admired sopranos, starred on the program at different times. Other musical personalities who gained national attention on this show were singer Ross Graham, the piano team of Banta and Rettenberg, tenor Frank PARKER, Robert Simmons, Rosario Bourdon, Dr. Frank Black, the Revellers Quartet, the Cavaliers Quartet, and the orchestras of Edwin Franko Goldman, Milton Rettenburg, and Paul LaValle. Guest stars from opera and the concert stage were regularly heard on the program. The show's announcer for many years was Ford BOND. When singer Jessica Dragonette made a sudden departure from this series to star on the PALMOLIVE BEAUTY BOX program, newspaper columnists and fans wrote thousands of letters criticizing her decision. The Petroleum Advisers for Cities Service sponsored the program.

CITIES SERVICE BAND OF AMERICA

1949–1950	NBC	Fri.	8 PM
1950–1955	NBC	Mon.	9:30 PM

This half-hour series evolved from the *Highways in Melody* program and starred Paul LAVALLE, its host and orchestra leader. It followed a format similar to CITIES SERVICE CONCERTS, except that popular instead of classical and semiclassical music was featured. Ford BOND was announced, and Cities Service Petroleum sponsored the program.

CITY HOSPITAL

1951–1953	CBS	Sat.	1:30 PM
1953–1956	CBS	Sat.	1 PM
1956–1958	CBS	Sat.	1:05 PM

"City Hospital, where life begins and ends; where around the clock—24 hours a day—men and women are dedicated to the war against suffering and pain,

One of radio's earliest soap operas was *Clara, Lu, and Em.* Pictured here are (from left) Louise Starkey (Clara), Isabel Carothers (Lu), and Helen King (Em). (NBC)

intent upon helping others no matter who they are." This was the inspiring opening of the half-hour *City Hospital* series. Set in a big-city hospital, the series starred Santos ORTEGA and then Melville Ruick as Dr. Barton Crane. Each week a different story concerning doctors and patients at Dr. Crane's hospital was presented. John Cannon was the program's announcer. Sponsors of the show included Arrid deodorant and Carter's Little Liver Pills.

CLARA, LU, AND EM

1931–1932	NBC Blue	Mon.–Fri.	10:30 AM
1932–1936	NBC Red	Mon.–Fri.	10:15 AM
1936–1942	(Off the air)		
1942–1943	CBS	Mon.–Fri.	11 AM
1943–1945	(Syndicated series. Various times and stations)		

Many say that this 15-minute, five-days-a-week series was radio's first daytime drama serial. About three small-town gossips, the program featured Louise Starey and then Fran ALLISON as Clara; Isobel Carothers and then Dorothy Day as Lu; and Helen King and then Harriet Allyn as Em. When the program was canceled in 1936, the public was outraged, and thousands wrote letters to NBC protesting the network's decision. The program was eventually returned to the airwaves in 1942. Don David was the show's final announcer. Sponsors of the show included Super Suds detergent, and Pillsbury flour.

CLARK, BUDDY (1911–1949)

Baritone pop singer Buddy Clark made numerous guest appearances on most major comedy-variety programs throughout the 1940s. Born in Boston, Massachusetts, he began his broadcasting career in 1934 and was a regular on *The* BEN BERNIE SHOW, *The Carnation Contented Hour,* and YOUR HIT PARADE. Two of Clark's best-known song hits are "On a Slow Boat to China" and "Contented." His untimely death at the age of thirty-eight ended a promising career at the height of his popularity.

CLARK, LON (1911–   )

Born in Minnesota, actor Lon Clark is perhaps best remembered as radio's supersleuth Nick Carter on the NICK CARTER, MASTER DETECTIVE series. Clark began to act on radio in 1941 after appearing in several stage productions as a singer and an actor. He was subsequently heard on such programs as *Wilderness Road,* BRIGHT HORIZON, and *The* MYSTERIOUS TRAVELER. When the *Nick Carter* series was canceled in 1957, Clark continued his stage and television careers. He also taught poetry, film, and Shakespeare at Adelphi University on Long Island, New York.

CLAUDIA (AKA CLAUDIA AND DAVID)

1941	CBS	Sat.	8 PM
1941–1947	(Off the air)		
1947–1948	(Syndicated series. Various times and stations)		

Rose Franken's hit play *Claudia* (also a 1943 film) became a half-hour weekly radio series with Patricia RYAN and later Kathryn Card playing the title role. Richard KOLLMAR and Paul Crabtree played Claudia's husband, David Naughton, and character actress Jane Seymour played her mother. The story concerned a sensitive young woman and her equally sensitive husband trying to adjust to life in a competitive, insensitive big-city atmosphere. Major supporting actresses were Peggy Allenby and Irene Hubbard; announcers were Charles Stark and Joe King, and Kenneth MACGREGOR and Carlo DEANGELO directed the series. The sponsor was Coca-Cola soft drink.

CLIQUOT CLUB ESKIMOS' ORCHESTRA, THE

1926–1927	NBC Red	Thurs.	10 PM
1927–1928	NBC Red	Thurs.	9 PM
1928–1930	NBC Red	Tues.	10 PM
1930–1933	NBC Red	Fri.	9 PM
1933–1935	(Off the air)		
1935–1936	NBC Red	Sun.	3 PM

This half-hour music-variety program, one of radio's earliest hit shows, featured banjoist Harry Reser and his band. Reser also acted as the show's host. Band members Raymond Knight, Merle Johnson, Jimmy Brierly, and Everett Clark, as well as the Six Jumping Jacks, Loretta Clemons, Speed Young, and Virginia Heyer, were regularly featured on the program. Phil Carlin was the program's announcer. Cal Kohl directed the show for many seasons. Cliquot Club sponsored the series. The show's theme music, which was composed by Reser, was an original song called "The Cliquot March."

CLUB FIFTEEN

1948–1951	CBS	Mon.–Fri.	7:30 PM
1951–1952	CBS	Mon., Wed., Fri.	7:30 PM
1952–1953	CBS	Mon., Tues., Wed., Fri.	7:30 PM

Club Fifteen was a 15-minute music program hosted by Bob CROSBY when it first went on the air. At various times, it starred singers Jo STAFFORD, Margaret Whiting, Giselle MacKenzie, the Modernaires, Patti Clayton, Evelyn Knight, the ANDREWS SISTERS, and Dick Haymes. Bob Crosby's Bobcats and the Jerry Gray orchestra offered musical accompaniments. *Club Fifteen* was directed by Cal Kuhl and Ace Ochs, and announced by Del SHARBUTT. The show's theme music varied according to who its star performer was. Campbell's soups was the program's sponsor.

COAST TO COAST ON A BUS (AKA THE CHILDREN'S HOUR; AKA HORN AND HARDART'S CHILDREN'S HOUR)

1924–1927	WJZ (NY)	Sun.	9 AM
1927–1940	NBC Blue	Sun.	9 AM
1940–1946	NBC	Sun.	10 AM
			9 AM
1946–1948	NBC	Sun.	9:30 AM

Coast to Coast on a Bus presented songs, dramatic sketches, and instrumental selections performed by gifted children. It was originally produced by pioneer broadcaster Ethel Park RICHARDSON. Performers who got their show-business start on this program included Estelle Levy (aka Gwen DAVIES), who became a regular on the LET'S PRETEND show; Jackie KELK, who later played Homer on *The* ALDRICH FAMILY; and Larry Robinson, who played Sammy on "The Goldbergs" TV series; and James "Jimmy" McCallion, Edwin Bruce, Joy Terry, Bill LIPTON, Billy Redfield, Ronald LISS, Michael "Mickey" O'DAY, Billy and Bobby Mauch, Ann Blyth, and Joan Tetzel. Milton CROSS was the show's host (called "the Conductor"), and Madge Tucker and Audrey Egan were featured as the Lady Next Door and Mumsy Pig. Ed HERLIHY was the program's host when it was known as *The* CHILDREN'S HOUR; he also hosted the Sunday-morning feature on television in the 1950s. *Coast to Coast on a Bus* was produced and directed by Madge Tucker. Tom De-Huff and Ted MacMurray also directed the series, and Walter Fleisher was the show's music director. The program's theme song was "On the Sunny Side of the Street."

COLBERT, JEAN (1918–   )

After appearing onstage in regional theater productions in the 1930s, actress Jean Colbert became one of radio's most active performers. Born in New York City, Colbert had featured roles on such popular daytime drama series as STELLA DALLAS, LIFE CAN BE BEAUTIFUL, *The* LIFE OF MARY SOTHERN, YOUNG DR. MALONE, PORTIA FACES LIFE, REAL STORIES FROM REAL LIFE, and AUNT JENNY. The actress also appeared on prime-time programs: FIRST NIGHTER, *The* LUX RADIO THEATER, and HOLLYWOOD HOTEL. In the cast of the original MERCURY THEATER production of "The War of the Worlds," Colbert retired from network radio in 1947 to raise her children but eventually became a talk-show hostess and news commentator for stations in Philadelphia, Cleveland, and Hartford. Her daily interview show, *The Jean Colbert Show,* was heard on WTIC in Hartford, Connecticut, well into the 1980s.

COLE, ALONZO DEAN (1897–1971)

Born in St. Paul, Minnesota, Alonzo Dean Cole was considered by many to be one of radio's most talented, if somewhat eccentric, writer and director. He created odd atmospheres in the studios where his shows were being broadcast. For his WITCH'S TALE series, Cole had a single microphone suspended from the ceiling in the center of the studio and used very dim lighting to "create the proper atmosphere" for his actors to read his eerie tales. He would often write scripts for the actors moments before they aired to add to the dramatic tension of the show. In addition to *The Witch's Tale,* Cole also steered *The* SHADOW and CASEY, CRIME PHOTOGRAPHER as well as many other programs to success.

COLGATE SPORTS NEWSREEL, THE (AKA BILL STERN'S SPORT'S NEWSREEL; BILL STERN'S SPORTSREEL)

1937–1938	NBC Blue	Sun.	(*)
1938–1939	NBC Blue	Thurs.	(*)
1939–1941	NBC Blue	Sun.	9:45 PM
1941–1943	NBC	Sat.	10 PM
1943–1951	NBC	Fri.	10:30 PM
1951–1952	NBC	Fri.	6:15 PM
1953	NBC	Mon.–Fri.	6:15 PM
1953–1956	ABC	Mon.–Fri.	6:30 PM

Sportscaster Bill STERN had one of the most popular sports and celebrity-interview programs on radio. Stern's 15-minute and half-hour *Colgate Sports Newsreels* presented profiles of legendary sports figures and others who were in some way connected with sports. He always began each profile saying either "portrait of an athlete" or "portrait of a man (or woman)". Stern's famous closing line was "That's our 3-0 [thirty-minute] mark for tonight!" He later added

interviews with entertainers. *Bill Stern's Colgate Sports Newsreel* was directed by Chuck Kebbe, Maurice Robinson, and Joseph Mansfield. Arthur Gary was the program's announcer. Original music was supplied by Murray Ross. In addition to Colgate toothpaste, Stern's sponsors later included Budweiser beer and Allstate insurance.

COLLEGE QUIZ BOWL

1953–1954	NBC	Sat.	8 PM
1954–1955	NBC	Wed.	8:45 PM

On this show, four-member teams from two different colleges competed with each other and attempted to answer questions asked by host Allen LUDDEN. The college that "buzzed-in" with answers to more questions than its opponents and had reached the highest number of points at the end of the half hour was judged "winner" and went on to compete with another college team at a later broadcast. This radio program later became a hit TV series, "General Electric College Bowl," also starring Ludden. Roger Tuttler was the program's announcer.

COLLIER HOUR, THE

1927–1932	NBC Blue	Sun.	8 PM
1932–1933	CBS	Mon.	8:45 PM

One of radio's first major variety shows, *The Collier Hour,* featured editors Jack Arthur, Arthur Hughes, and Phil Barrison from *Collier's Magazine.* Also actors, they served as the show's hosts. The hour-long show's orchestra was led by Ernest LaPrade. The program featured vocal and orchestral musical selections, comedy skits, and dramatic sketches. Actors Bill ADAMS, Jack Arthur, James Kelly, Joseph "Joe" Latham, John B. Kennedy, and Joseph Bell were heard regularly in various dramatic sketches. One of the show's most successful presentations was a serialized version of the famous FU MANCHU stories. This serialization featured host-actor Arthur HUGHES as the mysterious Fu Manchu. The program was produced by Malcolm La Prade and directed by Colonel Davis and Joseph Bell, and was heard on NBC's Blue network. The sponsor was *Collier* magazine.

COLLINS, RAY (1890–1965)

Orson Welles dubbed versatile American character actor Ray Collins "the best actor on radio." Born in Sacramento, California, Collins was heard on hundreds of radio programs throughout the 1930s, 1940s, and 1950s, including *America's Hour,* BULLDOG DRUMMOND, *The* CAVALCADE OF AMERICA, HILLTOP HOUSE, SPY SECRETS, AUNT JENNY, KAY KYSER'S KOLLEGE OF MUSICAL KNOWLEDGE, FLASH GORDON, JUST PLAIN BILL,

LIFE BEGINS, *The* PHILIP MORRIS PLAYHOUSE, WILDERNESS ROAD, *The* COLUMBIA WORKSHOP and, of course, Welles's MERCURY THEATER OF THE AIR.

Collins was a prosperous-looking, gray-headed gentleman who usually had a "knowing" smile on his face that became familiar to filmgoers in his many motion-picture appearances over the years. He was seen in such films as *The Magnificent Ambersons* (1942), *The Bachelor and the Bobbysoxer* (1947), *The Witness* (1949), *The Desperate Hours* (1953), and *Never Say Goodbye* (1956). Collins also acted on TV as Police Lt. Tragg in the "Perry Mason" series beginning in 1957.

COLLYER, CLAYTON "BUD" (1908–1969)

Actor, host, and announcer Clayton "Bud" Collyer was born in New York City and studied law at Fordham University before deciding on a career in show business. He was a singer on Broadway before he made his radio debut in the 1930s and was the original Clark Kent/Superman on *The Adventures of* SUPERMAN. Additional work gave him running roles or announcing positions on CAVALCADE OF AMERICA, ABIE'S IRISH ROSE (on which he played Abie), JUST PLAIN BILL, KITTY FOYLE, LIFE CAN BE BEAUTIFUL, PRETTY KITTY KELLY, *The* MAN I MARRIED, JOYCE JORDAN, GIRL INTERN, BELIEVE IT OR NOT, LIFE BEGINS, TERRY AND THE PIRATES (as heroic Pat Ryan), *The* GUIDING LIGHT, YOUNG WIDDER BROWN, and *The* ROAD OF LIFE. He also hosted the radio versions of the BREAK THE BANK and WINNER TAKE ALL quiz programs. Collyer was the voice of Superman in the *Superman* film cartoon series for many years. He also became familiar to TV viewers in the 1950s as host of quiz and panel shows "To Tell the Truth," "Beat the Clock," and "Feather Your Nest."

COLMAN, RONALD (1891–1958)

Academy Award–winning actor Ronald Colman was born in Richmond, Surrey, England. The very successful film actor starred in such classic silent and sound motion pictures as *Beau Geste* (1926), *A Tale of Two Cities* (1935), *Lost Horizon* (1937), *The Prisoner of Zenda* (1937), *Random Harvest* (1942), and *Champagne for Caesar* (1950). He won an Oscar as Best Actor for his performance in *A Double Life* (1947). On radio, Colman was a frequent guest star on *The* JACK BENNY SHOW and starred on *The* HALLS OF IVY with his wife, Benita Hume.

COLONNA, JERRY (1905–1987)

Walrus mustachioed, bug-eyed, loud-mouthed comedian Jerry Colonna was one of the major attractions on the BOB HOPE SHOW. Colonna, who was born in Boston, Massachusetts, of Italian-American parents, began his career on radio as a performer on *The* FRED ALLEN SHOW and also worked on the BING CROSBY SHOW before beginning his long association with Hope. In addition to working with Hope on radio, Colonna did 500 shows with Hope at various overseas military installations. Colonna also appeared on Hope's television program and was seen in the films *College Swing* and *Little Miss Broadway* (1938); *The Road to Singapore* (1940); *Sis Hopkins* (1941); *True to the Army, Star-Spangled Rhythms,* and *Ice Capades* (1942); *It's in the Bag* (1945); *The Road to Rio* (1947); *Meet Me in Las Vegas* (1956); and *Andy Hardy Comes Home* (1958).

COLUMBIA BROADCASTING SYSTEM (CBS)

In 1927, a young businessman named William S. PALEY bought several local, independent radio stations that he called the United Independent Broadcasters. One year later, the company's official name became the Columbia Broadcasting System. Almost immediately, CBS began to make broadcasting history. Paley believed that he could compete with the giant of the broadcasting industry, The Radio Corporation of America (which became the NATIONAL BROADCASTING COMPANY, NBC): he offered advertisers a wider audience for their products by advertising commercial messages over several stations rather than merely advertising local products on local outlets as his competitor, RCA, was doing. Paley's plan worked, and before long CBS became NBC's major competitor. Paley realized that the key to radio's future commercial success was to expand by offering programming free to affiliate stations in return for having a certain part of their schedule devoted to sponsoring network-produced shows. This opened the door for national, brand-name-product advertising. When CBS began, it had a mere 22 stations around the country, but that number of affiliates grew to 114 in a single decade because of Paley's attractive advertising policies. Ratings grew as well throughout the 1930s and 1940s as Paley secured the services of big-name radio stars from NBC, such as Kate SMITH, Bing CROSBY, and Jack BENNY, by offering them more lucrative financial compensation than NBC. Since the 1970s, CBS radio mainly produces syndicated programs, mainly news, for distribution to various independent stations around the country.

COLUMBIA WORKSHOP, THE (AKA CBS RADIO WORKSHOP)

1936–1937	CBS	Sat.	8 PM
1937–1938	CBS	Thurs.	10:30 PM
1938–1939	CBS	Sat.	8 PM
1939–1940	CBS	Thurs.	10 PM
1940	CBS	Sun.	8 PM
1940–1941	CBS	Sun.	10:30 PM
1941–1942	CBS	Mon.	10:30 PM

1942–1946	(Off the air)		
1946–1947	CBS	Sat.	2:30 PM
1947–1956	(Off the air)		
1956–1957	CBS	Fri.	8:30 PM
		Sun.	4:05 PM

To develop new writing talent for radio and to experiment with innovative techniques for presenting drama on the medium, CBS launched its half-hour, once-a-week *Columbia Workshop* series in 1936. The series presented works by such established literary figures as William Soroyan, Lord Dunsany, Irving Reis, Dorothy Parker, and Norman CORWIN, as well as works by untested, new writing talent.

Heard regularly on this sustained series were Orson WELLES, William CONRAD, Elspeth ERIC, Karl SWENSON, Mary Jane CROFT, Parley BAER, Stan FREBERG, Eric SEVAREID, Brooke Byron, Robert McQueeney, Jay Novello, John Sylvester, Ben WRIGHT, Richard Beals, Hans CONRIED, Lurene TUTTLE, Larry Haines, and Ken Lynch.

The program's announcers included Bob Pfeiffert, Hugh Downs, and Stu Metz. The production staff for *The Columbia Workshop* included such established radio personalities as Orson WELLES, William N. RONSON, Max Wylie, Douglas Coultier, and Davidson Taylor.

COLUMBO, RUGGERIO DE RUDOLPHO "RUSS" (1908–1934)

When he died at the age of twenty six—supposedly while cleaning a gun in his home—American-born Russ Columbo was one of the most famous singers in the United States, rivaling such crooners as Bing CROSBY and Rudy VALLEE in popularity. Called "the Radio Romeo," Columbo introduced such popular songs as "Prisoner of Love," "Stardust," and "More Than You Know" to the listening public. Also a violinist, a songwriter, and a bandleader, he first came to public attention as vocalist with Gus Arnheim's band, performing at the Coconut Grove in Los Angeles for many years. His handsome appearance eventually landed him a motion-picture contract and such films as *Wolf Song* (1929), *Hellbound* (1931), *Broadway Through a Keyhole* (1933) and *Wake Up and Dream* (1934). He was well on his way to movie stardom at the time of his death.

The circumstances surrounding Columbo's death were considered to be somewhat suspicious. The general public's grief at his death was as great as for silent-film star Rudolph Valentino, who had died several years earlier.

In addition to his very successful radio program, *The Russ Columbo Show,* Russ guest-starred on many popular radio music and variety shows in the early 1930s.

COMMAND PERFORMANCE

1942–1949	(Recorded and played overseas at various times)

Produced for the men and women in the military during World War II, this half-hour comedy-variety show featured major stars of Hollywood and Broadway as guest hosts and performers. Bob HOPE, Bing CROSBY, Don WILSON, and Harry VON ZELL were hosts.

The ANDREWS SISTERS, Dinah SHORE, Ethel MERMAN, Betty Grable, Dorothy LAMOUR, Ginny SIMMS, William BENDIX, Walter Pidgeon, Helen Forrest, Ella Mae Morse, Charles Boyer, the King Sisters, Judy GARLAND, Jimmy DURANTE, Marlene Dietrich, Rita Hayworth, Bette Davis, Carmen Miranda, Orson WELLES, Claudette Colbert, Peggy Lee, Linda Darnell, Martha Tilton, Woody Herman and his orchestra, Joan Leslie, Paulette Goddard, Louis Armstrong, Johnny Mercer, Ida Lupino, Cary Grant, Lionel BARRYMORE, John Charles Thomas, Fanny BRICE, Jack BENNY, Red SKELTON, Connee Boswell, Joe E. Lewis, Roy ROGERS, Carole Landis, Marilyn Maxwell, Tallulah BANKHEAD, and pianist Jose Iturbi made frequent appearances on the program to boost the troops' morale.

One hour-long *Command Performance* special—an original musical spoof of the DICK TRACY comic strip called "Dick Tracy in B Flat"—is notable for the range of important stars heard on it. Crosby played Tracy, Hope played the villain Flattop, and Dinah Shore played Tess Trueheart.

Also performing major roles on the show were Judy Garland as Snowflake, the Andrews Sisters as the Summers Sisters; and Frank Sinatra, Jerry COLONNA, Jimmy Durante, Frank Morgan, Cass DALEY, and Harry Von Zell. The show was produced by the U.S. War Department in cooperation with ARMED FORCES RADIO SERVICE. Producers, directors, and writers of this series varied from week to week and volunteered their services to the program.

COMO, PERRY (1912–　　)

Perry Como was born in Canonsberg, Pennsylvania, and was a barber before he became a singer. His smooth, easygoing, relaxed singing style made him one of America's most popular singers for more than forty years. Before his phenomenal television success in the 1950s, Como was a band singer with the Freddie Carlone orchestra, was heard on the FIBBER MCGEE AND MOLLY radio show as its weekly vocalist, and was one of the stars of *The CHESTERFIELD SUPPER CLUB* in the 1940s. The singer's own weekly radio program, *The Perry Como Show,* aired from 1953 through 1955 and later became a TV show. Como continues to make occasional public appearances.

CONRAD, WILLIAM (1920–1994)

Before his successes on TV as the star of the "Cannon," "Nero Wolfe," and "Jake and the Fat Man" programs in the 1970s and 1980s, actor William Conrad was the original Marshall Matt Dillon of GUNSMOKE on the radio. Born in Louisville, Kentucky, where he worked as a newspaper reporter, his family moved to Los Angeles, and at seventeen the ambitious young man asked for and received a job audition at radio station KMPC in Beverly Hills. Because of his adult-sounding, resonant, deep voice, Conrad was hired and soon moved on to network radio to become an active performer. Conrad was regularly heard on such celebrated radio series as ESCAPE, SUSPENSE, *The* SCREEN GUILD PLAYERS, *The* PHILIP MORRIS PLAYHOUSE, and *The* WHISTLER.

In addition to his work on radio and television, he became a character actor in Hollywood, usually playing the villain in such films as *The Killers* (1946), *Sorry, Wrong Number* (1948), and *Johnny Concho* (1956). Conrad produced and directed several films, including *My Blood Runs Cold* (1965) and *An American Dream* (1966) and has been heard as the speaking voice of several cartoon characters, most notably on "The Bullwinkle Show."

CONRIED, HANS (1917–1982)

Equally adept at playing comedy or serious dramatic roles, actor Hans Conried's voice was well known to radio listeners as the eccentric and very funny Professor Kropotkin on the MY FRIEND IRMA series, Oliver Honeywell on *The* GREAT GILDERSLEEVE, Mr. Hemingway on *The* JUDY CANOVA SHOW, and Uncle Baxter on *The* LIFE OF RILEY. Conried was born in Baltimore, Maryland, and attended Columbia University, where he decided to become an actor. His careful diction, ability to perform in various dialects, and acting versatility eventually led to his being heard on a wide variety of shows, including SUSPENSE, *The* ADVENTURES OF SAM SPADE, DETECTIVE, BURNS AND ALLEN, *The* MEL BLANC SHOW, ESCAPE, ONE MAN'S FAMILY, LIGHTS OUT, *The* FIRST NIGHTER, HOLLYWOOD HOTEL, *Signal Carnival, The Woodbury Playhouse, Saturday Night Party, The* LUX RADIO THEATER, and *The* SCREEN GUILD PLAYERS.

Tall and weedy in appearance, Conried also performed in such motion pictures as *Mrs. Parkington* 1944), *My Friend Irma* (1949), and *The Five Thousand Fingers of Dr. T* (1953). Perhaps best known to television audiences as Uncle Tanoose on "The Danny Thomas Show," he was also seen regularly on the "I Love Lucy" and "Lucy" programs and was the voice of many TV and film cartoon characters, including Mr. Darling in *Peter Pan*, "Faeries," "The Incredible Book Escape," "The Trolls and the Christmas Ex-

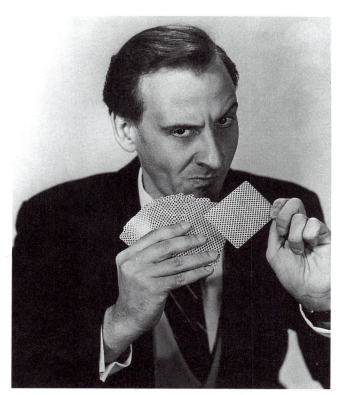

Hans Conried (CBS-TV)

press," "The Dudley-Do-Right Show," "The Adventures of Hoppity Hooper," "Christmas Is," "The Magic Pony," and several Dr. Seuss cartoons. Conried was featured in the Broadway musical comedy *Can Can* (1953) and toured the country in various stage productions.

CORRELL, CHARLES (1890–1972), AND GOSDEN, FREEMAN (1899–1982)

Charles Correll and Freeman Gosden were the original blackface AMOS AND ANDY characters in vaudeville and on radio.

A direct descendant of Confederacy President Jefferson Davis, Correll became almost as famous as his ancestor, playing Andy Brown and George "Kingfish" Stevens on the enormously popular *Amos and Andy* radio program. Born in Peoria, Illinois, where his Southern family had moved when the Civil War ended, Correll was hired as a part-time piano player at a silent-movie theater; he worked there evenings while working in construction during the day. When the Joe Bren theatrical touring company performed at the movie theater–vaudeville house and needed someone to fill in for an absent actor, Correll jumped at the chance, fell in love with performing, and joined the group.

Freeman Gosden, a native of Richmond, Virginia, was the son of a Confederate Army soldier. After a year in military school, Gosden decided to end his formal education to become a tobacco salesman. When World War I erupted, Gosden enlisted and served as a naval radio operator and electrician. At the war's end, he joined the Joe Bren Company, where he befriended Charles Correll during the Bren production *The Jollies of 1919.* Bren added circus and carnival performances in 1924, and Gosden and Correll worked together regularly as a clown-comedy team.

In 1925, the team performed on WQGA radio and found radio a perfect outlet for their particular brand of verbal humor. While performing they impressed a station official at WGN in Chicago so much that he offered them full-time positions. The pair developed a comedy series for WGN, *Sam and Henry,* in which they played two black men. Because both actors were from the South, they felt particularly comfortable imitating familiar African-American mannerisms and speech patterns. Although *Sam and Henry* was not an immediate success, the program gradually became a popular local attraction in the Chicago area. When their contract with WGN expired, Gosden and Correll, who felt they were underpaid, decided not to renew. WGN, however, owned the rights to *Sam and Henry,* so the team had to find new names.

WMAQ hired and paid them higher salaries. The pair still needed new names for their characters. One day on a WMAQ elevator, they overheard two passengers greeting another with, "Well, well, famous Amos," and "Well, well, handy Andy." Gosden and Correll knew they had found their characters' new names. In 1927, NBC signed Gosden and Correll to a long-term contract. With NBC's large promotional department's help, *Amos and Andy* became one of the most successful programs in radio history. Except for rare appearances on such programs as NBC's *Monitor* series, Gosden and Correll virtually retired from show business when *Amos and Andy* departed the airwaves in 1960, after thirty-four years on network radio.

CORWIN, NORMAN (1910–   )

One of radio's genuine, acknowledged creative geniuses, writer-producer-director Norman Corwin was born in Boston, Massachusetts, and educated at public schools. A newspaper reporter and editor before he was "discovered" by CBS Vice-President William B. Lewis, Corwin joined the CBS staff of program directors in 1938. After his apprenticeship, he was given a network program of his own, *Words Without Music,* which he wrote, produced, and directed. The show broke new ground in radio drama: its scripts relied heavily on sound and poetic materials.

As a result of the program's critical success, Corwin produced a big-budget variety-drama series, *Pursuit of Happiness,* which dealt mainly with "Americana" themes. It was followed by *Twenty-six by Corwin,* a

Norman Corwin (CBS)

program of original dramas, comedies, fantasies, and musical productions that gave the listening public everything from operas to documentaries, all written expressly for radio. Corwin's work was also presented on CBS's COLUMBIA PRESENTS CORWIN, PASSPORT FOR ADAMS, and the COLUMBIA WORKSHOP programs.

One of his most memorable radio scripts was "The Plot to Overthrow Christmas," which speculated on what might have happened if the world's most notorious villains—Nero, Lucretia Borgia, and even Lucifer himself—had plotted to eliminate Christmas. This play, like another Corwin comedy, "The Undecided Molecule," was written entirely in verse.

Because of his eloquent, poetic style, CBS commissioned Corwin to write a commemoration of the 150th anniversary of the Bill of Rights. World War II broke out shortly after, and the program became what radio historian Erik Barnouw called an unofficial "national manifesto of [the country's] war aims" and was rebroadcast several times. Subsequently, in 1945, Corwin wrote special programs about the end of the war; when Germany surrendered, he wrote "On a Note of Triumph"; when the war with Japan came to an end, his "14th August" was aired.

Corwin continues to be active as a writer and lecturer. His post-radio writing accomplishments include the screenplay for *Lust for Life,* which won him an

Academy Award nomination, and the Bill of Rights' 200th-anniversary broadcast, which won him an international gold medal.

COSTELLO, LOU

See ABBOTT AND COSTELLO.

COTSWORTH, STAATS (1908–1979)

Born in Oak Park, Illinois, actor Staats Cotsworth's best-remembered radio turn is the title role of CASEY, CRIME PHOTOGRAPHER. He was also heard regularly throughout the 1930s, 1940s, and 1950s on AMANDA OF HONEYMOON HILL (as the hero, Edward Leighton), BIG SISTER, The CAVALCADE OF AMERICA, FRONT PAGE FARRELL (playing Farrell), MARK TRAIL, MR. AND MRS. NORTH (playing police detective Bill Weigand), The RIGHT TO HAPPINESS, The SECOND MRS. BURTON, and WHEN A GIRL MARRIES. Shortly before his death, Cotsworth was featured on Himan Brown's CBS MYSTERY THEATER series. The actor was also active on the stage.

COUGHLIN, FATHER CHARLES EDWARD (1891–1974)

One of the most controversial personalities on radio in the 1930s was a Roman Catholic priest-turned-radio orator, Father Charles Edward Coughlin, "the fighting priest." Born in Detroit, Michigan, Coughlin's weekly program of inspirational and personal on-the-air comments on current world events was broadcast on WJR, Detroit, and then on the CBS network. His shows gained ever-wider listening audiences as his broadcasts became increasingly more political. Usually heard at 4 PM on Sunday, the program was dropped by CBS when Coughlin's pro-German, pro-Hitler comments became too sensitive for the network to keep him on the air. Originally a strong supporter of President Franklin D. Roosevelt, Coughlin turned on him and called him "a great liar and betrayer" when Roosevelt called for the nation's isolationist policies to end and encouraged the country's support of England in its war against Germany. Coughlin, whose listening audience had totaled millions, lost his popularity in the face of German aggression in Europe: attempts were even made on his life. When the United States finally declared war against Germany in 1941, the Roman Catholic Church set up a board to review Coughlin's radio scripts before each broadcast. Coughlin's popularity and influence were finally completely stifled, and he rapidly faded into obscurity. He later said, "I regret that I ever became involved in politics."

COULOURIS, GEORGE (1903–1989)

Born in Manchester, England, actor George Coulouris spent most of his career working in the United States. He appeared in several plays with Orson Welles's

Father Coughlin (CBS)

Mercury Theater in New York and then began to work on radio. In the late 1930s and 1940s, Coulouris was regularly heard on WELLES'S MERCURY THEATER ON THE AIR radio program. He was also featured on WE LOVE AND LEARN, YOUR FAMILY AND MINE, and in the title role on the BULLDOG DRUMMOND detective series for several seasons.

The versatile actor appeared in numerous films such as *Citizen Kane* (1941), *Watch on the Rhine* and *For Whom the Bell Tolls* (1943), *Between Two Worlds* and *None But the Lonely Heart* (1945), and *Murder on the Orient Express* (1974), playing a wide variety of characters' parts.

COUNT OF MONTE CRISTO, THE

1946–1947	Mutual		(Syndicated series. Various times and stations)
1947–1949	(Off the air)		
1949–1952	Mutual	Sun., Tues.	(Syndicated series. Various times and stations)

The Mutual network produced this syndicated, weekly, half-hour adventure serial based *The Count of Monte Cristo,* by Alexander Dumas. Actor Carlton YOUNG starred as Edmond Dantes, the Count of Monte Cristo, an aristocrat who fought for justice for others; and Parley BAER played his sidekick, Rene. Directed by Jaime DEL VALLE, the program's theme song was "The Sylvia Ballet."

COUNTERSPY (AKA DAVID HARDING, COUNTERSPY)

1942–1944	NBC Blue	Mon.	9 PM
1944–1945	NBC Blue	Wed.	8:30 PM
1945–1946	NBC Blue	Sun.	5:30 PM
1946–1948	ABC	Sun.	5:30 PM
1948–1950	ABC	Tues., Thurs.	7:30 PM

1950–1951	NBC	Sun.	5 PM
1951–1952	NBC	Thurs.	9:30 PM
1952–1953	NBC	Sun.	5:30 PM
1953–1954	Mutual	Sun.	4 PM
1954–1956	Mutual	Sun.	8 PM
1956–1957	Nutual	Fri.	8 PM

This long-running adventure series dealt with various wartime themes. When World War II ended, it concentrated mainly on the Cold War conflict between East and West. Don MACLAUGHLIN and House JAMESON starred as counterspy David Harding, and Mandel KRAMER played his assistant, Peters. The program's announcers included Bob Shepherd and Roger Krupp. Bill Sweets, Robert Steen, Victor Seydel, Marx Loeb, and Leonard Bass directed the series at different times. The producer of *Counterspy* was Phillips H. LORD, and many episodes of the show were written by Milton J. Kramer. Sponsors included Mail Pouch pipe tobacco, Shutter candy, Bromo quinine water, Pepsi Cola soft drink, Camel cigarettes, Eye-Gene eye cleaner, Doan's pain pills, and Gulf oil.

COUPLE NEXT DOOR, THE

1937–1938	Mutual	Mon.–Fri.	10:45 AM
1938–1958	(Off the air)		
1958–1959	CBS	Mon.–Fri.	2:30 PM
1959–1960	CBS	Mon.–Fri.	12:45 PM

The first 15-minute, Monday-through-Friday program to be called *The Couple Next Door* was a Chicago-based Mutual network series that featured Olan SOULE, Elinor Harriot, and Jack Brinkley. When the network moved operations to New York, Harold Vermilyea and Lillian Gish became the program's leads. The story concerned a typical small-town American couple and their family.

The most memorable program with this title, however, surfaced in 1958 on CBS and was written by and starred the talented Peg LYNCH: she had been responsible for the success of the popular ETHEL AND ALBERT series. Television had already begun to claim the home-entertainment audience, so Miss Lynch's *The Couple Next Door*, which costarred her *Ethel and Albert* partner, Alan BUNCE, played for only two seasons. Lynch and Bunce played the Pipers, and Francie Myers played their daughter Betsy. Jack Brinkley and James "Jimmy" Wallington announced the earlier version, and Stu Metz the later one. Kirby Hawkes was the earlier show's director. Oxydol detergent was the first version's sponsor; CBS sustained the second.

COURT OF MISSING HEIRS, THE

1937–1938	CBS	Sun.	10:30 PM
1938–1939	(Off the air)		
1939–1942	CBS	Tues.	8:30 PM
1942–1946	(Off the air)		
1946–1947	ABC	Wed.	8:30 PM

Actual unclaimed fortunes, both large and small, were the major attraction of this weekly series. Information about these legacies was given to listeners, who were then encouraged to claim them if they thought they might be the rightful inheritors. Jim Waters was this half-hour CBS series' host, and Everett SLOANE, Carl FRANK, Ed JEROME, Jeanette NOLAN, and Kenny DEL MAR were often heard in the casts of the dramatizations. Rosa Rio supplied appropriate organ music for the show. Tom Shirley announced the program, and John Loveton directed it. Sterling products (ironized yeast) and Skelly oil sponsored the series.

CRENNA, RICHARD (1927–   )

Actor Richard Crenna was born in Los Angeles, California. In the late 1940s and throughout the 1950s, he played numerous adolescent roles on several radio shows, but his voice became most well known to listeners as Walter Denton, Connie Brooks's favorite student on OUR MISS BROOKS. Crenna also played Oogie Pringle, Judy Foster's teenage boyfriend on A DATE WITH JUDY. He had running roles on BURNS AND ALLEN, *The* GREAT GILDERSLEEVE, *The* HARDY FAMILY ONE MAN'S FAMILY, *A* DAY IN THE LIFE OF DENNIS DAY and *The* ALDRICH FAMILY. His films include *Red Skies of Montana* (1952), *The Sand Pebbles* (1967), *Wait Until Dark* (1968), *Star* (1969), and *Body Heat* (1981). On television, Crenna appeared on "Our Miss Brooks," (1952) and "The Real McCoys" (1957), as well as in many made-for-TV movies.

CRESTA BLANCA CARNIVAL, THE

See JACK PEARL SHOW, *The.*

CRIME CLUES

See ENO CRIME CLUB.

CRIME DOCTOR

1940–1947	CBS	Sun.	8:30 PM

Ray COLLINS, House JAMESON, Everett SLOANE, and then John MCINTIRE starred as Dr. Benjamin Ordway the celebrated "crime doctor." Ordway was a former criminal who developed amnesia after a blow to the head and became a noted psychiatrist and a member of a parole board when he started his "new life." Edgar Stehli played District Attorney Miller on the half-hour series, Walter Vaughn was Harold Sayers and Walter GREAZA and Edith ARNOLD frequently played supporting roles on the show. Ken ROBERTS announced, and Paul Monroe directed the program which was written by Max Narcin. The program's sponsors included Philip Morris cigarettes and Revelation beauty products.

CRIME DOES NOT PAY

| 1949–1951 | Mutual | Mon.–Fri. | 8:30 PM |
| 1952 | Mutual | Mon. | 8:30 PM |

This well-received crime-adventure series featured several major Hollywood stars in leading roles: Cameron Mitchell, who was heard in a radio play called "A Piece of Rope"; Bela Lagosi in "Gasoline Cocktail"; and Alan Baxter in "Law of the Jungle." Actors well known for their work on radio, such as Myron MCCORMICK, Jean Muir, and Martin GABLE, were also regularly featured. Because it was syndicated to various local Mutual network stations, the program's director and writers went uncredited and sponsors varied according to where it was being heard.

CROFT, MARY JANE (c. 1920–   )

The talented actress Mary Jane Croft, heard on hundreds of radio programs throughout the 1940s and 1950s, was born in Muncie, Indiana. Her sensual and totally feminine voice made her popular as the leading lady as well as the "other woman" on various shows originating from the West Coast. She was Harriet on the BLONDIE series, Christine Abbott on ONE MAN'S FAMILY, and Mel's love interest Betty Colby on *The MEL BLANC SHOW*; she was also regularly featured on SAM SPADE, DETECTIVE, SUSPENSE, BEULAH, SHERLOCK HOLMES, ON STAGE, *Twelve Players*, MA PERKINS, FAMOUS JURY TRIALS, and MY TRUE STORY. Croft is perhaps best remembered, however, for supplying the sexy voice of the dog Cleo on the popular "Peoples Choice" (1951–1955) TV series.

CRONKITE, WALTER (1916–   )

Walter Cronkite, CBS's well-loved TV "Dean of Broadcasters," was for many years television's most familiar and popular news anchorman. Born in St. Joseph, Missouri, he attended the University of Texas before beginning his radio broadcasting career as a war correspondent with United Press International's news service. He joined the CBS radio news staff in 1950 and soon became that network's senior TV evening news anchorman. In addition to his news reporting on CBS radio in the 1940s and 1950s, Cronkite was also heard on the successful YOU ARE THERE (aka *CBS Is There*) series. He remained with CBS until he retired in the early 1980s.

CROSBY, BING (HARRY LILLIS CROSBY: 1901–1977)

Born in Tacoma, Washington, Crooner Bing Crosby got his nickname because as a child he always shouted "bing . . . bing" when he fired his toy guns while playing. After leaving college, he became a drummer in a small band and subsequently formed a vocal trio

Bing Crosby (CBS)

called the Rhythm Boys, with himself as lead singer. The trio attracted the attention of bandleader Paul Whiteman and eventually joined the Whiteman band as regulars. Before long, Crosby's easygoing singing style and All-American looks caught the attention of motion-picture scouts. He was screen-tested and signed for a series of short subjects, at the same time becoming a frequent guest performer on several radio shows. By 1934 he was starring on *The KRAFT MUSIC HALL*, a weekly musical variety program, and from 1946 until 1956 on his own BING CROSBY SHOW. Crosby's radio career lasted more than thirty years, his being one of the last major network shows. In addition to comedy-variety programs, he starred on the LUX RADIO THEATER, SCREEN GUILD PLAYERS, and other dramatic anthology shows. In the 1950s, Crosby reluctantly began to accept television dates, such as his occasional Christmas specials.

Among Crosby's song hits are "White Christmas," "When the Blue of the Night Meets the Gold of the Day," "High Hopes," and "Swingin' on a Star." As a major motion-picture star, he won an Academy Award for the film *Going My Way*. Among his other diverse films are the popular *Road* pictures (starring Bob HOPE and Dorothy LAMOUR), *Anything Goes* (1936), *Pennies from Heaven* (1938), *Holiday Inn* (1942), *The Bells of St. Mary's* (1945), *The Country Girl* (1955), and *High Society* (1956).

CROSBY, BOB (GEORGE R. CROSBY: 1913–1993)

Bing Crosby's younger brother Bob was born in Spokane, Washington, and was a major radio star in his own right from the 1930s to the 1950s. A bandleader and singer, he starred on his own BOB CROSBY SHOW featuring his Bobcats singing group, CLUB FIFTEEN, costarring the Andrews Sisters, and, for one summer season, on *The* KRAFT MUSIC HALL. In addition, he was a regular performer on *The* JACK BENNY radio and television shows for several seasons, replacing orchestra leader Phil HARRIS when he left the show to concentrate on his own series. Although his film career hardly rivaled Bing's, Bob did appear in several rather forgettable motion pictures in the 1930s and 1940s mainly as a "guest star" in such films as *The Big Broadcast of 1937.*

CROSS COUNTRY CHECKUP

1975–present	CBC	Mon.–Fri.	5:13 PM

This CANADIAN BROADCASTING CORPORATION program is Canada's only open-line, live, current-affairs radio series. The one-hour show is currently hosted by Dave Goldhawk, who engages Canadians around the country in telephone dialogues about a wide variety of contemporary concerns. Special guests have included cabinet ministers, foreign diplomats, social activists, politicians, dissidents, economists, and members of the Canadian public.

CROSS, MILTON (1897–1975)

Often called "the Dean of American Classical Music," New York–born music commentator and program host Milton Cross's soothingly familiar voice was heard on such popular radio shows as the AS & P GYPSIES SHOW, CHAMBER MUSIC SOCIETY OF LOWER BASIN STREET, INFORMATION PLEASE, *The* MAGIC KEY OF RCA and, most notably, *The* METROPOLITAN OPERA BROADCASTS, presented live from the New York opera house on Saturday afternoons during its season. Cross was also a general staff announcer at NBC for many years.

CROWLEY, MATT (1905–n.d.)

Born in New Haven, Connecticut, and a graduate of the Yale School of Drama, Matt Crowley was often featured as leading man on such daytime children's adventure serials as BUCK ROGERS IN THE 25TH CENTURY (as Buck), DICK TRACY (as Tracy), JUNGLE JIM (as Jim), MARK TRAIL (as Trail), and SUPERMAN (playing the role of Batman, a running character on the show).

His voice also made him a perfect romantic lead on daytime serial dramas: JOHN'S OTHER WIFE, MYRT AND MARGE, BRENDA CURTIS, AMANDA OF HONEYMOON HILL, PERRY MASON (as Perry's assistant, Paul Drake), *Pretty Kitty Kelly,* and *The Road of Life.* Crowley was also active as a stage, film (*Somebody Up There Likes Me* [1956]), and television actor.

CRUMIT, FRANK (1889–1943)

With his wife, Julia Sanderson, singer-host Frank Crumit was one of radio's most sought-after singing stars as well as a variety and quiz-show host. Crumit was born in Jackson, Ohio, and attended Culver Military Academy and then the University of Ohio, where he majored in engineering. Deciding to be a singer and entertainer, Crumit left Ohio in 1918 and went to New York, where he appeared on Broadway in the musical comedy *Betty Be Good* (1919). Crumit subsequently starred in such shows as *Tangerine* (1922) and *The Greenwich Village Follies* (1924). He met and married actress Julia Sanderson while they were both appearing in *Tangerine.* Together, the couple starred in several classic musical comedies, including the original Broadway productions of *No, No Nanette* (1925) and *Oh Kay* (1926).

When their Broadway careers began to wane, Sanderson and Crumit became radio performers in 1938, starring on *The Frank Crumit–Julia Sanderson Variety Show, The* BATTLE OF THE SEXES quiz program, and as guests on various music-variety programs throughout the 1940s.

CULLEN, BILL (1920–1990)

One of radio's busiest announcers and quiz- and panel-show moderators, Bill Cullen was born in Pittsburgh, Pennsylvania, and first worked in radio in that city in the mid-1930s. He hosted such radio game shows as FUN FOR ALL, HIT THE JACKPOT, WINNER TAKE ALL, and QUICK AS A FLASH, as well as announcing daytime serials such as THIS IS NORA DRAKE. In the 1950s, Cullen became one of television's earliest stars and was a panelist and host on such game shows as "I've Got a Secret," "Name That Tune," "The Price Is Right," "Where Was I?" and "Place the Face."

CURTAIN TIME

1938–1939	Mutual	Fri.	10:30 PM
1939–1945	(Off the air)		
1945–1946	NBC Blue	Thurs.	10 PM
1946–1947	ABC	Thurs.	10 PM
1947–1948	NBC	Sat.	7:30 PM
1948–1949	NBC	Wed.	10:30 PM

This weekly half-hour series of original radio plays was directed by Norman Felton and Blair Wallise

Joseph Curtin and Alice Frost in *Mr. and Mrs. North* (NBC)

and featured radio regulars such as Raymond Edward JOHNSON, Janet Logan, Spencer Bentley, Vivian Fridell, Olan SOULE, Beverly Younger, Art VAN HARVEY, Louise Fitch, Betty WINKLER, Harry Elders, and Beryl Vaughn. The show's music director was Joseph Gallichio, who wrote its original theme and any incidental music. Kix cereal and Mars candy bars sponsored the series.

CURTIN, JOSEPH (1910–1979)

Leading man Joseph Curtin was born in Cambridge, Massachusetts, and attended the Yale School of Drama. He is best remembered for playing Jerry North on the MR. AND MRS. NORTH mystery series. Curtin's costar on this series was actress Alice FROST. The actor's deep, romantic-sounding voice was also used to advantage on programs such as DAVID HARUM, ROSES AND DRUMS, SECOND HUSBAND, HILLTOP HOUSE, HER HONOR, NANCY JAMES, JOHN'S OTHER WIFE, MYRT AND MARGE, OUR GAL SUNDAY, and *The* THIN MAN (on which he played Nick Charles). Curtin also appeared in numerous Broadway and regional-theater productions including, in the 1930s, *The Merchant of Venice* and *Searching for the Sun*.

DAILY DILEMMA

| 1946–1948 | Mutual | Mon.–Fri. | (*) |

Cecil Roy wrote radio dramatizations for this half-hour quiz program, which always ended with a dilemma of one kind or another. Contestants selected from the studio audience had to try to say how they thought a particular problem being presented could be solved, such as whether a girl should go to a dance with a shy guy or with a more-popular fellow. A panel of judges, also selected from the studio audience, decided which of the diemmas would win the $50 cash prize as best dilemma of the day. Jack Barry was the show's host. Sponsors included Cuticura nail softener, Super Suds detergent, and Ex-Lax laxative.

DALEY, CASS (CATHERINE DAILEY: 1915–1975)

Buck-toothed, limber-limbed singing comedienne Cass Daley was born in Philadelphia, Pennsylvania. Considered one of the funniest women in America in the 1940s, she was known for half-shouting songs as she performed amusing bodily contortions. The comedienne was featured on MAXWELL HOUSE COFFEE TIME and The FITCH BANDWAGON, was a regular on the The Frank Morgan Show, and made frequent guest appearances on COMMAND PERFORMANCE and MAIL CALL. In the mid-1940s, The Cass Daley Show was a summer replacement. At the height of her popularity, Daley appeared in several motion pictures, including The Fleet's In (1941), Crazy House (1943), and Red Garters (1954) before falling into relative obscurity in the late 1950s due to alcoholism. She made a comeback

in the 1960s and had featured roles in the films The Spirit Is Willing (1967) and Norwood (1970) before an accident in her home ended her life.

DALY, JOHN (1914–1991)

Born in Johannesburg, South Africa, John Daly emigrated to the United States with his parents when he was ten years old. Daly was President Franklin D. Roosevelt's official radio announcer in 1940 and then became a CBS network newsman. He was frequently heard on CBS's radio drama YOU ARE THERE from 1947 through 1950 and on the same program on television in the early 1950s. In 1953, Daly host-moderated the TV panel show "What's My Line," remaining with the show for thirty years before retiring from show business.

DAMON, LESTER "LES" (1908–1962)

A leading man on many radio shows, Les Damon was born in Providence, Rhode Island, and was educated at Brown University and the Rhode School of Design before he decided to become an actor. Damon played Nick Charles on The THIN MAN and Mike Waring, the Falcon, on The FALCON radio detective series, in addition to being heard as the husband or boyfriend of various heroines on such daytime dramas as GIRL ALONE, HOUSEBOAT HANNAH, The ROAD OF LIFE, Manhattan Mother, MA PERKINS, The ROMANCE OF HELEN TRENT, LONE JOURNEY, PORTIA FACES LIFE, The RIGHT TO HAPPINESS, THIS IS NORA DRAKE, The WOMAN IN WHITE, and YOUNG DR. MALONE. On television, Damon was featured in the daytime serial dramas "As the World Turns" (1956–1957) "The

Guiding Light" (1956–1980), and "Kitty Foyle" (1958).

DAMROSCH, DR. WALTER (1862–1950)

Music authority Walter Damrosch was educated in various private schools, including the Conservatory of Music in New York City, where he was born. In 1885, he became the manager of the Metropolitan Opera Company, where his father had been the opera company's conductor, and held that position until 1891. In 1903, he managed the New York Philharmonic Orchestra. To promote classical music, Damrosch hosted an early-morning program called *The* MUSIC APPRECIATION HOUR, first heard on the NBC network in 1928. In addition to this series, Dr. Damrosch was also music conductor of the General Electric Symphony Orchestra in the late 1920s. Maestro Damrosch retired from his position as NBC's principal music consultant in 1946.

DAN HARDING'S WIFE

1936–1937	NBC Red	Mon.–Fri.	1:45 PM
1937–1938	NBC Red	Mon.–Fri.	12:30 PM
1938–1939	NBC Red	Mon.–Fri.	12 PM

This 15-minute weekday drama series was, according to its opening, "the dramatic story of Rhoda Harding and her struggles to cope with life after the death of her husband, Dan." Actress Isabel RANDOLPH starred as the widow, Rhoda Harding; and Merrill Fugit and Loretta Poynton played her children, Dean and Donna. Also heard on the series were Carl Hanson, Alice Goodkin, Gladys Heen, Herb Nelson, Tommye Birch, Templeton Fox, Cliff Soubier, Judith Lowry, and William Farnum. Les Griffith was the program's announcer. The series was written by Ken Robinson and directed by Ken MACGREGOR. Nabisco crackers sponsored the series.

DANDRIDGE, RUBY (1900–1987)

Born in Cleveland, Ohio, African-American actress Ruby Dandridge used her comedic, high-pitched voice and wonderful cackling laugh to advantage on such programs as *The* JUDY CANOVA SHOW (as Judy's maid Geranium) and BEULAH (as Beulah's friend Oriole). Dandridge also appeared in many films such as *Crossroads* (1942), *Cabin in the Sky* (1942) and *Tap Roots* (1948), usually playing domestics.

DANGEROUS ASSIGNMENT

1949	NBC	Sat.	9:30 PM
1950	NBC	Wed.	8 PM

1950–1951	NBC	Sat.	8 PM
		Fri.	9 PM
		Sat.	8:30 PM
1951–1953	NBC	Mon.	10:35 PM
1953	CBS	Wed.	10:35 PM

Film actor Brian Donlevy and then radio actor Lloyd Burell starred as Steve Mitchell, a soldier of fortune who found excitement and adventure as he traveled around the world. Helen Choate was featured as Mitchell's secretary on this action-packed series. A typical adventure had Mitchell investigating the theft of the crown jewels from the palace of the king of Bali. The series was written by Bob Ryan and directed by Bill Carne. NBC sustained the program for four years.

DANGEROUS PARADISE

1933–1934	NBC Blue	Mon., Wed., Fri.	8:30 PM
1934–1935	NBC Blue	Mon., Wed., Fri.	7:45 PM

Three days a week, the NBC Blue network presented this half-hour series about a romance-seeking young woman named Gail Brewster and her on-and-off boyfriend, Dan Gentry. Actress Elsie Hitz played Gail, and Nick Dawson played Dan. The program was sponsored by Woodbury facial soap. The writers and director of this series are unknown.

DATE WITH JUDY, A

1941–1942	NBC Red	Tues.	10 PM
1942–1943	NBC	Wed.	9 PM
1943–1949	NBC	Tues.	8:30 PM
1949–1950	ABC	Thurs.	8:30 PM

This half-hour weekly situation-comedy series was about a typical teenager named Judy Foster and remained popular among adolescents as well as adult listeners for eight years; a film of the same name was based on the series. Besides Judy and her squeaky-voiced boyfriend, Oogie Pringle, Judy's parents and her younger brother, Randolph, were also prominently featured. Dellie Ellis, Louise ERICKSON, and Ann Gillis played Judy; Erickson played the part the longest and initially took the part of Judy's best friend, Mitzi. Harry Harvey and Richard CRENNA played Oogie. Dix Davis played Randolph; Stanley Farrar and then Joseph KEARNS and John Brown played Judy's father, Melvyn Foster. Lois Corbett, Bea BENADERET, and Myra Marsh played Judy's mother, Dora, at different times. Also heard on the show were Mercedes MCCAMBRIDGE, Georgia Backus, and Fred Howard. Marvin MILLER, Bill GOODWIN, Ken NILES, and Ralph Langley were the show's announcers. The program was produced and directed by Helen Mack. Pepsodent toothpaste, Ipana toothpaste, Sal Hapatica

The original cast of *A Date with Judy:* (from left) Joseph Kearns, Bea Benaderet, Ann Gillis, and Dix Davis

antacid, Tums antacid, and Revere cameras were the show's sponsors.

DAVID HARUM

1936–1937	NBC Blue	Mon.–Fri.	10:45 AM
1937–1940	NBC Red	Mon.–Fri.	11 AM
1940–1941	NBC Red	Mon.–Fri.	11:45 AM
1941–1943	NBC Red	Mon.–Fri.	11:45 AM
	&		
	CBS	Mon.–Fri.	3 PM
1943–1946	NBC	Mon.–Fri.	11:45 AM
1946–1948	CBS	Mon.–Fri.	10:45 AM
1948–1949	CBS	Mon.–Fri.	3 PM
1949–1950	NBC	Mon.–Fri.	11:45 AM

Created by Frank and Anne HUMMERT, DAVID HARUM had a small-town, folksy setting; its kind, middle-aged banker-hero, David Harum, his friends, and his family became comfortably familiar characters to listeners, who identified with the leading characters' "all-American" values. Harum was benevolent and kind, and most episodes centered around his generosity toward neighbors and friends. Wilmer Walter, Craig McDonnell, and Cameron PRUD'HOMME played Harum. Also heard were Peggy Allenby and then Gertrude Warner as Susan Price Wells; Charme Allen and Eve Condon as Aunt Polly; and Paul Stewart, Lawson Zerbe, Joseph "Joe" Latham, James Van Dyke,

Joan Tompkins, Vivian SMOLEN, Junius Matthews, Arthur Maitland, Bennett KILPACK, William Shelley, Don Briggs, Florence Lake, Joseph CURTIN, Claudia MORGAN, Ethel Everett, and Paul Ford. Ford Bond was the series' announcer. The show was directed by Ed King, John Buckwalter, Martha Atwell, Arthur Hanna, and Lester Vail, and written by Noel B. Gerson, Johanna Johnson, John DeWitt, Charles J. Gussman, Mary W. Reeves, and Peggy Blake. *David Harum*'s theme song, "Sunbonnet Sue," was hummed by Stanley Davis as he accompanied himself on the guitar. Sponsors included Bab-O cleanser and Glim toothpaste.

DAVIES, GWEN (ESTELLE LEVY 1922–   )

New York City–born singer-actress Gwen Davies began to perform in stage variety shows when she was six years old. A regular performer on Yolanda Langworthy's *Arabesque* radio program one year later, she was in the original cast of *The Adventures of Helen and Mary,* later known as LET'S PRETEND. She remained with the show for twenty-three years.

In addition, Davies was heard on such radio programs as GANGBUSTERS, *Manhattan at Midnight,* EASY ACES, *The* FRED ALLEN SHOW, AUNT JENNY'S REAL LIFE STORIES, FORTY-FIVE MINUTES TO HOLLYWOOD, WE THE PEOPLE, *The* GOLDBERGS, *Rudy Vallee's* FLEISHMAN'S HOUR, *The* CHASE AND SANBORN HOUR (as Eddie Cantor's daughter), *The* AMERICAN SCHOOL OF THE AIR, *The* KATE SMITH SHOW, YOUNG WIDDER BROWN, HILLTOP HOUSE, *The Class of '41,* and *The* MERCURY THEATER OF THE AIR. Her most memorable performance is as Cosette, whom Jean Valjean adopts, in Orson Welles's miniseries production of "Les Miserables."

Davies sang hundreds of radio commercial jingles throughout the 1940s and 1950s, was vocalist with Bobby Sherwood's Band, and recorded with the Artie Shaw and Jan Garber orchestras. For many years, Davies was the voice of Casper, the Friendly Ghost, in hundreds of film cartoons.

DAVIS, ELMER (1890–1958)

News commentator Elmer Davis was born in Auroro, Indiana. His nightly radio commentaries on the news of the day were always insightful and, no matter how horrific things around the world were, Davis always seemed reassuringly calm and collected. His flat, rather unemotional Midwestern accent certainly added to the feeling that everything was going to be "okay after all"—especially during World War II.

Davis first came to the attention of the general public pinch-hitting for Hans V. KALTENBORN in 1939 and was heard on both ABC and CBS at different times. His longtime news-show sponsor was the Gillette safety razor. In 1942, Davis was appointed by

Joan Davis (NBC)

President Franklin D. Roosevelt to head the newly created Wartime Office of War Information Bureau. David continued to read the news of the day on radio for CBS until he retired.

DAVIS, JOAN (MADONNA JOSEPHINE DAVIS: (1907–1961)

Born in St. Paul, Minnesota, comedienne Joan Davis had a very successful career in vaudeville, radio, films, and on television. The perpetually vulnerable Joan, who always seemed to be putting her foot where it didn't belong, was one of the stars of *The* SEALTEST VILLAGE STORE variety program for several seasons and then starred on her own situation-comedy series, *Joannie Tea Room* and *I Married Joan,* both familiarly called *The* JOAN DAVIS SHOW. "I Married Joan" became a hit TV series in 1952. Davis also starred in many motion pictures, including *On the Avenue* (1937), *Sun Valley Serenade* (1941), *Show Business* (1944), and *If You Knew Susie* (1948).

DAWN BUSTER SHOW, THE

See DUPREE, HENRY.

DAY, DENNIS (EUGENE DENNIS MCNULTY: 1917–1988)

Irish-American tenor-actor-comedian Dennis Day first gained fame as the boyishly naive, seemingly simple-minded singer on *The* JACK BENNY SHOW. Born in New York City, Day attended Manhattan College in New

York and decided to become a singer shortly after he was graduated. Ultimately, he became the Benny program's longest-lasting vocalist, and he proved himself to be a versatile and talented comedian as well. The Benny Show eventually led to his own radio program, *A* DAY IN THE LIFE OF DENNIS DAY, which had a healthy five-year run. Dennis was also a frequent guest star on several TV music-variety programs, and was featured as the cartoon voice of Fred in *The Stingiest Man in Town* (based on Charles Dickens's *A Christmas Carol*) in 1978. Until shortly before he died, Day made personal appearances at various state fairs, in touring stage shows, and in nightclubs. He appeared in eight feature films, most notably *Music in Manhattan* (1944) and *Make Mine Laughs* (1949).

DAY IN THE LIFE OF DENNIS DAY, A

1946–1948	NBC	Wed.	8 PM
1948–1949	NBC	Sat.	10 PM
1949–1951	NBC	Sat.	9:30 PM

In 1946, Jack BENNY's popular vocalist, tenor Dennis Day, starred in this half-hour weekly radio show, in which Dennis Day played the same naive young bachelor character he had introduced on *The* JACK BENNY SHOW. Also heard on the program were Betty Miles and Barbara Eiler as Dennis's girlfriend, Mildred; "Dink" Trout and Bea BENADERET as Mildred's parents; and John Brown as Mr. Willoughby. Guest stars included Patty ANDREWS, Jimmy DURANTE, Rosemary Clooney, and others. Ken Carson announced the show. Frank O'Connor directed the series, which was written by Frank Galen. The program's sponsors were Luster Creme shampoo (featuring Luster Creme's singer, Ken Carson), Colgate dental cream, Cashmere Bouquet, and Palmolive shave cream. At one time the show's theme music was "Londonderry Air."

DeANGELO, CARLO (1895–1962)

Carlo deAngelo was born in Rome, Italy, and emigrated to the United States as a young boy. He began his show-business career as an entertainer and assistant film director before performing on radio's less-than-successful YOURS FOR A SONG show. DeAngelo eventually became a radio-program director and was responsible for the success of an impressive number of shows, including *Blackstone, the Magic Detective, The* ENO CRIME CLUB, *The* AVE MARIA HOUR, *Famous Trials of History, The* GIBSON FAMILY, *Charlie Wild, P.I., Circus Days,* ELLEN RANDOLPH, *The* FALCON, HILLTOP HOUSE, MANDRAKE THE MAGICIAN, *Of Human Bondage, The* O'NEILLS, PERRY MASON, and WE LOVE AND LEARN.

DEATH VALLEY DAYS

1930–1931	NBC Blue	Tues.	9:30 PM
1931–1932	NBC Blue	Mon.	8:30 PM
1932–1936	NBC Blue	Thurs.	9 PM
1936–1938	NBC Blue	Fri.	8:30 PM
1938–1940	NBC Red	Sat.	9:30 PM
1940–1941	NBC Blue	Fri.	8:30 PM
1941–1944	CBS	Thurs.	8:30 PM

Created by Ruth Woodman, *Death Valley Days* starred Tim Daniel Frawley, George Rand, Harry Humphrey, and John "Jack" MacBryde as the Old Rangler, Harvey Hays as the Old Prospector, John White as the Lone Cowboy, Edwin Bruce as Bobby Keen, Robert Haag as Sheriff Mark Chase, and Olyn Landick as Cassandra Drinkwater. Also heard regularly on this half-hour Western-adventure series were Frank Butler, Eunice Howard, Harlan Stone, Jane Gilbert, James Van Dyke, Eddie Firestone, Paul Nugent, Richard Barrows, Irene Hubbard, Charles Watson, Carl Kroenke, Milton Herman, Rosemarie Brancato, Helen Claire, Jack Arthur, Jean King, and Geoffrey Bryant. The show was retitled *Death Valley Sheriff* in 1944, and then it was simply called *The Sheriff* in 1945. Dresser Dahlstead, George Hicks, and John Paul King announced the program. Lillian Steinfeld directed the program in the early 1940s, and Ruth Adams Knight wrote many of the scripts for the show. Sponsors of the program included 20-Mule-Team Borax and Boraxo cleansers.

DE CAMP, ROSEMARY (1913–)

Best known as the sweet and loyal nurse Judy Price on the DR. CHRISTIAN show, actress Rosemary De Camp was born in Prescott, Arizona, was first heard on radio in 1933, and before appearing on *Dr. Christian* was featured on such programs as DOT AND WILL, TOM MIX, ONE MAN'S FAMILY, *Hollywood ScreenScopes, I Want a Divorce,* GANGBUSTERS, *The* GOLDBERGS, *The* SILVER THEATER, *The* LUX RADIO THEATER, BIG TOWN, and SCREEN GUILD PLAYERS. A popular character actress in such films as *Cheers for Miss Bishop* (1941) and *Yankee Doodle Dandy* (1942), De Camp usually played characters much older than she actually was: in *Yankee Doodle Dandy*, for example, she played James Cagney's mother even though she was several years younger than he. On television, De Camp played Cummings's sister on the long-running "Bob Cummings Show" in the 1950s.

DEFOREST, DR. LEE (1873–1961)

In 1906, Dr. Lee DeForest invented a three-element vacuum tube he called the audion, an elementary form of the modern radio tube that made it possible to receive wireless signals with more sensitivity than was possible with the electrolytic and carborundum

Vaughn de Leath (NBC)

able business practices, DeForest is still referred to as the "Father of Modern Radio," mainly because of his steadfast promotion of radio as an important means of long-distance communication.

DE LEATH, VAUGHN (1896–1943)

Singer Vaughn de Leath was born in Pulaski, Illinois. Her sultry, "bluesy" contralto voice made her a listening-audience favorite during radio's earliest years. De Leath, who made her radio debut in 1920, was called the "Original Radio Girl," and Dr. Lee DeForest claimed that she had "a voice perfectly suited for the radio microphone." In 1934, she had a popular morning show on WMCA in New York City and was subsequently featured on her own network program, *The* VAUGHN DE LEATH SHOW. A frequent guest star on *The Voice of Firestone*, the singer made numerous guest appearances on most 1930s major comedy-variety programs.

DELLA CHIESA, VIVIAN (1921–   )

Soprano Vivian Della Chiesa was born in Chicago, Illinois. Just out of high school, she defeated 3,800 others in a nationwide singing contest held by CBS. She subsequently starred on radio's *La Rosa Concerts*, *The* AMERICAN ALBUM OF FAMILIAR MUSIC, *The Saturday Night Party, Musical Footnotes, Then and Now, The*

types of tube then in use by wireless transmission systems.

Born in Council Bluffs, Iowa, DeForest became fascinated with machinery when he was a child, and by the time he was thirteen years old, he was already a fledgling inventor. After he was graduated from Yale University, he obtained a job with the Western Electric Company as a researcher. In 1902, he began public demonstrations of wireless telegraphy. In 1906, one year after DeForest's company went bankrupt, he was instrumental in broadcasting a live performance by Enrico Caruso from the stage of the Metropolitan Opera House in New York City, which he did to promote his sound-transmission systems. The broadcast attracted considerable press attention.

Despite his enthusiasm for radio transmission, DeForest continued to be a poor businessman: in order to keep his new company, DeForest Radio Telephone Company, solvent, he began to claim credit for inventions that others were far more instrumental in developing. Although he filed more than 200 patents, many of his claims were challenged. During World War I, DeForest conducted military research for the Bell Telephone Laboratories. Even though he was accused of having an enormous ego and engaging in question-

Vivian Della Chiesa (Courtesy of Miss Della Chiesa)

Contented Hour, and the *CBS American Melody Hour.* The soprano was also a frequent guest star on several music-variety programs and often appeared on the NBC SYMPHONY broadcasts as a soloist with Arturo Toscanini's orchestra. She continued to be active on the concert stage well beyond the end of her radio career. Della Chiesa was the first female entertainer to be honored by the prestigious Lambs Club.

DELMAR, KENNY (1910–1984)

Actor Kenny Delmar's most memorable radio character was Senator Beauregard Claghorn, the Southern windbag-politician resident of Allen's Alley on the FRED ALLEN SHOW. Claghorn became so popular that Delmar's character was given a series of his own. The versatile character actor, born in New York, appeared on the vaudeville circuit before entering radio. In addition to his Senator Claghorn role, Delmar was also featured in *The* THEATER GUILD OF THE AIR, *The* COURT OF MISSING HEIRS, JUNGLE JIM, *The* SHADOW, *The* LUX RADIO THEATER, and MYSTERY THEATER. A regular on the short-lived DANNY KAYE SHOW playing "Mr. Average Radio Listener," the actor also provided voices for many TV cartoon characters in "Tennessee Tuxedo and His Tales" (1963–1966), "The Adventures of Hoppity Hooper" (1964–1967), and "Underdog" (1964–1973). At the height of his Senator Claghorn popularity, Delmar starred in the film *It's a Joke, Son* (1947), the title of which was one of the senator's most quoted catch phrases.

DE MILLE, CECIL B. (1881–1959)

One of Hollywood's most celebrated directors, Cecil B. De Mille was born in Ashfield, Massachusetts. He became world-famous for directing such silent- and talking-film spectaculars as *King of Kings* (1927), *Cleopatra* (1934), *Union Pacific* (1939), *Reap the Wild Wind* (1942), *Samson and Delilah* (1949), *The Greatest Show on Earth* (1952), and *The Ten Commandments* (1956). On radio, De Mille hosted the successful dramatic anthology series *The* LUX RADIO THEATER from 1936 to 1954, although he did not actually direct any of its programs. He quit in 1954 rather than join the radio actor's union. De Mille also appeared as himself in several films.

DESMOND, CONNIE (1908–1983)

New York–born sportscaster Connie Desmond had one of radio's most recognizable voices. As the man who broadcasted the play-by-play accounts of the Brooklyn Dodger games, millions of people became familiar with his quick-paced, highly excited sportscasting style on both local and national sports broadcasts. Desmond also delivered the daily sports news

for several different networks such as NBC, CBS, and ABC.

DEVINE, ANDY (1905–1977)

Comic actor Andy Devine's gravelly, wheezy-sounding voice made him a perfect radio performer. Devine was born in Kingman, Arizona, and played professional baseball before becoming an actor. He was featured on *The* JACK BENNY SHOW for several seasons and was also a regular cast member on the LUM AND ABNER program. From 1951 until 1956, Devine co-starred with movie actor Guy Madison on the WILD BILL HICKOK Western-adventure series on both radio and television. He also made numerous guest appearances on most of the major comedy-variety shows including *The* CHASE AND SANBORN HOUR and *The* MAXWELL HOUSE COFFEE SHOW, and appeared in such films as *Stagecoach* (1939) and *The Red Badge of Courage* (1951). Devine hosted a successful daytime TV series for children called "Andy's Gang" in the 1950s.

DIAL DAVE GARROWAY (AKA THE DAVE GARROWAY SHOW)

1949–1959	NBC	Mon.–Fri.	11:15AM
1950–1953	NBC	Mon.–Fri.	11:45AM
1953–1954	NBC	Mon.–Fri.	2:20PM

This was NBC's answer to CBS's ARTHUR GODFREY TIME morning program. Garroway's easygoing manner and gentle humor rivaled Godfrey's, although his show never managed to steal Godfrey's loyal morning audience. Featured on Garroway's hour-long programs were singers Connie Russell, June Christie, Jack Haskell, Charlie Andrews, and Vivian Martin. Haskell and Ed Prentiss were the show's announcers. Sponsors included Dial soap and shampoo (hence the title of the show) and Chiffon soap flakes.

DICK TRACY, THE ADVENTURES OF

See ADVENTURES OF DICK TRACY, *The.*

DICKENSON, JEAN (1909–1989)

Soprano Jean Dickenson, a popular radio personality in the 1930s, was born in Montreal, Canada, and educated at Denver University and the Lamont School of Music. After concerts with the Milwaukee and Montreal symphonies, Dickenson made her operatic debut with the San Carlo Opera Company. The singer's first radio broadcast was on KOA, a local station in Denver, Colorado, but she became nationally known as one of the stars of the AMERICAN ALBUM OF FAMILIAR MUSIC, *The* PALMOLIVE BEAUTY BOX THEATER, and *The* HOUR OF CHARM. After her active career on radio ended, Dickenson continued to perform on the concert stage for many years until her retirement in the 1960s.

DIMENSION X (AKA X MINUS ONE)

1950–1951	NBC	Sun., Sat. Fri.	(*)	
1951–1955	(Off the air)			
1955	NBC	Sun., Thurs.	8 & 9 PM	
	NBC	Wed.	8 & 9:30 PM	
1956	NBC	Tues.	8:30 PM	
1956–1957	NBC	Wed.	9 PM	
1957–1958	NBC	Thurs.	8 PM	

Although science fiction would seem to be a perfect subject for radio dramas, there were few adult science-fiction series on the air during radio's golden years. One show, NBC's half-hour *Dimension X,* aired in the early 1950s, was one of the first programs to be recorded on tape for later broadcasting. Directed by Bob Warren and Fred Collins, the sustained *Dimension X* series featured, among its regular performers, Jack GRIMES, Joan Lazer, Jack Lemmon (during his brief radio tenure), Art CARNEY, Evie Juster, Jackson BECK, Mandel KRAMER, Everett SLOANE, Joan Alexander, Jan MINER, Claudia MORGAN, Bryna Raeburn, Joyce Gordon, Ronald LISS, Larry Haines, Santos ORTEGA, and Ralph Bell. Norman Rose was the show's announcer. Fred Weihe, among others, directed the program. The original series was on the air for only one year, but in the mid-1950s it was revived by NBC as *X Minus One.* Many of the actors heard on the original series were brought back. Previously recorded episodes of *Dimension X* were replayed on *X Minus One* as well.

DINAH SHORE SHOW, THE (AKA SONGS BY DINAH SHORE; CALL FOR MUSIC; IN PERSON, DINAH SHORE; BIRDSEYE OPEN HOUSE; and THE FORD SHOW)

1939–1940	NBC Blue	Sun.	7 PM
1940	NBC Blue	Fri.	10:15 PM
1940–1941	(Off the air)		
1941–1942	NBC Blue	Sun.	9:45 PM
1942–1943	NBC Blue	Fri.	8:15 PM
1943–1944	CBS	Thurs.	9:30 PM
1944–1945	NBC	Thurs.	6:30 PM
1945–1946	NBC	Thurs.	8:30 PM
1946–1947	CBS	Wed.	9:30 PM
1947–1948	(Off the air)		
1948	CBS	Fri.	10 PM
1948–1953	(Off the air)		
1953	NBC	Tues., Fri.	8 PM
1953–1954	(Off the air)		
1954–1955	NBC	Wed., Fri.	8 PM

After she left *The* EDDIE CANTOR SHOW, pop singer Dinah SHORE had several 15-minute and half-hour radio shows of her own that usually followed a similar format: In addition to her singing were occasional guest appearances by comedians such as Bob HOPE, Red SKELTON, Jack BENNY, and Eddie CANTOR. Regularly appearing with Dinah on her various programs were the Joe Lillie Singers, the orchestras of Paul

LAVALLE, Robert Emmett, Harry James, and Johnny Mercer. Announcers included Harry VON ZELL and Jack Rourke. Birds Eye frozen foods, Philip Morris cigarettes, Pabst Blue Ribbon beer, and Ford and Chevrolet automobiles sponsored Dinah's radio programs.

DISC DRIVE

1985–present	CBC	Wed.	3:05 PM

The CANADIAN BROADCASTING CORPORATION'S FM-stereo three-hour *Disc Drive* program has one of the networks largest listening audiences. Heard during late-afternoon "drive-home" hours, the show is hosted by Jurgen Gothe and features an eclectic variety of recorded popular, classical, folk, and jazz music—but never rock music—as well as intelligent, sometimes irreverent commentary on wine, food, and pop culture by Gothe. In 1988, the program won the Best Regular Radio Program gold medal at the New York International Radio Festival, beating out such stiff competition as the syndicated LARRY KING SHOW. The executive producer of *Disc Drive* is Janet Lea. The show's theme music is Rameau's "San Saranette."

DOC BARCLAY'S DAUGHTERS

1938–1940	CBS	Mon.–Fri.	1 PM

The late 1930s were banner years for daytime serial dramas and many programs were introduced to the listening public, many of which, including the 15-minute weekday *Doc Barclay's Daughters,* lasted only a few seasons. However, even these short-lived series managed to find a considerable audience. *Doc Barclay's Daughters* told of yet another small-town country doctor–widower and his family. Bennett KILPACK was heard as Doc Barclay; Elizabeth Reller, Mildred Robin, and Vivien SMOLEN played his daughters Connie, Mimi, and Marge. Janice Gilbert played Clarabelle Higgins, and Albert Hayes played Tom Clark. Also heard were Carlton YOUNG, Allan BUNCE, and Audrey Egan. The show's announcer was Tom Shirley. Stephen Gross and Lloyd Rosemond directed the program. The Personal Finance Company sponsored the series.

DOCTOR'S WIFE, THE

1952–1953	NBC	Mon.–Fri.	5:45 PM
1953–1954	(Off the air)		
1954–1955	NBC	Mon.–Fri.	3:45 PM
1955–1956	NBC	Mon.–Fri.	10:30 AM

This 15-minute weekday serial concerned physician Dr. Dan Palmer, who lived in a town called Stanton with his ever-patient and supportive wife, Julie. Donald Curtis, John Baragrey, and Karl WEBER played the doctor, and Patricia Wheel was his wife. (Baragrey later became one of television's most popular leading men on such shows as "Studio One" and "The Philco Playhouse.") The announcer on this series was Bob Schaerry. The show was sponsored by Ex-Lax laxative.

DON AMECHE SHOW, THE (AKA THE OLD GOLD SHOW)

| 1946–1950 | CBS | Mon.–Fri. | 5:30 PM |

When he left the CHASE AND SANBORN HOUR program, actor Don AMECHE became the star of a half-hour weekly series that bore his name. At first the show was a summer replacement for the popular RUDY VALLEE SHOW in 1946, but it was successful enough for NBC to keep it on the air for a full season the following year. Ameche's program featured dramatic skits as well as comedy sketches and musical selections. Marvin MILLER was the show's announcer, and the series was directed by Carlton Alsop and Howard Wiley. Many guest stars from film, the Broadway stage, and radio, such as Dorothy LAMOUR, Fred Astaire, Jimmy DURANTE, Edgar BERGEN, and Dinah SHORE, were heard on the program. The show's writers included George Faulkner, Henrietta Felstein, and Sid Zelinka. This final *Don Ameche Show* was sponsored by Drene shampoo.

DON WINSLOW OF THE NAVY

1937–1940	NBC Blue	Mon.–Fri.	5:15 PM
1940–1942	(Off the air)		
1942–1943	NBC Blue	Mon.–Fri.	6:15 PM

This 15-minute children's adventure serial was heard on the NBC's Blue network and originated from Chicago. Winslow was played by Bob Guilbert in the original Chicago edition and then by Raymond Edward JOHNSON when it originated in New York. Edward Davidson and John Gibson played Winslow's sidekick, Red Pennington; Betty Lou GERSON, Gertrude Warner, and Lenore Kingston played Mercedes Colby. Also heard on the show were Betty Ito as Lotus, Ruth Barth as Misty, and Gladys Heen in various roles. A typical *Don Winslow of the Navy* adventure during World War II had Don investigating an international Axis spy network for the government in such exotic places as Singapore, London, and Hawaii. Most of his investigations, however, took place on land rather than at sea, despite his being a navy man. Listeners remember the series' theme song, "Columbia, the Gem of the Ocean," almost as well as they remember the episodes. The program was directed by Ray Kremer and Al Barker. Sponsors included Kellogg's and Post Toasties breakfast cereals.

DONALD, PETER (1918–1979)

Multitalented radio performer Peter Donald was as comfortable as a comedian, announcer, or quiz-show host as he was in the role of dramatic actor. Donald also wrote for the *County Fair* series.

As an actor, Donald was featured on such daytime dramas as *The Grummits,* SECOND HUSBAND, STELLA DALLAS, *The* STORY OF MARY MARLIN, and YOUR FAMILY AND MINE. He was also a regular on the critically acclaimed MARCH OF TIME program and played the comic role of a stereotypical Irish-loudmouth funny man, Ajax Cassidy, on the FRED ALLEN SHOW. In 194? the 15-minute *Peter Donald Show* proved to be a short lived venture and was off the air before the season ended. For many years, Donald told jokes sent in by the listening audience on the CAN YOU TOP THIS comedy show. After network radio's demise, Donald worked as a voice-over performer for TV commercials and narrated industrial-film documentaries.

DOROTHY AND DICK

See KILGALLEN, Dorothy; KOLLMAR, Richard.

DOROTHY GORDON SHOW, THE (AKA THE CHILDREN'S CORNER)

| 1924–1937 | WEAF New York | (Times varied) | |
| 1937–1938 | CBS | Mon., Wed., Fri. | 5 P |

WEAF in New York City was the first radio station to broadcast Dorothy Gordon's 15-minute children story-hour program in 1924. Miss Gordon read familiar fairy tales and several original stories on her show which remained on the air throughout most of the 1930s. In 1938, Gordon decided to devote her time and talents to producing and directing children's stories and specials for NBC radio.

DOT AND WILL

| 1935–1937 | NBC Blue | (Various days and times) |

In the late 1930s, a number of radio daytime serials told of young couples attempting to make their way in post-Depression times. *Dot and Will* was one such series. Heard for 15 minutes each weekday, it featured Florence FREEMAN and James MEIGHAN as Dot and Will Horton, supported by radio veterans Helene Dumas, Allyn Joslyn, Ralph LOCKE, Rosemary DE CAMP, Effie Palmer, Sidney Smith, Irene Hubbard, Peggy Allenby, and Agnes MOOREHEAD. Ralph EDWARDS, Ford BOND, and Andre BARUCH announced the show. The director and writers of this series are unknown.

DOUBLE OR NOTHING

1940–1941	Mutual	Fri.	8 PM
1941–1945	Mutual	Fri.	9:30 PM
1945–1947	Mutual	Sun.	9:30 PM

1947–1948	CBS	Mon.–Fri.	3 PM
1948–1951	NBC	Mon.–Fri.	2 PM
1951–1953	NBC	Mon.–Fri.	10:30 AM

This long-running radio quiz program was on the air for twelve years, an unprecedented number for a game show. Contestants attempted to answer a series of questions, each time doubling their money from $20 to $40, $40 to $80, as soon as they answered each question correctly. Players were off the show when they missed a question. Walter Compton, John Reed KING, Todd Russell, and Walter O'Keefe hosted this series at one time or another. Fred Cole was the show's announcer. Harry Spears, John Wellington, and Thomas F. Vietor, Jr., directed the series, which was written by Gerald Rice, Harry Bailey, and Carroll Carroll. The show's theme song was "Three Little Words." Sponsors included Feen-A-Mint, Chooz breath candy, and Campbell's soup.

DOUGLAS, PAUL (PAUL FLEISCHER: 1911–1959)

Actor Paul Douglas was born in Philadelphia, Pennsylvania. Before he became one of the movies' most loveable tough guys, Douglas was a regular performer on radio. He announced the BUCK ROGERS IN THE 25TH CENTURY series, CHESTERFIELD PRESENTS, *The* CHESTERFIELD SUPPER CLUB, *The* FRED WARING SHOW, *The Fred Waring Pleasure Time, The Horn and Hardart's* CHILDREN'S HOUR, and BURNS AND ALLEN programs. Douglas had a running role on the ABIE'S IRISH ROSE situation-comedy series, but he is best remembered for his work in films. His memorable film debut was *A Letter to Three Wives* (1949); he then starred in *Clash by Night* (1952), *Executive Suite* (1954), and *The Mating Game* (1958) before he died of cancer at the height of his career.

DOWNEY, SR., MORTON (1896–1985)

The father of TV talk-show host Morton Downey, Jr., Morton Downey, Sr., was born in Wallington, Connecticut. Like Bing CROSBY, he began his career singing vocals with the Paul WHITEMAN band in the early 1920s. The Irish tenor became a star first on Broadway and then on radio, where he had one of the most listened-to programs, *The Coke Club,* in the late 1920s and then his own MORTON DOWNEY SHOW until the late 1940s. At the height of his popularity, Downey also appeared in several films, including what many believe was the first full-sound movie musical, *Syncopation* (1929), *Mother's Boy,* and *Lucky in Love* in the early 1930s.

DR. CHRISTIAN

1937–1938	CBS	Sun.	2:30 PM
1938–1939	CBS	Tues.	10 PM
1939–1954	CBS	Wed.	8:30 PM

Dr. Christian, a highly popular radio series about a small-town doctor, starred Danish-born actor Jean HERSHOLT as the kindly, old physician who had a talent for solving the medical and nonmedical problems of his patients. Lurene TUTTLE, Kathleen Fitz, Helen Kleeb, and Rosemary DE CAMP played his faithful nurse, Judy; De Camp, who played the part longest, is the Judy most listeners remember best. Art Gilmore was the program's announcer. The half-hour show's familiar theme music was "Rainbow on the River." *Dr. Christian* was directed by Neil Reagan and Florence Ortman and frequently written by Ruth Adams Knight. Each of its last few seasons on the air, a contest was held for the "best original script of the year." The listener who won received $2,000. The show's sponsors included Vaseline petroleum jelly, hair tonic, and lip ice.

DR. I.Q.

1939	NBC Blue	Mon.	10:30 PM
1939–1942	NBC Blue	Mon.	9 PM
1942–1944	NBC	Mon.	9:30 PM
1944–1949	NBC	Mon., Fri.	9:30 PM
1950	ABC	Wed.	8 PM

In this offbeat game show, selected members in the studio audience would ask Dr. I.Q. ("The Mental Banker") a question on any random subject. If the Dr. failed to answer the question correctly, the member of the audience who stumped him was given silver dollars, the amount increasing with the difficulty of the question asked. The questioner could receive as much as $250. Announcers were stationed throughout the audience; frequently you would hear one of them say, "I have a lady in the balcony" or "Down here in the third row center, Dr.!" Lew VALENTINE, Jimmy McClain, and Stanley Vainrib were heard at various times as Dr. I.Q. on this series, sponsored for many years by Mars candy bars. Allen C. Anthony was the show's major announcer. The half-hour program was the creation of Lee Segall. It was directed by Harry Halcomb and Paul Dumont. The show's theme song was "You Are My Lucky Star." A spin-off for younger listeners, DR. I.Q., JR., which also starred Lew Valentine, was heard in the mid-1940s but was canceled after less than a full season.

DR. I. Q., JR.

See DR. I.Q.

DR. KATE

| 1938–1940 | NBC Red | Mon.–Fri. | 10:45 AM |

The leading role on this 15-minute weekday series was originated by Cornelia Burdick and then played by Vicki VOLA. Dr. Kate had difficulty trying to balance her busy career as a doctor and her private life; this led to dilemmas and plot complications. Also heard on the series were Montgomery Mohn, Charles McAllister, Helen Kleeb, Earl Lee, and Everett Glass. The program's announcers were Sam Moore, Archie Presley, Leo Cleary, and Armand Girard. R. W. Stafford and Ward Byron directed the series, which was written by Hal Burdick. Its sponsor was the Sperry Flour Company.

DR. KILDARE

| 1950–1952 | (Syndicated series. Various stations and times) |

Metro-Goldwyn-Mayer studios produced a weekly radio series based on their popular *Dr. Kildare* films. The leading players were the MGM actors who appeared in the successful film series, Lionel BARRYMORE (as Dr. Gillespie) and Lew Ayres (as Dr. Kildare). Also recreating their screen roles were Alma Kruger as Nurse Molly Bird, Marie Blake as the hospital switchboard operator, and Nat Pendleton as her boyfriend. The series' announcer was Ken CARPENTER. Its directors were uncredited, but the scripts were written by Willis Goldbeck, Harry Ruskin, Lawrence Bachmann, and Ormand Ruthven, screenwriters for the original film series.

DRAGNET

1949–1950	NBC	Thurs.	10:30 PM
1950–1952	NBC	Thurs.	9 PM
1952–1953	NBC	Sun.	9:30 PM
1953–1955	NBC	Tues.	9 PM
1955–1956	NBC	Tues.	8:30 PM

Dragnet ranks as one of radio's most popular police shows. It began on radio, had two television incarnations (black-and-white beginning in 1952; color in 1967), and was made into two feature films (in 1954 with members of the television cast and as a spoof in 1987).

The series was noted for its stark, flat, conversationally subdued dialogue and the underplayed acting of the show's performers. Stories were taken from the Los Angeles Police Department files, and the technical advice of L. A. Police Chief William Parker was acknowledged at the end of each program. The show's closing line—"The story you have just heard is true; only the names have been changed to protect the innocent"—and its subsequent accounts of what happened to the people involved in the story made this program one of the most memorable and admired series on the air. Detective Joe Friday's catch phrase "Just the facts, ma'am" probably became as famous as the show itself.

Jack WEBB played the part of Police Detective Jo Friday, and his partner Sergeant Ben Romero wa played on radio by Barton YARBOROUGH. When Yar borough died unexpectedly, actor Ben Alexander be came Friday's new partner, Sergeant Frank Smith Also heard on the series regularly were Peggy Webbe as Ma Friday; and Tyler McVey, Harry Bartell, Her Ellis, Helen Kleeb, Georgia Ellis, Virginia Christine Virginia GREGG, Jeanette NOLAN, and John MCINTIRE *Dragnet*'s announcers were George Fenniman and Ha Gibney, and most of the episodes were directed b Jack Webb. James B. Moser, John Robinson, and Fran Burt scripted the series. The program's sponsors in cluded Fatima, L and M, and Chesterfield cigarette *Dragnet*'s famous "Dum-dee-dum-dum" theme musi was composed by Walter Schumann.

DRAGONETTE, JESSICA (1908–1980)

Soprano Jessica Dragonette was born on St. Valen tine's Day in Calcutta, India. She is almost as we remembered for her unusual name as she is for he superb singing. Her first major appearance as a singe was in the Max Reinhardt theatrical production (*The Miracle* (1923); Dragonette subsequently starred i stage productions of *The Student Prince* (1924) and *Th Grand Street Follies* (1926) before she made her radi debut. "The Greta Garbo of the airwaves," as sh was known, starred on several very successful musi variety programs in the 1930s and 1940s, including th

Jessica Dragonette (CBS)

CITIES SERVICE CONCERTS, *The Musical Comedy Hour*, SATURDAY NIGHT SERENADE, *The Philco Hour*, *The Ford Summer Show*, and *The* PALMOLIVE BEAUTY BOX SHOW. Her occasional guest appearances on the concert stage were always sold-out events, and the singer made cameo appearances in several films.

In 1935, Dragonette was voted Radio's Favorite Woman Star by *Radio Mirror* magazine. A devout Roman Catholic, Dragonette was decorated by Pope Pius XII with the *Pro Eccelsia de Pontifica* medal and the Lady Grand Cross of the Holy Sepulchre for her achievments in the entertainment world. She was also made an honorary colonel in the United States Army because of her bond-selling personal appearances during World War II. In 1967, Dragonette's autobiography, *Faith Is a Song*, was published.

DRAKE, GALEN (1906–1989)

California-born newscaster Galen Drake, known as "the housewives' favorite commentator," had several radio talk shows in addition to his daytime newscasting during the 1940s and 1950s. As the host of the popular GALEN DRAKE SHOW, heard weekdays at noon, Drake talked about everything from politics to entertainment. Eddie Safranski played with the NBC Band on the show; Milt Rosen wrote current-events material. Drake continued his broadcasting activities on New York City's WOR until shortly before his death.

DREFT STAR PLAYHOUSE, THE

| 1943–1945 | NBC | Mon.–Fri. | 11:30 AM |

This series presented successful films, adapted for radio in serialized, 15-minute five-days-a-week versions. Some of the films adapted for this series, such as *Kitty Foyle* and *How Green Was My Valley*, both based on long novels, took several weeks to read over the radio. Featured actors included Gale Page, Jane Wyman, Agnes MOOREHEAD, Maureen O'Sullivan, Mary Astor, Margo, Rosemary DE CAMP, and Les REMAYNE, who played roles they had not necessarily played in the original films. Announcers for the program were Terry O'Sullivan and Marvin MILLER. Lee Mitchel and Axel GRUENBERG directed the series, sponsored by Dreft dishwashing liquid. Various freelance writers wrote the scripts for the series.

DRYDEN, ROBERT (1916–   )

Unquestionably one of radio's most versatile and talented actors, native New Yorker Robert Dryden could play any type of role and was often heard as several different characters on a single radio program. He was equally adept at playing comic characters and archvillains and could sound convincingly like a young swain or a crotchety old man. After a brief stint in theater, Dryden became one of radio's busiest performers beginning in 1943, acting on: GANGBUSTERS, STUDIO ONE, *The* FORD THEATER, BIG TOWN, CASEY, CRIME PHOTOGRAPHER, *The* FALCON, *The* FAT MAN, *The* FBI IN PEACE AND WAR, SUPERMAN, WE LOVE AND LEARN, COLUMBIA PRESENTS CORWIN, *The* GREATEST STORY EVER TOLD, and FAMOUS JURY TRIALS. In the mid-1970s, Dryden was a regular cast member on Himan Brown's CBS MYSTERY THEATER series, and in 1976 he costarred with writer-actress Peg LYNCH on *The Little Things in Life*. He has also appeared in films and on such TV series as PBS's "American Playhouse" (1975) and the ANTA Matinee series (1970).

DUFF, HOWARD (1917–1989)

Actor Howard Duff was born in Bremerton, Washington, a suburb of Seattle. Beginning in 1941, Duff was heard on such radio shows as *Dear John*, *The* SCREEN GUILD PLAYERS, HOLLYWOOD STAR TIME, and SUSPENSE. It wasn't until Duff played Sam Spade on the ADVENTURES OF SAM SPADE, DETECTIVE series that he gained nationwide fame: his droll, wisecracking characterization made him a favorite radio performer and eventually led to a lucrative career in films and on television. Duff made his motion-picture debut in *Brute Force* (1947) and subsequently starred in *All My Sons* (1948), *Steel Town* (1952), and *Boys Night Out* (1962). On

Howard Duff as Sam Spade (NBC)

television, Duff starred on the "Mr. Adams and Eve" series (1957) with his wife, film actress Ida Lupino.

DUFFY'S TAVERN

1941–1942	CBS	Thurs.	8:30 PM
1942–1944	NBC	Tues.	8:30 PM
1944–1946	NBC	Fri.	8:30 PM
1946–1949	NBC	Wed.	9 PM
1949–1950	NBC	Thurs.	9:30 PM
1950–1951	NBC	Fri.	9:30 PM

Each episode of this hilarious program began: "Duffy's Tavern, where the elite meet to eat. Archie the manager speaking. Duffy ain't here. (Pause) Oh, hello, Duffy." The tavern's owner, Duffy, was never actually heard on this half-hour weekly series, but he made frequent calls to Archie to check up on how things were doing at his saloon. Other characters providing laughs included Duffy's daughter, known simply as "Miss Duffy," who had a classic Brooklyn accent; a slow-witted fellow named Clifton Finnegan; the tavern's black bartender, Eddie; Clancy the cop; Wilfred, who was Finnegan's kid brother; and Dolly Snaffle. Ed GARDNER starred as Archie; Shirley BOOTH, Florence HALOP, Gloria Erlanger, Florence Robinson, Sandra Gould, and Hazel Shermet played Miss Duffy; Charlie Cantor was Finnegan; Alan REED, Clancy the

Jimmy Durante (NBC)

Ed "Archie" Gardner and guest, the Lone Ranger (Brace Beemer), during a *Duffy's Tavern* rehearsal break. (NBC)

cop; Eddie Green, Eddie the waiter; Dick Van Patten, Wilfred; and Lurene TUTTLE, Dolly.

Benay Venuta, Tito Guizar, Bob Graham, and Helen Ward sang occasionally, and guest stars included Adolph Menjou, John Garfield, Joan Bennett, Esther Williams, Marlene Dietrich, Tony Martin, Vincent PRICE, Billie Burke, and Rex Harrison. The *Duffy's Tavern* orchestra was led by Joe Venuti, Reet Veet Reeves, and Matty Malneck. The show's announcers were James "Jimmy" WALLINGTON, Jay Stewart, Tiny Ruffner, Dan SEYMOUR, Marvin MILLER, Jack Bailey, Perry Ward, Alan REED, and Rod O'Connor. The program was directed by Tony Sanford, Rupert Lucas, Jack Roche, and Mitchell Benson and written by Ed GARDNER, Abe BURROWS, Larry Marks, George Faulkner, Lew Meltzer, Bill Manhoff, Raymond Ellis, Alan Kent, Ed Reynolds, Manny Sachs, Norman Paul, Dick Martin, and Vincent Bogert. The show's theme music was "When Irish Eyes Are Smiling." Bristol Meyers cigarettes, Shick razors, Ipana toothpaste, Eversharp razor blades, Sal Hapatica antacid, Vitalis hair dressing, Minit Rub liniment, Ingram's shave cream, Trushay deodorant, and Blatz beer were the program's sponsors.

In 1945, when *Duffy's Tavern* was at the height of its popularity, Paramount Pictures made a motion picture variety show featuring practically every star under contract to the studio at the time and starring Ed Gardner.

DUNNINGER THE MENTALIST

1943–1944	NBC Blue	Wed.	9 PM
1944–1945	(Off the air)		
1945–1945	NBC	Fri.	10 PM

"The Master Mentalist" Joseph Dunninger, who supposedly possessed amazing mind-reading abilities and had a half-hour radio program, read the minds of various people in the studio audience. Anyone who could prove that Dunninger had received any assistance during his performance was awarded $1,000. Featured on the program in between the mind-reading events were singers Bill Slater, Marilyn Day, and the Andy Love vocal group, with Mitchell Ayers and his orchestra. Announcers were Don Lowe and Roger Krupp. George Weist produced and directed the program, which was written by Marjorie D. Sloane. Sponsors included Lin-X, Kemstone oil, and Rinso cleanser.

DURANTE, JIMMY (1893–1980)

One of America's best-loved and most-admired entertainers, Jimmy Durante was born on the Lower East Side of New York City. He began his show-business career as a pianist at a Coney Island saloon in Brooklyn, eventually entered vaudeville, and appeared in Broadway's *Ziegfeld Follies of 1929* with his partners, Lou Clayton and Eddie Jackson. Later, Durante went solo and became enormously popular as a comedian and singer of novelty tunes. With his raspy voice, New York accent, and delightful malapropisms, Durante became a national entertainment institution onstage: in such films as *Cuban Love Song* (1932), *The Milkman* (1950), and *Jumbo* (1962); and on radio and television. Durante costarred on the *Durante and Moore* radio show with Garry Moore as Jimmy's straight man, and had his own very popular JIMMY DURANTE SHOW. Durante's songs "Ink-a-Dink-a-Doo" and "Umbriago," as well as his "Goodnight, Mrs. Calabash, wherever you are" closing statement, became his trademarks and kept audiences laughing for decades.

EASY ACES (AKA MR. AND MRS. ACE)

1931–1933	CBS	Mon-Wed-Fri.	10:15 AM
1933–1934	CBS	Mon.–Thurs.	1:30 PM
1934–1935	CBS	Mon.–Fri.	3:45 PM
1935–1936	NBC Red	Mon.–Wed.	7:30 PM
1936–1942	NBC Red	Tues.–Thurs.	7 PM
1942–1943	CBS	Wed.–Fri.	7:30 PM
1943–1945	CBS	Wed.	7:30 PM
1945–1948	(Off the air)		
1948–1949	CBS	Fri.	8:30 PM

Urbane, sophisticated Goodman ACE had a perfect comedic foil in his scatterbrained real-life wife, Jane, on his 15-minute and half-hour *Easy Aces* programs. Written by Ace to suit the unique vocal style and comedy talents of the pair, the *Easy Aces* series was always comically literate. He also wrote and even occasionally directed this series.

Goodman and Jane Ace on *Easy Aces* (NBC)

Heard in the supporting cast on various occasions were Mary Hunter, Ann Thomas, Peggy Allenby, James Van Dyke, Ethel Blume, Helene Dumas, and Paul Stewart. The show's theme song was "Manhattan Serenade." Ford BOND was usually the show's announcer. When the program was called *Mr. Ace and Jane*, Ken ROBERTS was its announcer. Lavoris mouthwash, Jad salts, Old English polish, and Anacin headache pills sponsored the show over the years.

ED SULLIVAN SHOW, THE

1932	CBS	Sun.	10 PM
1932–1941	(Off the air)		
1941	CBS	Sun.	6 PM
1941–1943	(Off the air)		
1943–1944	CBS	Mon.	7:15 PM
1944–1946	(Off the air)		
1946	ABC	Tues.	9 PM

Ed Sullivan had a variety program on the radio at various times, beginning as early as 1932. Heard in 15-, 30-, and 60-minute versions over the years, the show featured such guest stars as BURNS AND ALLEN, Eddie CANTOR, Jimmy DURANTE, Gladys Swarthout, Flo Ziegfeld, Jack PEARL, and others from films, the stage, and radio, and had a similar format to his later, famous TV show. Will Bradley's orchestra was featured, and sponsors were American safety razor, International Silver, Mennen shave cream, and Edgeworth pipe tobacco. There were numerous directors and writers of *The Ed Sullivan Show*, but they remained unrecorded.

ED WYNN SHOW, THE
See FIRE CHIEF, *The*.

EDDIE BRACKEN SHOW, THE

1945–1946	NBC	Sun.	8:30 PM
1946–1947	CBS	Sun.	9:30 PM

Movie actor-comedian Eddie Bracken, usually seen playing hard-luck small-town characters in films, brought his popular persona to CBS radio as the star of his own half-hour weekly *Eddie Bracken Show* in the mid-1940s. Bracken was ably supported by Ruth Perrot as Mrs. Pringle, Shirley BOOTH as Betty Mahoney, and William Demarest (who appeared with Bracken in the films *Hail the Conquering Hero* (1944) and *The Miracle of Morgan's Creek* (1944). Ann Rutherford and then Janet WALDO played Eddie's girlfriend on the show. John Wald was the announcer. *The Eddie Bracken Show* was produced by Mann Holmer and directed by Nat Wolff. Texaco oil sponsored the program.

EDDIE CANTOR SHOW, THE (AKA PABST BLUE RIBBON SHOW)

1931–1938	NBC Blue	(Various dates, times, and formats)
1938–1942	NBC Red	Wed.	9 PM
1942–1946	NBC	Wed.	9 PM
1946–1948	NBC	Thurs.	10:30 PM
1948–1949	NBC	Fri.	9 PM

The Mad Russian, Parkyakarkis, Rubinoff, and Mademoiselle Fifi were just a few of the amusing characters who were heard on the half-hour *Eddie Cantor Show.* Cantor had an energetic if somewhat frantic-sounding singing style and a fast-paced comedy delivery that proved perfect for the sound-oriented requirements of radio. But it was the many talented performers he assembled for his supporting cast that really made his show memorable: the hilarious, heavily accented Mad Russian played by actor Bert GORDON; the vocal performances of singers Dinah SHORE, Deanna Durbin, Margaret Whiting, Nora Martin, and Bobby Breen; comic actor Harry EINSTEIN as Greek food-stand operator Parkyakarkis; Lionel Stander and then Alan REED as the speaking voice of violinist David Rubinoff; Veola Vonn as the very funny, fluffy Mademoiselle Fifi; and the dithery banter of film comedienne Billie Burke. Announcers on the show included James "Jimmy" WALLINGTON and Harry VON ZELL. The program was directed by Abbott K. Spencer, Victor "Vick" Knight, and Manning Ostroff. The show's writers included Carroll Carroll, David Freedman, Bob Colwell, Phil Rapp, Barbara Hotchkiss, Matt Brooks, Ed Davis, Ed Belein, Izzy Elinson, Bob O'Brien, John Quillen, Everett Freeman, and Sam Harris. Eddie's theme song was "One Hour with You," and the show's many sponsors included Chase and Sanborn

coffee, Pebeco toothpaste, Texaco oil, Minit Rub liniment, Philip Morris cigarettes, Camel cigarettes, Sal Hepatica antacid, and Pabst beer.

EDDIE DUCHIN SHOW, THE (AKA THE LA SALLE SHOW; ARDEN HOUR OF CHARM; HOUR OF ROMANCE; and A DATE WITH DUCHIN)

1933–1934	NBC Blue	Tues., Thurs., Sat.	9:30 PM
1934–1936	(Off the air)		
1936–1937	NBC Red	Thurs.	4 PM
1937–1938	NBC Blue	Wed.	8 PM
1938–1939	NBC Red	Mon.	9:30 PM
1939–1940	Mutual	Thurs.	8 PM
1940–1946	(Off the air)		
1946–1947	NBC	Thurs.	9 PM
1947–1948	ABC	Mon., Wed., Fri.	4:30 PM

Pop-pianist Eddie Duchin had various 15-minute and half-hour shows on the air in the 1930s and 1940s, sponsored by Pepsodent toothpaste, Elizabeth Arden beauty products, La Salle automobiles, Cadillac cars, Pall Mall cigarettes, and Kreml dairy products. Ward Byron directed, Andre BARUCH announced, and Connee BOSWELL, Dinah SHORE, and Bing CROSBY guest-starred on the Duchin program. His numerous directors and writers went uncredited.

EDDY, NELSON (1901–1967)

Few singers enjoyed greater popularity than baritone Nelson Eddy. He was born in Providence, Rhode Island, and while studying to be a professional singer, he worked as a telephone operator, an artist, a reporter, and a newspaper copy editor. Eventually, he turned his attention to singing and began a successful stage, film, and radio career. On radio, Eddy starred on musical-variety programs such as *The* ELECTRIC HOUR, *Vicks Open House, Good News, The Ford Sunday Evening Hour, The* BELL TELEPHONE HOUR, and *The* CHASE AND SANBORN HOUR. In films, Eddy starred in musicals and operettas with soprano Jeanette MacDonald, the team becoming legends of the silver screen. Some of their films are *Naughty Marietta* (1935), *Rose Marie* (1936), *Maytime* (1937), *The Girl of the Golden West* (1938), *Sweethearts* (1938), *New Moon* (1940), *Bitter Sweet* (1940), and *I Married an Angel* (1942). Without MacDonald, Eddy appeared in *Rosalie* (1938), *The Chocolate Soldier* (1941), *The Phantom of the Opera* (1943), and *Knickerbocker Holiday* (1944) and was featured as the voice of Walt Disney's singing whale in *Make Mine Music* (1944). Songs associated with Eddy include "Sweethearts," "Indian Love Call," "Stouthearted Men," and "Song of a Vagabond." The singer contin-

Nelson Eddy (NBC)

ued to make personal appearances until shortly before his death.

EDGAR BERGEN–CHARLIE McCARTHY SHOW, THE

1949–1950	NBC	Sun.	8 PM
1950–1953	CBS	Sun.	8 PM
1953–1954	CBS	Sun.	9:30 PM

First featured on the CHASE AND SANBORN HOUR from 1937 through the early 1940s and then on his own half-hour *Edgar Bergen–Charlie McCarthy Show,* ventriloquist Edgar BERGEN used his impressive vocal talents to advantage as the voice of Charlie McCarthy, Mortimer Snerd, Effie Klinker, and others, each with a distinct character. McCarthy, a too-wise-for-his-age playboy, sported a tuxedo and top hat and wore a monocle in one eye. Snerd, the country bumpkin, was known for his slow speech and somewhat dim manner. Effie Klinker was a lovable old maid. These characters became the real stars of the Bergen show, even though everyone listening knew that without Bergen none of them would exist. Because of Bergen's talents, *The Chase and Sanborn Hour* and then *The Edgar Bergen–Charlie McCarthy Show* were among radio's top-rated programs.

For a while, Don AMECHE served as Bergen's maste of ceremonies. Also appearing on the program regu larly were Pat Patrick as Ersel Twang, a characte who spoke with a distinct whistle; Norman Field a Charlie's school principal; Barbara Jo ALLEN as th man-hungry Vera Vague; Richard Haydn as the priss Professor Lemuel Carp; and Eddie Mayhoff, Jin BACKUS, and Marsha Hunt. Many glamorous femal celebrities appeared on Bergen's show, most notably Rita Hayworth, Dorothy LAMOUR, Lana Turner, and Marilyn Monroe. Regular vocalists on the progran included Donald Dixon, Anita Ellis, and Anita Gor don. The show's orchestra was conducted by Ra Noble, who became a major character on the program Ken CARPENTER, Ben Alexander, Bill GOODWIN, and Bill Baldwin were Bergen's announcers. Earl Ebi wa the program's longtime director. Writers include Alan Smith, Robert Mosher, Zeno Klinker, Rolan MacLane, Royal Foster, Joe Connolly, Dick Mack Stanley Quinn, Joe Bigelow, and Carroll Carroll. Coca Cola soft drinks, Richard Hudnut shampoo, an Chase and Sanborn coffee sponsored the program.

EDWARDS, DOUGLAS (1917–1990)

Born in Ada, Oklahoma, Douglas Edwards decided when a teenager that he wanted to be a networ newsman. He made his broadcasting debut at the ag of 15 on WHET in Troy, Alabama. He continued t broadcast while studying at the University of Ala bama and then at the University of Georgia. Eventu ally, he caught the attention of CBS officials and joined their news staff in the 1940s. Edwards reported th news from overseas during World War II and wa the voice most listeners tuned in to hear for reportag of the Allied victory on V-E Day. Edwards later be came one of television's first major news anchorme and continued working at CBS-TV until the 1980s when he retired.

EDWARDS, JOAN (1918–1981)

Born in New York City, Joan Edwards became one o the pop-singing stars of YOUR HIT PARADE and wa also a frequent guest star on such 1940s–1950s music variety programs as *The* BOB BURNS SHOW, *The* BIN CROSBY SHOW, and DUFFY'S TAVERN. Edwards was als a regular vocalist on the *The* DANNY KAYE SHOW, *Th* CHESTERFIELD SUPPER CLUB, SHOW BOAT, *The* MAGI KEY, and *The Royal Gelatin Hour.*

EDWARDS, RALPH (1913–   )

Ralph Edwards, born in Merino, Colorado, was a bus CBS staff announcer in the 1930s and 1940s on such shows as *The* GUMPS, AGAINST THE STORM, LIFE CAI BE BEAUTIFUL, *The* ORIGINAL AMATEUR HOUR, VIC AN SADE, and *Headlines and Bylines.* His conversationa low-key approach to delivering commercial messages made him extremely popular among listeners. Edwards later produced and hosted TRUTH OR CONSEQUENCES on radio and then on television, as well as producing other TV shows such as "Place the Face" (1953) and "It Could Be You" (1962), and the "This Is Your Life" (1952) series, which he also hosted.

EDWARDS, SAM (1928–)

Sam Edwards began his busy acting career in the 1930s, singing and playing children's parts on radio station WOAI in San Antonio, Texas, where he was born. His family moved to California and before long he was heard on a network program his parents developed for NBC called *The Adventures of Sonny and Buddy*. Subsequently Edwards played on FATHER KNOWS BEST, *The* GUIDING LIGHT, GUNSMOKE, HAWTHORNE HOUSE and ONE MAN'S FAMILY. On the MEET CORLISS ARCHER situation-comedy series, he was Corliss's boyfriend, Dexter Franklin, and he appeared in such films as *Suppose They Gave a War and Nobody Came* (1971) and *Scandalous John* (1972). The actor's television credits include "The Burns and Allen Show," "The Jack Benny Show," and "The Twilight Zone."

EGLESTON, CHARLES (1884–1958)

Charles Egleston was born in Civington, Kentucky, and was a stage actor before he began acting on radio in 1929. His most memorable radio role was Shuffle Shober on the MA PERKINS daytime serial. Shuffle was Ma's best friend and longtime partner at her lumberyard. The actor played Humphrey Fuller on JUST PLAIN BILL and was also featured on UNCLE EZRA'S RADIO STATION, FIRST NIGHTER, and GATEWAY TO HOLLYWOOD.

EINSTEIN, HARRY (1904–1958)

Born in Boston, Massachusetts, Harry Einstein played the Greek food-stand owner Parkyakarkis on the EDDIE CANTOR SHOW from 1933 until 1945. In 1936, Einstein legally changed his name to Parkyakarkis, the character who became so popular that Einstein was given a radio show of his own, MEET ME AT PARKY'S. It ran for one season. In addition to *The Eddie Cantor Show*, Einstein was also regularly heard on *The* JIMMY DURANTE SHOW and *The* AL JOLSON SHOW.

ELECTRIC HOUR, THE

| 1944–1946 | CBS | Wed. | 10:30 PM |
| | | Sun. | 4:40 PM |

Baritone Nelson EDDY starred on this half-hour music-variety show, sponsored by the Electric Companies of America. Guest stars such as Risë Stevens, Gladys Swarthout, and Eileen Farrell appeared with Eddy: the orchestra which played mainly classical and semi-classical pieces, was conducted by Robert Ambruster. The show's announcer was Frank Graham.

ELLEN, MINETTA (1875–1965)

Actress Minetta Ellen was born in Cleveland, Ohio, and began her acting career onstage. She was best known for playing "Mother" Fanny Barbour on ONE MAN'S FAMILY, which she did for the entire run of the program (1932–1955). Minetta became so identified with that role that she had to limit her radio acting to appearing on just that one program.

ELLEN RANDOLPH (AKA THE STORY OF ELLEN RANDOLPH)

| 1939–1940 | NBC Red | Mon.–Fri. | 1:15 PM |
| 1940–1941 | NBC Red | Mon.–Fri. | 10:30 AM |

The Randolphs—Ellen, George, and Bobby—were the central characters on this 15-minute daytime drama series: Elsie Hitz and then Gertrude Warner played Ellen; John McGovern and then Ted Jewett played George; Jack "Jackie" Jordan was Bobby. Also heard on this series about a young married couple and their son were Macdonald CAREY, Helene Dumas, Jay Meredith, Coleen Ward, Bernard Lenrow, Florida Friebus, Ken Daigneau, John MCINTIRE, Bartlett "Bart" Robinson, Maurice Franklin, George Wallach, Eloise Ellis, and Effie Palmer. Announcers were Ford BOND and Marvin MILLER. Carlo DEANGELO, Jack Hurdle, and Harvey Lowell directed, and Margaret Sangster was its chief writer. Super Suds detergent and Cashmere Bouquet soap sponsored the series.

ELLERY QUEEN, THE ADVENTURES OF

See ADVENTURES OF ELLERY QUEEN, THE.

ELLIOT, WIN (1915–)

Radio announcer, host, master of ceremonies, and sportscaster, Win Elliot was born in Chelsea, Massachusetts. Entering radio shortly after he graduated from the University of Michigan, he hosted the QUICK AS A FLASH mystery-quiz program, the *County Fair* audience-participation show, *Magazine of the Air*, ONE MAN'S FAMILY, and JUVENILE JURY. Elliot also hosted "On Your Account" (1954), "To Tell the Truth" (1956), and "The Fireside Theater" (1949) on television.

ELSTNER, ANNE (1899–1981)

Born in Lake Charles, Louisiana, actress Anne Elstner became well known to radio listeners as the title character on the STELLA DALLAS daytime drama series. Elstner played Stella for the show's entire eighteen-year run. In addition to *Stella Dallas*, the actress was featured on *The* GIBSON FAMILY, *Brenda Curtis, Trouble House,* and *Wilderness Road.* When *Stella Dallas* departed the airwaves, Elstner bought and operated a popular restaurant in New Hope, New Jersey, until shortly before her death.

EMILY POST

1930–1931	CBS	Tues., Thurs.	10:15 AM
1931–1932	NBC Blue	Mon.	4 PM
1932–1933	NBC Blue	Tues., Thurs.	10:45 AM
1933–1934	(Off the air)		
1934	NBC Blue	Sun.	12 PM
1934–1936	(Off the air)		
1936–1937	NBC Blue	Mon.	4:30 PM
1937–1938	CBS	Tues., Thurs.	10:30 AM
1938–1939	NBC Red	Tues.	7:45 PM

Emily Post's etiquette book led to a regular 15-minute radio program in the early 1930s, on which she discussed such topics as how to set a proper table, wedding customs, and table behavior. Ken ROBERTS announced the show. Camay soap, DuPont chemicals, and the Florida Citrus Board sponsored it.

ENNIS, SKINNAY (1907–1963)

Bandleader Skinnay Ennis was born in North Carolina. While a student at the University of North Carolina, he roomed with musician Hal Kemp. The two young men joined the Kay KYSER band when they graduated from college, and Ennis sang many of the band's vocals. In 1937, Ennis formed his own band and became a major personality—leading the orchestras, as well as singing—on such radio programs as *The* ABBOTT AND COSTELLO SHOW and *The* BOB HOPE SHOW.

ENO CRIME CLUB, THE (AKA CRIME CLUES)

1931	CBS	Sat. Mon.–Fri.	6:45 PM
1932	CBS	Tues., Wed.	9:30 PM
1932–1933	(Off the air)		
1933–1934	NBC Blue	Tues.–Wed.	8 PM
1934–1936	NBC Blue	Tues.	8 PM

One of radio's earliest mystery anthology programs, *The Eno Crime Club* half-hour show starred Edward Reese and then Clyde North as Spencer Dean, the crime-solving crook hunter, and Jack McBride and Helen Choate as Dan Cassidy and Jane Elliott, his assistants. Dean founded a club devoted to solving crimes that the law couldn't solve.

Also appearing regularly on the show were Adele RONSON, Gloria Holden, Linda Carlon-Reid, Arline Blackburn, Ralph Sumpter, Georgia Backus, Ray COLLINS, Helene Dumas, Ruth Yorke, and before his film career, Brian Donlevy. Carlo DEANGELO directed, and Stewart Sterling and Albert G. Miller wrote the scripts for the series. The show was sponsored by Lever Brothers products.

ERIC, ELSPETH (c1918–   )

Born in Chicago, Illinois, Elspeth Eric was known on radio for her portrayals of gangsters' girlfriends, adventuresses, femme fatales, and occasionally love-blind victims on such programs as GANGBUSTERS, *The Molle Mystery Theater,* THIS IS YOUR FBI, INNER SANCTUM MYSTERIES, and THE FBI IN PEACE AND WAR. In addition to these shows, Eric played numerous "other women," best friends, villainesses, and troubled housewives on the popular daytime dramas THIS IS NORA DRAKE, BIG SISTER, CENTRAL CITY, FRONT PAGE FARRELL, JOYCE JORDAN, GIRL INTERN, *The Life and Loves of Dr. Susan,* ROSEMARY, *The* SECOND MRS. BURTON, VALIANT LADY, and YOUNG DR. MALONE. She was a regular on STUDIO ONE and in the repertory cast of the mystery-quiz show QUICK AS A FLASH. In the 1970s, Eric wrote several scripts for Himan Brown's CBS MYSTERY THEATER, on which she occasionally acted. In 1968, Eric was featured on the "Secret Storm" daytime TV series. Few radio actresses utilized vocal sound effects more expertly than Eric: in her many performances, she gasped, groaned, sighed, and purred to make listeners identify with the character's reactions.

Elspeth Eric (CBS/Photofest)

ERICKSON, LOUISE (1928–   )

One of several young radio ingenues in the 1940s and 1950s, actress Louise Erickson, who was born in Oakland, California, played the title role on *A DATE WITH JUDY*. Before starring in the situation-comedy series, Erickson had played Judy's best friend, Mitzi. She was also featured as Marjorie, Gildersleeve's niece, on *The GREAT GILDERSLEEVE*, until she was replaced due to a scheduling conflict with *A Date with Judy*. Erickson was also regularly featured on the *Dramas of Youth* series. The actress retired from show business when she was in her early twenties and settled down to raise a family.

ESCAPE

1947–1948	CBS	Wed.	10:30 PM
1948	CBS	Sat.	11:30 AM
1948–1949	CBS	Sat.	10:30 PM
1949–1950	CBS	Tues.	9:30 PM
1950	CBS	Sun.	3 PM
1950–1951	CBS	Fri.	10 PM
1951	CBS	Sun.	3 PM
1951	CBS	Wed.	9 PM
1951–1952	(Off the air)		
1952–1953	CBS	Sun.	9:30 PM
1953–1954	CBS	Sat.	10 PM

Escape usually presented protagonists in very difficult, almost impossible to overcome, situations. One famous story, "Three Skeleton Key," had three men trapped in a lighthouse as millions of rats from a deserted ghost ship covered the place, trying to get in as they searched for food. Another, "The Abominable Snowman," had its antagonist encounter a yeti in the Himalayas. William CONRAD and Paul Frees narrated the show, and Conrad often acted in many of the stories on the series. Other regulars were Luis VAN ROOTEN, Jay Novello, Harry Morgan, Jack WEBB, Sam EDWARDS, Virginia GREGG, Georgia Ellis, Parley BAER, Ben WRIGHT, Lawrence Dobkin, Elliott Reid, John Dehner, Vivi Janis, Edgar Barrier, Berry Kroeger, Byron Kane, Wilms Herbert, Frank LOVEJOY, Berry Kroeger, Jack Kruschen, and Barton YARBOROUGH. The program was produced and directed by William N. ROBSON and Norman Macdonnell, who were largely responsible for its success. The show's memorable theme music was "A Night on Bald Mountain" by Mussorgsky. The stories for the series were written by freelance writers. Richfield oil and Ford automobiles were the program's sponsors.

ETERNAL LIGHT, THE

1942–present	(Syndicated series. Various times and stations)

On the air continuously for more than forty-five years, the half-hour weekly *Eternal Light* program is the longest-running dramatic program on radio. This religious drama series was first heard on WJZ in New York and was produced by the Federation of Jewish Philanthropies. It has presented Bible stories, inspirational contemporary dramas, and even humorous comedies that have an inspirational message. Many notable radio actors have been heard on the series over the years, including Alexander SCOURBY, Adelaide Klein, Roger DeKoven, Edgar Stehli, Ronald LISS, Bernard Lenrow, and Norman Rose. The series was directed by Frank Papp and Anton M. Leader for many years and written by Morton Eishengrad, Virginia Mazer, and Joe Mindel.

ETHEL AND ALBERT (AKA THE PRIVATE LIVES OF ETHEL AND ALBERT)

1944–1945	ABC Blue	Mon.–Fri.	6:15 PM
1945–1946	ABC Blue	Mon.–Fri.	2:15 PM
1946–1947	ABC	Mon.–Fri.	2:15 PM
1947–1948	(Off the air)		
1948–1949	ABC	Mon.–Fri.	4:30 PM
1949–1950	ABC	Mon.	8 PM

Peg LYNCH was the talented woman who created, wrote, and starred as Ethel on this high-quality program. The half-hour stories centered around everyday events in the lives of a typical American married couple living in a fictitious small town called Sandy

Peg Lynch and Alan Bunce on *Ethel and Albert* (ABC/ Courtesy of Miss Lynch)

Harbor. It was unusual to hear anyone but the two major characters, Ethel and Albert, on the program because it was basically a two-person show. When the series first went on the air, actor Richard WIDMARK played the part of Albert opposite Miss Lynch. Widmark left the series for film stardom and was replaced by Alan BUNCE, who played Albert for the next twenty years on radio and television: "Ethel and Albert" was a featured segment on the Kate SMITH TV-variety show and was a weekly half-hour situation-comedy series in the mid-1950s. All told, the couple were on television for more than ten years. Lynch and Bunce assumed similar roles on radio in the late 1950s on *The* COUPLE NEXT DOOR. Child-impersonator Madeleine Pierce played the part of Ethel and Albert's baby, Susy. Julie Stevens, Raymond Edward JOHNSON, Leon JANNEY, Arnold STANG, and Don MCLAUGLIN occasionally played supporting roles. Over the years, *Ethel and Albert* was directed by Bob Cotton, William D. Hamilton, and others. Announcers on the program included George Ansbro, Fred Cole, Don Lowe, Cy Harrice, Glenn Riggs, and Herb Sheldon. The program's familiar theme songs were "Love Nest" and "Side by Side." The show was sustained by ABC for most of the years it was on the air.

ETHEL BARRYMORE THEATER, THE
See FAMOUS ACTOR'S GUILD, THE.

ETTING, RUTH (1897–1978)
Blues singer Ruth Etting, who was born in David City, Nebraska, was one of America's most famous vocalists of the 1920s and 1930s. Etting attended the Chicago Academy of Fine Arts as a young woman; when she was graduated, she starred on Broadway in *The Ziegfeld Follies* (1926), *Whoopie* (1928), and *Simple Simon* (1930) before becoming the star of the MUSIC THAT SATISFIES radio series in the early 1930s. On this program, Etting introduced several of her most popular song hits, including "Ten Cents a Dance," "Love Me or Leave Me," and "Mean to Me." In 1955, the singer was the subject of a motion-picture biography, *Love Me or Leave Me*, starring Doris Day as Ruth and James Cagney as her abusive gangster boyfriend-husband, Moe "The Gimp" Snyder.

See also RUTH ETTING SHOW, THE.

EVELYN AND HER MAGIC VIOLIN
See KLEIN, EVELYN KAYE.

EVELYN WINTERS (AKA THE STRANGE ROMANCE OF EVELYN WINTERS)

1944–1948	CBS	Mon.–Fri.	10:30 AM
1948–1949	CBS	Mon.–Fri.	2:45 PM
1949–1951	(Off the air)		
1951–1952	ABC	Mon.–Fri.	3:45 PM

The CBS network launched several new 15-minute serial dramas in the mid-1940s, but few of them became long-running hits. One of these was *Evelyn Winters*. Evelyn's "strange" romance was never very clearly defined, but it seemed to have something to do with a character named George Bennett, who could not forget his former wife long enough to marry Evelyn. Actress Toni Darnay starred as Evelyn; Karl WEBER and then Martin Blaine played George. Other actors who played regular supporting roles on this series were Kate McComb, Stacy Harris, Flora Campbell, Ralph Bell, James Lipton, Linda Carlon-Reid, Mary Mason, Vinton Hayworth, and John Moore. Larry Elliott was the show's announcer. The show was directed by Ernest Ricca and produced by Frank and Anne HUMMERT. It was written by Peggy Blake and H. L. Algyir. Sweetheart soap, Blu White bleach, and Philip Morris cigarettes sponsored the program.

EVEREADY HOUR, THE

| 1926–1930 | NBC Red | Tues. | 9 PM |

Originally a local half-hour program heard on WEAF in New York in 1923, *The Eveready Hour* made its network debut on NBC three years later. The first major variety show heard on radio, it featured such celebrated performers of the day as humorist Will ROGERS; comedians Weber and Fields and Eddie CANTOR; actor John Drew; cellist Pablo Casals; composer-pianist George Gershwin; film director D. W. Griffith; Beatrice Herford; the Two Black Crows; actors Richard Dix, Julia Marlowe, and Lionel Arwell; singer Belle Baker; and the Flonzaley String Quartet. Andre BARUCH, among others, was the show's announcer. Eveready batteries sponsored the series.

FABULOUS DR. TWEEDY
See FRANK MORGAN SHOW, *The*.

FACES OF LIFE
See RADIO PLAYHOUSE, *The*.

FACT A DAY ABOUT CANADA, A
Every day in the 1930s, usually after the news and weather had been presented, the CANADIAN BROADCASTING CORPORATION offered one feature that gave Canadian citizens a historical or sociological fact about their country. This was a popular feature on CBC for many years and is especially well remembered by Candians who were in school during the 1930s. Teachers often had their students write down the fact that was given and handed it in as the next day's homework assignment.

FADIMAN, CLIFTON (1904–   )
Clifton Fadiman was born in Brooklyn, New York. A respected educator, book critic, and newspaper columnist, Fadiman became one of radio's most celebrated moderators of information-oriented programs. Fadiman was first heard in 1924 when he reviewed books for a local station in New York City. It was, however, on the INFORMATION PLEASE! program, which he hosted from 1938 until 1948, that he became best known to radio listeners. Fadiman's calm, intelligent handling of his regular panelists gained the respect of the general public and radio critics alike. Fadiman also moderated *The* QUIZ KIDS whenever the regular host of that show, Joe Kelly, was unavailable. He did the same on *This Is Show Business, Mathematics* and *Alumni Fun*. In the 1950s, Fadiman hosted TV's

"Information Please!" and was a guest panelist on "I've Got a Secret" and "Masquerade Party." Fadiman also contributed to *Holiday* and *The New Yorker* magazines and is an editorial adviser for Simon & Shuster publishers.

FALCON, THE

1943	NBC Blue	Sat.	7 PM
		Wed.	7 PM
1943–1945	(Off the air)		
1945–1947	Mutual	Tues.	8:30 PM
1947–1948	Mutual	Mon.	8 PM
1948–1950	Mutual	Sun.	7 PM
1950–1952	NBC	Sun.	4 PM
1952–1954	Mutual	Mon.	8 PM

Mike Waring, aka *The Falcon*, was a crime-fighting private detective who battled the forces of evil with an occasional assist from two friends, Nancy and Renee. Typical *Falcon* plots had Waring solving the murder of a side-show freak; another the murder of a well-known actress. Featured actors included James MEIGHAN, Les DAMON, Berry Kroeger, Les TREMAYNE, and George Petrie in the title role; Joan BANKS and Ethel Everett played Waring's girlfriends Nancy and Renee, respectively. Also heard on the half-hour weekly series were Joan Alexander, Robert DRYDEN, and Mandel KRAMER. Ed HERLIHY and Russ Dunbar were the program's announcers. Bernard Schubert, Jr., produced the show, and Carlo DEANGELO, Stuart Buchanan, and Richard Lewis directed the series at various times. Jay Bennett wrote the show for several seasons. Sponsors included Gem razors and razor blades, Anahist nasal decongestant, Kraft salad oil, Miracle Whip salad dressing, and General Mills flour.

FALKENBERG, JINX (EUGENIA FALKENBURG: 1919–)

Several husband-and-wife daytime talk shows were very popular on radio in the forties and fifties. Among these were *Dorothy and Dick, The Fitzgeralds,* and the *Tex and Jinx Show,* starring Tex McCrary and model–actress Jinx Falkenberg. Falkenberg was born in Barcelona, Spain, where her U. S.-born father worked for the American Westinghouse Company. When Jinx was two-and-a-half years old, her father was transferred to Chile and then to Brazil, where she grew up. A tennis star in Brazil and then a swimming champion in Chile in her early teens, Jinx moved with her family to California when she was sixteen years old.

Her brunette good looks and statuesque figure shortly after led to a modeling contract with the John Robert Powers modeling agency. One of the world's most-photographed print models, Jinx was given a featured role in the 1941 Broadway musical *Hold On to Your Hats,* starring Al JOLSON and Martha Raye. She also appeared in such movies as *Latins from Manhattan* (1942), *Sing for Your Supper* (1942), *Tahiti Nights* (1944), and *Talk about a Lady* (1946).

In the late forties, Jinx and her husband, McCrary, began to host their popular early-morning radio talk show. The *Tex and Jinx Show* was known for its wide variety of celebrated guests from former first lady Eleanor ROOSEVELT to film comedian Groucho MARX. Performers, politicians, business leaders, and scientists were interviewed live on the daily show. In the mid-fifties, Tex and Jinx took their show to television; it was one of the first TV talk shows. Tex McCrary's Southern drawl, gentlemanly manners, and manly good looks, coupled with Jinx's beauty, charm, and intelligence, made the couple especially appealing to TV viewers and their TV show became as successful as their radio program, remaining on the air for many years. From the mid-1950s to the early 1960s, Jinx also made frequent guest appearances on TV panel shows "I've Got a Secret" and "Masquerade Party," but she gradually stepped out of the public spotlight and, with her husband, pursued private endeavors.

FAMILY HOUR, THE

See PRUDENTIAL FAMILY HOUR, *The.*

FAMILY THEATER

1947	Mutual	Fri., Sun.	10:30 PM
1947–1948	Mutual	Thurs.	10:30 PM
1948–1949	Mutual	Sat.	3:30 PM
1949–1951	Mutual	Wed.	9:30 PM
1951–1953	Mutual	Thurs.	9:05 PM
		Wed.	9 PM
1954	Mutual	Fri.	9:30 PM
1954–1956	(Off the air)		
1956	Mutual	Wed.	9:30 PM

Father Patrick Peyton, a Roman Catholic priest, was the host of this weekly half-hour dramatic anthology that presented wholesome stories suitable for the entire family. The major character usually overcame a moral or religious dilemma. Numerous Hollywood stars donated their services to this show: Bing CROSBY, Loretta Young, Bob HOPE, Gary Cooper, Irene Dunne, Spencer Tracy, Ethel BARRYMORE, Ray Milland, Macdonald CAREY, and Maureen O'Sullivan. Tony La Farra was the announcer. The sustained show was directed, at different times, by Dave Young, Mel Williamson, John Kelley, and Robert O'Sullivan. It was written by John Kelly and Robert O'Sullivan.

FAMOUS ACTOR'S GUILD (AKA ETHEL BARRYMORE THEATER)

| 1936–1937 | NBC Blue | Wed. | 8:30 PM |
| 1937–1941 | CBS | Tues. | 7:30 PM |

This weekly radio-drama series featured Ethel Barrymore and then Helen MENKEN as weekly hostesses. Other notables of the stage also hosted. The program presented half-hour original dramas and comedies written especially for radio, one of which was the SECOND HUSBAND serial-drama segment of the program. Ward Byron was the announcer. The series was sponsored by Bayer aspirin.

FAMOUS JURY TRIALS

1936–1937	Mutual	Mon.	10 PM
1937–1940	Mutual	Wed.	10 PM
1940–1944	NBC Blue	Mon.	10 PM
1944–1945	NBC Blue	Fri.	9 PM
1945–1946	NBC Blue	Sat.	8:30 PM
1946–1948	ABC	Sat.	8:30 PM
1948–1949	ABC	Sat.	7:30 PM

This long-running half-hour radio crime series presented a different trial, often of murderers, weekly; home listeners were invited to pretend they were on the jury. For many years, Maurice Franklin played the judge, and Roger DeKoven and DeWitt McBride narrated the stories. Also heard regularly were True Boardman, Raymond Edward JOHNSON, Alice FROST, Joe DESANTIS, Mandel KRAMER, Ted DeCorsia, Frank READICK, Byron Kane, Elspeth ERIC, and John Paul King. Peter Grant, Roger Krupp, and Hugh James were the announcers. The program's directors included Wylie Adams, Robert Nolan, Clark Andrews, Carl Eastman, and Charles Powers; for several seasons Milton J. Kramer wrote the show. Sponsors included Mennen shave cream, O'Henry candy bar, and General Mills flour.

FAT MAN, THE

| 1946–1950 | ABC | Fri. | 8:30 PM |
| 1950–1951 | ABC | Wed. | 8:30 PM |

The opening of this detective-mystery program became almost as famous as the show itself: "There he goes into the drugstore. He steps on the scale. Weight: 237 pounds! Fortune: Danger!!" J. Scott Smart played private detective Brad Runyon, whose speciality was solving murder cases with his formidable brain instead of his bulky body; this title character was loosely based on a character created by mystery writer Dashiell Hammett. Ed BEGLEY played Police Sergeant O'Hara, and Mary Patton played Brad's friend, Lila North. Actors regularly heard in supporting roles were Robert DRYDEN, Dan Ocko, Rolly Bester, and Margot Stevenson. Charles Irving announced the program, and Clark Andrews and Charles Powers directed. The music director was Bernard Green, and the scriptwriters were Robert Sloane and Dan Shuffman. Pepto-Bismol antacid, Unguentine ointment, and Camel cigarettes sponsored the program.

FATHER KNOWS BEST

1949–1951	NBC	Thurs.	8:30 PM
1951–1952	NBC	Thurs.	8 PM
1952–1954	NBC	Thurs.	8:30 PM

Before it became one of television's favorite family-oriented half-hour situation-comedy series, *Father Knows Best* was a long-running hit on NBC radio. As on TV in the mid-1950s, movie actor Robert Young starred. June Whitley played his radio wife, Margaret. Rhoda Williams, Ted Donaldson, and Norma Jean Nilsson played the Anderson children, Betty, Bud, and Kathy, respectively. Each week's domestic crisis was usually solved by the wise father, Jim Anderson, who was always fair and practical. Eleanor Audley and Herb Vigran played the Andersons' next-door neighbors, Elizabeth and Hector Smith; Sam EDWARD was the Smiths' son, Billy. Announcers were Marvin MILLER and Bill Forman. *Father Knows Best* was directed for radio by Ken Burton, Fran Van Hartenfeldt, and Murray Bolen and was written by Ed James. The show's sponsors were Maxwell House coffee, Post Toasties cereal and Postum instant coffee.

FAYE, ALICE (ALICE LEPPERT: 1912–   )

Motion-picture musical-comedy actress Alice Faye was born in New York City. She was a cabaret and vaudeville singer and dancer before she became a major movie star in such films as *George White's Scandals* (1934), *In Old Chicago* (1938), *Alexander's Ragtime Band* (19380, *Lillian Russell* (1940), *Fallen Angel* (1945), and *State Fair* (1961). Faye costarred with her husband, Phil Harris, on the PHIL HARRIS–ALICE FAYE SHOW—originally called *The* FITCH BANDWAGON—on radio and was a regular guest star on the JACK BENNY SHOW when Harris was a featured player on that show. In 1962, Faye retired from show business, but in 1974 she came out of retirement to star on Broadway in the musical comedy *Good News*. In recent years, Faye has toured the country lecturing about good health practices.

FBI IN PEACE AND WAR, THE

1944–1945	CBS	Sat.	8:30 PM
1945–1947	CBS	Thurs.	8:30 PM
1947–1948	CBS	Fri.	9:30 PM
1948–1952	CBS	Thurs.	8 PM
1952–1955	CBS	Wed.	8 PM
1955–1956	CBS	Wed.	8:30 PM
1956–1958	CBS	Sat.	6:05 PM

The Crime and adventure series *The FBI in Peace and War* presented stories "from the files of the Federal Bureau of Investigation" and was based on a book of the same title by Frederick L. Collins; however, it was not actually endorsed or approved by the FBI. The program featured actor Martin Blaine and then Jack Arthur as FBI Field Agent Shepherd, who narrated each week's story. Most of radio's busiest actors were heard on this program at various times, including Robert DRYDEN, Jackson BECK, Edith Arnold, Elspeth ERIC, Walter GREAZA, Frank READICK, Joseph DESANTIS, William J. Smith, Ed BEGLEY, Rosemary RICE, Grant Richards, Harold Huber, George Petrie, Charita Bauer, Ralph Bell, and John M. James. The show's announcers were Warren Sweeney, Andre BARUCH, and Len Sterling. It was directed by Betty Manderville and Max Marcin, and the music director was Vladamir Selinsky. The show's theme music was from the march in Prokofiev's *The Love of Three Oranges*. Sponsors were Lava soap, Wrigley's gum, Lucky Strike cigarettes, Nescafé, Brylcreem, Wildroot Cream Oil, and Wheaties cereal.

FELTON, VERNA (1890–1966)

Character-actress Verna Felton was born in Salinas, California. From the 1930s to the 1950s it was almost impossible to listen to the radio without hearing Felton's mature and versatile voice on one program or another. In show business since she was nine years old, when she played Little Lord Fauntleroy in a touring stage production, Felton was a regular on *The* JACK BENNY SHOW as Dennis Day's mother, A DAY IN THE LIFE OF DENNIS DAY, the LUX RADIO THEATER (in which she literally played hundreds of different roles), *The* JUDY CANOVA SHOW as Aunt Aggie, *The Ray Bolger Show*, *The* RED SKELTON SHOW as Junior's grandmother, *The* TOMMY RIGGS AND BETTY LOU SHOW as Mrs. McIntyre, *The* SEALTEST VILLAGE STORE as Blossom Blimp,

Verna Felton (ABC)

The screen guild players, *Hollywood Playhouse,* death valley days, *Texaco Town,* those we love, big town, burns and allen, and *The* adventures of philip marlowe, detective. Felton is perhaps best remembered as Spring Byington's friend, Hilda, on the *December Bride* radio and TV situation-comedy series in the mid-1950s. Felton was also a cartoon voice actress: many recognize her voice as that of the Fairy Godmother in Walt Disney's *Cinderella* (1950) (in which she sings "Bibbity-Bobbity-Boo"), as Aunt Sarah in *Lady and the Tramp* (1955), and as the Elephant in Disney's *The Jungle Book* (her last role, in 1967).

FENNELLY, PARKER (1892–1988)
Actor Parker Fennelly was born in Northeast Harbor, Maine. He became known to radio fans as Titus Moody, the hayseed New England farmer and inhabitant of Allen's Alley on the fred allen show, and to television commercial viewers as the longtime New England farm spokesman for Pepperidge Farm products. Fennelly had an active radio career, and in addition to his many years on *The Fred Allen Show,* he was regularly heard on *The* american school of the air; *Four Corners, U. S. A.* as Jonah Crowell; *Editor's Daughter* as Henry Foster; *Gibbs and Finney; General Delivery* as Gibbs; *Ma and Pa* as Pa; *Mother and Dad* as

Dad; *The Simpson Boys of Sprucehead Bay* as one of the Simpson boys; snow village as Dan'l Dickey; *The Stebbins Boys* as Esly; *Uncle Abe and David* as Uncle Abe; and on daytime serial dramas valiant lady, *Wilderness Road, Brenda Curtis,* ellen randolph, and your family and mine. Fennelly's many stage appearances include such Broadway productions as *Mr. Pitts* (1924) and such regional theater productions as *Our Town* (1950) and *Carousel* (1954). Fennelly acted in the motion picture *The Russians Are Coming, the Russians Are Coming* (1966), in which he reprised his hayseed New England farmer role.

FIBBER MCGEE AND MOLLY

1935	NBC Blue	Tues.	10 PM
1935–1936	NBC Blue	Mon.	8 PM
1936–1937	NBC Red	Mon.	9 PM
1937–1942	NBC Red	Tues.	9:30 PM
1942–1956	NBC	Tues.	9:30 PM

For more than twenty-one years, 79 Wistful Vista was the home address of radio's most famous married couple—lovable windbag Fibber McGee and his ever-loving and ever-patient wife, Molly. Fibber and Molly were played by Jim and Marian jordan, ex-vaudevillians who, in the mid-1930s, originally played similar characters on *The* breakfast club and *Smackouts.* Fibber, Molly, and their amusing friends and neighbors—Mayor La Trivia, Throckmorton P. Gildersleeve, Doc Gamble, the Old Timer, Teeny, Beulah, and Wallace Wimple—were among the beloved characters on the program. The running jokes on the show—the McGees' overcrowded hall closet, Fibber's numerous get-rich-quick schemes, and the friendly arguments Fibber always had first with Gildersleeve and then with Doc Gamble—are fond memories for thousands of listeners.

The cast of *Fibber McGee and Molly* was one of the most versatile on radio: Jim Jordan as both Fibber and Mort Toops; Marian Jordan as Molly, Sis, Teeny, Geraldine, Old Lady Wheedledeck, Mrs. Wearybottom, and Lady Vere-de-vere; Bill thompson as henpecked husband Wallace Wimple, the Old Timer (originated by Cliff arquette), Horatio K. Boomer (who sounded like W. C. Fields), Vodka, Nick Depopolous, and Uncle Dennis; Hal peary as next-door neighbor Throckmorton P. Gildersleeve; and Marlin hurt as Beulah, the maid. (The last two characters became so popular that they eventually had shows of their own, *The* great gildersleeve *and* beulah.) Gale gordon played Mayor La Trivia; Shirley mitchell, Alice Darling (a defense-plant worker rooming at the McGees' house during World War II); and Bea benaderet, Mrs. Carstairs. Also heard at various times on this half-hour program were Arthur Q. bryant as Doc Gamble, Gene Carroll as Lena the maid, and Isabel RANDOLPH as Mrs. Uppington; and Peggy Knudson, ZaSu Pitts, Lenore Kingstone, Bud Stephen, Elvia ALLMAN, Ransom SHERMAN, and Jess Kirkpatrick in supporting roles. The King's Men, a singing quartet, offered musical interludes; Rico Marchiello, Ted WEEMS, and Billy Mills led the orchestra. Clark Dennis and Harlow WILCOX, the show's longtime announcer, introduced the show. Don Quinn, later with Phil Leslie, wrote the *Fibber McGee and Molly Show* scripts, as he had for Jim and Marian Jordan's *Smackouts* program. Frank Pittman was the director. *Fibber McGee and Molly*'s sponsor for many years was the Johnson's Wax. Pet milk and the R. J. Reynolds Tobacco Company also sponsored the show.

FIDLER, JIMMIE (1899–1988)

Hollywood newspaper and magazine gossip columnist Jimmie Fidler was born in Brookhaven, Massachusetts. His 1930s–1940s radio show *Jimmy Fidler's Hollywood* offered the public news about their movie star favorites. The program, a five-minute spot sandwiched between news and regular evening programming, was on and off the air for more than sixteen years. Fidler was considered the most acerbic of the Hollywood gossip columnists: one of his trademarks was a four-bell rating system for judging films. He also wrote "open letters" to movie stars who were having scandalous extramarital affairs, publicly criticizing them for their behavior. Fidler also wrote a syndicated newspaper column until shortly before he died.

FIELDS, GRACIE

See GRACIE FIELDS SHOW, *The.*

FILLBRANDT, LAURETTE (1915–   )

Born in Zanesville, Ohio, Laurette Fillbrandt debuted on radio in 1934 and had leading roles on such Chicago-based series as *The* AFFAIRS OF ANTHONY in two roles, Jane Daly and Susan; BACHELOR'S CHILDREN, in which she played Ruth Ann Graham; and LI'L ABNER, as Daisy Mae. Fillbrandt was also prominently featured on such programs as *The* CHICAGO THEATER OF THE AIR, GIRL ALONE, *The* GUIDING LIGHT, DAN HARDING'S WIFE, LONE JOURNEY, MA PERKINS, MIDSTREAM, *The* WOMAN IN WHITE, ONE MAN'S FAMILY, SILVER EAGLE, MOUNTIE, *A* TALE OF TODAY, and TODAY'S CHILDREN. Fillbrandt was an NBC radio staff actress for several years before becoming a freelancer.

FIRE CHIEF, THE (AKA THE ED WYNN SHOW)

1932–1935	NBC Red	Tues.	9:30 PM
1935–1947	NBC Blue	Sat.	8 PM

Comedian Ed WYNN, billed as "The Perfect Fool," insisted on presenting his programs in front of a live studio audience to make his shows seem more like stage performances to those who were listening at home. Wynn even wore costumes and makeup so that his studio audiences would laugh louder. The result of these efforts was Wynn's comedy-variety show, *The Fire Chief,* which featured such guest performers from films and the stage as Ethel MERMAN, Alice FAYE, Bing CROSBY, and Rudy VALLEE. Donald VOORHEES and his orchestra appeared regularly; pianist Eddie Duchin and his orchestra and singer Evelyn Knight also performed.

"Fire Chief" was the trademark of the Texaco oil company, hence the show's title. The program was written by Wynn and Eddie Preble and directed by Preble. Its announcer was Graham MCNAMEE. When Texaco relinquished its sponsorship of Wynn's program, it became known as *The* ED WYNN SHOW and was sponored by Spud cigarettes. The production staff remained.

FIRESIDE CHATS, THE

1933–1945   (Times and stations varied)

Franklin D. ROOSEVELT was the first U.S. president to fully appreciate the power of radio in communicating his policies and promoting his political viewpoints. Shortly after being elected, President Roosevelt launched this periodic series in which he talked directly to listeners about subjects of national concern,

Laurette Fillbrandt (NBC/Courtesy of Miss Fillbrandt)

such as the impending war (World War II), the Great Depression, and the WPA (Work Projects Administration). He even talked about his dog, Fala, and other personal family matters. During a half-hour broadcast, the president was heard to have asked for a glass of water, which only added to the feeling of familiarity the program generated among listeners. Robert TROUT and James WALLINGTON were the program's announcers. Trout is generally credited with conceiving the show's title.

FIRST NIGHTER, THE

1930–1931	NBC Blue	Thurs.	8 PM
1931–1932	NBC Blue	Tues.	9 PM
1932–1933	NBC Blue	Fri.	9 PM
1933–1938	NBC Red	Fri.	10 PM
1938–1939	CBS	Fri.	8 PM
1939–1940	CBS	Fri.	9:30 PM
1940–1941	CBS	Fri.	8:30 PM
1941–1942	CBS	Fri.	9:30 PM
1942–1944	Mutual	Sun.	6 PM
1944–1945	(Off the air)		
1945–1946	CBS	Sat.	7:30 PM
1946–1947	(Off the air)		
1947–1949	CBS	Thurs.	10:30 PM
1949–1952	(Off the air)		
1952–1953	NBC	Tues.	10:35 PM

This weekly series of half-hour original radio dramas, supposedly broadcast from a "little theater off Times Square" in New York City, actually originated first from Chicago and then from Hollywood. At each show's beginning the First Nighter (the host) told the audience what and who they were going to hear that night. When the show premiered, Don AMECHE and June Meredith were its weekly stars. Betty Lou GERSON replaced Meredith for a short time, and then in 1936 Barbara LUDDY—the actress most people associate with *The First Nighter*—took over the leading female roles, with Les TREMAYNE as her leading man. In 1943, Tremayne left the series, and Olan SOULE became Luddy's weekly costar. They remained with the show until it left the air in 1953, playing almost every conceivable type of role—from debutantes to doughnut-shop drones, from playboys to plowboys. Among the supporting players were Charles P. Hughes, Bret MORRISON (who also played Mr. First Nighter), Marvin MILLER, Don Briggs, Rye Billsbury, Raymond Edward JOHNSON, Macdonald CAREY, Hugh STUDEBAKER, Herb Butterfield, William CONRAD, Sarah Selby, Verna FELTON, Willard WATERMAN, Sidney Ellstrom, Parley BAER, Rita Ascot, Bob Jellison, Frank Dane, Art Kohl, Cornelius Peeples, Ted Maxwell, Fred Sullivan, Ben WRIGHT, Cliff Soubier, and Jack Doty.

For many years, the show's announcer was Vincent Pelletier; Larry Keating and Rye Billsbury also an-

Les Tremayne and Barbara Luddy on the *First Nighter* (NBC)

nounced the program. *The First Nighter* was produced and directed by Joe Ardley. The weekly dramas and comedies were written for many years by Virginia Stafford Lynne, Edwin Halloran, George Vandel, Arch OBLER, and Dan Shuffman. Original music was composed by Frank Smith, and the series' theme music was "Neapolitan Nights." Sponsors of the program included Compana balm skin creme and Miller beer.

FITCH BANDWAGON, THE (AKA PHIL HARRIS–ALICE FAYE SHOW, THE)

1938–1942	NBC Red	Sun.	7:30 PM
1942–1945	NBC	Sun.	7:30 PM

The Fitch Bandwagon show changed formats several times. Initially a 15-minute music-variety program, it expanded to a full hour the year after its debut. The show originally featured Roby Reed and Irene Beasley; it included the Morin Sisters, the Ranch Boys, and Jerry Belcher, who interviewed such celebrities as Will ROGERS and Bing CROSBY. In 1937, *The Fitch Bandwagon* became a half-hour offering and concentrated on the "bandwagon" aspect of the show's title, featuring such big-name bands as Phil HARRIS's and Walter Sharp's orchestras. Dick POWELL became the master of ceremonies in 1938 and remained with the show for several years. Andy DEVINE was the resident comedian during these years. In the summer months, various stars and formats were used. Comedienne Cass DALEY and the RICHARD DIAMOND, PRIVATE DETECTIVE series were summer replacements for the regular program. In 1948, Phil HARRIS and his film-star wife Alice FAYE became the stars, and the format was changed once again to situation comedy. After one year, the show changed sponsors and its name became *The Phil Harris–Alice Faye Show*. The show's new sponsor was the Rexall drugstore chain. This program was produced and written for many years by Ward Byron. Fort Pearson, Dresser Dahlsted, Bill Forman, and Jack Costello were the show's announcers. Fitch shampoo was the "Fitch" in the original show's title and was its sponsor for many years. The program's *Fitch Bandwagon* theme music was "Smile for Me" and when Harris and Faye were starred, it became "That's What I Like About the South."

FITZGERALD, PEGEEN AND ED (PEGEEN: 1905–1990; ED: 1885–1972)

The Fitzgeralds was the longest-running, most successful early-morning husband-and-wife talk show of its day. Ed Fitzgerald, who had been a newspaper reporter and publicity man before becoming a radio celebrity, was born in Troy, New York; his wife, Pegeen, was born in Kansas. The couple conducted their radio broadcasts from their apartment in New York City. Their show was heard on the ABC network; when Fitzgerald died in the 1970s, Pegeen continued to host the show alone on WOR radio. Her gentle scolding—tempered with ever-loving patience—of her often cranky and acerbic husband made the couple familiar early-morning companions to thousands of housewives each weekday.

FITZGERALDS, THE

See FITZGERALD, PEGEEN AND ED.

FIVE STAR JONES

1935–1936	CBS	Mon.–Fri.	12:30 PM
1936	CBS	Mon.–Fri.	12:45 PM
1936–1937	NBC Blue	Mon.–Fri.	10:15 AM

Frank and Anne HUMMERT produced this 15-minute daytime series about a reporter at a fictional newspa-

per called *The Register*. The program starred John Kane as Tom "Five Star" Jones, the reporter, and Elizabeth Day as his wife, Sally. William "Bill" JOHNSTONE played *The Register*'s editor-in-chief, and Effie Palmer was featured as Ma Moran. The Hummerts also directed and wrote this series. Mohawk carpets and Oxydol detergent sponsored the program.

FIVE STAR THEATER

See MARX, GROUCHO.

FLEISCHMANN HOUR, THE

| 1929–1939 | NBC Red | Thurs. | 8 PM |

Singer Rudy VALLEE was the main attraction of this music-variety program that featured such well-known guest stars as Al JOLSON, Ethel MERMAN, ABBOTT AND COSTELLO, Jimmy DURANTE, John, Lionel, and Ethel BARRYMORE, and Weber and Fields. In the early 1930s, the one-hour and then half-hour show, which made Vallee a major star, featured singer Alice FAYE, later a film star, as its main female vocalist. Each program began with Vallee saying "Heigh-Ho, Everybody"; then he would sing a popular song of the day. Other songs, comedy sketches, and even occasional dramatizations were presented on the show. Regularly appearing in the supporting cast were Virginia GREGG, Andy DEVINE, Mary Boland, Abe Reynolds, Billie Burke, and Sara Berner. Announcers were Graham MCNAMEE, Frank Graham, Truman Bradley, James "Jimmy" WALLINGTON, and Marvin MILLER. Directors included Gordon Thompson, Tony Sanford, Art Daley, Howard Wiley, and Jim Wright. The show's writers were George Faulkner, Bob Colwell, A. L. Alexander, Henrietta Feldstin, Sid Zelinka, Sam Silver, R. Marks, and Carroll Carroll. Vallee later became the star of a radio variety show that bore his name, but it never rivaled the popularity of *The Fleischmann Hour*. His theme song was "My Time Is Your Time." The program's sponsor was Fleischmann's yeast. (See also RUDY VALLEE SHOW, *The*.)

FLETCHER, LUCILLE (1912–   )

Lucille Fletcher was born in Brooklyn, New York, and began to write for radio early in her career. Although she wrote for many radio shows, Fletcher is most noted for the scripts she wrote for the SUSPENSE series. One of her stories, "Sorry, Wrong Number," was one of the most critically acclaimed dramas ever presented on radio. In it, an invalid overhears a plot outlining her own murder. Another memorable radio drama Fletcher wrote for *Suspense* was "The Hitchhiker," which concerned a man who, at the beginning of a coast-to-coast automobile trip, sees a ghostlike figure by the side of the road hitching a ride. The figure actually turned out to be Death. Fletcher continues to write articles and books.

FLYNN, BERNADINE (1904–1977)

Born in Madison, Wisconsin, actress Bernadine Flynn is best known for her longtime performance as Sade in the domestic daytime comedy series VIC AND SADE. Flynn began her acting career on the stage and tried radio just as the medium was beginning to capture the public's interest. In addition to *Vic and Sade*, Flynn was also featured on the ENO CRIME CLUB and CHICAGO THEATER OF THE AIR series, as well as on the daytime serials *Welcome Valley, The* RIGHT TO HAPPINESS, and *Public Hero Number One*. Television viewers saw her on the "Hawkins Falls" (1950–1955) daytime drama series.

FLYWHEEL, SHYSTER, AND FLYWHEEL

See also MARX, GROUCHO.

FOLEY, RED (CLYDE JULIAN FOLEY: 1910– 1968)

For years, Red Foley was one of the most popular country-western performers in America. Born in Berea, Kentucky, he entered radio in the early 1930s when he was recruited by John Lair to appear on the popular NATIONAL BARN DANCE program. Foley played the guitar and sang with the popular Cumberland Ridge Runners. With numerous million-selling records to his credit—"Red River Valley" "Slowpoke"—Foley returned to *The National Barn Dance* in the early 1940s as master of ceremonies. In 1946, he served as master of ceremonies and principal performer on *The* GRAND OLE OPRY, which had by that time become a national network show. Foley was on the *Opry* until 1953 and made guest appearances on Gene Autry's MELODY RANCH and *The* ROY ROGERS SHOW; he was also featured on "The Country Music Jubilee" show on television in the 1950s. Foley continued to perform at state fairs and in concerts as well as to make recordings until shortly before his death in 1968.

FORBES, MURRAY (1907–1987)

Actor Murray Forbes was born and raised in Chicago, Illinois. On daytime radio he was best known for his role as MA PERKINS's hard-luck son-in-law, Willie Fitz, which he played throughout the series' long run. In addition, Forbes was heard on *The Foxes of Flatbush*, FU MANCHU, *Lives at Stake, Adventures in Health, Sally of the Movies, The* FIRST NIGHTER, GRAND HOTEL, WEL-COME VALLEY, GIRL ALONE, *Inside Story*, KNICKERBOCKER PLAYHOUSE, AUNT JENNY'S REAL LIFE STORIES, LONELY WOMAN, MARY MARLIN, and TODAY'S CHILDREN.

FORD THEATER, THE

| 1947–1948 | NBC | Sun. | 5 PM |
| 1948–1949 | CBS | Fri. | 9 PM |

The Ford motor company sponsored this one-hour weekly anthology series that dramatized great novels and plays for radio. Radio regulars Karl SWENSON and Mason ADAMS starred on the initial show, Mark Twain's *A Connecticut Yankee in King Arthur's Court*. In subsequent weeks, active radio performers such as Anne SEYMOUR, William J. Smith, Evelyn Varden, Les DAMON, Vicki VOLA, Claudia MORGAN, Barbara Weeks, Santos ORTEGA, Hugh MARLOWE, Les TREMAYNE, Fran CARLON, Arnold MOSS, Ed BEGLEY, Everett SLOANE, John LARKIN, and Shirley BOOTH starred in productions of such works as *On Borrowed Time, Ah! Wilderness, The Man Who Played God, Arsenic and Old Lace, The Count of Monte Cristo, Twentieth Century, The Informer, The Silver Cord, A Star Is Born, Laura*, and *Arrowsmith*. Fletcher MARKLE, the director of STUDIO ONE, in 1948 became *The Ford Theater*'s producer, director, and sometimes star performer. Markle's company from *Studio One*—Everett SLOANE, Miriam WOLFE, Robert DRYDEN, Hedley Rainnie, and Mercedes MCCAMBRIDGE—was heard weekly, and Louis Quinn, Hester Sondergaard, Alan Devitt, and Ronald LISS were frequently featured in the supporting cast. But another major change was that "name" Hollywood and Broadway stars played leading roles. *Madame Bovary*, the premiere production of CBS's *Ford Theater*, starred Marlene Dietrich, Claude Rains, and Van Heflin. Subsequent plays included *Double Indemnity* with Burt Lancaster and Joan Bennett; *Of Human Bondage* with Ray Milland and Joan Loring; *Wuthering Heights* with Montgomery Clift; *Skylark* with Bette Davis; *The Horn Blows at Midnight* with Jack BENNY; *Holy Matrimony* with Charles Laughton; and *Welcome Stranger* with Bing Crosby and Barry Fitzgerald. Other stars who appeared included Ingrid Bergman, Vincent PRICE, Ronald COLMAN, Jean Arthur, Bob HOPE, Claudette Colbert, Linda Darnell, Walter Huston, Lucille BALL, John Garfield, Joan Blondell, Gene Kelly, Geraldine Fitzgerald, Margo, Edward G. Robinson, Anne Baxter, Ida Lupino, and Burgess Meredith. The theme music for Markle's *Ford Theater* productions was Brahm's *Double Concerto for Violin and Cello*. The series' announcers were Nelson CASE, Kenneth Banghart, and Frank Martin. Incidental music was composed by Cy Feuer.

FORTY-FIVE MINUTES FROM HOLLYWOOD

1934–1936	CBS	Sat., Sun.	8 PM

Before the LUX RADIO THEATER came on radio, CBS offered this series of condensed half-hour versions of such movies as *Random Harvest, Little Women,* and *Anthony Adverse,* frequently starring relatively unknown radio performers in the major parts. The program, produced and directed by Tom Harrington, offered both dramas and musicals. Bert PARKS announced the program.

FRANCES LEE BARTON SHOW, THE (AKA KITCHEN PARTY)

1932–1933	NBC Red	Tues., Thurs.	11:15 AM
1933–1934	NBC Red	Thurs.	11:15 AM
1934–1935	NBC Red	Fri.	1:30 PM

Frances Lee Barton, a renowned cook, had this 15-minute program on the air in the early 1930s. The show gave listeners recipes and cooking tips, as well as useful kitchen information such as how to can fresh tomatoes and vegetables and how to set a proper table for a dinner party. Miss Barton produced, directed, and wrote the series. Swans Down cake flour and Calumet baking powder sponsored the show.

FRANCIS, ARLENE (ALINE KAZANJIAN: 1908–)

Born in Brookline, Massachusetts, Arlene Francis was one of radio's most active program hostesses and actresses. She began her broadcasting career in 1935 on WOR-Mutual in New York, hosting such game and quiz shows as BLIND DATE, *Fun for All,* HELPMATE, and WHAT'S MY NAME (the radio forerunner of TV's "What's My Line," on which she later appeared as a regular panelist). She also emceed the HOUR OF CHARM, starring Phil SPITALNY and his All-Girl Orchestra. As a dramatic actress, Francis starred as Betty on the BETTY AND BOB daytime serial and was heard on SECOND HUSBAND, CENTRAL CITY, MR. DISTRICT ATTORNEY, and *There Was a Woman.* For many years, she also hosted *The Arlene Francis Show,* a daily interview-talk program on WOR radio in New York, on which she interviewed actors, authors, and such celebrities as Henry Kissinger, Mercedes MCCAMBRIDGE, Saul Bellow, and Mary Margaret MCBRIDE.

FRANK, CARL (1909–1979)

Actor Carl Frank was born in Weehawkin, New Jersey, was first heard on radio on *The* RUDY VALLEE SHOW in 1937, and thereafter was Bob on BETTY AND BOB; the title character on the BUCK ROGERS IN THE 25TH CENTURY series; and Jerry Malone on YOUNG DR. MALONE. Frank was heard regularly on *The* COURT OF

MISSING HEIRS, *Her Honor Nancy James,* YOUR FAMILY AND MINE, GANGBUSTERS, BY KATHLEEN NORRIS, AUNT JENNY'S REAL LIFE STORIES, *The* SHADOW, *The* CAMPBELL PLAYHOUSE, *The* GOOD WILL HOUR, HOBBY LOBBY, and *Columbia Presents Corwin.* He was also the announcer on THIS IS YOUR FBI. In 1959, Frank was featured on "The Edge of Night" daytime television series.

FRANK MERRIWELL, THE ADVENTURES OF

See ADVENTURES OF FRANK MERRIWELL, *The.*

FRANK SINATRA SHOW, THE (AKA SONGS BY SINATRA; LIGHT-UP TIME; TO BE PERFECTLY FRANK)

1943–1947	CBS	Wed.	9 PM
1947–1949	(Off the air)		
1949–1950	NBC	Mon.–Fri.	7 PM
1950–1951	CBS	Sun.	5 PM
1951–1952	(Off the air)		
1952–1954	NBC	Tues., Thurs.	8:15 PM

Singer Frank SINATRA had several pop music shows with various names on the air in the 1940s, but all of these are usually referred to simply as *The Frank Sinatra Show,* which is how they were listed in magazine and newspaper radio-program listings. Judy GARLAND, Bing CROSBY, Bob HOPE, Lena Horne and others

Arlene Francis (NBC)

were heard on these programs with Frank. Regulars included the Pied Pipers, the Bobby Tucker Chorus, and Axel STORDAHL's Orchestra. Announcers were Marvin MILLER and Jerry Lawrence. Vimms vitamins, Max Factor makeup, Old Gold cigarettes, and Lucky Strike cigarettes sponsored these programs.

FRANKEL, HARRY "SINGING SAM" (1888–1948)

Born in New York City, Harry Frankel was a radio pioneer whose deep, distinctive, resonant bass voice became familiar to thousands of listeners. Frankel became best known as SINGING SAM, THE BARBASOL MAN on the show of that title and in the Barbasol shave cream commercials. Frankel made his radio debut in 1930 and was heard on many music-variety shows throughout the 1930s and 1940s. He continued singing the Barbasol jingles until he died in the late 1940s.

FREBERG, STAN (1926–   )

Satirist Stan Freberg was born in Los Angeles, California, but grew up in Pasadena, and had a short-lived prime-time network series on CBS radio in the late 1950s. He began his broadcasting career interviewing himself in man-on-the-street sketches on CBS's morning radio shows. In 1944, Freberg did the voices for several Warner Brothers cartoon characters and for Walt Disney Studios, Columbia Pictures, United Productions of America, and the United Press Association. His "St. George the Dragon" comedy record, which spoofed television's "Dragnet" series, sold well over a million copies. He appeared on several television shows in the 1950s and 60s and can still be heard on various NATIONAL PUBLIC RADIO comedy specials.

See also STAN FREBERG SHOW, The.

FRED ALLEN SHOW, THE (AKA LINIT BATH CLUB REVUE; TOWN HALL TONIGHT)

1932–1939	(Various shows, dates, and times)		
1939–1940	NBC Red	Wed.	9 PM
1940–1949	NBC	Sun.	8:30 PM

The Fred Allen Show, a half-hour program and for a short while in the late 1930s a one-hour program, featured Fred ALLEN, his wife, Portland HOFFA, organist Ann Leafat and her Wurlitzer, and actor Gale GORDON, when it was called *Town Hall Tonight*. Allen and his entourage performed spoofs such as "People You Don't Expect to Meet," and "The Workshop Players" (a takeoff on the COLUMBIA WORKSHOP series).

But it is best remembered for the "Allen's Alley" segment of the show. Each week, Allen and Hoffa knocked on the doors of Alley residents: Southern windbag-politician Senator Claghorn, played by

Kenny DELMAR; Irish loudmouth Ajax Cassidy, played by Peter DONALD; the heavily Yiddish-accented housewife Pansy Nussbaum, played by Minerva PIOUS; hayseed New England farmer Titus Moody, played by Parker FENNELLEY; and ham actor Falstaff Openshaw, played by Alan REED. They answered such questions as "Why does the Lone Ranger wear a mask?" and "What do you think of the current money crunch?"

In addition to these regular comic actors, the show featured the five singing De Marco Sisters, John BROWN, Charles CANTOR, Irwin Delmore, Shirley BOOTH, Kenny BAKER, Walter TETLEY, Sam Levene, Roy Atwell, and "Uncle Jim" Harkins, while guest stars included the ANDREWS SISTERS, Orson WELLES, Lauritz Melchoir, Beatrice Lillie, Tallulah BANKHEAD, Alfred Hitchcock, Bing CROSBY, Edgar BERGEN and, of course, supposed enemy but good friend and chief radio comedy competitor Jack BENNY. Announcers were James "Jimmy" WALLINGTON, Harry VON ZELL, and Kenny DELMAR. Victor "Vick" Knight and Howard Reilly directed the series. Music directors included Lou Katzman, Peter VAN STEEDEN, Lennie Hayton, Al GOODMAN, and Ferde Grofé. Writers for the show, in addition to Allen himself, included Larry Marks, Aaron Ruben, Nat Hiken, Herb Lewis, Harry Tugend, Arnold Auerbach, Herman Wouk, and Albert G. Miller. *The Fred Allen Show*'s theme song was "Smile, Darn Ya, Smile." Ipana toothpaste, Sal Hapatica antacid, V-8 juice, Blue Bonnet margarine, Shefford cheese, Linit bleach, Texaco oil, Tenderleaf tea, and Ford automobiles were the program's sponsors.

FRED WARING AND HIS PENNSYLVANIANS SHOW, THE

1931–1932	NBC	Mon.	(*)
1932–1933	CBS	Sun.	(*)
1933–1934	CBS	Wed.	10 pm
1935–1936	CBS	Tues.	9:30 & 9 PM
1938–1939	NBC Blue	Sat.	8:30 PM
1939–1944	NBC Blue	Sat.	7 PM
1944	NBC Blue	Thurs.	7 PM
1945	NBC Blue	Thurs.	10 PM
1945–1946	NBC	Thurs.	10 & 11 PM
1946–1947	NBC	Tues.	10 AM
1947–1949	NBC	Mon., Thurs.	10:30 PM
1949–1950	NBC	Sat.	10 AM
1950–1957	(Off the air)		
1957	ABC	Mon.–Fri.	10:30 PM

Orchestra leader Fred WARING and his Pennsylvanians were radio regulars for more than twenty-five years. With his orchestra, chorus, and various soloists, Waring was featured in hour-long and half-hour-long shows. For five years—from 1945 until 1950—Waring's company was the major attraction on *The* CHESTERFIELD SUPPER CLUB. Regular performers included

Fred Allen (with saxophone) and his "Allen's Alley" regulars (from left) Minerva Pious, Peter Donald, and Parker Fennelly (CBS)

Honey and the Bees; Stella and the Fellas; the Lane Sisters; tenor Gordon Goodman; soprano Jane Wilson; vocalists Donna Dae, Robert Shaw, Mac Perron, and Ruth Cottington; the piano team of Virginia Morley and Livingston Gearhart; guitarist Les Paul; and singer-comedienne Kay Thompson. Announcers included David Ross, Bob Considine, Paul DOUGLAS, and Bill Bivens. Writers were Frank Moore, Dave Harmon, Mike Dutton, and Bob Weiskopf; and Tom Bennett produced and directed. Waring's opening theme music was "I Hear Music," and his closing music was "Sleep." The show was sponsored by Old Gold cigarettes.

FREEMAN, FLORENCE (1911–1966)

New York City–born actress Florence Freeman was an English teacher before she entered show business as a radio actress in 1933. Playing on a host of shows, she was Mrs. Brown on ABIE'S IRISH ROSE; Dot on DOT AND WILL; Betty Harrison on *Jane Arden*; Dolores Winters on JOHN'S OTHER WIFE; and the title parts on VALIANT LADY, YOUNG WIDDER BROWN, and WENDY WARREN. She also acted regularly on *The* PAUL WHITEMAN SHOW, SHOW BOAT, ALIAS JIMMY VALENTINE, PEPPER YOUNG'S FAMILY, and AUNT JENNY'S REAL LIFE STORIES.

FROMAN, JANE (1907–1980)

Singer Jane Froman was born in St. Louis, Missouri. Her first singing job on radio was at station WLW in Cincinnati, and soon after, she became a vocalist with the Paul Whiteman Orchestra. In the early 1930s, the singer went to Hollywood and appeared in such films as *Stars Over Broadway* (1932), *Radio City Revels* (1933), *The Ziegfeld Follies of 1934* (1934), and *Keep Off the Grass* (1935). Froman later starred on the weekly radio program *Yours for a Song,* costarring opera singer Robert Weede, and subsequently on *The* PAUSE THAT REFRESHES ON THE AIR, *The Gulf Musical Playhouse,* and *The Jell-O Summer Show.*

Seriously crippled in an automobile accident, Froman's tragic but inspirational story was made into the film *With a Song in My Heart* (1952), starring Susan Hayward lip-synching to Froman's voice on the soundtrack. Froman continued to make personal appearances onstage, in nightclubs, and on television between operations until shortly before her death.

FRONT PAGE FARRELL

1941–1942	Mutual	Mon.–Fri.	1:30 PM
1942–1951	NBC	Mon.–Fri.	5:45 PM
1951–1954	NBC	Mon.–Fri.	5:15 PM

On this show, newspaperman David Farrell's domestic problems often overshadowed his work as a reporter and later as publisher of a small-town newspaper. Although this 15-minute drama series sometimes featured mystery and adventure, it usually centered around the everyday life of Farrell, his family, and his friends. Farrell's wife, Sally, gave him support at home. Fellow reporter Kay Barnett had adventures and domestic problems of her own to deal with. Richard WIDMARK first played Farrell. When he left the series to pursue a Hollywood career, the role was claimed by Carlton YOUNG and then by Staats COTSWORTH. Florence WILLIAMS and Virginia Dwyer played Sally; Betty GARDE was Kay Barnett. Also featured regularly were Evelyn Varden, Elspeth ERIC, George Sturgeon, Vivian SMOLEN, Athena Lorde, Peter Capell, Frank Chase, James Van Dyke, Robert Donley, William Shelly, James Monks, Eleanor Sherman, and Katherine Emmet. Announcers included Bill Bond, Mark Goodson, Ed Fleming, Dick Dunham, Don HANCOCK, and Larry Elliott. The show was produced by Frank and Anne HUMMERT and directed by Bill Sweets, Frank Hummert, Arthur Hanna, John Buckwalter, Richard Leonard, Ed Slattery, and Blair Wallister. It was written by the Hummerts and William Sweets. The show's theme song was "You and I Know." Anacin antacid, Black Flag bug spray, Kriptin, Bi-So-Dol antacid mints, Freezone, Aerowax automobile wax, Heet liniment, Chef Boy-Ar-Dee canned spaghetti, and Kolynos toothpaste were the program's sponsors.

FROST, ALICE (1910–   )

Born in Minneapolis, Minnesota, Alice Frost's most memorable radio role was Pamela North on the MR. AND MRS. NORTH detective series. Frost's unusual, very distinctive voice placed her on many radio programs, including starring roles in BIG SISTER, BRIGHT HORIZON, and *A* WOMAN OF COURAGE. Frost was also a regular on BUCK ROGERS IN THE 25TH CENTURY, *The* FRED ALLEN SHOW, FAMOUS JURY TRIALS, *The* MERCURY THEATER ON THE AIR, JOHNNY PRESENTS, TOWN HALL TONIGHT, SUSPENSE, *The* CBS WORKSHOP, and as one of the female stooges on STOOPNAGLE AND BUDD.

FU MANCHU (AKA THE COLLIER HOUR; THE SHADOW OF FU MANCHU)

1927–1933	CBS	Mon.	8 & 8:45 PM
1939–1949	(Syndicated series. Various stations and times)		

This mystery-adventure series was based on the Fu Manchu character created by novelist Sax Rohmer. First heard as a segment on CBS in the late 1920s and early 1930s, the series was off the air throughout most of the 1930s, returning in 1939. The title character, Fu Manchu, was actually the villain, and Malik, a French detective, was the series' hero. Malik tracked down and tried to destroy the elusive Fu, assisted by friends Nayland Smith and Dr. Petrie. Charles Warburton played Malik. John C. Daley and then Harold Huber were the most memorable of the Fu Manchus. Sunda Love and Charlotte MANSON were the slave girl, Karamench. *Fu Manchu* was the central character in a fifteen-episode film serial, *The Shadow of Fu Manchu,* in 1940. *Collier* magazine, first publisher of the Fu Manchu stories, sponsored the show. The segments were directed by Colonel Davis and written by Sax Rohmer.

See COLLIER HOUR, THE.

GABEL, MARTIN (1912–1986)

Martin Gabel's distinctive and distinguished theater-trained voice was well utilized on many radio programs throughout the late 1930s, 1940s, and 1950s. Born in Philadelphia, Pennsylvania, Gabel studied acting at the American Academy of Dramatic Arts and debuted on radio in 1934. He worked with Orson WELLES in the celebrated Mercury Theater in New York City, joining Welles at the microphone on that company's weekly radio series. In addition to that program, the actor was also heard regularly on BIG SISTER, GANGBUSTERS, *The* SHADOW, *The* CAVALCADE OF AMERICA, GRAND HOTEL, *CBS Presents Corwin*, and *The* MARCH OF TIME. Gabel was a guest panelist on TV shows "What's My Line?" and "I've Got a Secret" in the 1950s and 1960s.

GABEREAU

1985–1986	CBC	Mon.–Fri.	8 PM
1986–1987	CBS	Sat. Radio (AM)	1:08 PM
		Fri. Stereo (FM)	10 PM
1987–present	CBS	Mon.–Fri.	2:05 PM

Vicki Gabereau of the CANADIAN BROADCASTING CORPORATION interviews such celebrities as comedienne Roseanne Barr, writer Tom Robbins, ex-Rolling Stone Bill Wyman, and mountain-climber Sir Edmund Hillary, as well as ordinary citizens who have done some extraordinary things. Gabereau's ability to make her guests express themselves comfortably on her one-hour, five-days-a-week program has made her a favorite radio personality among her listeners. Bill Richardson is also heard, offering his particular brand of satire. Andre Rheaume talks about the popular-music scene around the world. On Wednesdays, Marge Mer-

kle, "the Answering Lady," is featured. The program's executive producer is Rosemary Allenbach.

GALEN DRAKE SHOW, THE

See DRAKE, GALEN.

Vicki Gabereau (CBC)

111

GANGBUSTERS (AKA G-MEN)

1935–1938	CBS	Wed.	10 PM
1938–1940	CBS	Sat.	8 PM
1940–1945	NBC Blue	Fri.	9 PM
1945–1946	NBC Blue	Sat.	9 PM
1946–1949	ABC	Sat.	9 PM
1949–1953	CBS	Sat.	9 PM
1953–1954	CBS	Sat.	8:30 PM
1954–1956	Mutual	Wed.	9 PM
1956–1957	Mutual	Wed.	8 PM

Called *G-Men* when first on the air, *Gangbusters* became the most popular crime-adventure show on radio. In stories that were both fact and fiction, gangsters, con artists, thieves, and their molls were pitted against the gangbusting cops of the show's title. Long before the "America's Most Wanted" TV show, this series described real-life wanted criminals at the end of each program. The roster of radio-acting regulars included Art CARNEY, Richard WIDMARK, Ethel Owen, Santos ORTEGA, Adelaide Klein, James "Jimmy" McCallion, Anne-Marie Gayer, Joe DeSantis, Athena Lorde, Barbara Lee, William J. Smith, Roger DeKoven, Linda Watkins, Don MCLAUGHLIN, Leon JANNEY, Robert Haag, Mason ADAMS, Larry Haines, Robert DRYDEN, Bill ZUCKERT, Lawson Zerbe, Ken Lynch, Bill LIPTON, Raymond Edward JOHNSON, Helene Dumas, Joan BANKS, Frank LOVEJOY, Mercedes MCCAMBRIDGE, Grant Richards, Elaine Rost, and George Petrie. Actresses Bryna Raeburn, Alice REINHEART, and Elspeth ERIC often played gun molls and female criminals: Eric, for one, was so convincing in these roles that convicts in maximum-security prisons formed two fan clubs in her honor.

The half-hour *Gangbusters* series was produced by Phillips H. LORD and directed by Paul Monroe, Harry Frazee, Jay Hanna, George Zachery, Bill Sweets, and Leonard Bass. The amazing sound effects, including machine-gun fire, explosions, gun battles, and car

Santos Ortega, Anne Marie Gayer, Grant Richards, and Jimmy McCallion during *Gangbusters* (CBS)

crashes, were executed by Ray Kremer, Jim Rogen, Jerry McCarthy, Bob Prescott, Ed Blainey, and Byron Winget. The show was narrated by Phillips H. Lord, Colonel H. Norman Schwartzkopf, John C. Hilley, and Dean Carlton. The Chief Investigator was played by Lewis J. Valentine. Announcers included Roger Forster, Art Hannes, Charles Stark, Frank Gallop, Don Gardiner, and H. Gilbert Martin. Phillips H. Lord, Stanley Niss, Brice Disque, Jr., and John Mole wrote the show. *Gangbusters* was sponsored by Chevrolet automobiles, Tide detergent, Kool cigarettes, Palmolive soap, *Cue* magazine, Sloan's liniment, Waterman's pens, and General Foods products.

GARDE, BETTY (1905–1989)

Actress Betty Garde was born in Philadelphia, Pennsylvania. Although an active stage and film actress before she entered radio in 1933, she came to be featured in a variety of roles: Kay Barnett in FRONT PAGE FARRELL, Lorenzo Jones's wife Belle in LORENZO JONES, the title role in *The Policewoman,* Mrs. Arden on *Jane Arden,* and Emily Abbott on WE, THE ABBOTTS. Garde was also regularly heard on PERRY MASON, *My Son and I, The* FAT MAN, AL PEARCE AND HIS GANG, *The* BIG STORY, *The* COLUMBIA WORKSHOP, STUDIO ONE, *McGarry and His Mouse,* GANGBUSTERS, INNER SANCTUM MYSTERIES, *The* HENRY MORGAN SHOW, MR. AND MRS. NORTH, and *The* THIN MAN.

On Broadway, Garde was the original Aunt Eller in *Oklahoma!* in the early 1940s, and appeared in *The Nervous Wreck* (1923), *Easy Come, Easy Go* (1932), and *The Poor Nut* (1935). The actress was also featured in many films, most notably as Wanda Skutnick in the film *Call Northside 777* (1948), and on television on the daytime series "Edge of Night" (1956) as Mattie Grimsley and "The World of Mr. Sweeney" (1954) as Mrs. Sweeney.

GARDNER ED (EDWARD PEGGENBURG: 1901–1963)

Ed Gardner was born in Astoria, New York. Before turning to writing for radio in 1930, Gardner was a fight manager, a pianist, and a typewriter and paint salesman. He was first heard on the air when he substituted for the star of *This Is New York.* Gardner used a very typical New York accent in his portrayal of a typical Brooklyn Dodger fan. Although he wrote scripts for the *First Line* radio program and directed the BURNS AND ALLEN, *Hollywood Good News, The* KRAFT MUSIC HALL, *Frank Fay Calling* and *The* TEXACO STAR THEATER shows, Ed Gardner is best known for starring on DUFFY'S TAVERN. For many years, Gardner played Archie, the manager of Duffy's Tavern, and in 1945 starred in the Paramount Pictures film based on

the series. Ed Gardner was considered by his peers to have had "one of the funniest minds in the business." Gardner retired from show business shortly after *Duffy's Tavern* left the air.

GARLAND, JUDY (FRANCES GUMM: 1922–1969)

Judy Garland was born in Grand Rapids, Minnesota. She made her first radio appearance on a small local station in Los Angeles after touring on the vaudeville circuit with her sisters in their singing act, The Gumm Sisters. After she starred in MGM's film classics *The Wizard of Oz* (1939) and *Meet Me in St. Louis* (1945), Garland appeared regularly on radio on *The* BOB HOPE SHOW, *Jack Oakie's College Good News, The* SHELL CHATEAU, *The* BOB BURNS SHOW, and *The* HARDY FAMILY. She was a weekly performer on Bing Crosby's KRAFT MUSIC HALL and BING CROSBY'S SHOW and the star of *The General Electric–Judy Garland Program* in 1952. Judy also contributed a great deal of her time and talent entertaining members of the armed forces on the COMMAND PERFORMANCE, MAIL CALL, and GI JOURNAL. Garland made "Somewhere over the Rainbow," "The Trolley Song," and "Have Yourself a Merry Little Christmas" famous.

GARROWAY, DAVE (1913–1982)

Born in Schenectady, New York, Dave Garroway began his radio career as an announcer at KDKA in Pittsburgh. After a stint in the navy, Garroway returned in 1942 to Chicago and hosted several programs for station WMAQ. The popularity of his local program eventually led to a network radio contract. On his early network radio shows, he hosted in the same casual, easygoing style that later made him one of TV's most successful program hosts. On TV, Garroway became famous as the first host of NBC's "Garroway at Large" TV variety show (1949) and NBC's "Today" show (1952). Becoming disillusioned by the business intrigues of the broadcasting industry and discouraged by its lack of gratitude for his contributions to the medium, Garroway left television. He took his own life in 1982.

GARRY MOORE SHOW, THE

| 1949–1959 | CBS | Mon.–Fri. | 3:30PM |

An hour-long program similar to Arthur Godfrey's morning show, *The Garry Moore Show* featured talk, music, and special guest stars such as Jimmy DURANTE, Judy GARLAND, and Ginny SIMMS. Besides Garry MOORE, host of the series, regulars included singer Eileen Wood, comedian Irving Miller, singer Ken Carson, and announcers Howard Petrie and then

Durwood Kirby, who later announced on Moore's TV variety show. Ransom Sherman wrote and directed many of the programs, which were sponsored by Camel cigarettes. Moore's theme music was the *William Tell Overture,* played in an offbeat style.

See also JIMMY DURANTE SHOW, *The.*

GASOLINE ALLEY

1941	NBC	Mon.–Fri.	6:45PM
1948–1949	Mutual	Fri.	(*)

Skeezix, Nina, Auntie Blossom, Wumple, Idaho Ida, Ling Lee, and the other characters from the early 1920s comic strip "Gasoline Alley" by Frank King were heard on this show, first in a 15-minute weekday and then a half-hour once-a-week format. The program's major characters lived in a poor section of a large unnamed American city. Episodes typically centered around one member of the community helping another to cope with a personal problem, such as a financial crisis or the loss of a job. James "Jimmy" McCallion, Billy Idelson, and Bill LIPTON played Skeezix; Janet Gilbert and Jean Gillespie played Nina Clock; Irna PHILLIPS played Auntie Blossom; Clifford Soubier played Wumple, Skeezix's boss; Hazel Dopheide played Idaho Ida; and Junius Matthews played Ling Wee, a Chinese waiter. Charles Schenck and John Cole were the program's directors. Kay Chase and Kane Campbell wrote the scripts for the series.

GAY MRS. FEATHERSTONE, THE (AKA THE BILLIE BURKE SHOW; FASHION IN RATIONS)

1943–1946	CBS	Sat.	11:30 AM
1946–1948	NBC	Wed.	8:30 PM

Billie Burke, well known as Glinda, the Good Witch, in the film *The Wizard of Oz* (1939), was the star of this radio show in the mid-1940s. First titled *The Billie Burke Show,* it was changed to *The Gay Mrs. Featherstone* the second year it was on the air. Supporting Burke on the series, about a featherbrained, dithery society woman, were Alan Hale, Lillian RANDOLPH, Earle Ross, Virginia Gilmore, and Marvin MILLER, who along with Tom Dickson were the program's announcers. Axel Gruenberg, Dave Titus, Ruth Brooks, and Paul West wrote scripts for the series, which Robert Hafter directed. Listerine toothpaste sponsored the series.

GAY NINETIES REVUE (AKA GASLIGHT GAIETIES)

1940–1941	CBS	Sat.	7:30 PM
1941–1944	CBS	Mon.	8:30 PM
1944–1945	NBC	Sat.	8 PM

Popular turn-of-the-century songs and comedy sketches were featured on this weekly half-hour music-variety show, set in a fictional gay-nineties music hall. Singer Beatrice KAYE sang such songs as "Under the Bamboo Tree," and "I'm Only a Bird in a Gilded Cage." Joe HOWARD and occasionally Billy M. Greene acted as master of ceremonies. Among the performers regularly heard on the series were Frank LOVEJOY as "Broadway Harry," Jack Arthur as "Danny Donovan," and Lillian Leonard, Michael O'Shea, Sally Sweetland, The Rockaway 4, Bill Days, Art Davies, Frank Halliday, and Harry Stanton. Occasionally featured were the Elm City Four (a barbershop quartet), the Four Clubman, and the Floradora Girls. Axel GRUENBERG directed on occasion, and Andre BARUCH announced the show. The show's orchestra was led by Ray BLOCH. Model pipe tobacco, Drene shampoo, and Teel shampoo were the program's sponsors.

GENE AND GLENN (AKA GENE AND GLENN WITH JAKE AND LENA)

1930–1932	NBC Red	Mon.–Sat.	8 AM
1932–1934	(Off the air)		
1934	NBC Red	Mon.–Fri.	7:15 PM
1934–1938	(Off the air)		
1938–1939	NBC Red	Mon.–Sat.	8:15 AM
1939–1940	NBC Red	Mon.–Fri.	8:30 AM
1940–1941	NBC Red	Mon.–Fri.	8:15 AM

Eugene Carroll and Glenn Rowell starred in this comedy-variety program that was heard for 15 minutes weekdays and some Saturdays as well. The show told of a music-and-comedy team who lived in a boardinghouse owned by Lena, played by Carroll. Her handyman, Jake, was played by Rowell. Typical shows centered around incidents that happened to the boardinghouse residents. Carroll and Rowell wrote and directed the series. Featured guest stars included Ed WYNN, Milton BERLE, and Ted Lewis.

GENE AUTRY SHOW, THE
See also MELODY RANCH.

GERSON, BETTY LOU (1914–   )
Betty Lou Gerson was born in Chattanooga, Tennessee, and debuted on radio in 1934. She soon became very successful as a result of her versatility—she could play many different parts—and her attractive, sexy voice, with which she could often sound quite seductive. She played Mercedes Colby in DON WINSLOW OF THE NAVY, Charlotte Brandon-Wilson in *The* GUIDING LIGHT, Julia Meredith in MIDSTREAM, Henrietta Dorne in MARY MARLIN, the title role on *The* WOMAN IN WHITE, and was featured on AUNT MARY, *The* ROAD OF LIFE, TODAY'S CHILDREN, *The* WHISTLER, *The* ADVENTURES OF PHILIP MARLOWE, *The* ADVENTURES OF NERO WOLFE, and INNER SANCTUM MYSTERIES. Gerson was also one of the featured performers on the CHICAGO

THEATER OF THE AIR, FIRST NIGHTER, ATTORNEY AT LAW, *Win Your Lady*, and ARNOLD GRIMM'S DAUGHTER. She later provided the voice for the cartoon character Cruella De Vil in Disney's *101 Dalmatians* (1961). On television, Gerson was featured on the "Morning Star" (1964–1965) daytime drama series.

GI JOURNAL

| 1942–1946 | (Various military national and foreign broadcasting facilities) |

During World War II, the half-hour *GI Journal* was produced for the entertainment of U.S. military personnel stationed around the world. Like COMMAND PERFORMANCE and MAIL CALL, GI JOURNAL was a music-and-comedy variety show designed to boost the morale of the troops and keep them abreast of what was happening in the country's entertainment industry. Many stars of Hollywood, Broadway, and radio—Judy Garland, Bing CROSBY, Bob HOPE, Mel BLANC, and Ransom SHERMAN—guest-hosted this series on a regular basis. Announcers Harlow Wilcox, Don WILSON, and Ken CARPENTER and writers, directors, and such cartoonists as Bill Maudlin patriotically volunteered their time to work on the show.

GIBSON FAMILY, THE

| 1934–1935 | NBC Red | Sat., Sun. | 9:30 PM |
| 1935–1936 | NBC Red | Sun. | 10 PM |

This half-hour weekly series about stagestruck youngsters trying to break into show business was one of the first radio programs to have original music and lyrics written especially for it, provided by Howard Dietz and Arthur Schwartz, who composed scores for the Broadway musicals *Three's a Crowd* (1930) and *A Tree Grows in Brooklyn* (1951). Heard on the radio show were Loretta Clemens, Jack Clemens, Al Dary, Adele RONSON, Anne Elstner, Bill ADAMS, Ernest Whitman, Warren HULL, Kate McComb, and John McGovern. Conrad Thibault and Lois Bennett provided the singing. The orchestra was conducted by Donald VOORHEES. James "Jimmy" WALLINGTON announced the program. Owen Davis created the series, wrote the scripts, and directed many of the show's episodes. The program was sponsored by Proctor and Gamble's Ivory soap and soap flakes.

GIBSON, JOHN (1905–1986)

Actor John Gibson was born in Oakland, California, and is remembered for playing Ethelbert, the bartender-friend of photographer Casey and reporter Ann Williams on CASEY, CRIME PHOTOGRAPHER. Gibson debuted on radio in 1925 and was also regularly heard on DON WINSLOW OF THE NAVY (as Red Pen-

nington), LONE JOURNEY, HOLLYWOOD HOTEL, *The* JACK BENNY SHOW, *The* FIRST NIGHTER, *The* LUX RADIO THEATER, FIBBER MCGEE AND MOLLY, *The* IRENE RICH DRAMAS, SCATTERGOOD BAINES, *Signal Carnival*, BIG TOWN, SILVER THEATER, *Hollywood Playhouse*, ONE MAN'S FAMILY, YOUR HIT PARADE, *The* MAN I MARRIED, *Michael and Kitty*, *The* MILTON BERLE SHOW, and TWO ON A CLUE. On television, Gibson was featured on the daytime TV serials "The Edge of Night" (1962–1972), "One Life to Live" (1984), and "Young Dr. Malone" (1981–1982). He also appeared on "Kraft Theater" (1954) and "Summer Stock" (1956).

GILLETTE CAVALCADE OF SPORTS

1947–1954	ABC	Fri.	10 PM
1954–1955	(Off the air)		
1955–1957	NBC	Fri.	10 PM

This program featured the "Fight of the Week," with boxing commentators Don Dunphy and Bill Corum. Sports specials, such as the coverage of the Joe Louis–Rocky Marciano bout in 1951 and Marciano's title-winning bout against Jersey Joe Walcott in 1952, were sponsored by Gillette Super-Speed razor, Gillette Blue razor blades, Gillette Foamy shaving cream, and Paper Mate pens.

GILMOUR'S ALBUMS

| 1956–present | CBC Stereo (FM) | Sat., Sun. | 6 & 12 PM |

Clyde Gilmour of *Gilmour's Albums*, the CANADIAN BROADCASTING CORPORATION's highest-rated music show, has been on the air for more than thirty-five years. The seventy-nine-year-old Gilmour continues to be the program's major attraction, in part because of his calm, soothing voice. Often playing pop, semiclassical, and classical recordings from his private collection, he entertains listeners each week with a wide variety of new and old records (though no rock music).

GINNY SIMMS SHOW, THE (AKA JOHNNY PRESENTS GINNY SIMMS; BORDEN PRESENTS GINNY SIMMS; THE COCA-COLA PROGRAM)

1941–1942	CBS	Fri.	9:55 PM
1942–1945	NBC	Tues.	8 PM
1945–1946	CBS	Fri.	7:30 PM
1946–1947	CBS	Fri.	9 PM
1947–1951	(Off the air)		
1951–1952	ABC	Sun.	10 PM

Originally a vocalist with Kay KYSER's band and a regular on KAY KYSER'S KOLLEGE OF MUSICAL KNOWLEDGE, singer Ginny SIMMS had several 15-minute and half-hour shows of her own throughout the 1940s. Known for her rich contralto pop voice, Simms popularized such songs as "Don't Ever Change," "St. Louis Blues," "Stardust," and "Frenesi." Her various shows, which were always called *The Ginny Simms Show*, featured Frank De Vol and his orchestra and the Buddy Cole Trio. This program was transmitted over the ARMED FORCES RADIO SERVICE and made Simms the favorite singer of millions of GIs during World War II. Don WILSON and Frank Graham were the program's announcers. Harry Saz directed Ginny's various programs. Philip Morris cigarettes, Bethany fabric mills, Coca-Cola soft drink, and Borden's dairy products were the show's sponsors.

GIRL ALONE

1935–1936	NBC Red	Mon.–Fri.	11 AM
1936–1937	NBC Red	Mon.–Fri.	12 PM
1937–1941	NBC Red	Mon.–Fri.	5 PM

The heroine of this 15-minute show, Patricia Rogers—played by veteran radio actress Betty WINKLER throughout the program's run—was a young, independent working woman who lived in her own apartment in a large unnamed American city, supported herself, and even managed to adopt an orphaned young girl. Supporting Winkler were Joan Winters, Fern Persons, Betty Caine, Sidney Ellstrom, Herb Nelson, Fred Sullivan, Don Briggs, Pat Murphy, Arthur Jacobson, June Travis, Dan Sutter, Hope Summers, Charles Penman, Michael Romano, Marylee Robb, Kathryn Card, Henry Hunter, Les DAMON, Karl WEBER, Syd Simons, Betty Lou GERSON, Janet Logan, Willard WATERMAN, Ted Maxwell, Laurette FILLBRANDT, Ian Keith, Bob Jellison, Fran CARLON, Art Kohl, Dan Gallagher, and Stanley Gordon. Announcers were Charles Lyon and Bob Brown. The series was written by Fayette Krum. Gordon Hughes and Blair Walliser directed the program. Sponsors included Kellogg's cereals and Quaker Oats. The program's theme song was "The Cecile Waltz."

GIVE AND TAKE

1945–1946	CBS	Sat.	10 AM
1946–1947	CBS	Mon.–Fri.	10 AM
	CBS	Sat.	2 PM
1947–1949	CBS	Sat.	2 PM
1949–1952	CBS	Sat.	1:30 PM
1952–1954	CBS	Sat.	11:30 PM

On this half-hour CBS quiz program, contestants would select items from a table full of prizes. They were then given $750 and could buy jewelry and merchandise up to that amount by correctly answering questions worth various dollar amounts. Money was subtracted from the $750 they had been given whenever they missed a question. The show was hosted by John Reed KING and then Bill CULLEN. Jack

Carney directed. The program's announcers were Jim Brown and Bill Cullen. Sponsors included Chef Boy-Ar-Dee food, Toni Home permanent, and Toni creme shampoo.

GLAMOUR MANOR

1944–1945	NBC Blue	Mon.–Fri.	12 PM
1945–1947	ABC	Mon.–Fri.	12 PM

Tenor Kenny Baker was the singing star and master of ceremonies of this 15-minute daytime comedy variety program that revolved around a mansion that had been turned into a health spa where characters would go to become glamorous. Featured in the supporting cast were Barbara Eiler as Barbara, Sam Hearn as Schlepperman, Elvia ALLMAN as Mrs. Biddle, Cliff ARQUETTE as Mrs. Wilson and Captain Billy, Bea BENADERET as Wanda Werewulf, and Tyler McVey, Lurene TUTTLE, Tom Carr, Terry O'Sullivan, Jack Bailey, Hal Stevens, and Charles Hale. Announcers for the series included Rod O'Connor, Don WILSON, and Terry O'Sullivan. The show was written by Carl Jampel, Walt Farmer, Sid Goodwin, Wright Esser, Charles Rinker, and Frank Moore. Ken Burton directed the program. Kenny Baker's theme song was "The Donkey Serenade." Sponsors were Ivory Snow soap powder and Crisco shortening.

GLENN MILLER SHOW, THE (AKA MUSIC THAT SATISFIES)

1939–1941	CBS	Tues., Thurs.	10 PM
1941–1942	CBS	Tues., Thurs.	7:15 PM

Swing bandleader Glenn Miller, whose dance band was one of the most successful musical groups in America, was the star of this 15-minute twice-a-week program. The show had been on the air for three years when Miller died in an airplane crash while traveling overseas to entertain troops during World War II. Featured on Miller's show were vocalists Frances LANGFORD and Marion Hutton. Some of the hit songs Miller popularized were "A String of Pearls," "Pennsylvania 6–5000," "In the Mood," and "Moonlight Serenade," which became his signature song. The program's announcer was Del SHARBUTT. Chesterfield cigarettes sponsored the series.

GLUSKIN, LUD (1899–1989)

Musical director Lud Gluskin was born in Poland and emigrated with his parents to the United States as a child. An outstanding musician and conductor, he led the orchestra and was the music director for *The KEN MURRAY SHOW*, many Norman CORWIN specials, and *The ADVENTURES OF SAM SPADE, DETECTIVE*. Gluskin was on the staff at CBS for many years and was musi-

director of countless CBS-TV and radio programs. He also conducted many concerts.

G-MEN

See GANGBUSTERS.

GODFREY, ARTHUR "RED" (1904–1983)

New Jersey–born Arthur Godfrey began his long and prosperous radio career at a small station, WFBP, in Baltimore, Maryland, where he sang and played his ukelele. After joining the NBC network announcing staff, he moved to CBS as host of its early-morning show. Godfrey discussed the current political and entertainment issues and interviewed guests. When President Franklin D. Roosevelt died in 1945, Godfrey's eloquent, unashamedly tearful radio coverage of the president's funeral touched the nation's heart and made Godfrey even more popular than he was before. He hosted the midmorning ARTHUR GODFREY TIME continuously from 1945 until 1972; ARTHUR GODFREY'S TALENT SCOUTS from 1946 until 1954, a variety talent show that featured instrumentalists and comedians; and in the 1950s, a weekly TV variety show, the "number-one" program in the country for several years. In the 1960s and 1970s, Godfrey made occasional guest appearances on various TV programs and even starred in a film, *The Glass Bottom Boat* (1966), playing Doris Day's father. Although Godfrey later battled cancer, he continued to perform on various TV specials for CBS until shortly before his death.

See ARTHUR GODFREY SUNDIAL SHOW, *The*.

GOFF, NORRIS (1904–1978) AND CHESTER LAUK (1901–1989)

Norris Goff and Chester Lauk gained fame as radio's LUM AND ABNER. Born and raised in Allene, Arkansas, which was very similar to the fictional small town Pine Ridge in their show, the two met in high school and later attended the University of Arkansas, where they often performed comedy routines in college variety shows. After college, the two young men opened a small store in Allene and, during their "off" hours, performed some of their comedy routines on a local radio station, KTHS, where the team first introduced their celebrated Lum and Abner characters. Network officials soon offered them a national show, which ran for twenty-two years.

GOLDBERGS, THE (AKA THE RISE OF THE GOLDBERGS)

1929–1930	NBC Blue	Wed.	7:15 PM
1930–1931	NBC Blue	Sat.	7:30 PM
1931–1932	NBC Red	Mon.–Sat.	7:45 PM
1932–1934	NBC Red	Mon.–Fri.	7:45 PM
1934–1935	CBS	Mon.–Fri.	5:45 PM

Gertrude Berg played Molly Goldberg on *The Goldbergs*. (CBS)

1935–1936	CBS	Mon.–Fri.	11 AM
1936–1937	NBC Red	Mon.–Fri.	12:15 PM
1937–1939	CBS	Mon.–Fri.	12:15 PM
1939–1940	CBS	Mon.–Fri.	1 PM
1940–1941	CBS	Mon.–Fri.	5:15 PM
	NBC	Mon.–Fri.	11:30 AM
1941–1945	CBS	Mon.–Fri.	1:45 PM
1945–1949	(Off the air)		
1949–1950	CBS	Fri.	8 PM

This long-running domestic comedy-drama program was the brainchild of talented Gertrude BERG, who wrote it and starred as Molly Goldberg, the quintessential Jewish mama. Originally called *The Rise of the Goldbergs*, the 15-minute and then half-hour story centered around the Goldbergs, a typical first-generation American Jewish family that included Mama Molly (Berg), Papa Jake (James Waters), their children Rosalie (Roslyn Silber) and Sammy (Alfred "Corn" Ryder and then Everett SLOANE), and their elderly Uncle David (Menasha SKULNIK). The program was different from other daytime drama series in that the family members were usually involved in relatively undramatic, everyday situations, such as deciding what everyone wanted for dinner or how to get

Sammy his first pair of long pants when the family had little money. Adele RONSON played David's daughter, who was usually away attending college. Other actors heard regularly included Arnold STANG, Eddie Firestone, Jr., Kate McComb, Tess Sheehan, Barbara Lee, Raymond Edward JOHNSON, Sidney Slon, Joan Tetzel, Zina Provendie, Joan Vitez, Garson Kanin, Minerva PIOUS, Joseph Cotten, Van Heflin, Philip Loeb, George Tobias, Georgia Burke, and Marjorie Main. The program's directors were Wes McKee and Henry Salinger, but Berg held the reins tightly when it came to everything concerning her program. *The Goldbergs'* theme music was Tosellio's "Serenade." Clayton "Bud" COLLYER, Alan Kent, and Art Millet were the show's announcers. *The Goldbergs* was sponsored by Duz and Oxydol detergents, Pepsodent toothpaste, and Sanka coffee.

GOOD WILL HOUR, THE

See JOHN J. ANTHONY SHOW, THE.

GOODMAN, AL (1891–1972)

Born in New York, Goodman was music director for programs such as *The BOB HOPE SHOW*, *The FRED ALLEN SHOW*, *Hit the Jackpot*, *The PRUDENTIAL FAMILY HOUR*, SHOW BOAT, YOUR HIT PARADE, and *The ZIEGFELD FOLLIES OF THE AIR*. He also composed and arranged music for many radio programs whose orchestras he conducted. From the early 1960s, Goodman was a music director and conductor on television and in the recording industry.

GOODMAN, BENNY (1908–1986)

Orchestra leader Benny Goodman, "the King of Swing," was born in Chicago, Illinois. Regularly heard on many big-band remote radio broadcasts during the 1930s and 1940s, he was one of the stars of the short-lived *Let's Dance* series. Goodman first took clarinet lessons at Huff House in Chicago when he was ten years old, later playing clarinet with various jazz groups in that city. In 1928, he went to New York City and performed in Paul Whiteman's, Ben Pollock's, and Ted Lewis's dance bands until 1934, when he formed his own orchestra. In 1939, Goodman wrote a book about jazz called *The Kingdom of Swing*, which added to his growing reputation as a first-class musician. In the 1940s, Goodman also made music history when he became the first swing musician to perform at New York City's legendary Carnegie Hall. He commissioned composer-cellist Bela Bartok to write "Contrasts" for him, and in concert he performed clarinet solos by contemporary American composers Aaron Copeland, Leonard Bernstein, and Morton Gould. During the later years of his life, Goodman concentrated on playing the clarinet at classical concerts, while continuing to perform in jazz and swing concerts around the world.

GOODWIN, BILL (1907–1959)

Announcer-actor Bill Goodwin was born in San Francisco, California, and studied law at the University of California. He decided to become an actor and appeared in a professional stage production of a play called *Broken Wing* (1929). After working with the Henry Duffy Players in Portland, Oregon, he joined radio station KFBK in San Francisco and, in 1930, CBS's KHJ in Los Angeles as a staff announcer. On the BURNS AND ALLEN SHOW, his Swan soap conversations with George and Gracie got almost as many laughs as the stars' jokes. Goodwin also had a regular comedy role on the EDGAR BERGEN-CHARLIE MCCARTHY *Show* in addition to his announcing chores on that show. He announced BLONDIE, *Feminine Fancies*, *The Louella Parsons Show*, AL PEARCE AND HIS GANG, *The CAMEL CARAVAN*, *The Park Avenue Penners*, and *The BOB HOPE SHOW* and he is featured in several motion pictures, such as *The Jolson Story* (1946), *Jolson Sings Again* (1950), and *Going Steady* (1958).

GORDON, BERT (BARNEY GORODETSKY: 1898–1974)

Best known as the Mad Russian on *The EDDIE CANTOR* and MILTON BERLE shows, comedian Bert Gordon was born in New York City. He became a vaudeville performer in 1914 and worked as an actor in both New York Yiddish theater productions and on Broadway in *George White's Scandals* (1921). The comic Russian character he played on Cantor's and Berle's radio shows was first introduced on *The JACK BENNY SHOW* in the early 1930s. Gordon also played the Mad Russian on the BEN BERNIE, PHIL BAKER, and LOU HOLTZ programs. Gordon's films include *The Amazing Colossal Man* (1957) and *The Magic Sword* (1962).

GORDON, GALE (CHARLES T. ALDRICH: 1905–1995)

Comedian–actor Gale Gordon was born in New York City. Radio listeners of the 1940s and 1950s recognized his voice as that of the ever-exasperated principal Mr. Conklin on the OUR MISS BROOKS situation-comedy series. Gale Gordon's radio credits extend to a wide variety of supporting characters on LUX RADIO THEATER, as well as BIG TOWN, *Dear John*, FIBBER MCGEE AND MOLLY (on which he played Mayor La Trivia), BURNS AND ALLEN, MY FAVORITE HUSBAND (as Rudolph Atterbury), *The Casebook of Gregory Hood*, *The GREAT GILDERSLEEVE*, *Johnny Madero, Pier 23*, DR. CHRISTIAN, *Star Theater*, *The JOE E. BROWN SHOW*, *The JUDY CANOVA SHOW*, JUNIOR MISS, THOSE WE LOVE, and *The Coronet Show*. As a young actor in Chicago, Gordon eve

Gale Gordon (CBS-TV)

played the heroic title role on the FLASH GORDON children's adventure serial. In addition to recreating Mr. Conklin on the "Our Miss Brooks" television series, Gordon is well remembered as bank president Mr. Mooney on "The Lucy Show" and "Here's Lucy."

GOSPEL SINGERS, THE

1933–1934	NBC Blue	Tues., Thurs., Sat.	10 AM
1934–1935	NBC Blue	Tues., Thurs., Sat.	10:15 AM
1935–1936	NBC Blue	Mon.–Sat.	10:15 AM
1936–1938	NBC Blue	Mon.–Fri.	11:45 AM
1938–1939	NBC Red	Mon.–Thurs.	9:45 AM
1939–1940	(Off the air)		
1940–1942	NBC Red	Mon.–Fri.	9:45 AM
1942–1943	(Off the air)		
1943–1944	NBC	Mon.–Fri.	1:15 PM

This religious program focused on singing hymns. The series was hosted by Edward MacHugh and featured a chorus of professional singers. When the half-hour program was canceled in 1939, the public outcry was so great that NBC put it back on the air for two more years. When it was canceled again, literally millions of listeners wrote to NBC demanding the show's return. The network obliged, and the show was back on the air for one final season. The program was sponsored by Ivory soap and flakes.

GOTHARD, DAVID (1911–1977)

David Gothard's rich, romantic baritone voice made him a major love interest on several daytime radio dramas. Born in Beardstown, Illinois, he was a stage actor before he began in radio in 1932 as an announcer. Gothard was a featured actor on BACHELOR'S CHILDREN, BIG SISTER, HILLTOP HOUSE, PAINTED DREAMS, CURTAIN TIME, LIGHT OF THE WORLD, *The* O'NEILLS, *The* RIGHT TO HAPPINESS, *The* ROMANCE OF HELEN TRENT (as the ever-patient and loving Gil Whitney), and *The* WOMAN IN WHITE. He also starred as Nick Charles on the prime-time *The* ADVENTURES OF THE THIN MAN mystery-adventure series.

GOULDING, RAY

See BOB AND RAY; BOB AND RAY SHOW, THE.

GOWDY, CURT (1919–   )

Newscaster Curt Gowdy had been a basketball star on the University of Wyoming's winning teams during 1941 and 1942; he soon began his sportscasting career by announcing basketball games in his hometown, Cheyenne, Wyoming. Gowdy's career was interrupted when he entered the military during World War II, but after his honorable discharge from the army, he was hired to announce games at Wyoming University. In 1949, Gowdy won a national competition for sports commentators conducted by NBC and became Mel ALLEN's partner on *Game of the Week*. Gowdy remained active with that network for many years thereafter, covering most of the major baseball, football, and basketball games.

GRACIE FIELDS SHOW, THE

1942–1943	NBC Blue	Mon.–Fri.	10:15 PM
1943–1944	Mutual	Mon.–Fri.	9:15 PM
1944–1945	NBC Blue	Tues.	9 PM
1945–1951	(Off the air)		
1951–1952	Mutual	Fri.	8:30 PM

British music-hall singer-comedienne Gracie Fields was a very successful performer on both sides of the Atlantic. Her weekly half-hour program was on American radio for three years in the early 1940s, and she returned in 1951 for another season. Fields's shows featured comedic songs and had a rather slight pseudobiographical story line. Guest stars Fred ALLEN, Jack BENNY, and Bing CROSBY were often featured in satirical sketches with the comedienne-singer. Regulars on her program were "the Arkansas Traveler" Bob BURNS and the Spartan Quartet. Bill GOODWIN and Don HANCOCK were Fields's announcers. Pall Mall cigarettes and Bristol-Meyers sponsored the program.

GRAND CENTRAL STATION

1937–1938	NBC Blue	Fri.	8 PM
1938–1940	CBS	Fri.	10 PM
1940–1941	NBC Blue	Tues.	9 PM
1941–1942	NBC Red	Fri.	7:30 PM
1942–1944	(Off the air)		
1944–1948	CBS	Sat.	1 PM
1948–1951	CBS	Sat.	12:30 PM
1951–1953	CBS	Sat.	1 PM

The half-hour *Grand Central Station* program had one of radio's best remembered openings: "As a bullet seeks its target, shining rails in every part of our great nation are aimed at *Grand Central Station! Grand Central Station*—heart of the country's greatest city. Drawn by the magnetic force—the fantastic metropolis—day and night, great trains rush toward the Hudson River, sweep down its eastern bank for 140 miles, flash briefly past the long red row of tenement houses south of 125th Street, dive with a roar into the two-and-one-half-mile tunnel which burrows beneath the glitter and swank of Park Avenue, and then . . . *Grand Central Station*—crossroads of a million private lives."

This dramatic anthology series presented original radio dramas, each featuring a story about one of the "million private lives" that passed through the train terminal. During World War II, one memorable story concerned a young sailor who had only two days to get home to visit his fiancée before he was shipped overseas.

Actors heard on the program included Arnold MOSS, Hume Cronyn, Nancy Coleman, Beverly Bayne, Charlotte MANSON, Adelaide Klein, Elaine Kent, Barbara Lee, Mary MASON, John Reed KING, Jim AMECHE, and Elliott Reid. Tom Shirley, George Baxter, and Ken ROBERTS were the show's announcers. The program was directed by William Rousseau, Ray H. Kremer, and Ira Ashley. Writers for the series included Martin Horrell, David Ragan, Dena Reed, Elinor Lenz, Ethel Abby, and Jay Bennett. Johnny Green was music director. Listerine mouthwash, Rinso cleanser, Pillsbury flour, Proctor and Gamble products, Toni home permanent, Cream of Wheat cereal, and Campbell's soups each sponsored the series.

GRAND HOTEL

1933–1934	NBC Blue	Sun.	5:30 PM
1934–1937	NBC Blue	Sun.	6:30 PM
1937–1938	NBC Blue	Sun.	8:30 PM
1938–1939	NBC Blue	Mon.	8:30 PM
1939–1940	CBS	Sun.	1:30 PM
1940–1944	(Off the air)		
1944–1945	NBC	Sat.	5 PM

Grand Hotel, a half-hour dramatic series that took place in a large metropolitan hotel, each week told stories about such hotel guests as a famous actress, a con artist, an ace airplane pilot, and a cowboy. Betty WINKLER played the hotel's telephone operator, the character who opened each show. Also heard on the series at different times were Don AMECHE, Raymond Edward JOHNSON, Don Briggs, Anne SEYMOUR, Phillips H. LORD, Betty Lou GERSON, Henry Hunter, Charles EAGLESTON, Henry Drew, Jean David, Jim AMECHE, Barbara LUDDY, Ted Maxwell, Jane WEBB, Cornelius Peeples, and Olan SOULE. Joe Ainley produced and directed, and Vincent Pelletier was the announcer. Campana Italian Balm skin moistener and Campbell's soups were the show's sponsors.

GRAND OLE OPRY, THE

1925–1941	(Various times and stations)		
1941–1942	NBC Red	Sat.	10:30 PM
1942–1951	NBC	Sat.	10:30 PM
1951–1954	NBC	Sat.	9:30 PM
1954–1955	NBC	Sat.	10:30 PM
1955–1956	NBC	Sat.	9:30 PM
1956–present	(Syndicated series. Various times and stations)		

The Grand Ole Opry—the most popular country-western radio program of all time—made its local Nashville debut on WSM in 1925, was an NBC network offering from 1939 until 1957, and then became a syndicated program that can still be heard on numerous stations throughout the country. Its first program originated from a small studio, but as the show's popularity increased, a theater was built especially to accommodate the large number of people who wanted to see the show "live" and paid the 25 cents admission to do so. The one-hour program's originators were George D. HAY and Jimmy Thompson, and its directors were Kenneth W. McGregor, Jack Stapp, and Ot Devine.

Very few country-western stars have not been heard on *The Grand Ole Opry* at one time or another. Some who performed regularly on the series included Red FOLEY, Ernest Tubb, Jimmy Riddle, the Cumberland Mountain Boys, Roy ACUFF, Gene AUTRY, Hank Williams, Eddy Arnold, Patsy Cline, and Loretta Lynn as well as comedians Rod Brasfield, Grandpa Jones, and "Cousin" Minnie PEARL. David Stone was the show's announcer in the late 1930s and early 1940s. Writers have included Dave Murray, Cliff Thomas, and Noel Digby. Over the years, sponsors have included Schick razors and blades, Coca-Cola soft drinks, Kellogg's cereals, Lava soap, R. J. Reynolds and Prince Albert tobacco, and Pet milk.

GRAND SLAM

1947–1953	CBS	Mon.–Fri.	11:30 PM

Mississippi-born Irene Beasley was the hostess of this quiz program that used the card game bridge as its model. Beasley, who debuted in 1931 and starred on *The Irene Beasley* and *The Zerone Jesters* shows, created *Grand Slam*. Like the card game, this half-hour show had two teams of two members each who bid for the right to answer a question and therefore score points. When a studio contestant failed to answer a question correctly, or "missed a trick," the prize was awarded to the listener who had submitted the question. Five correct answers won a contestant a $100 U.S. savings bond. Dwight WEIST was the show's announcer. Kirby Ayers and Victor Sack directed the show, and Beasley and Lillian Shoen wrote it. Wesson oil and Wonder bread sponsored the program.

GRAUER, BEN (1908–1977)

Radio personality Ben Grauer was born on Staten Island in New York City. As a young man, he worked as a film extra and then joined the NBC staff of announcers in 1930. Grauer hosted or announced such quiz, music, and panel shows as *Atlantic Spotlight, The* MAGIC KEY, *The Sealtest Sunday Night Party, The* BATTLE OF THE SEXES, *Pot O' Gold,* and *What Would You Have Done?* He was also the announcer on *Circus Days, The* HENRY MORGAN SHOW, INFORMATION PLEASE! GRAND CENTRAL STATION, MR. KEEN, *Tracer of* LOST PERSONS, *True Story,* KAY KYSER'S KOLLEGE OF MUSICAL KNOWLEDGE, and the WALTER WINCHELL SHOW. He is, however, probably best remembered as the longtime announcer of the NBC Symphony broadcasts, for his distinguished voice and staccato manner of speaking. Grauer also provided narration for films, most notably *Kon-Tiki* in 1951.

GREAT GILDERSLEEVE, THE

1941–1942	NBC Red	Sun.	6:30 PM
1942–1946	NBC	Sun.	6:30 PM
1946–1954	NBC	Wed.	8:30 PM
1954–1955	NBC	Sun., Thurs.	10:15 PM
1955–1956	NBC	Thurs.	8:30 PM

Throckmorton P. Gildersleeve was a popular character on the FIBBER MCGEE AND MOLLY SHOW. Because of this popularity, NBC created his own show. A blustering but good-hearted small-town water commissioner, Gildersleeve raised his orphaned niece and nephew, Marjorie and Leroy, with the help of his African-American maid, Birdie Lee Goggins. Hal PEARY starred as Gildersleeve for nine years. Due to contract disputes, Peary left the half-hour show, and Willard WATERMAN, who sounded amazingly like Peary, took over the role of Gildersleeve, playing the part for thirteen years until the program went off the air in 1956. Waterman also played the part on the TV version in 1955. The rest of the cast included Lillian RANDOLPH as Birdie; Walter TETLEY as Leroy; and Lurene TUTTLE, Marylee Robb, and Louise ERICKSON

Hal Peary as Gildersleeve with Walter Tetley and Louise Erickson (NBC)

as Marjorie. Peavey, the druggist, was played by Richard Legrand and then Forrest Lewis; Oliver Honeywell by Hans CONRIED; Floyd the barber by Arthur Q. BRYANT; Southern belle Leila Ransom by Shirley MITCHELL; Bronco Thompson by Richard CRENNA; Adeline Fairchild by Una Merkel; Eve Goodwin by Bea BENADERET and Cathy LEWIS; and Judge Hooker by Earl Ross. John Ward, Harlow WILCOX, Jim Bannon, Jay Stewart, and Bob Heistand were the program's announcers. Fran Van Hartenfeldt, Karl Gruener, and Cecil Underwood directed the series. Writers included John Whedon, Sam Moore, Virginia Safford Lynn, and Andy White. *The Great Gildersleeve* was sponsored by Kraft foods, General Mills products, Parkay margarine, Pabst beer, Velveeta cheese substitute, and Orange Crush drink.

GREATEST STORY EVER TOLD, THE

1947–1949	ABC	Sun.	6:30 PM
1949–1956	ABC	Sun.	5:30 PM

This half-hour religious program presented original stories set in biblical times and centered around the words and wisdom of Jesus Christ. Based on the popular book of the same title by Fulton J. Oursler, the series was written by Henry Denker and directed by Denker and Marx Loeb. The scripts always featured Christ's words as written in the Bible, spoken by actor Warren Parker. Robert DRYDEN, Ronald LISS, Abby LEWIS, and Roger DeKoven were frequently featured in the cast. Norman Rose announced, and Jacques Belasco was music director. The program was sponsored for many years by the Goodyear Tire and Rubber Company.

GREAZA, WALTER (1897–1973)

Walter Greaza was born in St. Paul, Minnesota, and served in the United States Navy during World War I before studying drama at the University of Minnesota. Greaza's mature, masculine voice made him perfect for authoritative roles in countless radio programs. He played regular running roles on BIG TOWN as Steve Wilson, CRIME DOCTOR as Dr. Ross, The FBI IN PEACE AND WAR, BUCK ROGERS in the 25th Century, and daytime serials LORA LAWTON and The RIGHT TO HAPPINESS. On television, Greaza starred on "Men in Action" and played Winston Grimsley on "The Edge of Night" daytime serial from 1956 until 1973.

GREEN HORNET, THE

1938–1939	Mutual	Tues., Thurs.	8:30 PM
1939–1940	Mutual	Tues., Thurs.	8 PM
1940–1941	NBC Blue	Mon., Wed.	8 PM
1941–1942	NBC Blue	Sat.	8 PM
1942–1943	NBC Blue	Sun.	4:30 PM
1943–1944	NBC Blue	Sat.	10:30 PM
1944–1945	NBC Blue	Tues.	7:30 PM
1945–1946	ABC	Tues.	7:30 PM
1946–1947	ABC	Sun.	4:30 PM
1947–1948	ABC	Tues.	7:30 PM
1948–1950	ABC	Tues., Thurs.	5 PM
1950–1953	Mutual	Mon., Wed., Fri.	5 PM

On this half-hour series, young publisher Britt Reid disguised himself as the Green Hornet and hunted down "the biggest game of all, public enemies who try to destroy America." The Green Hornet series was created and developed by the creators of The LONE RANGER, George W. TRENDLE and Fran STRIKER. Like the ranger, Reid had a "faithful companion," Kato, who aided him in his crime solving and served as his valet. Before World War II, Kato was Japanese; once the war began, he became Filipino. The Lone Ranger had his horse, Silver, for transportation, while the Green Hornet had his amazing car, Black Beauty, which buzzed like a hornet in flight. Al HODGE, Donovan Faust, Bob Hall, and then Jack McCarthy played Britt Reid; Raymond Hayashi, Rollon Parker, and then Mickey Tolan played Kato; and Lee Allman was featured as Reid's secretary, Lenore "Casey" Case. Also heard were Jim Irwin, Gil Shea, Jack Petruzzi, Harry Goldstein, Paul Hughes, Bill Saunders, Ernie Winstanley, and Lois Kibbee. Announcers were Charles Woods, Mike Wallace, Fred Foy, Fielden Farrington, Bob Hite, and Hal Neal. The series was produced by Ted Robertson and James Jewell and directed by Robertson and Charles Livingstone. Jewell also wrote for the show. The series' theme music was Rimsky-Korsakov's "The Flight of the Bumble Bee." Sponsors included General Mills products and Orange Crush drink.

GREENWOOD, CHARLOTTE (1891–1978)

Long-legged stage and film comedienne Charlotte Greenwood was born in Philadelphia, Pennsylvania. She became noted for her high-kicking comedy dancing and deadpan singing onstage in Linger Longer Letty (1919) and in the films Baby Mine (1927), Down Argentine Way (1940, Springtime in the Rockies (1943), and Oklahoma! (1956). The CHARLOTTE GREENWOOD SHOW was on the air in the mid-1940s. She was also a frequent guest star on such comedy-variety programs as The FLEISCHMANN'S HOUR, The CHASE AND SANBORN HOUR, and The FIRE CHIEF, throughout the 1930s and 1940s.

GREGG, VIRGINIA (1915–1986)

Greatly admired by members of her profession, actress Virginia Gregg was considered to be one of the best performers to ever step in front of a microphone. Born in Harrisburg, Illinois, she was regularly heard on DRAGNET, LET GEORGE DO IT, ONE MAN'S FAMILY, RICHARD DIAMOND, Private Detective, DR. KILDARE, LUM AND ABNER, Have Gun, Will Travel, and The ADVENTURES OF ELLERY QUEEN. The actress's voice was also used for various cartoon characters in The Night Before Christmas (1968), These Are the Days (1974), and Space Stars (1982). Gregg appeared on many TV episodes of "Gunsmoke" between 1955 and 1975, as well as in the films I'll Cry Tomorrow (1955), Judgment at Nuremberg (1961), Spencer's Mountain (1963), and Guess Who's Coming to Dinner (1967).

GREY, NAN (1918–1993)

Actress Nan Grey was born in Houston, Texas. During the 1930s, she appeared in such films as Dracula's Daughter (1936), Three Smart Girls (1936), and Sandy Is a Lady (1941). It is, however, as Kathy Marshall on radio's THOSE WE LOVE that the actress achieved her greatest recognition, playing her usual character, a romantic ingenue. Grey was also regularly heard on The LUX RADIO THEATER and the Corliss for Ponds Cream series.

GRIMES, JACK (1926–   )

A juvenile and later adult performer on many radio programs, Jack Grimes was born in New York City. First heard on Nila MACK's Saturday morning children's fairy-tale series, LET'S PRETEND, after Mack saw him on Broadway in the play Excursions (1937), he played Huck on the Adventures of Huckleberry Finn, Marty on The Affairs of Peter Salem, Archie in ARCHIE ANDREWS, and Junior on The LIFE OF RILEY. Grimes had running roles on BRIGHT HORIZON, DIMENSION X,

Joe and Mabel, JOYCE JORDAN, GIRL INTERN, *The* MAN I MARRIED, SECOND HUSBAND, and VALIANT LADY. An active cartoon voice-over actor, Grimes's perennially adolescent-sounding voice was heard in such cartoons as "Marine Boy" (1966) and "Speed Racer" (1967) and in the films *Pendulum* (1969) and *Cold Turkey* (1971). He played the undertaker, Mr. Whitehead, on TV's "All in the Family" in the 1970s.

GRUENBERG, AXEL (1902–1981)

Born in Riga, Latvia, Axel Gruenberg directed *The Affairs of Anthony,* AGAINST THE STORM, *The* BILLIE BURKE SHOW, MARY MARLIN, *Cameos of New Orleans, The* DREFT STAR PLAYHOUSE, GIRL ALONE, LONE JOURNEY, THIS IS YOUR LIFE, and TODAY'S CHILDREN in the 1930s and 1940s. In the late 1950s, he directed television episodes.

GUIDING LIGHT, THE

1937–1938	NBC Red	Mon.–Fri.	4:15 PM
1938–1940	NBC Red	Mon.–Fri.	3:45 PM
1940–1941	NBC Red	Mon.–Fri.	11:45 AM
1941–1942	NBC Red	Mon.–Fri.	3:30 PM
1942–1944	NBC	Mon.–Fri.	2:30 PM
1944–1947	NBC	Mon.–Fri.	2 PM
1947–1956	CBS	Mon.–Fri.	1:45 PM

The Guiding Light was one of only a few serial dramas to make the transition from radio to television. Originally, the show was an "inspirational" family series that featured a minister, Dr. John Rutledge, and his daughter, Mary, as its central characters. In time, the Bauer family became central to the program. Arthur PETERSON played Dr. Rutledge, and Sarajane Wells, Vivian Fridell, and Mercedes MCCAMBRIDGE each played Mary.

Actors in running roles on the program included Ed Prentiss, Hugh STUDEBAKER, John Barclay, Helen Buell, Jane Webb, Jerry Walters, Phillips H. LORD, Theodore Goetz, Charita Bauer (also on the TV series until the mid-1980s), Peggy Fuller, Murray FORBES, Karl Weber, Staats COTSWORTH, Gloria Blondell, Gertrude Warner, Charlotte Holland, Adelaide Klein, Nancy Douglas, Charlotte MANSON, Frank Dane, Herb Nelson, Phil Lord, Dora Johnson, Sam Wanamaker, Marvin MILLER, Raymond Edward JOHNSON, Betty Arnold, Eloise Kummer, Ken Griffin, Laurette FILLBRANDT, Henrietta Tedro, Willard WATERMAN, Bret MORRISON, Bill BOUCHEY, Lesley Woods, Mary Lansing, Betty Lou GERSON, Arnold MOSS, Michael Romano, Gladys Heen, Gail Henshaw, Frank Behrens, Jone Allison, Sunda Love, and Lyle Sudrow.

The program's longtime announcer was Clayton "Bud" COLLYER, but Herb Allen, Martin Block, Fort Pearson, Ed Prentiss, and Gene Baker also announced the series. *The Guiding Light* was produced and directed by Joe Ainley and written mainly by its creator, Irna PHILLIPS. Also directing the series were Charles Urquhart, Gordon Hughes, Gilbert Ralston, Carl Wester, Harry Bubeck, Howard Keegan, Gil Gibbons, and Ted MacMurray. The show's theme song was "Aphrodite." Sponsors of the program included Camay soap, Wheaties cereal, Duz and Tide detergents, Pang-o—the White Naptha soap, and Gleem toothpaste.

GULF SCREEN THEATER

See SCREEN GUILD PLAYERS.

GUMPS, THE

1934–1935	CBS	Mon.–Fri.	12:15 PM
1935–1937	CBS	Mon.–Fri.	12 PM

The popular comic strip *The Gumps* was a local program on WGN in Chicago before it became a 15-minute network radio series in the mid-1930s. Wilmer Walter played Andy Gump, Agnes MOOREHEAD played his wife, Min, and Jackie KELK was the Gumps' son, Chester. Written and directed by Himan BROWN and Irwin Shaw, the series focused on small-town America and the humorous situations the Gumps found themselves in. On the earliest version of the show, Jack Boyle played Andy Gump, Dorothy Denver Min Gump, and Charles Flynn, Jr., Chester Gump. Bess Flynn played the Gumps' maid, Tilda, on the series. Kayro syrup and Pebico toothpaste and tooth powder sponsored the program.

GUNSMOKE

1952–1953	CBS	Sat.	8:30 PM
1953–1954	CBS	Fri., Sat.	8:30 PM
1954–1955	CBS	Sat.	12:30 PM
		Sat.	8 PM
1955–1959	CBS	Sat.	12:30 PM
1959–1960	CBS	Sun.	6:30 PM
1960–1961	CBS	Sun.	6:35 PM

Gunsmoke, later a long-running TV program, was one of the last popular dramatic programs on network radio. On radio, William CONRAD played U.S. Marshall Matt Dillon; Parley BAER his deputy, Chester Proudfoot; Georgia Ellis, saloon owner–girlfriend Kitty Russell; and Howard McNear, Doc Adams. *Gunsmoke* was noted for its well-written scripts, natural acting, exciting music, and realistic and frequent sound effects. Such sounds as horses whinnying in the background and the creaking of plank floors helped to recreate the Wild West and the town of Dodge City.

In addition to its stars, the show boasted a repertory company of actors: Harry Bartell, Larry Dobkin, Jeanette NOLAN, Virginia GREGG, Vic Perrin, Barney Phillips, John Dehner, Lou KRUGMAN, Helen Kleeb, Jack

The cast of *Gunsmoke:* (sitting) Georgia Ellis, Howard McNear, (standing from left) William Conrad, and Parley Baer (CBS)

Kruschen, Herb Ellis, Paul Frees, Ben WRIGHT, Sam EDWARDS, Richard Beals and, on occasion, Hans CONRIED, Joseph KEARNS, Jeanne Bates, Lillian Buyeff, and Virginia Christine. Announcers on the series included George Walsh, George Fenneman, and Roy Rowan.

The half-hour program was created by John Mestor and developed by Norman Macdonnell, who also directed the series. Scripts were written by Herb Purdun, Les Crutchfield, Anthony Ellis, Marion Clark, John Dunkel, and Katherine Hite. Chesterfield cigarettes, 4-Way cold tablets, Buick automobiles, Post cereals, Post toasties cereal, Doan's pain pills, and Liggett and Meyers drugs were the show's sponsors.

GUY LOMBARDO SHOW, THE

1928–1929	CBS	Tues.	11 PM
1929–1932	CBS	Mon.	10 PM
1932–1934	(Off the air)		
1934–1935	NBC Red	Wed.	10 PM
1935–1936	CBS	Mon.	8 PM
1936–1938	CBS	Thurs.	8:30 PM
		Sun.	5:30 PM
1938–1939	CBS	Mon.	10 PM
1939–1940	CBS	Mon.	10 PM
	NBC	Fri.	10 PM
1940–1941	CBS	Mon.	10 PM
1941–1942	CBS	Wed.	11:30 PM
1942–1943	CBS	Mon.,	11:30 PM
		Wed.	
1943–1945	NBC	Sat.	10 PM
1945–1946	ABC	Tues.	9 PM
1946–1949	(Off the air)		
1949–1956	Mutual	Sat.	9:30 PM

Guy Lombardo and his Royal Canadians Orchestra were featured on several 15-minute and half-hour radio shows. Appearing with Lombardo were singers Kenny Gardner, Bill Flannagan, Mindy Carson, Don Mooney, ROSE MARIE, Billy Leach, and poet Ogden Nash. Lombardo's theme music was "Auld Lang Syne; other songs he made famous include "Always," "Enjoy Yourself," and "Harbor Lights." Announcers for his various shows included Andre BARUCH, A. A. Riggs, and David Ross. Sponsors included St. Joseph aspirin, Esso oil and gasoline, Bond clothes, Lady Esther face cream, Colgate Palmolive–Peet products, Robert Burns cigars, Ballantine beer, and Chelsea cigarettes.

HALEY, JACK (1899–1979)

Actor Jack Haley was born in Boston, Massachusetts and began his show-business career in vaudeville as half of the comedy team of Krafts and Haley. As a solo performer, he starred on Broadway in such musicals as *Gay Paree* (1926), *Good News* (1928), and *Follow Thru* (1930) and then in the films *Sitting Pretty* (1933), *Mister Cinderella* (1936), *The Wizard of Oz* (1939), as the Tin Man), and *People Are Funny* (1945). Haley was one of the stars of the popular SEALTEST VILLAGE STORE radio program, which also featured comediennes Eve ARDEN and Joan DAVIS at different times. He was one of the stars of the SHOW BOAT musical-variety series and made several guest appearances on "The Kraft Musical Hall" TV variety show in the late 1950s.

HALL, CLIFF (1894–1972)

One of radio's best-known straight men, Cliff Hall was born in Brooklyn, New York. He was Jack PEARL's foil "Sharlie," on *The* JACK PEARL SHOW, where Hall asked questions and made the statements that allowed top-banana Pearl to get laughs. Hall had one of the heartiest laughs himself, and his enjoyment of practically everything Pearl said became his trademark. Hall was also featured on the *Lucky Strike Program* and was a staff announcer at both CBS and NBC before he retired from show business in the early 1960s.

HALLMARK PLAYHOUSE, THE (AKA THE HALLMARK RADIO HALL OF FAME)

1948–1951	CBS	Thurs.	10 PM
1951–1952	CBS	Thurs.	8:30 PM
1952–1954	CBS	Sun.	9 PM

The Hallmark Greeting Card Company sponsored this half-hour dramatic anthology series, which presented plays, many of which were written especially for radio and starred major Hollywood and Broadway performers: "Woman with a Sword" with Ida Lupino, "The Desert Shall Rejoice" with John HODIAK, "Immortal Wife" with Loretta Young, "Morning Glory" with Elizabeth Taylor, "Goodbye, Mr. Chips" with Ronald COLMAN, "McCloud's Folly" with Robert Young, and "20,000 Leagues Under the Sea" with Louis Jourdan and Raymond Burr. James Hilton, author of *Lost Horizon,* and then actor Lionel BARRYMORE hosted the program. Frank Goss was the announcer, and the series was produced and directed by Dee Engelbach and written by Jean Holloway. The show's theme music was "Dream of Olwen." *The Hallmark Hall of Fame* later became a popular, if only occasional, TV offering. It featured such productions as "Peter Pan" (1955) with Mary Martin, which was repeated regularly for many years.

HALLS OF IVY, THE

1950–1951	NBC	Fri.	8 PM
1951–1952	NBC	Wed.	8 PM

Ronald COLMAN and his wife, Benita Hume, starred in this half-hour situation-comedy series that took place at a small American college. Colman played college president Dr. William Todhunter Hall, and Hume played his wife, Victoria Cromwell Hall. Dr. Hall spent most episodes trying to resolve the problems affecting his staff and his students. The show was humorous in tone, and the staff of professors consisted of broadly drawn caricatures, one bombastic, another acerbic, and all kept in check by Hall's wife, Victoria. Also heard in regular supporting roles were Willard WATERMAN as Mr. Merriweather, Herbert Butterfield as Clarence Wellman, Alan REED as Professor Heathcliff, Arthur Q. BRYANT as Professor Warren, and Gloria Gordon as the Halls' maid, Penny. The series was created especially for the Colmans by Don Quinn, who also wrote scripts for FIBBER MCGEE AND MOLLY. *The Halls of Ivy* was directed by Nat Wolfe. Ken CARPENTER was the show's announcer. The program's theme song was "The Halls of Ivy." Schlitz beer sponsored the series.

HALOP, BILLY (1920–1976)

Billy Halop was born in Brooklyn, New York, and debuted as a child actor on radio. He appeared on *The CHILDREN'S HOUR, BOBBY BENSON'S ADVENTURES* (playing the leading role of Bobby), HOME SWEET HOME, THIS IS YOUR FBI, SKIPPY, MARCH OF TIME, and LET'S PRETEND. Halop also appeared in several feature films, usually playing tough-teen roles, and was the leader of the original Bowery Boys in their early films, *Bowery Champs* (1944), *Bowery to Broadway* (1944), and *Bowery Buckaroos* (1947). On television, Halop played Mr. Munson, the owner of the taxi service on "All in the Family," in the 1970s.

HALOP, FLORENCE (1922–1986)

Billy Halop's sister Florence was born in Brooklyn, New York. A child actress, she made her radio acting debut on *The Children's Hour* and then appeared on the LET'S PRETEND programs. Halop was also featured as Polly Armstead on BOBBY BENSON'S ADVENTURES. As an adult, she played comic roles such as Miss Duffy on DUFFY'S TAVERN, Hortense on *The HENRY MORGAN SHOW*, Hotbreath Hoolihan on *The JIMMY DURANTE SHOW*, and Millie's mother on the TV version of MEET MILLIE. In the early 1980s, Halop was one of the stars of TV's "Night Court" but succumbed to cancer during the series' run.

HAMILTON, GENE (1910–   )

Best known as an announcer, Gene Hamilton was born in Toledo, Ohio, but began his show-business career as a band and pop singer. Hamilton's first major radio assignment as an announcer was on *The Armour Hour* program. He also announced for LUM AND ABNER, *The VOICE OF FIRESTONE*, *Kaltenborn Edits the News*, and CLARA, LU AND EM. For many years, he hosted the critically acclaimed *First Piano Quartet* radio series. Gene Hamilton's resonant voice also greeted listeners each week on the CHAMBER MUSIC SOCIETY OF LOWER BASIN STREET program.

HAMMERSTEIN'S MUSIC HALL

1934–1935	CBS	Sun.	2:30 PM
1935–1936	NBC Red	Mon.	8 PM
1936–1937	CBS	Tues.	8 PM
1937–1938	CBS	Fri.	8 PM

Ted Hammerstein was the host of this 30-minute program of popular music and variety entertainment. Regularly featured were Lucy McLaughlan, an unidentified singer who was known as "Lazy Dan the Minstrel Man," and Armida and Guy Robertson, who sang popular songs of the time, turn-of-the-century hits, and vaudeville tunes. The show was sponsored by Hills cold tablets and Kolynos toothpaste.

HANCOCK, DON (1910–1980)

One of radio's busiest announcers, Don Hancock was born in Anderson, Indiana. He was product spokesman and narrator for LIFE CAN BE BEAUTIFUL, *Music Box Hour, The CHILDREN'S HOUR, Just Entertainment,* GRAND CENTRAL STATION, *The Golden Theater,* and *The* ROMANCE OF HELEN TRENT. Hancock also announced the Major Bowes ORIGINAL AMATEUR HOUR talent program and worked on TV commercials and as a CBS staff announcer until his retirement in the late 1970s.

HAPPINESS BOYS, THE

1921–1926	(Various times and days)		
1926–1929	NBC Blue	Fri.	(*)
1929–1932	NBC Blue	Mon.	(*)
1939–1940	WMCA (NY)	Sun.	3 PM

The singing team of Billy Jones and Ernie Hare, known to radio listeners as The Happiness Boys, sang songs, told jokes, and were among radio's earliest stars. The team began to sing on radio together as early as 1921 on local station WJZ in New York. When Jones died, Hare continued for a year, billed as "Hare of Jones and Hare," but then retired. The Happiness Boys made "Side by Side" and "The Two of Us Together" famous and were known at various times as The Interwoven Pair, The Best Food Boys, and The Taystee Loafers, according to the product that was sponsoring them. The Happiness Boys programs were usually 15 minutes in length, and their theme was "How Do You Do."

HARPER, TRUMAN

See TRUMAN HARPER, THE RUMOR DETECTIVE.

HARRIS, ARLENE (1898–1976)

Comedienne-monologist Arlene Harris, known as "the Human Chatterbox," made her theatrical debut in 1916 onstage in *The Girl from Vagabondia* in Toronto, Canada, where she was born. Harris became a successful vaudeville performer but retired from the stage when she was seriously injured in an automobile accident in 1927. In 1934, Harris made her radio debut on WFWB in Hollywood and starred in a one-woman show on that station. Attracting considerable attention on that show, she became a regular on *The* AL PEARCE AND HIS GANG program and also played Baby Snooks's mother on *The* BABY SNOOKS SHOW. After leaving radio in the 1950s, Harris continued to work as a monologist performing her one-woman show on the stage and in various nightclubs.

HARRIS, PHIL (1906–1995)

Harris, who was born in Lafayette, Indiana, was originally a drummer before forming his own band. He was first heard on radio in 1932 and became a regular on *The Jack Benny Show*. In 1946, with his wife, film star Alice FAYE, Harris starred on the FITCH BAND-WAGON; the following year, he and Faye were heard on their own PHIL HARRIS–ALICE FAYE SHOW, which remained on the air for several seasons. Harris also

The Happiness Boys: (from left) Billy Hare and Ernie Jones (NBC)

appeared in several films, most notably *The High and the Mighty* (1954), and he voiced Baloo the Bear in the Walt Disney animated feature film *The Jungle Book* (1967). Since he retired in the early 1970s, Harris, known for his generosity, has tirelessly worked for many charities.

HARTZ MOUNTAIN CANARIES SHOW, THE (AKA THE AMERICAN RADIO WARBLERS)

| 1938–1945 | Mutual | Sun. | 11:45 AM |

Jess Kirkpatrick hosted this 15-minute musical program that featured a live orchestra and a studioful of singing canaries. Often, the shows were inadvertently funny: one incident involving the famous troupe of birds has become part of radio folklore. It was customary on the show for the canaries to chirp along with the orchestra to musical diversions such as "Ah Sweet Mystery of Life" and "To a Water Lily," the canaries often being louder than the music. One Sunday morning, the band played "I'm Only a Bird in a Gilded Cage," but for some reason the birds did not sing. When Kirkpatrick nervously announced, "And now the Hartz Mountain Orchestra will play 'When the Swallows Come Back to Capistrano' *without* the Hartz Mountain canaries," the canaries began to sing louder and stronger than they had ever sung before. The sponsor of the show was the Hartz Mountain birdseed company.

HARVEST OF STARS

1945–1947	CBS	Sun.	2 PM
1947–1948	NBC	Sun.	2:30 PM
1948–1949	CBS	Wed.	9:30 PM
1949–1950	NBC	Sun.	5:30 PM

The half-hour *Harvest of Stars* was one of radio's most listened-to musical-variety shows during the years it was on the air. Film actor Raymond Massey was the program's host and regularly played major roles on the series. Also heard at various times were singer James MELTON, the Howard BARLOW and Frank Bloch orchestras, and The Harvest Players, a group of actors who performed short dramatic sketches. The series was produced and directed by Glen Heisch, who also wrote many of the show's scripts. Don HANCOCK announced the series. It was sponsored by International Harvester farm machinery.

HARVEY, PAUL (PAUL H. ARANDT: 1918–)

Paul Harvey was born in Tulsa, Oklahoma. On the air since he was fifteen years old, he first worked on radio stations in Kansas, Kalamazoo, and Chicago. Harvey gained national prominence during the Cold

War when, as an ABC news reporter, he was arrested for breaking into the Atomic Energy Commission to get a story for ABC. His syndicated radio program *The Rest of the Story*, first aired in the 1930s, was heard on many stations throughout the United States until the mid-1980s. Harvey always began his broadcasts by saying, "Good morning, America, this is Paul Harvey." Though he retired in the mid-1980s, he occasionally gives special reports on ABC and for NATIONAL PUBLIC RADIO.

HASTINGS, BOB (1927–   )

Actor Bob Hastings has been active on both radio and television for more than fifty years. Born in Brooklyn, New York, Hastings began his career in the mid-1930s as Little Bobby Hastings, "the twelve-year-old boy soprano," when he was featured on The NATIONAL BARN DANCE. As a young adult, Hastings played Archie on The ADVENTURES OF ARCHIE ANDREWS for several years and was also heard regularly on A RIGHT TO HAPPINESS and X MINUS ONE. On television, the actor had regular roles on "MacHale's Navy" (1962) and "All in the Family" (1973–1983), as well as on the daytime serials "General Hospital" (1979–1986), "Kitty Foyle" (1958), and "The World of Mr. Sweeney" (1954–1955). Hastings also supplied the voices for such animated cartoons as "Gidget Makes the Wrong Connection" (1972), "C. B. Bears" (1977–1978), "Clue Club" (1976–1979), "The New Adventures of Superman" (1969–1970) as Superboy, "The Three Robonic Stooges" (1978–1981), and Batman (1981) as the title character.

HAWK, BOB (1907–d.   )

Comedian Bob Hawk was born in Creston, Iowa, and worked as a schoolteacher before entering show business. He became one of radio's most popular quiz-show hosts with a quiz program, *The* BOB HAWK SHOW, first heard on CBS in 1945. Hawk also hosted the successful TAKE IT OR LEAVE IT, *How Am I Doin'?*, and *Thanks to the Yanks* radio programs.

HAWTHORNE HOUSE

1935–1940	NBC Red	Mon.	8:30 PM

NBC decided to follow up its hit ONE MAN'S FAMILY with *Hawthorne House*. Like *One Man's Family*, this serialized dramatic show was about a San Francisco family, but unlike the rich characters of the earlier show, the Sherwood family was "a *formerly* wealthy family" that had fallen on hard times. Pearl King Tanner played Mother Sherwood, the family's widowed matriarch. Her somewhat self-centered, spoiled offspring were played at various times by Monty Mohn, Jack Moyles, Bobbie Dean, Florida Edwards, Eddie Firestone, Jr., and Sam EDWARDS. Actors Carl Kroenke and Ted Maxwell were frequently featured in supporting roles. Carlo DeANGELO directed the program. The half-hour once-a-week series was written by David Drummond, Ray Buffum, and Cameron PRUD'HOMME. Ken CARPENTER announced the program. The show's theme song was "Melody in G Flat" by Cadman. Wesson oil sponsored the series.

HAY, BILL (1877–1978)

Born in Dumfries, Scotland, Bill Hay became a staff announcer at station KPKK in Hastings, Nebraska, in the late 1920s. He eventually went to Chicago, at the time the center of the broadcasting industry. Hay became well known in 1929 as announcer for the AMOS AND ANDY program.

HAY, GEORGE D. (1895–1968)

Hay is credited with doing more than anyone else in the United States to promote country music's growth and popularity. Born in Attica, Indiana, he served as a reporter for *The Memphis Commercial Appeal* and read announcements for the newspaper's radio station, WMC, in the early 1920s. In 1924, Hay moved to Chicago's WLS, developing his broadcasting and dramatic talents as an announcer for the NATIONAL BARN DANCE and other radio shows. After *Reader's Digest* voted him the best general announcer in the United States, he was recruited to manage the newly founded radio station WSM in Nashville, Tennessee, in 1925. Always interested in country music, Hay began to promote that art form and with Harry Stone developed the idea of *The* GRAND OLE OPRY program on WSM. He ultimately became the show's master of ceremonies and leading force. The series was soon heard on national radio. Hay, who retired in the mid-1950s, was elected to the Country Music Hall of Fame in 1966.

HAYES, HELEN (HELEN BROWN: 1900–1993)

Actress Helen Hayes, dubbed the First Lady of the American Theater, was born in Washington, D.C., and attended the Sacred Heart Convent School. She appeared in such Broadway plays as *Victoria Regina* (1935), *Happy Birthday* (1946), and *A Touch of the Poet* (1958) and performed in such films such as *A Farewell to Arms* (1932), *The Sin of Madeleine Claudet* (1932), for which she won an Academy Award, *Anastasia* (1956), and *Airport* (1970). On radio, Hayes starred in *The* HELEN HAYES THEATER, a weekly dramatic anthology that was on the air at various times from 1935 until 1946. It featured a wide variety of programs from comedy and drama to romances in a half-hour format. Hayes was also regularly featured as a guest artist on *The* SILVER THEATER, *The* LUX RADIO THEATER, *The* FORD THEATER, and *The* THEATER GUILD ON THE AIR.

HAYES, PETER LIND

See PETER LIND HAYES SHOW, *The*.

HEART'S DESIRE

| 1946–1947 | Mutual | Mon.–Fri. | 3 PM |
| 1947–1949 | Mutual | Mon.–Fri. | 3:30 PM |

Ben Alexander, who later became famous as Friday's sidekick on DRAGNET, was the host of this half-hour audience-participation show that fulfilled a contestant's fondest material dream (within reason) if she or he could answer a series of questions correctly. Listeners sent in letters stating their heart's desire; the studio audience indicated its favorite heart-rending story by the enthusiasm of its applause. The winner could garner prizes worth up to $500. The program was sponsored by Philip Morris cigarettes.

HEARTS IN HARMONY

| 1942–1944 | (Syndicated series. Various stations and times) |

The United Service Organization, which organized shows and sent performers to military installations to entertain the troops during World War II, was the background for this dramatic series concerning a volunteer singer named Penny. A typical situation had Penny fall in love with a soldier who was just about to go into battle. Played by Jone Allison, Penny's singing voice was Anne Marlowe's. Also heard on this half-hour series were Alice Yourman, King Calder, Bill LIPTON, Billy Redfield, Bob Walker, George Matthews, and Ellen Maher. The show's announcer was Ed HERLIHY, and Martha Atwell directed. Kroger, who manufactured products for the military, sponsored the program.

HEATTER, GABRIEL (1890–1972)

New York City–born news commentator Gabriel Heatter became a newspaper reporter when he was only thirteen years old. His first radio appearance was as news commentator in the thirties after participating in a public debate with presidential candidate Norman Thomas. He received instant fame in 1936 for his descriptive, ad-libbed radio report of the execution of the Lindberg baby's kidnapper and murderer, Bruno Hauptmann. Heatter's commentaries were often criticized by U. S. presidents Franklin D. Roosevelt and Harry S. Truman, whom he often criticized on the air before, during, and after World War II. Heatter was heard by millions of Americans each weekday evening for many years, and he was also a foreign correspondent during World War II. In addition, he was a participant in the NBC Blue network's popular drama series WE, THE PEOPLE, which had originally been a feature on the *The* RUDY VALLEE SHOW. For most of the latter years of his career, Heatter was the major newscaster of the Mutual Broadcasting System. His often-quoted opening line on his programs was, "Ah, there's good news tonight." Heatter retired from broadcasting in 1960 but continued to be heard on a local radio station in Miami until he died.

HEDDA HOPPER SHOW, THE

1931–1932	CBS	Sun.	10 PM
1939–1942	CBS	Mon., Wed., Fri.	6:15 PM
1944–1945	CBS	Mon.	7:15 PM
1946–1947	CBS	Sat.	10:15 PM
1950–1951	NBC	Sun.	8 PM

On and off the air from the 1930s to the 1950s, *The Hedda Hopper Show* offered 15 minutes of Hollywood gossip by one of the two most famous newspaper and magazine movie gossip columnists of the day. First an actress, she gained enormous power in the movie capital because of her syndicated newspaper column (picked up around the country) and her radio programs; like her chief rival, Louella PARSONS, Hopper could either make or break a star's career or film. When she publicly criticized Ingrid Bergman for having an extramarital affair with Italian film director Roberto Rossinili, Bergman was blacklisted by the film industry for several years. Hedda's various radio sponsors over the years included Armour Treet canned meat, Sunkist lemons, and Ivory soap.

HEIDT, HORACE (1901–1986)

Born in Alameda, California, bandleader Horace Heidt was the music conductor on radio's *Answers by the Dancers*, *Treasure Chest*, *Pot of Gold*, and STOP ME IF YOU'VE HEARD THIS ONE. He also hosted *A Night with Horace Heidt*, a talent-search program similar to the more-successful ARTHUR GODFREY'S TALENT SCOUTS show. It was on Heidt's program that accordionist Dick Contino first surfaced and attracted considerable public attention. The winner of this show's talent contest returned the following week to compete with a new set of entertainers; Contino was the winner for months. Heidt also boosted the careers of such later-to-be-famous entertainers as comedian-actor Art CARNEY and singer Gordon MacRae. Heidt continued to play band dates and concerts until he retired from show business in the 1970s.

HELEN HAYES THEATER (AKA ELECTRIC THEATER, THE)

1935–1936	NBC Blue	Tues.	9:30 PM
1936–1937	NBC Blue	Mon.	8 PM
1937–1940	(Off the air)		
1940–1941	CBS	Sun.	8 PM
1941–1946	CBS	Sat.	7 PM
1946–1948	(Off the air)		
1948–1949	CBS	Sun.	9 PM

Helen HAYES, a veteran Broadway actress, starred on several weekly half-hour dramatic anthology series on radio that were called *The Helen Hayes Theater*. On her shows, Hayes acted a wide variety of parts in original and adapted-for-radio plays, occasionally reprising her most famous role of Victoria Regina. Appearing with Hayes at different times were leading men from theater and film, among them Cyril Ritchard, Peter Ustinov, and Joseph Cotten. Hayes's usual announcer was George Bryon. The *Helen Hayes Theater* was sponsored by Sanka coffee, Lipton tea, Textron products, and, during its *Electric Theater* years, by the Electric Power and Light company.

HELPMATE

| 1941–1942 | NBC Red | Mon.–Fri. | 10:30 AM |
| 1942–1944 | NBC | Mon.–Fri. | 10:30 AM |

This short-lived, 15-minute drama series starred Arlene FRANCIS and then Fern Persons in the leading role of Linda Emerson Harper, a young single woman trying to make it in the business world in a large unnamed American city. The supporting cast included Myron MCCORMICK, John LARKIN, Judith Evelyn, Santos ORTEGA, Ruth Perrot, Kathryn Card, Karl WEBER, Sidney Ellstrom, and Beryl Vaughn. Jack Costello was the program's announcer, and Margaret Lerwerth wrote and directed. Old Dutch cleanser and Delrich dairy products were the show's sponsors.

HENRY MORGAN SHOW, THE (AKA HERE'S MORGAN)

1940–1941	Mutual	Mon.–Fri.	6:45 PM
1941–1942	Mutual	Mon.–Fri.	7:15 PM
1942–1945	(Off the air)		
1945–1948	ABC	Thurs.	10:30 PM
1949–1950	NBC	Sun.	6:30 PM

Network officials were not at all sure that Morgan's somewhat droll, acerbic delivery would appeal to radio listeners when he first went on the air, but they were quickly proven wrong. Providing support were lateral-lisping Arnold STANG as Gerard, Florence HALOP as loud-mouthed Hortense, Art CARNEY as the coarsely comic "Athlete," Madeleine Lee as the haughty Mrs. Beethoven, and Alice Pearce as the girl with a perpetual cold, Daphne. Also heard on the show, which featured comedy sketches and interviews, were Durwood Kirby, Betty GARDE, Minerva PIOUS, and Maurice Gosfield. The 15-minute and then half-hour show's orchestra was led by Bernie Green and featured the Billy Williams Quartet. Announcers were Ben GRAUER, Art Ballinger, Charles Irving, David Ross, Joe Ripley, Dan Seymour, and Ed HERLIHY. Charles Powers directed the show, whose theme music was "For He's a Jolly Good Fellow." Writers included Morgan, Aaron Ruben, Joe Stein, and Carroll Moore, Jr. Eversharp razor blades, Adler Elevator shoes, Pall Mall cigarettes, Tootsie rolls candy and lollypops, Shell oil, Lifebuoy soap, Rinso cleanser, and Vimms vitamins were the program's sponsors that braved Morgan's assaults.

HERB SHRINER SHOW, THE

See HERB SHRINER TIME.

HERB SHRINER TIME (AKA THE HERB SHRINER SHOW)

| 1948–1949 | CBS | Mon.–Fri. | 5:45 PM |

Before he became a major television personality in the 1950s, Indiana-born humorist Herb Shriner had a comedy-talk radio program in which he used down-home humor to poke fun at the political scene of the time. Durwood Kirby was the announcer. Alka-Seltzer antacid and One-A-Day vitamins sponsored the program.

HERE'S TO ROMANCE

| 1943 | NBC Blue | Sun. | 6:05 PM |
| 1943–1945 | CBS | Thurs. | (*) |

Actor Jim AMECHE and singers Buddy CLARK and Dick Haymes hosted this musical-variety program that also featured singer Larry Douglas at one time and Ray BLOCH's orchestra and chorus. Song hits of the past as well as contemporary musical favorites were performed on this half-hour weekly series. Occasionally dramatic sketches were also presented. Lanny ROSS, Kenny BAKER, Dinah SHORE, the Pied Pipers, and others made guest appearances on the show. Evening in Paris perfume and face powder sponsored the show.

HERLIHY, ED (1910–   )

Born in Boston, Massachusetts, Ed Herlihy became a frequent radio announcer and product spokesman, master of ceremonies, and program host. Herlihy hosted the long-running CHILDREN'S HOUR program on both radio and television for more than seventeen years. Other radio shows he announced included TOWN MEETING OF THE AIR, GRAND CENTRAL STATION, MR. DISTRICT ATTORNEY, *The* BIG SHOW, DICK TRACY, *The* FALCON, *The* HENRY MORGAN SHOW, INFORMATION PLEASE!, JUST PLAIN BILL, LIFE CAN BE BEAUTIFUL, MR. DISTRICT ATTORNEY, *The* O'NEILLS, *The* THIN MAN, and VIC AND SADE. For many years, Herlihy was TV spokesman for Kraft cheese. Herlihy continues to be active as an announcer on radio and television.

HERMIT'S CAVE, THE

1940–1943   (Syndicated series. Various stations and times)

Similar in format to Alonzo Dean COLE's WITCH'S TALE series, *The Hermit's Cave* presented weird and unusual half-hour supernatural stories. Practically every program featured a ghost, ghoul, or insane criminal who terrorized the story's hero and/or heroine. The director and writers of the series went uncredited.

HERSHOLT, JEAN (1886–1956)

Actor Jean Hersholt was born in Copenhagen, Denmark, the son of theatrical parents. He starred in numerous American silent and sound films, such as *Greed* (1923), *Stella Dallas* (1925), *Abie's Irish Rose* (1929), *Seventh Heaven* (1935), and *Run for Cover* (1955). Hersholt made his radio debut in 1937, and his voice became well known as the compassionate DR. CHRISTIAN. The actor had already played the role in the film *Country Doctor* (1936). The radio series remained on the air throughout the 1940s. Hersholt was the president of the Academy of Motion Picture Arts and Sciences from 1947 until 1949 and an Academy Award for humanitarian achievement is named in his honor because of his efforts in behalf of his fellow performers.

HERTZ, HEINRICH RUDOLF (1857–1894)

The eventual development of vocal sounds transmitted via radio was advanced when German-born physicist H. R. Hertz confirmed James C. Maxwell's electromagnetism theory and experimented with electromagnetic waves. He demonstrated that these were long, transverse waves that traveled at the velocity of light and could be reflected, refracted, and polarized like light, thus making sound transmission possible. Hertz also investigated electric discharge in rarefied gases. His experiments paved the way for later developments in sound transmission.

HIGBY, MARY JANE (1916–1986)

Unofficially titled "the Queen of the Daytime Serials" by fellow actors and others in the broadcasting industry, actress Mary Jane Higby was born in St. Louis, Missouri. Higby began her radio acting career in Los Angeles after making brief stage appearances. While in Hollywood, she was heard on PARTIES AT PICKFAIR, *English Coronets,* and HOLLYWOOD HOTEL. Deciding that radio might be more lucrative in New York City, Higby established herself as one of the busiest radio actresses in that city, playing major roles on *The ROMANCE OF HELEN TRENT,* JOHN'S OTHER WIFE, PERRY MASON, STELLA DALLAS, MARY MARLIN, and THIS IS NORA DRAKE, in addition to her long-running starring role as Joan Davis on WHEN A GIRL MARRIES. The actress was also a regular on popular evening favorites such as MR. KEEN, TRACER OF LOST PERSONS, *Listening Post,* and *Joe Palooka.* In 1966, Higby wrote *Tune in Tomorrow,* one of the best accounts of the early days of radio.

HILDA HOPE, MD

1939–1940   NBC Red   Sat.   11:30 AM

This half-hour dramatic series starred Selena Royle as a doctor who balanced her profession and her private life, in which she strove to find romance and maintain a social life. In the show's regular supporting cast were Richard Gordon, Ann SHEPHARD, House JAMESON, and Vera Allen. The program's announcer was Nelson CASE. Frederick K. Cooper directed the series. Wheatena cereal was the show's sponsor.

HILDEGARDE (LORETTA SELL: 1906–   )

Singer Loretta Sell, known as "the Incomparable Hildegarde," was born in Adell, Wisconsin, near Milwaukee, to German-American parents. Early in her career, Hildegarde toured with the dancing De Marcos, and

"The Incomparable" Hildegarde (NBC)

with Bob Albright's and Gus Edwards's theatrical troupes. On Edwards's suggestion, she went to Paris in 1926 and attracted the attention of King Gustav of Sweden, who became her most ardent fan and champion. In London, Hildegarde headlined in various cabarets and appeared on the British Broadcasting Corporation (BBC). Returning to the United States in 1928, she appeared with William Gaxton in *Keep 'Em Laughing* (1928) and became a popular supper-club entertainer.

Hildegarde charmed her audiences with her bubbly personality, Continental-sounding, saucy singing voice, and such trademarks as her arm-length gloves, a single rose, and a long lace handkerchief—the end of which was wrapped around her finger. She called herself a "French chanteuse," although most of her witty and romantic songs were sung in English with only an occasional French phrase thrown in here and there.

Hildegarde made her radio debut on *The* FLEISCH-MANN HOUR. She later starred on *The* RALEIGH ROOM, a top-ten program for four years in the 1940s, and on NINETY MEN AND A GIRL; she also hosted the BEAT THE BAND quiz program.

In 1961, former first lady Eleanor Roosevelt, in her popular newspaper column, named Hildegarde "the First Lady of Supper Clubs." Hildegarde's nightclub act remained successful until well into the 1970s. She still makes occasional public appearances and published her memoirs—*Over Fifty—So What!*—in 1962.

HILLIARD, HARRIET (HARRIET HOCTOR: 1909–1994)

Harriet Hilliard was born in Des Moines, Iowa. She had an active career as a singer and actress on radio and in such films as *Follow the Fleet* (1936), *Canal Zone* (1942), and *Here Come the Nelsons* (1952). Hilliard was heard on radio on *The* JOE PENNER SHOW and *The* RED SKELTON SHOW before costarring in *The Adventures of* OZZIE AND HARRIET with her husband, bandleader Ozzie Nelson, and her sons, David and Ricky. The "Ozzie and Harriet Show" became a television situation comedy in 1954, again starring the four Nelsons. When the TV series left the air, Hilliard retired from show business. Her sons David and Ricky continued to perform, David as an actor and Ricky as a rock-and-roll star.

HILLTOP HOUSE

1937–1938	CBS	Mon.–Fri.	5:45 PM
1938–1940	CBS	Mon.–Fri.	10:30 AM
1940–1949	(Off the air)		
1949–1951	CBS	Mon.–Fri.	3:15 PM
1951–1955	CBS	Mon.–Fri.	3 PM
1955–1957	NBC	Mon.–Fri.	3:30 PM

This long-running drama was "the story of a woman who must choose between love and the career of raising other women's children." The 15-minute series starred velvety-voiced actress Bess JOHNSON as the head of an orphanage named Hilltop House. In 1941, the program was called *The Story of Bess Johnson;* when the actress decided to leave the series, it once again became known as *Hilltop House* and starred Grace MATTHEWS and then Jan MINER in the major role of Julie Erickson. In regular supporting roles were Jimmy Donnelly, Janice Gilbert, Charlottle MANSON, Linda Carlon-Reid, Vera Allen, Carlton YOUNG, Ray Walker, Ronald LISS, Spencer Bentley, Jack Rosleigh, Ethel Everett, Jackie KELK, Helen Coule, Norma Jane Marlowe, James Van Dyke, Edwin Bruce, and Don Briggs. Frank Gallop, Dan McDonald, and Gaylord Avory announced the series, which was directed by Carlo DEANGELO and Jack Rubin. William Sweets was the program's writer. *Hilltop House*'s theme song was Brahms's "Lullaby." Sponsors included Colgate toothpaste, Palmolive soap, Alka-Seltzer antacid, Miles Nervine pain reliever, One-A-Day vitamins, and Chooz breath mints.

HINT HUNT

1947–1949	CBS	Mon.–Fri.	4 PM

On the air every weekday, this 15-minute series offered women such household hints as how to remove stains on clothes and various cooking tips. It also included audience participation in which members of the studio audience could earn up to $50 worth of merchandise for providing a household tip or for dunking for apples or even clucking and walking like a chicken. Chuck Acree was the show's master of ceremonies. Armour Star foods and Chiffon soap flakes sponsored the program.

HIS HONOR, THE BARBER

1945–1946	NBC	Tues.	7:30 PM

One of Hollywood's most beloved character actors, quintessential Irishman Barry Fitzgerald was the star of this half-hour weekly radio drama series shortly after his popular success in the film *Going My Way* (1944) with Bing CROSBY. Fitzgerald played Judge Fitz, a small-town barber who also served as the county judge and became personally involved in the problems of his customers and those who stood before him at the bench. Fitzgerald was supported on the program by Barbara Fuller, Leo Cleary, William Greene, and Dawn Bender. The show's announcer was Frank Martin. The series was written and directed by Carlton E. Morse. Ballantine ale and beer were the sponsors.

HIT THE JACKPOT

1948–1950	CBS	Tues.	9:30 PM & 10 PM
		Sun.	7:30 PM

Hit the Jackpot was hosted by Bill CULLEN. When contestants answered five preliminary questions correctly, they could win up to $5,000 and then an additional $3,000 by answering a jackpot question. Questions were of a general nature, covering such topics as art and history; they increased in difficulty as a contestant neared the jackpot question. Al GOODMAN led the show's orchestra, and the Ray Charles Singers were featured on the program each week. The announcers for this half-hour weekly series included George Bryan and Richard Stark. Mark Goodson and Bill Todman, who later created many successful game and panel television shows, produced the series. The program was directed by Todman.

HOBBY LOBBY

1937–1938	CBS	Wed.	7:15 PM
1938	NBC	Sun.	7 PM (Summer series)
1938–1939	NBC Blue	Wed.	8:30 PM
1939–1940	CBS	Sun.	5 PM
1940–1943	CBS	Sat.	8:30 PM
1943–1946	CBS	Thurs.	9:30 PM
1946–1949	(Off the air)		
1949	Mutual	Sat.	4 PM

Dave Elman, who hosted *Auction Gallery*, also hosted this half-hour human-interest series. He introduced and chatted with celebrities and people with unusual hobbies such as collecting bottle-top caps, baseball cards, and soup-can labels. Some of the celebrities who appeared on the show were Milton BERLE and Clifton FADIMAN. Alan Kent and Carl Frank were the show's announcers. Addison Smith, H. Booraem, Edward Pola, and Joe Hill were the program's directors. The show was written by Ed Ettinger and Ray Naypole, Jr. Sponsors included Fels Naptha soap, Hudson paper products, and Colgate dental cream. The show's theme music was "The Best Things in Life Are Free."

HODGE, AL (1913–1979)

Actor-director Al Hodge was born in Detroit, Michigan, and began his network-broadcasting career as a member of the creative staff at WXYZ studios in Detroit. There, he directed such programs as CHALLENGE OF THE YUKON, The LONE RANGER, and NED JORDAN, SECRET AGENT. In 1936, Hodge was the first actor to play the Green Hornet at WXYZ; he also originated the role of Tex Mason on BOBBY BENSON'S ADVENTURES. Years later in New York, Hodge was heard on numerous daytime drama series such as MA PERKINS and The ROMANCE OF HELEN TRENT. Eventually, he became the star of one of television's first children's adventure programs, "Captain Video" (1949). He continued to be a busy voice-over announcer for television commercials until shortly before his death.

HODGES, RUSS (1911–   )

Sportscaster Russ Hodges was born in Dayton, Tennessee, and attended the University of Kentucky, where he played football. After several years of announcing local sports events in or near his home state, Hodges joined the ABC sports staff in the early 1940s. In 1945, he traveled 29,800 miles to broadcast twenty-seven "live" football games for ABC. Hodges reported Big Ten football games and Chicago baseball games for ABC and then moved to CBS, where he remained for many years. The sportscaster later became one of television's major boxing announcers in the 1950s and continued as a TV sportscaster until he retired in the 1980s.

HODIAK, JOHN (1914–1955)

John Hodiak, the son of Ukrainian immigrants, was born in Pittsburgh, Pennsylvania, and was heard on many of the early LONE RANGER broadcasts that originated there. In the 1930s, Hodiak played the title role on the L'IL ABNER comedy series and had leading parts on such daytime serial dramas as ARNOLD GRIMM'S DAUGHTER, BACHELOR'S CHILDREN, GIRL ALONE, LONE JOURNEY, The ROMANCE OF HELEN TRENT, and *Wings of Destiny*. In the 1940s, Hodiak had lead roles in motion pictures, most notably Alfred Hitchcock's *Lifeboat* (1943) opposite Tallulah BANKHEAD and MGM's *The Harvey Girls* (1946) opposite Judy GARLAND. The actor died after suffering a heart attack at the height of his career.

HOFFA, PORTLAND (1907–1990)

Named for her hometown, Portland, Oregon, actress Portland Hoffa enjoyed a moderately successful career in vaudeville before she married Fred ALLEN and became his costar on the TEXACO STAR THEATER. Hoffa became better known on *The FRED ALLEN SHOW*, where her weekly greeting of "Ohhhh, Mr. Al . . . len!" and her famous letters from her "Momma" became popular features; "Momma" would give her news from home and warn Hoffa about the perils of the big city. She retired from show business in the late 1940s.

HOLLYWOOD HOTEL (AKA HOLLYWOOD PREMIERE)

1934–1936	CBS	Fri.	9:30 PM
1936–1938	CBS	Fri.	9 PM
1938–1941	(Off the air)		
1941	CBS	Fri.	10 PM

The cast of *Hollywood Hotel:* (from left) Louella Parsons, Dick Powell, Frances Langford, and Ted Fio Rito (CBS)

This multifaceted half-hour music-variety-comedy-drama series starred motion-picture actor Dick POW-ELL during its best years, and also featured such Hollywood luminaries as Fred MacMurray, Herbert Marshall, and William Powell as hosts. Hollywood gossip columnist Louella PARSONS was cohostess and revealed the "most intimate secrets" of the Hollywood stars. The *Hollywood Hotel* orchestra was led by Raymond Paige and Ted Fio Rito. Regular singers on the show included Anne Jamison as "Jinnie, the soprano," Frank PARKER, Jean Sablon, and Frances LANGFORD. Other regulars were Igor Gorin, Barbara Lee, Jerry Cooper, Jone Williams, and Leo Carillo. Ken NILES, Lou Crosby, and Harlow WILCOX were the program's announcers. *Hollywood Hotel* was produced by Bill Bacher, directed by George MacGarrett, and written by Ed James. The program's theme music was "Blue Moon." Sponsors included Campbell soup and Life-buoy soap.

HOLLYWOOD PREMIERE

See HOLLYWOOD HOTEL.

HOLLYWOOD STAR PREVIEW (AKA HOLLYWOOD STAR PLAYHOUSE; HOLLYWOOD PLAYHOUSE; HOLLYWOOD STAR THEATER)

1947–1948	NBC	Sun.	6:30 PM
1948–1950	NBC	Sat.	8 PM

Half-hour adaptations of major Hollywood films such as *Random Harvest, Meet John Doe,* and *Now Voyager* and dramas written especially for radio were presented. Among the stars who acted as hosts were Charles Boyer, Jim AMECHE, Gale Page, Tyrone Power, Herbert Marshall, Ray Milland, Henry Fonda, Ronald COLMAN, Adolphe Menjou, Sydney Greenstreet, Jack CARSON, Rex Harrison, Helena Carter, Lionel BARRYMORE, Joan Lorring, Shelley Winters, Don Taylor, Richard Basehart, Patricia Neal, Wanda Hendrix, Douglas Fairbanks, Jr., and Betty Garrett. The program's musical director was Harry SOSNICK; its announcer was Ken Peters, and various freelance writers wrote scripts for the series. *Hollywood Star Preview* was sponsored by Anacin pain reliever and Kolynos toothpaste.

HOLLYWOOD STAR TIME

1944	NBC Blue	Mon.–Fri.	3:15 PM
1946–1947	CBS	Sun.	2:30 PM
		Sat.	8 PM
		Thurs.	10:30 PM

This weekly dramatic anthology offered half-hour adaptations of such popular films as JUNIOR MISS, starring Peggy Ann Garner, Barbara Whiting, and Allyn JOSLYN; *Hanover Square,* starring Linda Darnell and Vincent PRICE; *Seventh Heaven,* starring Tyrone Power and Jeanne Crain; and *Laura,* starring Gene Tierney and William Eythe. Harlow WILCOX and Harry VON ZELL announced the program. The director and writers of this series were uncredited.

HOLTZ, LOU (1893–1980)

Called "America's master of dialects" and one of vaudeville's best storytellers, comedian Lou Holtz was a familiar voice to radio listeners in the 1930s and 1940s. Born in New York City, he told jokes, often using his fictional friend "Lapidus"—an Eastern European–born Jewish man—as the central character. Holtz was a regular performer on The RUDY VALLEE SHOW and The KRAFT MUSIC HALL, and he continued to perform in various nightclubs around the country until he retired from show business in the early 1960s.

HOME SWEET HOME

1934–1936	NBC Red	Mon.–Fri.	3 PM
1935–1936	NBC Red	Mon.–Fri.	10:15 PM

This 15-minute drama series told of the problems of a married couple as they tried to establish a happy home for themselves and their young son during the Great Depression. The main characters, Fred and Lucy Kent, were played by Cecil Secrest and Harriet Mac-Gibbon. Billy HALOP played the Kent's son, Dick. Also featured on the show were Spencer Bentley and Joseph "Joe" Latham. Announcers were John Monks and George Ansbro. The sponsor of the series was Chipso.

HOP HARRIGAN

1942–1943	NBC Blue	Mon.–Fri.	5:15 PM
1943–1945	NBC Blue	Mon.–Fri.	4:45 PM
1945–1946	ABC	Mon.–Fri.	4:45 PM
1946–1950	Mutual	Mon.–Fri.	5 PM

Hop Harrigan, "America's ace of the airwaves," was the main character of this popular 15-minute children's adventure series. Hop was a pilot who had numerous adventures, many of them involving enemy agents during the World War II years. Chester STRATTON and Albert ALEY played Hop. Mitzi Gould played Hop's friend, Gail Nolan; and Kenny Lynch and Jackson BECK were heard as his friend and copilot, Tank Tinker. Glenn Riggs was the program's announcer. Jessica Maxwell, Allen DuCovney, and Jay Clark directed the series, which was written by Aley in its later years. General Foods products and Cocoa Marsh chocolate-drink mix sponsored the series.

HOPALONG CASSIDY

| 1949–1950 | Mutual | Sun. | 4 PM |
| 1950–1952 | CBS | Sat. | 8:30 PM |

Brought to radio in 1949 mainly because of the success of the early television series' films—which had originally been Saturday-matinee children's movie features in the 1930s and 1940s—the radio program starred William Boyd as Hoppy and Andy Clyde as his sidekick, California. (Both actors played the same parts on radio, television, and in films.) Hoppy's trusted horse was Topper. A typical *Hopalong Cassidy* episode involved Hoppy's tracking down bank robbers or kidnappers of the bank's female teller for ransom money. Of course, Hoppy always apprehended the outlaws and saved the damsels in distress. The radio series was sponsored by General Foods products, Post cereals, and Cella vineyards.

HOPE, BOB (LESLIE TOWNES HOPE: 1903–   )

Although he is considered one of the U.S.'s most successful and patriotic comedians, Bob Hope was actually born in Kent, England. His family settled in

Cleveland, Ohio, and after finishing his schooling, Hope worked as a shoe salesman, a telephone lineman, and even a boxer before deciding to become a performer. In New York City, his sheer brass and persistence eventually impressed a Broadway producer, and he was hired to appear in the musical comedy *The Ramblers* (1926) as its juvenile lead. By the early 1930s, he was a headliner in vaudeville and had starred on Broadway shows in *Roberta* (1931) and *Red, Hot, and Blue* (1936). He also guest-starred on several music-variety radio shows, such as Rudy Vallee's FLEISCHMANN HOUR SHOW. His comedy routines were so well received by the public that he was offered a weekly radio program of his own, *The* BOB HOPE SHOW, in the mid-1930s.

Hope's fast-talking, one-line jabs at politicians, pop culture, and society in general (especially contemporary events) made him one of show business's most topical comedians. His humor was often considered somewhat off-color, and self-righteous columnists such as Dorothy KILGALLEN often criticized his routines. Voluntary performances before various military units both in the United States and abroad during World War II, the Korean War, and the Vietnam conflict, however, brought him nothing but praise, though his devoted patriotism during the Vietnam War was greatly criticized by liberal citizens.

Hope appeared in many films, such as *The Big Broadcast* (1938); the celebrated *Road* films with Bing CROSBY and Dorothy LAMOUR; *The Paleface* (1947); and *The Seven Little Foys* (1955). One of the United States's most honored comedians, Hope received an honorary Academy Award for his work in films as well as for his long-time hosting of the Academy Award ceremonies. He also garnered countless good-citizenship awards from both local organizations and the national government. He received an honorary Doctor of Humane Letters from the University of San Diego in 1990 and was elected to the Comedy Hall of Fame in 1992.

HORACE HEIDT'S YOUTH OPPORTUNITY PROGRAM

| 1948–1951 | NBC | Sun. | 10:30 PM |

Similar to *The* ORIGINAL AMATEUR HOUR talent-contest program, this half-hour weekly program showcased young, unseasoned performers. The program was hosted by bandlader Horace HEIDT, whose band offered musical accompaniments for the performers. John Holbrook was the program's announcer. The series was sponsored by Philip Morris and Revelations cigarettes.

HOT COPY

1941–1942	NBC Red	Sat.	10:30 PM
1942	NBC	Mon.	11:30 PM
		Sat.	9:30 PM
1942–1943	(Off the air)		
1943–1944	NBC Blue	Sun.	3:30 PM
1944	NBC Blue	Sun.	5:30 PM

This half-hour series concerned the adventures and romances of syndicated newspaper columnist Patricia Murphy. Eloise Kummer and then Fern Persons played Murphy, and many of radio's Chicago-based actors, such as Fran CARLON, Mercedes MCCAMBRIDGE, Les TREMAYNE, and Willard WATERMAN, were heard in supporting roles on the series. The program was sponsored by O'Cedar furniture polish.

HOTEL FOR PETS

1954–1956	NBC	Mon.–Fri.	3:30 PM

A veterinarian's office was the setting for this 15-minute drama series that starred Charlotte MANSON as a veterinarian. Also heard were Frank McHugh, Lloyd Richards, and Abby LEWIS. In between the dramatic scenes, the show provided helpful hints about pet care. The program, whose director and writers were uncredited, was appropriately sponsored by Puss'N Boots cat food.

HOUR OF CHARM, THE

1934–1935	CBS	Thurs.	8 PM
1935–1936	CBS	Thurs.	9:30 PM
1936–1937	CBS	Sun.	9:30 PM
1937–1938	NBC Red	Mon.	9:30 PM
1938–1939	NBC Red	Mon.	9 PM
1939–1942	NBC Red	Sun.	10 PM
1942–1946	NBC	Sun.	10 PM
1946–1947	CBS	Sun.	4:30 PM
1947–1948	CBS	Sun.	5:30 PM

Phil SPITALNY and his All-Girl Orchestra starred on this hour-long musical program of semiclassical and classical music. The most famous performer on the show was violinist Evelyn Kaye KLEIN. Other popular performers on the program were singer Hollace Shaw (who was called "Vivien"), vocalists Maxene and Jeannie, Katherine Smith and her cornet, and percussionist Viola Schmidt. Arlene FRANCIS hosted *The Hour of Charm* for several seasons; Rosaline Greene and Barbara Lee were featured hostesses during later broadcasts of the show. Ron Rawson, Del SHARBUTT, Ken ROBERTS, and Richard "Dick" Stark were the program's announcers. The series was directed by Joseph Ripley, although David White directed during its peak years, the late 1930s and early 1940s. The theme songs on *The Hour of Charm* were "American Patrol" and "Isle of Golden Dreams." General Electric, Linit water

softener for the bath, and Electric Companies of America were the program's sponsors.

HOUSE, THE

1991–present	CBC Radio	Sat.	9:11 AM

The CANADIAN BROADCASTING CORPORATION's one-hour *The House* program covers Canada's political scene, concentrating on Parliament Hill in Ottawa. The show also presents interviews with people who are seeking to lobby or run for office. *The House* features Judy Morrison as hostess and reporters Ray Aboud and Bill Gillespie. The series' editor-director is Doug Caldwell.

HOUSE IN THE COUNTRY

1941–1943	NBC Blue	Mon.–Fri.	10:30 AM

House in the Country was "the story of a city couple's amusing problems when they moved to the country." This 15-minute drama series was unusual in that it concentrated mainly on lighthearted, simple domestic affairs rather than heavy-handed situations such as crime and infidelity. The series starred John Raby and then Lyle Sudrow as the husband and Joan BANKS and then Patsy Campbell as the wife. Raymond Knight, Ed Latimer, and Abby LEWIS were also heard on the program. Writer and director Raymond Knight claimed to have based it on his own personal experiences as a country homeowner. Announcers included Clayton "Bud" COLLYER and Hugh James.

HOUSE OF CHARM

1930s	(Syndicated series. Various stations and times)	

Beauty and charm expert Edythe Fern Melrose hosted this popular 15-minute daytime program for women. Melrose gave advice about how women should look and act to make themselves more attractive and thus be "everything (their) husbands wanted." Miss Melrose produced, directed, and introduced her own program.

HOUSE OF GLASS

1934–1935	NBC Blue	Wed.	8:30 PM
1935–1953	(Off the air)		
1953–1955	NBC	Fri.	9:45 PM

Gertrude BERG, creator, writer, director, and star of *The* GOLDBERGS, had far less success with her half-hour weekly *House of Glass* drama series. Berg first offered it in 1934 and then tried again in 1953. Both times, the show failed to prove popular with radio listeners. Businesswoman Bessie Glass, played by

Berg, owned a small retail shop and tried to make it on her own as a single, widowed mother. Also heard on the series were Helene Dumas as Ellen Mudge, Bessie's friend and co-worker in the shop, and actresses Arline Blackburn and Adele RONSON. The sponsors were Palmolive soap and Super Suds detergent.

HOUSE PARTY (AKA GENERAL ELECTRIC HOUSE PARTY; PILLSBURY HOUSE PARTY; ART LINKLETTER'S HOUSE PARTY)

1945–1946	CBS	Mon.–Fri.	4 PM
1946–1947	CBS	Mon.–Fri.	5 PM
1947–1951	CBS	Mon.–Fri.	3:30 PM
1951–1954	CBS	Mon.–Fri.	3:15 PM
1954–1956	CBS	Mon.–Fri.	3 PM

For eleven years, this audience-participation show entertained radio listeners and then continued to do so for eleven more years on television. Art LINKLETTER was the host of the half-hour series, on which contestants chosen from the studio audience were asked to play several games usually designed to make them look foolish: Linkletter used carefully constructed questions designed to goad the contestants into buffoonery. His "kids say the darndest things" segment of the show, in which he interviewed small children, was very popular among listeners. Another familiar feature was "What's in the House?" in which Linkletter gave difficult clues about an object inside a small house; the contestant had to guess what it was. For many years, Jack Slattery was the program's announcer. The series was produced and directed by John Guedel. The show's many sponsors included General Electric appliances, Pillsbury flour, Lever Brothers soap, Swift meats, Pharmacraft drugs, Dole pineapple, Curad foot pads, Formula 409 cough medicine, and Brach's candy.

HOUSEBOAT HANNAH

1936–1938	NBC Blue	Mon.–Fri.	10:45 AM
1938–1939	NBC Red	Mon.–Fri.	10:45 AM
1939–1941	NBC Red	Mon.–Fri.	10 AM

This 15-minute drama series originated in Chicago in the mid-1930s to early 1940s and featured some of that city's busiest actors, including Henrietta Tedro and Doris Rich. Also heard were Jim Andelin, William Rose, Virginia Dwyer, Les DAMON, John LARKIN, Bonnie Kay, Carl Kronke, Gil Faust, Ethel Owen, Earle George, Jeannie Jameson, Don Gallagher, Frank Darby, and Henry Saxe. Olan SOULE, Carlton Brickert, and Gene Baker were the show's announcers. Roy Winsor directed the program. The show's theme music was "The Last Rose of Summer." Lava soap sponsored the program.

HOW TO BE CHARMING

1936	NBC Blue	Mon., Wed., Fri.	4:30 PM
1936–1938	NBC Red	Mon., Wed., Fri.	11:30 AM

Phillip's Milk of Magnesia face cream sponsored this 15-minute series that featured beauty expert Beatrice DeSylvara, who gave women advice on how to improve their appearance with the help of Phillip's Milk of Magnesia face cream.

HOWARD, JOE (1878–1961)

One of vaudeville's most successful entertainers, New York City–born comic Joe Howard hosted the popular GAY NINETIES REVUE music-variety program. One of the country's most famous stage performers in the early twentieth century, he appeared as a headliner on the vaudeville circuit before he became the host of the popular music-hall revue. Howard retired from show business in the mid-1950s, when he was in his late seventies and lived until he was in his mid-eighties.

HOWARD STERN SHOW, THE

1976–present	(Syndicated series. Mornings in various cities)

Controversial broadcaster Howard Stern hosts this three-hour early-morning talk-comedy program, which first aired in Washington, D.C. His on-the-air profanity and frequent references to various unconventional sexual practices have given the show a large following—and a great deal of opposition from the Federal Communications Commission. Stern's costar is Robin Quivers, a sort of moderator-censor for Stern's shocking banter. The producer, Gary Dell'Abate (aka Boy Gary), frequently appears on the show, as does stand-up comedian-writer Jackie "the Jokeman" Martling. The program currently airs from WXRK (K-Rock) in New York and is simulcast every weekday morning across the country.

Outrageous guests include drag queens, lesbians, prostitutes, and occasionally rock and porn-film stars. Celebrities such as exercise-diet expert Richard Simmons, novelty singer Tiny Tim, and sex-scandal personality Jessica Hahn also appear. Visits to the fictional "homo room in the basement of his studio building," frequent phone calls from his often angry wife and his mother—both of whom criticize Stern for remarks they consider too personal for him to have made—as well as his calls to lawyers, politicians, famous actors, and others in the news keep his fans listening. Stern's controversial best-selling autobiography, *Private Parts* (1993), as well as his often-discussed plans to star in a feature film as his character Fart Man are often discussed on the show.

HUGHES, ARTHUR (1893–1982)

Character actor Arthur Hughes was born in Illinois and as a stage actor appeared in *The Guardsman* (1924) and *Caprice* (1926) before becoming a radio actor in the late 1920s. Hughes played the title roles on MR. KEEN, TRACER OF LOST PERSONS, and JUST PLAIN BILL. He was regularly featured on the JUNGLE JIM series and played supporting roles on many of radio's major dramatic programs. In 1968, Hughes had a featured role in the Broadway musical comedy *How Now, Dow Jones* and later he appeared in the films *Bananas* and *The Great Gatsby*.

HUGHES, DONALD "DON" (1918–1990)

Born in New York City, actor Don Hughes was the son of vaudeville and musical-comedy performers Beth Stone and Frank Hughes. When he was twelve years old Don, who attended the Professional Children's School in New York City, appeared in the Broadway play *The Enemy* (1931). He subsequently became a regular cast member on radio's *The Adventure of Helen and Mary,* later known as LET'S PRETEND. The young actor remained with *Let's Pretend* as a regular performer until the show left the air in 1954. Hughes was also a regular on the short-lived *Danny and Rollo* series and in the 1950s turned his attention to writing scripts for such children's adventure series as MARK TRAIL and TOM CORBETT, SPACE CADET.

HULICK, WILBUR "BUDD" (1915–d)

Comedian-actor Wilbur Hulick was born in Asbury Park, New Jersey. Prior to his radio career, Hulick was a vaudeville comic. He was then featured on radio series such as *The Adventures of Mr. Meek,* on which he played the leading role of Mortimer Meek; *Hook 'n' Ladder Follies,* playing Stringbean Crachet; STOOPNAGLE AND BUDD, as Budd, his most famous radio role. With Arlene Francis, he cohosted WHAT'S MY NAME. The comedian was also heard on *The Gulf Program* and *The Minute Man* shows.

HULL, WARREN (1903–1974)

Radio panel and game-show host Warren Hull was born in Gasport, New York, and was master of ceremonies and quiz-master on programs such as *Spin to Win* and STRIKE IT RICH. He also announced *The* GIBSON FAMILY, SHOW BOAT, *Vicks Open House, Log Cabin Jamboree,* YOUR HIT PARADE, *Melody and Madness,* and VOX POP. On television, Hull hosted a popular TV version of "Strike It Rich" in the 1950s.

HUMAN SIDE OF THE NEWS, THE

1932–1952   CBS, NBC, & ABC   7 PM

Edwin C. Hill, a well-respected newsman and commentator, anchored this 15-minute, early-evening news program. In addition to AMOCO, sponsors over the years included Barbasol shave cream, Seurutan laxative, Band-Aid adhesive bandages, Dolcin pain tablets, Lucky Strike cigarettes, and the Pan-Am Coffee Bureau.

HUMMERT, FRANK AND ANNE (FRANK: 1882–1966, ANNE: 1905–)

The prolific husband-and-wife team Frank and Anne Hummert created, produced, supervised, and sometimes directed many of radio's most memorable programs. Hummert was born in St. Louis, Missouri, and his wife was born in Baltimore, Maryland. The couple were well known in the industry for the strict rules and regulations they imposed on their casts and crews, such as insisting that everyone who worked on one of their programs turn in their scripts at the end of each broadcast to prevent other producers and writers from studying them.

A partial list of the series they were responsible for includes: *The* AMERICAN ALBUM OF FAMILIAR MUSIC, *Four Star Jones,* EASY ACES, MR. KEEN, TRACER OF LOST PERSONS, DOC BARCLAY'S DAUGHTERS, ORPHANS OF DIVORCE, LITTLE ORPHAN ANNIE, SECOND HUSBAND, ALIAS JIMMY VALENTINE, AMANDA OF HONEYMOON HILL, MARY NOBLE BACKSTAGE WIFE, DAVID HARUM, FRONT PAGE FARRELL, JOHN'S OTHER WIFE, JUST PLAIN BILL, LORENZO JONES, MR. CHAMELEON, MYSTERY THEATER, OUR GAL SUNDAY, *The* ROMANCE OF HELEN TRENT, STELLA DALLAS, YOUNG WIDDER BROWN, REAL STORIES FROM REAL LIFE, and *Evelyn Winters.*

HURT, MARLIN (1905–1947)

Born in DuQuoin, Illinois, Marlin Hurt worked as a coal miner and cigarmaker before he became a musician and a vocalist with the Vicent Lopez Orchestra. Hurt turned to acting in 1938, and his talent for dialects and a wide range of voices made him a much-sought-after performer on radio. He played Dick, a part he had originally performed on the PLANTATION PARTY show, on the *The Affairs of Tom, Dick and Harry* radio series in the mid-1930s. Hurt also began to specialize in playing female characters on radio. He was Fibber and Molly's black maid, Beulah, on the FIBBER MCGEE AND MOLLY SHOW and became so popular that he was given a spin-off series called BEULAH. Hurt was also heard as Mademoiselle Levy on *The* RED SKELTON SHOW. At the height of his success, Hurt died suddenly of a heart attack at 42 years of age.

HUSING, TED (1901–1962)

Sportscaster-announcer Ted Husing was born in Demming, New Mexico, but grew up in Gloversville, New York. He began his radio broadcasting career in 1924 at WHN in New York City after winning an announcing competition and in 1927 joined the CBS staff of announcers. Chief product spokesman on programs such as BURNS AND ALLEN, *The* MARCH OF TIME, and *The Saturday Night Swing Club,* he gained a reputation as "the world's greatest sportscaster" to people working in the sports field. Ralph EDWARDS once remarked that "Marconi invented radio, but Ted Husing knew what to do with it."

HYMNS OF ALL CHURCHES

1935–1936	Mutual	Mon.–Fri.	9 AM
1936–1937	CBS	Mon.–Fri.	10:30 AM
1937–1938	CBS	Mon., Tues., Thurs.	1:15 PM
1938–1940	NBC Red	Mon., Tues., Thurs.	2:45 PM
1940–1941	CBS	Mon., Tues., Thurs.,	9:45 AM
1941–1943	NBC Red	Mon.–Thurs.	2:45 PM
1943–1945	NBC	Mon.–Fri.	2:45 PM
1945–1946	ABC	Mon., Fri.	10:30 AM & 2:45 PM
1946–1947	ABC	Mon., Thurs.	10:30 AM

This 15-minute program presented inspirational organ music by the Joe Emerson Choir. Originally part of the *Gold Medal Pleasure Time* series, the show then became the *General Mills Hour.* Gold Medal flour, Softasilk flour, and Bisquick biscuit mix were sponsors.

I DEAL IN CRIME

| 1946–1947 | ABC | Mon. | 9 PM |
| | | Sat. | 8:30 & 8 PM |

On this half-hour mystery series, film actor William Gargan was hard-boiled private detective Ross Nolan, who had a talent for getting into trouble with the law. In supporting roles were Betty Lou GERSON, Hans CONRIED, Mitzi Gould, Lurene TUTTLE, Joseph KEARNS, and Ted DeCorsia. The program was directed by Leonard Rieg.

I LOVE A MYSTERY

1939–1940	NBC Red	Mon.–Fri.	7:15 PM
1940–1941	NBC Blue	Mon.	8 PM
1941–1943	(Off the air)		
1943–1944	CBS	Mon.–Fri.	7 PM
1944–1949	(Off the air)		
1949–1950	Mutual	Mon.–Fri.	7:45 PM
1950–1952	Mutual	Mon.–Fri.	10:15 PM
1952–1953	Mutual	Mon.–Fri.	10:30 PM

Carlton E. MORSE's 15-minute and, for a while, half-hour weekly *I Love a Mystery* featured private detectives Jack Packard, Doc Long, and Reggie Yorke of the San Francisco–based "A-1 Detective Agency" as its major characters. The original adventure series premiered in 1939 and starred Michael RAFETTO as Jack, Barton YARBOROUGH as Doc, and Walter Patterson as Reggie; they were also regular cast members on Morse's ONE MAN'S FAMILY series. Gloria Blondell was featured as their secretary, Jerry Booker. Frequently, Kathleen Wilson, Cathy and Elliott LEWIS, and Barbara Jean Wong were in the supporting cast. Famous segments included "The Thing That Cries in the Night," "The Temple of the Vampires," and "Bury Your Dead, Arizona."

Five years after it went off the air, CBS and then the Mutual network brought the show back by popular demand with a new cast that included Russell Thorson and then Robert DRYDEN as Jack, Jim Boles as Doc, Tony Randall as Reggie, and Althena Lorde as their secretary, Mary Kay Brown. Mercedes MCCAMBRIDGE and Wally Maher became regulars on the second version of the show. The program's original announcer was Dresser Dahlstead. Fleischmann's yeast, Proctor and Gamble products, Chase and Sanborn coffee, Ivory soap, and Oxydol detergent were the show's sponsors. *I Love a Mystery*'s theme music was "Valse Triste."

I LOVE LUCY

| 1951–1952 | CBS | Tues. | 9:30 PM |

Lucille BALL and her "I Love Lucy" TV cast—husband Desi Arnaz as Ricky Ricardo and William Frawley and Vivian Vance as Fred and Ethel Mertz—had this half-hour radio show following the tremendous suc-

The stars of *I Love a Mystery:* (from left) Russell Thorson, Tony Randall, John Boles (Courtesy of Carlton E. Morse)

cess of the TV situation comedy. Unfortunately, *I Love Lucy* proved less appealing when heard rather than seen and lasted less than one season. Bob Carroll, Jr., and Madelyn Pugh wrote the scripts for both media, Jess Oppenheimer directed, and Johnny Jacobs announced. Philip Morris cigarettes was the sponsor.

I WAS A COMMUNIST FOR THE FBI

1952–1954   (Syndicated, Mutual-produced series. Various times)

As the Cold War between the U.S. and the then U.S.S.R. was beginning, this syndicated half-hour weekly radio series capitalized on the country's festering anticommunist attitudes. It starred motion-picture actor Dana Andrews as double agent Matt Cvetic, who infiltrated various communist organizations in order to spy for the U.S. government. The series was based on a popular book of the same name. A few of the program's episode titles reveal the basic theme: "The Red Ladies," The Red Waves," and "The Reds Among Us.

IDEAS

1965–1993   CBC   Mon.–Fri.   9:05 PM

Lester Sinclair hosted this CANADIAN BROADCASTING COMPANY one-hour series that provided Canadians with innovative, thought-provoking, and challenging behind-the-scenes stories. They concerned current events, the humanities, popular culture, the arts—and gossip. For example, if the prime minister's political mission to Washington, D.C., slighted his wife, *Ideas* would be much more interested in the prime minister's slighted wife than in his political accomplishments. Sinclair was the host of this program from 1983. Also heard on the program were philospher Farrel Christensen and historian Seth Felman.

INFORMATION, PLEASE!

1938–1940	NBC Blue	Tues.	8:30 PM
1940–1943	NBC Red	Fri.	8:30 PM
1943–1946	NBC	Mon.	9:30 PM
1946–1947	CBS	Wed.	10:30 PM
1947–1952	Mutual	Fri.	9:30 PM

"Wake up, America! It's time to stump the experts," the weekly half-hour *Information, Please!* program began. Clifton FADIMAN moderated this popular panel show. Listeners sent in questions, hoping a panel of intellects would not be able to answer them. If the listeners succeeded, a cash register rang, and they received a set of the *Encyclopedia Britannica*, as well as cash prizes. The panel of experts consisted of John Kieran and Franklin P. Adams, and, for a while, pianist Oscar Levant. John Erskine, Hendrick Willem Van Loon, Warden Lewis E. Lawes, and Stuart Chase

(From left) John Kieran, Clifton Fadiman, and Franklin P. Adams from *Information, Please!* (CBS)

were occasional guest panelists. The program's announcers were Ed HERLIHY, Milton CROSS, and Ben GRAUER. *Information, Please!* was produced and directed by Dan Golenpaul and Wilfred S. King. Canada Dry soft drinks, Lucky Strike cigarettes, Heinz foods, Parker pens, and Mobil oil sponsored the program.

INNER SANCTUM MYSTERIES

1940–1941	NBC Blue	Tues.	9:30 PM
1941–1943	NBC Blue	Sun.	8:30 PM
1943–1944	CBS	Sat.	8:30 PM
1944–1946	CBS	Tues.	9 PM
1946–1950	CBS	Mon.	8 PM
1950–1951	ABC	Mon.	8 PM
1951–1952	ABC	Sun.	8 PM

Producer-director Himan BROWN made *The Inner Sanctum Mysteries* program one of the most successful mystery-horror series on the air. Each week, host Raymond Edward JOHNSON—then for many years, Paul MACGRATH, and, for a short time, House JAMESON—welcomed listeners through "the squeaking door" into the "inner sanctum," where eerie tales of ghosts, ghouls, murder, and mayhem held listeners spellbound for a half-hour each week. Hollywood horror stars Boris Karloff, Peter Lorre, Laird Cregar, and Claude Rains often guest-starred; Karloff's episodes were the most memorable. In the mid-1940s, Brown also used Helen Hayes, Clifton Webb, Miriam Hopkins, and Raymond Massey in leading roles, but the mainstays were his repertory company of radio actors, including Mercedes MCCAMBRIDGE, Arnold MOSS, Everett SLOANE, Elspeth ERIC, Lawson Zerbe, Arline Blackburn, Wendy Barrie, Karl SWENSON, Anne SEYMOUR, Larry Haines, Santos ORTEGA, Alice REINHEART, Ann SHEPHARD, Lesley Woods, Adele RONSON, Charlotte Holland, Mason ADAMS, Kenneth Lynch, Arthur Vinton, Myron MCCORMICK, Claudia MORGAN, and Barbara Weeks. Carter's Little Liver Pills, Lipton teas and soups, Bromo Seltzer antacid, Mars candy, and Palmolive shave cream sponsored the show over the years. Mary Bennett was the Lipton tea spokeswoman for several seasons, and Ed HERLIHY, Dwight WEIST, Allen C. Anthony, and Norman BROKENSHIRE announced. The series was written by Gail and Harry Ingram, among others.

IRENE RICH DRAMAS (AKA WOMAN FROM NOWEHERE)

1933–1934	NBC Blue	Wed., Fri.	7:45 PM
1935–1936	NBC Blue	Fri.	8 PM
1936–1938	NBC Blue	Sun.	9:45 PM
1938–1941	NBC Blue	Sun.	9:30 PM
1941–1944	CBS	Sun.	6:15 PM

Stage and screen star Irene RICH displayed remarkable versatility as an actress on this half-hour anthology series of original radio plays. Also featured were regular performers John Lake, Larry Nunn, Florence Baker, Melville Ruick, Wally Maher, Betty Moran, Ray Montgomery, Janet Beecher, Gerald MOHR, and J. Arthur Young. When Rich's program moved to the CBS network, it became known as *Woman from Nowhere*. Announcers included Herb Allen, Ed HERLIHY, Frank Goss, and Marvin MILLER. George Hughes directed the program. Sponsors included Welch's grape juice and Ry-Krisp diet wheat crackers.

IT CAN BE DONE

See WELCOME VALLEY.

IT PAYS TO BE IGNORANT

1942	WOR	Thurs.	8 PM
1942–1944	Mutual	Mon.	10 PM
1944–1948	CBS	Fri.	9 PM
			10 PM
1948–1949	CBS	Sat.	9:30 PM
		Sun.	9:30 PM
1949–1950	CBS	Tues.	9:30 PM
1950–1951	CBS	Wed.	9 PM
	NBC	Wed.	9 PM (Summer)

This half-hour comedy program, a spoof of serious panel programs such as INFORMATION, PLEASE!, featured a panel of supposedly dim-witted characters who were asked simple questions like "Who is buried in Grant's tomb?" Its moderator and host was former vaudeville comic Tom Howard. At first, networks were reluctant to air the show because of its "insulting" title, but eventually WOR—a local station in New York and one of the MUTUAL network of stations—took a chance. The program was a success there for two years and then moved to CBS. The panel of "expert" fools on the show was comprised of three very different and colorful performers: Lulu McConnell, a loud-mouthed comedienne; George Shelton, a typical Brooklyn comic and Tom Howard's former comedy partner; and Harry McNaughton, a dry, dimsounding Englishman. The program, the brainchild of Howard's daughter Ruth, was written by Tom HOWARD and Ruth Howell. The show was directed by Herbert S. Polesie. Al Madru and the Esquires and then the Corncobbers, a Spike Jones–like unconventional orchestra, provided vocals and musical interludes on the show. Announcers were Ken ROBERTS, Bruce Elliott, and Richard "Dick" Stark. Sponsors included Piels beer and Philip Morris and Revelations cigarettes.

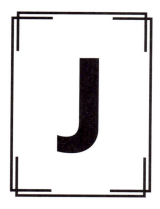

JACK AND LORETTA CLEMENS SHOW, THE

1934–1935	NBC Red	Sun.	11:15 AM
1935–1936	NBC Blue	Mon.	11 AM
1936–1938	NBC Blue	Mon., Wed., Fri.	1:45 PM
1938–1939	CBS	Mon.–Fri.	2:15 PM

In the mid to late 1930s, Jack and Loretta Clemens had one of radio's first successful husband-and-wife talk shows. The couple chatted about the latest hit movies, the problems they were having with their children, and menus for the day's meals; they even offered occasional variety entertainment by singers and comedians. The 15-minute program was sponsored by Kirkman's soap flakes and Kirkman's soap.

JACK ARMSTRONG, THE ALL-AMERICAN BOY

1933–1936	CBS	Mon.–Fri.	5:30 PM
1936–1940	NBC Red	Mon.–Fri.	5:30 PM
1940–1942	Mutual	Mon.–Fri.	5:30 PM
1942–1945	NBC Blue	Mon.–Fri.	5:30 PM
1945–1948	ABC	Mon.–Fri.	5:30 PM
1948–1950	ABC	Mon.–Fri.	5:30 PM

One of the most memorable features of the *Jack Armstrong, the All-American Boy* children's adventure serial was its opening theme song, sung by a barbershop quartet:

> Wave the flag for Hudson High, Boys,
> Show them how we stand!
> Ever shall our team be champions!
> Known throughout the land!
> Rah Rah Boola Boola Boola
> Boola Boola Boola Rah Rah Rah!

When the announcer proclaimed, "Wheaties, breakfast food of champions, presents *Jack Armstrong, the All-American Boy!*" youngsters prepared for 15 minutes of exciting adventure. This show was the longest-running program of its kind, remaining on the air for a continuous seventeen years.

Jack Armstrong was a typical middle-class American teenager who attended Hudson High School and had a talent for involvement in extraordinarily exciting adventures. During World War II, Jack's escapades frequently involved tracking down Axis spies and traitors. Several actors played Jack, beginning with St. John Terrell in 1933. Others included Jim AMECHE (1933–1938), Charles Flynn (1938–1939), and Michael Rye, aka Rye Billsbury (1943–1950). His friends Billy—originally played by Murray McLean and then by John Gannon, Roland Butterfield, Milton Guion, and Dick York—and Betty—played by Scheindel Kalish, aka Ann SHEPHARD, Sarajane Wells, Loretta Poynton, and Patricia Dunlap—shared his adventures. Other actors heard on the program included James Goss, Robert Barron, Ken Christy, William Greene, Leo Curley, Naomi May, Arthur Van Slyke, Olan SOULE, Don AMECHE, Jack Doty, Frank Dane, Frank Behrens, Ken Griffin, Herb Nelson, Cornelius Peeples, Herb Butterfield, and Marvin MILLER.

The series was created and written by Robert Hardy Andrews and announced by David Owen, Tom Shirley, Franklyn MacCormack, Bob McKee, Truman Bradley, and Paul DOUGLAS. The series was directed at different times by Pat Murphy, James Jewell, Ted MacMurray, Ed Morse, and David Owen. Contributing writers included Colonel Pashcal Strong, Talbot Munday, Irving J. Crump, James Jewell, and Lee Knopf. The program's longtime sponsor, Wheaties cereal, introduced a jingle that became almost as famous as the *Jack Armstrong* program's opening:

Have you tried Wheaties?
They're whole wheat with all of the bran,
Won't you try Wheaties?
For wheat is the best food of man!
They're crispy and crunchy the whole year through.
Jack Armstrong never tires of them
And neither will you.
So just buy Wheaties
The best breakfast food in the land!

JACK BENNY SHOW, THE

1932–1933	CBS	Thurs.	8 PM
1933–1934	NBC Red	Sun.	10 PM
1934–1936	NBC Red	Sun.	7 PM
1936–1937	NBC Blue	Sun.	7 PM
1937–1941	NBC Red	Sun.	7 PM
1941–1948	NBC	Sun.	7 PM
1948–1958	CBS	Sun.	7 PM

The regulars on the Jack BENNY Show included his wife, Mary LIVINGSTONE; a valet named Rochester, played by actor Eddie ANDERSON; announcer Don WILSON; bandleaders Phil HARRIS and then Bob CROSBY; and tenors Frank PARKER, Kenny BAKER, Dennis DAY, Larry Stevens, Michael Bartlett, and James MELTON. Together they kept *The Jack Benny Show* at the top of the ratings from the early 1930s until the mid-1950s, when Benny began to concentrate on the TV version of his show. Other performers who helped make Benny's half-hour program a success were Artie Auerbach as Mr. Kitzel; actresses Sara Berner and Bea BENADARET, who played two Brooklyn-born telephone operators, Mabel and Gertrude; Jane Morgan and Gloria Gordon as two of Benny's elderly adoring fans, Emily and Martha; and actors Mel BLANC, Frank NELSON, Joseph KEARNS, Carl Kroenke, Sheldon Leonard, the Sportsmen Quartet, Butterfly McQueen (as Livingstone's maid), Verna FELTON, Dix Davis, Sam Hearn, Frank Fontaine, and Lois Kibbee. Screen tough girl Iris Adrian also played various supporting parts on the program but is best remembered as the drugstore waitress who shouted, "Wait a minute!" even louder than Benny did.

(First row from left) Jack Benny, Mary Livingstone, Dennis Day, Eddie "Rochester" Anderson, and Don Wilson during the *Jack Benny Show* (NBC)

The show was replete with comic imagery that has become classic radio lore: Benny's pet polar bear, Carmichael, who ate the gas man and guarded Benny's safe in the basement of his home; the wheezing and sputtering sounds of Benny's ancient Maxwell car (actually Mel Blanc's wonderful vocal sound effects); Benny's legendary "cheapness" and his never-changing age—thirty-nine. But it was Jack Benny whose perfect comic timing and wonderful radio characterization kept the show at the top of the ratings for twenty-six years.

In addition to longtime announcer Don Wilson, the show was also announced by George Hale, Charles Buck, Paul DOUGLAS, and Alois Havulla. Irving Fein and Hilliard Marks produced, and Robert Ballin and Hilliard Marks directed the program. The show's talented writers included Sam Perrin, Milt Josefsberg, George Balzer, John Tackaberry, Bill Morrow, Jack Douglas, and Ed Beloin. Benny's theme songs were "Love in Bloom" and "Hooray for Hollywood." Jell-O and Lucky Strike cigarettes were long-term sponsors, and Canada Dry soda, Chevrolet automobiles, Grape-Nuts Flakes cereal, Grape Nuts Wheat Meal cereal, Herbert Tareyton, and filter-tipped Tareyton cigarettes also sponsored the program at various times.

JACK BERCH SHOW, THE

1937	CBS	Tues., & Thurs.	1 PM
		Mon., Wed., Fri.	9:30 AM
1937–1939	(Off the air)		
1939–1940	NBC Blue	Mon., Wed., Fri.	11:30 AM
1940–1942	(Off the air)		
1942	(Syndicated series. Various stations and times)		
1942–1943	(Off the air)		
1943–1944	Mutual	Mon.–Fri.	1:15 PM
1944–1945	ABC	Mon.–Fri.	11:45 AM
1945–1946	ABC	Mon.–Fri.	4 PM
1946–1951	NBC	Mon.–Fri.	11:30 AM
1951–1954	ABC	Mon.–Fri.	12 PM

Jack Berch hosted this 15-minute show, which featured household hints, occasional interviews with film stars such as Robert Taylor and Van Johnson, and menu suggestions. The show was sponsored at various times by Knox gelatin, Sweetheart soap, Kellogg's cereals, Prudential Insurance, Gulf spray, and Fels-Naptha.

JACK CARSON SHOW, THE (AKA THE CAMPBELL SOUP PROGRAM)

1943–1947	CBS	Wed.	8 PM
1947–1948	NBC	Thurs.	9:30 PM
1948–1949	CBS	Fri.	8 PM
1949–1955	(Off the air)		
1955–1956	CBS	Mon.–Fri.	9:05 PM

Actor Jack CARSON had several programs on the air over the years, but the series he is best remembered for was a half-hour situation comedy that revolved around his fictitious home life. Featured were Jane Morgan as Old Lady Foster, Mel BLANC as Hubert Peabody, Arthur Treacher as the butler, Eddie Mars as Carson's press agent, Elizabeth Patterson as Aunt Sally, Dave Willock as Carson's nephew, Tugwell, Norma Jean Nilsson as the little girl next door, and Irene RYAN, Hal PEARY, Barbara Jo ALLEN (as Vera VAGUE), Kay St. Germain, and Randy Stuart. Del SHARBUTT and Howard Petrie were Jack's announcers. The *Jack Carson Show* was produced by Victor "Vick" Knight and Sam Fuller, directed by Larry Berns and Sam Fuller, and written by Henry Taylor, Jack Rosem Marvin Fisher, Jack Douglas, Leonard Levinson, Fred S. Fox, Larry Marks, and Lou Fulton. Campbell's soup was the program's sponsors.

JACK KIRKWOOD SHOW, THE

| 1944–1946 | CBS | Mon.–Fri. | 7 PM |

This 15-minute music-variety program featured comedy sketches, musical selections, and jokes. It starred Jack KIRKWOOD and featured such regulars as Lillian Lee, Don Reid, Jean McKean, Lee Albert, and Gene LaValle, as well as Irving Miller's Orchestra. James "Jimmy" WALLINGTON was the show's announcer. Joseph Manfield directed the show, and Kirkwood and Ransom Sherman were its writers. Ivory soap and Oxydol detergent sponsored the program.

See also MIRTH AND MADNESS.

JACK PEARL SHOW, THE (AKA CRESTA BLANCA CARNIVAL; LUCKY STRIKE PROGRAM)

1932	CBS	Sun.	10:30 PM
1932–1933	NBC	Thurs.	10 PM
1933–1934	NBC	Sat.	9 PM
1934	NBC	Wed.	8 PM
1935	CBS	Wed.	10 PM
1936	NBC	Mon.	9:30 PM (Summer)
1937–1948	(Off the air)		
1948–1949	NBC	Wed.	8:30 PM
1949–1951	(Off the air)		
1951	NBC	Tues.	9:30 PM (Summer)

On and off the air many times during a twenty-year period, *The Jack Pearl Show* always managed to attract a sizeable enough listening audience to demand its return to the airwaves whenever it was canceled. Comedian Jack PEARL starred as Baron Munchausen, who had a comically heavy German accent and regularly said such things as "Vas you dere, Sharlie?" and "You make me soo madt!" His long-winded and often-interrupted stories kept people laughing. Cliff HALL was Pearl's ever-patient straight man. Also heard were Tommy Dorsey and his Orchestra, Morton Bowe, comedienne Mae Questel, and soprano Mimi Benzell. Sponsors of *The Jack Pearl Show* included Lucky Strike cigarettes, Royal desserts, Raleigh cigarettes, Kool cigarettes, and Pet milk.

JACK SMITH SHOW, THE (AKA THE OXYDOL PROGRAM; THE TIDE PROGRAM)

1946–1953	CBS	Mon.–Fri.	7:15 PM

Not to be confused with "Whispering" Jack SMITH— radio's singing star of the 1930s—"Smilin'" Jack SMITH was a radio pop singer of the 1940s and 1950s. Regular performers on "Smilin'" Jack's 15-minute program included singers Margaret Whiting, Dinah SHORE, and Ginny SIMMS. Don HANCOCK, Bob Stevenson, and Rod O'Connor were the show's announcers. Oxydol detergent, Spic and Span floor cleaner, Tide detergent, and Lilt hair products were the sponsors.

JAMESON, HOUSE (1903–1971)

House Jameson was born in Texas. After he was graduated from Columbia University in New York City in 1924, he took acting lessons in New York City and appeared on Broadway and in numerous stock-company and touring productions. Jameson's wonderful diction and pleasant baritone voice helped him become one of the medium's most successful character actors. From 1930, he was heard on such varied programs as RENFREW OF THE MOUNTED POLICE, YOUNG WIDDER BROWN, *Brave Tomorrow*, THIS DAY IS OURS, *Columbia Presents Corwin*, INNER SANCTUM MYSTERIES, BY KATHLEEN NORRIS, and WE THE PEOPLE. He also played the title role of Dr. Ordway on the CRIME DOCTOR series. Jameson's most memorable radio characterization, however, was as Henry Aldrich's father, Sam, on the popular ALDRICH FAMILY series. In addition to his stage and radio work, Jameson was also seen in feature films, most notably *Naked City (1948)* and *The Swimmer (1969)*, playing businessmen, politicians, and fathers.

JANNEY, LEON (1917–1980)

Born in Ogden, Utah, Lean Janney attended the Hollywood Children's Professional School and eventually became a major juvenile film star. From 1930 to 1934, Janney played the title character in the *Penrod* film series, adapted from Booth Tarkington's books. As early as 1939, Janney was heard, first as a juvenile actor and then as an adult, on various radio programs: he played Chick on the CHICK CARTER, BOY DETECTIVE mystery series, Number-One Son on CHARLIE CHAN, Jerry Feldman on PEPPER YOUNG'S FAMILY, and Richard Parker on *The* PARKER FAMILY. He was also frequently heard on GANGBUSTERS, STUDIO ONE, and

CHANDU THE MAGICIAN. In 1954, Janney was blacklisted by the House Un-American Activities Committee because of his supposed involvement with various communist front organizations. By 1960, he had managed to vindicate himself and subsequently appeared on such daytime TV dramas as "From These Roots" (1960–1961) and "Another World" (1964–1965).

JENKINS, GORDON (1911–1984)

Master music conductor and arranger Gordon Jenkins was born in St. Louis, Missouri. Perhaps best known for his work in the recording industry, he was also active on radio from the 1930s through the 1950s. Jenkins was music director of *The Dick Haymes Show, Men with Wings, Signal Oil Concerts, Little Ole Hollywood, Cavalcade of Hits,* and *Time and Tempo.* He also guest-conducted many other music-variety programs. Jenkins conducted and arranged music for recordings by Frank SINATRA, Perry COMO, Peggy Lee, Jo STAFFORD, and others.

JERGEN'S JOURNAL (AKA KAISER–FRAZER NEWS; WALTER WINCHELL SHOW, THE)

1932–1938	NBC Blue	Sun.	9:30 PM
1938–1945	NBC Blue	Sun.	9 PM
1945–1954	ABC	Sun.	9 PM
1954–1955	Mutual	Sun.	6 PM

News commentator–gossip columnist Walter WINCHELL began each half-hour or 15-minute broadcast by saying, "Good evening, Mr. and Mrs. North and South America and all the ships at sea. Let's go to press!" He then delivered—in rapid-fire succession—various news stories and "flashes," interrupted by the sound of telegraph bleeps between items. They were usually sensational and often concerned political and entertainment-world celebrities, such as the elderly Vice President Albin Barkley's marriage to a much younger woman and Rita Hayworth's announced marriage to Ali Kahn. When Jergens hand lotion and face cream dropped its sponsorship of the program, Dryad deodorant, Kaiser–Frazer automobiles, and Richard Hudnut shampoo took over.

JEROME, EDWIN "ED" (1886–1959)

Actor Edwin "Ed" Jerome was born in New York City. After appearing on the stage for many years, he collected an impressive list of radio acting credits from 1934, including AUNT JENNY'S REAL LIFE STORIES, BY KATHLEEN NORRIS, CAROL KENNEDY'S ROMANCE, CAVALCADE OF AMERICA, *The* COURT OF MISSING HEIRS, *The* MARCH OF TIME, MR. KEEN, TRACER OF LOST PERSONS, *Spy Secrets, The* ADVENTURES OF DICK TRACY, FAMOUS JURY TRIALS, *Society Girl,* ORPHANS OF DIVORCE, SECOND HUSBAND, GANGBUSTERS, JUST PLAIN

BILL, THE MAN I MARRIED, RICH MAN'S DARLING, *The THEATER GUILD OF THE AIR*, WHEN A GIRL MARRIES, WOMAN OF AMERICA, and the title role on the *Blackstone the Magician* series. Television viewers saw Jerome in "Love of Life" (1951–1953), "Studio One," "The Kraft Theater," and Perry Mason."

JESSEL, GEORGE (1898–1981)

George Jessel was born in the Bronx, New York. Beginning his career in vaudeville as a singer and a comedian, he became a Broadway star in 1925 in Al Jolson's *The Jazz Singer*. Jessel then appeared on virtually every major comedy-variety radio program and was often featured on the FRED ALLEN SHOW. His own series, *The George Jessel Show*, was on the air for a brief time in the early 1940s. Telephone conversation-monologues with his "Momma," first introduced in vaudeville, were popular attractions on these shows. Jessel also appeared in the film *My Mother's Eyes* (1930), based on one of his hit songs. Called the unofficial toastmaster general of the United States, Jessel often presided over events as keynote speaker and frequently introduced guest speakers at countless banquets, state dinners, and show-business "roasts."

JIGGS AND MAGGIE

See BRINGING UP FATHER.

JIMMY DURANTE SHOW, THE

1943–1945	CBS	Fri.	10 PM
1945–1947	CBS	Fri.	9:30 PM
1947–1948	NBC	Wed.	10:30 PM
1948–1950	NBC	Fri.	9:30 PM

It was on radio that Jimmy DURANTE made famous such remarks as "Everybody wants to get into de act," and "Goodnight Mrs. Calabash, wherever you are." First working with comedian Garry MOORE as his straight man and then by himself, Durante's half-hour radio program presented Hotlips Hoolihan, played by actress Florence HALOP; Vera VAGUE (Barbara Jo ALLEN); comic actor Candy Candido's deep-descending voice saying, "I'm feeling migh-ty looooow!" and actors Elvia ALLMAN, Joseph KEARNS, Arthur Treacher, Sara Berner, and Don AMECHE. Durante's announcer for many years was Howard Petrie. The orchestra was led by Xavier Cugat and then Roy Bargy. Georgia Gibbs was Durante's longtime vocalist. The *Jimmy Durante Show* was directed for many years by Phil Cohan and then Stanley Davis, and was written by Sid Zelinka, Leo Solomon, Sid Reznick, Jack Robinson, Ray Sommers, and Stanley Davis. Theme songs were "Ink-a-Dink-a-Doo" and "You Gotta Start Off Each Day with a Song." Sponsors over the years included Camel cigarettes and Rexall drugstores.

JIMMY FIDLER IN HOLLYWOOD

See FIDLER, JIMMY.

JOAN DAVIS SHOW, THE

See LEAVE IT TO JOAN.

JOANIE'S TEA ROOM

See LEAVE IT TO JOAN.

JOE E. BROWN SHOW, THE

| 1938–1939 | CBS | Sat. | 7:30 PM |
| 1939 | CBS | Thurs. | 7:30 PM |

Film and stage comedian Joe E. Brown, who literally had one of the biggest mouths in show business, was the star of this half-hour radio program. His mouth was so large that he often stuffed whole doughnuts into it as part of his act. Regulars on this comedy-and-music variety show were Margaret McCrae, Frank Gill, Bill Demberg, and Paula Winslow. Don WILSON was the program's announcer. Post Toasties cereal sponsored the series.

JOE PENNER SHOW, THE (AKA THE BAKER'S BROADCAST; THE PARK AVENUE PENNERS; THE TIP TOP SHOW)

1933–1936	NBC Blue	Sun.	7:30 PM
1936–1938	CBS	Sun.	6 PM
1938–1939	CBS	Thurs.	7:30 PM
1939–1940	NBC Blue	Thurs.	8:30 PM

Originally called *The Baker's Broadcast*, this show became so popular that the name was changed to *The Joe Penner Show*. On this half-hour situation comedy, Penner played the part of the "black sheep" of the rich Park Avenue Penner family. His pet phrases, "You wanna buy a duck?" "Don't ever DO that!" and "You nasty man!" were much repeated by fans across the country. In support were actresses Gay Seabrook, Margaret Brayton, Martha Wentworth, and Stephanie Diamond. Also heard were Dick Ryan, Monk Monsel, and the orchestras of Ozzie NELSON and Jimmy Grier, with vocals by Gene AUSTIN, Harriet HILLIARD, and Joy Hodges. *The Joe Penner Show* was directed by Gordon Thompson and written by Carroll Carroll, George Wells, Hal Fimberg, Matt Brooks, Bob Phillips, Arnold G. Maguire, Parke Levy, Eddie Davis, and Don Prindle. Bill GOODWIN and Lou Crosby were the program's announcers. Sponsors included Cocomalt chocolate-drink mix, Fleischmann's yeast, Baker's coconut, Huskies dog food, and Ward baking products.

JOHN J. ANTHONY SHOW, THE

1945–1946	Mutual	Mon.–Fri.	1:45 PM
1946–1952	(Off the air)		
1952–1953	Mutual	Sun.	9:30 PM

"Does your husband love you as much as he did the day you were married? Has the war created new problems for you in your marriage? To answer these and other personal problems brought in by your friends and neighbors, Carter's Little Liver Pills presents John J. ANTHONY in a program of 15-minute weekday sessions of helpful advice." Directors were numerous over the years. George Putnam was the program's announcer. Arrid deodorant and Carter's Little Liver Pills sponsored the series.

JOHNNY (JOHN ROVENTINI: 1910–   )

Johnny, the diminutive page boy whose perfect B-flat "Call for Philip Morris" became one of radio's most memorable commercial message signatures, was born in Brooklyn, New York. A perfectly proportioned midget, Johnny was a bellhop at the Hotel New Yorker in New York City in 1933 when a Philip Morris cigarette-company advertising executive heard him calling for various residents of the hotel and decided he would be perfect as the company's signature radio spokesman. Johnny remained with the Philip Morris company for more than twenty years and was featured on *The* PHILIP MORRIS PLAYHOUSE, JOHNNY PRESENTS, and other shows sponsored by Philip Morris.

Philip Morris cigarettes' living trademark, "Johnny" Roventini (Philip Morris)

JOHNNY PRESENTS

1933–1940	NBC Red	Tues.	8 PM

This half-hour program, sponsored by Philip Morris cigarettes, featured product spokesman JOHNNY Roventini as its host. A true variety show, *Johnny Presents* changed formats over the years, depending on the whims of the Philip Morris Company. Beverly Freeland, Genevieve Rowe, Floyd Shermam, and Glenn Cross were featured. The Three Harmonies and the Johnny Green and Ray BLOCH orchestras provided the music for the show. The program also presented occasional dramatic sketches, such as "The Perfect Crime" "Hughesreel" with Rush Hughes and "The Story Comes to Life," as special features. Joseph Latham, Spencer Bentley, and Adelaide Klein often played roles in these sketches. R. Schuebel directed the series in the late 1930s. The program's announcer for several years was Charles O'Connor. The show's theme music was "On the Trail."

JOHN'S OTHER WIFE

1936–1940	NBC Red	Mon.–Fri.	10:15 AM
1940–1942	NBC Blue	Mon.–Fri.	3:30 PM

No daytime serial on radio has been the butt of more spoofs and jokes because of its title. The "other wife" of this daytime serial drama referred to John's secretary, not his mistress; John's relationship with his secretary was *strictly* professional. Several actors played John on the program, including Hanley STAFFORD, Matt CROWLEY, Luis VAN ROOTEN, Richard KOLLMAR, William Post, Jr., and Joseph CURTIN. John's wife, Elizabeth, was played by Adele RONSON and then Erin O'Brien Moore. His secretary, Martha Curtis, was played by Phyllis Welch and then Rita Johnson. Other actors included Lynda Kane, Elaine Kent, John Kane, James Van Dyke, Ruth Yorke, Alan BUNCE, Vivia Ogden, Franc (pronounced *France*) Hale, Mary Jane HIGBY, Stella Adler, Linda Watkins, Alexander Kirkland, Irene Hubbard, Kingsley Colton, Macdonald CAREY, Florence FREEMAN, Helene Dumas, Alice REINHEART, and others. The series was produced by Frank and Anne HUMMERT and written by Bill Sweets and Doris Halman, among others. James Fleming was the announcer. The theme music for the show, "The Sweetest Story Ever Told," was whistled and played on the guitar by Stanley Davis. Sponsors of this program included Angelus cosmetics, Kolynos toothpaste, BiSodol antacid mints, and Old English wax.

JOHNSON, BESS (1902–1975)

Actress Bess Johnson, who was born in Chicago, Illinois, had a lovely, velvety-smooth voice, which was used when she spoke as Lady Esther on several pro-rams sponsored by Lady Esther face cream. At one me, Johnson was such a popular daytime performer hat she had a daytime serial drama series named or her, *The Story of Bess Johnson* (originally HILLTOP OUSE). The actress was featured on many other se- es, including MARY MARLIN, TODAY'S CHILDREN, and RUE CONFESSIONS. As Lady Esther, Johnson was eard on *The Lady Esther Serenade* and *The Lady Esther CREEN GUILD PLAYERS*. The actress also appeared on he "Search for Tomorrow" (1951–1954, 1960–1961) elevision series.

OHNSON FAMILY, THE

1936–1938	Mutual	Mon.–Fri.	9:15 PM
1938–1939	Mutual	Mon.–Fri.	5:15 PM
1939–1940	Mutual	Mon.–Fri.	4:45 PM
1940–1945	Mutual	Mon.–Fri.	7:15 PM
1945–1950	Mutual	Mon.–Fri.	4:15 PM

his 15-minute series told about an African-American mily living in a small Southern town called "Chica- ola." Jimmy Scribner, a Caucasian, played all the arts on the show. The show's characters dealt with sues pertaining to living in a ghetto situation, such s finding the necessary money to buy a Christmas inner. In 1950, the show was canceled because civil- ghts groups protested what they felt was unflat- ring, racial stereotyping. Harlow WILCOX announced he program. The show's theme music was "My Old entucky Home" and "Listen to the Mockingbird." It as directed by J. C. Lewis, Cecil Underwood, Rich- rd Lewis, and Tom Slater. Scribner wrote the scripts or the series. Interesting enough, the United States avings Bond drive sponsored the program at one me.

OHNSON, RAYMOND EDWARD (1911–   )

erhaps best known as "Your host, Raymond" on ie INNER SANCTUM MYSTERIES, Raymond Edward ohnson was born in Kinosha, Wisconsin. His radio areer began with the help of actress Bess JOHNSON fter he taught drama, voice, and diction at the Good- an Dramatic School, the University of Indiana, and osary College. In addition to *Inner Sanctum Mysteries,* ohnson was prominently featured on *Brave Tomorrow,* TUDIO ONE, CAVALCADE OF AMERICA, DIMENSION X, ON WINSLOW OF THE NAVY (in the title role), FAMOUS JRY TRIALS, GANGBUSTERS, *The* GOLDBERGS, *The* GUID- JG LIGHT, JOYCE JORDAN, GIRL INTERN, LIGHTS OUT, ANDRAKE THE MAGICIAN (playing Mandrake), MR. ISTRICT ATTORNEY, MYRT AND MARGE, NICK CARTER, ASTER DETECTIVE, *The* PHILIP MORRIS PLAYHOUSE, UICK AS A FLASH, STELLA DALLAS, *The* STORY OF MARY ARLIN, *The* TELEPHONE HOUR (as Alexander Graham ell), TODAY'S CHILDREN, and VALIANT LADY. Illness rced the actor into retirement in the early 1970s.

JOHNSTONE, WILLIAM "BILL" (1908–   )

Born in Brooklyn, New York, actor William Johnstone played the leading role of Lamont Cranston (aka The Shadow) on *The* SHADOW and was also regularly fea- tured on *The* CAVALCADE OF AMERICA, BIG SISTER, *There Was a Woman*, FAMOUS JURY TRIALS, MRS. WIGGS OF THE CABBAGE PATCH, *The* PHILIP MORRIS PLAYHOUSE, PORTIA FACES LIFE, VALIANT LADY, *Wilderness Road,* NERO WOLFE, SUSPENSE, and *The* LUX RADIO THEATER. The actor also appeared as Judge Lowell on daytime television's "As the World Turns" from 1957 until 1978.

JOLSON, AL (ASA YOELSON: 1886–1950)

Singing legend Al Jolson was born in St. Petersburg, Russia, and made his Broadway stage debut as a child in *Children of the Ghetto* in 1899. He subsequently appeared in such musical comedies as *Dancing Around, Robinson Crusoe, Jr, Sinbad,* and *Big Boy* in the early 1900s. On radio as early as 1927, Jolson was the star of *The* KRAFT MUSIC HALL music-variety series for several years, became the star attraction on *The* SHELL CHATEAU program, and made frequent guest appear- ances on many comedy-variety programs in the 1930s and 1940s. He became known for performing in black face on-stage and for singing such songs as "Swanee," "Mammy," "Alexander's Ragtime Band," and "The Anniversary Song." Jolson made his film debut in *The Jazz Singer* in 1927, which was the first film with synchronized sound. He also starred in *The Singing Fool* (1928), *Mammy,* and *Rose of Washington Square* (1939). A fictionalized version of his life was presented in the film *The Jolson Story* (1946) and its sequel, *Jolson Sings Again* (1949). Although Jolson was played by actor Larry Parks, he did sing for himself on the films' soundtracks. His last radio broadcast on September 1950 was an interview on *The Louella Parson's Show,* while entertaining the troops in Korea.

JONES, ALLAN (1908–1992)

Radio, stage, and film star Allan Jones was born in Old Forge, Pennsylvania. He was a featured performer on *The* CHICAGO THEATER OF THE AIR, the SHOW BOAT, and the *Fred Astaire* radio programs; his most famous song was "The Donkey Serenade," his theme song. Some of Jones's films were *A Night at the Opera* (1935), *Show Boat* (1936), *A Day at the Races* (1937), *The Boys from Syracuse* (1940), *One Night in the Tropics* (1940), and *Honeymoon Ahead* (1945).

JONES, SPIKE (LINDLEY ARMSTRONG JONES: 1911–1965)

Radio was the perfect medium for displaying the unique musical talents of bandleader Spike Jones and his City Slickers band. Born in Kentucky, Jones began his career as a serious musician but formed his own comedy band in the mid-1930s. They played humorous renditions of such familiar songs as "Tea for Two" and "The Waltz of the Flowers," as well as original comedy songs like "In the Feurer's Face," using such wild sounds as horns honking, bells ringing, glass breaking, belches, screams, and howls. Spike had his own radio program, *The* SPIKE JONES AND HIS CITY SLICKERS SHOW, and guest-starred on many music-variety programs, such as *The* CHESTERFIELD SUPPER CLUB, *The* FRED ALLEN SHOW, and *The* BING CROSBY SHOW. Spike's vocalist, Dorothy Shay, "the Park Avenue Hillbilly," often accompanied the band on their guest appearances. Besides such films as *Thank Your Lucky Stars* (1943), *Bring on the Girls* (1945), and *Fireman, Save My Child* (1955), the Jones band starred on television's "The Colgate Comedy Hour" and "The Spike Jones Show" in the early 1950s.

JORDAN, JIM AND MARIAN (JIM: 1897–1988; MARIAN: 1898–1961)

Jim Jordan, who became world-famous as Fibber McGee on radio and in films, was born in Peoria, Illinois. His career as a vaudeville singer was interrupted by the draft into World War I. After discharge, Jordan married his childhood sweetheart, Marian Driscoll, who was also born in Peoria. As a young girl, Marian had studied piano, voice, and violin; the

couple began to work as a song-and-dance comedy team in various midwestern vaudeville theaters. The Jordans first worked on radio at station WIBO in Chicago in 1924, billed as "The Singing O'Henry Twins"; at WENR, they were featured on *The A Scouts* and later appeared in a dramatic series called *The Smith Family.*

In 1931, the Jordans performed their first Fibber McGee and Molly comedy routine on *The Smackou* and this domestic comedy sketch soon appeared o such network shows as *The* BREAKFAST CLUB, *Saturda Night Jamboree,* and KALTENMEYER'S KINDERGARTE Regularly heard on *The* NATIONAL FARM AND HOM HOUR, the couple developed their own series in 193 FIBBER MCGEE AND MOLLY, which ran for more tha twenty-one continuous years. In demand as film star the couple next appeared in several motion pictur in the 1930s and 1940s, including *Look Who's Laughin* (1941) and *Heavenly Days* (1944). After their show le the air, the couple occasionally appeared as Fibbe McGee and Molly on the NBC *Monitor* series. I the mid-1970s, after Marian's death, Jordan hosted program about radio's past popular shows on a loc Los Angeles radio station.

JOSTYN, JAY (1905–1977)

Midwesterner Jay Jostyn began to work on radio the early 1930s, becoming best known in the title ro of MR. DISTRICT ATTORNEY. He was also featured such programs as *Foreign Assignment* (with *Mr. Distri Attorney* costar Vicki VOLA), HILLTOP HOUSE, OUR GA SUNDAY, *The* PARKER FAMILY (as Mr. Parker), SECON HUSBAND, MRS. WIGGS OF THE CABBAGE PATCH, POPE THE SAILOR, *The* LIFE OF MARY SOUTHERN, and TH DAY IS OURS. Jostyn had the kind of firm, masculi voice that made people believe that whatever he sai was honest and true; therefore, he was the perfe actor to play district attorneys, judges, and patriarch At one point in his radio career, Jostyn is reported have played forty-eight upright characters on thirt six programs in just one week.

JOYCE JORDAN, GIRL INTERN (AKA JOYCE JORDAN, M.D.)

1938–1940	CBS	Mon.–Fri.	3 PM
1940–1944	CBS	Mon.–Fri.	2:15 PM
1944–1945	CBS	Mon.–Fri.	2 PM
1945–1948	NBC	Mon.–Fri.	10:45 AM
1948–1951	(Off the air)		
1951–1952	ABC	Mon.–Fri.	3 PM
1952–1955	(Off the air)		
1955–1956	NBC	Mon.–Fri.	10:15 AM

This 15-minute drama series focused on the profe sional and domestic problems of a doctor in a big-ci hospital. Five actresses played Joyce: Rita Johnso

Jim and Marian Jordan were better known as Fibber McGee and Molly. (NBC)

Ann Shephard and Raymond Edward Johnson on *Joyce Jordan, M.D.* (CBS)

Sheindel Kalish (aka Ann SHEPHARD), Betty WINKLER, Elspeth ERIC, and Gertrude Warner. Joyce Jordan spent most episodes grappling with failed romances and the difficulties she had as a woman in a male-dominated profession. Others who appeared on the show included Myron MCCORMICK, Charlotte Holland, Lesley Woods, John Raby, Ethel Owen, Ed Latimer, Alan Devitt, Patricia RYAN, Raymond Edward JOHNSON, Joseph JULIAN, Richard WIDMARK, Frank Behrens, Santos ORTEGA, Ruth McDevitt, Jack GRIMES, Les TREMAYNE, Larry Robinson, Irene Hubbard, Virginia "Ginger" Jones, Louise Fitch, James Monks, Charles "Chuck" Webster, Edwin Bruce, Butterfly McQueen, Horace Braham, Amanda RANDOLPH, Virginia Dwyer, Michael Fitzmaurice, Aileen Pringle, Frank LOVEJOY, Ed BEGLEY, Vera Allen, Mary Jane HIGBY, and Larry Haines. The announcers were Ken ROBERTS, Ed HERLIHY, Richard Stark, and Ron Rawson. Produced by Himan Brown and directed by Ted Corday, Arthur Hanna, and Mende Brown, the program was written by Ralph Berkey, Henry Selinger, and Julian Funt. The theme music was "Poem." Sponsors included Colox tooth powder, Solidified Albolene face cream, Satina flour, LaFrance bleach, Minute tapioca, Postum instant coffee, Crisco shortening, and various Lever Brother products.

JUDY AND JANE

| 1932–1935 | NBC Blue | Mon.–Fri. | (*) |
| 1941–1942 | (Syndicated series. Various stations and times) | | |

This 15-minute serial drama presented the problems of two young women trying to find love and happiness in a Depression-laden, trouble-filled world. Judy

was played by actresses Joan Kay and Margie Calvert, and Jane by Donna Reade, Margaret Evans, Irene WICKER, and Betty Ruth Smith. Wicker also played Joyce on the series, and Marvin MILLER played Dr. Bishop. Jack Brinkley was the announcer, and Harry Holcomb and Jim Whipple directed and wrote the program. The series' sponsor was Folgers coffee.

JUDY CANOVA SHOW, THE

1943–1944	CBS	Tues.	8:30 PM
1944–1947	NBC	Sat.	10 PM
1947–1949	NBC	Sat.	9:30 PM
1949–1951	NBC	Sat.	10 PM
1951–1952	NBC	Sat.	9:30 PM
1952–1953	NBC	Thurs.	10 PM

For ten years, comedienne–country singer Judy CANOVA presented such memorable characters as Aunt Aggie (played by veteran radio character-actress Verna FELTON); Judy's housekeeper, Geranium (Ruby DANDRIDGE); her Mexican friend Pedro (Mel BLANC); her neighbor Mr. Hemingway (Hans CONRIED); Joe Crunchmuller (Sheldon Leonard); Mrs. Atwater (Ruth Perrott); and Count Benchley Botsford (Joseph KEARNS). Also appearing were Gale GORDON, Sharon Douglas, the Sportsmen Quartet, and Bud Dant's Orchestra.

Canova's comic country songs were also highlights of the program. Flashbacks to her hillbilly home always began with her "Howdy, Luuuu-kie!" greeting to actor Mel Blanc as her country-bumpkin cousin; Pedro's "Pardon me, señorita, for talking in your face," and Canova's sign-off song, "Go to sleeep-y, little baby," were also well-received moments on the show. The *Judy Canova Show* was directed by Joe Rines and written by Fred Fox and Henry Hoople. Howard Petrie was the announcer. The sponsors were Palmolive soap, Colgate tooth powder, Super Suds detergent, Colgate dental cream, and Halo shampoo.

JULIAN, JOSEPH (1911–1982)

Joseph Julian was born in New York City and during the 1930s, 1940s, and 1950s was heard on thousands of radio programs playing both heroes and villains: on BIG SISTER, he played Pete Kirkwood; on BRIGHTER DAY, Michael West; and on LORENZO JONES, Sandy Mattson. Julian was also regularly heard on such programs as LIFE CAN BE BEAUTIFUL, JOYCE JORDAN, GIRL INTERN, INNER SANCTUM MYSTERIES, BOSTON BLACKIE, *The* ADVENTURES OF SUPERMAN, *The* GREATEST STORY EVER TOLD, NERO WOLFE, *The* GOLDBERGS, *The General Electric Theater*, and CASEY, CRIME PHOTOGRAPHER. Although he was a staunch anticommunist, Julian was mistakingly listed in the government's Red Channel publication of suspected communist sympathizers; he spent years trying to clear his name of this accusation and eventually managed to exonerate himself and return to acting. Julian also performed as a voiceover for TV and radio commercials and dubbed foreign films.

JUNGLE JIM

1935–1952   (Syndicated series. Various stations and times)

Set in the jungles of Africa, the 15-minute children's adventure serial *Jungle Jim* was on the air for more than seventeen years. One particularly memorable, and typical, sequence had Jim and his jungle sidekick, Kolu, rescuing a candidate for cannibalism. Matt CROWLEY played Jim, and Juano Hernandez was heard as Kolu. Also heard were Franc (pronounced *France*) Hale as Shanghai Lil, Irene Winston as Tiger Lil, Owen Jordan as Tom Sun, Arthur HUGHES as Singh-Lee, Jack Lloyd as Van, and Vicki VOLA and Kenny DELMAR in various supporting roles. Glenn Riggs was the program's announcer. The series was produced by Jay Clark and directed by Stuart Buchanan and Irene Fenton. Gene Stafford wrote the scripts for the series. It was based on the "Jungle Jim" comic strip created by Alex Raymond.

JUNIOR MISS

1942–1943	CBS	Wed.	9 PM
1943–1948	(Off the air)		
1948–1950	CBS	Sat.	11:30 AM
1950–1952	(Off the air)		
1952–1954	CBS	Thurs.	8:30 PM

Novelist Sally Benson's popular heroine Judy Graves was the major character of this weekly half-hour situation-comedy radio series about the everyday problems faced by a typical American teenage girl at school, at home, and among her friends. In the early 1950s, movie star Shirley Temple, in her teens at the time, played Judy; Barbara Whiting, Judy's best friend Fuffy in the 1945 film *Junior Miss* (which inspired the radio series) replaced Temple in the role of Judy. K. T. Stevens, Barbara Eiler, and Peggy Knudson played Judy's older sister, Lois; Gale GORDON and then Elliott LEWIS, her father, Harry; Sarah Selby and Margaret Lansing, Judy's mother, Grace; Myra Marsh, the Graves' maid, Hilda; and Priscilla Lyon and then Beverly Wills, Fuffy Adams. The program's announcers were Durwood Kirby and Ben Gage. Fran Van Hartenfeldt produced the series, and William Royal directed it. The program was written by Jack Rubin, Herbert Little, Jr., David Vieter, and Charles Sinclair. Proctor and Gamble products, Rayve home permanent, and Rayve Creme shampoo sponsored the show.

JUNIOR NURSE CORPS

1936–1937	CBS	Mon., Wed., Fri.	5 PM
1937–1938	NBC Red	Mon., Fri.	5 PM

This show presented incidents experienced by the founder of modern nursing, Clara Barton, as they occurred at one of America's first military hospitals. On one memorable episode, Barton wrote a letter to the wife of a soldier who had lost both of his hands in battle. The series starred Sunda Love as Clara Barton and featured Jess Pugh as army doctor Major Drucker. The 15-minute program was sponsored by Sunbrite cleanser.

JUST PLAIN BILL

1935–1936	CBS	Mon.–Fri.	7:15 PM
1936–1937	CBS	Mon.–Fri.	11:30 AM
1937–1940	NBC Red	Mon.–Fri.	10:30 AM
1940–1941	NBC Blue	Mon.–Fri.	3:45 PM
1941–1942	NBC Red	Mon.–Fri.	5:30 PM
1942–1951	NBC	Mon.–Fri.	5: 30 PM
1951–1954	NBC	Mon.–Fri.	5 PM
1954–1955	NBC	Mon.–Fri.	3:45 PM

Just Plain Bill was the story of small-town barber Bill Davidson and his daughter, Nancy, who lived in Hartsville. The kind of man everyone came to with their problems, Bill would then try to help solve them. The 15-minute series was created by Frank and Anne HUMMERT. Arthur HUGHES played Bill, and Ruth Russell and then Toni Darney played his daughter, Nancy. Also heard were Curtis Arnall, Arline Blackburn, Adelaide Klein, James MEIGHAN, Ray COLLINS, Bill Quinn, baby impersonators Madeleine Pierce and Sarah Fussell, Joseph "Joe" Latham, Elaine Kent, Tess Sheehan, Bill LYTELL, Macdonald CAREY, Ann SHEPHARD, Teri Keane, Charles EGLESTON, Cliff Carpenter, Ara Gerald, Leo Curley, Anne ELSTNER, Bud COLLYER, Guy Sorel, and Audrey Egan. Announcers on the program included Andre BARUCH, Ed HERLIHY, Roger Krupp, Tom Shirley, Hugh James, Don Pardo, and Fielden Farrington. Directing the series were Martha Atwell, Norman Sweetser, Gene Eubank, Arthur Hanna, Blair Walliser, and Ed King. Robert Hardy Andrews and David Davidson wrote scripts for the program over the years. The theme music was "Darling Nellie Gray," which opened the show, and "Polly Wolly Doodle," which closed it. It was played on a harmonica and whistled by Hal Brown. *Just Plain Bill*'s sponsors included Kolynos toothpaste, Anacin pain reliever, Clapp's baby food, Old English wax, Aeromist nasal spray, Black Flag bug killer, BiSoDol shaving cream, and Heet liniment.

JUVENILE JURY

1946	Mutual	Sat.	8:30 PM
1946–1948	Mutual	Sun.	8 PM

1948–1952	(Off the air)		
1952–1953	NBC	Sun.	6:30 PM

Jack Barry hosted this half-hour program that featured a panel of child "jurors," never fewer than four in number, who were asked how they would solve a particular child-oriented problem such as how to spend allowances wisely, when to do homework, how to get along with teachers, and how to get around doing household chores. The children included Johnny McBride, Charlie Hankinson, Robin Morgan, Jerry Weissbard, Peggy Bruder, Glenn Mark Arthur, Dickie Orian, Patsy Walker, Elizabeth Watson, Billy Knight, and Laura Mangels at different times. John Scott was the program's announcer. The show was produced and directed by Dan Ehrenreich. Guest stars Eddie CANTOR, Red SKELTON, and Milton BERLE made occasional appearances on the show.

KALISH, SCHEINDEL

See SHEPHARD, ANN.

KALTENBORN, HANS V. (1878–1965)

News commentator Hans V. Kaltenborn was born in Milwaukee, Wisconsin, of German-American parentage. He began to broadcast in 1922 and trained himself in the art of total recall—he was able to commit to memory speeches of political figures after hearing them only once. This gift allowed him to quote from the speeches at length during his broadcasts and to comment on the speeches freely instead of using prepared scripts. Because he spoke fluent German, Kaltenborn was assigned to cover the dictator Adolph Hitler's rise in the mid- to late 1930s. His ability to report word for word what Hitler said made him one of the United States's most respected and valued newsmen in pre–World War II America. In the 1930s and 1940s, *Kaltenborn Edits the News* became radio's most popular newscast. His daily commentaries were always insightful and informative, and he is said to have been the favorite newsman of Presidents Roosevelt and Truman, even though Truman was known to have mimicked his unusual clipped delivery from time to time. This was especially true when Kaltenborn predicted that Thomas E. Dewey would defeat Truman in his bid for the presidency in 1947. Called the "dean of American news commentators" by the press, Kaltenborn was the first newscaster to express his own opinions about news happenings—for that time, an innovative, somewhat daring thing to do. His fame and prestige continued to grow throughout and well after World War II, and his influence extended into the Cold War years.

KALTENMEYER'S KINDERGARTEN

1935–1937	NBC Red	Sat.	5:30 PM
1937–1938	NBC Red	Sat.	7 PM
1938–1940	NBC Red	Sat.	6 PM

Bruce Kamman starred as Professor August Kaltenmeyer, D.U.N., on this program, which was billed as "the Nonsense School of the Air." During its earliest years, the half-hour show featured comedy, stories, and music. Johnny Wolfe played "Yohnson"; Marian JORDAN, Gertie Glump; Jim JORDAN, Mickey Donovan; Merrill Fugit, Percy Van Schuyler; Sidney Ellstrom, Chauncer the Bum; and Cecil Roy, Daisy Dean. Also heard were Billy White, Cliff Petersen, Floyd Holm, and Douglas Craig as the escorts and Betty: these characters, in a typical episode, would randomly appear at Kaltenmeyer's school, quickly turning the classroom into a roomful of silly dunces. The program was written by Harry Lawrence. Shortly before the outbreak of World War II, German Professor Kaltenmeyer suddenly became Professor Ulysses S. Applegate, undoubtedly due to the anti-German sentiment that was emerging in this country. Kaltenmeyer's familiar weekly farewell, "*Auf widesehen und adieu*," was dropped altogether. Quaker Oats cereal sponsored the program.

KATE HOPKINS, ANGEL OF MERCY

| 1939–1941 | CBS | Mon.–Fri. | 2:45 PM |
| 1941–1943 | CBS | Mon.–Fri. | 4:45 PM |

This 15-minute drama series centered around Kate Hopkins, a nurse confronting the problems of a big-city hospital. Helen Lewis and then Mary MacDonald played Kate. Also heard were Ned WEVER, Clayton

"Bud" COLLYER, Peggy Allenby, Raymond Edward JOHNSON, Constance Collier, and Templeton Fox. The program was directed by Jack Hurdle and written by Chester McCraken and Gertrude BERG. Ralph EDWARDS announced the series, which was sponsored by Maxwell House coffee.

KATE SMITH SHOW, THE (AKA KATE SMITH SINGS; NEW STAR REVUE; THE A & P BANDWAGON; THE KATE SMITH HOUR)

1931–1932	CBS	Mon., Wed.	8:30 PM
		Thurs., Sat.	
1932–1933	CBS	Mon., Wed.	8 PM
1933–1934	(Off the air)		
1934	CBS	Mon., Wed.,	8 PM
		Fri.	
1934–1935	CBS	Mon.	8:30 PM
1935–1937	CBS	Tues.–Thurs.	7:30 PM
1937–1938	CBS	Fri.	8 PM
1938–1939	CBS	Thurs.	8 PM
1939–1944	CBS	Fri.	8 PM
1944–1945	CBS	Sun.	7 PM
1945–1946	CBS	Fri.	8:30 PM
1946–1947	CBS	Sun.	6:30 PM
1947–1948	(Off the air)		
1948–1949	Mutual	Fri.	12:15 PM
1949–1960	(Various stations and times)		

Originally called *The A and P Bandwagon,* singer Kate SMITH's nighttime radio show introduced Irving Berlin's stirring "God Bless America" in 1938; this song, along with her theme song, "When the Moon Comes over the Mountain," became inextricably identified with the singer. Some of the biggest names in show business, such as Greta Garbo, Bert Lahr, John Barrymore, and Mary Boland, made their initial radio appearances on Smith's program, and many later-to-become famous entertainers, such as ABBOTT AND COSTELLO, Arthur Allen, Parker FENNELLY, Johnny Wil-

Kate Smith (CBS)

liams and the Smart Set, Ezra STONE, and Henny Youngman, first received national attention by appearing on her show. Ted Collins, Smith's manager, often served as the program's host, and her longtime announcer was Andre BARUCH. Tom Shirley also announced the show. Jack Miller led her orchestra for many years, and Tony Gale was her personal music arranger. Bunny Coughlin and Bob Lee were the show's directors. Sponsors of *The Kate Smith Show* included La Palina cigars, Hudson paper products, A&P supermarkets, Calumet baking powder, Swans Down cake flour, Sanka instant coffee, Jell-O puddings, and Post's Grape Nuts cereal.

See also KATE SMITH SPEAKS.

KATE SMITH SPEAKS (AKA KATE SMITH'S NOONDAY CHATS)

| 1938–1951 | CBS | Mon.–Fri. | 12 AM |

"It's high noon in New York and time for Kate SMITH," Ted Collins (her manager) announced at the beginning of this 15-minute talk show. Guests from the political and entertainment worlds appeared with Smith and Collins, who produced and directed. Sponsors were Sanka cofee, Diamond Crystal salt, Swans Down cake flour, Sure-jell gelatin, and Cain's mayonnaise.

See also KATE SMITH SHOW, THE.

KATIE'S DAUGHTER

| 1947–1948 | ABC | Mon.–Fri. | 11:15 AM |

Katie's Daughter is the story of Nana Harris, a lovely young actress, who lives on Park Avenue and whose mother, Katie Harris—Hamburger Katie—runs a restaurant on the waterfront. This is the story of two worlds that asks the question, How far should a mother sacrifice to give her daughter advantages in life she herself never had? Similar to the STELLA DALLAS program, *Katie's Daughter* was a 15-minute series that starred Anne Marie Gayer as Nana and Grace Cooper as Katie, Nana's hardworking, if somewhat common, mother. Kenneth Banghart was the series' announcer. Sweetheart soap and Blu White bleach were its sponsors. The writers and director of the series are unknown.

KAY KYSER'S KOLLEGE OF MUSICAL KNOWLEDGE

1938–1941	NBC Red	Wed.	10 PM
1941–1946	NBC	Wed.	10 PM
1946–1947	NBC	Wed.	10:30 PM
1947–1948	NBC	Sat.	10:30 PM
1948–1949	ABC	Mon.–Fri.	11 AM

Kay Kyser and Mervyn "Ish Kabibble" Bogue (NBC)

Bandleader Kay KYSER hosted this half-hour variety-music-quiz program. In addition to playing such songs of the day as "Praise the Lord and Pass the Ammunition," and "Who Wouldn't Love You," Kyser conducted a comic music-quiz segment using a mock college-campus setting. The format of the *Kollege of Musical Knowledge* was rather simple. The questions, referred to as "midterms," were easy to answer and usually had a humorous slant. If a contestant from the studio audience couldn't answer the question, Kyser would provide a broad hint. Then, when the contestant finally answered the question, Kyser would ask, "How did he get that?" During a question-and-answer segment on the show, if the contestant answered answered a true or false question correctly, Kyser would call out, "That's right; you're wrong!"

Adding to the proceedings were musician Mervyn Bogue, better known as Ish Kabibble, a strange fellow who had bangs that hung down to his eyebrows and spoke in a deliberate manner; singer Ginny SIMMS, a popular attraction on the program; Trudy Erwin; Sully Mason; baritone Harry Babbitt, who had numerous hit recordings both with Kyser's band and on his own; singer Georgia Carroll; actress Shirley MITCHELL; the Town Criers; and the King Sisters (Alice, Donna, Yvonne, and Louise). Kyser's theme song was "Think-

ing of You." Verne Smith, Dick Jones, Ken NILES, Bud Heistan, and Bill Forman were the program's announcers. Frank O'Connor produced the series; William Warwick, John Cleary, Harry Saz, and Ed Cashman directed. Writers for the show included Richard Dana and Martin Stark. Colgate dental cream, Palmolive soap, Palmolive shave cream, Lustre Cream shampoo, Colgate tooth powder, and Pillsbury flour were the sponsors.

KAYE, BEATRICE (BEATRICE KUPPER: 1907–1986)

Singer Beatrice Kaye was born in New York City and became one of the stars of the popular GAY NINETIES REVUE program in the 1940s, singing in a style reminiscent of music-hall and vaudeville performers at the turn of the century. Debuting as a professional singer when she was six years old, she sang such turn-of-the-century hits as "In the Good Old Summertime," "On the Sidewalks of New York," "Under the Bamboo Tree," and "Only a Bird in a Gilded Cage." Kaye was also a frequent performer on the FRED ALLEN radio program and replaced his show during a summer with *The Beatrice Kaye Show*. Featured in such Broadway shows as *What's in a Name* (1920), *Secrets* (1922), and *Rain or Shine* (1928), the singer was also seen in the film *Billy Rose's Diamond Horseshoe* (1945). Kaye retired in the late 1950s but made a comeback in such films as *Underworld, USA* (1961) and *A Time for Dying* (1962).

KAYE, DANNY

See DANNY KAYE SHOW, THE.

KAYE, SAMMY (1910–1987)

Bandleader Sammy Kaye was born in Cleveland, Ohio, and graduated from Ohio State University with a degree in engineering, but he decided to become a professional musician. Proficient at playing the violin, the bass horn, the saxophone, the banjo, the guitar, and the trumpet after having played them all throughout his school years, Kaye formed his own band. In addition to numerous big-band, late-night remote radio broadcasts, Kaye hosted *Sunday Serenade, The* SAMMY KAYE SHOW, and SO YOU WANT TO LEAD A BAND. Among the songs his orchestra made famous were "Harbor Lights," "There Will Never Be Another You," and "Remember Pearl Harbor." Kaye continued to play nightclub and concert dates until he retired in the 1970s.

KEARNS, JOSEPH (1907–1962)

One of the most recognizable voices on radio during the 1930s and 1940s belonged to Joseph Kearns, a versatile and talented actor who was comfortable in comedies as well as dramas. His clipped voice and manner of speaking were unmistakable to those who heard him. Kearns was featured on countless programs from the 1930s to the 1950s and is said to have worked on as many as fifty shows a week. Known as the host of SUSPENSE, he also appeared regularly on LIGHTS OUT, The ADVENTURES OF SAM SPADE, DETECTIVE, The JACK BENNY SHOW, GUNSMOKE, The LUX RADIO THEATER, The SCREEN GUILD PLAYERS, The WHISTLER, The JUDY CANOVA SHOW (playing Count Benchley Botsford), The JIMMY DURANTE SHOW, and BURNS AND ALLEN. On television, Kearns was the ever-exasperated next-door neighbor Mr. Wilson on the original "Dennis, the Menace" series in 1960.

KEIGHLEY, WILLIAM (1889–1984)

Film director William Keighley was born in Philadelphia, Pennsylvania. When motion-picture producer-director Cecil B. DeMille abandoned his hosting chores on the popular LUX RADIO THEATER program because of a contract dispute, Keighley, who had directed such first-rate films as *Bullets and Ballots* (1936), *The Prince and the Pauper* (1937), *The Adventures of Robin Hood* (1938), *The Man Who Came to Dinner* (1941), *George Washington Slept Here* (1942), and *The Street With No Name* (1948), took over the job. He was the host of *Lux Radio Theater* from 1945 until 1955.

KEILLOR, GARRISON

See PRAIRIE HOME COMPANION, THE.

KELK, JACKIE (1922–   )

An actor whose ever youthful-sounding voice typecast him in juvenile roles well into his adult years, Jackie Kelk was born in Brooklyn, New York. One of his earliest radio assignments was *The Fannie Brice–Baby Snooks Show* in 1933, but he became known for playing Homer Brown, Henry Aldrich's best friend on *The ALDRICH FAMILY*. When he was a child, Kelk was also heard on *Coast to Coast on a Bus* and was featured on such programs as *Dick Tracy* (playing Junior Tracy), *The GUMPS* (playing Chester Gump), TERRY AND THE PIRATES (playing Terry Lee), SUPERMAN (playing Jimmy Olson), and daytime drama series HILLTOP HOUSE, HELLO PEGGY, AMANDA OF HONEYMOON HILL, and ROSEMARY.

KEN MURRAY SHOW, THE (AKA THE LIFEBUOY SHOW)

1932–1936	CBS	(*)	(*)
1939–1940	CBS	Thurs.	8:30 PM

Ken MURRAY was the host of this half-hour music-comedy-variety show in the 1930s. Featured on Murray's show were actress-comedienne Eve ARDEN, who was Murray's straight woman, Shirley Ross, Marlyn Stuart, and singer Phil Regan. A popular character on the program was Oswald, played by Tony Labriola. His prissy mannerisms, overblown articulation, and foppish ways were loved by listeners. Murray's orchestra leaders were Lud GLUSKIN and Russ Morgan. The program was written by Ken Englund and David Freedman. Lifebuoy soap and Rinso cleanser sponsored the program.

KIERAN, JOHN (1892–1982)

One of the regular panelists on the popular INFORMATION, PLEASE series, John Kieran was born and educated in New York City, graduated from the City College of New York, and then became a staff writer for *The New York Times*. A well-read and very intelligent man, Kieran had a highly retentive mind that enabled him to answer many questions on *Information, Please* that stumped other experts. He remained on the show from 1938 until 1948, the entire time it was on the air. Afterward, Kieran wrote special articles and features for various newspapers and frequently lectured at colleges and universities around the country.

KILGALLEN, DOROTHY (1913–1965)

Newspaper columnist Dorothy Kilgallen was born in Chicago, Illinois, but grew up in Brooklyn, New York. She became a radio celebrity when her "Voice of Broadway" newspaper column became an on-the-air gossip-news feature. From 1947 to 1949, Kilgallen had a morning show of her own, *The Dorothy Kilgallen Show*, on which society gossip and show business were discussed, sponsored by Windex glass cleaner and Drano drain cleaner. She was a regular panelist on LEAVE IT TO THE GIRLS, and later, with her husband, actor Richard "Dick" KOLLMAR, hosted an early-morning talk show, *Dorothy and Dick*, which originated from the couple's New York City townhouse. Kilgallen later became a well-known face as a regular panelist on the "What's My Line" television series.

KILPACK, BENNETT (1883–1962)

Bennett Kilpack, who was born in England, first worked on American radio in 1927. His mature, patient, and gentle voice made him the perfect actor for the title roles of the kindly David Harum and Mr. Keen. A busy character actor, Kilpack was also heard on several daytime serial drama series, including SETH PARKER, MRS. WIGGS OF THE CABBAGE PATCH, ALIAS JIMMY VALENTINE, and YOUNG WIDDER BROWN, as well as on the BELIEVE IT OR NOT evening series.

KING, JOHN REED (1915–1979)

One of radio's most popular program hosts, John Reed King was born in Wilmington, Delaware, and attended Princeton University. He worked as an announcer on many radio programs and was the host of such quiz and panel programs as BREAK THE BANK, CHANCE OF A LIFETIME, THE MISSUS GOES A-SHOPPIN', DOUBLE OR NOTHING, and GIVE AND TAKE. King announced the OUR GAL SUNDAY, BOBBY BENSON, CAROL KENNEDY'S ROMANCE, and *The Crysler Air Show* series. King continued to perform voice-overs for radio and TV commercials until he retired in the early 1970s.

KING, LARRY (LARRY ZIEGER: 1933–   )

Broadcaster Larry King was born in Brooklyn, New York, and began his broadcasting career in 1957 on a 250-watt radio station in Miami. *The* LARRY KING SHOW is currently a Mutual Broadcasting System production and is heard on more than 400 stations nationally. A *Guinness* record holder, King has interviewed more than 30,000 people on his syndicated radio program since it went on the air in 1978.

King has been the recipient of numerous awards for his radio work, including the Peabody Award from the National Association of Radio Broadcasters in 1985 and the Jack Anderson Investigative Reporting Award. In 1986, he was named Best Radio Talk-Show Host by the *Washington Journalism Review*, and in 1990 he earned the National Association of Broadcasters' Marconi Award as Network Radio Personality of the Year.

In addition to his radio show, King hosts CNN's television program, "Larry King Live," and writes a

Larry King (Courtesy of Larry King)

weekly column "Larry King's People" in *USA Today*. King was inducted into the National Association of Broadcasters' Broadcasting Hall of Fame in 1992.

KING, WAYNE (1901–1985)

Wayne King, known as "the Waltz King," was born in Savannah, Illinois, and worked his way through college playing the clarinet in a college dance band. After he graduated from the University of Illinois, King learned to play the saxophone and joined the Al Short orchestra in Chicago. In 1924, after forming his own orchestra, he appeared on radio station KYW in Chicago and was eventually heard on big dance-band remote broadcasts and then on *The Lady Esther Serenade* program. King and his band continued to make regular personal appearances until he retired from active performing in the 1960s.

KINSELLA, WALTER (1901–1975)

Best remembered as Harrington, the faithful assistant to the D.A. on MR. DISTRICT ATTORNEY, actor Walter Kinsella was born in Ireland. Specializing in roles that required an Irish accent, he also played Patrick Murphy on the ABIE'S IRISH ROSE series, Pat Patton on *The* ADVENTURES OF DICK TRACY; Mike on *Joe and Mabel*; Mike McNally on *Leave It to Mike*; Happy McCann on MARTIN KANE, PRIVATE EYE; Sergeant Mullins on MR. AND MRS. NORTH; the general manager on CIRCUS DAYS; and Gus Grady on STELLA DALLAS.

KIRKWOOD, JACK (1896–1964)

A talented performer who was equally adept at playing comic or serious roles, Jack Kirkwood was heard as Santa Claus and as various comic characters on *The* BOB HOPE SHOW. Kirkwood was also featured on HAWTHORNE HOUSE and had a leading role on MIRTH AND MADNESS, as well as his own JACK KIRKWOOD SHOW from 1944 until 1946.

KITTY FOYLE

| 1942–1944 | CBS | Mon.–Fri. | 10:15 AM |

A best-selling novel by Christopher Morley and an award-winning 1940 film, *Kitty Foyle* became a 15-minute drama series shortly after the film was released. Actress Julie STEVENS played the title role of Kitty, the daughter of a working-class father, who spent most episodes dealing with her love affair with a wealthy fellow named Wyn Strafford, played by Clayton "Bud" COLLYER. Stratton's rich mother despised Kitty and warned her son about marrying below his class, but that did not keep Strafford from pursuing Kitty. Kitty believed that there was dignity in good, honest work and, in the end, she kept her job and worked instead of marrying Strafford. The radio version proved less successful than it had been in print and on film, and the series was canceled after two seasons on the air. Phil Lord played a major supporting role. The radio series was written by Doris Halman and Al Barker. Mel ALLEN announced the show, and General Mills flour was the program's sponsor.

KITTY KEENE

1937	NBC Red	Mon.–Fri.	4:45 PM
1937–1938	CBS	Mon.–Fri.	4:30 PM
1938–1939	NBC Red	Mon.–Fri.	11:45 PM
1939–1941	NBC Red	Mon.–Fri.	5 PM

Created and written by Dat Keene and Wally Norman, this 15-minute drama series originated in Chicago and starred Beverly Younger, Gail Henshaw, and then Fran CARLON as Kitty Keene, a young single woman trying to survive in a male-dominated business office in a large city. Also heard on this series were Bob BAILEY, Dick Wells, Patricia Dunlap, Herb Nelson, Angeline Orr, Carlton KaDell, Dorothy Gregory, Louise Fitch, Virginia "Ginger" Jones, Mary Patton, Janet Logan, Josephine Gilbert, Phil Lord, Loretta Poynton, Herb Butterfield, and Ian Keith. Jack Brinckley and Don Donaldson were the program's announcers. *Kitty Keene* was directed by Roy WINSOR, George Fogle, and Win Orr and was written by Lester Huntley. The show's theme song was "None But the Lonely Heart." The show was sponsored by Dreft cleaner.

KLEIN, EVELYN KAYE (1920–)

For many years, Evelyn and Her Magic Violin was the major musical attraction on the HOUR OF CHARM program, which starred Phil SPITALNY and his All-Girl Orchestra. Born in New York City of Hungarian-American parents, Evelyn won a gold medal for her violin playing while she was a student at the Juilliard School of Music in New York City. After studying at the Damrosch Insitute as a scholarship student, Evelyn won the Fontainebleu Grand Prix, the MacDowell Club Award, and the National Arts Club competition and made her professional debut as a concert violinist at Carnegie Hall in the 1930s. On attending one of Evelyn's concerts, orchestra leader Phil Spitalny was so impressed with the young musician's talent that he asked her as a solo artist to join an all-girl orchestra he was forming. Evelyn accepted, and the orchestra made its debut at the Capitol Theater in New York City in 1934. This led to a long-term contract for the orchestra to appear on *The Hour of Charm* program. Eventually, Evelyn married Spitalny; after their radio program was canceled, they continued to make concert appearances and were featured guest stars on several television music-variety programs in the 1950s.

KNICKERBOCKER PLAYHOUSE

1939	CBS	Sun.	10 PM
1939–1940	CBS	Wed.	9 PM
1940–1942	NBC Red	Sat.	8 PM

"Good evening. Come in. Welcome backstage to *Knickerbocker Playhouse*," this dramatic anthology series began. Similar to *The* FIRST NIGHTER program in format, *Knickerbocker Playhouse* was set in a fictitious theater and presented weekly, original half-hour dramas written especially for radio. Elliott LEWIS was the program's weekly star, with such regulars as Marvin MILLER, Betty WINKLER, and Barbara LUDDY appearing in the supporting cast. The program was directed by Richard G. Jennings, Joe Ainsley, George Fogle, and Owen Vinson. Dick Wells was the show's announcer. Sponsors included Drene and Special Drene shampoo and Teel shampoo.

KOLLMAR, RICHARD (1910–1971)

Best known to listeners as Blackie on the prime-time BOSTON BLACKIE syndicated radio mystery series, actor Richard Kollmar was born in Ridgefield, New Jersey. Heard in such daytime program roles as Michael West on BIG SISTER and its spin-off, BRIGHT HORIZON,

Evelyn Kaye Klein and her "Magic Violin" (CBS)

Kollmar also played David on CLAUDIA AND DAVID, John Perry on JOHN'S OTHER WIFE, Barry Markham on LIFE CAN BE BEAUTIFUL, Dennie Pierce on PRETTY KITTY KELLY, and Phil Stanley on WHEN A GIRL MARRIES. He was frequently featured on *The* PALMOLIVE BEAUTY BOX THEATER and *The* LIFE OF MARY SOTHERN. For many years, Kollmar costarred on the early-morning talk show *Dorothy and Dick* with his wife, Dorothy KILGALLEN. His acting career waned when dramas departed the airwaves in the 1950s.

KOSTELANETZ, ANDRE (1901–1980)

Music conductor Andre Kostelanetz was born in St. Petersburg, Russia, and attended the St. Petersburg Conservatory of Music. While still in his teens, Kostelanetz became the conductor of the Imperial Grand Opera in Russia. In 1922, at twenty, Kostelanetz emigrated to the United States and shortly after debuted on American radio. He subsequently conducted orchestras for *The Sweetheart Hour, Southern Melodies, The* ZIEGFELD FOLLIES OF THE AIR, *Five Star Revue, Threads of Happiness, The Pontiac Program, Buick Presents,* CHESTERFIELD PRESENTS, and *Tune-Up Time.* Kostelanetz became conductor of the New York Philharmonic Orchestra in 1952, a position he held until shortly before his death.

KRAFT MUSIC HALL, THE

1933–1940	NBC Red	Thurs.	10 PM
1940–1941	NBC Red	Thurs.	9 PM
1941–1946	NBC	Thurs.	9 PM
1941–1949	NBC	Thurs.	9 PM

Kraft foods sponsored this musical-variety program that featured various stars and formats over the many years it was on the air. The program's earliest stars included entertainer Al JOLSON, orchestra leader Paul WHITEMAN, and program host Deems TAYLOR, who broadcast a two-hour local program from New York City. When the program became a network show, Whiteman, singer "Ramona" (whose real name remained unknown), and Johnny Mercer were the stars.

In 1936, the show's new star, Bing CROSBY, moved the program to Hollywood. Comedian Lou HOLTZ became very popular with its listening public, as did comedian-singer Eddie Foy, and singers Jack Fulton, Nelson EDDY, Dorothy Kirsten, and Roy Bargy. Among Crosby's other frequent guests were actress-singer Mary Martin, singer Connee BOSWELL of the BOSWELL SISTERS, comedian-pianist Victor Borge, singer Peggy Lee, the ANDREWS SISTERS, Dorothy LAMOUR, Judy GARLAND, and Bob HOPE. Featured as regular supporting players were "the Arkansas Traveler" Bob BURNS, comedian Jerry Lester, and film star George Murphy. For one year, bandleader Jimmy Dorsey led the Kraft orchestra and hosted the show, and then for the remainder of its run, John Scott

Trotter was the show's conductor. The Merry Maid and Hal supported Crosby with backup vocals.

Announcers on the program included Don WILSON, Ed HERLIHY, Roger Krupp, and for many years Ken CARPENTER. Carroll Carroll was one of the original writers of the series; his work was so effective that most listeners thought that Crosby's show was being ad-libbed. The program was directed by Carl Kuhl, Manny Mannheim, Ezra MacIntosh, Ed Gardner, and Bob Brewster. Crosby left the show when Kraft refused to allow him to record his programs for later broadcast and became the star of a new program called *The* BING CROSBY SHOW. During several summer seasons, the *Kraft Music Hall* starred his younger brother, Bob CROSBY, and motion-picture character actors Frank MORGAN and Don AMECHE. These shows featured Robert Ambruster and his Orchestra.

See also AL JOLSON SHOW, THE; PAUL WHITEMAN SHOW, THE.

KRAMER, MANDEL (1917–1989)

New York City–born Mandel Kramer had a long and distinguished career as a radio actor and television commercial spokesman. Kramer appeared on MARY NOBLE, BACKSTAGE WIFE, COUNTERSPY, DIMENSION X, *The* FALCON, FAMOUS JURY TRIALS, MR. AND MRS. NORTH (as Mahatma McGloin, the cab diver), PERRY MASON (as Lieutenant Tragg), QUICK AS A FLASH, *The* SHADOW, STELLA DALLAS, TERRY AND THE PIRATES, THIS IS YOUR FBI, TRUE DETECTIVE, GANGBUSTERS, and YOURS TRULY, JOHNNY DOLLAR (as the title character). Kramer had featured roles on several TV series as well, most notably "The Verdict Is Yours" (1954–1957) and "The Edge of Night" (1959–1979). Kramer continued to be active as a voice-over performer until shortly before his death.

KRUGMAN, LOU (1914–1992)

Actor Lou Krugman was born in New York City. While attending high school, he was heard on local radio station WODA in Paterson, New Jersey. After a relatively short period of stage acting in New York, Krugman continued in radio on such programs as *The Buster Brown Gang Show, Dear Mom,* and *The* ROMANCE OF HELEN TRENT. Krugman moved to the West Coast and was heard on several Hollywood-based radio programs, most notably GUNSMOKE and ESCAPE, usually in villain roles. Krugman was also featured in many films, such as *To the Ends of the Earth* (1948) and *I Want to Live* (1958). His television credits include appearances on "Dragnet" and "Gunsmoke" from 1955 to 1975.

KYSER, KAY (1906–1985)

Bandleader Kay Kyser (also known as "the Professor" or "Fes") was born in Rocky Mountain, North Carolina. He formed his first orchestra in 1926 while he was a student at the University of North Carolina, and, after graduation, played at various dance engagements across the country, several of which were broadcast from late-night supper clubs. In the late 1930s, the bandleader became a radio star. In addition to his successful KAY KYSER'S KOLLEGE OF MUSICAL KNOWLEDGE, one of the most listened-to shows on the air in the late 1930s and 1940s, Kyser and his band guest-starred on DUFFY'S TAVERN and The RED SKELTON SHOW. Kyser greeted his listeners by saying, "Evenin' folks! How y'all?"—this became one of his trademarks. At the height of their popularity, Kyser and his band appeared in such films as *That's Right, You're Wrong* (1939), *Swing Fever* (1943), and *Carolina Blues* (1944). In 1950, *Kay Kyser's Kollege of Musical Knowledge* became a television show, but after four years, the bandleader decided to retire from show business.

LADD, ALAN (ALAN WALBRIDGE: 1913–1964)

Born in Hot Springs, Arkansas, Alan Ladd was a busy radio actor before he became a major motion-picture star in the early 1940s. He played supporting roles on *The* LUX RADIO THEATER and other shows that originated on the West Coast. He had minor roles in films, most notably *Citizen Kane* (1941), until he achieved movie stardom with his impressive performance as a baby-faced killer in Paramount's *This Gun for Hire* (1942), followed by films with Veronica Lake—*The Blue Dahlia* (1944) *Saigon* (1948)—and his best work, *Shane* (1953). Ladd's wife, former Hollywood actress-turned-agent Sue Carroll, guided his career and was largely responsible for his film stardom.

In 1948, Ladd starred on a radio series called BOX 13, playing private investigator Dan Holiday. The show had a two-year run before Ladd's busy moviemaking schedule forced him to abandon the series. The actor continued to work on radio, however, guest-starring frequently on *The* LUX RADIO THEATER and *The* SCREEN GUILD PLAYERS.

LADIES BE SEATED

1944–1946	NBC Blue	Mon.–Fri.	3:30 PM
1946–1949	ABC	Mon.–Fri.	3 PM
1949–1950	ABC	Mon.–Fri.	12 PM

Ed and Polly East, Johnny and Penny Olson, and Tom Moore hosted this audience-participation program at different times. Contestants on the 15-minute show could win prizes of $300 in merchandise by answering questions, singing, playing an instrument, or reciting a story or a poem. Audience applause decided the winner of each show. Produced by Philip Patton and directed by George Wiest, the show had George Ans-

bro as announcer. Quaker Oats cereals and Philip Morris cigarettes sponsored the program.

LADIES FAIR

1949–1950	Mutual	Mon.–Fri.	2 PM
1950–1954	Mutual	Mon.–Fri.	11 AM

Ladies Fair presented 15-minute segments on cooking and housekeeping tips of general interest. Professional shoppers, cooks, marital experts, and similar guests regularly appeared on the program. Holland Engle and Don Gordon hosted the show. Tabcin pain reliever sponsored the program.

LADY ESTHER SCREEN GUILD PLAYERS, THE

See SCREEN GUILD PLAYERS, *The.*

LAKE, ARTHUR (ARTHUR SILVERLAKE: 1906–1987)

Actor Arthur Lake was born in Corbin, Kentucky made his show-business debut working in a traveling circus with his parents, and was featured in a silent screen version of *Jack and the Beanstalk* (1917). Most identified with the role of Dagwood Bumstead, Lake played the character in twenty-eight *Blondie* films, as well as on radio and television. Chic Young's popular comic-strip couple was first dramatized on screen in 1937. Two years later, BLONDIE began a long run as a situation-comedy series on radio from 1939 to 1950. *Blondie* was introduced to television viewers in the early 1950s.

LAMOUR, DOROTHY (DOROTHY KAUMEYER: 1914–)

Singer-actress Dorothy Lamour was born in New Orleans, Louisiana. She was first heard on radio in 19 when she sang with the Herbie Kaye Orchestra and guest-starred on most of the major music-variety programs in the 1930s and 1940s, including *The* BOB HOPE SHOW, *The* LUX RADIO THEATER, *The* EDGAR BERGEN–CHARLIE MCCARTHY CHASE AND SANBORN SHOW, and DUFFY'S TAVERN. In the 1940s, Lamour starred on a short-lived radio series of her own, *The Dorothy Lamour Show.* During World War II, she frequently hosted COMMAND PERFORMANCE and MAIL CALL, produced for the armed forces overseas.

In films, Lamour's dark, exotic good looks afforded her roles in *Jungle Princess* (1936), *Hurricane* (1937), and the *Road* pictures with Bob HOPE and Bing CROSBY. She also had a major role in the Academy Award–winning *The Greatest Show on Earth* (1952). Lamour made occasional guest appearances on television on a talk or award shows and such shows as *The Love Boat.*

LAND OF THE LOST

1943	(Syndicated series. Various stations and times)		
1944–1945	ABC	Sat.	11 AM & 10:30 AM
1944–1946	NBC Blue	Tues.	7 PM
1946–1947	Mutual	Sat.	11:30 AM
1947–1948	ABC	Sat.	11:30 AM

Created and written by Isabel Manning Hewson, this children's adventure-fantasy serial starred Junius Matthews and then Art CARNEY as Red Lantern, a big red fish who lived in an underwater house. Isabel and Jimmy, played by Betty Jane Tyler and Ray Ives, used Red Lantern as their guide on various under-the-sea adventures. Other underwater characters such as sharks, whales, and octopuses were encountered by the children (and the listeners) on this show. Also featured on the half-hour series in supporting roles were Jim Boles, Althena Lorde, Ann Thomas, Tom Eldridge, Lee Marshall, and Kay Marshall. Michael Fitzmaurice was the program's announcer, and the series was directed by Cyril Armbrister.

LANGFORD, FRANCES (1914–   )

Pop singer Frances Langford was born in Lakeland, Florida. In 1932, she signed to appear on a Tampa radio station for thirteen weeks for a cigar manufacturer who had heard her sing at an American Legion party. This led to an appearance on *The* RUDY VALLEE SHOW. Vallee subsequently signed the singer as a regular on his weekly program and Langford later became the weekly vocalist on *The* BOB HOPE SHOW—she also went on tour with Hope when he entertained the military at bases all over the world during World War II. Other radio programs that Langford was featured on included HOLLYWOOD HOTEL, *The Old Gold Show,* and *The* TEXACO STAR THEATER. While appearing

on *The Old Gold Show,* Langford and actor Don Ameche introduced a series of short skits about a constantly bickering married couple—appropriately called "The Bickersons." This led to a radio show of that name. In addition to singing on various comedy-variety programs, Langford appeared in such films as *Every Night at Eight* (1935), *Hollywood Hotel* (1937), *Yankee Doodle Dandy* (1942), *The Bamboo Blonde* (1945), and *The Glenn Miller Story* (1954).

LANNY ROSS SHOW, THE (AKA MARDI GRAS; THE PACKARD HOUR)

1928–1930	NBC Red	Sat.	11 PM
1930–1931	NBC Red	Sun.	11 PM
1931–1932	NBC Blue	Thurs.	9:30 PM
1932–1937	(Off the air)		
1937–1938	NBC Red	Tues.	9:30 PM
1938–1939	(Off the air)		
1939–1940	CBS	Mon., Wed., Fri.	11 AM
1940–1942	CBS	Mon.–Fri.	7:15 PM
1942–1946	(Off the air)		
1946	CBS	Mon.–Fri.	7 PM
1946–1948	(Off the air)		
1948–1949	Mutual	Mon.–Fri.	11:45 AM
1949–1951	Mutual	Mon.–Fri.	12:15 PM
1951–1952	Mutual	Mon.–Fri.	10 AM

Singer Lanny ROSS, who was called "the Troubadour of the Moon," starred in several music-variety shows, presenting popular and semiclassical selections. His shows had both 15-minute and half-hour formats in which he sang along with his guests. Regulars on Lanny's various programs included singers Evelyn Knight and Louise Carlyle, the Buddy Weed Trio, the Al Fannell Trio, and the Will Lutrin Orchestra. Jean Paul King, Jimmy Blaine, John Scott, and Nelson CASE were the show's announcers. Maxwell House coffee, Log Cabin syrup, Oxydol detergent, Ivory soap, Packard automobiles, Franco-American canned spaghetti, and Dictograph recording machines are just a few of Ross's many sponsors. His theme song was "Blue Moon." Numerous directors and writers worked on Ross's programs.

LARKIN, JOHN (1913–1965)

Versatile actor John Larkin was born in Kansas City, Missouri. A graduate of the University of Missouri, Larkin was Perry Mason on the PERRY MASON program when it was a daytime radio series. He also played Buck on the BUCK ROGERS IN THE 25TH CENTURY series; Mark Trail on the MARK TRAIL series, and lead roles on such daytime dramas as MARY NOBLE, BACKSTAGE WIFE, LONE JOURNEY, MA PERKINS, PORTIA FACES LIFE, *The* RIGHT TO HAPPINESS, *The* ROAD OF LIFE, *The* ROMANCE OF HELEN TRENT, and STEPMOTHER. On television, Larkin played Mike Karr on the daytime television series "The Edge of Night" from 1956 until 1962. Illness forced the actor's retirement.

LARRY KING SHOW, THE

1978–present   (Syndicated series. Various stations)

The Larry King Show was first aired from Miami by the Mutual Broadcasting System on twenty-eight stations beginning in January 1978 as an experiment. Today, *The Larry King Show,* syndicated across the country, is heard on more than 400 stations, making it the most popular radio program on the air.

King's guests on his first show were Don Shula, Miami Dolphins football coach, and comedian Jackie Gleason. Since that broadcast, he has interviewed major personalities from business, entertainment, and the literary world to celebrated criminals. King has also interviewed major politicians, including Presidents Bush and Clinton and members of Congress and the Supreme Court.

LASSIE

1947–1948	ABC	Sun.	3 PM
1948–1949	NBC	Sat.	5:45 PM
1949–1950	NBC	Sat.	11 AM

The success of the MGM film *Lassie Come Home* (1943) eventually led to a half-hour *Lassie* radio series in 1947. Animal imitator Earl Keen barked as the star dog, Lassie, who heroically rescued people in trouble, cornered criminals, and had occasional exciting adventures in the wild. Lassie's owners were played by Betty Arnold and Marvin MILLER. Charles Lyon was the program's announcer, Frank Ferrin and Harry Stewart produced the show, and Stewart directed it. The radio series was written by Hobe Donavan. Appropriately, Red Heart dog food sponsored the series.

LAUK, CHESTER

See LUM AND ABNER.

LAVALLE, PAUL (1908–   )

Born in the small town of Beacon, New York, musician Paul Lavalle became one of radio's most successful music conductors. Lavalle led the orchestras on the CITIES SERVICE CONCERTS and CHAMBER MUSIC OF LOWER BASIN STREET. He also wrote musical arrangements for such programs as *The* CHESTERFIELD SUPPER CLUB and CLUB FIFTEEN in the 1940s. Lavalle continued to work as a music arranger and conductor for many television shows until he retired in the early 1980s.

LAVENDER AND OLD LACE

1934–1935	CBS	Tues.	8 PM
1935–1936	CBS	Sun.	5 PM
1936	NBC Blue	Wed.	8:30 PM

This half-hour music-variety program starred such celebrated concert and opera singers as Frank MUNN, Lucy Monroe, William Meeder, and Bernice Claire.

Bayer aspirin sponsored the series. The show's director and writers were uncredited.

LAZY DAN, THE MINSTREL MAN

1933–1934	CBS	Sun.	1:30 PM
1934–1935	CBS	Sun.	2 PM
1935–1936	CBS	Fri.	7:15 PM
1936	CBS	Tues.	8 PM

Former minstrel-show headliner Irving Kaufman starred on this half-hour music-variety show, heard in 15-minute and half-hour versions. The show nostalgically recalled nineteenth- and early-twentieth-century minstrel shows by presenting the standard minstrel format: comic banter between the "interlocutor" and members of the chorus, as well as such songs of the Old South as "Dixie." The names of the show's announcer, director, and writers were unrecorded. Old English wax sponsored the program.

LEAVE IT TO JOAN (AKA THE JOAN DAVIS SHOW)

1943–1945	NBC	Thurs.	8:30 PM
1945–1947	CBS	Mon.	8:30 PM
1947–1948	CBS	Sat.	9 PM
1948–1950	CBS	Fri.	9 PM

Comedienne Joan DAVIS starred on this half-hour situation comedy, playing the awkward, foot-in-the-mouth character she had popularized on radio's SEALTEST VILLAGE STORE and in such films as *Sun Valley Serenade* (1941). On the show, Davis had encounters with bill collectors, was locked in her hall closet for hours, ruined a dinner that her husband's boss and his wife were invited to eat at her home, and generally made life complicated for her long-suffering husband. Davis's costar on the radio show was Jim BACKUS as her husband, a role he repeated for the comedienne's television show, which debuted in 1952. Appearing on the radio show with them were Verna FELTON and Shirley MITCHELL. Andy Russell was Joan's vocalist at one time. Harry VON ZELL and Bob Lamond were the program's announcers. The series was produced and directed by Dick Mack. Sealtest ice cream, Swan soap, and Roi-Tan cigars sponsored the show.

See also SEALTEST VILLAGE STORE, THE.

LEAVE IT TO THE GIRLS

| 1945–1949 | Mutual | Sat. | 9 PM |

On this half-hour program, a panel of women—at various times consisting of Arlene FRANCIS, Constance Bennett, Robin Chandler, Binnie Barnes, Dorothy KILGALLEN, Florence Pritchard, Lucille BALL, and Eloise McElhone—answered questions and chatted about subjects of interest to women, usually concerning problems women had with members of the opposite sex. In humorous discussions, these women talked about such subjects as men's irresponsibility and behavior. Maggie McNellis was the program's hostess and moderator. A male celebrity, such as Fred ALLEN, Milton BERLE, or Oscar Levant, was usually featured to attempt to defend the male point of view, while the all-girl panel assaulted him verbally. The program was produced by Martha Rountree and directed by Joan Sinclaire and Jean Wright.

LET GEORGE DO IT

1946–1954   Mutual   Mon., Wed., Fri.   9:30 PM

George Valentine was the master sleuth on this half-hour detective series, starring Bob Bailey in the title role. The mysteries usually had P. I. Valentine taking on a murder case that invariably had some amusing twist to it. Virginia GREGG and then Frances Robinson played Valentine's secretary. Prominently featured in the cast regularly were Ed BEGLEY and Olan SOULE. The program was written and directed by David Victor and sponsored by Chevron gasoline stations.

LET'S PRETEND (AKA THE ADVENTURES OF HELEN AND MARY)

1931–1933	CBS	Sat.	10:30 AM
1933–1938	CBS	Sat.	10:30 AM
1938	CBS	Tues., Thurs.	6 PM
1938–1939	CBS	Mon., Thurs.	5 PM
1939–1940	CBS	Sat.	12:30 PM

The "Let's Pretenders": (standing from left) Arthur Anderson, Gwen Davies, Jack Grimes, Bill Lipton; (kneeling from left) Michael O'Day, Mary Jane Tyler; (sitting from left) Miriam Wolfe and Nila Mack; (sitting on floor) Sybil Trent (CBS)

1940–1941	CBS	Sat.	1 PM
1941–1943	CBS	Sat.	11:30 AM
1943–1945	CBS	Sat.	11:05 AM
1945–1946	CBS	Sat.	11:30 AM
1946–1949	CBS	Sat.	11 AM
1949–1953	CBS	Sat.	11:05 AM
1953–1954	CBS	Sat.	10:35 AM
			2:30 PM

Unquestionably one of the most celebrated children's programs of its time, *Let's Pretend,* originally called *The Adventures of Helen and Mary,* was the brainchild of Yolanda Langworthy and was taken over and steered by writer-director Nila MACK. For a half hour each week for more than twenty-three consecutive years, such fairy tales as "Cinderella," "Sleeping Beauty," "Beauty and the Beast," and "Jack and the Beanstalk" were adapted for young listeners. The show garnered many awards for Mack and CBS, among them the Motion Picture Daily award for "best children's program on the air" in 1929, 1940, 1944, and 1946; the Women's National Radio Committee's best children's radio show in 1939; and the Peabody Award for outstanding children's program in 1943. Harry Swan was the program's original host (he was later replaced by William "Uncle Bill" ADAMS). Swan played a character named Captain Bob as well as all of the animal roles heard on the program until Brad Barker and Donald Bain began to supply those characterizations. *Let's Pretend* was broadcast for many years from Radio Playhouse 3 in New York City, which is currently CBS's Ed Sullivan Theater. Many children joined the cast and remained with the show well into their adult years: Albert ALEY, Arthur ANDERSON, Vivian Block, Kingsley Colton, Gwen DAVIES (Estelle Levy), Marilyn Erskine, Jack GRIMES, Billy and Florence HALOP, Don HUGHES, Jackie KELK, Bill LIPTON, Ronald LISS, Michael O'DAY, Patricia Peardon, Bob READICK, Patricia RYAN, Walter TETLEY, Sybil TRENT, Mary Jane Tyler, and Miriam WOLFE. Others heard on the show were Donald Buka, Daisy Aldan, Rita Lloyd, Jack "Jackie" Jordan, Evie Juster, Robert Lee, Jimsey Sommers, Sidney Lumet (later a film director), the Mauch twins, Anne Marie Gayer, Lorna Lynn, and Larry Robinson. For years the show resisted sponsorship until CBS yielded to economic pressures; Cream of Wheat cereal was the show's first sponsor. The program's theme music, "Komzak's Fairy Tales," was given lyrics that were sung at the beginning of each broadcast by Gwen Davies and Sybil Trent.

When the song ended, the show's host decided with various cast members' help how they would be transported to Let's Pretend land. A different mode of transportation was chosen each week, such as "on a duck's back," "by airplane," or "in a car." The show's many announcers included Warren Sweeney, Bert PARKS, Jackson Wheeler, Frank Gallop, Jim Campbell, Peter Thomas, Hugh O'Connor, Douglas Edwards, and John Tillman. Original musical bridges and special music were composed and/or conducted by Emery Deutsch, Sidney Raphael, Leon Goldman, and Maurice Brown.

LEWIS, ABBY (CAMELIA ALBON LEWIS 1910–)

Actress Abby Lewis was born in Misilla Park, New Mexico. After she graduated from the University of New Mexico, Lewis studied speech and drama and appeared in many stage productions before she entered radio. The actress played Ada Overton on *The* ROAD OF LIFE, Mrs. Garrett on BRIGHTER DAY, and Clarabelle Hopkins on *A* HOUSE IN THE COUNTRY, and was frequently heard on FAMOUS JURY TRIALS, MY TRUE STORY, LIGHT OF THE WORLD, *The* GREATEST STORY EVER TOLD, BELIEVE IT OR NOT, WHEN A GIRL MARRIES, MARY NOBLE BACKSTAGE WIFE, YOUNG WIDDER BROWN, BIG TOWN, FRONT PAGE FARRELL, *The* FORD THEATER, COUNTERSPY, QUIET PLEASE, DAVID HARUM, GANGBUSTERS, *The* SHADOW, *The* MERCURY THEATER, YOU ARE THERE, MYSTERIOUS TRAVELER, AND SHERLOCK HOLMES. On television, Lewis was featured on "Famous Jury Trials," "Mama" and "The Philco Playhouse" as well as on numerous commercials.

Abby Lewis (CBS)

Cathy Lewis (CBS)

LEWIS, CATHY (1918–1968)

Born in Spokane, Washington, Cathy Lewis moved to Chicago, where she found work as a radio actress on FIRST NIGHTER and A TALE OF TODAY. She became known for her attractive-sounding voice and excellent articulation. In the early 1940s, she moved to Hollywood, married radio actor-director Elliot LEWIS, and continued her radio career, playing Jane Stacy, Irma's roommate, on MY FRIEND IRMA and roles on hundreds of SUSPENSE shows. Lewis was also a regular performer on the SAM SPADE, DETECTIVE series. With her husband, she costarred on the weekly dramatic anthology ON STAGE, playing all of the female leading roles, and was a regular on Carlton E. Morse's I LOVE A MYSTERY series. Lewis had major roles on several TV shows, including "My Friend Irma" in 1952, "Fibber McGee and Molly" in 1959, and "Hazel" in 1962. Her last TV appearance was an episode of "F Troop" in 1965, playing an aging Indian princess.

LEWIS, ELLIOTT (1917–1991)

Multitalented radio actor, director, and producer Elliott Lewis was born in New York City. Debuting on radio in 1936, he played every conceivable type of role, from comedy parts on The JACK BENNY SHOW, MAISIE, The AL JOLSON SHOW, and the PHIL HARRIS–ALICE FAYE SHOW—as the usually "tipsy" musician

Frank Remley—to serious roles on SILVER THEATER, SAM SPADE, Detective, The Casebook of Gregory Hood, I LOVE A MYSTERY, and ONE MAN'S FAMILY. Lewis also played a major role on the BROADWAY IS MY BEAT detective series as the assistant "fellow detective" and was regularly featured on KNICKERBOCKER PLAYHOUSE and SUSPENSE. In the 1950s, Lewis directed and produced *Suspense* and also produced, directed, and starred on a weekly dramatic anthology, *On Stage,* co-starring his wife, Cathy LEWIS. Lewis tried to bring some radio-drama magic back to the airwaves in the 1970s with a series of adaptations of great works of literature, such as *Ivanhoe* and *A Connecticut Yankee in King Arthur's Court,* on a program called *The Sears Playhouse.*

LEWIS, FULTON, Jr. (1903–1977)

Calm-sounding, intelligent, and articulate news commentator Fulton Lewis, Jr., was born in Washington, D.C., and educated at the University of Virginia. The author of a syndicated newspaper column "Washington Sideshow," Lewis founded the Radio Correspondents Association after becoming a broadcaster on WOI in Washington. For many years, Lewis was the chief news commentator for the Mutual Broadcasting System and continued to be heard on WOR in New York City well into the 1970s.

LIFE BEGINS AT EIGHTY

1948–1949	Mutual	Sun.	3:30 PM
1949–1952	(Off the air)		
1952–1953	ABC	Wed.	8:30 PM

Senior citizens above eighty years of age were given a chance to air their views and entertain radio listeners on this half-hour comedy-panel discussion show. The show consisted of the jokes and remembrances these senior citizens would tell about themselves and their lives and showed just how sharp people over eighty can be. Designed as a counterpart to JUVENILE JURY, both programs were hosted by Jack Barry. Among the regular panel members on *Life Begins at Eighty* were Fred Stein, Eugenia Woilland, Joseph Rosenthal, and Georgiana P. Carhart. The program was produced by Dan Ehrenreich (aka Dan Enright) and directed by Diana Bourbon. Geritol vitamin supplement, Serutan laxative, and Campbell's soup sponsored the show. Ken ROBERTS announced the series. The show's theme song was "Melody in F."

LIFE CAN BE BEAUTIFUL

1938–1939	CBS	Mon.–Fri.	1:15 PM
1939–1941	NBC Red	Mon.–Fri.	9:45 AM
	& CBS	Mon.–Fri.	1:15 PM
1941–1947	CBS	Mon.–Fri.	1 PM
1947–1954	NBC	Mon.–Fri.	3 PM

Affectionately called "Elsie Beebee" (L.C.B.B.), the abbreviation for the show's title by radio actors who enjoyed working on it, *Life Can Be Beautiful* revolved around Papa David Solomon, a benevolent, elderly man and his employees—also his wards—Carol "Chichi" Conrad and Stephen Hamilton, who worked at "The Slightly Read Bookshop." Papa David, a homespun philosopher, possessed abundant sense and was a wonderful friend to anyone who happened to need his help. Ralph LOCKE played Papa David Solomon, Alice REINHEART and Teri Keane played Chichi, and Earl Larrimore and then John Holbrook played Stephen Hamilton. Also heard at various times were Carl Eastman, Paul Stewart, Adelaide Klein, Richard KOLLMAR, Dick Nelson, Roger DeKoven, Peggy Alleby, Ian Martin, Ruth Yorke, Mitzi Gould, Agnes MOOREHEAD, Clayton "Bud" COLLYER, Ruth Weston, Charles "Cuck" Webster, Ed BEGLEY, Sidney Smith, Ethel Owen, Humphrey Davis, Elsie Hitz, Minerva PIOUS, Gavin Gordon, and Joseph JULIAN. Announcers included Ralph EDWARDS, Vinton Hayworth, Ron Rawson, Ed Roberts, Bob Dixon, Don Hancock, Ed HERLIHY, Carl Bixby, and Don Becker. The program was directed by Chick Vincent, Storrs Haynes, and Oliver Barbour. It was written by Don Becker. Sponsors of the series included Ivory soap flakes, Camay soap, Ivory soap, Crisco oil, Spic and Span floor cleaner, Tide detergent, and Ivory snow detergent.

LIFE OF MARY SOTHERN, THE

1935–1936	Mutual	Mon.–Fri.	11:45 PM
1936–1937	Mutual	Mon.–Fri.	5:15 PM
1937–1938	CBS	Mon.–Fri.	5:15 PM

When the theme music "Just a Little Love, a Little Kiss" swelled and the announcer stated that *The Life of Mary Sothern* was on the air, listeners heard the story of a woman's struggle to survive and find love in the trouble-filled modern world. The 15-minute drama starred Linda Carlon-Reid, Minabelle Abbott, and Betty Caine as Mary Sothern, and featured Florence Golden, Charles Seel, Bess McCammon, Jay JOSTYN, Jerry Lesser, Mary Patton, Leon JANNEY, Jeanne Colbert, Rikel Kent, and Bess Cameron. Jack Zoller and Joseph Julian played Mary's love interest, Danny Stratford. Ken ROBERTS was the program's announcer. Chick Vincent directed. Pebeco toothpaste and Hinds Honey and Almond Fragrance cream sponsored the show.

LIFE OF RILEY, THE

1944–1945	NBC Blue	Sun.	10 PM
1945–1948	NBC	Sat.	8 PM
1948–1951	NBC	Fri.	10 PM

William BENDIX, who played Chester A. Riley on a half-hour radio program, was known from the television situation-comedy series *The Life of Riley*, although film character-actor Lionel Stander originated the role of Riley when the radio program first went on the air in 1944. Riley was a typical blue-collar American factory worker. His family consisted of wife, Peg; their son, "Junior"; and their daughter, "Babs." The show was one of the few radio programs that dealt with domestic crises—quite often financial difficulties were discussed—but it did so in a comedic format. Grace Coppin, Georgia Backus, and then Paula Winslow played Riley's wife, Peg; Jack GRIMES, Scotty Beckett, Conrad Binyon, and Tommy Cook, Riley's son, Junior; and Peggy Conklin, Sharon Douglas, and Barbara Eiler as his daughter, Babs. John Brown played an amusing character named Digger O'Dell, "friendly undertaker." Also heard on the show were Dink Trout as Waldo, Charlie CANTOR as Uncle Buckley, Elvia ALLMAN and then Shirley MITCHELL as Olive "Honeybee" Gillis, John Brown doubling as Gillis, and Hans CONRIED as Uncle Baxter. Few people who heard the series can forget Riley's catchphrase, "What a revoltin' development dis is," or Digger O'Dell's catchphrase, "You're looking well, Riley. Very natural!" The show's announcers included James "Jimmy" WALLINGTON, Ken CARPENTER, Ken NILES, and Harry VON ZELL. The show was directed by Al Kaye, Marx Loeb, and Don Bernard. It was written by Ruben Ship, Ashmead Scott, Alan Lipscott, Robert Sloane, and Leonard Bercovici. The program's sponsors were American Meat Institute, Teel shampoo, Ivory soap flakes, Dreft detergent, Prell shampoo, Drene shampoo, Lava soap, and Pabst Blue Ribbon beer.

LIFE WITH LUIGI

1948–1949	CBS	Sun.	8:30 PM
1949–1950	CBS	Sun.	9:30 PM
1950–1953	CBS	Tues.	9 PM

The leading character of this half-hour situation-comedy series was a childlike, innocent, gentle Italian immigrant named Luigi Basco. Luigi, who spoke broken English, was a bit like a child in a candy shop in his view of the world. Because he was in a new country, everything was new and exciting to him. This was communicated by the expert acting delivered by veteran character-actor J. Carrol NAISH. Alan REED was Luigi's sponsor and restaurant-owner boss, Pasquale. Pasquale brought Luigi to America from Italy hoping that Luigi would marry his obese, unattractive, constantly giggling daughter, Rosa, played by Jody Gilbert. Mary Shipp played Luigi's night-school English teacher, whom he had a crush on. Other students in his class included Horowitz, played by Joe Forte; Schultz, played by Hans CONRIED; and Petersen played by Ken Peters. The show's theme music was "Oh, Marie," but Luigi always sang "America, I Love

ou" during the program. Announcers included Bob
amond, Bob Stevenson, and Charles "Charlie" Lyon.
fe with Luigi was created, produced, and directed by
y Howard and written by Lou Derman. The sponsor
as Wrigley's spearmint gum.

IFEBUOY PROGRAM, THE

| 1936–1939 | CBS | Tues. | 8:30 PM |

zz singer Al JOLSON starred on this half-hour com-
dy-music program after he left SHELL CHATEAU. Reg-
larly appearing on the program with Jolson were
omedienne Martha Raye and Harry "Parkyakarkis"
INSTEIN. Guest stars such as Eddie CANTOR, George
SSEL, and George BURNS and Gracie ALLEN appeared
rith Jolson. Tiny Rufner was the show's announcer.
ifebuoy soap and Rinso cleanser sponsored the
eries.

IGHT OF THE WORLD

1940–1942	NBC Red	Mon.–Fri.	2 PM
1942–1943	NBC	Mon.–Fri.	2 PM
1943–1946	CBS	Mon.–Fri.	10:15 AM
1946–1950	NBC	Mon.–Fri.	2:45 PM

ight of the World was a 15-minute show that voiced
strong moral message. Topics such as how to live
rith decency and honor were presented dramatically;
he show leaned toward religious solutions to the
roblems, although it was not officially a religious
rogram. Bret MORRISON and David GOTHARD nar-
ated the series; regularly featured were versatile
ctors Sanford Bickart, Chester STRATTON, Florence
VILLIAMS, Humphey Davis, Eric Dressler, Mitzi
ould, Louise Fitch, Barbara Fuller, William "Bill"
DAMS, James Monks, Peggy Allenby, James McCal-
on, Lynne Rogers, Linda Carlon-Reid, Virginia
ayne, Jack Arthur, Dan Sutter, Elaine Rost, and Er-
est Graves. The announcers on the series were Stuart
1etz, James Fleming, and Ted Campbell. Created and
roduced by Don Becker and Basil Loughrane, *Light
f the World* was directed by Don Cope, Chick Vincent,
nd Oliver Barbour. The scripts were written by Mar-
aret Sangster, Don Becker, and others.

IGHTS OUT (AKA THE DEVIL AND MR. O)

1935–1939	NBC Red	Wed.	12:30 AM
1939–1942	(Off the air)		
1942–1943	CBS	Tues.	8 PM
1943–1945	(Off the air)		
1945	NBC	Sat.	8:30 PM
1945–1946	(Off the air)		
1946	NBC	Sat.	10 PM
1946–1947	(Off the air)		
1947	ABC	Wed.	9:30 PM

It is later than you think! This is the witching hour.
t is the hour when dogs howl and evil is let loose on
a sleeping world. Want to hear about it? Then turn
out your lights," the *Lights Out* program began, and
then, after a pause, the announcer said, "Lights out . . .
everybody!" A typical *Light's Out* story was "Murder
Castle," in which a young woman found herself
trapped in a castlelike house by a madman. He would
lure innocent young women to his home on the pretense of offering them a job and then kill them. This
young woman was able to escape and bring him to
justice.

Although Wyllis Cooper was the creator of this
memorable anthology of horror tales and wrote many
of its early scripts, Arch OBLER is the program's best-
remembered contributor. Obler wrote, directed, and
even acted in many of the stories. In its earliest years,
the program originated from Chicago and featured
Hans CONRIED, Mercedes MCCAMBRIDGE, Cathy LEWIS,
Elliott LEWIS, Virginia GREGG, Joseph KEARNS, Betty
WINKLER, Raymond Edward JOHNSON, Bea BENA-
DERET, Edgar Barrier, Tex Maxwell, Sidney Ellstrom,
Irene Tedrow, Lou Merrill, Gloria Blondell, Wally
Maher, Earle Ross, Tom Lewis, and Templeton Fox.
Frank Martin and George Stone were the show's an-
nouncers. Ironized yeast, Energine vitamin supple-
ment, Snow White bleach, and Eversharp-Schick
razors sponsored the program.

LI'L ABNER

| 1939–1940 | NBC Red | Mon.–Fri. | 5:30 PM |

Cartoonist Al Capp's hillbilly comic-strip characters
were the focus of this 15-minute late-1930s comedy
program. In Dogpatch, U.S.A., located in the Ozark
Mountains, lived a big, bumbling but handsome hillbilly, played by John HODIAK. Hazel Dopheide and
Clarence Hatzell played Abner's Mammy and Pappy
Yokum; and Laurette FILLBRANDT acted as his girlfriend, Daisy Mae. Durwood Kirby was the program's
announcer. The series was written by Charles
Gussman, produced by Wynn Wright, and directed
by Ted MacMurray.

LIMBAUGH, RUSH (1951–   )

Broadcaster Rush Limbaugh was born in Cape Girar-
deau, Missouri, to a family of lawyers. His first broadcast, at the age of sixteen, was done after school at his
hometown radio station. After finishing high school,
Limbaugh joined the staff of ABC at Pittsburgh's
KWV as a disc jockey. Later, he directed group sales
for the Kansas City Royals baseball team. In 1983,
Limbaugh became a radio political commentator for
KMBZ in Kansas City, and a year later he hosted a
daytime talk show on KFBK in Sacramento, California,
which led to his current syndicated program. Limbaugh's ultraconservative political and social views
have made him one of the country's most controver-

Rush Limbaugh (Courtesy of Rush Limbaugh)

sial radio personalities. As of this writing, Limbaugh is heard on 575 radio stations around the country.

See also RUSH LIMBAUGH SHOW, *The.*

LINCOLN HIGHWAY

1940–1942	NBC Red	Sat.	11 AM

Hosted by actor John MCINTIRE, *Lincoln Highway* was a half-hour dramatic anthology that presented stories about everyday events that happened to ordinary people in both rural areas and big-city environs. Heard on this series were Ethel Barrymore, Joe E. BROWN, Harry Carey, Claude Rains, Victor Moore, Gladys George, Henry Hull, Luther Adler, Burgess MEREDITH, Joan Bennett, Betty Field, Luise Rainer, and Raymond Massey. Don Cope, Maurice Lowell, and Theodora Yates directed the series, which was written by various freelance writers. The program was sponsored by Shinola shoe polish.

LINDA'S FIRST LOVE

1937–1942	(Syndicated series. Various stations and times)		
1942–1943	NBC	Mon.–Fri.	9:15 AM
1943–1950	(Syndicated series. Various stations and times).		

"This is the true-to-life story of a girl in love with the world around us . . . and in love with wealthy, young Kenneth Woodruff. She is a shop girl, and he a wealthy young man. The romance is frowned upon by Linda's family, and Linda faces the world with her dreams of happiness . . . alone! Should Linda go on fighting for Kenneth despite the opposition of his dictatorial mother, or should she return to faithful, steady Danny Grogan?" Arline Blackburn played Linda, Frank LOVEJOY was Danny Grogan, and Mary Jane HIGBY was Linda's mother on this series. Roger Forster and Andre BARUCH were the program's announcers. The series was written and directed by Martha Atwell. Its theme music was "If You Are But a Dream." Kroger's coffee was the sponsor.

LINDLAHR FOOD AND NUTRITION SHOW, THE

1936–1937	Mutual	Mon.–Fri.	12 PM
1937–1938	Mutual	Thurs.	12 PM
1938–1941	Mutual	Mon., Wed., Fri.	12 PM
1941–1945	Mutual	Mon., Wed., Fri.	9:15 AM
1945–1947	Mutual	Mon.–Fri.	11:45 AM
1947–1948	Mutual	Mon.–Fri.	12:15 PM
1948–1950	Mutual	Mon.–Fri.	11:15 AM
1950–1951	ABC	Mon.–Fri.	10:45 AM
1951–1953	ABC	Mon.–Fri.	12:15 PM

Nutritionist Victor H. Lindlahr had a popular program in both 15-minute and half-hour versions on the air for seventeen years. The show offered good advice about healthy and nutritious eating, best food buys, the importance of taking vitamins, and good health in general. Lindlahr's sponsor for many years was Serutan ("Nature's spelled backwards") laxative.

LINE UP, THE

1950–1953	CBS	Tues.–Fri.	(*)

William "Bill" JOHNSTONE starred as Lt. Ben Guthrie, and Wally Mayer played Sgt. Matt Robb on this 15-minute action series about events that occurred in the police precinct of a large American city. Members of the police department tracked down and apprehended criminals and put them in a lineup for identification by eyewitnesses to their crimes. Also heard regularly were Ed BEGLEY, John MCINTIRE, Walter Catlett, Dave Young, and Howard McNear. The program was produced and directed by Jaime Del Valle.

LINKLETTER, ART (1912–   )

Art Linkletter debuted as a radio announcer at station KGB in San Diego in 1933 and is best remembered as host of PEOPLE ARE FUNNY, on radio from 1942 and on television from 1952. His easygoing interviewing style encouraged people to recount silly arguments with their spouses or the facts about their collection of a x-foot-diameter ball of string. Most memorable was the "kids [under five years of age] say the darndest things" segment. Linkletter also hosted the audience-participation program *House Party* and *What's Doin', Ladies,* which were also on the air in the 1940s. *People Are Funny* became a television mainstay in the 1950s and for many years. Linkletter also produced shows for TV.

LIPTON, WILLIAM "BILL" (1926–)

In 1937, when Brooklyn-born actor Bill Lipton was eleven years old, he debuted on a local radio program, aired on WOR in New York City, called *Rainbow House.* He was subsequently featured on programs such as LET'S PRETEND, GASOLINE ALLEY (playing the lead role of Skeezix), and CHICK CARTER, BOY DETECTIVE (playing Chick). By the time he had become a young adult, he was also featured on YOUNG DR. MALONE, *The* ROAD OF LIFE, *The* MARCH OF TIME, MRS. MINIVER, and *The* COLUMBIA WORKSHOP. In 1960, Lipton entered politics and became Senator Stuart Symington's radio and television adviser. Not long after, he was stricken with Parkinson's disease. His physical disabilities gradually forced him into retirement, though he remained an active member on the board of directors of the Oregon chapter of the American Parkinson's Disease Association.

LISS, RONALD (1931–1969)

Few child actors were more consistently employed than curly-headed "Ronnie" Liss. Born in New York City, he was six years old when he first stepped in front of a microphone to play his violin and sing. He was featured on Madge Tucker's COAST TO COAST ON A BUS children's variety show and on Nila Mack's LET'S PRETEND children's fairy-tale series; on the first, Liss sang the show's opening theme-song line, "The white rabbit line . . . jumps anywhere, anytime!"

Liss continued on radio throughout his teens and into his young adult years, playing Bobby on BRIGHT HORIZON, Buddy on BUCK ROGERS IN THE 25TH CENTURY, Tiny Tim on HILLTOP HOUSE, Batman's sidekick, Robin, on *The* ADVENTURES OF SUPERMAN, and Scotty on MARK TRAIL. He was also featured on STUDIO ONE, *The* FORD THEATER, and TWO ON A CLUE. Remaining active on radio throughout the 1950s, Liss was also involved in television production until his untimely death at the age of thirty-nine.

LISTENING POST

| 1944–1948 | ABC | Tues.–Fri. | 10:45 AM |

Bret MORRISON, probably best remembered as *The* SHADOW, hosted this 15-minute dramatic anthology series of human-interest stories, previously published in *The Saturday Evening Post* magazine. Usually involving people who had overcome obstacles in their lives, such as illness or financial setbacks, characters on this series were played by Everett SLOANE, Mary Jane HIGBY, Myron MCCORMICK, Joan Tetzel, Ethel Owen, and Clayton "Bud" COLLYER, and others, as well as by such special guest stars as Fredric March and Martha Scott. The program was directed by Henry Klein and James Sheldon and written by Ben Kagen, Gerald Holden, and Noel B. Gerson.

LITTLE ORPHAN ANNIE

1935–1936	NBC Blue	Mon.–Fri.	5:45 PM
1936–1940	NBC Red	Mon.–Fri.	5:45 PM
1940–1943	Mutual	Mon.–Fri.	5:45 PM

Long before *Annie* was a hit Broadway musical and film, Harold Gray's Little Orphan Annie comic strip character was a long-running radio series. The title character was an adventure-seeking little girl who, with her dog, Sandy—and often with the help of her long-lost-but-finally-found father, Daddy Warbucks—became involved in many exciting escapades for 15 minutes each weekday. Each *Little Orphan Annie* radio program opened with a theme song that became almost as famous as the show itself:

> Who's that little chatterbox,
> The one with all those curly locks?
> Who can she be?
> It's Little Orphan Annie!
> She and Sandy make a pair.
> They never seem to have a care.
> Cute little she,
> Little Orphan Annie!

Annie was originally played by actress Shirley Bell and then by Janice Gilbert. Henry Saxe, Stanley Andrews, and Boris Aplan were Daddy Warbucks. Also heard in the cast were Allan Rourke as Joe Corntassle, Herry O'Meara, and Henrietta Tedro as Mr. and Mrs. Silo, Olan SOULE as Aha, the Chinese cook, Hoyt Allen as Clay, who invented the secret decoding device so Annie's listeners could decode product-oriented messages sent from Annie at the end of the show such as "Drink your Ovaltine." Sandy, the dog, was played by actor Brad Barker. Often heard in supporting roles were St. John Terrell, Cornelius Peeples, Harry Cansdale, and James Monks. For many years, the program was directed by Robert Wilson and Alan Wallace. It was written by Roland Martini, Day Keene, Wally Norman, and Ferrin N. Fraser. Ovaltine choco-late-flavored health drink sponsored *Little Orphan An-*

nie, which was one of the first programs to offer premiums such as decoding badges, rings, milk shakers, and mugs to young listeners who sent in a dime and a label from an Ovaltine jar. The series' announcer was Pierre Andre.

LITTLE THINGS IN LIFE, THE

See RADIO PLAYHOUSE, THE.

LIVE LIKE A MILLIONAIRE

1950–1952	NBC	Mon.–Fri.	2:30 PM
1952–1953	ABC	Mon.–Fri.	11 AM

Jack McCoy and John Nelson hosted this half-hour quiz program in which contestants answered questions about historical and current events in an attempt to earn the top prize of "living like a millionaire"—which was an evening on the town in New York City, complete with dinner for two at a fine restaurant, tickets to a Broadway show, and limousine service for the evening. General Mills products sponsored the program.

LIVES OF HARRY LIME, THE (AKA THE THIRD MAN)

1951–1952	(Syndicated series. Various stations and times)

Orson WELLES gave an impressive performance in the 1949 film *The Third Man,* which was set in post–World War II Vienna. The film starred Joseph Cotten as Rollo Martins, a down-and-out pulp Western writer, and Welles as Harry Lime, a childlike and opportunistic soldier of fortune who sold defective medications for a profit. In the radio series, however, Welles turned Lime from a villain to a hero, apprehending international jewel thieves, spies, and dangerous murderers. This half-hour weekly, early-1950s radio series, first heard on the BBC in England, featured the same Anton Caras zither music played in the movie as musical bridges. Welles directed the series, but the writers were uncredited.

LIVINGSTONE, MARY (SADYE MARKS: 1908–1983)

Mary Livingstone was born in Vancouver, Canada, and grew up in Los Angeles. In 1927, she married comedian Jack BENNY and appeared with him on *The* JACK BENNY PROGRAM on radio in the mid-1930s. Livingstone also made guest appearances with Jack on several music-comedy-variety programs such as *The* FRED ALLEN SHOW and *The* FLEISCHMANN HOUR and starred with him in several LUX RADIO THEATER adaptations of films. Mary modestly claimed that she

was "not really much of an actress," but her expe comic timing and flawless delivery of comedy lines the *Benny Show* proved otherwise. Never particular comfortable with performing, she retired from sho business after making a few appearances on Benny television show: she was unable to adjust to pe forming live, without a script, in front of an audienc Livingstone and Benny had been married for 47 yea when Benny died in 1974. Mary lived in relati seclusion until her death nine years later.

LOCKE, RALPH (c1885–1956)

Eastern Eurpean–born character actor Ralph Loc was active in Yiddish theater in New York and on t Broadway stage before he entered radio. He playe various ethnic-Jewish roles on many radio progran in the 1930s and 1940s, but is best remembered Papa David Solomon, the kindly owner of t "Slightly Used Book Store," on the daytime dran series LIFE CAN BE BEAUTIFUL. Locke was also featur on DOT AND WILL, *The* ENO CRIME CLUB, *The* PALMOLI BEAUTY BOX THEATER, DEATH VALLEY DAYS, GANGBU TERS, BIG SISTER, YOUR FAMILY AND MINE, YOUNG D MALONE, and SECOND HUSBAND, mainly playing ethn roles.

LOMAX, STAN (1899–1987)

Sportscaster Stan Lomax was born in Pittsburg Pennsylvania. He had one of the longest-lasting ar most productive careers on radio, broadcasting pla by-play baseball game actions and dispensing spor news throughout the 1930s and 1940s. His rapid-fi delivery earned him a reputation as one of the faste talking yet accurate sports reporters on radio.

LOMBARDO, GUY (1902–1977)

For more than forty years, the Guy Lombardo Orche tra played "the sweetest music this side of heaven Lombardo was born in London, Ontario, Canad When he was twenty-one years old, he formed h first orchestra and performed with his three brothe at his mother's ladies' club meetings. From the 195 through the 1950s, Lombardo and his Royal Canac ans Orchestra played jazz and swing tunes on nume ous radio programs, including frequent big-band, lat night remote broadcasts from various nightclul around the country. *The Bob Burns Pantela Progra* and other guest appearances on comedy-varie shows soon followed. His annual New Year's E broadcasts from New York City were a "must" fi many Americans, with Lombardo and his Royal Can dian Orchestra playing their version of "Auld Lar Syne" at the stroke of midnight on December 31.

See also GUY LOMBARDO SHOW, *The.*

ONE JOURNEY

1940–1941	NBC Red	Mon.–Fri.	11:30 AM
1941–1943	NBC Red	Mon.–Fri.	10:45 AM
1943–1946	(Off the air)		
1946–1947	CBS	Mon.–Fri.	2:30 PM
1947–1951	(Off the air)		
1951–1952	ABC	Mon.–Fri.	11 AM

he fictional town of Lewiston, Montana, was the etting for the *Lone Journey* drama series about the omestic and social difficulties of living in a remote ural community. The program starred Les DAMON, eese Taylor, Staats COTSWORTH, and Henry Hunter s Wolfe Bennett, the program's hero; and Claudia ORGAN, Betty WINKLER, Betty Ruth Smith, Eloise ummer, Olive Deering, Charlotte Holland, and Les-y Woods starred as his wife, Nita Bennett. Also eard regularly were Warren Mills, Nancy Osgood, mes MEIGHAN, John HODIAK, Betty Caine, Nancy larshall, Cliff Soubier, Richard Coogan, DeWitt lcBride, Geraldine Kay, John Larkin, Cleveland owne, Laurette FILLBRANDT, Henry Hunter, and Nel-on CASE. The announcers included Durwood Kirby, elson Case, Henry MORGAN, and Richard Stark. The rogram was directed by Axel GRUENBERG, Ted lacMurray, Roy WINSOR, and Martin Magner and so at times written by Magner. Dreft detergent, Lava oap, Carnation evaporated milk and Lever Brothers roducts sponsored the series.

ONE RANGER, THE

1933–1936	Mutual	Mon., Wed., Fri.	8 PM
1936–1941	Mutual	Mon., Wed., Fri.	7:30 PM
1941–1942	NBC Blue	Tues.	7:30 PM
1942–1945	NBC Blue	Mon., Wed., Fri.	7:30 PM
1945–1955	ABC	Mon., Wed., Fri.	7:30 PM
1955–reruns	ABC	Mon., Wed., Fri.	7:30 PM

A fiery horse with the speed of light, a cloud of dust nd a hearty 'Hi yo, Silver!' *The Lone Ranger* rides gain!" This famous opening introduced one of radio's est-remembered Western adventure series. Wearing is black mask as a disguise, the Lone Ranger fought keep the southwestern United States free of outlaws nd other bad elements for more than twenty years n radio and television. A former Texas Ranger whose ntire company had been massacred by renegade Indi-ns, John Reid was left for dead but was found by onto and nursed back to health. He became the one Ranger. The half-hour program was created by eorge W. TRENDLE and Fran STRIKER and was based n Striker's comic-book character. The radio series as broadcast from WXYZ in Detroit.

First played by George Stenius (aka George Seaton) nd then by Jack Deeds and Earle Graser, the best-emembered Ranger is Brace BEEMER, who played the part for thirteen consecutive years (1941–1954). Prior to 1941, he substituted as the Ranger and was also the show's announcer. John Todd played Tonto for most of the show's run, but Jim Jewell was also heard in the role. Regular supporting players included WXYZ staff actors Paul Hughes, Elaine Alpert, Ernie Winstanley, Rollon Parker, Harry Goldstein, Lee All-man, and Bill Saunders. Clayton Moore and Jay Sil-verheels played the Ranger and Tonto on TV.

The show's dramatic theme music was the overture to *William Tell* by Rossini; the often-heard musical bridges between scenes were from Liszt's "Les Pre-ludes" and Tchaikovsky's 1812 Overture. Announcers included Beemer, Harold True, Charles Woods, Fred Foy, Harold Golder, and Bob Hite. For many years, the series was produced and directed by James Jewell. Other directors included Al HODGE, Ted Robertson, and Charles Livingstone. The show's many writers included Striker, Felix Holt, Bob Green, Shelly Stark, Bob Shaw, Dan Beatty, Tom Dougall, and Gibson Scott Fox. General Mills was the program's sponsor for many years, and the program sold products such as Silvercup bread, Bond bread, Cheerios cereal, Wheaties cereal, Kix cereal, Betty Crocker cake mixes and Merita bread (in seven Southern states).

LORA LAWTON

1943–1945	NBC	Mon.–Fri.	10 AM
1945–1946	NBC	Mon.–Fri.	10:15 AM
1946–1950	NBC	Mon.–Fri.	11:45 AM

The durable *Lora Lawton* drama series was originally set in the Midwest but later moved to Washington, D.C., when its heroine moved to the nation's capital to work for a politician. She remained unmarried, harboring an unrequited love for her boss. Joan Tomp-kins and then Jan MINER starred as Lora. Also heard on the series were James MEIGHAN, Ned WEVER, Ethel Wilson, James Van Dyke, Marilyn Erskine, Fran CAR-LON, Lawson Zerbe, Walter GREAZA, Paul MCGRATH, Carol Summers, and Kate McComb. Produced by Frank and Anne HUMMERT, *Lora Lawton* was directed by Martha Atwell, Arthur Hanna, and Fred Weihe. It was written by Elizabeth Todd. Ford Bond was the show's announcer. Bab-O cleanser, Glim toothpaste, and Aunt Polly's Noodle Soup sponsored the program.

LORD, PHILLIPS H. (1902–1975)

Radio actor and producer Phillips H. Lord was born and raised in Hartford, Vermont, and after attending Andover Academy and then Bowdoin College, Lord went to New York City determined to pursue an acting career. Having difficulty obtaining the stage roles he wanted, he found that radio was willing to hire him because he spoke in a cultured, articulate manner that appealed to broadcasting officials of the time. He played leading roles on the SETH PARKER and *Country Doctor* radio shows. Then, in the mid-1930s, Lord's interests shifted to producing. He was responsible for such radio successes as GANGBUSTERS, BY KATHLEEN NORRIS, MR. DISTRICT ATTORNEY, *Sky Blazers, Treasury Agent,* WE THE PEOPLE, *The Black Robe,* COUNTERSPY, and POLICEWOMAN.

LORENZO JONES

1937–1940	NBC Red	Mon.–Fri.	11:15 AM
1940–1942	NBC Red	Mon.–Fri.	4:30 PM
1942–1952	NBC	Mon.–Fri.	4:30 PM
1952–1954	NBC	Mon.–Fri.	5:30 PM
1954–1955	NBC	Mon.–Fri.	5:15 PM

"We all know couples like lovable, impractical Lorenzo Jones and his devoted wife, Belle. Lorenzo's inventions have made him a character to the town . . . but not to Belle, who loves him. Their struggle for security is anybody's story. But somehow, to Lorenzo, it has more smiles than tears," the 15-minute serial *Lorenzo Jones* began. Although Lorenzo worked as a mechanic at Jim Barker's garage, he was really an inventor at heart. Most of his inventions, such as a ground-level wheel that walked dogs in circles, seemed absurd at the time the show was aired, but several—such as his outdoor vacuum cleaner, which had people doubled over with laughter in the 1940s— are now facts of life.

The program starred Karl SWENSON and John Raby as Lorenzo, and Betty GARDE and then Lucille WALL as Belle. Also in the cast were Nancy Sheridan, Mary Wickes, Grace Keddy, Elliott Reid, Ethel Owen, John Brown, Frank Behrens, Jean McCoy, Louis Hector, Irene Hubbard, Roland Winters, Art CARNEY, Chester STRATTON, Joe JULIAN, Helen Walpole, Coleen Ward, Ann SHEPHARD, and Doris Rich. The program's announcers were Jean Paul King, Don Lowe, Roland

Lorenzo Jones: Karl Swenson and Betty Garde (NBC)

Winters, George Putnam, and Ken ROBERTS. Lloyd Rosenmond and Ernest Ricca directed the program, which was written by Mathilde and Theodore Ferro. The theme music for *Lorenzo Jones* was "Finiculi, Funicula." Phillips Milk of Magnesia's antacid tablets, face cream, and toothpaste, Bayer aspirin, Ironized yeast tablets, Dreft detergent, Fab detergent, Colgate dental cream, Palmolive soap, Hazel Bishop lipstick, and Dr. Lyon's tooth powder sponsored the show.

LOUISIANA HAYRIDE, THE

1948–1953			(Syndicated show. Saturday evenings)
1953–1954	CBS	Sat.	9 PM
1954–present			(Syndicated show. Saturday evenings)

On April 3, 1948, a Shreveport, Louisiana, radio station—KWKH—launched a live country-western program, *The Louisiana Hayride,* featuring country singers and comedians. The brainchild of station manager Henry Clay, the show was picked up by stations throughout the southern and southwestern United States and was soon heard on twenty-five regional radio stations. Broadcast from the Shreveport Municipal Auditorium stage, the show introduced an impressive number of country-western performers to the American public: Hank Williams (on the show the first year it was aired), Elvis Presley (his radio debut), Johnny Cash, Slim Whitman, Johnny Horton, Red Sovine, Webb Pierce, the Tennessee Mountain Boys (featuring Kitty Wells), Patsy Montana, comic "Cousin" Wilbur Four, Loretta Lynn (her radio debut at 19 years of age), and pianist Floyd Cramer. The show's announcers were Frank Page and Nat Stuckey. In 1953, the CBS radio network launched its "Saturday Night-Country Style" program and picked up *The Louisiana Hayride* for all of the United States to hear. One year later, however, the show returned to syndication. The Far East Network of the ARMED FORCES RADIO SERVICE broadcast the show to troops stationed in Vietnam in the 1960s and 1970s. For many years *The Louisiana Hayride* was directed by Henry Clay. The program had numerous local sponsors.

LOVEJOY, FRANK (1912–1962)

Actor Frank Lovejoy was born in the Bronx in New York City. He made his radio debut in 1934 on FORTY-FIVE MINUTES FROM HOLLYWOOD and subsequently played the title role on *The* AMAZING MR. MALONE, Lucky Stone on NIGHT BEAT, and Nick Fowler of CALLING ALL DETECTIVES. Daytime serial listeners heard Lovejoy on such programs as YOUR FAMILY AND MINE, STELLA DALLAS, JUST PLAIN BILL, BRAVE TOMORROW, SECOND HUSBAND, and BRIGHT HORIZON.

Lovejoy was also prominently featured on the evening series *The* GAY NINETIES REVUE, *Deadline Dramas*, GANG-BUSTERS, *The* SHADOW, JOHNNY PRESENTS, *The* COLUMBIA WORKSHOP, *The* ADVENTURES OF SAM SPADE, DETECTIVE, and *Texas Village.* Film-star Lovejoy appeared in such films as *Home of the Brave* (1949), *In a Lonely Place* (1950), *The Sound of Fury* (1951), *I Was a Communist for the FBI* (1951), *The Hitchiker* (1952), *Rereat Hell* (1952), *House of Wax* (1953), *Beachead* (1954), and *Strategic Air Command* (1955). On television, Lovejoy starred in the "Man Against Crime" (1956) and "Meet McGraw" (1957) series.

LUDDEN , ALLEN (1918–1981)

Wisconsin-born master of ceremonies and moderator Allen Ludden was a drama and English teacher before he decided to enter radio. Ludden originated and hosted COLLEGE QUIZ BOWL, a radio program in which colleges competed against each other for various scholarships. It later became a popular television series. Ludden also produced and hosted several teen-oriented panel shows for NBC, including *Mind Your Manners.* He is best known, however, as the host of the "Password" television series, aired from the 1960s into the 1980s. Ludden died while "Password" was still on the air.

LUDDY, BARBARA (1908–1979)

Actress Barbara Luddy was born in Chicago, Illinois. One of Chicago's busiest radio actresses throughout the 1930s, she was the leading lady for seventeen years of the FIRST NIGHTER program, on which she played every conceivable part in comedies, dramas, and adventure stories. Luddy was heard regularly on CHICAGO THEATER OF THE AIR, GRAND HOTEL, *Great Gunns* (playing Veronica Gunn), LONELY WOMAN, *The* ROAD OF LIFE, and *The* WOMAN IN WHITE. Consistently voted Favorite Radio Actress in *Radio Mirror* and *Radio Guide* fan-magazine polls, the actress was also an active voice-over performer for many characters in feature-length film cartoons. She was the speaking voice for Lady in *Lady and the Tramp* (1955), for Rover in *101 Dalmations* (1961), and for Kanga in *Winnie the Pooh* (1966).

LUM AND ABNER

1935–1936	Mutual	Mon., Wed., Fri.	7:15 PM
1936–1937	NBC Blue	Mon.–Fri.	7:30 PM
1937–1938	CBS	Mon., Wed., Fri.	6:45 PM
1938–1939	CBS	Mon., Wed., Thurs., Fri.	7:15 PM
1939–1940	CBS	Mon., Wed., Fri.	7:15 PM
1940–1945	NBC Blue	Mon.–Thurs.	8:15 PM
1945–1947	ABC	Mon.–Thurs.	8 PM
1947–1953	CBS	Mon.–Fri.	5:45 PM

On the air continuously for twenty-two years, the 15-minute and sometimes half-hour *Lum and Abner* show

Chester Lauk and Norris Goff as *Lum and Abner* (NBC)

centered around two small-town men who owned the Jot 'em Down Store in Pine Ridge, Arkansas. Pine Ridge was originally a fictitious town, but in 1936, the village of Waters, Arkansas, officially changed its name to Pine Ridge in honor of the radio program. Many people, especially in rural areas, strongly identified with the various characters on the show. Chester LAUK and Norris GOFF, who created the characters and the show, starred as Lum and Abner. Lauk was also heard as Grandpappy Peabody, Snake Hogan, and Cedric Wehunt; Goff also played Dick Huddleston the postmaster, Doc Miller, and Squire Skimp. Also heard were Edna Best, Cornelius Peeples, ZaSu Pitts, Andy DEVINE, and Cliff ARQUETTE. Opie Cates led the program's orchestra at one time, and Gene Hamilton, Del SHARBUTT, Carlton Brickert, Lou Crosby, Wendell NILES, Gene Baker, and Roger Krupp were the show's announcers over the years. The series was produced and directed for many years by Larry Berns. Also directing were Robert McInnes, Forrest Owen, William L. Stuart, and Bill Gay. The show's writers included Jay Sommers, Betty Boyle, Roz Rogers, Hugh Wedlock, Jr., and Howard Snyder. Quaker Oats cereal, Ford automobiles, Horlick's malted milk, Alka Seltzer antacid, One-A-Day vitamins, Miles Nervine pain

The original stars of the film *So Proudly We Hail:* (from left) Veronica Lake, Claudette Colbert, and Paulette Goddard, re-created their film roles on *Lux Radio Theater.* (CBS)

medicine, and the General Motors Company sponsored the show, whose theme music was "Evalana."

LUX RADIO THEATER, THE (AKA LUX PRESENTS HOLLYWOOD)

1934–1935	NBC Blue	Sun.	2:30 PM
1935–1954	CBS	Mon.	9 PM
1954–1955	NBC	Tues.	9 PM

Nearly every major Hollywood film star in the 1930s, 1940s, and 1950s made at least one appearance on *The Lux Radio Theater* program (see Appendix D for a listing). This hour-long weekly show featured radio adaptations of popular movies, whenever possible featuring the film's original stars. When the show debuted in 1934, the scripts were mainly adaptations of Broadway plays and novels, but in 1936 the show turned to film adaptations. Anthony "Tony" Stanford (1934–1935), film director Cecil B. DEMILLE (1935–1945), William KEIGHLEY (1945–1951), and Irving Cummings (1951–1955) hosted the program. *The Lux Radio Theater* was consistently voted "Favorite Dramatic series" in various magazine polls. Frequently heard in supporting roles were radio regulars Verna FELTON, Frank NELSON, Anne Sargent, Gloria Gordon, Wally Maher, Aileen Pringle, child actress Norma Jean Nilsson, Willard WATERMAN, Gerald MOHR, Joseph KEARNS, Lurene TUTTLE, Eddie Marr, Florence Lake, Margaret Brayton, Lou Merrill, Jeff CHANDLER, How-

ard DUFF, Alan LADD, and Gale GORDON. Announcers on the show were Melville Ruick, John Milton Kennedy, Frank Goss, and Ken CARPENTER; the program's directors included Anthony Stanford, Frank Woodruff, Fred MacKaye, and Earl Ebi. Regular writers were Charles S. Munroe, Ed James, Sanford Barnett, Stanley Richards, Carroll Carroll, and True Boardman. Lux soap sponsored the programs for most of the years it was aired, but Rinso Blue bleach-detergent and Spry shortening were the sponsors during the show's last years.

(See also Appendix D.)

LYNCH, PEG (1917–)

Writer-actress Peg Lynch was born in Lincoln, Nebraska. She began her broadcasting career in 1938 as a jack-of-all trades at a small-town Minnesota radio station. Moving on to Chicago, Lynch wrote a radio show for women before her move to New York in 1944, where officials at the newly formed independent Blue network asked her to develop a new program. The result was the ETHEL AND ALBERT show, similar to those she had written in Chicago, about the married life of a typical American couple. As writer and leading actress, Lynch was primarily responsible for the show's enormous success. The show moved to television in the 1950s and returned to radio at the end of the decade with the new title *The* COUPLE NEXT DOOR. In the 1960s, Lynch produced and costarred with film actor Eddie Bracken in more than a hundred husband-and-wife promotional spots for the American Banking Association. In the mid-1970s, Lynch starred and wrote all of the scripts for *The Little Things in Life*, a 15-minute segment of *The* RADIO PLAYHOUSE. Currently, she performs *Ethel and Albert* at various colleges and universities, and continues to entertain fans, who find her scripts as original and relevant today as when they were first aired. Lynch's *Ethel and Albert* scripts are among the Samuel French play-publishing company's best-selling plays.

LYTELL, BERT (1888–1954)

Actor Bert Lytell played the title role on the ALIAS JIMMY VALENTINE adventure series and was a regular performer on *The* KATE SMITH SHOW. Lytell is best remembered, however, as the host of the STAGE DOOR CANTEEN, aired during World War II to boost troop morale. The actor also starred in such motion pictures as *To Have and to Hold* (1917), *Lady Windermere's Fan* (1926), *The Lone Wolf* (1931), *Blood Brothers* (1930), and *Stage Door Canteen* (1943), which was based on the radio show. Lytell was also seen as Father Barbour on the television version of Carlton E. Morse's "One Man's Family" series in 1949.

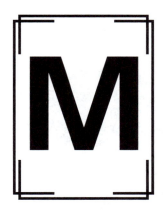

MA PERKINS

1933–1934	NBC Red	Mon.–Fri.	3:00 PM
1935–1937	NBC Red	Mon.–Fri.	3:15 PM
	Mutual	Mon.–Fri.	11:30 AM
1937–1938	NBC Blue	Mon.–Fri.	10:15 AM
	NBC Red	Mon.–Fri.	3:15 PM
1938–1939	CBS	Mon.–Fri.	2 PM
	NBC	Mon.–Fri.	3:15 PM
1939–1942	NBC Red	Mon.–Fri.	3:15 PM
1942–1943	NBC	Mon.–Fri.	3:15 PM
1943–1950	CBS	Mon.–Fri.	1:15 PM
	NBC	Mon.–Fri.	3:15 PM
1950–1960	CBS	Mon.–Fri.	1:15 PM

"And now, Oxydol's own *Ma Perkins*," the announcer introduced this 15-minute drama series. *Ma Perkins* was on the air for more than twenty years, with the title character continuously played by Virginia PAYNE. A kind, lovable, loving widow, Ma was the devoted mother of two grown daughters, Fay and Evey. She owned the Rushville Center Lumber Yard, and—with the help of her longtime friend and partner, Shuffle Shober—tried to keep it and her family in order. Several actresses played Fay over the years, including Rita Ascot, Marjorie Hannan, Cheer Brentson, Laurette FILLBRANDT, and Margaret Draper. Evey was played by Dora Johnson, Laurette Fillbrandt, and—for fifteen years—by Kay Campbell. Shuffle was played by Charles EGLESTON for twenty-five years and by Edwin Wolfe for two years. Evey's trouble-prone husband, Willy Fitz, was played by Murray FORBES. Also heard were Cecil Roy, Herb Nelson, Lenore Kingstone, Arthur Young, Bobby Ellis, Constance Crowder, Fran CARLON, Louise Fitch, Marilor Neumayer, Beverly Younger, Don Gallagher, Carl Kroenke, Maurice Copeland, Angeline Orr, Dan Sut-

ter, Forrest Lewis, Les TREMAYNE, Nanette Sergeant, Beryl Vaughn, Rye Pillsbury, Helen Lewis, Casey Allen, Gilbert Faust, Edwin Wolfe, Patricia Dunlap, and Elaine Roessler.

Jack Brinkley, Dick Wells, Marvin MILLER, Dan Donaldson, Bob Brown, and Bob Pfeiffer were the program's announcers. The series was created and originally written by Robert Hardy Andrews, directed by Lester Vail (who also produced the series), Edwin Wolfe, George Fogle, Philip Bowman, and Roy Winsor, and written by Orin Tovrov, Lee Gebheart, Natalie Johnson, and Lester Huntley. Proctor and Gamble's Oxydol laundry powder, Sta-Puf fabric softener, and Kellogg's All-Bran cereal were the show's sponsors.

MACGREGOR, KENNETH (1905–1968)

Born in Brockton, Massachusetts, Ken MacGregor first entered radio in 1934. One of the many talented people who directed *The* CHICAGO THEATER OF THE AIR, MacGregor also directed such diverse programs as the country-and-western show *The* GRAND OLE OPRY, the situation-comedy series *Archie Andrews*, mystery-detective series *City Desk* and *The Molle* MYSTERY THEATER, the dramatic anthology PALMOLIVE BEAUTY BOX THEATER, the variety show SHOW BOAT, the wartime program *Thanks to the Yanks*, and daytime serial dramas WHEN A GIRL MARRIES and PRETTY KITTY KELLY. He also directed such diverse prime-time programs as BELIEVE IT OR NOT, *The Jack Haley Show*, *The Wonder Show*, *The* JOE PENNER SHOW, SKY BLAZERS, and STRANGE AS IT SEEMS.

MACK, CHARLIE

See MORAN AND MACK.

MACK, NILA (1891–1953)

Born in Arkansas City, Kansas, Nila Mack was the writer, director, and major force behind CBS's children's radio program LET'S PRETEND. A precocious child, Mack sang, danced, and played the piano at local theaters in Arkansas City. She studied dramatics, French, and elocution in Boston. She first acted in local stock-company productions in Boston and then on tour. Mack married actor Roy Briant and they put together a vaudeville act. Moving to Hollywood, she worked as a silent-film actress and her husband was a scenario writer for several years. After Briant died in 1922, she moved to New York and worked on radio in The THEATER GUILD OF THE AIR, *Nit Wits* and *Night Club Romances*. In 1930, she was hired by CBS to direct *The Adventures of Helen and Mary* (later renamed *Let's Pretend*) and became one of the few women directors in radio. She also directed *Sunday Mornings at Aunt Susan's,* a one-hour program featuring Elaine Ivan as Aunt Susan, and the "Tales from Far and Near" segment of The AMERICAN SCHOOL OF THE AIR series. It was mainly due to Mack's expert writing and her ability to direct child actors that the *Let's Pretend* series became the most critically acclaimed, award-winning children's program on the air. Mack also directed CBS's children's quiz program *The March of Games* (with Arthur Ross as quizmaster and Sybil Trent as the drum majorette) and the adult daytime drama series *Mrs.* MINIVER.

MACLAUGHLIN, DON (1907–1986)

Before he began to act on television in the mid-1950s, Iowa-born actor Don MacLaughlin was one of radio's busiest performers. Leading-man MacLaughlin played Jim on CHAPLAIN JIM, David Harding on COUNTERSPY, and Jed on TENNESSEE JED. He was also heard regularly on GANGBUSTERS, ETHEL AND ALBERT, *The* ROAD OF LIFE, *The* FBI IN PEACE AND WAR, *The* ROMANCE OF HELEN TRENT, and WE LOVE AND LEARN. MacLaughlin became well known to television viewers as Chris Hughes, patriarch of the Hughes family, on the soap opera "As the World Turns" from 1956 until 1986.

MACON, DAVID HARRISON (1870–1952)

One of *The* GRAND OLE OPRY'S favorite performers, "Uncle" Dave Macon did not become a professional entertainer until he was in his fifties. Born in Smart Station, Tennessee, Macon moved to Nashville when he was thirteen years old. For the next forty years, he worked as a farmer and for a freight corporation, occasionally performing as an amateur singer and guitarist. In 1924 Macon decided it was time to pursue a performing career full-time and went to New York for the first of what would be numerous recording sessions. Late in 1925, he became a performer on *The Grand Ole Opry* program and introduced such songs as "The Dixie Dewdrop," which became his nickname. After twenty-five years on the program, Macon retired. The country music–legend star was elected to the Country Music Hall of Fame posthumously in 1966.

MAGGIE AND JIGGS

See BRINGING UP FATHER.

MAGIC KEY, THE (AKA THE MAGIC KEY OF RCA)

1935–1939	NBC Blue	Sun.	2 PM

Milton CROSS and Ben GRAUER hosted this one-hour music program that also featured commentaries by musicologist John B. Kennedy. Basically a classical and semiclassical music concert series, the program featured some of the world's most distinguished singers and instrumentalists, such as James MELTON, Dorothy Kirsten, Risë Stevens, Jerome Hines, and Yehudi Menuin in weekly, on-the-air concerts. Andre BARUCH announced the show. RCA records and phonographs sponsored the program.

MAGIC VOICE, THE

1932–1933	CBS	Tues., Sat.	8:15 PM
1933–1936	(Off the air)		
1936–1937	NBC Blue	Mon.–Fri.	4:45 PM

During the 1930s, actress Elsie Hitz was said by *Radio Guide* fan magazine to have had "the most beautiful voice on radio." Starring on *The Magic Voice*, Hitz read romantic stories and poems on this 15-minute program. Actor Nick Dawson also appeared on the series as the show's announcer. The program was sponsored by Ex-Lax laxative and Chipso soap flakes.

MAGNIFICENT MONTAGUE, THE

1950–1951	NBC	Fri.	9 PM

Actor Monty Woolley, an impressive stage (1939) and screen (1941) performer who played the cantankerous Sheridan Whiteside in *The Man Who Came to Dinner*, starred in this series. The role was that of droll, acerbic, not-unlike-Sheridan-Whiteside former Shakespearean actor Edwin Montague, the reluctant star of a weekly radio series that he felt was unworthy of his talents. Montague's wife, Lily Bohème Montague, was played by Anne SEYMOUR and Agnes, the maid, by Peri Kelton. The half-hour situation-comedy series was written and directed by Nat Hiken. Don Pardo was the series' announcer. Sponsors of the program included Anacin pain reliever, RCA Victor records and phonographs, and Chesterfield cigarettes.

MAIL CALL

1942–1950 (Various times)

This half-hour program was broadcast at various military bases across the United States and around the world during World War II. Among the guest hosts and regular visitors to this variety show were Bob HOPE, Bing CROSBY, the ANDREWS SISTERS, Judy GARLAND, Jimmy DURANTE, Peggy Lee, Norma Shearer, Jack CARSON, Nelson EDDY, Mel Torme, Don WILSON, Tallulah BANKHEAD, organist Ethel Smith, Danny KAYE, Harry Moore, Ann Rutherford, and Johnny Mercer. Wilson, Harry VON ZELL, and Ken CARPENTER announced the series, which was produced by the ARMED FORCES RADIO SERVICE.

MAISIE, THE ADVENTURES OF

See ADVENTURES OF MAISIE, The.

MAJOR BOWES' FAMILY HOUR

See PRUDENTIAL FAMILY HOUR, The.

MAJOR BOWES' ORIGINAL AMATEUR HOUR

See ORIGINAL AMATEUR HOUR.

MAJOR HOOPLE

1942–1944 NBC Blue Mon. 7:05 PM

The characters on this show were originally introduced in Gene Ahern's "Our Boarding House" comic strip in 1921. The cast included Arthur Q. BRYANT as Major Amos Hoople, an overstuffed, boorish, self-styled philosopher; Patsy Moran as his wife, Martha; and Franklin Bresee as the major's precocious nephew, Little Alvin. Also heard on this half-hour series were Mel BLANC as Mr. Twiggs and John Battle in a variety of roles. Lou Bring's and Walter Greene's orchestras provided music for the program. The series was written by Phil Leslie. It's director and sponsors are unknown.

MALONE, TED (FRANK A. RUSSELL: 1908–1989)

Radio host and journalist Ted Malone began his broadcasting career in 1927 at radio station KMBC in Kansas City, Missouri, where he was born. Malone later starred on BETWEEN THE BOOKENDS from 1935 until 1956, on which he read poems and made personal, down-to-earth observations about life in general, such as the value of having a good friend and how people should take the time to appreciate such little things in life as a beautiful sunset or a sweet rose. Host of the YANKEE DOODLE QUIZ program and author of a monthly column, "Between the Bookends," for *Radio Mirror* magazine, Malone was a war correspondent during World War II for the ARMED FORCES RADIO SERVICE and was the only American broadcaster to cover Queen Elizabeth II's coronation live from London. In 1957, Malone produced an Academy Award–winning short-subject film called *The Day of the Painter*. He broadcast a local show produced at WKRG in Mobile, Alabama, until January 2, 1987.

MAN BEHIND THE GUN, THE

| 1942–1944 | CBS | Wed., Sun. | 10:30 PM |
| | | Sat. | 7 PM |

This half-hour program was developed to boost U.S. citizens' morale during World War II and featured the actual experiences of members of the armed services, such as individual acts of heroism in battle and away-from-home encounters of military with ordinary citizens of faraway places. Jackson BECK narrated the stories. Heard regularly were Myron MCCORMICK, William Quinn, Frank LOVEJOY, Elizabeth Reller, Larry Haines, and Paul Luther. The program was produced and directed by William N. ROBSON and written by Ranald MacDougall. Van Cleave's orchestra provided the music for the program. The program was sustained by CBS.

MAN CALLED X, A

1944	NBC Blue	Mon., Sat.	9:30 PM (Summer)
1944–1945	NBC Blue	Sat.	10:30 PM
1945	NBC	Tues.	10 PM (Summer)
1945–1946	(Off the air)		
1946	NBC	Tues.	10 PM
1946–1947	(Off the air)		
1947	CBS	Thurs.	10:30 PM
1947–1948	CBS	Sun.	8:30 PM
1948–1950	(Off the air)		
1950–1951	NBC	Fri.	8:30 PM
		Sat.	8:30 PM
1951–1952	NBC	Fri.	9:30 PM
		Fri.	8 PM
		Fri.	9:30 PM
		Mon.	10:30 PM
		Tues.	10:30 PM

This half-hour weekly series told of soldier-of-fortune Ken Thurston, who tracked down dangerous criminals who were usually engaged in some sort of espionage work. Thurston's favorite hangout was the exotic Cafe Tambourine in Cairo, Egypt. He was assisted in his crime-solving efforts by his unnamed girlfriend, who had one of the most ear-piercing screams on radio. Film actor Herbert Marshall played Thurston, and his girlfriend was played by GeGe Pearson. Leon Belasco played Thurston's assistant, Pagan Zeldschmidt. Wendell NILES was the program's announcer. Jay Richard Kenny produced the series, and Jack Johnstone and William N. ROBSON were the program's directors. Milton Merlin wrote the scripts for the show. Sponsors included Lockheed aircraft manufacturers, Pepsodent toothpaste, Frigidaire refrigerators, Anacin pain reliever, and RCA Victor records and phonographs.

MAN I MARRIED, THE

1939–1940	NBC Red	Mon.–Fri.	10 AM
1940–1942	CBS	Mon.–Fri.	11:15 AM

This NBC 15-minute radio soap opera concerned the marital woes of Evelyn Waring, whose husband was considered weak. The role of Evelyn Waring was played by a number of actresses, including Vicki VOLA, Gertrude Warner, Dorothy Lowell, Lesley Woods, Betty WINKLER, and Barbara Lee. Van Heflin and Clayton "Bud" COLLYER played Evelyn's husband, Adam Waring, who was sometimes drunk, unable to hold a job, and was dominated by his mother. Also heard on the program were Ethel Owen, Santos ORTEGA, Rikel Kent, Fran CARLON, Fred Lewis, Jack GRIMES, Betty Worth, Arnold MOSS, Raymond Edward JOHNSON, Walter Vaughn, Spencer Bentley, Ed JEROME, and John Gibson. Announcers on the series were Del SHARBUTT and Howard Petrie. Oliver Barbour directed the series, which was written by Carl Bixby and Don Becker. Basil Loughrane was in charge of the production. Oxydol detergent and Campbell's soup sponsored the program.

MANDRAKE THE MAGICIAN

1940–1942	(Syndicated series. Various times and stations)

First introduced in 1934, Lee Falk and Phil Davis's comic-strip hero, *Mandrake the Magician,* arrived on radio in 1942 with Raymond Edward JOHNSON playing the famous crime-solving magician, who trapped enemy spies by using his special magic abilities. Juano Hernandez was featured as Mandrakes's assistant, Lothar, and Francesca Lenni played his girlfriend, Narda. The series was produced by Henry Souvaine and directed by Carlo DEANGELO.

MANHATTAN MERRY-GO-ROUND

1932–1933	NBC Blue	Sun.	3:30 PM
1933–1942	NBC Red	Sun.	9 PM
1942–1949	NBC	Sun.	9 PM

Manhattan Merry-Go-Round began each show with the following theme song:

> Jump on the Manhattan Merry-Go-Round
> We're touring alluring old New York town!
> Broadway to Harlem . . . a musical show
> The orchids that you rest at your radio.
> We're serving music . . . songs and laughter
> Your happy heart will follow after.

> And we'd like to have you all with us
> On the Manhattan Merry-Go-Round!

These lyrics became almost as familiar to listeners a the program itself during the seventeen years th series was on the air. The half-hour music show fea tured such artists as Thomas L. Thomas, Conrad Th bault, Pierre Le Kreun, Marion McNanus, Rache Carlay, Dennis Ryan, Marion McManus, Barry Rob erts, Glenn Cross, Dick O'Connor, Rodney McClen nan, and the Jerry Mann Voices, as well as the Me About Town singing groups. Victor Arden's, Do Donne's, and Andy Sanella's orchestras were feature at different times. Ford Bond and Roger Krupp hoste the series, which was created and produced by Fran and Anne HUMMERT. Paul Du Mont directed the se ries. Dr. Lyon's tooth powder was the program longtime sponsor.

MANSON, CHARLOTTE (1917–   )

Actress Charlotte Manson was born in New York Cit and attended New York University. While attendin college, Manson appeared with the Washingto Square Players in productions of *A Midsummer Night Dream* (playing Hermia), *As You Like It* (playing Rosa lind), and *Hamlet* (playing Ophelia). She repeate these performances when the company toured Grea Britain in the late 1930s. When Manson graduate she appeared in the film *East Side Story* (1938) and o Broadway in *Ringside Seat* (1938). She was subse quently signed to a contract as an NBC radio sta actress, her first show being *Parade of Programs.* Mar son appeared on NBC's experimental television pro ductions in the late 1930s. Other NBC radio and CBS and Mutual network radio programs followed. Mar son was prominently featured on such programs a SOCIETY GIRL, MARY NOBLE, BACKSTAGE WIFE, *America Woman, The* BRIGHTER DAY, *The* SHADOW OF FU MAN CHU, *MGM Screen Test, The* GUIDING LIGHT, HOTEL FO PETS, *The Joe DiMaggio Story, The* ROMANCE OF HELE TRENT, *The* ROAD OF LIFE, STEPMOTHER, THIS IS NOR DRAKE, TRUE CONFESSIONS, and the TWENTY QUESTION quiz program as the Ronson cigarette-lighter girl. Th actress was particularly proud of her work on th drama series *America's Women in the Air,* which tol of females serving their country as pilots durin World War II. Manson is, however, best remembere for playing Patsy Bowen for more than ten year on the long-running NICK CARTER, MASTER DETECTIV series. She appeared on TV's "The Untouchables (1960).

MARCH OF TIME, THE

1931–1933	CBS	Fri.	10:30 PM
1933–1935	CBS	Fri.	9 PM

1935–1936	CBS	Mon.–Fri.	10:30 PM
1936–1937	CBS	Thurs.	10:30 PM
1937–1938	NBC Blue	Thurs.	8:30 PM
1938–1939	NBC Blue	Fri.	9:30 PM
1939–1942	NBC Blue	Thurs.	8 PM
1942	NBC Blue	Fri.	9 PM
1942–1944	NBC	Thurs.	10:30 PM
1944–1945	ABC	Thurs.	10:30 PM

The *March of Time* series dramatized contemporary news events. The show's first story, taken from newspaper headlines of the time, was "Big Bill" Thompson's renomination as mayor of Chicago. Thereafter, news figures such as Franklin D. ROOSEVELT, Adolf Hitler, Winston Churchill, and Joseph Stalin were presented each week. The narrators on this half-hour weekly series included Ted HUSING, Harry VON ZELL, and Westbrook Van Voorhis. When he was a character on one of the dramas being presented, Franklin D. Roosevelt was played by either Bill ADAMS, Art CARNEY, or Staats COTSWORTH. Agnes MOOREHEAD, Nancy Kelly, or Jeanette NOLAN played Eleanor ROOSEVELT over the years. Other actors included Edwin "Ed" JEROME as Stalin and Haile Selassie, Dwight WEIST as Hitler, Ted DeCorsia as Benito Mussolini, Maurice TARPLIN as Churchill, Elliott Reid as King Farouk, and Jack Smart as Huey Long. Also heard were Myron MCCORMICK, Althena Lorde, the Mauch twins, Claire Niesen, Kate McComb, Barbara Lee, John Kane, Cal Tinney, Adelaide Klein, John MCINTIRE, Georgia Backus, Karl SWENSON, Kenny DELMAR, Everett SLOANE, Martin GABEL, Gary MERRILL, and Agnes Young. Donald VOORHEES and Howard BARLOW led the program's orchestra. Arthur Pryor, Jr., produced and directed the program for many years. Also directing were Don Stauffer, Homer Fickett, William Spear, and Lester Vail. Writers included Richard Dana, Brice Disque, Jr., Carl Cramer, Paul Milton, and Garrett Porter. *Time* magazine, Remington-Rand typewriters, Wrigley's gum, and Electrolux vacuum cleaners were among the sponsors.

MARCONI, GUGLIELMO (1874–1937)

One of the world's most celebrated physicists, Italian-born Guglielmo Marconi was the inventor of a successful system of radio telegraphy and founder of the Marconi Wireless Company. Marconi applied the principles of electromagnetism to the problem of transmitting messages through space and explored the commercial possibilities of electrical communication without wires to an unlimited number of receivers at the same time, therefore paving the way for modern radio broadcasting. Marconi won the Nobel Prize in 1909, and when he died, he was given a state funeral by the Italian government and two minutes of silence on telegraph and wireless telephone services throughout Europe.

MARIE, THE LITTLE FRENCH PRINCESS

1933–1935	CBS	Mon.–Fri.	2 PM

Himan BROWN produced and directed this 15-minute series, which he claimed was "the first daytime drama series on radio," although Frank and Anne HUMMERT also claimed that they had created the first daytime radio serial with ORPHANS OF DIVORCE. *Marie, the Little French Princess* concerned a foreign-born, former princess who settled in the United States and was determined to live happily as an ordinary citizen. Ruth Yorke played Marie, and James MEIGHAN played her love interest, Richard. Also heard were Allyn Joslyn, Alma Kruger, Helen Choate, and Porter Hall. The announcer for this series was Andre BARUCH. Louis Phillipe-Angelus cosmetics sponsored the program.

MARION TALLEY SHOW, THE

1936–1937	NBC Red	Fri.	10:30 PM
1937–1938	NBC Red	Sun.	5 PM

Metropolitan Opera soprano Marion Talley starred on this half-hour program of classical and semiclassical music that featured Josef Koestner and his Orchestra. From the concert and opera stages, James MELTON, Lauertiz Melchoir, Risë Stevens, and Gladys Swarthout regularly guest-starred with Talley. Ry-Krisp diet rye thins sponsored the series.

MARK TRAIL

1950–1951	Mutual	Mon., Wed., Fri.	5 PM
1951–1952	ABC	Mon.–Fri.	5:15 PM

Mark Trail was one of the last 15-minute weekday children's adventure serials to be introduced on network radio. Originally a comic strip by Ed Dodd, first seen in 1946, Mark Trail was a conservationist and outdoorsman, and the radio show promoted conservation and protection of wild life and forests. Matt CROWLEY, John LARKIN, and Staats COTSWORTH starred as Trail. Ben Cooper and then Ronald LISS were heard as his young companion, Scotty. Also heard were Joyce Gordon and then Amy Sidell as their friend, Cherry. Jackson BECK and Glenn Riggs were the program's announcers. Frank Maxwell and Drex Hines directed the series. Writers included Albert ALEY, Donald HUGHES, and others. Kellogg's cereals sponsored the series.

MARKLE, FLETCHER (1921–1991)

Canadian-born Fletcher Markle was brought to the United States in 1946 to direct and occasionally star on a CBS summer-replacement version of Orson WELLES' MERCURY THEATER ON THE AIR. Like Welles, Markle was a "triple threat" in that he was an actor, a producer, and a director. When the summer ended, Markle was rewarded with a one-hour dramatic anthology of his own on CBS, STUDIO ONE. The following year, he was also given charge of The FORD THEATER series. During his STUDIO ONE and Ford Theater years, Markle directed and subsequently married actress Mercedes MCCAMBRIDGE. He either produced and/or directed such TV programs as the situation-comedy version of the hit Broadway play and movie Life with Father and several productions on the "Studio One" television program. He continued to work on television until he retired in the late 1970s.

MARLOWE, HUGH (HUGH HIPPLE: 1911–1982)

Actor Hugh Marlowe was born in Philadelphia, Pennsylvania, and began his show-business career as a stage actor, appearing on Broadway in the play Arrest That Woman (1931). Entering radio as an announcer in 1931, he subsequently played detective Ellery Queen on The ADVENTURES OF ELLERY QUEEN, Jim Curtis on Brenda Curtis, and Gann Murray on OUR GAL SUNDAY. He was also featured on Amateur Gentleman, HOLLYWOOD HOTEL, The SHELL CHATEAU, and many other programs. Marlowe was seen in several motion pictures, most notably as playwright Lloyd Richards in the film classic All About Eve (1950), as well as in Mrs. Parkington (1944), The Day the Earth Stood Still (1951), Monkey Business (1952), and Thirteen Frightened Girls (1964). Marlowe also repeated his radio role of Ellery Queen on a television series of the same title, "The Adventures of Ellery Queen."

MARRIAGE FOR TWO

1949–1951	NBC	Mon.–Fri.	10:30 AM
1951–1952	ABC	Mon.–Fri.	4:15 PM

"Marriage for Two is the story of a romantic-but-wise girl's marriage to an affectionate but irresponsible young man," this 15-minute drama series stated at the beginning of each program. Teri Keane played Vikki Hoyt, the romantic young woman, and Staats COTSWORTH played her incorrigible husband, Roger. John Tillman was the show's announcer. Kraft cheese sponsored the series.

MARTHA DEANE SHOW, THE

See MARY MARGARET MCBRIDE SHOW, The.

MARTHA WEBSTER

See LIFE BEGINS AT EIGHTY.

MARTIN KANE, PRIVATE EYE

1949–1951	Mutual	Sun.	4:40 PM
1951–1953	NBC	Sun.	4:30 PM

Fictional private detective heroes came and went on the airwaves, but one sleuth managed to remain on the air for five consecutive years and to survive a successful transition from radio to television in the early 1950s. He was Martin Kane, Private Eye, a hard-boiled, tough-talking P.I. who solved murders and found missing relatives on such episodes as "The Case of the One-Armed Bandit," "The Girl with the Green Eyes," and "Blues of the City." Kane was played at various times on this half-hour weekly radio series by motion-picture stars William Gargan, Lee Tracy, and Lloyd Nolan. His assistant, Happy McMann, was played by Walter KINSELLA. Nichola Saunders played Sgt. Ross on the series. Ted Hedinge wrote and directed the program. The program's announcer was Fred Uttal. The United States tobacco company sponsored the program.

MARX, GROUCHO (JULIUS MARX: 1890–1977)

Like his brothers, Harpo, Chico, Gummo, and Zeppo comedy legend Groucho Marx was born on New York City's Lower East Side. Encouraged by their stagestruck mother, Minnie, and their uncle Al Shean of the vaudeville team of Gallagher and Shean, the Marx Brothers appeared in vaudeville and eventually became a major comedy team on the Broadway stage and in such films as Monkey Business (1931), Horse Feathers (1932), A Night at the Opera (1935), A Day at the Races (1937), and Duck Soup (1933). Gummo did not work in films; Zeppo co-starred in a few films but quit to become an agent. Groucho was the only Marx brother to become a radio star as well, although in the early 1930s he appeared in twenty-six episodes of "Flywheel, Shyster, and Flywheel" with his brother Chico, on the short-lived FIVE STAR THEATER program. Many of the routines the brothers performed on this show were later seen in Marx Brothers' films. On his own, Groucho made many guest appearances on such programs as The FLEISCHMANN HOUR and The ED SULLIVAN SHOW. For many years, he was the host of the comedy-quiz show YOU BET YOUR LIFE, first heard on radio in 1950 and simulcast on both radio and television. Groucho starred on Blue Ribbon Town, The CIRCLE, and in a Norman Corwin Presents drama called "The Undecided Molecule" on radio. In the 1970 Groucho, after years of being retired, made a comeback and appeared in a comedy concert at Carnegie Hall that was recorded for posterity.

MARY LEE TAYLOR SHOW, THE

1933–1935	CBS	Tues., Thurs.	11 AM
1935–1936	CBS	Tues., Thurs.	12:15 PM
1936–1943	CBS	Tues., Thurs.	11 AM
1943–1948	CBS	Sat.	10:30 AM
1948–1949	NBC	Sat.	10 AM
1949–1954	NBC	Sat.	10:30 AM

The 15-minute Mary Lee Taylor Show was the longest running cooking program on radio. Its host, nutritionist and master chef Mary Lee Taylor, offered recipe and food-shopping and cooking tips. John Cole was the show's announcer. Pet milk sponsored the series.

MARY MARGARET MCBRIDE SHOW, THE (AKA THE MARTHA DEANE SHOW)

1934–1937	Mutual	Mon.–Fri.	12 PM
1937–1938	CBS	Mon.–Fri.	12 PM
1938–1939	CBS	Mon., Wed., Fri.	12 PM
1940–1941	CBS	Mon.–Fri.	12 PM
1941–1942	NBC Red	Mon.–Fri.	1 PM
1942–1949	NBC	Mon.–Fri.	1 PM
1949–1951	ABC	Mon.–Fri.	1 PM
1951–1954	ABC	Mon.–Fri.	2 PM

Mary Margaret MCBRIDE was the first lady of network radio talk shows for almost twenty years. Originally known as WOR-Mutual's "Martha Deane," a stock name used for all of WOR's female celebrity interviewers for many years, McBride first attracted national attention when the one-hour program became a feature of the Mutual network roster of shows. When she left Mutual and went to work for the CBS network, McBride began to use her own name. During her many years on the air, McBride interviewed authors such as James Thurber, Fannie Hurst, Thor Heyerdahl, and Quentin Reynolds; actors such as Bob HOPE, Jimmy DURANTE, Danny KAYE, Mary Martin, and Elizabeth Taylor; politicians such as Vice President Alben Barkley and President Harry S Truman; Swiss bell ringers, screwball inventors, trapeze artists, hog callers, and flagpole sitters. General Omar Bradley conversed with McBride about the difficulties of being a general on a broadcast during World War II; actress Lilli Palmer spoke about having a baby while German bombers were blitzing London; author John Hershey discussed the occupation of Japan as the war ended; Henry Morganthau talked about his plans for removing Germany's postwar industrial power; and aviatrix Amelia Earhart talked about her successful flights and the upcoming one from which she never returned. McBride's easygoing interviewing style made both guests and listeners feel as if they were visiting with an old friend. Her announcer for many years was Vincent Connolly, although Ken ROBERTS served as her announcer in the late 1930s to early 1940s. Carol Irwin was McBride's longtime director. Her sponsors over the years included Minute tapioca, LaFrance bleach, Dromedary dates, Sweetheart soap, Borden's Hemo health drink, Dazzle bleach, and Tender Leaf tea.

MARY MARLIN

See STORY OF MARY MARLIN, THE.

MARY NOBLE, BACKSTAGE WIFE

1935–1936	Mutual	Mon.–Fri.	11:30 AM
1936–1937	NBC Blue	Mon.–Fri.	4:15 PM
1937–1942	NBC Red	Mon.–Fri.	4 PM
1942–1954	NBC	Mon.–Fri.	4 PM
1954–1959	CBS	Mon.–Fri.	12:15 PM

One of radio's most enduring 15-minute serial dramas, *Mary Noble, Backstage Wife* told of a small-town girl from Iowa who met and married the famous actor Larry Noble, who was adored by millions. The series was voted "Radio's Best Daytime Serial Progam" in 1941 by readers of *Movie-Radio Guide* magazine; *Radio Mirror*'s reader's poll judged it "favorite daytime radio serial" for five consecutive years in the 1940s. *Mary Noble, Backstage Wife* was so popular that radio personalities BOB AND RAY regularly spoofed the series on their program in a skit they called *Mary Backstayge, Noble Wife*.

Vivian Fridell and then Claire Niesen played Mary; Ken Griffin, James MEIGHAN, and Guy Sorel played Larry; and Ethel Owen played Larry's mother. Also heard were Eloise Kummer, Patricia Dunlap, Gail Henshaw, Norman Gottschalk, Leo Curley, Ethel Wilson, Charles Webster, Joyce Howard, George Petrie, Paul Luther, Carlton KaDell, Bess McCammon, Charme Allen, Sherman Marks, Virginia Dwyer, Mandel KRAMER, Hoyt Allen, Vicki VOLA, Virginia "Ginger" Jones, Lesley Woods, Eileen Palmer, Don Gallagher, Dan Sutter, Luise Barclay, Louise Fitch, Henrietta Tedro, Charlotte MANSON, Marvin MILLER, Elmira Roessler, Anne BURR, Dorothy Sands, Susan Douglas, John McGovern, Betty Ruth Smith, and Bartlett "Bart" Robinson.

The show's announcers included Edward Allen, Stuart Dawson, Harry Clark, Bob Brown, Pierre Andre, Ford BOND, Roger Krupp, and Sandy Becker. Frank and Anne HUMMERT produced this series, and directors included Blair Walliser, Richard Leonard, Joe Mansfield, Fred Weihe, Richard Leonard, DeWitt McBride, Lou Jacobson, and Les Mitchel. Writers were Frank and Anne HUMMERT, Doris Halman, Elizabeth Todd, Phil Thorne, Ned Cramer, and Ruth Borden. The series was sponsored by Dr. Lyon's toothpaste and tooth powder, Bayer aspirin, Energine vitamin supplement, Haley's M–O laxative, Mulsfield Coconut Oil shampoo, Astring-O-Sol cleanser, Double Danderine shampoo, and Blue Cheer detergent. The series' theme music was "Stay as Sweet as You Are" and "The Rose of Tralee."

MARY SMALL SHOW, THE (AKA LITTLE MISS BAB-O; SURPRISE PARTY; MARY SMALL REVUE; IMPERIAL TIME)

1934–1935	NBC Red	Sun.	1:30 PM
1935–1936	NBC Blue	Wed., Fri.	6:15 PM
1936–1937	NBC Blue	Fri.	7 PM
1937–1941	(Off the air)		
1941–1942	Mutual	Mon.	10:15 PM
1942–1943	CBS	Tues., Thurs.	10:45 PM

| 1943–1945 | NBC Blue | Sun. | 5 PM |
| 1945–1946 | ABC | Sun. | 5 PM |

Mary SMALL was a child of five when her show first went on the air and an adult when it left the air twelve years later. On her 15-minute show, Small sang popular songs of the day as well as of the past. Ray BLOCH led the show's orchestra. Small's announcer for many years was Clayton "Bud" COLLYER. Sponsors included Bab-O cleanser, Clark gum, and Spud Imperial cigarettes.

MATTHEWS, GRACE (1910–   )

Actress Grace Matthews was born in Toronto, Ontario, Canada. She is perhaps best remembered as one of several actresses who played the part of Margo Lane, the SHADOW's girlfriend. She also played the title role in BIG SISTER, Liz Dennis on *The* BRIGHTER DAY, and Julie Erickson on *Hilltop House* and was a member of the supporting cast on HEARTS IN HARMONY. In the 1970s, Matthews was heard on Himan Brown's CBS MYSTERY THEATER. On television, she was featured on "The Guiding Light" (1968–1969) daytime drama series.

MAXWELL HOUSE COFFEE TIME (AKA MAXWELL HOUSE GOOD NEWS)

| 1940–1941 | NBC Red | Thurs. | 8 PM |
| 1941–1944 | NBC | Thurs. | 8 PM |

This hour-long comedy-variety series featured numerous show-business luminaries as guest hosts, including Metro-Goldwyn-Mayer president Louis B. Mayer, singer Nelson EDDY, dancer-actor Ray Bolger, comedienne Fannie BRICE as BABY SNOOKS, and movie stars Robert Young, Spencer Tracy, Alice FAYE, Mickey Rooney, Judy GARLAND, Norma Shearer, Joan Crawford, Tony Martin, and Melvyn Douglas. Actor Frank MORGAN and comedienne Cass DALEY were summer-replacement stars for one season, and John Conte was also one of the show's long-term hosts. *Maxwell House Coffee Time's* announcer was Abbott Tessman. It was written by Paul Henning, Keith Fowler, Phil Rapp, and Ed James. The show's theme music was "You and I."

MAXWELL, JAMES CLERK (1831–1879)

Scottish-born physicist James C. Maxwell discovered the existence of an electromagetic field in our atmosphere. This discovery led to experiments that concluded that electric and magnetic energy traveled in transverse waves that prorated at a speed equal to that of light. Maxwell subsequently began to investigate heat in general and the kinetic theory of gases. In addition to his work as a physicist, Maxwell taught at Edinburgh and Cambridge universities and was a professor at Marischal College in Aberdeen, Scotland.

MAYOR OF THE TOWN

1942	NBC	Sun.	7 PM
1942–1943	CBS	Wed.	9 PM
1943–1944	(Off the air)		
1944	CBS	Mon.	9 PM
1944–1945	CBS	Sat.	7 PM
1945–1947	CBS	Sat.	8:30 PM
1947–1948	ABC	Wed.	8 PM
1948–1949	Mutual	Sun.	7:30 PM

Veteran actor Lionel BARRYMORE was the star of this half-hour comedy-drama program about a small-town, Middle America mayor who became deeply involved in the problems and lives of his constituency, helping someone who was, for example, out of work or someone who has been arrested for a minor crime; as a subplot, he also helped to raise an orphaned boy. In spite of his cranky demeanor, the mayor had a heart of gold, and the people in the town felt they could go to him with their problems. Conrad Binyon played the mayor's ward, Butch, and Agnes MOOREHEAD played his housekeeper, Marilly. Priscilla Lyon played the mayor's niece, Holly Ann. Frank Martin and Carlton Kadell announced the program. The series was directed by Jack Van Nostrand, and for many years it was written by Jean Halloway. Sponsors included Lever Brothers soap, Rinso cleanser, Mutual benefits life insurance, and Noxzema skin and shaving creams.

MCBRIDE, MARY MARGARET (AKA "MARTHA DEANE"): (1899–1976)

Radio interviewer Mary Margaret McBride was born in Paris, Missouri, and educated at the University of Missouri. She began her career as a newspaper features writer in the mid-1920s, moved to radio in 1934, and became known as Martha Deane—the stock name used by New York radio station WOR for its celebrity interviewers. In 1937, McBride moved her interview show to CBS and began to use her own name. The premier interviewer of her day, McBride interviewed such notable figures as Groucho Marx, Jack Benny, and actor Fanny Hearst. In 1941 she left CBS and went to NBC, and in 1950 to ABC. She was named "the most important woman in the United States" by the United Nations in the 1950s, and thousands of fans attended a spectacular tribute to her in Madison Square Garden in New York City, which, according to *The New York Times,* had "never been equaled in numbers of fans" attending similar tributes. After more than twenty years on network radio, McBride retired from the national airwaves but continued to broadcast on a local station near her home. She au

Mary Margaret McBride (NBC)

Mercedes McCambridge (Warner Brothers)

thored twelve books, including *A Long Way from Missouri* (1959) and *Out of the Air* (1960).

See also MARY MARGARET MCBRIDE SHOW, *The*.

MCCAMBRIDGE, MERCEDES (1918–   )

Academy Award–winning actress Mercedes McCambridge was born in Joliet, Illinois, and began her acting career while still in her teens as an NBC contract radio actress in Chicago in the late 1930s. An NBC executive thought that McCambridge's unusual voice was perfect for radio. Over the years, she was regularly heard on LIGHTS OUT, INNER SANCTUM MYSTERIES, STUDIO ONE, *The* FORD THEATER, I LOVE A MYSTERY, *The* CBS MYSTERY THEATER, MURDER AT MIDNIGHT, ONE MAN'S FAMILY, *The* ADVENTURES OF DICK TRACY, MIDSTREAM, A TALE OF TODAY (as Flora Little), *The Arch Obler Theater*, THIS IS NORA DRAKE (as Peg Martinson), ARMSTRONG THEATER OF TODAY, *This Is the Show, Everyman's Theater*, STELLA DALLAS, *The* ROMANCE OF HELEN TRENT, and GANGBUSTERS. McCambridge also played the leading roles of Rose in ABIE'S IRISH ROSE, Ruth Evans Wayne on BIG SISTER, Mary Rutledge on *The* GUIDING LIGHT, Betty on BETTY AND BOB, and the star roles in DEFENSE ATTORNEY and FAMILY SKELTON. During her long and distinguished career on radio, no less an authority than Orson WELLES called McCambridge "the world's greatest radio actress."

On television, McCambridge was seen on several major dramatic anthologies such as "Studio One" and "The Kraft Theater," and was the star of the "Wire Service" television series. In 1949, McCambridge received the Academy Award for Best Supporting Actress in the film *All the King's Men* and was nominated a second time in 1956 for *Giant*. Onstage, McCambridge starred in *Who's Afraid of Virginia Woolf?* (1964), *'Night Mother* (1985), and *Lost in Yonkers* (1992). One of McCambridge's most publicized performances was as the voice of the devil in the film *The Exorcist* (1973). She was also featured in *Johnny Guitar* (1954), *Suddenly Last Summer* (1960), and *Angel Baby* (1961). The actress is the author of two books that document incidents in her personal and professional life: *The Two of Us* (1960) and *The Quality of Mercy* (1981), "Mercy" being her nickname).

MCCONNELL, ED "SMILIN' ED" (1892–c1960)

Atlanta-born singer, homespun philosopher, writer, and children's show host Ed McConnell left home shortly after he graduated from college and, against his parents' wishes, began to work as a vaudeville performer. He performed on several local radio stations in Georgia in 1925 before joining NBC's roster of stars. Known to his audiences as "Smilin' Ed,"

McConnell appeared on such shows as *Ballad's Over Ready Biscuit Program* and SMILIN' ED AND HIS BUSTER BROWN GANG.

MCCORMICK, MYRON (1908–1962)

Radio, stage, and film actor Myron McCormick, born in New York City, was the original Luther Billis in the musical play *South Pacific* (1949). Previously, he had appeared on Broadway in *State of the Union* (1945). McCormick also made numerous films, including *Winterset* (1937), *One Third of a Nation* (1939), *Jigsaw* (1949), *Jolson Sings Again* (1950), *No Time for Sergeants* (1958), and *The Hustler* (1961). On radio, McCormick played leading men as well as villains: Robert Shellenberger on CENTRAL CITY, Steve Harper on HELPMATE, and Paul Sherwood on JOYCE JORDAN, GIRL INTERN. He was also a regular on LISTENING POST, *The* MARCH OF TIME, and *The* MAN BEHIND THE GUN; and he played Adams on PASSPORT FOR ADAMS and Walter Manning on PORTIA FACES LIFE. Other radio work included appearances on Fletcher MARKLE's STUDIO ONE and FORD THEATER dramatic anthologies.

MCCRARY, TEX

See FALKENBERG, JINX.

MCDANIEL, HATTIE (1895–1952)

One of America's most famous African-American character actresses, Hattie McDaniel was born in Wichita, Kansas. She is best known for her Academy Award–winning performance as Mammy in *Gone With the Wind* (1939) but was also featured in *Nothing Sacred* (1937), *Margie* (1946), *Song of the South* (1947), and *Mr. Blandings Builds His Dream House* (1948). On radio, the actress starred as BEULAH and was a regular on SHOW BOAT, *The* BILLIE BURKE SHOW, and *Blueberry Hill*.

MCGRATH, PAUL (1904–1978)

Actor Paul McGrath was born in Chicago, Illinois. For many years he was the host of INNER SANCTUM MYSTERIES, although Raymond Edward JOHNSON is probably better remembered in that role. McGrath played a variety of roles ranging from villains to lovers on daytime serials such as BIG SISTER, *The* BRIGHTER DAY, LORA LAWTON, THIS LIFE IS MINE, WHEN A GIRL MARRIES, and YOUNG DR. MALONE. He was also heard on *The Casebook of Gregory Hood* in the title role. On television, McGrath was featured on the daytime serial dramas "First Love" (1954–1955) and "The Guiding Light" (1967).

MCINTIRE, JOHN (1907–1990)

Character actor John McIntire was born in Spokane, Washington. He was also well known for his radio work. He and his wife, actress Jeanette NOLAN, were members of a repertory company of actors on the MARCH OF TIME series. He was also featured on MEET THE MEEKS, *The* CAVALCADE OF AMERICA, *The* CRIME DOCTOR (in the leading role of Dr. Benjamin Ordway), *Ellen Randolph*, *The* MERCURY THEATER ON THE AIR, SUSPENSE, *The* PHILIP MORRIS PLAYHOUSE, WE, THE ABBOTTS, and *The* ADVENTURES OF SAM SPADE, DETECTIVE. McIntire also appeared in numerous films, notably *The Asphalt Jungle* (1953), *Summer and Smoke* (1962), and *Rough Night in Jericho* (1967), and starred on such television shows as "The Naked City" (1958) and "Wagon Train" (1961).

MCKAY, JIM (JAMES MCMANUS: c1928–   )

Born in Philadelphia, Pennsylvania, sportscaster Jim McKay's long-running active career in broadcasting began when this writer for *The Baltimore Sun* hosted a program called *Sports Parade* for radio station WMAR. He then went to CBS to host *The Real McKay* show. Since the 1950s, he has broadcasted sports events on radio and television. McKay was the first sportscaster to receive an Emmy award for his play-by-play reports on television.

MCNAMEE, GRAHAM (1889–1942)

Washington, D.C.–born Graham McNamee announced and hosted *The Atwater Kent Auditions,* which gave amateur talent an opportunity to be heard on

Hattie McDaniel (CBS)

national radio; the *Behind the Mike Show,* which went behind the scenes in broadcasting; and *The* ORIGINAL AMATEUR HOUR, another talent-search program. He was also an announcer who interviewed players and special guests at numerous World Series and other baseball games. McNamee announced *The Texaco Fire Chief, The Royal Gelatin Hour, The Time of Your Life, The Royal Crown Revue,* and *Four Star News.* He is most famous, however, for announcing Charles Lindbergh's triumphant return to America after his celebrated nonstop trans-Atlantic flight to Europe in 1927.

MCNEILL, DON (1907–   )
Born in Galina, Illinois, Don McNeill was the long-lasting host of a popular early-morning program, *The* BREAKFAST CLUB. McNeill's easygoing, down-to-earth, chatty style made him a favorite of people all across America, who looked forward to having their morning coffee with him every day. Before hosting *The Breakfast Club,* McNeill was an NBC staff announcer and introduced a number of programs originating from Chicago in the 1930s, including *Memory Time, The Pontiac Program, Climalene Carnival, Tea Time at Morrells,* and *Avalon Time.* He tried TV for a time, but returned to radio until his retirement in the 1970s.

MEET CORLISS ARCHER

1943–1944	CBS	Thurs.	8 PM
1944–1945	CBS	Thurs.	9:30 PM
1945–1946	CBS	Sun.	4:30 PM
1946–1952	CBS	Sun.	9 PM
1952–1954	ABC	Fri.	9:30 PM

Meet Corliss Archer was the story of a teenage girl who was "coming of age." It presented her problems with boyfriends, parents, and teachers. This half-hour situation-comedy series starred Janet WALDO, Priscilla Lyon, and Lugene Saunders as Corliss; Fred Shields and Bob BAILEY as her father; Irene Tedrow and Helen Mack as her mother; Sam EDWARDS, David Hughes, and Irwin Lee as her boyfriend, Dexter Franklin; Tommy Bernard as her pain-in-the-neck little brother, Raymond; and Barbara Whiting as Corliss's best friend, Mildred. Announcers on the program included Bud Heistand, Del SHARBUTT, Ken CARPENTER, and Jack Hartz. Created by F. Hugh Herbert, the series was directed by Bert Prager and written by Carroll Carroll, Herbert, and Jerry Adelman. Sponsors were Campbell's soup and Electric companies of America.

MEET ME AT PARKY'S

1945–1947	NBC	Sun.	10:30 PM
1947–1948	Mutual	Sun.	9 PM

The character of Nick Parkyakarkis, the Greek-born owner of a short-order beanery who spoke in fractured English, was first introduced by actor Harry

EINSTEIN on *The* EDDIE CANTOR SHOW. Parkyakarkis became so popular that Einstein was made the star of his own comedy radio show, *Meet Me at Parky's.* Joan Barton played Nick's cashier; Ruth Perrott, a hilarious character named Prudence Rockbottom; and Sheldon Leonard, his usual con-artist type of role as Orville Sharp. Also heard were Frank NELSON, Leo Carey, and vocalists Peggy Lee, Betty Jane Rhodes, Dave Street, and Patty Bolton. Art Gilmore was the show's announcer. The program was directed by Maurice Morton and Hal Fimberg, and written by Fimberg and Harry Einstein. The *Meet Me at Parky's* orchestra was conducted by Opie Cates. The show was sponsored by Old Gold cigarettes.

MEET MILLIE

1951–1952	CBS	Sun.	9:30 PM
1952–1954	CBS	Thurs.	8 PM

A sultry blonde with a pronounced pout, film actress Audrey Totter [*The Lady of the Lake* (1946) and *Unsuspected* (1947)] starred on the half-hour radio situation-comedy series *Meet Millie,* in which she played a single working girl. Her mother, who was always trying to get her married, was played by Bea BENADERET. The series became a hit on television in 1951 with Elena Verdugo and Florence HALOP playing Millie and her mother. Actor Marvin Kaplan was featured on both the radio and television versions, playing Millie's comically meek neighbor, Alfred E. Prinzmetal. In supporting roles were Bill Tracy, Rye Billsbury, and Earle Ross. Bob Lamond was the program's announcer. Brylcreem hair dressing, Nescafé instant coffee, and Lava soap sponsored the radio series.

MEET THE MEEKS (AKA THE ADVENTURES OF MORTIMER MEEK; THE LIFE OF MORTIMER MEEK; MEET MR. MEEK)

1940–1942	CBS	Wed.	7:30 PM
1942–1947	(Off the air)		
1947–1949	NBC	Sat.	11 AM

This comedy program was about mild-mannered, henpecked Mortimer Meek, whose inability to make such decisions as what to have for dinner constantly enraged his nagging wife. Meek was played by Wilbur "Budd" HULICK, Forrest Lewis, and Frank READICK; Adelaide Klein and then Fran ALLISON played his wife. In the supporting cast were Beryl Vaughn, Doris Dudley, Elmira Roessler, and Cliff Soubier. Dan SEYMOUR was the program's announcer. The show's writers and director are unknown. Lifebuoy soap and shave cream and Allsweet sponsored the series.

MEET THE PRESS

1947–1949	Mutual	Fri.	10 PM
1949–1951	Mutual	Fri.	9:30 PM

1951–1952	(Off the air)		
1952–1954	NBC	Sun.	10:30 PM
1954–1956	NBC	Sun.	8 PM

Each episode of this series featured a panel of journalists who asked extemporaneous questions of a prominent guest from the political world. Martha Rountree and Lawrence Spivak were the original hosts of the long-running series, although Bill Slater also hosted at times during its first years on radio. When it became a radio feature, most of NBC's major news commentators hosted the one-hour program at one time or another, including Rountree, Ben Grauer, and Spivak. The radio series was directed by Rountree and Ray Hervey. The program has been a fixture on NBC television since 1947.

MEIGHAN, JAMES (1906–1970)

Actor James Meighan was born in New York City and graduated from Carnegie Institute of Technology. On radio he starred as Jimmy Valentine on ALIAS JIMMY VALENTINE and as Mike Waring, the Falcon, on *The* FALCON. In addition, Meighan played leading roles on such programs as AGAINST THE STORM, MARY NOBLE, BACKSTAGE WIFE, BY KATHLEEN NORRIS, *City Desk*, DOT AND WILL, *I Love Linda Dale*, JUST PLAIN BILL, LORA LAWTON, LONE JOURNEY, MARIE, THE LITTLE FRENCH PRINCESS, ORPHANS OF DIVORCE, *The* ROMANCE OF HELEN TRENT, SECOND HUSBAND, and *Special Agent*.

MELODY RANCH (AKA GENE AUTRY'S MELODY RANCH; THE GENE AUTRY SHOW)

1940–1943	CBS	Sun.	6:30 PM
1943–1945	(Off the air)		
1945–1946	CBS	Sun.	5:30 PM
1946–1949	CBS	Sun.	7 PM
1949–1953	CBS	Sat.	8 PM
1953–1956	CBS	Sun.	6 PM

The half-hour weekly *Melody Ranch* featured songs by cowboy star Gene AUTRY, as well as a weekly adventure story that, in addition to Autry, featured Pat Buttram as his comic sidekick. Jim Boles, Wally Maher, and Tyler McVey played various supporting roles on the show's stories, in which Autry tracked down outlaws and helped those in need of justice. Other musical performers heard were the Cass County Boys, the Pinafores, the Gene Autry Blue Genes, Alvino Ray, Carl Cotner's Melody Ranch 6, Johnny Bond, the King Sisters (Donna, Alice, Yvonne, and Louise), and Mary Ford. Lou Crosby and Wendell NILES were the program's announcers. Bill Burch produced and directed the series for many years, and it was written by Ed James. Autry's popular theme song was "Back in the Saddle Again." Wrigley's Doublemint gum sponsored the show.

MELROSE, EDYTHE FERN

See HOUSE OF CHARM, THE.

MELTON, JAMES (1904–1961)

Renowned opera tenor James Melton was born in Moultrie, Georgia, made his radio debut in 1927 on the ROXY'S and HIS GANG *Show,* and was one of the long list of tenors featured on the JACK BENNY SHOW. Melton also starred on such radio music-variety series as *The* HARVEST OF STARS, *The* VOICE OF FIRESTONE, *Circus Night, The Sealtest Sunday Night Party, The* PALMOLIVE BEAUTY BOX *Theater, The Song Shop, The* TELEPHONE HOUR, and *The* CHICAGO THEATER OF THE AIR.

MENKEN, HELEN (1901–1966)

Stage and radio actress Helen Menken was born in New York City. Active on the stage, Menken was seen in Broadway productions of *Seventh Heaven* (1922) and *The Old Maid* (1934). She was one of the founders of the celebrated Stage Door Canteen in New York City, a place where the armed services could get free food and entertainment before going off to fight in World War II. STAGE DOOR CANTEEN became a radio program in the 1940s, with Menken often appearing as the show's hostess. Although primarily active on Broadway, Menken managed to find time to appear on several radio programs—including *The* KATE SMITH HOUR, where she acted in various dramatic sketches and performed monologues, and SECOND HUSBAND, in which she originated the role of Brenda Cummings. The actress was frequently heard on such popular dramatic anthology programs as *The* THEATER GUILD ON THE AIR. Menken portrayed herself in the film version of *Stage Door Canteen* (1943).

MERCURY THEATER ON THE AIR, THE (AKA THE CAMPBELL PLAYHOUSE)

1937	Mutual	Sun.	9 PM
1938–1941	CBS	Mon. & Sun.	9 PM
		Fri.	8 PM

Orson WELLES's successful theatrical productions at his Off-Broadway Mercury Theater in New York City in the mid-1930s led to this weekly hour-long series of radio adaptations of classic literary works. *The Mercury Theater of the Air* featured a repertory cast of supporting actors who played different roles each week. Members of the company—many of whom also appeared in his stage productions—included Joseph Cotten, Peggy Allenby, Everett SLOANE, Agnes MOOREHEAD, Ray COLLINS, Martin GABEL, Arthur ANDERSON, John MCINTIRE, Karl SWENSON, Kenny DELMAR, and George COULOURIS. The company's radio tryout was in 1937 on the Mutual network, where

Orson Welles during his *Mercury Theater of the Air* days (CBS)

the players presented a six-part adaptation of Victor Hugo's *Les Miserables*. Welles wrote, directed, and starred in the play, which featured such later-to-be radio notables as Gabel, Moorehead, Alice FROST, Betty GARDE, Collins, Estelle LEVY (Gwen Davies), Adelaide Klein, William JOHNSTONE, Allenby, Sloane, Virginia Welles, Frank READICK, and Hiram Sherman.

Welles became nationally famous, however, when he presented a sensational adaptation of H. G. Wells's science-fiction novel *The War of the World* on *The Mercury Theater* broadcast on October 30, 1938, Halloween Eve. The adaptation was written as a series of news flashes and had listeners believing that what they were hearing was an actual Martian invasion. The resulting press coverage led to a motion-picture contract for Welles.

Ernest CHAPPELL was the program's announcer. Campbell's soups, Lady Esther cold cream, and Pabst Blue Ribbon beer were the show's sponsors.

See also APPENDIX D.

MEREDITH, BURGESS (1909–   )

Born in Cleveland, Ohio, film, television, and stage actor Burgess Meredith was one of radio's most prominent performers. After working as a store clerk, a Wall Street runner, a vacuum-cleaner salesman, and a sailor, Meredith began to study acting in New York City. He worked with Orson WELLES at the Off-Broadway Mercury Theater and became a regular member on MERCURY THEATER ON THE AIR. Meredith was also heard in the title role of the *Red Davis* daytime serial drama, later known as PEPPER YOUNG'S FAMILY. He also acted on *Columbia Presents Corwin*, LINCOLN HIGHWAY, and THEATER GUILD ON THE AIR. Film fans are familiar with Meredith's work through appearances in *Winterset* (1936—his film debut), *The Story of GI Joe* (1945), *Hurry Sundown* (1967), *Day of the Locust* (1975), and *Rocky* (1976). His extensive television work includes commercial narrations, appearances as the Penguin on "Batman" in the 1960s, and roles on "Robert Montgomery Presents" (1950), "The General Electric Theater" (1953), and "The Big Story" (1950), which he hosted.

MERMAN, ETHEL (ETHEL AGNES ZIMMERMAN: 1908–1984)

Broadway's song-belting musical comedy diva Ethel Merman, who was born in Astoria, Queens, in New York City, began her performing career in 1930 after working as a secretary. She rose to instant stardom, singing such blockbuster hits as "Blow Gabriel, Blow" and "You're the Top" in the Broadway musical *Anything Goes* (1934), and subsequently starred in *DuBarry Was a Lady* (1939), *Annie Get Your Gun* (1946), and *Gypsy* (1959). Merman starred on her own *Ethel Merman Show* in 1949–1950 and was a frequent guest star in the 1940s on *The* KRAFT MUSIC HALL, *The* TEXACO STAR THEATER, COMMAND PERFORMANCE, and MAIL CALL. She also costarred in such films as *Kid Millions* (1934), *There's No Business Like Show Business* (1954), and *It's a Mad, Mad, Mad, Mad World* (1963). Among Merman's frequent television appearances were memorable performances on *The Ford 50th Anniversary Show* (1955), where she sang duets with Mary Martin, and on *The Judy Garland Show* (1963), where she sang with GARLAND and Barbra Streisand.

MERRILL, GARY (1915–1990)

Actor Gary Merrill was born in Hartford, Connecticut, and attended Bowdoin and Trinity colleges before becoming a radio, stage, and film actor. He was a regular cast member on *The* MARCH OF TIME, played Mike Nelson on *The* RIGHT TO HAPPINESS, and Stanley on *The* SECOND MRS. BURTON. Merrill's films include *Twelve O'Clock High* (1949), *All About Eve* (1950), *Decision Before Dawn* (1951), and *Phone Call from a Stranger* and *Blueprint for Murder* (1953). In the 1960s, Merrill was also heard as a voice-over narrator for television commercials and documentaries.

METROPOLITAN OPERA BROADCASTS

Live performances from New York City's celebrated Metropolitan Opera House have been a constant Saturday and Sunday afternoon feature on many radio stations around the country since 1931; at that time, the first live Metropolitan Opera broadcast—the opera *Hansel und Gretel*—was heard on the NBC network of stations. In between the opera's acts, moderator Olin Downes conducted an opera quiz in which he would ask celebrity guests such as mezzo-soprano Risë Stevens, pianist Oscar Levant, and composer John Carlo Menotti opera-centered questions; and musicologist Boris Goldovsky often interviewed opera celebrities. The program's longtime host and announcer was Milton CROSS. Texaco sponsored the broadcasts. Currently, live Metropolitan Opera broadcasts can be heard on NATIONAL PUBLIC RADIO stations. *The Metropolitan Opera Auditions* was also a popular series that was heard on NBC and later on ABC over a twenty-one-year period. On the show, unknown opera singers auditioned for contracts with the company.

MEYER THE BUYER

Mid-1930s	(Syndicated series. Various stations and times)

Traditional Jewish humor prevailed on this half-hour situation-comedy series. The show featured several actors using heavy Yiddish accents and stereotypes that today many people would find offensive, portraying people who worked in the New York City garment industry. Harry Hershfield, panel-member/comedian on CAN YOU TOP THIS, starred as Meyer. Others in the cast included Alan REED as Mayor Mizznick, owner of a dress-manufacturing business; Adele RONSON as Irma Mizznick, his daughter; Paul DOUGLAS as Lawyer Friedman; Ethel Holt as his model, Mollie; Nick Adams as Uncle Ben; Dot Harrington as Beatrice; Geoffrey Bryant as Milton Mizznick; and Ruth Yorke as the company's secretary. The series' director and writers are unknown.

MGM THEATER OF THE AIR

1949–1952	(Syndicated series. Various stations and times)

For three years, MGM Studios produced a weekly hour-long series of radio adaptations of films in a format similar to the LUX RADIO THEATER. From October 1949 until April 1951, the program was syndicated around the country. The Mutual Broadcasting System purchased the series in May 1951 and for the next year rebroadcast the previously recorded programs.

See APPENDIX D.

MICHAEL SHAYNE, PRIVATE DETECTIVE

1944–1947	Mutual	Tues.	8 PM
1948–1950	Mutual	Sat.	5 PM
1950–1952	(Off the air)		
1952–1953	ABC	Tues.	9:30 PM
		Fri.	8 PM

Based on a mystery novel character created by Brett Haliday, *Michael Shayne, Private Detective* starred Wally Maher for a short while and then Jeff CHANDLER for a longer period of time as the red-headed, tough-talking shamus, Shayne. A somewhat violent show, Shayne always seemed to be "slugging" someone or getting "slammed" himself. Featured on the half-hour series regularly was actress Gloria Blondell as Shayne's secretary. The writers and director of this series were uncredited.

MIDSTREAM

1938–1939	Mutual	Mon.–Fri.	4:15 PM
1939–1940	NBC Red	Mon.–Fri.	4:45 PM
1940	NBC Blue	Mon.–Fri.	10:45 AM and 5:15 PM
1940–1941	NBC Blue	Mon.–Fri.	10:45 AM and 2:45 PM
1941	NBC Blue	Mon.–Fri.	11:45 AM and 2:45 PM

"*Midstream!* Where the currents of life are swiftest, where the problems of life are greatest, where the temptations of life are strongest! This is the story of Charles and Julia Meredith, who have reached the halfway mark between the distant shores of birth and death!" So began this series. Its stories usually involved midlife crises such as the "seven-year itch" or the difficulties of finding employment in middle age. Hugh STUDEBAKER, Louis Levy, Russell Thorson, and Sidney Ellstrong starred as Charles Meredith; Fern Persons and Betty Lou Gerson played Judith Meredith. Prominent in the cast at times were Mercedes MCCAMBRIDGE, Mary Jane CROFT, Laurette FILLBRANDT, Lenore Kingston, Helen Behmiller, Alice Hill, Elliott LEWIS, Henry Hunter, Sharon Grainger, Bill BOUCHEY, Willard Farnum, Marvin MILLER, Lesley Woods, Olan SOULE, Jane Green, Bob Jellison, and Josephine Gilbert. Gene Baker was the program's announcer, and Gordon Hughes directed the show. It was written by Pauline Hopkins. Teel and Drene shampoos sponsored the program.

MILDRED BAILEY SHOW, THE (AKA MUSIC 'TIL MIDNIGHT; PLANTATION ECHOES)

1933–1934	CBS	Sat.	6:15 PM
1934–1935	NBC Blue	Mon., Wed., Fri.	7:15 PM
1935–1944	(Off the air)		
1944–1945	CBS	Fri.	11:30 PM

Pop-blues singer Mildred Bailey's rich contralto voice made her one of America's favorite performers. On her music shows in 15- and 30-minute formats, she performed such songs as "Stormy Weather" and "Birth of the Blues." Vicks vaporub was one of her most loyal sponsors.

MILLER, MARVIN AKA "CHARLIE WARREN" (1913–1985)

Marvin Miller was born in St. Louis, Missouri, and was graduated from Washington University before entering radio. His list of radio credits is indeed formidable: *The* ANDREWS SISTERS SHOW, AUNT JEMIMA, AUNT MARY, MARY NOBLE, BACKSTAGE WIFE, BEAT THE BAND, BEULAH, *The* BILLIE BURKE SHOW, CAPTAIN MIDNIGHT, *The* CISCO KID, A DATE WITH JUDY, *The* DON AMECHE SHOW, FATHER KNOWS BEST, *The* GAY MRS. FEATHERSTONE, GREAT GUNNS, *The* GUIDING LIGHT, HAROLD TEEN, JACK ARMSTRONG, ALL-AMERICAN BOY, KNICKERBOCKER PLAYHOUSE, MIDSTREAM, ONE MAN'S FAMILY, *The* RAILROAD HOUR, *The* RED SKELTON SHOW, *The* ROAD OF LIFE, *The* ROMANCE OF HELEN TRENT, SCATTERGOOD BAINES, THAT BREWSTER BOY, TODAY'S CHILDREN, *The* WHISTLER, and *Song by Sinatra (The* FRANK SINATRA SHOW). Despite all these credits, Miller is probably best known for playing Michael Anthony, the "ever-faithful secretary" of John Beresford Tipton, on "The Millionaire" (1954) television series. Miller used the pseudonym "Charlie Warren" during a contractual conflict between two sponsor-employers when he announced the NBC Blue network's *Madison Square Boxing* program, broadcast from Chicago. Announcer Don Donaldson also used the "Charlie Warren" name when the network moved the program to New York.

Marvin Miller (NBC)

MILTON BERLE SHOW, THE

1944–1945	CBS	Wed.	10:30 PM
1945–1946	(Off the air)		
1947–1948	NBC	Tues.	8 PM
1948–1949	ABC	Wed.	9 PM

Milton BERLE never enjoyed the success on radio that he had on television, although he had several opportunities to do so. Berle's first weekly radio comedy show remained on the air for just one season. After he became one of television's earliest stars, he hosted a second comedy program—and again it failed, perhaps because Berle's comedy was more visual than aural. Bert GORDON (the Mad Russian), singer Eileen Barton, and talented character actors Pert Kelton, Jack Albertson, Arnold STANG, Mary Shipp, John GIBSON, Ed BEGLEY, Arthur Q. BRYANT, and Jackson BECK offered Berle formidable support, as did the Murphy Sisters singing group and Ray BLOCH and his orchestra. The program's announcers were Frank Gallop, Roland Winters, and Ken ROBERTS. His shows were written and directed by Martin A. Ragaway and Hal Block. Berle's radio sponsors over the years included Eversharp-Schick razors, Philip Morris and Revelation cigarettes, and Texaco oil.

MINER, JAN (1919–   )

Actress Jan Miner was born in Boston, Massachusetts, and performed regularly on radio before embarking on an extensive stage, film, and television career. She played Ann Williams on CASEY, CRIME PHOTOGRAPHER and was the title character on LORA LAWTON. Miner was also heard regularly on BOSTON BLACKIE, PERRY MASON (as Della Street), HILLTOP HOUSE, and DIMENSION X. After the demise of drama on radio, Miner became a busy character actress onstage at Joseph Papp's New York Festival and at the American Shakespeare Festival in Stratford, Connecticut. She worked with numerous repertory companies all across the country and performed with the Public Theater in New York City. In films, the actress was a supporting player in *The Swimmer* (1968) and played Lenny Bruce's mother in *Lenny* (1974). Anyone who has watched television during the last twenty years would immediately recognize Miner as Madge the Manicurist in the Palmolive dishwashing detergent commercials.

MIRTH AND MADNESS (AKA THE JACK KIRKWOOD SHOW)

| 1943–1945 | NBC | Mon.–Fri. | 9 AM |

Jack Kirkwood and then Ransom Sherman hosted this 15-minute variety program that featured dramatic and comedy sketches as well as musical selections. As the theme song "Hi, Neighbor" played, the show's announcer would say, "Hey you! Are ya listenin'?" and the audience knew they were about to have "a half-hour of fun-filled entertainment." Heard on this series were Lillian Lee, Don Reid, Jean McKean, Tom Harris, Billy Grey, Ransom SHERMAN, Lee Bridie, Mike McTooch, and Herb Sheldon. Irving Miller and Jerry Jerome led the show's orchestra. The program was directed by Joseph Mansfield and written by Jack Kirkwood and Ransom Sherman.

MISSUS GOES A SHOPPIN', THE

1944–1945	CBS	Mon.–Sat.	8:30 AM
1945–1949	CBS	Sat.	8:30 AM
1949–1950	CBS	Sat.	9:45 AM

John Reed KING hosted this daytime quiz show on which a female contestant would try to answer a series of trivia questions in order to "shop" for various prizes such as groceries, jewelry, and clothing with the money she had won. The 15- and 30-minute program were sponsored by Hormel food products.

MITCHELL, SHIRLEY (c. 1920–   )

Born in Toledo, Ohio, actress Shirley Mitchell attended the University of Michigan. On radio, she played for several seasons the flirtatious Southern belle Leila Ransom, one of the heartthrobs on *The* GREAT GILDERSLEEVE. Mitchell was a regular cast member of FIBBER MCGEE AND MOLLY, in which she played Alice Darling, a defense-plant worker who roomed with them during World War II. On *McGarry and His Mouse*, she was featured as "the mouse," Kitty Archer. Mitchell also appeared regularly on KAY KYSER'S KOLLEGE OF MUSICAL KNOWLEDGE, *The* RED SKELTON SHOW, WILLY PIPER, *The* RUDY VALLEE SHOW, *The* SEALTEST VILLAGE STORE, *Young Love*, and ROMANCE. Frequently heard as various cartoon characters for animated films such as *Cathy's Last Resort* (1988), the actress performed in numerous television commercials for such companies as Oscar Meyer, Hormel, and AT&T.

MODERN CHILD CARE

| 1936–1938 | CBS | Mon., Wed., Fri. | 11:45 PM |

Dr. Alan Roy DaFoe, the world-famous Canadian physician who delivered the Dionne quintuplets in 1934, hosted this 15-minute program about health care and the proper social upbringing of children. The program was sponsored by Lysol disinfectant.

MODERN ROMANCES

1949–1951	ABC	Mon.–Fri.	11 AM
1951–1952	ABC	Mon.–Fri.	10:45 PM
1952–1954	(Off the air)		
1954–1955	ABC	Mon.–Fri.	11 AM

Each week this 15-minute program presented a different story, such as the "Dear John" letter situation, adapted from the pages of *Modern Romances* magazine. Actress Gertrude Warner, playing Helen Gregory, hosted the program and narrated each week's story. Also hosting at various times were Kathi Norris and Eloise McElhone. Bob Sabin was the show's announcer. William Marshall and Joe Graham directed the program, and Margaret Sangster, Ira Marion, Lillian Shoen, and Don Witty wrote the show's scripts. Pepto-Bismol antacid, Unguentine medicated ointment, and Ex-Lax laxative sponsored the program.

MOHR, GERALD (1914–1968)

Born in New York City, actor Gerald Mohr's dark suave looks, pencil-thin mustache, and perpetual smirk got him cast as "heavies," slick con men, and—occasionally—heroes in such films as *The Monster and the Girl* (1941), *Lady of Burlesque* (1943), *Ten Tall Men* (1951), *The Eddie Cantor Story* (1953), and *Funny Girl* (1968). He played *The Lone Wolf* in the 1940s film series. However, his rich, resonant baritone voice garnered Mohr numerous romantic leading roles on hundreds of radio programs where he would not be typecast by appearance. The actor starred as tough-guy-detective Phillip Marlowe on *The* ADVENTURES OF PHILIP MARLOWE, *Private Detective*; as Nero Wolfe's assistant, Archie, on NERO WOLFE; and in the romantic lead roles on dramatic anthologies *The* LUX RADIO THEATER, HOLLYWOOD STAR THEATER, SCREEN ACTOR'S

Gerald Mohr (United Artists)

GUILD, and ROMANCE. Mohr died in Stockholm while filming a pilot for an unnamed television series that costarred his Swedish-born wife.

MOLASSES 'N' JANUARY, AKA PICK AND PAT (PICK MALONE 1892–1962; PAT PADGETT 1903–   )

For a while in the early 1930s, comedians Malone and Padgett almost rivaled AMOS AND ANDY in radio popularity. The team, who worked together in vaudeville, were originally heard on radio in 1929 on the *WOR (New York) Minstrels* show, where they did a blackface act. First billed as Pick and Pat, they changed their professional names to Molasses 'n' January, the names of popular characters they played on NBC's SHOW BOAT in 1932. In 1941, the team resumed their Molasses 'n' January names when they starred on a program called *Dr. Pepper Parade*. Molasses 'n' January were last heard on radio during World War II as "America's advisers on the home front" in a 5-minute comedy segment that was heard weekdays on CBS.

MONITOR

1955–1957	NBC	Fri.	(evenings)
		Sat.	(afternoons)
		Sun.	(evenings)
1957–1961	NBC	Fri., Sat., Sun.	(afternoons)
1961–1974	NBC	Sat., Sun.	(afternoons)

This program began: "*Monitor*, a continuing service in sound. A new dimension in radio, *Monitor* brings you your story . . . yours because you wrote it . . . part of it, at least!" In the mid-1950s, when major network-produced radio programs were no longer being presented, NBC attempted to rekindle the spark of radio's former glory days by offering this weekend radio series that featured news, comedy, talk, and music. Past and present radio stars, including BOB AND RAY, Arlene FRANCIS, FIBBER MCGEE AND MOLLY, John Chancellor, Hugh Downs, Lindsay Nelson, Walter Kiernan, Lorla Lynn, Tedi Thurman, Morgan Beatty, Ray Shaerer, James Fleming, Clifton FADIMAN, Leon Pearson, Skitch Henderson, Ed McMahon, Ted Webbe, Frank Blair, Chet Huntley, Barbara Walters, Dave GARROWAY, Gene Rayburn, the Art Van Damme Quartet, cartoonist Al Capp, Barry Nelson, Jonathan Winters, and Henry MORGAN. John Cameron SWAYZE was the program's major news commentator during the show's early years. American Motors and Barbasol shave cream were just two of the show's many sponsors.

MONSIEUR HERCULE POIROT, THE ADVENTURES OF

See ADVENTURES OF MONSIEUR HERCULE POIROT, THE.

MOONSHINE AND HONEYSUCKLE

| 1930–1933 | NBC | Sun. | (*) |

Moonshine and Honeysuckle was one of the earliest daytime drama serials on radio. A half-hour country-comedy show, it featured Louis Mason as Clem Betts, a young mountaineer; Claude Cooper as his pal, "Peg Leg" Gaddis; and Anne Elstner as Peg Leg's wife, "Cracker." Also heard were Virginia Morgan, Jeanie Begg, John Milton, Anne Sutherland, and Sara Haden. The series, which was written by Lulu Vollmer, was very rural in flavor and featured homespun country humor. Henry Stillman directed the program.

MOORE, GARRY (THOMAS GARRISON MORFIT: 1915–1993)

Born in Baltimore, Maryland, comedian–program host Garry Moore made his radio debut on *The RANSOM SHERMAN SHOW* in 1935: on this show, a female listener from Pittsburgh won a contest by giving him his professional name. The name stuck, and he subsequently became comedian Jimmy DURANTE's straight man and comedy partner on *The JIMMY DURANTE–GARRY MORE SHOW*. A distinctive-looking young man with a boyish crew cut and a fast-paced comic delivery, Moore remained with Durante for several years and then became the star of his own GARRY MOORE SHOW. Moore also hosted *The CAMEL CARAVAN*, BEAT THE BAND, TAKE IT OR LEAVE IT, and BREAKFAST IN HOLLYWOOD. In 1950, Moore made his television debut on a daytime variety show, *The Garry Moore Show*, which remained on the air until 1958. He also hosted quiz-panel show "I've Got a Secret" and, in 1958, an evening comedy-music-variety show featuring Carol Burnett, Marion Lorne, Durwood KIRBY, Denise Lor, and Ken Carson. Moore retired in 1964, but in 1966 he returned to TV for two seasons, retiring once and for all in 1968.

MOOREHEAD, AGNES (1906–1974)

Character actress Agnes Moorehead was born in Clinton, Massachusetts, and attended the American Academy of Dramatic Arts in New York City. Heard on local radio as early as 1925 and one of Orson Welles's original MERCURY THEATER ON THE AIR company, she played Margo Lane on *The SHADOW*, Marilly on *The MAYOR OF THE TOWN* opposite Lionel Barrymore, Homer Brown's mother on *The ALDRICH FAMILY*, the mother-in-law on BRENDA CURTIS, Maggie on BRINGING UP FATHER, and The Dragon Lady on TERRY AND THE PIRATES. Moorehead was also a frequent performer on such programs as *The MARCH OF TIME*, *There Was a Woman*, *Spy Secrets*, BELIEVE IT OR NOT, STRANGE AS IT SEEMS, CAVALCADE OF AMERICA, LIFE BEGINS AT

Agnes Moorehead during the broadcast of "Sorry, Wrong Number"

EIGHTY, BIG SISTER, *The* BEN BERNIE SHOW, *The Mighty Show*, AUNT JENNY'S REAL LIFE STORIES, THIS DAY IS OURS, *The* PHIL BAKER SHOW, *The* ADVENTURES OF BULL-DOG DRUMMOND, LIFE CAN BE BEAUTIFUL, and GRAND CENTRAL STATION.

The actress also made numerous appearances on SUSPENSE, most notably as Mrs. Albert Smythe-Stevenson, the complaining invalid-socialite who was slated for murder in Lucille FLETCHER's classic radio chiller, "Sorry, Wrong Number." Moorehead's performance was so compelling that she was invited to repeat the role each year on the *Suspense* series.

The actress's stage, film, and television appearances were as numerous as those she made on radio. She was seen on Broadway in *Don Juan in Hell* (1949) and *Gigi* (1973), on film as Orson Welles's mother in *Citizen Kane* (1941), and in *The Magnificent Ambersons* (1942), *Jane Eyre* (1943), *Tomorrow the World* (1944), *Dark Passage* (1947), *Magnificent Obsession* (1954), *Raintree County* (1957), *How the West Was Won* (1962), and *Hush . . . Hush Sweet Charlotte* (1964). On television, Moorehead is best remembered for playing Samantha's witch-mother, Endora, on the "Bewitched" (1964) series. In the mid-1970s, shortly before her death, Moorehead returned to radio on the first program of Himan BROWN's CBS MYSTERY THEATER series.

MORAN AND MACK (MORAN—SWOR, JOHN (1883–1965) AND SEARCHY, GEORGE (1881–1949); MACK—SELLERS, CHARLES (1882–1949)

In radio's earliest days, white performers who entertained in blackface and used African-American dialects were used as commonly on the airwaves as they had been onstage in minstrel shows in the nineteenth and early twentieth centuries. One of the most successful blackface duos heard on radio were "the Two Black Crows." Originally, the parts were played by two Kansas-born comedians named John Swor and Charles Sellers, but when Swor left, he was replaced by comedian George Searchy and the team changed their name to Moran and Mack. In addition to their own *Two Black Crows* show, the original team starred on *The* EVEREADY HOUR and *The Majestic Theater* programs. On Broadway, the original team had starred in *Over the Top* in 1917, *The Ziegfeld Follies* in the 1920s and *the Greenwich Village Follies* in 1924 and 1926. In 1927, Moran and Mack made several hit comedy recordings and were featured in the films *Two Flaming Youths* (1927) and *Why Bring That Up?* (1929). Moran and Mack split up in 1929, original team member Swor was reunited with Sellers, and they appeared in such films as *Anybody's War* (1930). The team continued to perform together until Sellers was killed in an automobile accident in 1935. George Searchy, who had, by this time taken the name of "Moran" to capitalize on his Moran and Mack fame, continued to perform as a solo artist and was seen in the W. C. Fields films *My Little Chickadee* (1940) and *The Bank Dick* (1940).

MORGAN, CLAUDIA (1912–1974)

Actress Claudia Morgan, daughter of actor Ralph Morgan and niece of actor Frank MORGAN, was born in New York City. She is best remembered for playing Nora Charles on the *Adventures of the* THIN MAN radio series and was Christy Allen Cameron on AGAINST THE STORM, Nita Bennett on LONELY JOURNEY, Clarissa Oakley on DAVID HARUM, and Carolyn Kramer Nelson on *The* RIGHT TO HAPPINESS. The actress was also heard on the dramatic anthology GRAND CENTRAL STATION and was frequently featured on INNER SANCTUM MYSTERIES, ON STAGE, *Accent on Youth*, and DIMENSION X. In the 1970s, Morgan was occasionally heard on Himan BROWN's CBS MYSTERY THEATER.

MORGAN, EDWARD P. (1910–1993)

Newscaster Edward P. Morgan first came to the attention of radio listeners in 1941 when, as a correspondent for the United States Press International, he reported the murder of Leon Trotsky in Mexico. After working as a war correspondent throughout World

War II, he joined the ABC news staff and became one of that network's top newscasters and anchormen until well into the mid-1960s. Morgan's relaxed, easygoing delivery was distinctly different from the rapid-fire news-report style of most radio newsmen in the 1930s and 1940s.

MORGAN, FRANK (FRANCIS PHILIP WUPPERMAN: 1890–1949)

New York–born character actor Frank Morgan was the original "Daddy" when Fannie BRICE first introduced her popular BABY SNOOKS character to radio listeners on the ZIEGFELD FOLLIES OF THE AIR and MAXWELL HOUSE COFFEE TIME programs. He also hosted The KRAFT MUSIC HALL and *Old Gold Show*, and for several seasons starred on his own FRANK MORGAN SHOW. In addition to his world-famous portrayal of the title role in the film *The Wizard of Oz* (1939), the actor appeared in many silent and sound motion pictures during his distinguished career, such as *Tortilla Flat* (1942), *Any Number Can Play* (1949), and *Key to the City* (1950), released the year after he died of a heart attack.

MORGAN, HENRY (HENRY LERNER VAN OST: 1915–1994)

New York–born Henry Morgan first attracted public attention with a 15-minute, early-evening radio show on WOR—Morgan played unusual records from his own collection and often poked fun at his sponsors, which delighted his listeners but cost him sponsors such as Adler elevated shoes. Network officials were intrigued with his obvious audience appeal and high ratings in New York City. On his own national, prime-time program, *The* HENRY MORGAN SHOW, he continued to make refreshingly candid comments about such sponsors as Life Savers candy and especially Schick razors. When Morgan was told on the air that his show was dropping in the ratings, he said, "Frankly, I don't think it's my show! I think it's their razor!" In the 1950s and 1960s, Morgan became a panelist on several television game shows, including "What's My Line?" (1953) and "The Great Talent Hunt" (1958), on which he often displayed his acerbic wit. Dissatisfied with television work, Morgan retired in the early 1980s.

MORNING EDITION

1979–present   NPR   Mon.–Fri.   6 AM

A daily three-hour news program, NATIONAL PUBLIC RADIO's *Morning Edition* gives in-depth news reports, insightful and provocative interviews, and special features about nature, the environment, and various hu-

Bob Edwards (Max Hirshfeld)

man-interest stories. The program features Bob Edwards as its anchorman. Well-informed reporters and special commentators such as Nina Tottenberg, Elizabeth Arnold, and Washington correspondent Carl Kasell—whose voice is the first one heard when the program goes on the air—deliver this on-air magazine. For many years, special features such as Bob Kanter's "Bird Watch," later called "Nature Watch," have been offered daily.

MORNINGSIDE

1981–present   CBC   Mon.–Fri.   9:05 AM

Millions of listeners have tuned in for years to hear one of the best-loved and most familiar voices in Canada say, "Good morning, I'm Peter Gzowski and this is *Morningside*." Gzowski has hosted this three-hour current-affairs program on the CANADIAN BROADCASTING CORPORATION for more than ten years. He has had conversations with prominent Canadians as well as dancers, activists, musicians, merchants, writers, actors, and farmers. *Morningside* uses a wide variety of forms, such as daily sketches, monologues, and live broadcasts of stage shows. The program also presents panel discussions about politics, books, sports, and Canadian arts and culture in general. In 1986, Gzowski was named an Officer of the Order of Canada for his service to the nation as a newscaster

Morningside host Peter Gzowski (CBC)

and radio-program host. Current special features on the program include "Vinyl Cafe" on Mondays, "The Best of . . ." on Tuesdays and Thursdays, and "My Kinda Jazz" on Fridays. The program has had many producers and directors. Paul Kennedy has also been heard as the show's host.

MORRISON, BRET (1912–1978)

Bret Morrison, born in Chicago, Illinois, made his network-radio acting debut in a promotional adaptation of the film *Dracula* and was subsequently regularly heard on Chicago-based programs *The* CHICAGO THEATER OF THE AIR, *Vanity Fair*, ATTORNEY AT LAW, *Win Your Lady*, GREAT GUNNS, and as the man who introduced *Mr.* FIRST NIGHTER. Hoping to become a film actor, Morrison moved to Hollywood in the mid-1930s, continuing to work on West Coast radio. He became a regular performer on PARTIES AT PICKFAIR and other Hollywood-based programs. When a career in films failed to materialize, Morrison went to New York City, where he was heard as THE SHADOW and on *The* GUIDING LIGHT, *The* ROAD OF LIFE, ARNOLD GRIMM'S DAUGHTER, *The* ROMANCE OF HELEN TRENT, *The* STORY OF MARY MARLIN, and *The* WOMAN IN WHITE. Throughout the 1960s and into the 1970s, Morrison dubbed foreign films. He was also occasionally heard on Himan BROWN's CBS MYSTERY THEATER in the mid-1970s.

MORRISON, HERB (1906–1989)

Herb Morrison, who was born in Fairmont, Pennsylvania, began his career as a newspaper journalist, and later became a radio broadcaster in Pittsburgh. His vivid, emotional on-the-air, on-the-score description of the explosion of the German dirigible the *Hindenburg* in 1937 brought instant fame. After years of working as an announcer and a newscaster, he became one of the first television news directors at station WTAE in Pittsburgh. He continued to work as a station-break announcer and commerical spokesman until he was well in his seventies. In 1975, Morrison was sent across the country by Universal Studios to help promote its film *Hindenberg* (1975), which starred George C. Scott.

MORSE, CARLTON E. (1901—1993)

One of radio's most respected creative-writing talents because of the natural way he wrote dialogue, Carlton E. Morse was born in Jennings, Louisiana, and raised on a farm in Oregon. He became one of NBC's most valuable staff members while working at that company's San Francisco headquarters. The creator and major force behind such celebrated series as the long-running serial ONE MAN'S FAMILY on radio and on television and the mystery-detective program I LOVE A MYSTERY, Morse also wrote and directed HIS HONOR THE BARBER and *Family Skeleton*.

MOSS, ARNOLD (1910–1989)

Actor Arnold Moss was born in Brooklyn, New York, and became well known for the many motion-picture and television roles he played as well as for those he created for radio. Moss had a deep, rich, and resonant voice and was a regular on GRAND CENTRAL STATION and a frequent guest star on INNER SANCTUM MYSTERIES and *The Mighty Show*. Radio audiences also remember Moss as a major character on daytime radio programs AGAINST THE STORM, JANE ARDEN, VALIANT LADY, MANHATTAN MOTHER, BIG SISTER, *The* GUIDING LIGHT, and *The* STORY OF MARY MARLIN. He also starred in the *Cabin B-13* and *The* FORD THEATER series. In the 1970s, Moss was regularly featured on Himan BROWN's CBS MYSTERY THEATER series. An active member of the Phoenix Theater in New York City in the 1950s and 1960s, Moss was also featured in regional theater productions. He is seen in the films *Temptation* (1946), *Salome* (1953), *Bengal Brigade* (1954), and *Gambit* (1966). A memorable television appearance by Moss was a "Star Trek" episode in which he played a villainous Shakespearean actor touring the universe as Shakespeare's *King Lear*.

MOSTLY MUSIC

| 1980s– present | CBC | Mon.–Fri. | 9:05 AM |
| | | | 10:05 PM |

Every weekday and weeknight, host Ken Winters broadcasts concerts from all over Canada on the CA-NADIAN BROADCASTING CORPORATION's *Mostly Music* series. The show features the Toronto Symphony Orchestra, currently under the direction of Gunther Herbig; the Montreal Symphony Orchestra, conducted by Charles Dutoit; and the Vancouver Symphony Orchestra, conducted by Sergui Commissiona. Other orchestras are also featured at various times. The show's executive producer is Charlotte Cheng.

MOYLAN SISTERS, THE (PEGGY JOAN: 1934–; MARIANNE: 1932–   )

The singing Moylan Sisters were born in New York City. Even as children they sang *three-part harmony* (!) and were billed as "The Angels of the Airwaves" when they made their radio debuts in 1938 on *The* CHILDREN'S HOUR. Marianne and her younger sister Peggy Joan starred on their own 15-minute Sunday afternoon music program *The Moylan Sister Show* in 1939 under contract to NBC: at the time, they were, respectively, seven and five years old. The Moylan Sisters were also frequent guest stars during the early 1940s on *The* FRED ALLEN SHOW and *The* ALEC TEMPLETON SHOW.

MOYLAN SISTERS SHOW, THE

See MOYLAN SISTERS, THE.

MR. AND MRS. ACE

See EASY ACES.

MR. AND MRS. NORTH, THE ADVENTURES OF

See ADVENTURES OF MR. AND MRS. NORTH, THE.

MR. ANTHONY–THE GOODWILL HOUR (AKA A. L. ALEXANDER'S GOODWILL COURT)

1936–1937	Mutual	Sun.	10:30 AM
1937–1944	Mutual	Sun.	10 AM
1944–1961	(Syndicated series. Various stations and times)		

First heard during the earliest days of commercial radio, this program was originally hosted by Albert L. Alexander in 1936. *The Good Will Court* dispensed legal and marital advice to listeners who wrote in questions. When the New York Supreme Court, on the recommendation of the New York County Lawyers Association, ruled that legal advice should not be given on the radio, the program's format changed

and *The Good Will Court* became *Alexander's Mediation Board*. Instead of giving legal advice, Alexander gave social advice. He still discussed marital problems, for example, but dispensed advice on a personal rather than a legal basis. A similar half-hour program, presided over by John J. ANTHONY (whose real name was Lester Kroll), was called *Mr. Anthony–The Goodwill Hour*, which dispensed advice on the air. Anthony would consistently reprimand guests for "touching the microphones" and sharply tell them "not to use any names, please!" Roland Winters announced the show. The series was produced and directed by Thomas Vieters, Jr.

MR. CHAMELEON

1948–1951	CBS	Wed.	8 PM
1951–1952	CBS	Thurs.	9 PM
1952–1953	CBS	Fri.	8:30 PM

The title character on this half-hour series was a master of disguises and used this ability to aid him in bringing various criminals to justice. Versatile actor Karl SWENSON played Mr. Chameleon, and Frank Butler portrayed his assistant, Dave Arnold. Richard Keith was heard as the police commissioner on the series. *Mr. Chameleon* was produced by Frank and Anne HUMMERT, directed by Richard Leonard, and written by Marie Baumer. The program's announcers were Roger Krupp and Howard Claney. Bayer aspirin and Dr. Lyon's tooth powder sponsored the program.

MR. DISTRICT ATTORNEY

1939	NBC Red	Tues.	10 PM
1939–1940	NBC Blue	Sun.	7:30 PM
1940–1941	NBC Red	Wed.	9:30 PM
1941–1951	NBC	Wed.	9:30 PM
1951–1954	ABC	Fri.	9:30 PM

"Mr. District Attorney: Champion of the people, defender of truth, guardian of our fundamental rights of life, liberty, and the pursuit of happiness," the announcer said at the beginning of each half-hour *Mr. District Attorney* program. The show revolved around the D.A. of a large American city and his pursuit of justice when such crimes as murder, theft, and confidence games were committed. Dwight WEIST was the first *Mr. District Attorney*, followed by Raymond Edward JOHNSON, but Jay JOSTYN, who played Mr. District Attorney the longest (twelve years), is best remembered in the role. In the 1950s, film actor David Brian played the part for the final two years of its run.

Playing major roles opposite Jostyn were Vicki VOLA as faithful secretary and assistant Edith Miller and Walter KINSELLA and then Len Doyle as his chief investigator, Harrington. In supporting roles were

Eleanor Silver, Arlene FRANCIS, Maurice Franklin, Craig McDonnell, Geoffrey Bryant, Amy Seidell, Frank LOVEJOY, Paul Stewart, and Thelma Ritter. Announcing the program were Ed HERLIHY, Ben GRAUER, Fred Uttal, Mark Hawley, and Bob Shepherd.

Mr. District Attorney was created and directed by Edward Byron and produced by Phillips H. LORD. Writers included Byron, Harry Herman, Finis Farr, Jerry McGill, Jerry Devine, and Robert J. Shaw. Bristol Myers products and Pepsodent toothpaste were the program's longtime sponsors, but Ipana toothpaste, Sal Hapatica antacid, Vitalis hair dressing, Bufferin pain reliever, Ingram shaving cream, Sentry hair tonic, and Mum deodorant also sponsored the program.

MR. KEEN, TRACER OF LOST PERSONS

1937–1942	NBC Blue	Tues.–Thurs.	7:15 PM
1943–1947	CBS	Thurs.	7:30 PM
1947–1951	CBS	Thurs.	8:30 PM
1951–1953	NBC	Thurs.	8:30 PM
1953–1954	CBS	Fri.	8 PM
1954–1955	CBS	Mon.–Fri.	10 PM

Although three actors played the part of Mr. Keen on the half-hour program, Bennett KILPACK played the part longest and is the performer most identified with the role. Phil Clark and Arthur HUGHES also played Mr. Keen, with Hughes in the role during the show's final years. Florence Malone played Mr. Keen's secretary, Miss Ellis, and Jim Kelly played his faithful assistant, Mike Clancy. William J. Smith, Arline Blackburn, Adelaide Klein, and Joseph "Joe" Latham were frequently heard in the supporting cast. The announcers included Larry Elliott, James Fleming, and Jack Costello. The series was produced by Frank and Anne HUMMERT, directed by Richard Leonard, and written by David Davidson. The show's theme song was, quite appropriately, "Someday I'll Find You." Sponsors of this program included Anacin pain reliever, Kolynos toothpaste, BiSoDol antacid mints, Heet liniment, Aerowax wax, Hill's cold tablets, Chesterfield cigarettes, Dentyne chewing gum, and RCA Victor records, radios, and phonographs.

MR. PRESIDENT

1947–1948	ABC	Thurs.	9:30 PM
1948–1950	ABC	Sun.	2:30 PM
1950–1953	ABC	Wed.	(*)

Each week on this show, film actor Edward ARNOLD portrayed a different United States president in a story pertaining to his personal life. The respective president was never revealed until the end of the half-hour dramatization, and listeners were encouraged to try to guess who it was as the story unfolded. The

show became a favorite of millions of listeners and was required listening for many schoolchildren across the country. Produced and directed by Dick Wooller Joe Graham, Dwight Hauser, and Leonard Reeg, was written by Jean Holloway. Fred Cole announced the series, which was sustained by the ABC network Various public-service announcements were made during the half-hour it was aired.

MRS. WIGGS OF THE CABBAGE PATCH

1935–1936	CBS	Mon.–Fri.	10:45 AM
1936–1938	NBC Red	Mon.–Fri.	10 AM

Alice Caldwell Rice's popular novel *Mrs. Wiggs of th Cabbage Patch* was adapted for radio as a 15-minut drama serial. It featured Betty GARDE and then Ev Gordon in the title role of Mrs. Wiggs, a kindly coun trywoman who found time to help everyone. Rober Strauss played Pa Wiggs, and Andy Donnelly wa Billy Wiggs. Other actors included Joseph "Joe" La tham, William "Bill" JOHNSTONE, James Van Dyke Vivia Ogden, Agnes Young, Alice FROST, Marjori Anderson, and Frank Provo. George Ansbro was th show's announcer. The series was produced and di rected by Frank and Anne HUMMERT. Jad Effervescen salts and Old English wax sponsored the program.

MUNN, FRANK (PAUL OLIVER: 1895–1953)

Tenor Frank Munn was born in New York City and worked in an embroidery factory before embarkin on a professional singing career, first in vaudevill and then on the concert stage and on radio's *Th* AMERICAN ALBUM OF FAMILIAR MUSIC. Munn, know as "the golden voice of radio," sang light opera and semiclassical songs such as "Londonerry Air" and "Ah, Sweet Mystery of Life." In addition to appearin on *The American Album of Familiar Music,* the singe was heard on LAVENDER AND OLD LACE in the earl 1930s and frequently guest-starred on *Waltz Time* and other music programs. Munn continued to perform a concerts until shortly before his death.

MURDER AND MR. MALONE

1947–1948	ABC	Sat.	9:30 PM
1948–1949	ABC	Sat.	8:30 PM
1949–1950	ABC	Wed.	8 PM
1951	ABC	Fri.	9 PM

Frank LOVEJOY was given star billing as Mr. Malone on this half-hour detective-mystery series. Malone who was also played by actor Gene Raymond, was a worn-out shamus who had hard luck finding payin clients: he took cases no one else seemed to want Larry Thor announced the program. William Rous eau directed the series, which was written by Craig Rice.

MURRAY, KEN (DON COURT: 1903–1988)

Comedian Ken Murray was born in New York City and was the longtime star of a Los Angeles stage show called *Ken Murray's Blackouts*. He was a true variety performer and usually played a funny "straight man," a little like Bud Abbott of ABBOTT AND COSTELLO. On radio, Murray starred on *The* KEN MURRAY SHOW in 1932 and again in 1939. He was also regularly featured on the TEXACO STAR THEATER and the *Which Is Which* quiz show. The star of his own "Ken Murray Show" on television as early as 1950, Murray starred on TV's "The Colgate Comedy Hour" (1950–1954) and was a panelist on "I've Got a Secret" and "Masquerade Party."

MURRAY, LYN (LIONEL BREESE: 1910–1989)

Born in London, England, orchestra leader Lyn Murray was was music conductor on *The* DANNY KAYE SHOW, *The* ADVENTURES OF ELLERY QUEEN, *Watch the Lords Go By, Heinz Magazine of the Air, The Chrysler Show of the Air, Sunday Night Party, Rippling Rhythm Revue,* YOUR HIT PARADE, *The* HALLMARK PLAYHOUSE, and *Music from the House of Squibb*. Murray was considered by many people in the music business (including Ray NOBLE and Al GOODMAN) to be one of the best music directors on radio because he was an expert in classical and popular music and an excellent conductor as well.

MURROW, EDWARD R. (1908–1965)

Born in Greensboro, North Carolina, Edward R. Murrow was one of radio and television's most respected newscasters. He majored in political science, speech, and international relations at Washington State College, and as a news staffer and then as chief of news services at CBS, Murrow brought news of the horrors of World War II into American homes. His broadcasts from London as the city was being bombed by the Nazis made him internationally known. Murrow later became CBS's major news commentator and was heard on HERE IT NOW, a program that replayed famous news events. Murrow was one of the first newsmen to criticize Senator Joseph McCarthy on both radio and television for his destructive anti-Communist crusade. In 1951, he hosted television's "See It Now" and later the very popular "Person to Person" series on which he interviewed such celebrities as the Duke and Duchess of Windsor, Jacqueline Kennedy, and Israeli President Ben Gurion. Radio listeners fondly remember Murrow's famous opening, "This

Edward R. Murrow (CBS)

. . . is the news," as well as his equally famous closing, "Good night, and Good luck!"

MUSIC APPRECIATION HOUR, THE

| 1928–1942 | NBC | Mon.–Fri. | (*) |

Unquestionably one of radio's most enduring classical and semiclassical music programs, *The Music Appreciation Hour* was hosted for more than fourteen years by musicologist-conductor Dr. Walter DAMROSCH. This hour-long early-morning series presented recorded music and offered commentaries by Dr. Damrosch; it even became required listening for many schoolchildren throughout the United States. The program was produced and directed by Damrosch.

MUSIC THAT SATISFIES

| 1932–* | CBS | Mon.–Sat. | (*) |
| 1944–1945 | CBS | Tues., Wed., Thurs. | 7:15 PM |

Arthur TRACY, radio's celebrated "Street Singer," was the star of this 15-minute program of semiclassical and popular music. Also appearing were Bing CROSBY, the BOSWELL SISTERS, and singers Ruth ETTING and Monica Lewis. Norman BROKENSHIRE was the program's announcer. The series was sponsored by Chesterfield cigarettes, whose boast that they produced the "cigarette that satisfies" led to the show's title. The show was heard on NBC's Red network of stations.

MUSIC WITH THE HORMEL GIRLS

1949–1950	ABC	Sun.	6:30 PM
1950–1951	NBC &	Sun.	3 PM
	CBS	Sat.	2 PM
1951–1953	CBS	Sat.	2 PM
1953–1954	CBS	Sat.	1:30 PM

Similar to the hour-long HOUR OF CHARM program in that it featured only women in the cast and orchestra, *Music with the Hormel Girls* starred Betty Dougherty, Elina Hart, and Mary Ellen Domm as mistresses of ceremonies. Marilyn Wilson was the show's announcer. Songs from operettas and musical comedies were presented. Hormel foods, makers of Spam meat, Dinty Moore stew, and Hormel chili, sponsored the series.

MUTUAL BROADCASTING SYSTEM, THE

The Mutual Broadcasting System was formed in 1934 when four privately owned eastern and midwestern radio stations joined together to make themselves available to advertisers at a group rate. The stations were WGN in Chicago, owned by *The Chicago Tribune* newspaper; WOR in New York City, owned by Bamberger's Department Store; WLW in Cincinnati, owned by Powel Crosley, Jr.; and WXYZ in Detroit, owned by George W. TRENDLE. WXYZ made its popular LONE RANGER program available to its partners, and the new network of stations was off to an impressive beginning with a sizable listening audience. First called the Quality Network, the company changed its name to the Mutual Broadcasting System in 1935. Mutual never had central ownership like CBS and NBC, but the participating stations were heavily affiliated. After two years, other stations began to join the cooperative venture, and many new shows, such as *The* SHADOW and NICK CARTER, MASTER DETECTIVE, were introduced to its growing list of programs. By 1940, there were 118 Mutual affiliates; by 1941 that number had increased to more than 200. In the 1950s, however, the Mutual network was plagued by scandal. From 1956 until 1959, ownership of the network changed six times, with one management convicted of stock manipulation and another accused of selling a guarantee of favorable mention to Dominican Republic dictator Rafael Trujillo. Because of this and ever-increasing disenchantment with the company's board of directors, more than 130 stations dropped their Mutual affiliation and in the early 1960s the network was disbanded altogether.

Lucille Ball and Richard Denning in *My Favorite Husband* (CBS)

MY FAVORITE HUSBAND

1948–1950	CBS	Sun.	6 PM
1950–1951	CBS	Sat.	9:30 PM

Comedienne Lucille BALL starred on this half-hour weekly situation comedy about a wife named Liz Cooper, who—like Lucy on "I Love Lucy"—had a talent for getting into trouble. Her ever-patient, loving husband, George, was first played by film star Lee Bowman and then for most of the series' run by Richard Denning. The series was written by the same people who later made "I Love Lucy" a hit television show—Bob Carroll, Jr., and Madelyn Pugh. It was also written by its director, Jess Oppenheimer. Heard in supporting roles were Ruth Perrott as Katie, the maid; Gale GORDON as George's boss, Rudolph Atterbury; Bea BENADERET as Iris Atterbury; Hans CONRIED as the Cooper's next-door neighbor, Mr. Wood, who had eleven children and was always tired; and Frank Nelson, who played various roles on the show. *My Favorite Husband* was based on a book by Isabel Scott Rorick called *Mr. and Mrs. Cugat* (1928). Bob Lamond was the program's announcer. Sponsors included Jell-O, Sanka instant coffee, LaFrance bleach, Pepsodent toothpaste, Swan soap, Spry shortening, Eye-Gene eye cleaner, Camel cigarettes, Cavalier cigarettes, Arrid deodorant, Carter's Little Liver Pills, and Toni home permanent.

MY FRIEND IRMA

1947–1951	CBS	Mon.	10 PM
1951–1952	CBS	Sun.	6 PM
1952–1954	CBS	Tues.	9:30 PM

On this half-hour radio situation-comedy series, Irma Peterson and Jane Stacy were working women who

omed together in Mrs. O'Reilly's boardinghouse in
large American city. The only thing they had in
ommon was that they were both secretaries; other-
ise they were exact opposites. Irma was a stereotypi-
l sexy-but-dumb blonde whose illogical behavior
as a constant source of frustration to her roommate
ne, a bright and very practical brunette. Marie WIL-
N and Cathy LEWIS played Irma and Jane. Their
ndlady was played by Gloria Gordon. A fellow
arder, Professor Kropotkin—one of the most popu-
r characters on the show—was portrayed by veteran
dio performer Hans CONRIED. Also heard in regular
les were John Brown as Irma's slick-talking boy-
iend, Al; Alan REED as Irma's ever-exasperated boss,
r. Clyde; Leif Erickson as Jane's rich boyfriend,
ichard Rhinelander III; and Myra Marsh and Gale
RDON as Richard's snobbish, rich parents. The
ow's orchestra was led by Lud GLUSKIN. Cy Howard
irected the series, which was written by Parke Levy,
anley Adams, Roland MacLane, and Jack Denton.
he show's theme song was "Friendship." Wendell
ILES, Frank Ringman, Johnny Jacobs, and John Ca-
so announced the series.

1Y LITTLE MARGIE

1952–1954	CBS	Sun.	8:30 PM
1953–1955	CBS	Sun.	8:30 PM
	Mutual	Thurs.	9:30 PM

his half-hour program, also a hit on television,
arred motion-picture actress Gale Storm as Margie,
working girl who lived at home with her widowed
ther, Verne Albright, played by Charles Farrell. Marie's father was a handsome, debonaire fellow who
ways got mixed up with various women. In many
isodes, Margie struggled to keep her father out of
oman trouble. Also heard on the series were Gil
tratton, Jr., as Freddie Wilson; Doris Singleton as
oberta Townsend; and Will Wright as George Hon-
ywell, Margie's boss. Johnny Jacobs was the pro-
ram's announcer. Sponsors included Philip Morris
garettes and Parliament cigarettes.

1Y TRUE STORY

1943–1944	NBC Blue	Mon.–Fri.	3:15 PM
1944–1945	NBC Blue	Mon.–Fri.	10 AM
1945–1956	ABC	Mon.–Fri.	10 AM
1956–1960	NBC	Mon.–Fri.	10:05 AM
1961–1962	Mutual	Mon.–Thurs.	8:15 AM

his show adapted stories from *True Story* magazine
nd serialized them in five-day-a-week installments.
he 15-minute stories usually involved an act of hero-
m or some sort of a frightening experience such as
eing lost in the wilderness, but always had a roman-

tic twist to it. Featuring Adele RONSON, Curtis Arnall,
Ethel Everett, Abby LEWIS, Court Benson, Jane Amar,
Nancy Guild, Evie Juster, Charles Warburton, and
Sidney Slon, the program was directed by Martin
Andrews, Charles Warburton, and George West and
written, for many years, by Margaret Sangster. The
program's theme song, "My True Story" was played
by organist Rosa Rio. Glenn Riggs and Ed HERLIHY
announced the series. The show was sponsored by
Libby's baby food, Phillips Milk of Magnesia antacid,
Sterling drugs, and Bayer aspirin.

MYRT AND MARGE

1931–1936	CBS	Mon.–Fri.	7 PM
1936–1942	CBS	Mon.–Fri.	10:15 AM

One of radio's earliest 15-minute serial dramas, *Myrt
and Marge* concerned a hard-boiled, experienced stage
actress named Myrt and her innocent young fellow
trooper, Marge, as they experienced such events as
auditioning for the same role in a play or falling in
love with the same man. Myrt was played by Myrtle
VAIL, who also created and wrote the series. Actresses
Alice Yourman and Toni Gilman played Myrt on
those rare occasions when Miss Vail was indisposed.
Marge was played by Vail's real-life daughter, Donna
Dammerel Fick. When Donna died in childbirth, the
part was taken over by Helen Mack, Alice Goodwin,
and Lucy Gilman. Other actors included Santos OR-
TEGA, Ray Hedge, Betty Jane Tyler, Arthur Elmer,
Marie Nelson, Henry Saxe, Leo Curley, Michael Fitz-
maurice, Linda Carlon-Reid, Charlotte MANSON,
Charles Flynn, Vivian Fridell, Henrietta Tedrow, Da-
vid Ross, Olan SOULE, Joseph Curtin, Ed BEGLEY, Ken
Griffin, Sunda Love, Jeanne Juvelier, Alan Devitt, Cliff
ARQUETTE, Jackson BECK, Roger DeKoven, Alan REED,
Joe Latham, Raymond Edward JOHNSON, Robert
Walker, Matt CROWLEY, Maurice TARPLIN, and Doro-
thy Dix. The program was produced and directed by
Bob Brown and also directed at times by Lindsay
MacHarrie, Jack Mullen, Ted Barash, and John Gunn.
The show's theme music was "Poor Butterfly." An-
nouncers included Davis Ross, Jean Paul King, Del
SHARBUTT, Vinton Hayworth, Tom Shirley, Andre
BARUCH, and Don MACLAUGHLIN. In addition to Vail,
Cliff Thomas wrote scripts for the series. Wrigley's
gum, Concentrated Super Suds detergent, Colgate
dental cream, and Halo shampoo sponsored the series.
See also VAIL, MYRTLE.

MYSTERIOUS TRAVELER, THE

1943–1944	Mutual	Sun.	7 PM
1944	Mutual	Sun.	3:30 PM
1944–1945	Mutual	Sat.	9:30 PM

Mysterious Traveler: (from left) Bill Zuckert, Lon Clark, Roger DeKoven, Ed Begley, Maurice Tarplin, Jimmy Wallington and Jackson Beck (Mutual Broadcasting System)

1946	Mutual	Sun.	4 PM
1946–1947	Mutual	Sun.	7 PM
1947–1948	Mutual	Tues.	8 PM
1948–1949	Mutual	Thurs.	9:30 PM
1949–1951	Mutual	Wed.	9 PM
1951	Mutual	Fri.	9 PM
1951–1952	Mutual	Tues.	9:30 PM

On this half-hour weekly show, the Mysterious Traveler related his encounters as he traveled around the country by train. "I take this same train each week at this time," the Traveler, who was played by actor Maurice TARPLIN, would say. He would then warn his listeners to "keep a hypo handy for emotional emergencies," because most of the stories involved mystery and adventure. One particularly frightening story heard on the series involved a homocidal maniac's attempt to lure unsuspecting women into his house on the pretense of giving them housekeeping work.

Regularly featured performers were Bill ZUCKERT, Lon CLARK, Roger DeKoven, Ed BEGLEY, Jackson BECK, Vicki VOLA, Robert DRYDEN, James Stevens, Larry Haines, Ralph Bell, Arthur Shirley, and Jan MINER. James "Jimmy" WALLINGTON was the program's announcer for most of the time the series was on the air. The show was directed by Jock MacGregor and written by Robert A. Arthur and David Kogan. The

music for the program was conducted by Emerso Bentley.

MYSTERY THEATER (AKA THE MOLLE MYSTERY THEATER; MYSTERY THEATER WITH MARK SABRE)

1943–1944	NBC	Sun.	9 PM
1944–1945	NBC	Tues.	9 PM
1945–1947	NBC	Fri.	10 PM
1951–1953	ABC	Wed.	8 PM
1953–1954	ABC	Wed.	9:30 PM

Molle shaving cream initially sponsored this weekl series of mystery dramas, which usually featured murder. Bernard Lenrow and Geoffrey Bond were th hosts during the Molle years. Toward the end of it run, the half-hour show was changed to *Hearthston of the Death Squad.* Heard on the series regularly wer Frank READICK, Robert DRYDEN, Bernard Lenrow, an Elspeth ERIC. The series was produced by Frank an Anne HUMMERT and directed by Martha Atwell, Er nest Ricca, Frank K. Telford, Day Tuttle, Kenneth W MACGREGOR, and Henry Howard. In 1952, *The Myster Theater* resurfaced with a leading character name Mark Sabre. Les DAMON and Robert Carroll starred Sabre. Also heard were Walter Burke and Rober Westerfield as Tim Maloney. This version of the *Mys tery Theater* was announced by Roger Foster. Writers for both *The Molle Mystery Theater* and *The Mystery Theater with Mark Sabre* included Frank and Anne HUMMERT, Edward Francis, Lawrence Menkin, Bill Wyman, Joseph Russell, Jay Bennett, Peter Lyon, and

Charles Tazewell. Sponsors included Bayer aspirin, Phillips Milk of Magnesia antacid, Ironized yeast, Dr. Lyon's tooth powder, and Double Danderine shampoo.

See also CBS MYSTERY THEATER.

NAGEL, CONRAD (1896–1971)

Actor Conrad Nagel was born in Keokuk, Iowa. He made his radio debut in 1938 and became the host of such radio programs as *The* RADIO READER'S DIGEST, *The Passing Parade, Seventy Six Revue, The* ALEX TEMPLETON SHOW, and *The* SILVER THEATER, on which he occasionally played the leading male roles. Nagel also guest-starred on many Hollywood-based dramatic anthologies such as LUX RADIO THEATER and SCREEN GUILD PLAYERS. The actor first appeared in films in 1920 and subsequently starred in silent- and sound-screen classics *Little Women* (1919), *Quality Street* (1927), *East Lynne* (1931, and *Navy Spy* (1937). Nagel continued to appear in films until the late 1950s, when he retired.

NAISH, J. CARROLL (JOSEPH CARROLL NAISH 1900–1973)

Actor J. Carroll Naish was born in New York City of Irish descent. He served in the military during World War I before becoming an actor. Naish became best known as Luigi Basco, the lovable Italian immigrant-hero on the popular LIFE WITH LUIGI radio situation-comedy series. In addition, he made guest appearances on such dramatic anthologies as LUX RADIO THEATER, SCREEN GUILD PLAYERS, and *Suspense,* which originated in Hollywood. On television, Naish played the famous Oriental-Hawaiian detective Charlie Chan in the 1950s. Very active in films, he appeared in *Anthony Adverse* (1936), *Beau Geste* (1939), *The Southerner* (1945),*Annie Get Your Gun* (1950), and *The Hanged Man* (1964).

NATIONAL BARN DANCE

1924–1933	WLS	Sat.	9:30 PM
1933–1936	NBC Blue	Sat.	9:30 PM
1936–1941	NBC Blue	Sat.	9 PM
1941–1942	NBC Red	Sat.	9 PM
1942–1946	NBC	Sat.	9 PM
1946–1948	(Off the air)		
1948–1950	ABC	Sat.	10 PM
1950–1960	(Syndicated series. Various times and stations)		

This half-hour country-western music and comedy program was originally heard in 1924 on WLS in Chicago, a powerful 50,000-watt station that could be picked up over a large part of the United States and Canada. In 1933, it could be heard on sixty NBC affiliated stations. *The National Barn Dance* was aired from the Eigth Street Theater in Chicago, where the entire stage was transformed into a hayloft every Saturday night. For many years, Joe Kelly hosted the program of regularly featured and guest performers. Pat Barrett played Uncle Ezra, who always said "Give me a toot on the tooter, Tommy" just before he'd go into his clippety-clop dance steps. Luther Ossiebrink was heard as Arkie, the Arkansas Woodchopper, and Hoyt Allen played Pokey Martin. Also heard on this long-running country show were the Hoosier Hot shots, the Prairie Ramblers, cowgirl Patsy Montana, Pat Buttram, Lulu Belle, and Scotty (who were Myrtl "Lulubelle" Cooper and Scotty Wiseman), Malcolm Claire, the Cumberland Road Runners, Louise Massey and the Westernaires, the Vass Family, Ken and Pau Trietsch, the Wisconsin Honey Bees (Verne, Lee, and Mary), Betty Ross, Grace Wilson, Bob Atcher, Dolph

DeWitt, Homer and Jethro, Red Blanchard, the Dinning Sisters (Ginger, Jean, and Lou), Lee and Mary Trio, "Little" George Gable, "the twelve-year-old boy soprano" Bobby Hastings, Bob Ballentine, Linda Parker (the Sunbonnet Girl), Janie and Connie, Joe Parsons, Sally Foster, Skip Farrell, Eddie Peabody, Joe Parsons, Grace Wilson, Henry Burr, Ted Morse, and the Novelodeons. Gene AUTRY and Red FOLEY were heard on this show early in their careers. The orchestra was led by Glenn Welty. Jack Holden was the program's announcer for many years. The show was produced and written by Peter Lund and Jack Frost and also produced by Walter Wade and Ed Freckman. Bill Jones and W. A. Wade, among others, directed the series. Alka Seltzer, One-A-Day vitamins and Phillips Milk of Magnesia sponsored the series of programs. The show's theme song was "Hail, Hail, the Gang's All Here."

NATIONAL BROADCASTING COMPANY (NBC)

The Radio Corporation of America is one of the largest electronics conglomerates in the United States, and the National Broadcasting Company is one of that company's subsidiaries. In 1919, the General Electric Company, of which RCA was a subsidiary at that time, acquired the MARCONI Wireless Telegraph Company of America from a British-owned company. Marconi Wireless was the only company capable of handling commercial transatlantic radio communication. In 1919 General Electric took it over, with the assistance of the United States Navy, which wanted to keep any new radio technology under American control. For the next fifty years, RCA was led by David SARNOFF, who managed to build his company into one of the largest communications conglomerates in the world. Although Westinghouse in 1920 was the first company to present a commercial broadcast, Sarnoff followed close behind with the first sports broadcast that same year. In 1926, the National Broadcasting Company was formed to carry on RCA's broadcasting activities. When the Federal Commissions Act was passed in 1934, the government began to treat radio as if it were a public utility: its Federal Communications Commission (FCC) doled out licenses, imposed minimum requirements for local community programming, and tried to discourage broadcasting companies from offering the public too many commercials. By 1941, RCA owned two networks, the Blue and the Red, and the FCC—wishing to discourage monopolies in the broadcasting industry—told RCA that it had to get rid of one of its networks. The Blue network was sold to businessman Edward J. Noble in 1943 and eventually became the American Broadcasting Company (ABC); the Red network re-mained NBC's sole radio property. In 1986, the General Electric Company acquired the Radio Corporation of America and its subsidiary, NBC, although most of its local stations had long before been sold to independent owners.

NATIONAL FARM AND HOME HOUR, THE

1929–1930	NBC Blue	Mon.–Fri.	1 PM
1930–1931	NBC Blue	Mon.–Sat.	1:15 PM
1931–1942	NBC Blue	Mon.–Fri.	12:30 PM
1942–1945	NBC Blue	Mon.–Fri.	12:30 PM
1945–1956	NBC	Sat.	1 PM

As "Stars and Stripes Forever" blasted its patriotic tones, rural American listeners prepared to hear *The National Farm and Home Hour,* which offered information about new farm products, crop growing, animal care, useful products for the home by name, child rearing, homemaking, house repair, and so forth. Entertainment was provided by the Cadets male quartet, Jack Baus and the Cornbusters, and Mirandy of Persimmons Holler. The 15-minute show featured Don AMECHE and Raymond Edward JOHNSON, the Forest Ranger. W. E. Driggs directed the show, which was produced by Herbert Layeau. Montgomery Ward was the program's earliest sponsor, and Allis-Chalmers farm equipment and the United States Department of Agriculture paid production costs for the show during its final years.

NATIONAL PUBLIC RADIO (NPR)

There are well over 400 National Public Radio "member" stations nationwide, and people have been tuning in to them for more than twenty years. Approximately 12 million people listen to National Public Radio programs daily in the United States and parts of Canada. These noncommercial, public-supported stations can be heard in forty-eight states, Puerto Rico, and Washington, D.C., and are partners in a national nonprofit organization (NPR). Many of radio's first stations, established at various colleges and universities in the 1920s, were noncommercial and educational in their programming. In the late 1940s, the Federal Communications Commission (FCC) set aside a segment of FM radio time for the exclusive use of educational stations; many of these still exist today. In 1967, Congress passed the Public Broadcasting Act, authorizing the creation of the Corporation for Public Broadcasting to encourage the growth and development of noncommercial radio. National Public Radio was formally created in 1970 to provide leadership in national news gathering and production and to act as the first permanent, nationwide intercommunication among noncommercial stations. National Public Radio's first program was live coverage of the Senate

National Public Radio's legal correspondent, Nina Totenberg (Michael Geissinger)

Vietnam hearings in 1971. Other shows followed, including ALL THINGS CONSIDERED, an evening news magazine; MORNING EDITION, an early-morning news magazine; WEEKEND EDITION, a weekend news show; and PERFORMANCE TODAY, a daily program of recorded classical music. The list of NPR regular programs includes *World of Opera, Heat* with John Hockenberry, *Afropop Worldwide, Car Talk* with Ray and Tom Magliozzi, *Pass the Word,* and *Bluestage.* Because each independent educational radio station has much program autonomy, local stations can present radio drama, comedy, live community concerts, talk shows, and special-interest features. STAR WARS, Garrison Keillor's PRAIRIE HOME COMPANION, and various serialized programs produced by both the CANADIAN BROADCASTING CORPORATION and the British Broadcasting Corporation are available to NPR member stations.

NBC SYMPHONY, THE

1937–1940	NBC Blue	Sat.	10 PM
1940–1941	NBC Blue	Sat.	10:30 PM
1941–1942	NBC Blue	Sat.	9:30 PM
1942–1947	NBC	Sun.	5 PM
1947–1953	NBC	Sat.	6:30 PM

David SARNOFF, National Broadcasting Company founder and president, believed that one of radio's most important functions was to provide culture, particularly good music programs. In 1936, under Sarnoff's direction, NBC formed the NBC Symphony orchestra to present such entertainment on a weekly basis. Its first conductor was Maestro Arturo Toscanini, one of the world's most respected musicians. Pierre Monteaux also led the NBC orchestra. Dr. Frank Black offered musical commentaries. The finest musicians were assembled to play in the orchestra, and the symphony became one of America's best classical music organizations. A specially designed studio was constructed for the program at Radio City in New York City, where NBC's main studios were located. Ben GRAUER announced for most of the years the NBC Symphony was on the air. General Motors and House of Squibb drugs sponsored the series.

NBC THEATER, THE

See SCREEN DIRECTOR'S PLAYHOUSE.

NBC UNIVERSITY THEATER OF THE AIR, THE

1948–1949	NBC	Fri.	9 PM
	NBC	Sun.	2:30 PM
	NBC	Sat.	6:30 PM
1949–1950	NBC	Sun.	2 PM
1950–1951	NBC	Sun.	3 PM
		Thurs.	10 PM
		Sun.	10:30 PM
		Sat.	6:30 PM
		Wed.	10:30 PM

This hour-long dramatic anthology series presented adaptations of great works of literature and was required listening for many students. *NBC University Theater of the Air* featured many talented performers such as Alfred Lunt, Lynn Fontanne, Helen HAYES, and Burgess MEREDITH. Some of the novels and plays adapted for this series were Henry James's *Portrait of a Lady,* and *The Ambassadors,* D. H. Lawrence's *Sons and Lovers,* Ibsen's *Hedda Gabler,* Maxwell Anderson's *Dark Laughter,* Fielding's *Tom Jones,* Katherine Porter's *Noon Wine,* Graham Greene's *England Made Mad,* Edith Wharton's *The House of Mirth,* Thomas Hardy's *The Mayor of Casterbridge,* Anatole France's *The Crime of Sylvester,* and Chekhov's *The Darling.* Many NBC staff announcers, directors, and writers worked on this series, and practically every radio actor in New York performed on the NBC-produced series.

NED JORDAN, SECRET AGENT

1938	(Syndicated series. Various stations and times)		
1939–1940	Mutual	Thurs.	9:30 & 8:30 PM 10 PM
1941–1942	Mutual	Sun.	10:30 PM
1942	Mutual	Sat.	2 PM

The half-hour children's adventure serial *Ned Jordan, Secret Agent* first went on the air prior to United States involvement in World War II. Jack McCarthy starred as Jordan, a special agent for the railroad. When the United States entered the war, Ned went to work for the government as a secret-service agent. Al HODGE, later known as television's *Captain Video*, was the program's director. The syndicated program was written by various freelance writers and sponsored by a variety of local companies depending upon where it was heard.

NELSON, FRANK (1911–1986)

Actor Frank Nelson was born in Denver, Colorado. He was best known as the Floorwalker and various other officious characters on *The* JACK BENNY SHOW. Nelson usually greeted Benny with the long, drawn-out and unctuous "Yeeeeees?" He was also active on hundreds of other radio shows, such as BLONDIE (as Herb Woodley, Dagwood and Blondie's next-door neighbor), *The* EDDIE CANTOR SHOW, MEET ME AT PARKY'S, BURNS AND ALLEN, *The* DANNY KAYE SHOW, BABY SNOOKS SHOW, and *The* LUX RADIO THEATER. A busy commercial voice-over performer during the last years of his career, he spoke for numerous cartoon characters in such animated television shows and films as "The Mouse and His Child" (1977), "The Little Rascals' Christmas Special" (1982), "Puff, the Magic Dragon" (1978), "Thanksgiving in the Land of Oz" (1980), "The All New Popeye Hour" (1978–1981), "Baggy Pants and the Nit Wits" (1977–1978), "The Oddball Couple" (1975–1977), and "The Snorks" (1984–1985).

NELSON, OZZIE (OSWALD NELSON 1906–1975)

Popular bandleader Ozzie Nelson was born in Jersey City, North Dakota, and attended Rutgers University. He intended to study law, but always interested in music, he entered show business instead. Ozzie led the orchestras on *The Feg Murray Show, The* JOE PENNER SHOW, *The* RED SKELTON SHOW, and BELIEVE IT OR NOT. However, he is best remembered for *The* ADVENTURES *of* OZZIE AND HARRIET radio and television series. Ozzie, Harriet, and their sons David and Ricky played themselves on the series.

NERO WOLFE, THE ADVENTURES OF

See ADVENTURES OF NERO WOLFE, THE.

NEW YORK PHILHARMONIC

1927–1935	(Various formats and times)		
1935–1950	CBS	Sun.	3 PM
1950–1951	CBS	Sun.	1 PM
1951–1956	CBS	Sun.	2:30 PM
1956–1957	CBS	Sun.	3 PM
1957–1958	CBS	Sun.	3:05 PM
1958–1960	CBS	Sat.	8:30 PM
1960–1963	CBS	Sat.	9:15 PM
1963–1964	Mutual	Sun.	3 PM
1964–1966	Mutual	Sat.	8:30 PM

This show presented classical music by the world's most celebrated composers. Georges Enesco led the New York Philharmonic when the orchestra first went on the air in the late 1920s. Bruno Walter, Arturo Toscanini, and Leonard Bernstein also conducted. Deems TAYLOR, Frank Gallop, and Milton CROSS acted as weekly hosts. Sponsors included U.S. Rubber, Standard Oil of New Jersey, and Willy's Motors.

NEWSCASTERS

In the 1920s, most Americans relied almost entirely on their newspapers to get the news of the day or week. But as radio increasingly found its way into more homes, broadcasting stations began to realize that they could get the news to the public faster and more concisely by periodically reading condensed news stories over the airwaves. News reports throughout radio's history have been broadcast early in the morning (usually at 7 AM), at noon, and at night (10 or 11 PM). This is a format that is practiced to this day by most television networks, too. Throughout the 1930s, 1940s, and 1950s, newscasts were usually 5 minutes in length and then expanded to 15 minutes. The broadcasts by special newscasters and commentators were given increasingly more air time; when an important news event was taking place—such as invasion during World War II or an election—strict time slots were not adhered to.

The earliest newscasters were usually technicians who happened to be working at the first small stations. As these stations were bought up by the large networks, huge news departments were formed and news personalities began to have names that went with their previously anonymous voices. Some of the more celebrated radio newsmen included Gabriel HEATTER, Floyd Gibbons; Hans V. KALTENBORN, Paul HARVEY, Boake Carter, Fulton LEWIS, Jr., Herbert MORRISON, Drew PEARSON, and Edward R. MURROW, whose broadcasts from war-torn London were a major contributing factor in making Americans aware of pre–World War II events. At this time, fewer than ten thousand Americans had television receivers in their homes, so people had to rely on their radios for the latest war news. Newscaster Johnny Carpenter reported the action live from various European battlefronts to millions of American households.

Other newscasters whose voices became immediately identifiable by radio listeners included John Charles DALY, Cedric Adams, Morgan BEATTY, Bob

Considine, John Vandercook, B. S. Bercovici, Don Gardiner, George Hicks, Walter Kiernan, Fulton Oursler, Elmer Peterson, Quentin Reynolds, Eric SEVAREID, Mike Douglas, Walter CRONKITE, Lisa Sergio, Robert TROUT, Cedric Foster, Harrison Wood, Frank Edwards, George Sokolsky, Howard K. SMITH, John Cameron SWAYZE, Martin Agronsky, Pauline Fredericks, Everett Holles, Cecil Brown, Cal Tinney, Taylor Grant, Ray Henle, Felix Morley, Ned Brooks, and Upton Close. Currently in the United States NPR, ABC, CBS, and NBC provide syndicated national news coverage to local radio stations who purchase the service.

NICK CARTER, MASTER DETECTIVE

1943	Mutual	Sun.	5:30 PM
		Tues.	9:30 PM
		Wed.	8:30 PM
1943–1944	Mutual	Sat.	7 PM
1944–1945	Mutual	Sun.	3:30 PM
1945–1946	Mutual	Sun.	6 PM
1946–1952	Mutual	Sun.	6:30 PM
1952–1953	Mutual	Sun.	6 PM
1953–1955	Mutual	Sun.	4:30 PM

"Yes, it's another case for that most famous of all manhunters . . . the detective whose ability at solving crime is unequaled in the history of detective fiction: *Nick Carter, Master Detective!*" these broadcasts began. This mystery-adventure series' entire run starred actor Lon CLARK as Carter. Helen Choate and then Charlotte Manson played Patsy Bowen, Carter's girlfriend and assistant crime solver. Ed Latimer was heard as Sergeant "Mattie" Mathison; John Kane played Scrubby; and John RABY, Bill LIPTON, Joseph "Joe" Latham, Raymond Edward JOHNSON, James Kreiger, and Bryna Raeburn were heard in the supporting cast.

An urbane, sophisticated private detective, Nick Carter used logical deductions to expose criminals and solve his cases. This quality endeared him to mystery-loving fans, who read and listened to every detective-mystery story they could. To the delight of his many fans, at the end of each show, Nick always related to his girlfriend, Patty, just how he had been able to track down the murderer or thief.

The series was produced and directed by Jock MacGregor and written by Milton J. Kramer, David Kogan, John McGreevey, Ferrin N. Frazer, Norman Daniels, and Alfred Bester. Ken Powell and Michael Fitzmaurice were the program's announcers. Sponsors included Lin-X starch, Mem-tone face cream, Old Dutch cleanser, Delrich dairies, and Libby's baby food.

NIGHTBEAT

| 1950–1952 | NBC | Fri. | 10 PM |

Actor Frank LOVEJOY starred as Randy "Lucky" Stone, a hard-boiled city reporter for the fictional *Chicago Star* newspaper, who had a talent for stumbling upon murder and adventure in his attempts to report the news. Supporting players included Jeff Corey, Larry Dobkin, Lurene TUTTLE, Herb Butterfield, Joan BANKS, Vivi Janis, Georgia Ellis, Ben WRIGHT, William CONRAD, and Lou Merrill. The half-hour series was produced and written by Russell Hughes and also directed by Warren Lewis. Don Rickles was the program's announcer. Wheaties cereal sponsored the series.

NIGHTFALL

| 1980–1983 | CBC & NPR (Syndicated series. Various NPR stations in the United States) |

This half-hour series, produced by the CANADIAN BROADCASTING CORPORATION and heard in Canada, was rebroadcasted on NATIONAL PUBLIC RADIO stations throughout the United States. Adaptations of contemporary and classic short stories such as "The Body Snatchers" by P. L. Stevenson and John Graham's "Love and the Lonely One" featured Canadian actors Neal Munro, Graham Haley, Robert Christy, Wendy Thatcher, Elva May Hoover, Mignon Elkins, Jay Bowen, John Stocker, and Eric House. The program was produced and directed by Bill Howell.

NILES, KEN (1907–1988)

Ken Niles, whose brother Wendell was also a radio announcer, introduced hundreds of programs to the listening public during the 1930s and 1940s. Born in Twin Valley, Minnesota, he announced such varied programs as The ABBOTT AND COSTELLO SHOW, BURNS AND ALLEN, BIG TOWN, GATEWAY TO HOLLYWOOD, The DANNY KAYE SHOW, HOLLYWOOD HOTEL, and PARTIES AT PICKFAIR. Niles continued to work as a voice-over announcer until he retired in the early 1980s.

NILES, WENDELL (1904–1994)

Announcer-writer-producer Wendell Niles was born in Twin Valley, Minnesota, and attended the University of Montana and then New York University before entering radio as an orchestra leader in 1923. Niles, the brother of Ken Niles, announced The CHASE AND SANBORN HOUR, MELODY RANCH, AL PEARCE AND HIS GANG, The Old Gold–DON AMECHE SHOW, and many other programs. Niles also narrated many film shorts and "coming attraction" movie trailers for most of the major motion-picture studios.

NOBLE, RAY (1908–1978)

Born in Brighton, England, orchestra leader Ray Noble is perhaps best remembered as the witty British band leader who exchanged jokes with Edgar BERGEN and Charlie McCarthy on The CHASE AND SANBORN HOUR and EDGAR BERGEN–CHARLIE MCCARTHY SHOW. After attending Dulwich College in Sussex, England, Noble joined the British (RCA) Victor Company in 1927 as a musician. He began to lead various orchestras for that company and in 1933 traveled to the United States with his own orchestra to fulfill an engagement at the celebrated Rainbow Room in New York City. He made radio appearances on BURNS AND ALLEN as well as on numerous big-band remote broadcasts and even appeared in several films, including *Here We Go Again* (1942) and *Second Fiddle* (1940). Noble retired from show business in the mid-1960s.

NOBLETTE, IRENE

See RYAN, IRENE.

NOBODY'S CHILDREN

1939–1940	Mutual	Sun., Sat.	2:30 PM
1940–1941	Mutual	Sun.	10 PM
1941–1942	Mutual	Sun.	7:30 PM

This half-hour series, originating in Los Angeles's KHJ's Mutual network outlet, gave orphans a chance to be adopted by a responsible and caring family. The orphans told their stories on the air and were always accompanied by a special guest star, who made an appeal to members of the listening audience to adopt them. As a result of these broadcasts, many children were successfully placed in happy homes. However, the FCC and various lobby groups protested that the series was too much like "a slave market," and the program was eventually taken off the air. Walter White, Jr., was the program's host; the matron who introduced each guest and child was played by Georgia Fifield. Robert Mitchell's Boys' Choir performed on the show. Guest celebrites included Bob HOPE, James Cagney, Joe E. BROWN, Jack BENNY, and Barbara Stanwyck. Bill Kennedy was the program's announcer.

NOLAN, JEANETTE (1911–)

Character actress Jeanette Nolan was born in Los Angeles, California. On radio, Nolan played Nicolette on Carlton E. Morse's ONE MAN'S FAMILY and was also a regular supporting player on SUSPENSE, *The* ADVENTURES OF SAM SPADE, DETECTIVE, *The* CAVALCADE OF AMERICA, *The* COURT OF MISSING HEIRS, LIFE BEGINS AT EIGHTY, *The* MARCH OF TIME (often playing Eleanor ROOSEVELT), *The* PHILIP MORRIS PLAYHOUSE, and GUNSMOKE. Although she also appeared in many films, Nolan's most famous movie role was as Lady

Jeanette Nolan (CBS-TV)

Macbeth in Orson Welles's *Macbeth* (1948). Her other films were *No Sad Songs for Me* (1950), *The Big Heat* (1953), *April Love* (1957), and *Chamber of Horrors* (1978). She has been featured on such television series as "Gunsmoke" "Dragnet" (1952–1958) and "Jake and the Fat Man" (1991). Nolan is still active in films and on television.

NORTHERN MESSENGER

1930s–present   CBC   Mon.–Sun.   (Various times)

The CANADIAN BROADCASTING CORPORATION (CBC) broadcasts to the farthest northern regions of Canada via its *Northern Messenger* service. This service covers a vast area of 4 millions square kilometers of bush, muskeg, tundra, and barren lands in regions that include the Northwest Territories, the Yukon, the James Bay area, and the Arctic Circle. The northern service provides a blend of local, regional, and national programming, enabling listeners living in these remote regions to keep in touch with one another and the world.

OBLER, ARCH (1910–1987)

According to newspaper and magazine critics, Arch Obler was the United States's foremost radio mystery writer in the 1930s, 1940s, and 1950s. Obler, who was born in New York and educated at the Hyde Park School and the University of Chicago, began to write for radio in Chicago in the mid-1930s. He was responsible for such programs as LIGHTS OUT and *The Arch Obler Theater* because of his well-written scripts and expertise as a director. He also authored more than 200 short stories. Obler's scripts always realized the full potential of sound to create effective radio drama, and he always insisted on absolutely authentic sound effects on his shows. In addition to his own series, Obler wrote scripts for such nonmystery programs as GRAND HOTEL, EVERYMAN'S THEATER, IRENE RICH DRAMAS, *The Gelatin Hour, The* MAGIC KEY OF RCA, and *Your Hollywood.* He later produced several films, including the first three-dimensional motion picture, *Bwana Devil,* in 1952.

O'DAY, MICHAEL "MICKEY" (1920–1982)

One of the many talented child actors who began their careers performing on the COAST TO COAST ON A BUS and LET'S PRETEND radio programs, Michael O'Day, was born in Newark, New Jersey. Like other children who appeared on these shows, he continued his career on radio as he grew older. O'Day was Richard Parker on *The* PARKER FAMILY, the Newsboy on BIG TOWN, Neddie Evans, the son of BIG SISTER Ruth Evans, and Jinky on *Robinson Crusoe Jr.* Before he reached adulthood, O'Day was also heard on *The* KRAFT MUSIC HALL, FORTY-FIVE MINUTES TO HOLLYWOOD, CAVALCADE OF AMERICA, *The* ALDRICH FAMILY, *The* LANNY ROSS SHOW, *The* MARCH OF TIME, and his

own short-lived *Michael O'Day Show.* O'Day disc-jock eyed for a local station in New Jersey in the earl 1960s.

OFFICIAL DETECTIVE

1947	Mutual	Sun.	2:15 PM
		Tues.	8:15 PM
1947–1948	Mutual	Tues.	8:30 PM
		Sat.	1:30 PM & 2 PM
1949–1952	Mutual	Tues.	8:30 PM
		Sun.	8 PM
1952–1953	Mutual	Sun.	6:30 PM
1953–1957	(Syndicated series. Various stations and times)		

According to its opening, the half-hour *Official Detec tive* series was "dedicated to the men who guard you safety and protect your home, your police depart ment!" This program accurately and realistically de picted a typical police department's procedures with regard to tracking down criminals. When the show first went on the air, Joe McCormack starred as Detec tive Dan Britt. He was replaced by veteran radio actor Ed BEGLEY, and Begley by Craig McDonnell. Actor Louis Nye, later famous as a regular on "The Steve Allen Show" on television, played the police sergeant Also heard were Bill ZUCKERT, Charles "Chuck" Web ster, and Alan Stevenson. Dwight WEIST announced the series. It was directed by Wynn Wright and writ ten by Jack Bentkover and William Wells. The show was heard in syndication on most Mutual stations.

O'KEEFE, WALTER (1901–1983)

Singer, comedian, and radio-program host Walter O'Keefe was stricken with infantile paralysis as a young man. While in the hospital, he wrote a play and sent it to producer-writer John Golden, who encouraged him with favorable comments. Upon his release from the hospital, O'Keefe decided to continue his career in show business and went to New York City. After appearing at Texas Guinan's nightclub and in Barney Gallant's Greenwich Village nightclub as a singer, O'Keefe went to Hollywood, where he wrote songs for films. He appeared on *The* PAUL WHITEMAN SHOW performing with a group called the Rhythm Boys in 1930 and eventually became a singer-soloist and then a radio-show host on *The* BATTLE OF THE SEXES and DOUBLE OR NOTHING. O'Keefe quietly retired from show business in the late 1950s.

OLD GOLD SHOW, THE
See DON AMECHE SHOW, THE.

OLIVIO SANTORO SHOW, THE

| 1940–1941 | NBC Blue | Mon.–Fri. | 7:15 PM |

One unlikely performer who became a radio star for a short period of time was Olivio Santoro, the Boy Yodeler. Olivio was a talented young teen who played the guitar, sang, and yodeled. His 15-minute weekday program followed the popular MOYLAN SISTERS' program and, therefore, he was guaranteed a considerable audience. After announcer Glenn Riggs introduced the show, Olivio sang, and of course yodeled. The show's theme song was sung to the tune of "Ta-Ra-Ra-Boom-De-Ay":

> Scrapple o-del-ay-de-ay
> Comes from Phil-a-del-phi-ay!
> Eat Philadelphia Scrapple, friends
> With that advice, my story ends!

When the boy yodeler retired from the airwaves, one of the most asked questions among show business people was "What the hell ever happened to Olivio Santoro?" It has been reported that Olivio eventually became a very successful businessman. The *Olivio Santoro Show's* sponsor was Scrapple, a breakfast side dish of heavily breaded sausage patties.

OLMSTED, NELSON (1914–1992)
Actor Nelson Olmsted was born in Minneapolis, Minnesota, but grew up in Texas. Considered one of the best storytellers on radio, he had a one-man show on which he read stories and played all the parts. A wonderful reader, he breathed new life into stories by O. Henry, de Maupassant, Poe, and other masters of the short story. The program was called STORIES BY OLMSTED. The actor was also heard on *The World's Greatest Stories* and *Nelson Olmsted's Sleep No More.* In addition, he played the parts of Paul Martel on AR-

NOLD GRIMM'S DAUGHTERS, Joe Houston on BACHELOR'S CHILDREN, and Edgar Lee on *In Care of Aggie Horn,* as well as acting on *The* CHICAGO THEATER OF THE AIR, which originated in Chicago in the late 1930s.

ON STAGE

1952–1953	CBS	Thurs.	8:30 PM
1953–1954	CBS	Wed.	8:30 PM
1954	CBS	Wed., Thurs.	9 PM

Husband and wife Elliott and Cathy LEWIS starred on this half-hour weekly dramatic anthology that displayed their acting versatility in comedies, suspense stories, mysteries, thrillers, romances, and adventure tales. Also heard were Clayton Post, GeGe Pearson, Peggy Allenby, Ben Wright, Tony Barrett, Edgar Barrier, Harry Bartel, Peggy Webber, John MCINTIRE, John Dehner, Barney Phillips, Byron Kane, and William CONRAD. George Walsh was the program's announcer. Elliott Lewis was the show's director. The program was sustained by CBS.

ONE MAN'S FAMILY

1933–1934	NBC Red	Sat.	11 PM
1934–1935	NBC Red	Wed.	10:30 PM
1935–1938	NBC Red	Wed.	8 PM
1938–1941	NBC Red	Thurs.	8 PM
1941–1942	NBC Red	Sun.	8:30 PM
1942–1945	NBC	Sun.	8:30 PM
1945–1949	NBC	Sun.	3:30 PM
1949–1950	NBC	Sun.	3 PM
1950–1957	NBC	Mon.–Fri.	7:45 PM
1957–1959	NBC	Mon.–Fri.	2:30 PM

One of the first and best of radio's family serial dramas, Carlton E. MORSE's *One Man's Family* had a large following of faithful listeners who literally grew up with the major characters on the series—the Barbour family and their friends. The Barbour family's story enfolded in "chapters" and "books," and by the time the series left the air in 1959, Chapter 30 of Book 134 had been aired.

The family home was a large, comfortable house overlooking San Francisco Bay and the Golden Gate Bridge in an area called Sea Cliff. Henry and Fanny's five children were Paul, Hazel, their twins Clifford and Claudia, and their youngest son, Jack.

Actor J. Anthony SMYTHE played Father Barbour, an investment broker, the entire time the series was on the air. Minetta ELLEN was Fanny for most of the show's run, with Mary Adams playing the part for the last three years. Michael RAFFETTO was Paul, the ex–World War I army pilot and eldest son of the Barbours; Bernice Berwin, Hazel; Barton YARBOROUGH, Clifford; Kathleen Wilson and then Floy Margaret Hughes, Barbara Fuller, and Laurette FILLBRANDT played Claudia; and Page Gilman played Jack, the

One Man's Family: (clockwise from top) Winifred Wolfe, Kathleen Wilson, Bernice Berwin, J. Anthony Smythe, Minetta Ellen, Michael Raffetto, Barton Yarborough, Anne Shelley, and (center) Page Gilman (Courtesy of Carlton E. Morse)

youngest child. For many years, Winifred Wolfe portrayed Paul's adopted daughter, Teddy. Ann Shelly and then Mary Lou Harrington were Claudia's troubled daughter, Joan. Claudia's English husband, Nicholas Lacey, was acted by Walter Paterson and then by Tom Collins, Dan O'Herlihy, and Ben WRIGHT. Father Barbour's favorite grandchild, Margaret, Hazel's youngest child, was played by Dawn Bender; Hazel's twin sons Pinky and Hank were played by several young actors, including Richard Svihus, Dix Davis, Billy Idelson, Eddie Firestone, Jr., Tommy Bernard, George Pirrone, Conrad Binyon, and Dickie Meyers. Among the radio actors heard in supporting roles were Janet WALDO, Jack Edwards, Jr., Ruth Perrott, Anne Stone, Jay Novello, William Greene, Wally Maher, Bill BOUCHEY, Russell Thorson, (who also played Paul on the program's last few years), Virginia GREGG, Jeanne Bates, Anne Whitfield, Tyler McVey, Sharon Douglas, Jeanette NOLAN, Lenore Ledoux (who played various baby roles on the show), Mary Jane CROFT, Marvin MILLER, Hans CONRIED, Richard

CRENNA, Ted DeCorsia, Larry Dobkin, Rosemary DE CAMP, Alice REINHEART, Barbara Jean Wong, Luis VAN ROOTEN, Helen Kleeb, Forrest Lewis, James "Jimmy" McCallion, Francis X. Bushman, Elliott LEWIS, John MCINTIRE, and Mercedes MCCAMBRIDGE.

The show was directed at one time by Carlton E Morse, the program's creator and only writer, and Michael Raffetto, Clinton Twiss, Charles Buck, and George Fogle. Announcers included William An drews, Ken CARPENTER, and Frank Barton. *One Man's Family's* memorable theme music was Brahms's "Destiny Waltz" and "Patricia" by Paul Carson. Sponsors were Wesson oil, Snow Drift detergent, Kentucky Winner tobacco, Standard Brands foods, Tender Lea tea, Chase and Sanborn coffee, Alka Seltzer antacid Bactine disinfectant, Tabcin pain reliever, Toni home permanent, Sweetheart soap, Blu White bleach Fleischmann's yeast, and Miles Laboratories.

O'NEILLS, THE

1935–1936	CBS	Mon., Wed., Fri.	7:30 PM
1936–1937	NBC Red	Mon.–Fri.	3:45 PM
1937–1938	NBC Blue	Mon.–Fri.	11 AM
	& Red		3:45 PM
1938–1939	NBC Red	Mon.–Fri.	12:15 PM
	& CBS		2:45 PM
1939–1940	NBC Red	Mon.–Fri.	12:15 PM
1940–1941	NBC Red	Mon.–Fri.	12:15 PM
	CBS		5:30 PM
1941–1942	CBS	Mon.–Fri.	5:30 PM
1942–1943	NBC Red	Mon.–Fri.	10:15 AM

One of the earliest 15-minute drama serials on radio *The O'Neills* was first heard in 1935. The series fea tured Kate McComb, Vivia Ogden, and then Luise Barclay as Mother O'Neill, a widowed Irish immigran bringing up her brood of three alone in a fictitiou American town called Royalton. A benevolen woman, Mother O'Neill was the one everyone in the town came to for help. Heard in continuing roles were Arline Blackburn, Ethel Everett, Mary Patton, Jimmy Donnelly, James Van Dyke, Effie Palmer, Betty WINK LER, Betty Caine, Violet Dunn, Janice Gilbert, Jack Rubin, Claire Niesen, Betty GARDE, Jimmy Tanney GeGe James, Julian Noa, Santos ORTEGA, Joe JULLIAN Marjorie Anderson, David GOTHARD, Roger De Koven John McGovern, Lawson Zerbe, Josephine Hull, Sel ena Royle, Jack Rubin, Helen Claire, Jack "Jackie" Jordan, Roy Fant, Jane West, and Chester STRATTON Announcing the program were Ed HERLIHY, Alan Kent, and Craig McDonnell. Jack Rubin and Carlo DEANGELO directed the series, and Jane West and Jack Rubin were the program's writers. Sponsors of thi program included Silver Dust, Ivory soap and Ivory soap flakes. The program's theme song was "The Londonderry Air."

OPEN DOOR, THE

| 1943–1944 | CBS | Mon.–Fri. | 10:30 AM |
| 1944 | NBC | Mon.–Fri. | 12 PM |

he setting of this drama series was a fictional Ameri-
an college called Jefferson University. Dr. Alfred T.
orf, an actual college professor, starred as Eric Han-
on, the Dean of Students who solved mysteries at
nd around the campus. Heard on this 15-minute
rogram in regular roles were Barbara Weeks and
en Florence FREEMAN as Liza Arnold; Edwin Bruce
Timmy; Martin Blaine as Ivan Jones; Charlotte
olland as Corey Lehman, Dean Hansen's secretary;
nd John Brown, Ethel Intropidi, Jane Houston, Joan
lexander, and Alexander SCOURBY. Arnold MOSS was
e show's announcer. Royal Gelatin, Royal Pudding,
nd Tender Leaf tea sponsored the series. Professor
orf also directed the series, which was written by
ndra Michael and Dona Folliet. The program's
eme song was "Sim Sala."

OPEN HOUSE

| 1986–1993 | CBC | Sat., Sun. | 8:11 (Stereo-FM) |
| | | | 7:05 (Radio-AM) |

he CANADIAN BROADCASTING CORPORATION's two-
our series Open House, hosted by Marguerite Mac-
onald, covered a wide variety of subjects such as the
eaning of dreams, the value of humor in different
ultures, and the spiritual connection between Cana-
ians and their land. The show also explored beliefs
nd how they affect personal and social relationships
nd presented interviews, documentaries, dramas, po-
ry, and storytelling centered on people and human
alues. The show was produced by Dave Redell.

ORCHESTRA LEADERS

rom the 1920s through the 1940s, variety-comedy
rograms always had a full orchestra to provide the
pening, closing and interval music as well as musical
ccompaniment for the songs performed. Often, the
usic conductors were well-known dance-band lead-
rs or classically trained musicians who had led large
oncert stage orchestras. Prime-time dramatic antholo-
ies such as The LUX RADIO THEATER, The FORD THE-
TER, and The MERCURY THEATER ON THE AIR always
ad full orchestras to provide the theme music and
usical bridges heard between scenes. Occasionally,
rominent bandleaders such as Paul WHITEMAN,
ammy KAYE, Ozzie NELSON, and Wayne KING re-
eived radio star status and had shows of their own.
ther successful orchestra leaders were Horace HEIDT,
incent Lopez, Phil HARRIS, Bob CROSBY, Ted WEEMS,
avier Cugat, Ray NOBLE, Freddie Rich, Jolly Coburn,
nd Don Redmond. World-renowned classical-music

conductors such as Arturo Toscanini (who led the
famous NBC Symphony orchestra), Howard Barlow
(of The VOICE OF FIRESTONE), and Arthur Fiedler (who
led the Boston Pops Orchestra) became even more
famous for their work on radio than they were for
their concert stage performances.

ORGANISTS

Instead of assuming the expense of a full orchestra
and conductor to play theme songs, musical bridges,
and closing music, many radio producers opted to
have a single, talented organist supply all of the music
for a particular program. Daytime serial dramas, children's adventure shows, and mystery and horror programs commonly employed organists. A list of some
of radio's most prominent organists and their respective programs includes Sybil Bock (Lum and Abner),
Lou Bring (MAJOR HOOPLE), Paul Carson (ONE MAN'S
FAMILY), Gaylord Carter (AMOS AND ANDY), Milton
Charles (BACHELOR'S CHILDREN), Sybil Chism (ONE
MAN'S FAMILY), John Duffy (LASSIE), John Gart (BRIGHT
HORIZON), Dolph Gobel (ETHEL AND ALBERT), Martha
Green (ONE MAN'S FAMILY), Skitch Henderson (Smile
Time), George Henninger (MODERN ROMANCES), Eddie
House (MYRT AND MARGE), Chester Kingbury (HILLTOP
HOUSE, The SECOND MRS. BURTON), Eddie Layton (nu-
merous shows), Ann Leaf (LORENZO JONES), Richard
Leibert (BIG SISTER, The SECOND MRS. BURTON, STELLA
DALLAS, WHEN A GIRL MARRIES), Herschel Leucke (LIFE
CAN BE BEAUTIFUL, WE LOVE AND LEARN), William
Meeder (PEPPER YOUNG'S FAMILY, The RIGHT TO HAPPI-
NESS), Charles Paul (The ROAD OF LIFE, The SHADOW,
THIS IS NORA DRAKE, YOUNG DR. MALONE), Rosa Rio
(BETWEEN THE BOOKENDS, The SHADOW, CAVALCADE OF
AMERICA, COURT OF MISSING HEIRS, DEADLINE DRAMA,
ETHEL AND ALBERT, FRONT PAGE FARRELL, HANNIBAL
COBB, LORENZO JONES, MY TRUE STORY, MYRT AND
MARGE, Rosa Rio Rhythms, WHEN A GIRL MARRIES),
Ted Steele (Society Girl), Henry Sylvern (NICK CARTER,
MASTER DETECTIVE, PHILO VANCE), Elsie Thompson
(AUNT JENNY, The SHADOW), Jack Ward (The MAGNIFI-
CENT MONTAGUE), Doc Whipple (MA PERKINS), Lew
White (ETHEL AND ALBERT), John Winters (MR. KEEN,
TRACER OF LOST PERSONS, MYRT AND MARGE, WHEN A
GIRL MARRIES, YOUNG WIDDER BROWN), and George
Wright (ARCHIE ANDREWS).

ORIGINAL AMATEUR HOUR, THE (AKA MAJOR BOWES AND HIS ORIGINAL AMATEUR HOUR)

1935–1936	NBC Red	Sun.	8 PM
1936–1945	CBS	Thurs.	9 PM
1945–1948	(Off the air)		
1948–1949	ABC	Wed.	8 PM
1949–1952	ABC	Thurs.	9 PM

"The weekly wheel of fortune . . . Around and around she goes and where she stops, nobody knows," the host of this series, Major Edward BOWES, announced at the beginning of each program. First heard on local station WHN in New York in 1934, this one-hour and later half-hour program was graduated to network status on the CBS and then the ABC network. Radio's foremost amateur-talent-contest show, *The Original Amateur Hour* was also hosted by movie character actor J. C. Flippen (1948) and then by Ted Mack (1949–1952), who was also the star of the television version of the series. Every conceivable type of "talent" was showcased on this show from spoon and washtub players to opera and pop singers. One star, Frank Sinatra, received his first national exposure on this program in 1941. Produced by Lou Goldberg, the show was directed by Bob Reed, Lloyd Marx, and John Gordon. Graham MCNAMEE, Paul Carlin, Norman BROKENSHIRE, Jimmy WALLINGTON, Ralph EDWARDS, Dan SEYMOUR, Dennis James, Tony Marvin, Warren Sweeney, and Don HANCOCK announced the series over the years. The show's theme songs were "Stand By" and Irving Berlin's "There's No Business Like Show Business." Chase and Sanborn coffee, Chrysler automobiles, and Old Gold cigarettes sponsored the program.

ORPHANS OF DIVORCE

1939	NBC Blue	Mon.	7 PM
1939–1942	NBC Blue	Mon.–Fri.	3 PM

This half-hour and then 15-minute drama series was one of many shows produced by Frank and Anne HUMMERT. The "orphans" were played by Richard Gordon, Claire Wilson, Patricia Peardon, and Warren Bryan. The woman who adopted them, Nora Worthington, was played by Margaret Anglin and then by Effie Palmer. Rather advanced for its time, *Orphans of Divorce* dealt with the problems children of divorced parents have and was an accurate reflection of society's dim view of divorce in the 1930s and 1940s. Divorce was an unusual occurrence, and all children of divorced parents were considered victims at the time. They were called "orphans" because, like real orphans, they were without at least one parent. Appearing on the series in supporting roles were James MEIGHAN, Louis Hall, Geraldine Kay, James Krieger, Vivia Ogden, Joan Tompkins, Charita Bauer, Richard Keith, Joseph JULLIAN, Louis Hall, Richard Keith, and Henry Neely. Stuart Metz announced the program. Richard Leonard directed the series, and Doris Halman was the show's major writer. The program's theme song was "I'll Take You Home Again, Kathleen." *Orphans of Divorce* was sponsored by Dr. Lyon's tooth powder.

ORTEGA, SANTOS (1900–1976)

New York City–born character actor Santos Ortega began his acting career on the stage at the age of seventeen and went on to play leading and supporting roles in radio. Few actors played roles as diversified as Ortega's. He was Nero Wolfe on *The ADVENTURES OF NERO WOLFE*, Hannibal Cobb on *Hannibal Cobb, Detective*, Charlie Chan on *The ADVENTURES OF CHARLIE CHAN*, Bulldog Drummond on *The ADVENTURES OF BULLDOG DRUMMOND*, Perry Mason on PERRY MASON, and Commissioner Weston on *The SHADOW*. The actor played the title role on the unsuccessful *Roger Kilgore, Public Defender* series and had regular-running roles on THIS DAY IS OURS, BIG SISTER, BRIGHT HORIZON, JOYCE JORDAN, GIRL INTERN, MYRT AND MARGE, and OUR GAL SUNDAY. In addition, Ortega was a regular on QUICK AS A FLASH, THIS IS YOUR FBI, and INNER SANCTUM MYSTERIES. Ortega continued his busy acting career on television and was featured on "The Brighter Day" (1954–1955) and "As the World Turns" (1956–1976).

OUR DAILY FOOD

1930–1931	NBC Red	Mon.–Sat.	9:45 AM
1931–1932	NBC's Red & Blue	Mon.–Sat.	9:45 AM
			10:30 AM

Both Red and Blue networks of NBC presented this series, which concerned food tips, recipes, food programs for schools, and other related information. Hosted by a fictitious character named Colonel Goodbody (whose real identity was never revealed), the series was sponsored by the A & P food-chain company.

OUR GAL SUNDAY (AKA RICH MAN'S DARLING)

1936–1937	CBS	Mon.–Fri.	11:45 AM
1937–1959	CBS	Mon.–Fri.	12:45 PM

Titled *Rich Man's Darling* at first, this long-running 15-minute soap opera originally asked the question "Can a girl from a mining town out West find happiness as the wife of a wealthy and titled Englishman?" Sunday, the poor girl from the West, was originally played by Peggy Allenby, then by Dorothy Lowell and finally by Vivian SMOLLEN, who is best remembered in the role. Alistair Duncan and then Karl SWENSON played Lord Henry Brinthrope, Sunday's English husband. Also heard in supporting roles were Jay JOSTYN, Carleton YOUNG, Doris Rich, Barbara Lee, Joseph "Lee" Latham, Spencer Bentley, Elaine Kent, Charita Bauer, Vicki VOLA, Santos ORTEGA, Florence Robinson, Jay Meredith, Hugh MARLOWE, Fran CARLON, Ruth Russell, Ann SHEPHARD, James Monks, John McGovern, Katherine Emmett, Louis Hall, Ara Ge-ald, Irene Hubbard, John RABY, and Charlotte Lawrence. Art Millett, James Fleming, John A. Wolfe, Bert PARKS, Charles STARK, Warren Sweeney, Clyde North, Ed Fleming, and John Reed KING, announced the program. The series was produced by Anne and Frank HUMMERT and directed by the Hummerts, Frank Gross, Stephen Goss, and Art Hanna. Writers included Jean Carroll and Helen Walpole. Sponsors were Anacin pain reliever, Old English wax, 3-in-1 oil, Black Flag insect killer, Kolynos toothpaste, BiSoDol antacid mints, and Chef Boy-Ar-Dee canned foods. The show's theme song was "The Red River Valley."

OUR MISS BROOKS

1948–1949	CBS	Sun.	9:30 PM
1949–1954	CBS	Sun.	6:30 PM
1954–1955	CBS	Sun.	8 PM
1955–1956	CBS	Sun.	8:05 PM
1956–1957	CBS	Sun.	7:30 PM

The main character on this show, Connie Brooks, was a single high-school English teacher who taught at Madison High School; had a room at Mrs. Davis's boardinghouse; was madly in love with science teacher Mr. Boynton; was the constant thorn in the side of her ever-exasperated principal-boss, Osgood Conklin; and had a favorite student, Walter Denton, who chauffeured her back and forth from school. Film actress Eve ARDEN played Connie Brooks on both a radio and television (1952–1958) version of this program and became forever identified with the role. Jeff CHANDLER played Boynton; Gale GORDON played Conklin; Richard CRENNA played Denton; Jane Morgan played Connie's landlady, Mrs. Davis; and Gloria McMillan and Leonard Smith played Harriet Conklin and Stretch Snodgrass. The series was produced by Larry Berns and directed by Al Lewis. Verne Smith and Bob Lamond were the show's announcers. The sponsors included Palmolive soap, Lustre Cream shampoo, Colgate tooth powder and dental cream, Palmolive brushless shaving cream, Vel hair-setting lotion, White Rain shampoo, Deep Magic beauty cream, Toni home permanent, Anacin pain reliever, and Kolynos toothpaste.

OZZIE AND HARRIET, THE ADVENTURES OF
See ADVENTURES OF OZZIE AND HARRIET, THE.

PAIGE, RAYMOND (1900–1965)

Wisconsin-born musician-conductor Raymond Paige was orchestra leader on the HOLLYWOOD HOTEL music-variety series. Paige, who as a young man led a dance band, was also the music director of *Salute to Youth, Musical America, Hollywood Mardi Gras,* and STAGE DOOR CANTEEN. In addition, he conducted the Los Angeles Philharmonic and the Standard Symphony orchestras for several seasons until his retirement in the early 1960s.

PAINTED DREAMS

1935–1936	Mutual	Mon.–Fri. 12:45 PM
1936–1940	(Off the air)	
1940–1941	NBC Blue	Mon.–Fri. 10 AM

Radio actress and writer Irna PHILLIPS played Mother Moynihan, a kind, loving friend of those in need, on this 15-minute radio soap opera. The series featured Ireene WICKER as her daughter. Also heard were Jane Green, Sally Smith, Alice Hill, Ed Prentiss, and Pat Murphy. The episodic stories eventually ended with Mother Moynihan solving a social or personal problem of one kind or another. When Phillips's ever-increasing writing assignments began to interfere with her acting, actress Bess Flynn assumed the role of Mother Moynihan. Many people claim that *Painted Dreams* was actually the first soap opera on radio, but this is difficult to substantiate because many shows began as local programs before they became network offerings. Don Gordon was the series' announcer. Kellogg's cereals, Cal-Aspirin pain reliever, and Chipso soapflakes sponsored the program.

PALEY, WILLIAM S. (1901–1990)

When William S. Paley was in his late teens, his family moved from Chicago to Philadelphia, where he attended the Wharton School of Finance at the University of Pennsylvania. With his bachelor's degree in business administration, Paley joined the family business as its vice president in charge of promotion. Fascinated with the new medium that was just beginning to surface—radio—Paley was convinced of its great potential as a way to promote his father's cigar company. He signed one of radio's earliest advertising contracts in 1929. That same year, Paley bought a small network of independent stations and named his new network the COLUMBIA BROADCASTING SYSTEM (CBS). Paley slowly built his new company into one of the country's leading radio and television networks. From the late 1930s until well into the 1940s, Paley secured the services of such great radio performers as Jack BENNY, AMOS AND ANDY, Al JOLSON, Edgar BERGEN, Kate SMITH, and Bing CROSBY. During World War II, he served as an Office of War Information supervisor and later as chief of radio in the OWI's Psychological Warfare Department. After the war, Paley once again devoted his time to his broadcasting empire and encouraged and supported Edward R. MURROW in his efforts to make CBS the leading news and information network. In 1966, he waived his company's mandatory retirement rule so that he could remain active as chairman, a position he held until 1983. He was forced to retire in 1986 but was restored as chairman shortly after. The great power he had formerly wielded, however, was not restored, and Paley had to contend with people who for the first time in his company's history, owned more CBS stock than he did. Four years later, Paley died.

PALMOLIVE BEAUTY BOX THEATER (AKA PALMOLIVE RADIO HOUR)

1927–1928	NBC Red	Fri.	10 PM
1928–1929	NBC Red	Fri.	9:30 PM
1929–1931	NBC Red	Wed.	8:30 PM
1934–1936	NBC Blue	Tues.	10 PM
1936–1937	CBS	Wed.	9:30 PM

Kenneth W. MACGREGOR directed this half-hour music-variety series, which at its height starred soprano Jessica DRAGONETTE. Also heard at various times were Frank MUNN (billed as Frank Oliver), Gladys Swarthout, Josephine Antoine, and John Barclay. Comedian Benny Fields was also featured on the series. It was on this program that Fanny BRICE (as BABY SNOOKS) and her "Daddy" received their most widespread exposure. Virginia Rea played a character named Olive Palmer (Palm-olive scrambled), spokeswoman for Palmolive soap. The program also featured Al Goodman's orchestra. *Palmolive Beauty Box Theater* offered many premiums as giveaways, such as the Dionne quintuplets paper-doll book and various mugs, pamphlets, and trinkets. Jean Paul King was the show's longtime announcer.

PARKER FAMILY, THE

1939–1940	CBS	Thurs.	7:15 PM
1940–1942	NBC Blue	Sun.	9:15 PM
1942–1944	ABC	Fri.	9:45 PM

A typical American teenage boy, Richard Parker, was the central character on this half-hour situation-comedy series, featuring Michael O'DAY and then Leon JANNEY in the leading role. Interested in girls, an average student in high school, and from a middle-class family, Richard Parker grappled with the usual problems facing teenagers, such as girlfriend problems, finding money to buy nice Christmas presents, and dealing with the school bully. Also heard were Jay JOSTYN and Linda Carlon-Reid and later Marjorie Anderson as Mr. and Mrs. Parker, Richard's parents; Mitzi Gould and Patricia Ryan as Nancy and Elly Parker; Roy Fant as Grandpa Parker; and Aileen Pringle and Fern Persons in supporting roles. Harry Clarke and Erik Rolfe announced the show. The series was created and produced by Don Becker and directed by Oliver Barbour, Blayne Butcher, and Chick Vincent. It was written by Ed Wolfe, Chick Vincent, Ben Kagen, Priscilla Kent, and Vera Oldham. The show's theme song was "Deep Purple." Woodbury soap sponsored the series.

PARKER, FRANK (1906–   )

Born in New York City, tenor Frank Parker starred in such Broadway shows as *Little Nelly Kelly* (1922),

My Princess (1924), and *No, No Nanette* (1925) before working in radio. Parker was one of the original singers on the early radio A AND P GYPSIES program and starred on *The* EVERREADY HOUR in 1926. Primary singer on HOLLYWOOD HOTEL, as well as being one of JACK BENNY'S tenors, the singer also starred on the *Woodbury Soap Hour* music variety series in the mid-1930s and was featured on *The* BURNS AND ALLEN SHOW and *The* EDDIE CANTOR SHOW. In the 1950s, Parker became well known to television viewers as the leading tenor on "Arthur Godfrey and his Friends" for several years.

PARKS, BERT (1915–1992)

Master of ceremonies for the annual Miss America Beauty Contest on television from 1954, Georgia-born Bert Parks was one of radio's busiest announcers and game-show hosts. This CBS staff announcer for many years introduced *The* EDDIE CANTOR SHOW and many late-night remote-band broadcasts for that network. He became the star of BREAK THE BANK and STOP THE MUSIC, both of which he also hosted on television. Other shows Parks announced included FORTY-FIVE MINUTES FROM HOLLYWOOD, *Hammerstein's Music Hall*, *The* CAMEL CARAVAN, *Luncheon at the Waldorf*, *The* KATE SMITH SHOW, MCGARRY AND HIS MOUSE, OUR GAL SUNDAY, RENFREW OF THE MOUNTED POLICE, and SECOND HONEYMOON.

PARSONS, LOUELLA O. (LOUELLA ROSE OETTINGER 1884–1972)

Internationally known Hollywood gossip columnist Louella Parsons was born in Freeport, Illinois. She had a syndicated column in the Hearst chain of newspapers for many years before she brought her gossip column to the airwaves in 1928. It was said that Louella and her fellow Hollywood gossip reporter Hedda Hopper had so much power in Hollywood that they could "make" or "break" a star or a film by a mere mention in their columns. Louella was the star of a regular daily gossip program, *The Louella Parsons Show*, heard in the early-evening hours. For a while, Parsons was also the cohost with actor Dick POWELL of HOLLYWOOD HOTEL, which presented drama and musical variety entertainment and featured some of the biggest stars in Hollywood as guests. Parsons continued writing her syndicated newspaper gossip column until shortly before her death.

PARTIES AT PICKFAIR

1934–1935	NBC Blue	Wed.	7 PM
1935–1936	CBS	Tues., Sun.	9 PM

Silent-film star Mary Pickford hosted this weekly half-hour radio program from her Hollywood mansion,

Pickfair. Each week, the listening audience was "invited" into her home via the airwaves to hear dramatic sketches featuring Pickford and such film actors as Bette Davis, Douglas Fairbanks, Jr., William Powell, and Constance and Joan Bennett. Actor Eric Snowden both played Pickford's butler Alvin and announced the show. Regularly heard as "guests" and supporting actors in the various sketches were Mary Jane HIGBY, Bret MORRISON, Ted Osbourne, Lou Merrill, and James Eagles. Many of the famous actors were also interviewed by Pickford. Al Lyons led the show's orchestra; the Paul Turner Singers were also regularly featured. The series was created and produced by Nat Wolfe and Marion Parsonette, directed by Eric Snowden, and written by Jerry Cady. It was sponsored by an amalgam of ice-box manufacturers. Their slogan was "Cold alone is not enough!"

PAT NOVAK, FOR HIRE

1946–1949	ABC	Sun.	7 PM
		Sat.	9 PM & 8 PM

Before he became well known as Joe Friday on DRAGNET, actor Jack WEBB was the star of the relatively popular, highly stylized *Pat Novak, For Hire,* a half-hour detective series, for three years. He both directed the program and played the title role. Tudor Owen was heard as his sidekick, "Jocko" Madigan. Novak, a private detective who took cases no other sleuth in Los Angeles wanted, specialized in surveillances. Also heard on the series were John Galbraith (as the inspector) and Raymond Burr in various supporting roles. Hal Gibney announced the program, which was written by Richard Breen.

PAUL WHITEMAN SHOW, THE (AKA MUSICAL VARIETIES; PAUL WHITEMAN PRESENTS; PAUL WHITEMAN CONCERTS; FOREVER TOPS; PAUL WHITEMAN HOUR; PAUL WHITEMAN PROGRAM; PAUL WHITEMAN TEEN CLUB; PAUL WHITEMAN VARIETIES)

1929–1930	CBS	Tues.	9 PM
1930–1931	(Off the air)		
1931–1932	NBC Blue	Fri.	10 PM
1932–1933	NBC Red	Mon.	9:30 PM
1933–1935	(Off the air)		
1935–1936	NBC Blue	Sun.	9:45 PM
1936–1937	(Off the air)		
1937–1939	CBS	Fri.	8:30 PM
1939–1943	(Off the air)		
1943	NBC	Sun.	8 PM
1943–1946	(Off the air)		
1946	ABC	Mon.	9:30 PM
1947–1948	ABC	Sun.	9 PM
1948–1949	(Off the air)		
1949–1950	ABC	Tues.	8 PM
1950–1951	(Off the air)		
1951–1952	ABC	Mon.	9 PM
1952–1953	ABC	Tues.	8:30 PM
1953–1954	ABC	Thurs.	9 PM

"The King of Jazz," orchestra leader Paul WHITEMAN had several half-hour programs with various names on the air from the late 1920s until well into the 1950s. At one time, song stylist Evelyn Knight was featured on Whiteman's program, as were singers Bing CROSBY, Morton DOWNEY, and Gene AUSTIN. Numerous guest stars appeared on Paul's shows, and he is credited with "discovering" many of the entertainment industry's biggest names, such as George Gershwin, Oscar Levant, Rudy VALLEE, and Allan JONES. Alan Kent was Whiteman's longtime announcer. Whiteman's theme music was Gershwin's "Rhapsody in Blue" after Whiteman introduced the selection at a Carnegie Hall concert. The show's various sponsors included Old Gold cigarettes, Pontiac automobiles, Buick automobiles, Kraft cheese, Woodbury face cream, Chesterfield cigarettes, Chase and Sanborn coffee, and Nescafé instant coffee.

See also KRAFT MUSIC HALL, *The.*

PAUSE THAT REFRESHES ON THE AIR, THE

1935	NBC Red	Fri.	10:30 PM
1935–1948	(Off the air)		
1948–1949	CBS	Sun.	6:30 PM

Coca-Cola sponsored this half-hour series of classical and semiclasscial music selections, the title of the program taken from one of their advertising slogans. Frank Black, sixty-five musicians and 25 vocalists, Andre KOSTELANETZ, Albert Spaulding and his orchestra, and singers Ginny SIMMS and Jane FROMAN were featured on the program at different times. Ken CARPENTER announced the series. The director and writer of the program are unknown.

PAWLEY, EDWARD (1904–1988)

Actor Edward Pawley was born in Chicago, Illinois, and after working as a staff announcer in that city, he became an actor and frequent performer on such radio programs as *The* MARCH OF TIME and *The* CAVALCADE OF AMERICA from the 1930s through the 1950s. Pawley became best known as Steve Wilson, the major character on BIG TOWN, even though Hollywood actor Edward G. Robinson originated the role on the air in the late 1930s.

PAYNE, VIRGINIA (1910–1977)

Actress Virginia Payne was born in Cincinnati, Ohio. In 1933, at the age of 23, her first important acting job was playing MA PERKINS on network radio, Payne played Ma Perkins for the next twenty-seven years. When the series finally left the air, in 1960, Payne was actually the age she was supposed to have been when *Ma Perkins* first aired. Payne was also heard regularly on *The* CARTERS OF ELM STREET, *The* FIRST NIGHTER, LIGHT OF THE WORLD, *Lonely Women*, TODAY'S CHILDREN, and *The* CAVALCADE OF AMERICA. The actress continued her acting career playing character roles in touring productions of *Carousel, Oklahoma!, Long Day's Journey into Night, Becket,* and *Life with Father* in the 1960s and 1970s, and appeared on Broadway with Carol Burnett in the musical comedy *Fade Out, Fade In* in 1962. Payne was also heard on radio once again in the 1970s on Himan BROWN'S CBS MYSTERY THEATER series.

PEARCE, AL (1898–1961)

Comedian Al Pearce was born in San Francisco, California. He began his show-business career as a musician when he was fifteen years old but became a salesman when music jobs failed to materialize. Eventually, he returned to show business as a comedian. His first radio work was reading commercials on *The Happy-Go-Lucky Hour* in 1929. One of the first comics to realize the potential of verbal humor on radio, Pearce gathered together a wonderful, ear-pleasing company of regular performers such as Bill Comstock, Bill WRIGHT, Artie AUERBACH, Morey Amsterdam, Marie Green and her Merry Men, and Phil Hanna, who acted as prototypes for many comedy-show characters that followed on other programs. With Pearce playing a zany character named Elmer Blurt, the program—originally called *Watch the Fords Go By* because it was sponsored by the Ford Motor Company—was an instant hit. In addition to *Al Pearce–Watch the Fords Go By* (aka AL PEARCE AND HIS GANG), Pearce was also heard on *Happy Go Lucky* and *Blue Monday Jamboree.*

PEARL, JACK (JACK PEARLMAN: 1895–1982)

New York–born comedian Jack Pearl became famous for playing a character named Baron Munchausen, who was based on an actual teller of tall tales, Baron von Munchausen, on one of the most popular shows on radio, *The* JACK PEARL SHOW. People all over the country imitated the heavy German accent and quoted the Baron's humorous expression, "Vas you dere, Sharlie?" As the war with Germany approached, the humor of the Munchausen character lost favor with the public and Pearl's popularity began to diminish. In addition to *The Jack Pearl Show,* Pearl was also heard on *The Lucky Strike Program* and *The* ED SULLIVAN SHOW, on which he first introduced his Baron Munchausen character to radio audiences. He was also featured in the Broadway shows *Artists and Models* (1926) and *The Ziegfeld Follies of 1931.*

PEARL, MINNIE (SARAH OPHELIA COLLEY: 1912–   )

Country-western comedienne Minnie Pearl is well known to fans of the "HeeHaw" television series

(1966 and still in syndication). Born in Centerville, Tennessee, Pearl was a dance and drama teacher before she decided to become a professional entertainer. Her man-hungry spinster character, invented for *The* GRAND OLE OPRY radio program, made the show a success and her a star. Her trademarks were her "store-bought" hat—price tag still on it "so that people would know how much (she) had paid for it"—and her boisterous greeting, "Hoooooooow-deee!" In addition to her appearances on *The Grand Ole Opry,* Pearl toured with the WSM touring unit known as "The Camel Caravan," which performed at various military bases around the world during World War II. On *The Grand Ole Opry,* Pearl often worked with her longtime friend and stage companion Roy ACUFF. Pearl was elected to the Country Music Hall of Fame in 1975.

PEARSON, DREW (1897–1969)

Born in Evanston, Illinois, Drew Pearson worked as a newspaperman, a college instructor, and a seaman before becoming a broadcaster. He teamed up with Robert Allen for a time, but for most of his years on radio, Pearson was strictly a solo act. As a newsman on radio from 1935, Pearson became especially adept at making such accurate political predictions of who would win a political election or whether a certain

(From left) Jack Pearl and Cliff Hall (NBC)

bill would or would not pass through Congress. His predictions proved to be 85 percent correct, an astounding feat by today's standards. For many years, Pearson also wrote a widely read syndicated newspaper column called "Washington Merry-Go-Round," a behind-the-scenes look at politicians and politics.

PEARY, HAL (1908–1985)

Actor Hal Peary was born in San Leandro, California. He began his career on radio as a thirteen-year-old singer billed as "The Oakland Tribune's Boy Caruso." Although he became best known for playing Water Commissioner Throckmorton P. Gildersleeve on radio's *The* GREAT GILDERSLEEVE program—a role he had originated on FIBBER MCGEE AND MOLLY—Hal Peary was also a regular on *Flying Time,* GIRL ALONE, *Inside Story,* DON WINSLOW OF THE NAVY, *Hollywood Playhouse,* TEXACO STAR THEATER, FIRST NIGHTER, *Roads of Romance,* LITTLE ORPHAN ANNIE, GRAND HOTEL, LIGHTS OUT, *The* STORY OF MARY MARLIN, TOM MIX, WELCOME VALLEY and ONE MAN'S FAMILY. Because of the popularity of his Gildersleeve characterization, Peary also played the role in several feature-length films: *The Great Gildersleeve* (1940), *Gildersleeve's Bad Day* (1941), *Gildersleeve on Broadway* (1942), and *Gildersleeve's Ghost* (1944). His other film credits include *County Fair* (1940), *Look Who's Laughing* (1941), and *Seven Days Leave* (1942). Peary became an active cartoon voice-over actor and was heard on such television programs as "Gerald McBoing-Boing" (1951–1956), "Rudolph and Frosty's Christmas in July" (1976), "The Bullwinkle Show" (1959–1961), "The Lone Ranger" (1966–1969), and "Roman's Holiday" (1973).

PENNER, JOE (JOSEF PINTER: 1904–1941)

Comedian Joe Penner emigrated to the United States from Hungary with his parents when he was nine

Joe Penner (NBC)

years old. He worked as a newsboy and a piano salesman before he became a comedian. His first show-business appearances were in vaudeville and various stage revues, where Penner developed his oddball comedy-character routines. His first radio appearance was *The* RUDY VALLEE SHOW in 1933. Eventually given his own radio show, Penner's comedy catchphrases, "Wanna buy a duck," "You nasty man!" and "Don't ever *do* that!" were being repeated all around the country. In spite of his notoriety, Joe's popularity proved short-lived. His show, first heard in 1936, was off the air by 1940, perhaps due to Penner's failing health. The comedian died in 1941 before his fortieth birthday while he was touring in the musical comedy *Yokel Boy.*

PENTHOUSE PARTY

1934–1935	NBC Blue	Wed.	8:30 PM
1935–1936	CBS	Sun.	10:30 PM
1936–1941	(Off the air)		
1941	CBS	Fri.	10 PM
	NBC	Wed.	9:30 PM

Writer Mark Hellinger was the host of this half-hour talk-variety program, *Penthouse Party,* which featured Ilka Chase, Bert PARKS, Yvette Harris, and Hal Kemp's orchestra as regulars. Popular song hits of the day, as well as pop song hits of the past, were presented along with comedy sketches and chats about historical events and current films. Andre BARUCH was the show's announcer. Its director and writers are unknown. The series was sponsored by ENO effervescent salt and Camel cigarettes.

PEOPLE ARE FUNNY

1942–1943	NBC	Fri.	10 PM
1943–1945	NBC	Fri.	9:30 PM
1945–1948	NBC	Fri.	9 PM
1948–1951	NBC	Tues.	10:30 PM
1951–1954	CBS	Tues.	8 PM
1954–1956	NBC	Tues.	8 PM
1956–1959	NBC	Wed.	8:05 PM

This half-hour program was similar to TRUTH OR CONSEQUENCES in that it made contestants reveal amusing anecdotes about themselves. Unlike that show, however, *People Are Funny* concentrated on interviews with contestants rather than on stunts. Art BAKER hosted, followed by Art LINKLETTER, who retained that job when the series went to television in 1956. Announcers on the program included Rod O'Connor, Ted Myers, Herb Allen, and Allen C. Anthony. The program was produced and directed by John Gruedel and written by Linkletter, Gruedel, Jack Stanley, and Johny Murray. Sponsors included Wings cigarettes, Raleigh cigarettes, Salem cigarettes, Kool cigarettes, Mars candy, Pamper fabric softener, and Prom and Toni home permanents.

PEPPER YOUNG'S FAMILY (AKA RED ADAMS; FOREVER YOUNG)

1933–1934	NBC Blue	Mon.–Fri.		8:45 PM
1934–1935	NBC Blue	Mon., Wed., Fri.		7:30 PM
1936–1937	NBC Red	Mon.–Fri.		3 PM
1937–1938	NBC Blue	Mon.–Fri.		10:30 AM
	NBC Red	Mon.–Fri.		3 PM
1938–1939	NBC Blue	Mon.–Fri.		11:15 AM
	NBC Red	Mon.–Fri.		3 PM
1939–1940	NBC Blue	Mon.–Fri.		11:30 AM
	NBC Red	Mon.–Fri.		3:30 PM
1940–1941	NBC Blue	Mon.–Fri.		11 AM
	NBC Red	Mon.–Fri.		3:30 PM
1941–1942	NBC Red	Mon.–Fri.		11:15 AM
1942–1944	CBS	Mon.–Fri.		2:45 PM
	NBC	Mon.–Fri.		3:30 PM
1944–1954	NBC	Mon.–Fri.		3:30 PM
1954–1955	NBC	Mon.–Fri.		4:45 PM
1955–1956	NBC	Mon.–Fri.		4:30 PM
1956–1959	NBC	Mon.–Fri.		3:45 PM

Originally called *Red Adams, Red Davis,* and then *Forever Young,* this 15-minute series ran longest under the title *Pepper Young's Family.* When the program was called *Red Davis,* Burgess MEREDITH, Betty Wragge, Jack Roseligh, and Marion Barney played the Davis family, a typical American family who had settled in a small midwestern town. When the title was changed to *Pepper Young's Family,* Curtis Arnall, Lawson Zerbe, and, for most of the series' run, Mason ADAMS played "Pepper" Young. Betty Wragge remained on the series as Pepper's sister, Peggy. Jack Roseleigh, Bill ADAMS, and then Thomas Chalmers played Sam Young. Marion Barney continued as Pepper's mother. The program also featured actors Alan Bunce, Elliott Reid, Mary Patton, Eunice Howard, child impersonator Madeleine Pierce, Leon JANNEY, Spencer Bentley, Tess Sheehan, Charles "Chuch" Webster, K. T. Stevens, John Kane, Jean McCoy, Peter Fernanedez, Thomas Chalmers, William "Bill" JOHNSTONE, Margaret Draper, Maureen McManus, Burt Brazier, Edwin Wolfe, Leo Curley, Jean Sothern, Cecil Roy, Tony Barrett, Arthur Vinton, and Irene Hubbard in supporting roles. Richard "Dick" Stark, Martin Block, Stuart Metz, Bill Lazar, Bob Dixon, Red BARBER, and Alan Kent announced. The series was directed by Chick Vincent, John Buckwalter, and Ed Wolfe, and Elaine Sterne CARRINGTON wrote the scripts. The show's theme music was "Au Matin." Camay soap, PandG The White Naptha soap, Crisco shortening, Duz detergent, Golden Fluffo pie crust, Tide and Joy detergents sponsored the show.

PERFORMANCE TODAY

1987–present	NPR	Mon.–Fri.	(*)

NATIONAL PUBLIC RADIO'S popular *Performance Today* program, aired for three hours daily, is hosted by Martin Goldsmith. It presents recorded classical music, as well as interviews with musical authorities, performers, and contemporary composers such as Morton Gould, Alfred Schnitke, and Marilyn Horne. According to NPR, "the program is designed to broaden listeners' appreciation of classical music and to explore the myths that classical music is outdated and stodgy, belonging only in music museums."

PERRY MASON

1943–1955	CBS	Mon.–Fri.	2:15 PM

Before it became one of television's longest-running mystery-detective programs in 1957, "Perry Mason" was a 15-minute drama series on radio. As on the television series, Mason was a lawyer who defended the innocent who had been wrongly accused of crimes. The radio series, based on the stories of Earl Stanley Gardner first published in the early 1930s, starred Barlett Robinson, Santos ORTEGA, Donald Briggs, and John LARKIN as Perry. Larkin played the role the longest and was said to have been deeply disappointed when Raymond Burr was cast for the television version. Gertrude Warner, Jan MINER, and Joan Alexander played Perry's secretary, Della Street; and Matt CROWLEY and Charles Webster played Perry's investigating assistant, Paul Drake. Other regulars included Arthur Vinton as Sergeant Dorset; Mandel KRAMER and Frank Dane as Lieutenant Tragg; Betty GARDE as Peg Neeley; Maurice Franklin as the judge; and Mary Jane HIGBY as Mary Blade. Adele RONSON was frequently featured in the supporting cast. Richard "Dick" Stark and Bob Dixon announced the program. *Perry Mason* was produced for radio by Tom McDermott and Leslie Harris and directed by Art Hanna, Carlo deAngelo, Carl Eastman, Hoyt Allen, and Ralph Butler. The series was written by Irving Vendig, Dan Shuffman, Eugene Wang, and Earl Stanley Gardner. General Foods products sponsored the program.

PETERSON, ARTHUR (1912–1952)

Actor Arthur Peterson was born in Mandan, North Dakota, to theatrical parents. In 1930, after years of acting in numerous stage productions, he made his radio debut in Minneapolis. When *The* GUIDING LIGHT series debuted on radio, Peterson played the central character, Protestant minister the Reverend Doctor John Rutledge, for several years, until the series became less inspirational and more sensational. Peterson was featured on BACHELOR'S CHILDREN, IT CAN BE DONE, GIRL ALONE, FIRST NIGHTER, *The* STORY OF MARY MARLIN, WOMAN IN WHITE, *The* BARTON FAMILY, SILVER EAGLE, MOUNTIE, and TOM MIX.

PHIL BAKER SHOW, THE

1931–1933	CBS	Sun.	9 PM
1933–1935	NBC Blue	Fri.	9:30 PM
1935–1939	CBS	Sun.	7:30 PM

In addition to its star, Phil Baker, this half-hour comedy show featured Ward Wilson and then Sid Silvers as Beetle the Heckler, Harry McNaughton as Bottle the Butler, Ward Wilson as Ferdinand, Agnes MOOREHEAD as Mrs. Sarah Heartburn, and Artie AUERBACH (later Mr. Kitzel on *The* JACK BENNY SHOW), Oscar Bradley, and Mabel Albertson. The show presented comedy sketches, amusing interviews, and songs. Frank Shields and Hal Kemp led the show's orchestra, Harry VON ZELL was the program's announcer, Ira Ashley directed, and Sam Perrin and Phil Baker wrote the scripts. Phil Baker's theme song was "Rolling Along." The show was sponsored by Gulf oil.

PHILCO RADIO HALL OF FAME, THE (AKA THE PHILCO HALL OF FAME)

1943–1945	ABC	Sun.	9 PM
1945–1946	(Off the air)		
1946	ABC	Sun.	6 PM

Although this half-hour series was only a summer-replacement show, major stars of Hollywood, Broadway, and radio—including Jimmy DURANTE, Bob HOPE, singers Helen Forrest and Lina Romay, Fred ALLEN, opera tenor Lauritz Melchoir, Brian Donlevy, singer Ginny SIMMS, Red SKELTON, Jack HALEY, Groucho MARX, and news commentator Lowell THOMAS made regular guest appearances. The program used a variety-show format. At one time during its run, orchestra leader Paul WHITEMAN was the weekly star. Ken CARPENTER was the show's announcer. Philco radios and phonographs sponsored the series.

PHILIP MARLOWE, THE ADVENTURES OF

See ADVENTURES OF PHILIP MARLOWE, *The*

PHILIP MORRIS PLAYHOUSE, THE.

1939–1943	CBS	Fri.	9 PM
1943–1948	(Off the air)		
1948–1949	CBS	Fri.	10 PM
1949–1951	(Off the air)		
1951–1952	CBS	Thurs.	9:30 PM
1952–1953	CBS	Sun.	8:30 PM

This half-hour program presented dramatic adaptations of celebrated short stories and novels such as Poe's "The Tell-Tale Heart," Dickens's *Great Expectations,* and de Maupassant's "The Necklace." Regularly featured actors included Ray COLLINS, Charlie CANTOR, Alan REED, Bill JOHNSTONE, John MCINTIRE, Jeanette NOLAN, Ann Thomas, Barbara Weeks, Ward Wilson, and Raymond Edward JOHNSON. When the series was revived in 1948 and again in 1953, Hollywood stars Marlene Dietrich, Dan Dailey, Vincent PRICE, and Gloria Swanson were frequent guests. William Spier, Jack Johnstone, and Charlie Martin directed the series at different times. Philip Morris

cigarettes sponsored the show. Their trademark was page-boy, midget JOHNNY (Johnny Roventini), whose "Call for Philip Moor-rees!" became one of radio's most famous advertising attention-getters. Art Ballinger and Ken ROBERTS were the show's announcers. Johnny Green was the program's music director. Revelation cigarettes also sponsored the series for a time.

PHILLIPS, IRNA (1901–1973)

Writer and actress Irna Phillips, "the grand lady of soap operas," was born in Chicago, Illinois, attended Northwestern University, and taught high school and college drama and English before she entered radio in 1938 as an actress. Phillips either originated or wrote such programs as *The* GUIDING LIGHT, BRIGHTER DAY, *Lonely Women,* PAINTED DREAMS, *The* RIGHT TO HAPPINESS, *The* ROAD OF LIFE, TODAY'S CHILDREN, WELCOME VALLEY, and *The* WOMAN IN WHITE. As an actress, Phillips was featured on *Gasoline Alley* as Auntie Blossom. She also created and wrote several television daytime serial dramas, including "Today's Children," "Another World," "As the World Turns," "The Brighter Day," "Days of Our Lives," and "Love Is a Many-Splendored Thing."

PHILO VANCE

1945	NBC	Thurs.	7:30 PM (Summer)
1948–1950	(Syndicated series. Various stations and times)		

Sophisticated detective and expert private detective Philo Vance first appeared in numerous mystery novels and films. On radio first as a half-hour weekly summer-replacement series in 1945 and then as a syndicated show in 1948, Philo Vance solved murders committed at fashionable, high-society parties as well as backstage at the opera. Jackson BECK and film-and-stage star Jose Ferrer played Vance at different times. The cast included George Petrie as District Attorney Markham, Joan Alexander and Frances Farras as Vance's secretary, and Humphrey Davis as Sergeant Heath. The series was produced by Frederic W. Ziv and directed by Jeanne K. Harrison. It was written by Robert J. Shaw and Kenny Lyons.

PHRASE THAT PAYS, THE

1953–1955	NBC	Mon.–Fri.	11:30 AM

On this half-hour quiz program, hosted by Ted Brown and later by Red Benson, a contestant chosen from the studio audience was given three clues to identify a well-known phrase. Like today's popular "Wheel of Fortune" television series, prizes were awarded based on the clue that led to the identification of the phrase. If the contestant failed to guess the phrase correctly, the listener who sent in the phrase and clues won the prize. Colgate-Palmolive toothpaste and soap sponsored the program.

PICK AND PAT
See MOLASSES AND JANUARY.

PICKENS, JANE (1909–1992)
Jane Pickens was a member of the famous singing trio the Pickens Sisters (Jane, Patti, and Helen). The sisters were born in Macon, Georgia, and were heard on many early music-variety radio programs in the early 1930s, singing the popular songs of the day. When Patti and Helen decided to leave show business in the mid-1930s, Jane Pickens became a soloist and a major attraction on *The* BEN BERNIE SHOW and *The* CHAMBER MUSIC SOCIETY OF LOWER BASIN STREET. Married into a wealthy family, Pickens continued to sing on various fund-raising shows and was active on behalf of many charities.

PIOUS, MINERVA (1904–1979)
Born in Odessa, Russia, actress Minerva Pious first acted on the Yiddish stage in New York City in the mid-1920s and eventually became one of radio's most sought-after character comediennes, versatile enough to play all sorts of roles in various dialects. Pious was Pansy Nussbaum on *The* FRED ALLEN SHOW and played other character roles in other skits on that program as well. Equally adept at serious drama and comedy, Pious was heard on *Columbia Presents Corwin*, EASY ACES, DUFFY'S TAVERN, PHILIP MORRIS PLAYHOUSE, *The* GOLDBERGS, *The* HENRY MORGAN SHOW, and LIFE CAN BE BEAUTIFUL. Audiences saw Pious in such Broadway plays as *Love in Our Time, Dear Me, The Sky Is Falling,* and *The Last Analyst* and on screen in *The Ambassador's Daughter* (1956) and *Love in the Afternoon* (1957). On television, the actress was a regular on the Merv Griffin and Les Crane talk shows and had featured roles on the soap operas "The Edge of Night" (1964) and "Another World" (1968).

PLANTATION PARTY (AKA THE DUKES OF PADUCAH)

| 1936–1943 | NBC Blue | Wed. | 8:30 PM |

This half-hour music-comedy-variety program with a country-western slant featured Whitey Ford as master of ceremonies, a singing group called Tom, Dick, and Harry (Bud Van Doren, Marlin HURT, and Gordon Van Doren), the Doring Sisters, accordionist Larry Wellington, bass Michael Stewart, and the Westerners. Charles Lyon was the show's announcer, and Tom Wallace directed the show. Bugler tobacco sponsored the series.

POND'S PROGRAM, THE

| 1932–1934 | NBC | Fri. | 9:30 PM |

This half-hour program, narrated by Eleanor ROOSEVELT, consisted of semiclassical and classical musical selections, interspersed with commentaries on various social problems during the Great Depression. Governor Franklin Delano ROOSEVELT's wife was well placed to comment on issues such as the war pending in Europe and the Works Progress Administration. Leo Reisman and his orchestra and vocalist Lee Wiley were featured. Pond's cold cream sponsored the program.

POPEYE THE SAILOR

| 1935–1936 | NBC Red | Mon., Wed., Fri. | 7:15 PM |
| 1936–1938 | CBS | Mon., Wed., Fri. | 7:15 PM |

E. C. Segar's cartoon character, Popeye the Sailor, on the air for 15-minute segments, had Det Poppen and then Floyd Buckley as Popeye. Olive Le Moy, Miriam WOLFE (who also played The Sea Hag), and Mae Questel played Olive Oyl; Johnny Donnelly, Matey the newsboy; Jackson BECK played Bluto; Charles Lawrence, Whimpy; and Don Costello, Everett SLOANE, James Kelly, and Jean Kay had supporting roles. Similar in style and content to the cartoon, but with a different cast, Popeye spent most episodes fighting with the thug Bluto over the slim beauty Olive Oyl. Kelvin Keech was the show's announcer. Wheatena cereal sponsored the series.

PORTIA FACES LIFE

1940–1941	NBC Red	Mon.–Fri.	4 PM
1941–1942	NBC Red	Mon.–Fri.	5:15 PM
1942–1944	NBC	Mon.–Fri.	5:15 PM
1944–1945	CBS	Mon.–Fri.	2 PM
1945–1952	NBC	Mon.–Fri.	5:15 PM

The heroine of this daytime series, Portia Blake Manning was a lawyer and a widowed mother who was trying to raise a son on her own, with occasional romances. Lucille WALL starred as Portia. Ray Ives, Larry Robinson, Alastair Kyle, and Edwin Bruce played Dickie Blake, her son, and Joan BANKS played Arline Manning. Other regulars included Raymond Ives, Edwin Bruce, Myron MCCORMICK, Carlton YOUNG, Bartlett "Bart" Robinson, Don Briggs, Esther Ralston, Roseline Greene, Anne SEYMOUR, Henriette Tedro, Doris Rich, Walter Vaughn, Selena Royle, Kenneth Lynch, Peter Capell, John LARKIN, William "Bill" JOHNSTONE, James Van Dyke, Elizabeth Reller, Santos ORTEGA, Virginia "Ginger" Jones, Luise Barclay, Lyle Sudrow, Nancy Douglas, Ethel Intropidi, Les DAMON, Karl SWENSON, and Marjorie Anderson. The series was produced by Don Cope and Tom McDermott and directed by Hoyt Allen, Mark Goodson (later a successful game-quiz show producer), Beverly Smith, and Paul Knight. Hector Chevigny wrote the series. Announcers for the program were George Putnam, Jack Costello, and Ron Rawson. *Portia Faces Life* was sponsored by Post Toasties cereal, Grape Nuts Flakes cereal, Grape Nuts Wheat Meal, Maxwell House coffee, LaFrance bleach, and Jell-O puddings.

POWELL, RICHARD "DICK" (1904–1963)

Actor Dick Powell was born in Mountain View, Arkansas, and began his show-business career as a chorus boy on Broadway as well as a featured singer. In the 1930s, a motion-picture contract got him lead roles in such musicals as the now-classic *42nd Street* with frequent costar Ruby Keeler. In 1944, Powell's performance in the mystery-detective film *Murder My Sweet* changed the direction of his career. Thereafter, he mainly played serious tough-guy roles and became well known on radio as Richard Diamond, the singing detective on RICHARD DIAMOND, *Private Detective.* In addition to working on radio musical comedies such as HOLLYWOOD HOTEL, *Campana Serenade* and *The* FITCH BANDWAGON, he starred on ROGUES GALLERY. After becoming an active television director and producer, Powell formed a production company called Four Star Productions, which produced a number of hit television shows such as "Climax" (1954), "Dick Powell's Zane Grey Theater" (1955), and "Four Star Playhouse" (1958).

PRAIRIE HOME COMPANION, A

1977–1980s	APR(Various times and APR and NPR stations)
1994–present	NPR(Various times and NPR stations)

Each week, Garrison Keillor, a cracker-barrel philosopher–feature writer, takes his listeners to his mythical hometown, Lake Wobegon, a typical small, mainly Scandinavian-American community in Minnesota. Lake Wobegon was "the town time forgot and the decades (could) not improve ... where the women (were) strong, the men good-looking, and the children above average," Keillor stated at the beginning of each show. The program's fictional sponsor was Powdermilk biscuits, which "came in the big blue box or in the brown bag with stains that indicate freshness." Other bogus sponsors were Bertha's Kitty Boutique, which encouraged cat ranching; the Fearmonger Show, which served paranoids and offered "a safety toilet seat a yard high" to be "out of reach of snakes"; the Chatterbox Cafe, which served strawberry cream pie "that made grown men cry and lose all ambition in life"; the Open Clothes Shop; Ralph's Pretty-Good Grocery, which claimed, "If you can't find it at Ralph's, you probably can get along without it"; and Bob's Bank, which stated, "Never a borrower or lender be. Save at the sign of the sock." The music on the program, a mixture of jazz, bluegrass, Western swing, light opera, and ethnic, was played by the Butch Thompson Trio, Stoney Lonesome and the Bluegrass Band, and various others, using pianos, zithers, harp-sichords, fiddles, dulcimers, banjos, and mandolins. After several years and several less-than-well-received radio and PBS-TV shows, Garrison Keillor returned with his program to the nation's public radio airwaves by popular demand in 1994. The new show used the same basic format as Keillor's previously successful radio series.

PRETTY KITTY KELLY

1937–1940	CBS	Mon.–Fri.	10 AM

The heroine of this 15-minute series, Kitty Kelly, had been a criminal's girlfriend in Ireland, was arrested and was put on trial for the murder of Police Inspector Conway. Acquitted, Kitty emigrated to America and tried to make a new life for herself in a small American town. Arline Blackburn and then Fran CARLON starred as Kitty. Clayton "Bud" COLLYER played her respectable American boyfriend, Michael Conway. Also heard were Helen Choate, Bartlett "Bart" Robinson, Dennis Hoey, Linda Carlon-Reid, Eunice Howard, Tess Sheehan, Barbara Lee, James Van Dyke, Ethel Intropidi, Richard KOLLMAR, Florence Malone, Artells Dickson, Lucille WALL, Luis Van ROOTEN, Charme Allen, Matt CROWLEY, Virginia "Ginger" Jones, and Louis Hector. The show's theme song was "Kerry Dance." Andrew Stanton announced, Ken MACGREGOR directed, and Frank Dahn wrote the scripts for the series. Wonder bread and Hostess cupcakes sponsored the series.

PRICE, VINCENT (1911–1993)

Motion-picture actor Vincent Price was born in St Louis, Missouri. A graduate of Yale University with a degree in fine art, Price decided to become an actor while he was furthering his art studies in London. Returning to the United States, Price appeared in several plays, such as *Angel Street* (1941), before he debuted in films. In his early movie career, he played major roles in such classic motion pictures as *Laura* (1944), *Leave Her to Heaven* (1945), and *Dragonwyck* (1946). Price brought his velvety, precise speaking voice to radio with a major role on a mystery-adventure series called *The Croupier.* He later played Simon Templer, the Saint, on *The* SAINT series and made many guest appearances on SUSPENSE, ESCAPE, and *The* LUX RADIO THEATER. During his later film career, Price was mostly featured in such low-budget horror films as *House of Wax* (1953), *The Fall of the House of Usher* (1961), *Tales of Terror* (1962), and *House of a Thousand Dolls* (1967). His last film, however, was *The Whales of August,* a superb film costarring Lillian Gish and Bette Davis. PBS viewers saw him host the "Mystery" series, and he was a frequent commercial product spokesman.

PRIME TIME

1980s–present	CBC	(*)	(*)

On this CANADIAN BROADCASTING CORPORATION'S program, host Geoff Pevere spends one hour each weeknight probing pop culture and the arts. Guests join Pevere on the phone or in the studio to discuss topics ranging from sexism in advertising to a look at the few family-oriented movie theaters that still exist in Canada. The program also presents documentary dramas on specific topics and people. The executive producer is Dave Downey.

PROFESSOR QUIZ

1936–1938	CBS	Sat.	9 PM
1938–1940	CBS	Fri.	7:30 PM
1940–1941	CBS	Thurs.	10:15 PM
1941–1946	(Off the air)		
1946–1947	ABC	Thurs.	7:30 PM
1947–1948	ABC	Sat.	10 PM

This successful half-hour and later 15-minute quiz program was hosted by Dr. Craig Earl, better known as Professor Quiz. The show is reported to have been radio's first quiz program. On the show, guests asked the professor quiz questions, trying to stump him. If they succeeded, they won a cash prize of $25. The announcers on this program were Robert TROUT and Arthur GODFREY. The show was directed by Ed FITZGERALD and Robert Jennings. Sponsors of the program included Kelvinator refrigerators, Noxzema skin cream, Teel shampoo, Velvet pipe tobacco, Drene shampoo, and AMOCO oil and gasoline.

PRUDENTIAL FAMILY HOUR, THE (AKA THE PRUDENTIAL FAMILY HOUR OF STARS; MAJOR BOWES' FAMILY HOUR; TED MACK FAMILY HOUR; CAPITOL FAMILY HOUR)

1941–1948	CBS	Sun.	5 PM
1948–1949	CBS	Sun.	6 PM

Although Major Edward BOWES and Ted Mack hosted programs using the *Family Hour* title and a program called *The Capitol Family Hour* was also on the air briefly, it is *The Prudential Family Hour* program that is the best-remembered *Family Hour* series. The respected musical commentator Deems TAYLOR and for a short time actor Jose Ferrer hosted this 45-minute program of musical selections, featuring such celebrated personalities as contralto Gladys Swarthout, baritone Ross Graham, soprano Patrice Munsel, and pop singer Jack SMITH. On Major Bowes' *Family Hour* program, child singer Belle "Bubbles" Silverman—opera and concert soprano Beverly Sills—was the show's featured vocalist. The Prudential program's orchestra was conducted by Al GOODMAN. Frank Gallop and Truman BRADLEY were the program's announcers. The *Family Hour's* theme music was "Intermezzo" when Prudential sponsored the series and "Clair de Lune" on Bowes' program. During Prudential's sponsorship of the show, 10-minute dramatizations of the lives of the composers Beethoven, Edvard Grieg, Franz Schubert, Antonin Dvořák, and others were presented. The Prudential Insurance Company and Capitol records sponsored the Bowes show. Tony La Franzo announced the Bowes' *Family Hour*, which was directed by Dave Young, Mel Williamson, John Kelly, and Robert O'Sullivan and written by Kelly and O'Sullivan. *The Prudential Family Hour* series was written and directed by William N. ROBSON.

PRUD'HOMME, CAMERON (1892–1967)

Radio actor and writer Cameron Prud'homme was born in San Francisco, California, and began his career on radio in 1931 playing the title role of DAVID HARUM. In addition, he was heard on ONE MAN'S FAMILY, DEATH VALLEY DAYS, *Laugh with Ken Murray, Log Cabin Dude Ranch, Dr. Kate,* HAWTHORNE HOUSE, *Dangerous Road,* and THEATER GUILD OF THE AIR. Prud'homme also wrote scripts for such series as HAWTHORNE HOUSE and acted in such films as *The Rainmaker* (1958).

PURSUIT

1949–1950	CBS	Tues.	10:30 PM
1950–1951	CBS	Wed.	10:30 PM
1951–1952	CBS	Tues.	9:30 PM

"A criminal strikes and fades quickly back into the shadows of his own dark world. And then the man from Scotland Yard, the relentless dangerous pursuit when man hunts man!" The half-hour *Pursuit* mystery-adventure series starred Ted DeCorsia and then Ben WRIGHT as Inspector Peter Black of Scotland Yard. Don Baker and Bob Stevenson announced, and William N. ROBSON produced and directed. Sponsors included Ford automobiles, Energine vitamin supplement, Double Danderine shampoo, Bayer aspirin, Phillips' Milk of Magnesia antacid, Haley's M-O antacid, Molle shaving cream, and Dr. Lyon's tooth powder.

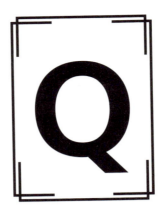

QUEEN FOR A DAY

1945–1947	Mutual	Mon.–Fri.	2:30 PM
1947–1950	Mutual	Mon.–Fri.	2 PM
1950–1951	Mutual	Mon.–Fri.	2:30 PM
1951–1958	Mutual	Mon.–Fri.	11:30 AM

Women from the studio audience were selected to compete against each other on this 15-minute program by telling a personal story that could earn them the title of "queen for a day." The event they related could be some heroic act or simply an amusing, usually poignant, incident from their lives. One woman described the difficulties of raising fifteen children with no husband. Others often related heart-rending stories of wartime separation of loved ones called overseas to fight. The winning storyteller of the day was selected by the studio audience by applause and could receive as much as $2,500 in gifts and cash. Bud Williams, Harry Mynatt, and Jack Bailey hosted this series, and Gene Baker, Mark Houston, and Fort Pearson were the program's announcers. James Morgan, Bud Ernst, and Lee Bolen directed the show. Sponsors over the years included Alka Seltzer antacid, One-A-Day vitamins, Old Gold cigarettes, and Philip Morris cigarettes.

QUICK AS A FLASH

| 1944–1949 | Mutual | Sun. | 5:30 PM |
| 1949–1951 | ABC | Mon.–Fri. | 11:30 AM |

On this half-hour series, three contestants were selected from the studio audience and seated at a table with different-colored lights and buzzer buttons in front of them. As a series of questions were asked, a contestant tried to be the first to ring his or her buzzer and answer a question or solve a puzzle based on a mystery drama sketch. If he or she answered incorrectly, the sketch continued to the end, and the remaining panelists were asked to try to solve the mystery. The final sketches featured a well-known radio-program guest detective such as ELLERY QUEEN, NERO WOLFE, BULLDOG DRUMMOND, The SHADOW, and The FALCON; the actors who played the parts on their respective radio shows appeared in the sketches. A repertory cast of actors—including Elspeth ERIC, Santos ORTEGA, Jackson BECK, Julie STEVENS, Charles Webster, Joan Alexander, Mandel KRAMER, and Raymond Edward JOHNSON—also appeared. Ken ROBERTS, Win ELLIOT, and Bill CULLEN were the hosts of this series, which was directed by Richard Lewis. Announcers included Frank Gallop and Cy Harrice. The show was directed by Richard Lewis and written by Louis M. Heyward, Mike Sklar, and Eugene Wang. Helbros watches sponsored the series, as did Aunt Jemima pancake mix and Ammident toothpaste.

QUIET, PLEASE

1947–1948	Mutual	Sun.	3:30 PM
1948	Mutual	Mon.	9:30 PM
1948–1949	ABC	Sun.	5:30 PM

This excellent, albeit relatively short-lived, half-hour sustained series of mystery and suspense stories was written, produced, and directed by Wyllis Cooper and starred Ernest CHAPPELL as a different major character each week. Well-remembered stories such as "The Thing on the Fourble Board," about an oil rigger who encounters a strange being at the top of an oil well, were told in a first-person narrative by Chappell and were exceptionally well written and outstandingly acted. The theme music for *Quiet Please!* was the second movement of César Franck's Symphony in D Minor, which became closely identified with the program for many years.

QUIRKS AND QUARKS

| 1979–present | CBC | Sat. | 12:08 PM |

Jay Ingram hosts this popular CANADIAN BROADCASTING CORPORATION current-affairs program, which discusses such topics as virtual reality, monster birds, a person's height and ancestry, the Nobel Prize, why some dogs bark unnecessarily, the search for extraterrestrial life, and how cheese and sunlight prevent tooth decay. The program, which won the Canadian Science Writers' Award in 1991, is produced by Anita Gordon, coauthor of the book *It's a Matter of Survival.*

QUIZ KIDS, THE

1940–1941	NBC Blue	Wed.	8 PM
1941–1945	NBC Blue	Sun.	7:30 PM
1945–1946	ABC	Sun.	7:30 PM
1946–1949	NBC	Sun.	4 PM
1949–1951	NBC	Sun.	3:30 PM
1951–1953	CBS	Sun.	4:30 PM
1953–1954	CBS	Sun.	5:30 PM

Joe Kelly was the host of this half-hour radio series, which featured some of the brightest youngsters in America as regular panelists. These "quiz kids" were asked questions most adults would probably have difficulty answering, such as to define the words *antimacassar, sarong, dinghy,* and *aperture.* The "kids" were all under sixteen years of age and were paid for their appearances on the show. Several of them became nationally known celebrities because of their unusual mental abilities. The children who appeared on this series over the years included Gerard Darrow, Joan Bishop, Van Dyke Tiers, Mary Ann Anderson, Charles Schwartz, Louis Jean Ashbeck, George Coklas, Cynthia Cline, Joan Alizier, Virginia Booze, Richard Kosterlitz, Linda Wells, Lloyd Wells, Mary Clare McHugh, Marvin Zenkere, Clem Lane, Jr., Emily Anne Israel, Robert Walls, Jack Beckman, Davida Wolffson, Edith Lee James, Richard Williams, Geraldine Hamburg, Jack Lucal, Paul Kirk, Tim Osato, Muriel Deutsch, Elizabeth Wirth, Lucille Kevill, Barbara Hitchinson, Gloria Jean, Jack French, Gloria Hunt, Nancy Coggenshall, Arthur Haelig, Richard Frisbie, Nanni Kahn, Frank Mangin, Jr., William Wegener, Claude Brenner, Lois Karpf, Shelia Brenner, Pat Chandler, Corinne Shapira, Sally Bogolub, Joan McCullough, Nancy Bush, Joann Cohen, Lois Jean Hesse, Harve Bennett Fischman, Ruth Duskin, Joel Kupperman, Patrick Owen Conlon, Ruel "Sparky" Fischman, Lonny Lunde, Shelia Conlon, Gunther Hollander, Andre Aerne, Nancy Wong, Norman "Skippy" Miller, Richard Weixler, John C. Pollock, Rochelle Liebling,

Quiz Kids Ruth Duskin and Joel Kupperman visit the Lone Ranger (Brace Beemer) and his horse, Silver. (NBC)

Naomi Cooks, and Robert Burns. The announcers on this program included Fort Pearson, Roger Krupp, and Ed Scott. The series was produced by Louis G. Cowan, directed by Jack Callahan, Riley Jackson, Forrest Owen, Ed Simmons, and Clint Stanley, and written by John Lewellen and Maggie O'Flaherty. Sponsors included Alka Seltzer antacid and One-A-Day vitamins.

QUIZ OF TWO CITIES

| 1944–1946 | Mutual | Sun. | (*) |

"Is Chicago ready? Is New York ready? Then make way for *The Quiz of Two Cities,* brought to you by Listerine toothpaste, the prescription for your teeth!" On this game show, two contestants representing different American cities competed against each other by trying to be the first to answer a question and win a prize. The cities featured on the half-hour show were New York vs. Chicago, Minneapolis vs. St. Paul, and San Francisco vs. Los Angeles. The program was produced by Dan Enright and directed by Ray Kremer. Michael Fitzmaurice was the host and coordinator of the program. Announcer-hosts included Reid Kilpatrick, Mark Goodson, Hale Sparks, Clayton "Bud" COLLYER, and Holland Engle.

RADIO CITY PLAYHOUSE

    1948–1949   NBC   Sat.   10 PM & 10:30 PM
    1949–1950   NBC   Sun.   5 PM

Active radio performers such as Bill ADAMS, Santos ORTEGA, William CONRAD, Joseph KEARNS, Mary Jane HIGBY, and Gertrude Warner and such film stars as Ronald COLMAN, James Stewart, Anita Louise, Robert Taylor, and Barbara Stanwyck were heard on the weekly adaptations of stories written by such authors as James Hilton, Ernest Hemingway, and O. Henry. On one memorable broadcast, an incident similar to Orson Welles's *War of the Worlds* was dramatized by RADIO CITY PLAYHOUSE: When a jet pilot crashes through the sound barrier and goes backward in time, an actual Air Force defense drill was executed on the air as a sound effect. Many listeners believed the drill signal they heard was "the real thing" and that the broadcast was reporting an actual event. Numerous callers reported that they saw "the lights of enemy aircraft" and heard "unexplainable noises coming from the air." Actors Bill LIPTON and John LARKIN were the major performers on this much-publicized broadcast. Fred Collins was the show's announcer. The program was produced by Richard McDonough and directed by Harry Junkin. Its theme music was "Shangri-La."

RADIO PLAYHOUSE, THE

    1976–1977   (Syndicated series. Various stations
                      and times)

In 1976, DCA Productions produced a one-hour program consisting of four daily syndicated 15-minute shows, heard on many stations throughout the United States. On this attempt to bring back daytime radio drama, the four 15-minute shows were *The Faces of Life,* in which a young woman confronts life and love in the 1970s; *The Little Things in Life,* a domestic comedy about life's little frustrations, written by and starring Peg LYNCH and costarring Robert DRYDEN as her husband; *The Author's Studio,* serialized versions of famous novels and plays, such as *Becky Sharp;* and *To Have and to Hold,* three generations of a family caught up in "the conflict between the traditional and the new morality." The executive producer of *The Radio Playhouse* was Dick Cox. Some of the performers heard on these programs were Dolores Sutton, Joyce Gordon, Larry Haines, Charita Bauer, Arthur ANDERSON, Rosemary RICE, Margaret Hamilton, Evie Juster, Arnold STANG, and Roger DeKoven.

RADIO READER'S DIGEST

    1942–1945   CBS   Sun.   9 PM
    1945–1946   CBS   Sun.   2 PM
    1946–1948   CBS   Thurs.   10 PM

This half-hour dramatic anthology presented adaptations of stories from *Reader's Digest* magazine, mainly from their "Life in these United States" features. Actors Richard KOLLMAR and Les TREMAYNE were the program's host-announcers; each story was narrated by film star Conrad NAGEL. Heard regularly were Ethel Barrymore, Edwin Bruce, Edgar Staley, Van Heflin, and Will Geer. The program was produced by Anton Leader and Carl Schullinger and directed by Robert Nolan. Martin Magner wrote many of the scripts. Sponsors included Campbell's soups and Hallmark cards.

RADIO SHOW, THE

1981–present	CBC	Sat.		2:08 PM

CBC's one-hour *The Radio Show* features comedian "Captain Jack" Fare, and offers its listeners interviews, comedy sketches, and send-ups of favorite Canadian institutions, including the show itself. Danny Finkelman and Joy Fielding give comic reviews of current books, Bernadette Hardaker reports on the environment, and "Scoop" Jordon is the show's investigative reporter. The program often presents unusual events, including a mock telethon urging the audience to call in and pledge their local population in a bid to claim "over one billion listeners"; the British Brewery expedition to excavate, translate, and eventually brew beer according to King Tut's recipe; the annual Kelowna, B.C., architecture contest to build a bridge out of spaghetti; and the mysterious case of Albert Einstein's missing brain. The show's producer-director is Gary Graves.

RAFFETTO, MICHAEL (1899–1990)

Actor Michael Raffeto was born in Pleasantville, California, and appeared in several silent films before entering radio. His deep, masculine voice made him one of writer-producer Carlton E. MORSE's favorite performers. Raffetto played Paul on ONE MAN'S FAMILY and Jack Packard on Morse's I LOVE A MYSTERY. Raffetto also directed several episodes of *One Man's Family* and wrote a short-lived series called *The Arms of the Law*. In 1948, he played a major supporting role in the film *A Foreign Affair*. The actor retired from show business shortly thereafter.

RAILROAD HOUR, THE

1948–1949	ABC	Mon.	8 PM
1949–1954	NBC	Mon.	8 PM

Baritone Gordon MacRae, star of the film classics *Oklahoma!* (1955) and *Carousel* (1956), and pop singer Dinah Shore were the stars of this hour-long music-variety series. Orchestra leaders were John Rarig and Carmen Dragon, and the choral director was Norman Luboff. Fran Van Hartenfeld and Ken Burton directed the show, and Jean Holloway was one of its major writers. Marvin MILLER was the program's announcer. The theme song was, appropriately, "I've Been Working on the Railroad"—the sponsor was America's Railroads.

RALEIGH ROOM, THE

See HILDERGARDE.

RANDOLPH, AMANDA (1902–1967)

African-American character actress Amanda Randolph was born in Cleveland, Ohio. Her list of radio-show credits includes both situation-comedy and dramatic-anthology series: the title role on AUNT JEMIMA, a domestic on ABIE'S IRISH ROSE, various roles on AMOS AND ANDY (most notably Sapphire's overbearing mother), and frequent appearances on STUDIO ONE and *The* FORD THEATER. Like her sister, Lillian RANDOLPH, Amanda was occasionally featured on the BEULAH radio series.

RANDOLPH, ISABEL (1890–1973)

Actress Isabel Randolph was born in Chicago, Illinois, to theatrical parents. A character actress who specialized in playing haughty, overbearing socialites, Randolph—who many people thought was English—played Mrs. Uppington on FIBBER MCGEE AND MOLLY and was a regular performer on DAN HARDING'S WIFE, ONE MAN'S FAMILY, *The* STORY OF MARY MARLIN, *A* TALE OF TODAY, and WELCOME VALLEY. On television, Randolph was featured on "The Bob Cummings Show" (1955), "I Love Lucy" (1951–1956), "The Dick Van Dyke Show" (1961–1966), and "Our Miss Brooks" (1952–1953). Her films include *Heavenly Days* (1944), *The Great Gildersleeve* (1943), *Look Who's Laughing* (1941), and *If You Knew Susie* (1948).

RANDOLPH, LILLIAN (1915–1980)

Like her older sister Amanda RANDOLPH, African-American actress Lillian Randolph was born in Cleveland, Ohio, and played Birdie Lee Goggins on *The* GREAT GILDERSLEEVE, various characters on AMOS AND ANDY (including the formidable Madame Queen), and the title role on BEULAH. Randolph's film credits include *The Great Gildersleeve* film series in the 1940s, *Little Men* (1941), *Child of Divorce* (1946), and *Once More Darling* (1949).

RATHBONE, BASIL (1892–1967)

Actor Basil Rathbone, world famous as Sherlock Holmes, was born in Johannesburg, South Africa, to British parents, immigrated to England in 1912, and played various Shakespearean roles in the West End and regional theaters. His first major role in a talkie, after many silent films, in *The Last Mrs. Cheyney* (1929), led to numerous classics, including *David Copperfield* (1935), *Anna Karenina* (1935), and *The Adventures of Robin Hood* (1938). In 1939 he played Sherlock Holmes for the first time in *The Hound of the Baskervilles;* he played the role in fourteen subsequent films and on *The* ADVENTURES OF SHERLOCK HOLMES radio series. Rathbone's innate charm and excellent diction led to increasing radio work in leading roles on TALES OF FATIMA, *The Circle, Scotland Yard's Inspector Burke,* and STARS OVER HOLLYWOOD. His guest appearances in-

Basil Rathbone as Sherlock Holmes (CBS)

clude *The* LUX RADIO THEATER and SCREEN GUILD PLAYERS.

READICK, FRANK, JR. (c1908–1955)

Actor Frank Readick, whose parents and grandparents were actors, was born in Denver, Colorado, and was the second of several actors to play The SHADOW on radio. Readick was also heard on *The Adventures of* MR. MEEK in the title role; *America's Hour*, a World War II special produced by CBS in 1942 to recruit women to help in the war effort; BUCK ROGERS IN THE 25TH CENTURY, *The* CAVALCADE OF AMERICA, *The* FBI IN PEACE AND WAR, FAMOUS JURY TRIALS, *The* MARCH OF TIME (playing New York mayor Jimmy Walker), FORTY-FIVE MINUTES FROM HOLLYWOOD (often portraying film actor James Cagney), and the title role on both *Joe Palooka* and SMILIN' JACK. A regular member of Orson Welles's MERCURY THEATER ON THE AIR, he was heard in the legendary "War of the Worlds" broadcast and appeared in Welles's film *Journey into Fear* (1942).

READICK, ROBERT "BOB" (1926–1985)

Born in New York City, actor Bob Readick, whose father, Frank, was a popular radio actor, appeared in such Broadway shows as *George Washington Slept Here*

(1940) and *All in Favor* (1942) but was also active on radio. Debuting on CBS's LET'S PRETEND in 1939, he was a regular on that show until 1954. Readick also had regular roles on *The* SECOND MRS. BURTON, THIS IS NORA DRAKE, and AUNT JENNRY's *Real Life Stories*. In the 1940s and 1950s, he played the title roles on YOURS TRULY and JOHNNY DOLLAR as well Marlene Dietrich's leading man on her *Cafe Instanbul* program. In the 1970s, Readick was occasionally featured on Himan BROWN's CBS MYSTERY THEATER program.

REAL STORIES FROM REAL LIFE

| 1944–1947 | Mutual | (*) | (*) |

This 15-minute daytime drama series, produced by Frank and Anne HUMMERT and directed by Ernest Ricca, was different from other soap operas in that its serialized stories were on the air for just one week. They always centered around romance or a domestic crisis, such as divorce or child-rearing problems. Mary Jane HIGBY, Anne SEYMOUR, Elspeth ERIC, Gertrude Warner, James MEIGHAN, John Raby, Julie STEVENS, Alice REINHEART, Les TREMAYNE, and Robert DRYDEN were often featured on the series.

RED DAVIS

See PEPPER YOUNG'S FAMILY.

RED RYDER, THE ADVENTURES OF

See ADVENTURES OF RED RYDER, THE.

RED SKELTON SHOW, THE

1939–1940	NBC Blue	Wed.	8:30 PM
1940–1941	NBC Red	Wed.	8:30 PM
1941–1942	NBC Red	Tues.	10:30 PM
1942–1948	NBC	Tues.	10:30 PM
1948–1949	NBC	Fri.	9:30 PM
1949–1951	CBS	Sun.	8:30 PM
1951–1952	CBS	Wed.	9 PM
1952–1953	NBC	Tues.	8:30 PM

On this popular half-hour part-variety and part-situation-comedy show, Red SKELTON played his celebrated comic roles: the mean-widdle kid Junior, Clem Kadiddlehopper, Deadeye the comic cowboy, Willy Lump-Lump, J. Newton Numskull, and Bolivar Shagnasty Harriet HILLIARD, the show's vocalist, and later Lurene TUTTLE played Junior's mother and Red's girlfriend, Daisy June. In addition, Hilliard played Calamity Jane and Mrs. Willy Lump-Lump on the series. GeGe Pearson was regularly heard as Sara Drew, Mrs. Bolivar Shagnasty, Mrs. J. Newton Numskull, and occasionally Mrs. Willy Lump-Lump. Character actress Verna FELTON was prominently featured as Junior's grandmother, and female impersonator Marlin HURT played Mademoiselle Levy. Also heard were singers "Wonderful" Smith, Tommy Mack, and Anita Ellis. Ozzie NELSON and David Rose led the show's orchestra. Jack Simpson produced the program, and Keith McLeod directed it. Announcers included John Holbrook, Patrick McGeehan, Truman BRADLEY, Del King, Marvin MILLER, Rod O'Connor, and Bob Dixon. The program was written by Edna Skelton, Jack Douglas, Ben Freedman, and Johnny Murray. Sponsoring the show were Avalon cigarettes, Raleigh cigarettes, Sir Walter Raleigh pipe tobacco, Tide detergent, Norge refrigerators, and Blue Star razor blades.

REED, ALAN (TEDDY BERGMAN: 1908–1977)

Born in New York City, actor Alan Reed is best known as the voice of cartoon character Fred Flintstone, a part he played for nineteen years from 1960 until his death in 1979. Reed appeared in more than fifty motion pictures, including *Days of Glory* (1944), *Perfect Strangers* (1950), *Kiss of Fire* (1955), and *Tarnished Angels* (1958). And was one of radio's most versatile and prolific performers, playing Daddy to comedienne Fannie Brice's BABY SNOOKS; Falstaff Openshaw, the poetry-reading "ham" actor on the Allen's Alley segment of *The* FRED ALLEN SHOW; Luigi's boss Pasquale on LIFE WITH LUIGI; and Clancy the Cop on DUFFY'S TAVERN. Reed was also a regular on *The* EDDIE CANTOR SHOW, *The* JACK PEARL SHOW, *The* BOB HOPE SHOW, MY FRIEND IRMA (playing Irma's boss, Mr. Clyde), ABIE'S IRISH ROSE (as Abie's father, Solomon Levy), MAXWELL HOUSE COFFEE TIME, *Fun in Swing Time*, and *The* ZIEGFELD FOLLIES OF THE AIR. An accomplished dramatic actor, Reed was often heard on SUSPENSE, *Flash Gordon*, MYRT AND MARGE, VALIANT LADY, AL PEARCE AND HIS GANG, THE COLLIER'S HOUR, *The* PHILIP MORRIS PLAYHOUSE, *The* SHADOW, *The* ADVENTURES OF SAM SPADE, DETECTIVE, and PHILIP MARLOWE, PRIVATE DETECTIVE. Besides his Fred Flintstone cartoon-voice characterization, Reed was the voice of characters in such feature-length animated films as Disney's *Alice in Wonderland* (1951) and *Lady and the Tramp* (1955), and played several vocal roles in the "Touche Turtle" (1962) cartoon series.

REINHEART, ALICE (1910–1993)

Actress Alice Reinheart was born in San Francisco, California. In addition to her stage, film, and television work, she had an impressive list of radio credits. She played Chichi, Papa David Solomon's employee and ward, on LIFE CAN BE BEAUTIFUL and was the leading lady on WE, THE ABBOTTS, *City Desk*, and ROMANCE. She also appeared on GANGBUSTERS, THIS DAY IS OURS, FAMOUS JURY TRIALS, JOYCE JORDAN, SILVER THEATER, MYSTERY THEATER, MY TRUE STORY, YOUNG DR. MALONE, PRETTY KITTY KELLY, TWENTY THOUSAND YEARS IN SING SING, CAVALCADE OF AMERICA, MARCH OF TIME, PERRY

Alan Reed (CBS)

Alice Reinheart (NBC)

MASON, The ADVENTURES OF THE THIN MAN, The FALCON, The ADVENTURES OF ELLERY QUEEN, The SHADOW, INNER SANCTUM MYSTERIES, GRAND CENTRAL STATION, I LOVE A MYSTERY, ONE MAN'S FAMILY, STARS OVER HOLLYWOOD, The WHISTLER, Heartbreak Theater, CASEY, CRIME PHOTOGRAPHER, and AMANDA OF HONEYMOON HILL. Filmgoers saw Reinheart in The Lieutenant Wore Skirts (1956) and A Housed Is Not a Home (1957). On television, Reinheart made guest appearances on "I Dream of Jeannie" (1965), "Make Room for Daddy" (1955–1960), and "The Donna Reed Show" (1958–1966). She acted in Broadway productions of Parapet (1922), The Mask and the Face (1924), Journey to Jerusalem (1940), and Leaf and Bough (1944).

RELIGIOUS PROGRAMS

Christian evangelists such as Aimee Semple McPherson and the mesmerizing Billy Sunday were popular attractions on radio in the late 1920s and throughout the 1930s with their "hell, fire, and brimstone" messages. Catholic priest Father Charles Edward Coughlin had a controversial pro-German "keep America out of the war" weekly program on the air in the mid- to late 1930s that received a large radio audience. Several weekly dramatic shows with a religious slant have also been very popular over the years, including The GREATEST STORY EVER TOLD, The ETERNAL LIGHT (sponsored by the Federation of Jewish Philantrophies), and The AVE MARIA HOUR (sponsored by the Catholic Friars at Greymoor). Soap operas such as The GUIDING LIGHT and LIGHT OF THE WORLD began their radio runs as inspirational daytime serials, but as time went on they abandoned religious themes and concentrated on more domestic concerns. In recent years, both the celebrated evangelists such as Billy Graham and the infamous Jim Baker have once again begun to preach over the American and Canadian airwaves on television as well as radio.

RENFREW OF THE MOUNTED POLICE

1936–1937	CBS	Tues., Fri., Sat.	6:45 PM
1937–1938	NBC Blue	Mon.–Fri.	6:45 PM
1938–1940	NBC Blue	Sat.	6:30 PM

Although on the air for only four seasons, this 15-minute weekday and then half-hour weekly children's adventure serial is inexplicably one of the shows best remembered by old-time radio fans. Actor House JAMESON played law-enforcement officer Inspector Douglas Renfrew of the Royal Canadian Mounted Police, who tracked down dangerous criminals and located children lost in the wilderness of Canada's northern provinces. Joan Baker was heard as his friend Carol Girard. Brad Barker played the many animals heard on the program, including Renfrew's dog. The

series was created, directed, and written by Laurie York Erskine. Bert PARKS was the program's announcer.

RICE, ROSEMARY (c1925–   )

Before she became Katrin on the television serie "Mama" from 1949 until 1958, Rosemary Rice, wh was born in Montclair, New Jersey, was a frequent per former on radio. Usually playing ingenues and young leading-lady roles—including Betty on ARCHIE AN DREWS, Susan Wakefield on The RIGHT TO HAPPINES Kathy Cameron on WHEN A GIRL MARRIES, and Jill Ma lone on YOUNG DR. MALONE—she was regularly hear on LIFE CAN BE BEAUTIFUL, The THEATER GUILD OF TH AIR, LET'S PRETEND, The CAVALCADE OF AMERICA, Th SECOND MRS. BURTON, The FBI IN PEACE AND WAR, M. PERKINS, GRAND CENTRAL STATION, NBC THEATER, SU PENSE, and STUDIO ONE. The actress had the lead role Francie in Fletcher Markle's award-winning produc tion of A Tree Grows in Brooklyn on the Studio One radi series. In the 1970s, Rice was featured on Hima BROWN'S CBS MYSTERY THEATER series and was a princ pal actress on TO HAVE AND TO HOLD. Early in her ca reer, Rice appeared in several successful Broadwa productions, including Junior Miss (1941), Dear Rut (1945), and Mr. Roberts (1947). She recorded origin and classic children's songs and stories and won Grammy for her album Learning to Tell Time wit Grandson Clock. In addition to appearing in "Mama" o television, Rice was also featured on "The Kraft Th ater" (1954), "Studio One" (1956), and "The Edge Night" (1962), as well as on television commercials fo products such as Campbell's soup, Lady Clairol ("If have only one life to live, let me live it as a blonde" Lux soap, Shell oil, and Buick, Ford and Plymouth au tomobiles, winning a television-commercial Cle award for her efforts.

RICH, IRENE (IRENE LUTHER: 1891–1988)

Actress Irene Rich was born in Buffalo, New Yor made her first film appearance in 1919 in the siler movie The Trap, and subsequently became one the screen's major stars, appearing in films such Desperate Trials (1921), Compromise (1925), and Craig Wife (1928). Rich debuted in radio in 1933 and wa subsequently heard on such programs as Dear Joh Glorious One, The WOMAN FROM NOWHERE, and he own IRENE RICH DRAMAS anthology series. She als worked in regional theater and on Broadway i George M. Cohan's long-running mystery play Seve Keyes to Baldpate and appeared in such sound films Strangers May Kiss (1931), Down to Earth (1932), an This Time for Keeps (1941). In 1933, Rich's spons Welch's grape juice hosted a forty-second birthda party for her that "anyone was invited to attend and in 1934 *Variety* called Rich "a radio personality probably without counterpart."

RICH MAN'S DARLING

See OUR GAL SUNDAY.

RICHARD DIAMOND, PRIVATE DETECTIVE

1949	NBC	Sun.	7 PM
1949–1950	NBC	Sat.	7:30 PM
1950	NBC	Wed.	10 PM
1950–1951	NBC	Sat.	8:30 PM
1951–1952	ABC	Fri.	8 PM
1952–1953	(Off the air)		
1953	CBS	Sun.	7:30 PM

Motion-picture actor Dick POWELL and then Steve Dunne played Richard Diamond, a tough-talking, smooth-with-the-ladies, singing private detective on this half-hour weekly mystery show. At the end of each program, Powell always managed to find the time to sing a song for his girlfriend, one of *Richard Diamond*'s trademarks. Featured were Ed BEGLEY (as Police Lieutenant Levinson), Virginia GREGG (as Diamond's rich girlfriend, Helen Asher), and Wilms Herbert (as Helen's butler). Gloria Blondell, Betty Lou GERSON, Jane Morgan, Hy Averback, Jack Kruschen, Herb Butterfield, Jay Novello, Jeanne Bates, and Ted DeCorsia were often featured in the supporting cast. Bill Forman announced the show. The program was directed by Jaime DelValle, William Rousseau, and Richard Sanville. Blake Edward wrote the scripts. The music for the show was under the direction of Frank Worth. Rexall drugs and Camel cigarettes sponsored the program.

RICHARDSON, ETHEL PARK (1883–c1960)

Pioneer broadcaster Ethel Park Richardson was born in Deckerd, Tennessee. An early writer, producer, and actress on radio, Richardson made major contributions to the medium while working at the fledgling National Broadcasting Company in the late 1920s and early 1930s: most notably, she produced a series of radio plays based on American folk tales and songs such as Johnny Appleseed, Barbara Allen, and Paul Bunyon. When she ran out of folk-story material, Richardson turned to Shakespeare and adapted his plays for radio, using country-hillbilly settings and dialogue. Many later-to-be-famous performers made their radio debuts on Richardson's programs, including Agnes MOOREHEAD, singing cowboy Tex Ritter, and soap-opera star Anne ELSTNER. Her contribution to folk music consisted of recording, and therefore preserving, numerous songs, such as "Barbara Allen" and "On Top of Old Smoky," that might otherwise have been lost to future generations of Americans.

RIGGS, TOMMY (1908–1957)

Born in Pittsburgh, Pennsylvania, ventriloquist-comedian Tommy Riggs worked in vaudeville as a comedian-ventriloquist and then turned to radio in the mid-1930s; he appeared on The RUDY VALLEE SHOW, performing in his own voice and introducing a character named Betty Lou in a comedy sketch. Though Betty Lou never actually existed as a dummy, the act was an immediate success and led to many more radio guest appearances. Eventually Riggs was offered a show of his own, *The* TOMMY RIGGS AND BETTY LOU SHOW. Illness caused Riggs to retire from show business at the height of his career, and he died of cancer when he was only 49 years old.

RIGHT TO HAPPINESS, THE

1939–1940	NBC Blue	Mon.–Fri.	11:15 AM
1940–1941	NBC Blue	Mon.–Fri.	10:15 AM
1941–1942	CBS	Mon.–Fri.	1:30 PM
1942–1955	NBC	Mon.–Fri.	3:45 PM
1955–1956	NBC	Mon.–Fri.	4 PM
1956–1957	CBS	Mon.–Fri.	2 PM
1957–1960	CBS	Mon.–Fri.	2:05 PM

One of the longest-running 15-minute drama series on the air. *The Right To Happiness*s heroine Carolyn Kramer Nelson was played by Claudia MORGAN and then by Eloise Kummer. Doris Cameron was played by Selena Royle, Constance Crowder, and finally by Irene Hubbard. Ruth Bailey played Rose Kransky, a down-to-earth, somewhat common young woman with a heart of gold. Regularly featured on the series were radio actors Charles "Chuck" Webster, Billy Redfield, Art Kohl, Hugh STUDEBAKER, Julian Noa, Dick Wells, Don MACLAUGHLIN, Alice Yourman, Kenneth Daigneau, Peter Capell, Carl Kroenke, Jerry Macy, Sidney Ellstrom, Anne Sargent, Maurice Franklin, Dora Johnson, child impersonator Sarah Fussell, Kevin McCarthy, Gary MERRILL, Peter Fernandez, Reese Taylor, Carlton Kadell, Sarajane Wells, Frank Behrens, Ed Prentiss, David GOTHARD, Sunda Love, Mary Patton, Bernadine Flynn, Lucy Gilman, Pat Murphy, Virginia Dwyer, Les DAMON, Charita Bauer, Alexander SCOURBY, Rosemary RICE, Ian Martin, Luise Barclay, Staats COTSWORTH, John LARKIN, Virginia "Ginger" Jones, Bill LIPTON, Bill Quinn, Ethel Owen, Gertrude Warner, and Helene Dumas. The series was produced by Paul Martin, Carl Wester, Kathleen Lane, and Fayette Krum and directed by Frank Papp, Charles Urquhart, Joseph Bell, Carl Wester, Howard Keegan, Art Hanna, and Gil Gibbons. Irna PHILLIPS and John M. Young were the show's chief writers. Announcing the program were Ron Rawson, Michael Fitzmaurice, Don Gordon, Marvin MILLER, and Hugh Conover. Gilbert Ralston directed the program in the late 1930s and early 1940s, and sponsors included

Crisco shortening, Ivory soap, Duz detergent, Dreft detergent, Spic and Span floor cleaner, Blue Cheer detergent, Joy dishwashing liquid, Tide detergent, and Columbia phonographs and records. The show's theme song was "Song of the Soul" by Breil.

RIN-TIN-TIN

1930–1931	NBC Blue	Sat.	8:15 PM
1931–1932	NBC Blue	Thurs.	8:15 PM
1932–1933	NBC Blue	Thurs.	8:30 PM
1933–1934	CBS	Sun.	7:45 PM
1934–1955	(Off the air)		
1955	Mutual	Sun.	5 PM

Brad Barker, an actor known for playing various animals on many radio programs throughout the 1930s and 1940s, played the part of filmdom's most famous dog-hero, Rin-Tin-Tin, on this radio show. The adventure series, heard in both 15- and 30-minute formats, had actor Francis X. Bushman as the wonder dog's owner and Lee Duncan, who actually owned the real Rin-Tin-Tin, in the supporting cast. Rin-Tin-Tin spent episodes tracking down criminals and performing acts of heroism, such as saving a drowning child. The canine hero returned to the airwaves on television in 1954 and then in a half-hour radio program. Over the years, the show was appropriately sponsored by Ken-L Ration dog food and Milk-Bone dog biscuits.

RIPLEY, ROBERT (1893–1949)

Born on Christmas Day in Santa Rosa, California, Robert Ripley was working for *The New York Evening Globe* newspaper as a cartoonist when he first got the idea for his "Believe It Or Not" cartoon-column, which illustrated and reported odd, fantastic facts (how deep the deepest part of the world's oceans is) and incidents (how Columbus actually thought he had reached India when he had in fact landed on a Caribbean island) as well as depicting two-headed men and previously unseen animals. The newspaper feature became so popular that a BELIEVE IT OR NOT radio show was produced, with Ripley serving as the program's host. In addition to Ripley's strange and unusual facts, dramatizations of certain items were also presented. Ripley received more than a million letters a year for more than twenty years from people who thought they had unusual stories or circumstances to report, according to NBC. This is more mail than any individual has received in history to this date. Ripley wrote and drew his syndicated column until his death.

RISE OF THE GOLDBERGS, THE

See GOLDBERGS, THE.

ROAD OF LIFE, THE

1937–1938	NBC Blue	Mon.–Fri.	11:15 AM
	NBC Red	Mon.–Fri.	4:45 PM
1938–1939	CBS	Mon.–Fri.	9:30 AM
	NBC Red	Mon.–Fri.	4:45 PM
1939–1940	NBC Red	Mon.–Fri.	11:45 AM
	CBS	Mon.–Fri.	1:30 PM
1940–1941	NBC Red	Mon.–Fri.	11:15 AM
	CBS	Mon.–Fri.	1:45 PM
1941–1942	NBC Red	Mon.–Fri.	10:45 AM
	CBS	Mon.–Fri.	1:45 PM
1942–1945	NBC	Mon.–Fri.	11 AM
1945–1949	NBC	Mon.–Fri.	10:30 AM
1949–1954	NBC	Mon.–Fri.	3:15 PM
1954–1956	CBS	Mon.–Fri.	1 PM
1956–1959	CBS	Mon.–Fri.	1:45 PM

Once "the story of a widowed Irish-American mother and the trouble she had raising her children on her own," this long-running, 15-minute drama series was eventually set in a typical American big-city hospital. During the 1940s, Dr. Jim Brent, played by Ken Griffin, Matt CROWLEY, Don MACLAUGHLIN, David Ellis, and Howard Teichmann, was the series' major character. The nurse who paged Dr. Brent at the opening of each program was played by Jeanette Dowling and then by Angel Casey. Marion Shockley and then Lesley Woods played Dr. Jim's wife, Carol. Heard as Helen were Peggy Allenby, Betty Lou GERSON, Muriel Bremmer, and then Janet Logan. Other supporting players included Gowan Stephenson, Jack Rosleigh, Percy Hemus, Carlton KaDell, Hope Summers, Doris Rich, Vivian Fridell, Lawson Zerbe, Effie Palmer, Marvin MILLER, Barbara Fuller, Charlotte MANSON, Frank Dane, Willard WATERMAN, Jeanette Dowling, Guy Sorel, Ethel Wilson, Joseph "Joe" Latham, Sarajane Wells, Evelyn Varden, Louise Fitch, Anne Sargent, Ethel Everett, Reese Taylor, Helen Lewis, Frank Behrens, Harry Elders, Jack Bivens, Bill Griffis, Gladys Heen, Angeline Orr, Dorothy Sands, Russell Thorson, Bill LIPTON, Abby LEWIS, Bret MORRISON, Barbara LUDDY, Nanette Sargeant, Mary Patton, Art Kohl, John LARKIN, Julie STEVENS, Lyle Sudrow, and Sam Wanamaker. Clayton "Bud" COLLYER, Ron Rawson, Gene Baker, Nelson CASE, Dick Joy, James Fleming, Stu Metz, and George Bryan announced the series. *The Road of Life* was produced by Carl Wester, Walt Ehrgott, Kay Lane, and Feyette Krumm. Charles Schenck, Charles Urquhart, Walter Gorman, Elizabeth Howard, Stanley Davis, and Gil Gibbons directed the program at various times. The program's theme music was the first movement of Tchaikovsky's Sixth Symphony ("Pathetique"). Sponsors included Chipso detergent, Oxydol detergent, Ivory soap flakes, Duz detergent, Crisco shortening, Ivory soap, Hazel Bishop lipstick, Drene shampoo, and Spic and Span floor cleaner.

ROBERT Q. LEWIS SHOW, THE

1947–1948	CBS	Sun.	2 PM
1948–1949	CBS	Sun.	5 PM
1949–1950	CBS	Fri.	8 PM
1950–1952	CBS	Fri.	9:30 PM

1952–1953	CBS	Sat.	9:45 AM
1953–1954	CBS	Sat.	10:15 AM
1954–1956	CBS	Sat.	11 AM

Robert Q. Lewis, a popular television personality in the 1950s, was one of radio's leading daytime variety–talk show hosts. Lewis's 15-minute, half-hour, and hour-long programs featured Tom Mahoney, character actress Doro Merande, Cam Andrews, and the Chordettes. Similar in format to *The* ARTHUR GODFREY SHOW, this program was first on the air in the early-evening hours but drew a larger audience as a morning feature. Sponsors of the program included Pine Sol disinfectant-cleaner, Perma Starch, Kasco Dog Ration dog food, Suave shampoo, Helene Curtis Shampoo Plus Egg, Royal Crown Cola, Van Kamp tuna, and Gala bleach.

ROBERTS, KEN (PAUL TROCHWON: 1908–   )

Ken Roberts's precise diction and rich baritone voice made him one of radio's most popular announcers. Roberts was born in New York City and entered radio as an announcer in 1931. He is perhaps best remembered as the chief spokesman for Philip Morris cigarettes. The list of radio programs Roberts announced include QUICK AS A FLASH (which he also hosted), *The* PHILIP MORRIS PLAYHOUSE, *The* MARY MARGARET MCBRIDE SHOW, HOBBY LOBBY, *Lady Esther Serenades*, AL PEARCE AND HIS GANG, *The* BABY SNOOKS SHOW, EASY ACES, GRAND CENTRAL STATION, IT PAYS TO BE IGNORANT, JOYCE JORDAN, GIRL INTERN, BRENDA CURTIS, *The Sophie Tucker Show, The* SHADOW, and THIS IS NORA DRAKE. Roberts also announced several successful television programs, most notably the "Candid Camera" show in the 1950s. Roberts continued to record voice-over announcements for numerous television products until his retirement in the 1980s.

ROBSON, WILLIAM N. (1906–1995)

Born in Pittsburgh, Pennsylvania, William N. Robson was the creative genius who guided the *Suspense* program for approximately three years. On the production staff of CBS radio during the 1930s and 1940s, Robson was a director who understood radio as the sound-oriented medium that it is. With a natural sense for what would work on radio, William Robson was able to handle scripts deftly and get the most out of actors' voices. In addition to directing SUSPENSE, Robson directed BIG TOWN, *The* COLUMBIA WORKSHOP, MAN BEHIND THE GUN, ESCAPE, *A* MAN CALLED X, *The* PRUDENTIAL FAMILY HOUR, and *The* RADIO READER'S DIGEST.

ROCKY FORTUNE

| 1953–1954 | NBC | Tues. | 9:30 PM |
| 1954–1955 | CBS | Wed. | 9 PM |

In the mid-1950s, shortly before his comeback as a dramatic actor in films, singer Frank SINATRA starred on a short-lived half-hour weekly radio detective-adventure series called *Rocky Fortune.* He played a street-tough private eye who solved various crimes for a colorful assortment of unusual clients. He was replaced at the season's end by actor Jack Hoyles. Frequently heard supporting Sinatra were Jeanne Bates, Jack Mather, and Barney Phillips. The show was directed by Lucy Love and written by George Lefferts.

When Moyles played Rocky Fortune, he was the owner of the Cafe Tambourine in Cairo, Egypt, a club not unlike Rick's Cafe Americaine in the film *Casablanca* (1941). The series was moved from NBC to CBS, was directed by Gordon T. Hughes, and written by Gomer Kool and Larry Roman. Larry Thor was the show's announcer.

ROGERS, ROY (LEONARD SLYE: 1912–   )

Billed as "the King of the Cowboys," American country-western cowboy singer-actor Roy Rogers was born in Cincinnati, Ohio. With his horse, Trigger, and his wife, singer-actress Dale Evans, Rogers starred in dozens of pot-boiler, second-feature Western films on radio and television. Working in a shoe factory and as a fruit picker, Rogers's talent as a singer and guitarist led him to sing on local radio shows in the Cincin-

Roy Rogers, Dale Evans, and Trigger (Republic Pictures)

nati area in the early 1930s. Republic Pictures thought his clean-cut, all-American looks would make him a popular cowboy star and soon had him starring in such films as *Tumbling Tumbleweed* (1935), *The Arizona Kid* (1939), and *The Yellow Rose of Texas* (1944). On radio he starred on *The* ROY ROGERS SHOW for more than a decade and then on "The Roy Rogers Show" on television. Later, Rogers and Evans made—and still make—frequent guest appearances at rodeos and state fairs across the country and guest-starred on television's "The Chevy Show" in 1961. Roy still makes occasional public appearances on television and on the stage.

ROGERS, WILL (1879–1935)

Oklahoma-born humorist Will Rogers was one of the United States's favorite entertainers because he talked simply about things everyone in his audience had in common as he swung his lariat. Rogers starred in *The Ziegfeld Follies of 1919* on Broadway and subsequently appeared in the films *A Connecticut Yankee in King Arthur's Court* (1930), *State Fair* (1933), *David Harum* (1934), *In Old Kentucky* (1935), and others; on radio he appeared on *The* EVERREADY HOUR and made guest appearances on *The* ZIEGFELD FOLLIES OF THE AIR. A shrewd observer of politics and the American people, Rogers's popularity with the public was such that it was even suggested that he run for president of the United States. A well-known philanthropist, he insisted that any fees he received for his radio appearances be donated to the American Red Cross. The star died tragically in an airplane crash in 1935.

ROGUE'S GALLERY

1945	NBC	Sun.	7:30 PM (Summer)
1945–1946	Mutual	Thur.	8:30 PM
1946	NBC	Sun.	7:30 PM (Summer)
1947	NBC	Sun.	7:30 PM (Summer)
1950–1951	ABC	Wed.	9 PM

Movie star Dick POWELL played private eye Richard Rogue on this half-hour pre–RICHARD DIAMOND detective-mystery series. Originally a summer-replacement show for *The* FITCH BANDWAGON, *Rogue's Gallery* stayed on the air for an additional year. In 1946, the show was once again presented as a summer replacement for *The Fitch Bandwagon*; the following season it returned to the airwaves with motion-picture actor Barry Sullivan in the leading role. Then in 1951, after a three-year absence, the series again returned with actor Paul Stewart as Rogue. The show was originally produced and directed by Dee Engelbach and subsequently produced by Charles Varda and directed by Clark Andrews and Jack Lyman. The series was written by Roy Buffum.

ROMANCE

1943–1946	CBS	Tues.	8:30 PM
1946–1948	CBS	Sat.	7:30 PM
1948–1950	CBS	Tues.	9 PM
1950–1953	(Off the air)		
1953–1954	CBS	Thurs.	9 PM
1954–1956	CBS	Sat.	10:05 PM

The stories presented on this series always centered around romantic encounters, adventures, and love affairs. Radio regulars heard on this series included William CONRAD, Georgia Ellis, Will Wright, Herb Ellis, Shirley MITCHELL, Harry Bartell, Barney Phillips, Lamont Johnstone, Junius Matthews, John Dehner, Jack Moyles, Virginia GREGG, Jack Kruschen, Larry Dobkin, and Ben WRIGHT. The series was produced and directed by Norman MacDonald. It was sponsored for many years by Wrigley's spearmint gum and also by Colgate toothpaste, Palmolive soap, and Jergen's lotion.

ROMANCE OF HELEN TRENT, THE

1933–1936	CBS	Mon.–Fri.	2:15 PM
1936–1937	CBS	Mon.–Fri.	11:15 AM
1937–1960	CBS	Mon.–Fri.	12:30 PM

On the air continuously for more than twenty-seven years, *The Romance of Helen Trent* told "the story of a woman who sets out to prove ... that romance can live on at thirty-five ... and even beyond." Fashion designer Helen Trent, whose many lovers usually met with untimely ends due to accidents or wartime military service, was played over the years by Virginia Clark (who originated the role), Betty Ruth Smith, and Julie STEVENS. Helen's various lovers were played by David GOTHARD (perhaps her longest-lasting suitor), Marvin MILLER, William Green, Carlton Ka Dell, Cornelius Peeples, Reese Taylor, Grant Richards, Olan SOULE, and Roy Gabler. In ongoing featured roles were Hilda Graham, Ed Latimer, Sarah Burton, Florence Robinson, Alice Hill, Lou KRUGMAN, Marie Nelson, Katherine Emmet, Bess McCammon, Loretta Poynton, Selena Royle, Vivian Fridell, Virginia "Ginger" Jones, Bartlett "Bart" Robinson, Patricia Dunlap, Herb Nelson, Charlotte MANSON, Bernice Silverman, Hal Studer, Hope Summers, Alice Goodkin, William Green, Reese Taylor, Donna Reade, Alan Hewitt, Nanette Sargeant, Bill BOUCHEY, Spencer Bentley, Lesley Woods, Mary Jane HIGBY, Cathleen Cordell, Doris Rich, Mitzi Gould, Helene Dumas, Janet Logan, Les TREMAYNE, Don MACLAUGHLIN, and Ed Prentiss. Chicago announcers included Don HANCOCK and Pierre Andre. The New York announcer was Fielden Farrington. Blair Walliser, Les Mitchel, Ernest Ricca, and Richard Leonard directed the program. The show was written by Ruth Borden, Martha Alexander, Ronald

Dawson, and Marie Banner. The series' theme song was "Juanita." When *The Romance of Helen Trent* went off the air in 1956, *Time* magazine ran an obituary for the show, naming it "the oldest of all soap operas." *The Romance of Helen Trent's* formidable list of sponsors included Old English wax, Fly-ded bug killer, Angelus lipstick, Clapp's baby food, Kolynos toothpaste, BiSoDol antacid mints, Black Flag bug killer, various Lever Brothers products, Campana face cream, Scott paper, Aerowax, Wizard Wick room deodorizer, and Hopper's White Clay Pack facial mask.

RONSON, ADELE (c. 1918–)

Actress Adele Ronson was born in New York City and educated at Columbia University. She appeared on Broadway and in regional theater productions of *Road to Rome*, *The Portrait of Dorian Gray*, and *The Legend of Leona* in the 1920s and 1930s. Debuting on radio in 1930, Ronson played Wilma Deering on BUCK ROGERS IN THE 25TH CENTURY for several years and Uncle David's "college girl" daughter on *The* GOLD-BERGS. The actress also played major roles on *The* ENO CRIME CLUB, *On Broadway*, MY TRUE STORY, INNER SANCTUM MYSTERIES, PERRY MASON, MR. KEEN, TRACER OF LOST PERSONS, *The* GIBSON FAMILY, *The Little Things in Life*, JOHN'S OTHER WIFE, MEYER THE BUYER, and WE LOVE AND LEARN.

ROOSEVELT, ELEANOR

See STARRING MRS. ROOSEVELT; POND'S PROGRAM.

ROOSEVELT, FRANKLIN D.

See FIRESIDE CHATS.

ROSE OF MY DREAMS

| 1946–1948 | CBS | Mon.–Fri. | 2:45 PM |

This 15-minute drama series was "the story of two sisters: Rose, who is sweet and kind, and Sarah, who is devious and scheming, and their attempts to win the heart of an Englishman, a man who toys with both of them." Mary Rolfe and Charita Bauer played the sisters, and Joseph CURTIN was the romantic Englishman. Larry Elliott was the series' announcer. Sweetheart soap and Blu White bleach sponsored the program.

ROSEMARY

| 1944–1945 | NBC | Mon.–Fri. | 11:15 AM |
| 1946–1955 | CBS | Mon.–Fri. | 11:45 AM |

This series told of a young woman trying to succeed as a single woman living in a typical, large American city. *Rosemary* starred Betty WINKLER and then Virginia Kaye as the title character. Featured in the cast

were Sidney Smith, Joan Alexander, Ethel Owen, Charles Penman, Patsy Campbell, Ed Latimer, James Van Dyke, Elspeth ERIC, Helen Choate, Jone Allison, Jackie KELK, Bill ADAMS, Marion Barney, Lesley Woods, Joan Lazer, Larry Haines, Ethel Wilson, Robert READICK, Casey Allen, and George Keane. Announcers included Gil Herbert, Joe O'Brien, Ed HERLIHY, and Bob Dixon. The series was produced by Tom McDermott and directed by Carl Eastman, Hoyt Allen, Leslie Harris, Theodora Yates, Ralph Butler, and Charles Fisher. The program was written by Elaine Sterne CARRINGTON. Dash detergent, Ivory Snow, Prell shampoo, Camay soap, and Tide detergent sponsored the series.

ROSES AND DRUMS

| 1932–1933 | CBS | Sun. | (*) |
| 1934–1936 | NBC Blue | Sun. | (*) |

The American Civil War was the background for this historical drama series. The half-hour program, noted for its historical accuracy, related stories of heroism, romance, and adventure related to two Army officers, one a Northerner and one a Southerner. Reed Brown, Jr., played Captain Gordon Wright, the Union officer; John Griggs played Captain Randy Claymore, the Confederate officer. Also heard playing the soldiers' friends and family members were Florence WILLIAMS, Betty Love, Helen Claire, Pedro de Cordoba, De Wolf Hopper, Osgood Perkins, Walter Connolly, Guy Bates Post, Richard Mansfield, and Jack Rosleigh. Professor M. W. Jennings of the University of Chicago checked the scripts, which were written by various uncredited authors, for historical accuracy. Herschel Williams directed the series.

ROSS, DAVID (1881–1975)

Born in New York City, David Ross was equally adept at announcing and hosting radio programs. From as early as 1926, Ross introduced or hosted *Arabesque*, *Coke Club*, *The* FRED WARING SHOW, *The* HENRY MORGAN SHOW, MYRT AND MARGE, *The Old Curiosity Shop*, *The Studebacker Champions*, *Time to Shine*, CHESTERFIELD PRESENTS, TAKE IT OR LEAVE IT, and *Poet's Gold*. Ross was also a talented poet, and his poetry appeared in *The New Republic*, and *The Nation*. For many years, Ross was the "Bob" of *The True Story Hour with Mary and Bob*.

ROSS, LANNY (LANCELOT PATRICK ROSS: 1906–1988)

Singing star Lanny Ross was born in Seattle, Washington. Ross's father, Douglas, was a noted Shakespearean actor, while his mother was a professional pianist and ballet-dancer Anna Pavlova's accompanist. Lanny graduated from Yale University and then studied law at Columbia University. In 1928, while attending law school, he paid his expenses by singing on the radio and was so successful that he began a career in show business. Soon he was the featured singer of MAXWELL HOUSE COFFEE TIME and then SHOW BOAT. For several seasons, Ross, known as "the troubador of the moon," was the leading male singer on YOUR HIT PARADE before Frank Sinatra took over. During his earliest years on radio, Ross's speaking voice was supplied by actor Allyn Joslyn, but, as his career progressed, his speech improved and he eventually spoke for himself.

ROXY AND HIS GANG

1922–1927	(*)	(*)	(*)
1927–1928	NBC Blue	Mon.	7:30 PM
1928–1930	NBC Blue	Sun.	2 PM
1930–1931	NBC Blue	Sun.	11 PM
1932–1934	(Off the air)		
1934–1935	CBS	Sat.	8 PM

The first radio program to actually broadcast "live" from a theater, *Roxy and His Gang* originated from the stage of the Roxy Theater in New York City and then from the stage of Radio City Music Hall. On his first hour-long broadcast, Roxy theater owner Samuel L. Rothafel (known as Roxy) led the show's orchestra. Although he couldn't read music, he knew the general tempo of songs and managed to conduct the orchestra effectively. Among the musical celebrities heard on the show were the Fred WARING and Erno Rappe orchestras; singers Marie Gambarelli and "Wee" Willy Robyn; tenors James MELTON, Jan Peerce, and Harold Van Duzee; baritones Leonard Warren, Bomby Bomberger, and Douglas Stanbury; bass Peter Hanover; contraltos Beatrice Belkin, Florence Mulholland, and Adelaide De Loca; and sopranos Caroline Andrews, Betsy Ayers, and Gladys Rice. The Roxy Male Quartet was also regularly featured on the program. Phil Carlin was the show's announcer. Rothafel produced and directed the series, which his Roxy Theater sponsored.

ROY ROGERS SHOW, THE

1944–1945	Mutual	Tues.	8:30 PM
1945–1946	(Off the air)		
1946–1947	NBC	Sat.	9 PM
1947–1948	(Off the air)		
1948–1951	Mutual	Sun.	6 PM
1951–1952	NBC	Fri.	9 PM
1952–1955	NBC	Thurs.	8 PM

Movie cowboy star Roy ROGERS and his gang had several popular half-hour radio programs on the air, always featuring songs sung by Rogers, as well as exciting Western drama-adventure segments. The gang consisted of singer-actress Dale Evans (later Rogers's wife), character actors Gabby Hayes and Pat Brady, Forrest Lewis, and Bob Nolan. Also featured were the singing groups the Whipporwills and the Sons of the Pioneers, Roy Williams and the Riders of the Purple Sage orchestra, Rogers's wonder horse Trigger, his dog Bullet, and announcer-narrator Marvin MILLER. Billed as "the King of the Cowboys," Rogers's theme song was "Happy Trails" (often sung with Dale Evans). Announcers were Lou Crosby and Verne Smith. *The Roy Rogers Show* was produced and directed at different times by Tom Hargis, Art Rush, Fran Van Hartenfeldt, and Ralph Rose and was written by Ray Wilson. Sponsors included Goodyear tires, Alka-Seltzer antacid, Quaker Oats cereal, Post cereals, and Dodge automobiles.

ROYAL CANADIAN AIR FARCE, THE

1972–present	CBC	Sat., Sun.	10:35 AM (Stereo-FM)
			1:08 PM (Radio-AM)

After more than twenty years on the air, the CANADIAN BROADCASTING CORPORATION'S *Royal Canadian Air Farce Show* remains one of Canada's favorite half-hour comedy programs. The show offers a "cheeky" and unabashed satirical slant on the rich and famous, politics, government, sports figures, authority figures, and religion. Often poking fun at such political figures as Canadian Prime Minister Trudeau, the show also lampoons Americans and bewails the notion that Canadians are simply "Invisible Americans." The troupe consists of Roger Abbott, Don Ferguson, Luba Goy, and John Morgan.

The Royal Canadian Air Farce: (from left) Don Ferguson, Luba Goy, John Horgan, and Roger Abbott (CBC)

RUDY VALLEE SHOW, THE (AKA THE FLEISCHMANN HOUR; THE SEALTEST PROGRAM; THE SEALTEST VILLAGE STORE; VILLA VALLEE; VALLEE VARIETIES)

1929–1941			(Various shows not called but best known by the public as *The Rudy Vallee Show*)
1941–1942	NBC Red	Thurs.	10 PM
1942–1943	NBC	Thurs.	9:30 PM
1944–1946	NBC	Thurs.	10:30 PM
1946–1947	NBC	Tues.	8 PM

Singer and heartthrob Rudy VALLEE had several programs on the air over the years that had different titles but were usually referred to as *The Rudy Vallee Show*. As the singing-star-host of *The* FLEISCHMANN HOUR in 1929, Vallee set the standard for musical comedy–variety radio shows that followed. Over the years, Vallee introduced many celebrated performers: English comedienne Beatrice Lillie, Ezra "Henry Aldrich" STONE, Edgar BERGEN and his dummy Charlie McCarthy, Brazilian singer-bombshell Carmen Miranda, ventriloquist Tommy RIGGS, Eddie CANTOR, Milton BERLE, Phil BAKER, Olson and Johnson, singer-actress Alice FAYE, and Bob BURNS. Vallee also presented dramatic sketches on his program, and among his most popular guests were John Barrymore, Helen Hayes, Ethel Barrymore, Eva LaGallienne, and Walter Huston. His theme song was "My Time Is Your Time."

Following his long-running success as the host of *The Fleischmann Hour*, Vallee starred on several other programs in the 1940s, all of which were called *The Rudy Vallee Show*. Regulars on these programs included actors John and Ethel Barrymore, comedienne Joan DAVIS, Monty Woolley, and Sara Berner as a comic character named Conchita Shapiro. The show's announcers included James "Jimmy" WALLINGTON, Dresser Dahlstead, Knox Manning, Carol Hurst, and Marvin MILLER. *The Rudy Vallee Show* was directed by Gordon Thompson, Tony Sanford, Art Daly, Howard Wiley, and Jim Wright. Vallee's writers were George Faulkner, Bob Colwell, A. L. Alexander, Henrietta Feldstein, Sid Zelinka, Sam Silver, R. Marks, and Carroll Carroll. In addition to Fleischmann's yeast, sponsors included Sealtest dairy products, Philip Morris cigarettes, and Drene shampoo.

RUSH LIMBAUGH SHOW, THE

1988–present	(Syndicated series. Various stations and times)

One of America's highest-rated radio talk shows, the two-hour *Rush Limbaugh Show* is controversial, reactionary, and politically to the right.

RUTH, BABE

See ADVENTURES OF BABE RUTH, THE.

RUTH ETTING SHOW, THE (AKA THE DEMI-TASSE REVUE)

1932–1933	CBS	Mon., & Thurs.	9 PM
1933–1934	(Off the air)		
1934–1935	NBC Blue	Thurs.	7:45 PM

Popular blues singer Ruth ETTING was the hostess and singing attraction on this variety-music program, heard in both 15- and 30-minute formats and sponsored by Kellogg's Pep cereal, Chesterfield cigarettes, MJB coffee, and Dodge automobiles.

RYAN, IRENE (IRENE NOBLETTE: 1902–1973)

Actress Irene Ryan was born in El Paso, Texas. Television situation-comedy devotees remember the character actress–comedienne as Granny on the long-running series "The Beverly Hillbillies" (1962–1968). Before her success on that program, however, Ryan maintained careers on radio and in films. Ryan used her maiden name, Irene Noblette, for her radio work and was first heard in the late 1920s on *Circus Night* as a singer and a comedienne. She was a regular performer on *The* BOB HOPE SHOW, *The* JACK CARSON SHOW, and *The* TEXACO STAR THEATER, and was also heard on *Fun in Swing Time*, CAREFREE CARNIVAL, *Royal Crown Revue*, and THE FLEISCHMANN HOUR. With her husband, Tim Ryan, she costarred on *The Tim and Irene Show*. Ryan's film work included *Melody for Three* (1941), *San Diego, I Love You* (1944), *Diary of a Chambermaid* (1946), *Meet Me After the Show* (1951), and *Blackbeard the Pirate* (1952).

RYAN, PATRICIA (1921–1949)

Actress Patricia Ryan was born in London, England, but settled in New York City. In 1929, Ryan was hired to play Helen on Yolanda Langworthy's radio show for children, *The Adventures of Helen and Mary*. CBS staffer Nila MACK took over as the head writer and director of this series shortly after its debut and eventually renamed it LET'S PRETEND. Ryan remained on the show for the next twenty years. She was later featured on WE THE PEOPLE, *The* AMERICAN SCHOOL OF THE AIR, JOYCE JORDAN, GIRL INTERN, *The* PARKER FAMILY, *The* ALDRICH FAMILY, and GIRL ALONE. She won the much-sought-after title role of CLAUDIA, based on a novel and film of the same name. In 1949, the 27-year-old actress, pregnant with her first child, was playing the female lead opposite film actor Glenn Ford on a CAVALCADE OF AMERICA dramatization about author Nathaniel Hawthorne when she suddenly became ill and was rushed to the hospital. Ryan died of a cerebral hemorrhage the same night.

SAINT, THE

1945–1947	NBC	Sat.	7:30 PM
	CBS	Wed.	8 PM (Summer)
1947–1950	Mutual	Sun.	7:30 PM
1950–1951	NBC	Sun.	7:30 PM

Sophisticated, urbane private detective, Simon Templer (aka "The Saint"), created by British mystery writer Leslie Charteris, was the leading character on this half-hour weekly series. On a typical episode of *The Saint,* Templer solved the murder of a thug who, with a group of fellow gangsters, had stolen an old car that had $400,000 hidden in it. Program titles such as "Murder in the Theater," "A Confession Before a Crime," and "The Conley Silver-Mine Murders" suggest the content of other adventures in the series. The Templer–Saint part was played by film stars Edgar Barrier, Brian Aherne, Tom Conway, and Barry Sullivan, but it was Vincent PRICE—the actor who played the role in the late 1950s—who is best remembered. Larry Dobkin, John Brown, Ken Christy, Louise Arthur, Theodore von Etz, and Joe Forte were regular supporting players. Dick Joy was the program's announcer. The radio series was produced and written by author Charteris and directed by Bill Rousseau. Later *The Saint* television series starred British actor Roger Moore.

SALTER, HARRY (1899–1984)

Music director–conductor Harry Salter was born in Bucharest, Romania. He was first heard on radio shortly after he immigrated to the United States in 1927, at which time he made a strong impression. Salter led the orchestras on several musical quiz programs, including *Melody Puzzles,* NTG AND HIS GIRLS, STOP THE MUSIC, and HOBBY LOBBY. In addition, Salter was the music director of MR. DISTRICT ATTORNEY, *Your Unseen Friend,* YOUR HIT PARADE, WHAT'S MY NAME, and *The Amazing Mr. Smith.* He was also ABC's music director well into the 1970s.

SAM SPADE, DETECTIVE, THE ADVENTURES OF

See ADVENTURES OF SAM SPADE, DETECTIVE, THE.

SAMMY KAYE SHOW, THE (AKA SAMMY KAYE'S SHOWROOM; SAMMY KAYE'S SUNDAY SERENADE ROOM)

1937–1938	CBS	Sun.	8:30 PM
1938–1939	(Off the air)		
1939–1940	NBC Red	Mon.	7:30 PM
1940–1941	(Off the air)		
1941–1942	NBC Red	Sun.	2 PM
1942–1943	(Off the air)		
1943–1944	CBS	Wed.	8 PM
1944–1945	NBC Blue	Sun.	1:30 PM
	Mutual	Thurs.	8:30 PM
1945–1946	NBC Blue	Sun.	1:30 PM
1946–1950	(Off the air)		
1950–1951	ABC	Sun.	1 PM
1951–1952	ABC	Sun.	5 PM
1952–1953	NBC	Sun.	12 PM
1953–1954	ABC	Mon.–Fri.	8:15 PM
1954–1956	ABC	Sun.	9:35 PM

Sammy KAYE and his "Swing and Sway with Sammy Kaye" orchestra were heard on a half-hour radio show featuring Tommy Ryan, Don Cornell, Laura Leslie, Tony Russo, Sally Stewart, the Vass Family, the Kay Choir, Bill Williams, Arthur Wright, Tony Alamo, Barbara Benson, Don Rogers, Clyde Burke, Jimmy Bram, and the Kaydettes. Also heard at times was sportscaster Red BARBER. Gene Hamilton was Kaye's longtime announcer. John Cleary directed the program. *The Sammy Kaye* programs were sponsored at different times by Sensation cigarettes, Tangee orange drink, Old Gold cigarettes, Rayve shampoo, Richard Hudnut shampoo, and Sylvania radios and televisions.

See also SO YOU WANT TO LEAD A BAND.

SANDERSON, JULIA (JULIA SACKETT: 1887–1975)

Singer-actress-radio show hostess Julia Sanderson was born in Springfield, Massachusetts. At fifteen, Sanderson decided that she wanted to be an actress and left home for New York City to pursue her dream of becoming a musical-comedy stage star. After months of auditions, producer Charles Frohman hired her to play the ingenue lead in his musical comedy *Sunshine Girl* (1914). She was also acclaimed for her Broadway performances in *No, No, Nanette* (1925) and *Oh, Kay* (1926). While appearing in the musical comedy *Tangerine*, Sanderson met and married her third husband, leading man Frank CRUMIT. In 1928, Sanderson and Crumit starred on such radio programs as BATTLE OF THE SEXES, *Blackstone Plantation, Universal Rhythms,* and *The Frank Crumit–Julia Sanderson Show.* After Crumit died in 1943, Sanderson continued to work on radio as hostess of the short-lived *Let's Be Charming* program, but retired from show business in the mid-1940s.

SARNOFF, DAVID (1891–1971)

One of America's foremost businessman-broadcasting executives, David Sarnoff was born in Uzlian, Russia. When he was fifteen years old, Sarnoff taught himself the Morse code and got a job with the MARCONI WIRELESS COMPANY of America. In 1912, he picked up signals from a sinking ship, the *Titanic.* For seventy-two consecutive hours, Sarnoff relayed the names of the ship's survivors to newspapers around the world, receiving instant fame and recognition for his work.

When the Radio Corporation of America acquired the American Marconi Wireless Company, Sarnoff became one of RCA's fast-rising corporate stars. In 1922, he formulated the concept of creating a network of local affiliated stations to "serve as nonprofit, public-service facilities, with no advertising allowed." In actuality, Sarnoff's interest in radio was strictly financial. The more radio stations his company owned, the more he could promote RCA's radios, phonographs, and recordings. In 1926, at Sarnoff's urging, RCA formed the NATIONAL BROADCASTING COMPANY; by 1930 Sarnoff was the president of the company, a position he held until 1949. From 1947 until 1970, shortly before his death, Sarnoff was the chairman of the board of the Radio Corporation of America and, of course, the National Broadcasting Company.

SATURDAY AFTERNOON OPERA

1981–present   CBC   Sat.   1:30 PM

Each Saturday afternoon, the CANADIAN BROADCASTING CORPORATION Stereo (FM) network presents this opera program, hosted by Howard Dyck. The show presents live performances and recordings by opera companies in Manitoba, Vancouver, Edmonton, and Calgary. *Saturday Afternoon Opera* also broadcasts performances from the Canadian Opera Company and New York City's Metropolitan Opera House.

SATURDAY NIGHT ON CBC

1980–present   CBC   Sat.   1:30 PM

The CANADIAN BROADCASTING CORPORATION's Saturday evening lineup of shows is presented under the banner of *Saturday Night on CBC.* It includes *Coast to Coast* at 6:15 PM (hosted by Goeff Edwards); *Say It with Music* at 7:05 PM (hosted by Richard Ouzoumian); *Finkelman's 45's* at 8:08 PM (hosted by Danny Finkelman); *A-Propos* at 10:08 PM (hosted by Jim Corcoran); and *Saturday Night Blues* at 11:08 PM (hosted by Holger Petersen).

SATURDAY NIGHT SERENADE

1936–1938	CBS	Sat.	9:30 PM
1938–1947	CBS	Sat.	9:45 PM
1947–1948	CBS	Sat.	10 PM

Literally millions of Americans tuned in their radios each Saturday night to hear the popular half-hour and for a short while 15-minute *Saturday Night Serenade* program, starring one of the medium's most admired sopranos, Jessica DRAGONETTE. She sang classical and semiclassical selections such as arias from *La Bohème* and *La Traviata* and such operetta favorites as "I Love You Truly" and "Because." Also appearing were Bill Perry, the Emil Coty Serenaders, and pop singers Vic Damone and Hollace Shaw. The *Saturday Night Serenade* orchestra was led by Gustave Haenschen and Howard BARLOW. At one time, the Sammy KAYE Band was featured. Mary Eastman, William "Bill" ADAMS, and Bill Perry hosted at different times. The series was produced, directed, and written by Roland "Chick" Martini. Bob TROUT announced the series. Pet milk was the show's longtime sponsor.

SCARLET QUEEN, THE VOYAGE OF

1947–1948	Mutual	Thurs.	8:30 PM & 10 PM
1948	Mutual	Sat.	9:30 PM

The half-hour, transcribed *Voyage of the Scarlet Queen* adventure series was set in the mid-1800s on a five-mast sailing ship that sailed to exotic ports of call with occasional pirate raids and threats of mutiny disrupting the voyages. Each episode was narrated by ship's master Philip Carey as he wrote the ship's log. Carey was played by actor Elliott LEWIS. Also heard regularly in the supporting cast were Ed Max, Gloria Bondell, Cathy LEWIS, John Dehner, Jack Kruschen, William CONRAD, and Ben WRIGHT. On occasion, film juvenile Roddy MacDowall was heard as the ship's cabin boy. The Mutual network syndicated the series, which had various sponsors according to where in the country it was being heard. Jaime Del Vallee and Elliott Lewis directed the program, and Lewis also wrote many of the show's episodes. The show's announcer was Larry Thor.

SCATTERGOOD BAINES

1937–1939	CBS	Mon.–Fri.	11:15 AM
1937–1942	CBS	Mon.–Fri.	5:45 PM
1942–1949	(Off the air)		
1949–1950	(Syndicated series. Various times and stations)		

Actor Jess Pugh and then Wendell Holmes starred as a small-town, good-natured character named Scattergood Baines on this 15-minute drama series set in the fictitious town of Cold River. The program captured the atmosphere of rural, small-town America perfectly, but although it had a loyal and large listening audience, it was canceled by CBS in 1942 to make way for "more serious" daytime dramas. In 1949, the series was revived and placed in syndication but did not attract a sizable enough audience. John Howard played Hippocrates Brown, Francis "Dink" Trout was Pliny Pickett, and Catherine McCune and Arnold Robertson played Clara and Ed Potts. Forrest Lewis played several characters, including J. Wellington Keats, Agamemnon, and Ernie Baker. Also heard were John Hearne, Louise Fitch, Charles "Chuck" Grant, Boris Aplan, Janet Logan, Marvin MILLER, Jean McCoy, Burton Wright, Viola Berwick, Arnold Robertson, Patricia Conley, Bob Bailey, Barbara Fuller, Dorothy Gregory, Eileen Palmer, Norma Jean Ross, George Watson, and Roger Krupp. George Walsh and Bob Emrick were the show's announcers. The original series was directed by Walter Preston and Nelson Shawn. Wrigley's spearmint gum sponsored the show.

SCOURBY, ALEXANDER (1914–1985)

Considered by many people in broadcasting to have one of the best male voices on radio, Alexander Scourby, born in New York City, was trained as a stage actor and had a formidable list of radio credits—including AGAINST THE STORM, The RIGHT TO HAPPINESS, The SECOND MRS. BURTON, YOUNG WIDDER

BROWN, The OPEN DOOR, The THEATER GUILD ON THE AIR, and The ETERNAL LIGHT. Scourby's motion-picture appearances, usually as characters with less than admirable intentions, included *Affair in Trinidad* (1952), *The Big Heat* (1953), and *Seven Thieves* and *The Big Fisherman* (1959). On television, Scourby had a running role on "All My Children" (1976–1977) and was also a voice-over performer, narrating numerous documentaries and commercial announcements.

SCREEN DIRECTORS' PLAYHOUSE (AKA THE NBC THEATER)

1949–1950	NBC	Thurs.	9 PM
1950–1951	NBC	Thurs.	10 PM

Each week, a different motion-picture director such as Alfred Hitchcock or Sam Wood introduced a radio adaptation of one of his films, such as *Notorious* or *Casanova Brown* on The Screen Director's Playhouse series. Barbara Stanwyck, Joseph Cotten, James Stewart, and others starred in leading roles, not necessarily recreating their original roles. James "Jimmy" WALLINGTON was the series' announcer. Pabst Blue Ribbon beer, Anacin pain reliever, and RCA Victor radios, phonographs, and records sponsored the show. Originally a summer-replacement show, the series proved popular enough among listeners for NBC to make it a permanent weekly offering when the summer of 1949 ended.

See APPENDIX D.

SCREEN GUILD PLAYERS (AKA GULF SCREEN GUILD THEATER; LADY ESTHER SCREEN GUILD PLAYERS)

1939–1941	CBS	Sun.	7:30 PM
1941–1947	CBS	Mon.	10 PM
1947–1948	CBS	Mon.	10:30 PM
1948–1949	NBC	Thurs.	10 PM
1949–1950	NBC	Thurs.	9 PM
1950–1951	ABC	Thurs.	8 PM

Motion-picture stars who appeared on the *Screen Guild Players* program received no salaries: their fees were donated to various Screen Actor's Guild (the screen actor's union) charities. Like The LUX RADIO THEATER radio adaptations of feature films such as *Casablanca* and *The Maltese Falcon* were the standard fare. Unlike *The Lux Radio Theater*, however, the dramas were only a half hour in length instead of one full hour, which often resulted in some amusingly abbreviated versions of the original screen hits, the plots having been reduced to their barest bones. Although the program actually went on the air in January 1939, only continuous listings from September 1939 onward have been located by vintage radio-program catalogists and collectors. The premiere on January 8, 1939, had a variety

arbara Britton and Gregory Peck starred in a *Screen ctor's Guild* adaptation of *Arrowsmith*. (CBS)

rmat featuring George Murphy, Judy GARLAND, and ck BENNY. It was followed by Spencer Tracy and livia de Havilland in a radio play, "Three Days larch"; and Robert Taylor and Jeanette MacDonald n "Clotilda." On February 26, BURNS AND ALLEN were atured in another variety-show offering; Paul Muni nd Josephine Hutchinson starred in "Bridge of lercy"; and a comedy, "Tailored by Tony," starred mes Stewart and Carole Lombard, among others. fter Gulf oil relinquished its sponsorship of the rogram in 1942, Lady Esther face cream, and later amel cigarettes, became the show's sponsors. George lurphy hosted many of the series' earliest programs, ut Roger Pryor was its most enduring host. Oscar radley led the program's orchestra. Michael Roy, ohn Conte, and Harry VON ZELL were among the low's announcers.
See APPENDIX D.

EA HOUND, THE

1942–1944	ABC	Mon.–Fri.	5 PM
1946–1947	Mutual	Mon.–Fri.	5 PM
1948	ABC	Mon.	5 PM
1948–1951	(Off the air)		
1951	ABC	Mon.–Fri.	5 PM

Captain Silver, Jerry, Carol Anderson, and Tex were the major characters on this adventure program, produced for listeners under fourteen years of age. This half-hour and then 15-minute series was set on the high seas and was mainly concerned with voyages of a sailing ship, *The Sea Hound.* Kenneth Daigneau played Captain Silver, Bob HASTINGS was Jerry, Janice Gilbert was Carol Anderson, Allan Devitt was Kukai, and Walter Vaughn was Tex. The show was directed by Cyril Ambrister and written by Floyd Miller and Frank C. Dahm.

SEALTEST VILLAGE STORE, THE (AKA THE VILLAGE STORE; AT THE VILLAGE STORE)

1943–1948   NBC   Thurs.   9:30 PM

Radio and motion-picture comedienne Joan DAVIS and stage and film star Jack HALEY originally starred in this half-hour program, Haley as the proprietor-host at the fictional Sealtest store. When Davis left the show, Eve ARDEN costarred with Haley. Jack CARSON ultimately replaced Haley as the show's host, and Arden remained as his costar. The program, sponsored by Sealtest dairy products, had a variety–situation comedy format and featured such guest stars as Tallulah BANKHEAD, Jack BENNY, and Ed GARDNER. Ray NOBLE was the program's music director for a time. Regulars on the show were Verna FELTON as Blossom Blimp and Sharon Douglas as Penelope. Dave Street was vocalist during Haley's tenure on the show. *The Sealtest Village Store* program was produced and directed by Bob Reid and written by Si Wills.

SECOND HUSBAND (AKA THE ETHEL BARRYMORE THEATER)

1937–1941	CBS	Tues.	7:30 PM
1941–1946	CBS	Mon.–Fri.	11:15 AM
1946–1955	(Off the air)		
1955–1956	CBS	Mon.–Fri.	11:45 AM

Stage actress Ethel Barrymore hosted and Helen MENKEN starred on this serial drama when it first aired in 1937. Menken was subsequently replaced by actress Kathleen Cordell as Brenda Cummings, who, "when widowed, remarried and tried to start a new life for herself." On this half-hour evening offering, later five-days-a-week daytime serial, Joseph Curtin played Brenda's "second husband," Grant Cummings, Ralph LOCKE was Milton Brownspun, and Carleton YOUNG, Ralph Lee Robertson, Mercer McCloud, Janice Gilbert, Charita Bauer, Tommy Donnelly, and Jack GRIMES were Brenda's stepchildren. Jay JOSTYN, Arlene FRANCIS, William Podmore, Ethel Owen, Joy Hathaway, Jacqueline DeWit, Judy Blake, Dick Nelson, Vinton Hayworth, Stefan Schnabel, Peter DONALD, Virginia Dwyer, Rod Hendrickson, Collen Ward, John Thomas,

Helen Menken, John Thomas, and Virginia Dwyer on *Second Husband* (CBS)

and Skippy Homeier played supporting roles. Frank and Ann HUMMERT produced the series, which was written by Helen Walpole, Nancy Moore, David Davidson, Bill Bixby, and Elizabeth Todd. Andre BARUCH, Vinton Hayworth, and Frank Gallop were the program's announcers. Lester Vail produced and directed the series; Ed Wolfe also directed the program for several seasons. Bayer aspirin sponsored the evening version of *Second Husband;* the daytime version was sponsored by Dr. Lyon's toothpaste, Phillips' Milk of Magnesia antacid, and Energine vitamin supplement. The show's theme songs were "If Love Were All" and "Diane."

SECOND MRS. BURTON, THE

1946–1956	CBS	Mon.–Fri.	2 PM
1956–1958	CBS	Mon.–Fri.	2:15 PM
1958–1960	CBS	Mon.–Fri.	1:45 PM

Many women identified with the problems of Terry Burton, the "second" Mrs. Burton, on this long-lived 15-minute drama series. The "first" Mrs. Burton referred to Terry's meddlesome mother-in-law—the cause of most of the heroine's problems who constantly told Terry how to raise her children and take care of her husband. Over the years, Sharon Douglas, Claire Niesen, Patsy Campbell, Jan MINER, and Teri Keane played Terry Burton; Evelyn Varden, Charme Allen, and Ethel Owen played her mother-in-law; Dwight WEIST played Terry's husband, Stan; and Dix Davis, Edwin Bruce, Ben Cooper, and Larry Robinson played their son, Brad. Heard in supporting roles were Joan Alexander, Karl WEBER, Gary MERRILL, Alice FROST, Elspeth ERIC, King Calder, Robert "Bob" READICK, Alexander SCOURBY, Doris Rich, Rod Hendrickson, Staats COTSWORTH, Madaline Lee, Helen Coule, Les TREMAYNE, Bartlett "Bart" Robinson, Betty

Caine, Craig McDonnell, Cathleen Cordell, Anne Stone, Larry Haines, and Arline Blackburn. Harry Clark, and Hugh James were the show's announcers. The series was produced and directed by Ira Ashley for many years; it was also produced by Lindsay MacHarrie and directed by Beverly Smith, Viola Burns, and Stuart Buchanan. Hector Chevigny, among others, wrote many of the show's scripts. The series many sponsors included Postum health drink, Swans Down cake mixes, Post Toasties cereal, LaFrance bleach, Instant Maxwell House coffee, Jell-O puddings, Dial soap, Dial shampoo, Columbia phonographs, and Instant Chase and Sanborn coffee.

SETH PARKER (AKA SUNDAY EVENING AT SETH PARKER'S; CRUISES OF SETH PARKER)

1929–1933	NBC	Sun.	(*)
1933–1934	NBC Blue	Tues.	10 PM
1934–1935	(Off the air)		
1935–1936	NBC Blue	Sun.	10:30 PM
1936–1938	(Off the air)		
1938–1939	NBC Blue	Sun.	7:30 PM

This half-hour series, a combination serial drama and music-variety show, starred Phillips H. LORD as Seth an ordinary American citizen who lived in the fictional town of Jonesport, Maine. *Seth Parker* was created, written, and directed by Lord and featured his wife, Sophia M. Lord, as Seth's wife, Lizzie. This program was noted for its small-town humor and down-home hymn-singing sessions, as well as for stories about the harm gossip can do and the various domestic hardships that can befall families—such as the death of a loved one or an accident. The program also featured Effie Palmer and then Barbara Bruce as Ma Parker, Seth's mother; Joy Hathaway and then Erva Giles as Jane; and Richard Hunter, Bennett KILPACK, Edward Wolters, William Jordan, Richard Maxwell, Gertrude Foster, James Black, John Kulick, Norman Price, and Edwin Dunham as various towns people and hymn singers. Polly Robertson was the pianist organist on the show. The program's sponsor and announcer are unknown.

SEVAREID, ERIC (1912–1992)

Before he became one of television's most respected news reporters and commentators, Eric Sevareid was a familiar voice on radio. Born in Velva, North Dakota, Sevareid joined the CBS news staff as a war correspondent during World War II after reporting for *The Minneapolis Journal* newspaper. Sevareid wrote his first book, *Canoeing with Cree,* in 1935 and subsequently wrote three books about his battleground experiences during World War II, as well as *Not So Wild a Dream* (1946), *In One Ear* (1952), and *Conversations with Eric Sevareid* (1976). After years of appearing on CBS radio nd television as a correspondent and commentator, Sevareid became one of CBS's editors and "elder tatesmen." He served as consultant to CBS from the ime of his retirement in 1977 until his death in 1992.

SEYMOUR, ANNE (1909–1988)

American character actress Anne Seymour, who was born in New York City, came from a theatrical family: her father was a stage actor and director, and her mother, May Davenport Seymour, and her uncle, John D. Seymour, were well-known stage performers. Seymour first appeared on the stage with Helen Hayes when she was twelve years old in *To the Ladies*. After her radio acting debut in 1932, she became the leading lady on GRAND HOTEL, *The* MAGNIFICENT MONTAGUE, *The* STORY OF MARY MARLIN (on which she played Mary), and *A* WOMAN OF AMERICA, playing Prudence Dane. Seymour was also featured on OUR GAL SUNDAY, AGAINST THE STORM (on which her mother, May Davenport Seymour, played her mother), *The* FORD THEATER, *The* FIRST NIGHTER, IT CAN BE DONE, *The Inside Story*, and INNER SANCTUM MYSTERIES. The actress, who had a highly recognizable deep voice, made her film debut as the teacher-wife of the fictional Southern Governor Willy Stark's in the Academy Award–winning motion picture *All the King's Men* (1949). Seymour subsequently appeared in *Man on Fire* (1957),

Anne Seymour with her uncle, actor John D. Seymour

Home from the Hills (1959), *Sunrise at Campobello* (1960), and *Blindfold* (1966). On television she was a regular performer on "Empire" (1962).

SEYMOUR, DAN (1914–1982)

Announcer Dan Seymour was born in New York City and made his radio debut in 1935. Seymour was the "Danny" with whom Aunt Jenny conversed at the beginning and end of the AUNT JENNY daytime drama series. He also delivered the commercial announcements on the show. In addition to announcing *Aunt Jenny*, Seymour was the chief product spokesman on such shows as *The* ALDRICH FAMILY, *The* HENRY MORGAN SHOW, BOBBY BENSON, ORIGINAL AMATEUR HOUR, *Meet the Dixons*, STOP ME IF YOU'VE HEARD THIS ONE, *Tune-up Time, Sing It Again*, and WE THE PEOPLE. Seymour's comfortable manner of speaking made him a particular favorite among listeners, who normally took announcers somewhat for granted. He received numerous fan letters from women who thought he sounded like "the perfect American male."

SHADOW, THE

1930–1931	CBS	Thurs.	9:30 PM
1931–1932	CBS	Tues.	10 PM
1931–1932	CBS	Thurs.	9:30 PM
1932	CBS	Tues.	10 PM
1932–1933	NBC	Wed.	8:30 PM
1934–1935	NBC	Mon., Wed.	6:30 PM
1935–1945	Mutual	Sun.	5:30 PM
1945–1954	Mutual	Sun.	5 PM

"Who knows what evil lurks in the hearts of men? The Shadow knows!" this popular mystery series began. The series, created by Harry Charlot, was about a bon vivant who, while in the Orient, learned the secret of how to make himself invisible and used this knowledge to track down and bring to justice various evil-doers. In the show's later years, the Shadow was Lamont Cranston, who, with "his lovely companion Margo Lane," spent many years bringing criminals to justice. But when the series was first aired in 1930, Lamont Cranston didn't exist. In the early episodes, the Shadow character alternated between being both villainous and heroic. At the end of each half-hour show, everyone in America was convinced that "the weed of crime [bore] bitter fruit" and that "crime [did] not pay!" Jack La Curto was the first actor to play the Shadow on radio, but it was Frank READICK, Jr., who made the character a national sensation with his venomously sinister laugh. Readick was followed by Orson WELLES, William "Bill" JOHNSTONE, Bret MORRISON (whose voice is perhaps best remembered as the Shadow because he played the part the longest), John Archer, and Steve Courtleigh. Margo Lane was played by Margot Stevenson, Agnes MOOREHEAD,

Bret Morrison as The Shadow (Mutual)

Marjorie Anderson, Gertrude Warner, Laura Mae Carpenter, Lesley Woods, and finally Grace MATTHEWS. Commissioner Weston of the police department was played by Dwight WEIST, Ken ROBERTS, Arthur Vinton, Kenny DELMAR, Santos ORTEGA, and Ted DeCorsia. The show's many announcers included Andre BARUCH, Don HANCOCK, Carl Caruso, Jean Paul King, Sandy Becker, Ken ROBERTS, and Frank McCarthy. Writers included William Sweets, Peter Barry, Jerry McGill, Alonzo Dean COLE, Joe Bates Smith, Stedman Coles, Robert Arthur, Max Ehrlich, and Sidney Slon. Bill Tuttle and Chick Vincent directed the series in the late 1930s and early 1940s and established the best-remembered "tone" of the program. In 1994, there was an unsuccessful *Shadow* feature film starring Alec Baldwin as Cranston/the Shadow, but it did not receive either public or critical acclaim. Blue Coal, Street and Smith (who published *The Shadow* magazine), Perfect-O-Lite bulbs, B. F. Goodrich tire company, Bromo Quinine antacid, and Wildroot Cream-Oil hair

dressing sponsored the series. The theme song of *The Shadow* was "Omphale's Spinning Wheel."

SHADOW OF FU MANCHU

See FU MANCHU.

SHAKESPEARE ON RADIO

The plays of William Shakespeare were occasionally presented on radio and can be heard, though infrequently, on various stations affiliated with the NATIONAL PUBLIC RADIO. Except for those rare occasions when they were presented by a dramatic anthology series, such as *The* LUX RADIO THEATER or *The* THEATER GUILD ON THE AIR, Shakespeare's works were rarely heard on radio because officials were convinced that the public would not understand the language.

In 1937, CBS presented a summer series of hour-long radio adaptations of Shakespeare's plays starring some of Hollywood's major film stars. Actor Burgess Meredith starred on the first program in an adaptation of *Hamlet*, which received favorable critical acclaim; subsequent productions met with less enthusiasm. Edward G. Robinson played Petrucchio in a dismally miscast production of *The Taming of the Shrew*, and Humphrey BOGART played Hotspur in *Henry IV, Part One and Two*, sounding as if he were a New York playboy. Tallulah BANKHEAD and Orson WELLES overacted in *Twelfth Night*, and Walter Abel, Thomas Mitchell, and Claude Rains were heard in a considerably better adaptation of *Julius Caesar*. Rosaline Russell, Leslie Howard, and Elissa Landi were featured in *As You Like It, King Lear*, and *Much Ado About Nothing*. The critics were less than impressed overall with what one of them called "CBS's pathetic attempt to bring culture to the masses via their radio network." In a desperate attempt to find something they could use for publicity purposes to promote the series, CBS network officials decided to conduct live interviews with ordinary people on the street to hear their opinions of the show. The people questioned were screened beforehand to make sure they said positive things about the series. "I think it's wonderful," one man said on a *live* broadcast, but he quickly ad-libbed, "I don't understand a word they're saying, but I think it's wonderful."

Occasionally, other dramatic anthologies presented Shakespeare's plays, such as *The* LUX RADIO THEATER's and *The* THEATER GUILD ON THE AIR's adaptations of *Macbeth* with Maurice Evans and Judith Anderson, *Romeo and Juliet* with Dorothy McGuire and Evans, *Hamlet* with John Gielgud, and *Julius Caesar* with Evans and Basil RATHBONE.

SHARBUTT, DEL (1912–)

Announcer Del Shabutt was born in Cleburne, Texas, made his broadcasting debut in 1929, and was the announcer on *The* JACK CARSON SHOW, *The* JACK PEARL SHOW, LAVENDER AND OLD LACE, *The Song Shop,* HOBBY LOBBY, MYRT AND MARGE, HOUR OF CHARM, *Melody and Madness, The* LANNY ROSS SHOW, LUM AND ABNER, YOUR HIT PARADE, and CLUB FIFTEEN. For many years, Sharbutt announced *Amos and Andy.* He continued to work on radio as an NBC staff announcer until his retirement in the 1980s.

SHELL CHATEAU, THE

1935–1937   NBC Red   Sat.   9:30 PM

This half-hour comedy-variety series starred Broadway singer Al JOLSON and featured Walter WINCHELL's celebrity gossip, as well as movie character actor Wallace Beery, comedians Smith Ballew, Joe Cook, and Victor Young and his Orchestra, featuring Peggy Gardner and Jack Stanton as vocalists. Singer Nadine Connor starred on the program for a while, with actress Mary Jane HIGBY supplying her speaking voice. Cal Kuhl and Herb Polesi directed the series. The program's opening theme song, sung to the tune of "About a Quarter to Nine," became almost as popular as the show itself. Harlow WILCOX was the program's announcer. *Shell Chateau* was written by Bob Colwell, Ed Rice, and Carroll Carroll. It was sponsored by Shell oil.

SHELTON, GEORGE (1884–1971)

Comedian, program panelist, and writer George Shelton was born in New York City. Shelton was first heard on radio in 1933 on *The Chesterfield Program,* after performing his comedy routines for many years on the vaudeville stage as a member of the Shelton and Howard comedy team. The comedian was also featured on MUSIC THAT SATISFIES, *The Sealtest Saturday Night Party,* and *The* RUDY VALLEE SHOW, but he is best remembered as a dim-witted panelist on IT PAYS TO BE IGNORANT. Shelton continued to write comedy material for other comedians until shortly before he died.

SHEPHARD, ANN (SCHEINDEL KALISH: 1915–d.)

At the height of her radio acting career, Scheindel Kalish—who was born in Chicago, Illinois—changed her name to Ann Shephard, feeling that it sounded "less foreign." The actress worked onstage for several years and debuted on radio in 1933. She played the title role on JOYCE JORDAN, GIRL INTERN and was regularly heard on INNER SANCTUM MYSTERIES, *The* KATE SMITH SHOW, ELLEN RANDOLPH, AUNT JENNY'S Real Life Stories, HILLTOP HOUSE, HILDA HOPE, MD, GRAND CENTRAL STATION, BIG SISTER (as Hope Melton Evans), JACK ARMSTRONG, *All-American Boy* (as Betty

Fairchild), JUST PLAIN BILL (as Bessie), LORENZO JONES (as Margaret), and OUR GAL SUNDAY. Shephard had a lovely and feminine, if somewhat fraught-filled, voice that was perfect for playing young women with serious problems such as dying husbands, children who were in accidents or sick, and elderly parents who needed to be nursed back to health.

SHERIFF, THE (DEATH VALLEY SHERIFF)

1945–1951   NBC Blue & ABC   Fri.   9:30 PM

Originally called *Death Valley Days,* then *Death Valley Sheriff,* and finally *The Sheriff,* this weekly half-hour Western-adventure series was about a law officer in the Old West. It starred Bob Warren, Robert Haag, and finally Donald Briggs as Sheriff Mark Chase of Canyon County, California. Actor Olyn Landick was featured as Cassandra Drinkwater, better known as "Cousin Cassie." Also appearing regularly was Helen Claire. The program was directed by Walter Scanlan, John Wilkinson, and Florence Ortman. Dresser Dahlstead was the program's announcer. 20 Mule Team Borax and Boraxo cleaners sponsored the series.

See also DEATH VALLEY DAYS.

SHERLOCK HOLMES, THE ADVENTURES OF

See ADVENTURES OF SHERLOCK HOLMES, THE.

SHERMAN, RANSOM (1898–1985)

Born in Appleton, Wisconsin, writer and actor Ransom Sherman graduated from the University of Michigan before he debuted on radio in 1923 as a variety performer. He was heard on such shows as *The Three Doctors, Club Matinee, Laugh Doctor,* and MIRTH AND MADNESS and was also a regular on *The* FIBBER MCGEE AND MOLLY SHOW, *The Sunbride Smile Parade,* and *Quicksilver.* As a radio performer, Sherman also had his own program, *The* RANSOM SHERMAN SHOW, from 1939 until 1942. Filmgoers saw Sherman in *Are You with It?* (1948), *Whiplash* (1949), and *Pretty Baby* (1950).

SHORE, DINAH (FRANCES ROSE SHORE: 1917–1994)

Singer Dinah Shore was born in Winchester, Tennessee, and started singing on local radio stations at the age of ten. After attending Vanderbilt University, earning a B.A. degree in sociology in 1936, Shore decided to pursue a career as a professional singer. First a featured vocalist on *The* EDDIE CANTOR SHOW in 1939, she subsequently became the star of CHAMBER MUSIC SOCIETY OF LOWER BASIN STREET in 1942. For a time, she performed on YOUR HIT PARADE and starred on several DINAH SHORE SHOWS, popularizing such songs as "Blues in the Night," and "Buttons and Bows." During World War II, Shore made numerous appearances at various U.S.O. (United Service Organizations) shows and entertained troops at military installations all around the world. She was also one of the armed forces' COMMAND PERFORMANCE radio program's most frequent guests. On television, Shore had a twice-a-week, 15-minute musical show as early as 1951. In 1956, her evening musical-variety show for Chevrolet made its debut and became one of television's most popular prime-time programs, remaining on the air until 1962. After her variety show departed the airwaves, Shore hosted a daytime, daily TV talk show that was the forerunner of such programs as *The Oprah Winfrey Show* and *The Sally Jessie Raphael Show*. At the height of her popularity Shore was also featured in several films, including *Thank Your Lucky Star* (1943), *Up in Arms* (1944), *Belle of the Yukon* (1944), *Till the Clouds Roll By* (1946), and *Aaron Slick from Punkin Crick* (1952). Shore continued both her singing career and her Dinah Shore Open Women's Golf tournament activities until illness forced her to retire.

SHOW BOAT

1932–1937	NBC	Thurs.	8 PM
1939–1940	NBC	Sun.	10:30 PM
1940	NBC Blue	Fri.	9 PM
1940–1941	NBC	Mon.	9:30 PM

Edna Ferber's 1926 novel about a riverboat captain and his family whose show boat traveled up and down the Mississippi River was turned into a hit stage musical in 1927 and again in 1994, a half-hour radio program in 1932, and was a film in 1936 and 1951. On the radio version of *Show Boat*, Charles Winninger was Captain Henry, the show's host; he was replaced by Frank McGuire. Irene Hubbard played Aunt Maria; Hattie MCDANIEL played Mammy; and Pat Padgett and Pick Malone played minstrel performers MOLASSES 'N' JANUARY. Muriel Wilson provided the singing voice and Rosaline Greene the speaking voice of the show's ingenue, Mary Lou. Also featured in the cast were Winifred Cecil, Annette Henshaw, Lanny ROSS, Cal Tinney, Ethel Everett, Conrad Thibault, Jules Bledsoe, Frank Willoughby, Ross Graham, Sam Hearn, "Tiny" Ruffner, Jack HALEY, Virginia Verrill, Warren HULL, Nadine Connor, Dick Todd, Helen Jepson, Honey Dean, the Show Boat Four, Louise Massey and the Westerners, and the orchestras of Donald VOORHEES and Al GOODMAN. At one point the show's sponsor, Maxwell House Coffee, decided to abandon the show-boat theme altogether and make the locale of the series a tent show. But a program called *The* GIBSON FAMILY had already used that background, so the show boat setting was reinstated. Eventually, *Show Boat* was replaced by a pro-

gram called *Hollywood Good News*, which wa produced in conjunction with the MGM film studic and starred singer Lanny ROSS (who was one of th stars of *Show Boat*) and then Allyn JONES. And BARUCH announced the show. *Show Boat* was directe by Kenneth W. MACGREGOR and written by Sam Pe rin, Ruth Adams Knight, Arthur B. Phillips, and otl ers. *Show Boat* was the prototype for many hit comed variety shows that followed, such as *Maxwell Hou Coffee Time* and *The Shell Chateau*. The show's them song was, appropriately, "Here Comes the Sho Boat."

SHUTTA, ETHEL (1897–1976)

Singer-actress Ethel Shutta, who was born in Ne York City, shared the microphone with Jack BENNY his costar in the early 1930s when Benny's radio care was just beginning. Shutta had been heard on sever radio programs before she teamed up with Benr and was a popular singer and comedienne on tl Broadway stage and in vaudeville. Playing comic i genue parts when she was young, Shutta was be known for her vaudeville sketches and dancing. Yea later, in 1971, she came out of retirement to appear Stephen Sondheim's musical *Follies* (1971), in whi she sang a show-stopping number, "Broadway Baby Shutta died shortly after touring with *Follies* throug out the United States.

SILVER EAGLE, MOUNTIE

| 1951–1952 | ABC | Thurs. | 7:30 PM |
| 1952–1953 | ABC | Tues.–Thurs. | 7:30 PM |

This half-hour radio adventure series for young aud ences was about a law-enforcement officer in Canada Northwest territories who tracked down escaped co victs and tried to enforce conservation. The show, o of the last programs of its kind to debut on radi starred Jim AMECHE as Canadian Mountie Jim We Michael Romano and then Jack Lester as Joe Bideau John Barclay and then Jess Pugh as Inspector Argyl Clarence Hartzell as "Doc"; and Ed Prentiss and the Bill O'Connor as the program's narrator. Heard in tl supporting cast were Charles Flynn, Fern Persor Cornelius Peeples, Paul Barnes, Beverly Younger, D Bivens, Everett Clark, Geraldine Kay, Johnny Coor Leo Curley, Eloise Kummer, Laurette FILLBRAND Maurice Copeland, Don Gallagher, Harry Elders, A VAN HARVEY, Frank Dane, Alma Platts, Elmira Ro sler, and Vera Ward. The announcers were Ken N dine and Ed Cooper. James Jewell was produc director, and chief writer of the series; Bob Wools also directed. Richard Dix was music director of *Sil Eagle, Mountie*.

SILVER THEATER, THE (AKA SILVERTOWN THEATER)

1937–1941	CBS	Sun.	5 PM & 6 PM
1941–1943	CBS	Thurs.	6
1943–1944	CBS	Sun.	6 PM

CBS presented this dramatic anthology series featuring guest stars from Broadway and Hollywood, hosted by film actor Conrad NAGEL and sponsored by the International Silver Company. The show presented original half-hour radio plays and adaptations of literature and such classic films as *The Silver Cord, Tom Sawyer,* and *Random Harvest* performed by Lee Tracy, Helen Hayes, Rosalind Russell, Joan Crawford, Douglas Fairbanks, Henry Fonda, Gail Patrick, and others. James Jewell produced and directed the program; Bob Woolson and Glenhall Taylor directed the show at various times as well. The series' announcers were Dick Joy and Roger Krupp, and Milton Rettenberg was music director. The scripts for *The Silver Theater* were written by James Lawrence, Gibbon Scott Fox, Thomas Eldridge, Richard Thorne, John T. Kelly, and True Boardman.

SIMMS, GINNY (VIRGINIA SIMMS: 1913–1994)

Attractive brunette singer Ginny Simms was born in San Antonio, Texas, but grew up in California and studied piano and voice as a child. While attending Fresno State Teacher's College, Simms sang in a trio with two of her sorority sisters; when she finished her schooling, she soloed on local radio shows in the Los Angeles area, attracting the attention of bandleader Kay KYSER. She joined his band as a featured vocalist in the late 1930s and was heard on KAY KYSER'S KOLLEGE OF MUSICAL KNOWLEDGE. Simms became a frequent guest star on DUFFY'S TAVERN, *The* BOB BURNS SHOW, and *The* BING CROSBY SHOW and was frequently featured on the Armed Forces' COMMAND PERFORMANCE. She also starred on her own GINNY SIMMS SHOW. During and for many years after World War II, Simms entertained military personnel stationed at U.S. installations at home and abroad. In addition to her radio-show appearances and recordings, Simms was also featured in several motion pictures—including *Playmates* (1941), *Seven Days' Leave* (1942), *Shady Lady* (1945), and *Night and Day* (1946). Simms popularized such songs as "Don't Ever Change," "St. Louis Blues," "Stardust," and "Frenesi." The singer made occasional guest appearances on such TV variety shows as "The Colgate Comedy Hour" and "Ed Sullivan's Toast of the Town" in the 1950s.

SINATRA, FRANCIS "FRANK" (1915–   )

Born in Hoboken, New Jersey, pop singer and film star Frank Sinatra ("Old Blue Eyes) has had a long and successful career as both a singer and an actor. After winning first place on the Major Bowes' ORIGINAL AMATEUR HOUR program as a member of a singing group, "The Hoboken Four," seventeen-year-old Sinatra became a band singer. A slender, sensitive-looking young man who had a soulful, crooningly romantic singing style, Sinatra soon attracted the attention of millions of teenage girls around the world, who, attending his personal appearances, would swoon and faint at the mere sound of his voice. In the 1940s, Sinatra starred on YOUR HIT PARADE and was subsequently heard on various FRANK SINATRA SHOWS and on such major comedy and variety programs as *The* BING CROSBY SHOW, *The* BOB HOPE SHOW, and COMMAND PERFORMANCE during World War II. Sinatra starred in numerous motion pictures during his long career, including *Higher and Higher* (1943), *Anchor's Aweigh* (1945), *From Here to Eternity* (1953), for which he won a Best Supporting Actor Academy Award, *A Hole in the Head* (1959), *Von Ryan's Express* (1965), and *The First Deadly Sin* (1980). A living legend, Sinatra continues to make appearances and sing his old classics to large audiences and is occasionally seen on television specials and awards shows.

See also FRANK SINATRA SHOW, *The.*

SINCLAIR MINSTRELS PROGRAM, THE

| 1932–1936 | NBC Blue | Mon. | 9 PM |

Minstrel shows featuring Caucasian performers portraying African-American characters in comedy sketches and songs had been a popular convention in the United States since the mid-1800s and flourished in vaudeville in the 1920s and 1930s. One successful half-hour minstrel show on radio in the 1930s was *The Sinclair Minstrel Show,* sponsored by Sinclair oil. Gene Arnold and then Gus Van were the program's hosts. Featured regularly were Malcolm Claire as Spare Ribs, William J. Smith, and the Sinclair Minstrel Men (Bill Childs, Cliff Soubier, and Fritz Clark). The series was written, produced, and directed by Gene Arnold.

SINGIN' SAM, THE BARBASOL MAN (AKA REMINISCIN' WITH SINGIN' SAM)

1930–1931	CBS	Tues., Thurs.	8:15 PM
1931–1933	CBS	Mon., Wed., Fri.	8:15 PM
1933–1934	(Off the air)		
1934–1935	CBS	Mon.	10:30 PM
1935–1936	CBS	Tues., Mon.	7:30 PM
1936–1937	NBC Blue	Fri.	8:15 PM
1937–1939	(Off the air)		
1939–1942	(Syndicated series. Various times and stations)		
1942–1943	Mutual	Mon., Wed.	8 PM
1943–1944	Mutual	Tues., Thurs.	8 PM

| 1944–1945 | (Off the air) |
| 1945–1947 | (Syndicated series. Various stations and times) |

Singin' Sam the Barbasol Man, played by Harry FRAN-KEL, was one of radio's first major characters and became a radio institution for seventeen years as Barbasol shaving cream's singing spokesman. Whenever this 15-minute show was taken off the air, it was always brought back by popular demand for one more season. On the show, Sam sang popular songs of the past and hit musical-comedy as well as such operetta basso-profundo selections as "Sleep in the Deep" and "Swing Low, Sweet Chariot." His well-known Barbasol shaving cream theme song was sung to the tune of "Tammany."

SINGING LADY, THE (AKA THE SINGING STORY LADY)

1931–1932	NBC Blue	Mon.	5 PM
1932–1936	NBC Blue	Mon.–Fri.	5:30 PM
1936–1939	NBC Blue	Mon.–Thurs.	5:30 PM
1939–1940	NBC Blue	Mon.–Fri.	5:15 PM
1940–1941	NBC Blue	Mon.–Fri.	5 PM
1941–1945	(Off the air)		
1945	Blue (ABC)	Mon.–Fri.	5:45 PM

Ireene WICKER was the hostess of this children's radio program that featured such songs as "Mary Had a Little Lamb" and "Jack and Jill" as well as such stories as "Jack and the Beanstalk" and "Cinderella." The program was suitable for listeners under seven years of age. Bob Brown was the show's announcer. The 15-minute and later half-hour series was produced and written by Wicker and directed by Charles Warburton and Charles Bishop. Milton Rettenberg was the show's music director. Kellogg's cereals was the program's longtime sponsor.

SINGLETON, PENNY (DOROTHY MCNULTY: 1912–   )

Born in Philadelphia, Pennsylvania, actress Penny Singleton became well known as the title character of the hit motion picture and radio series BLONDIE. Singleton started in vaudeville after attending the Alex McClue talent school and then Columbia University. Her first major Broadway play was a 1928 production of the musical comedy *Good News,* and she then appeared in the plays *Walk a Little Faster* (1932) and *Hey Nonny-Nonny* (1934). In Hollywood, Singleton was seen in *After the Thin Man* (1936), *Blondie* (1938), *Go West, Young Lady* (1936), and *Young Widow* (1946). When she left the *Blondie* series in 1950, Singleton crusaded for performers' rights as an activist for the American Guild of Variety Artists.

SINGO

| 1942–1944 | NBC Blue | Tues.–Thurs. | 1:45 PM |

Singer "Welcome" Lewis hosted this half-hour musical quiz program, in which listeners sent in a combination of any three song titles that, when put together, told a story. The contestants had to tell a story based on the songs they heard. Game winners finally had to split the four-dollar prize money with a member of the wartime armed forces. Lewis and Art Gentry—who also served as vocalists on the program—often sang duets that, if identified properly, paid the contestant double, or eight dollars. George Ansbro was the show's announcer.

SISTERS OF THE SKILLET (AKA THE QUALITY TWINS)

1930–1932	NBC Blue	Tues., Thurs., Fri.	8:45 PM
1932–1936	(Various stations and times)		
1936–1937	NBC Blue	Mon., Wed., Fri.	7:45 PM
	CBS	Tues., Thurs.	11:15 AM
1937	CBS	Tues., Thurs.	11:15 AM

The 15-minute *Sisters of the Skillet* comedy series starred Ed East and Ralph Dumke at different times. Proctor and Gamble and Knox gelatin sponsored the program. Because no information or recordings of this program have survived, it is impossible to give an accurate description of the show's format or to name its production personnel or sponsors.

$64 QUESTION, THE (AKA TAKE IT OR LEAVE IT)

1940–1947	CBS	Sun.	10 PM
1947–1950	NBC	Sun.	10 PM
1950–1956	NBC	Sun.	10 PM

Called *Take It Or Leave It* when it first aired on radio, the half-hour *$64 Question* is perhaps better remembered as television's "The $64,000 Question," hosted by Hal March. In 1955, the series was simulcast on both radio and television. Among the hosts on the show when it was called *Take It Or Leave It* were comedian Phil BAKER, Bob HAWK, Garry MOORE, Jack Paar, and Eddie CANTOR. Contestants chosen from the studio audience selected a category from a game board and attempted to answer questions, doubling their earnings with each correct answer until they reached the $64 maximum. Money not won was added to the following week's jackpot. The program's announcers were David Rose, Ken NILES, Jay Stewart, and Hy Averback. The radio show was directed by Harry Spears and Betty Manderville, written by Edith Oliver, and sponsored by Revlon beauty products, Eversharp pens, and Eversharp-Schick razors and blades.

KELTON, RED (RICHARD SKELTON: 1913–)

Born in Vincennes, Indiana, comedian Red Skelton was the son of a circus clown and his performer-wife. Red began his show-business career in a touring minstrel act and later appeared in tent shows, in various summer and winter stock-company productions, and on the vaudeville circuit. Skelton debuted on radio on The RUDY VALLEE SHOW in 1937 and proved so popular that MGM Studios signed the comedian to a long-term film contract. Skelton subsequently appeared in such films as *Having Wonderful Time* (1938), *DuBarry Was a Lady* (1943), *The Show Off* (1946), *The Clown* (1953), and *Those Magnificent Men in Their Flying Machines* (1965). On his radio show, The RED SKELTON SHOW, the comedian introduced such characters as Willy Lump-Lump, Junior (the mean "widdle" kid), and Clem Kadiddlehoffer to the listening public. Skelton claimed that he especially enjoyed guest starring on the JUVENILE JURY program, which starred bright children who answered difficult questions in a direct, simple manner, saying that he was "really just a child at heart" himself. Skelton was also active on television from 1951 until 1971 as the star of CBS's "Red Skelton Show." As of this writing, he continues to perform and make public appearances.

SKIPPY

1931–1932	NBC	Mon.–Sat.	5:15 PM
1932–1933	CBS	Mon.–Sat.	5:30 PM
1933–1934	CBS	Mon.–Fri.	5 PM
1934–1935	CBS	Mon.–Fri.	5:45 PM

In the 1920s, Percy Crosby's newspaper comic strip, *Skippy*, about a typical small-town American boy was extremely popular. Radio capitalized on the comic strip's success and presented a 15-minute children's program featuring the character. The series was one of the earliest programs produced by Frank and Anne HUMMERT. Played by Franklin Adams, Jr., Skippy had many adventures as he encountered criminals and befriended unusual characters. His best friend, Socky, was played by Francis Smith; another friend, Jim Lovering, was played by the actor St. John Terrell. David Owen directed the program, which was written by Robert Hardy Andrews and Roland Martini. Sponsors of the show included General Mills flour and Phillips' Milk of Magnesia antacid.

SKIPPY HOLLYWOOD THEATER, THE

1940–1950	(Syndicated series. Various stations and times)

The *Skippy Hollywood Theater* was one of the most popular syndicated programs on the air throughout the 1940s. The stories heard on this dramatic anthology ranged from adventure to romance and were written especially for the series. Skippy Peanut Butter sponsored this program of half-hour plays that featured major Hollywood stars in leading roles; making regular guest appearances on this series were Peter Lorre, Jane Withers, Joan Bennett, Vincent PRICE, Anita Louise, Paulette Goddard, Herbert Marshall, Basil RATHBONE, and Dana Andrews.

SKULNIK, MENASHA (1892–1970)

Born in Warsaw, Poland, Menasha Skulnik became one of the American Yiddish Theater's most important performers. The Yiddish Theater was flourishing in New York City at the turn of the century, and catered to the theatrical tastes of millions of Yiddish-speaking immigrants who had settled in and around New York City. Skulnik's formidable comic talents eventually led to his being offered roles in such English-language plays as *The Fifth Season* (1944), *Uncle Willie* (1952), *Come Blow Your Horn* (1961), and *Zulu and the Zayda* (1966). On radio, he usually played amusing but stereotypical Jewish characters: Skulnik was Uncle David on The GOLDBERGS and the comic, henpecked Mr. Cohen on ABIE'S IRISH ROSE in the early 1940s.

SKY KING

1946–1947	ABC	Mon.–Fri.	5:30 PM
1947–1950	ABC	Tues.–Thurs.	5:30 PM
1950–1954	Mutual	Tues.–Thurs.	5:30 PM

One of the last children's adventure programs on radio to feature an aviator hero (similar to other radio heroes, such as SMILIN' JACK, CAPTAIN MIDNIGHT, and TERRY AND THE PIRATES) was *Sky King*. On this 15-minute show, Sky King was a ranch owner who used his airplane to round up his cattle and track down dangerous rustlers and other outlaws. The series, which originated in Chicago, featured Jack Lester, Earl Nightingale, and finally Roy Engel as Sky King, Beryl Vaughn as Penny, Jack Bivens as Chipper, and Cliff Soubier as Sky King's ranch foreman. The program was written by Abe BURROWS and Roy WINSOR. It was sponsored by Mars candy.

SLOANE, EVERETT (1909–1965)

A character actor for many years, Everett Sloane was born in New York City, made his film debut in Orson WELLES's classic film *Citizen Kane* in 1941, and subsequently appeared in numerous films and television programs. He was heard on literally thousands of radio programs throughout the 1930s, 1940s, and 1950s. This very versatile actor could play all sorts of parts—young or old, hero or villain—and his voice could sound enticing and romantic or unattractive. Sloane played various roles on STUDIO ONE, FORD THEATER, MERCURY THEATER ON THE AIR, MARCH OF TIME, and CAVALCADE OF AMERICA, and was also featured as Denny, Drummond's faithful valet and crime-solving assistant on The ADVENTURES OF BULLDOG DRUMMOND, Sammy Goldberg on The GOLDBERGS, and Shirley Booth's love interest on Hogan's Daughter. The actor was also regularly featured on THIS IS NORA DRAKE, BIG SISTER, The ROAD OF LIFE, and VALIANT LADY and was an oft-time supporting player on The SHADOW, FLASH GORDON, COURT OF MISSING HEIRS, The Danny Kaye Show, DIMENSION X, and INNER SANCTUM MYSTERIES, among others. In the late 1950s, Sloane starred on the television series "Official Detective" and appeared on "Studio One," "Kraft Theater," "Omnibus," and "Playhouse 90." In addition to Citizen Kane, Sloane was also seen in the films Journey into Fear (1942), The Men (1950), The Big Knife (1953), Patterns (1956), Home from the Hills (1959), and The Disorderly Orderly (1965).

SMALL, MARY (1922–   )

Singer Mary Small was born in Baltimore, Maryland. As a child in 1932, Small was featured as a jingle singer, "Little Miss Bab-O," advertising the cleanser. She subsequently became the child star of her own MARY SMALL SHOW. As a teenager, she vocalized on the BEN BERNIE and The MAGIC KEY OF RCA shows and continued to make guest appearances on numerous music-variety radio programs throughout the 1940s and 1950s. The singer later became one of television's earliest singing stars with a 15-minute program on the air in the late 1940s to the early 1950s, and again sang commercials for various radio and television sponsors.

SMILIN' ED AND HIS BUSTER BROWN GANG (AKA THE BUSTER BROWN SHOW; THE SMILIN' ED MCCONNELL SHOW)

1929–1932	CBS	(*)	(*)
1932–1933	CBS	Sun.	2 PM
1933–1934	CBS	Wed.	12:30 PM
1934–1936	CBS	Sun.	6:30 PM
1936–1937	NBC Red	Sun.	5:30 PM
1937–1938	NBC Blue	Sun.	5:30 PM
1938–1939	NBC Blue	Tues., Thurs.	10:30 PM
1949–1940	CBS	Mon.–Fri.	4:45 PM
	NBC Red	Sat.	11:45 PM
1940–1941	NBC Red	Sat.	11:45 PM
1941–1944	(Off the air)		
1944–1951	NBC	Sat.	11:30 AM
1951–1952	NBC	Sat.	9:30 AM
1952–1953	ABC	Sat.	11 AM

Based on the comic-strip character by R. F. Outcault, the half-hour and 15-minute Buster Brown Gang show was produced by Buster Brown shoes, which used the character as its trademark. The program, which debuted on radio in 1929, starred the genial and jolly Ed MCCONNELL as its host. Early in his radio career, McConnell was primarily a singer, but as time went on, he sang less and spent more time story-telling. He also played the piano and captivated children with his easygoing style and sense of fun. Wonderful characters who were from the comic strip or originated on the radio show included Froggie the gremlin, Squeakie the mouse, and Tige the dog. McConnell would narrate a story that always featured one of four heroes: the Arabian boy, Baba; Ghangi, a Hindu boy; Little Fox, a Native American lad; and Kulah, a boy who had a "Jug Genie" (an Arabian Nights– type genie who lived in a jug instead of a lamp) as his friend and assistant. Robby Ellis, Tommy Cook, Tommy Bernard, Billy Roy, Jimmy Ogg, and Peter Rankin played the four young heroes at various times, and Lou Merrill was the Jug Genie. Also heard on the show were Jerry Marin as Buster Brown, Bud Tollefson as the dog Tige, and supporting actors June Foray, John Dehner, Lou KRUGMAN, and Marvin MILLER. McConnell played the part of Froggie as well as acting as the program's host. Arch Presby and Norman Barr were the show's announcers. The series was produced by Frank Perrin and written and directed by Hobart Donovan and Perrin.

SMILIN' JACK

1935–1939   (Syndicated series. Various stations and times)

Actor Frank READICK starred as airplane pilot and adventurer Smilin' Jack on this 15-minute weekday children's adventure serial, based on the comic strip drawn and written by Zack Mosley. Smilin' Jack was an airplane pilot who tracked down criminals and, during World War II, spies as he flew his airplane around the world. Other actors who were heard on the show included Jackson BECK, Ted DeCorsia, and Gertrude Warner. Tom Shirley was the show's announcer. This adventure series was one of several aviation-oriented serials (SKY KING, Sky Blazers, and CAPTAIN MIDNIGHT) that were on radio in the late 1930s. The series was directed by Alan Wallace.

SMITH, HOWARD K. (1914–   )

During World War II, Howard K. Smith was chief of the CBS European news staff because of his expertise on Germany, which he began to develop in 1936 when he realized that the world was about to go to war with that country. In 1939, when war did indeed break out, Smith was in London with the United Press Bureau. Traveling to Berlin as a CBS radio corresponent in 1941, he began his attacks against Nazism and as ultimately expelled from Germany. His expulsion om Germany resulted in his becoming one of the orld's best-known newsmen. From there he went to ngland, where he continued his attacks on Germany nd reported war news. After the war, Smith returned the United States; in the late 1950s he became CBS's nief Washington commentator and began to appear n television. He remained active as a television news ommentator when radio became America's major ource of "over-the-airwaves" news. Smith is considred by those in the industry to be one of the "deans" f television and radio news broadcast.

MITH, KATE (1907–1985)

obust singer Kate Smith was born in Greenville, irginia, and became one of radio's great stars. Smith rew up in Washington, D.C., and to please her family ttended nursing school after she graduated from igh school. Her heart, however, was set on becoming professional singer. During World War I, Smith egan to sing at various army training camps in and round Washington, D.C., and finally decided to go New York City to pursue a career in show business. he sang on the general vaudeville circuit and any-vhere else she could get a job until 1929, when she ad a featured role in Eddie Dowling's Broadway how *Honeymoon Lane* and then in *Flyin' High.* Her owerful voice and light-footed dancing were a show-topper, and Smith returned to vaudeville as a head-ner billed as "the Songbird of the South."

Debuting both on radio and on Broadway in 1929, he was continuously on the air thereafter until well nto the 1950s. She then began to concentrate on elevision and concert appearances. In addition to her ATE SMITH HOUR, a music-variety radio program also alled *The A&P Bandwagon* for a time, Smith hosted a aily noontime talk program, KATE SMITH SPEAKS. In 939, her variety program was named one of the top-en shows in America in radio fan magazine polls.

In the 1940s, Smith introduced a song written by omposer Irving Berlin, "God Bless America," which he sang in the film *This Is the Army.* The song became ne of the patriotic anthems of World War II. Her heme song, however, was "When the Moon Comes ver the Mountain." Toward the end of her career, Kate Smith often sang the national anthem at various porting and special political events and is well re-nembered for these appearances by post-golden-lays-of-radio audiences.

MITH, "SMILIN' JACK" (c. 1915–)

est known as "the singer with a smile in his voice" n the 1940s and 1950s, Smilin' Jack Smith was born in eattle, Washington, and starred on several successful radio programs such as *Songs by Smith* and *The* JACK SMITH SHOW. In addition, Smith was a frequent guest star on several of radio's music-variety shows and had a 15-minute weekly evening television program on the air in the late 1950s. He eventually left radio in the early 1960s to concentrate on business interests.

SMITH, "WHISPERING JACK" (1898–1950)

It was Whispering Jack's soft, crooning singing style that gave him his nickname and set the standard for many song stylists who followed, most notably Gene AUSTIN and Bing CROSBY. Born in New York, Smith began his show-business career in 1915 as part of a singing quartet and was a song plugger for Irving Berlin in 1918. One of radio's first singing stars, he was heard over the airwaves as early as 1925, had several programs on the air throughout the 1930s, but retired from show business long before "Smilin' Jack" SMITH made his radio debut. Yet people often con-fused the two Smiths and thought they were the same performer. Whispering Jack Smith's last radio show was in 1941 on WEAF, a local station in New York.

SMOKE DREAMS

| 1938–1939 | NBC Blue | Tues. | 10:45 PM |
| 1939–1940 | NBC Red | Sun. | 2 PM |

"The Dreamer" Virginio Marusco and his orchestra and various music guest artists such as Connee BOS-WELL, Mary SMALL, Dick Haymes, and Bea Wain were featured on *Smoke Dreams,* a weekly program that presented popular and semiclassical musical selec-tions. Charles Wood announced the 15-minute and then half-hour series. It was directed by Art Trask. At a time when disc-jockey shows that played hit recordings of popular songs were rare, programs like *Smoke Dreams* were—besides the few times songs were featured on hit comedy-variety shows—the only way people could hear new songs. The M. Fenrich Com-pany sponsored the series.

SMOLEN, VIVIAN (c. 1920–)

New York City–born actress Vivian Smolen attended Brooklyn College before embarking on a career in show business. Smolen had a warm, sweet-sounding, young female voice that allowed her to be cast as ingenues and young leading ladies. She played Veron-ica Lodge, one of teenage Archie's love interests, on ARCHIE ANDREWS and had regular, running roles on daytime dramas FRONT PAGE FARRELL and DOC BAR-CLAY'S DAUGHTERS. For many years, Smolen played the major role of Stella's rich daughter, Laurel ("Lolly Baby"), on STELLA DALLAS, but it is as the title charac-ter on OUR GAL SUNDAY that Smolen is best remem-bered. Actress Dorothy Lowell originated the role in

1937 and played it until Smolen took it over in the mid-1940s. Smolen then acted on the show until it left the air in 1959. After radio drama's demise in the early 1960s, Smolen tried television acting but felt uncomfortable working in the new medium. Except for occasional television commercials and voice-over narrations, Smolen rarely made appearances after the mid-1960s.

SMYTHE, J. ANTHONY (1875–1965)

Born in San Francisco, California, J. Anthony Smythe played the patriarch Father Barbour on the long-running radio drama series ONE MAN'S FAMILY for the entire twenty years the program was on the air. Smythe had been a stage actor before a crippling accident caused him to abandon legitimate theater and concentrate on radio acting. As a staff actor at NBC's San Francisco studios, Smythe had worked with the creator and writer of *One Man's Family*, Carlton E. MORSE, on many previous productions. Ultimately, his comfortable and grandfatherly, if somewhat stuffy-sounding, voice made him the perfect choice to play the part of Father Barbour on the series. So identified with this role did Smythe become, in fact, that he literally would not be accepted in any other part by the listening public during the rest of his career in the role. When the show finally left the air, he was the age he was supposed to be when the program debuted. He quietly retired from show business.

SNOW VILLAGE (AKA SNOW VILLAGE SKETCHES; SOCONYLAND SKETCHES)

1928–1936	NBC	(*)	(*)
1936–1937	NBC Red	Sat.	9 PM
1937–1942	(Off the air)		
1942–1943	NBC	Mon.–Fri.	11:30 AM
1943–1946	(Off the air)		
1946	Mutual	Sun.	11 AM

Listeners demanded that this "comfortable" and "homey" half-hour and 15-minute series, set in the New England town of Four Corners, be returned to the airways each time it left. *Snow Village* featured characters that could be seen in typical, small American towns of the time, such as the local greengrocer, the milkman, the town gossip, the post-office clerk, and the strict-but-excellent teacher. Arthur Allen played a kindly, old Dan'l Hickey, and Parker FENNELLY played his friend, Hiram Neville—characters they had developed on such programs as *Four Corners, USA; Gibbs and Finney; General Delivery; The Simpson Boys of Sprucehead Bay; Smalltown Boys; The Stebbins Boys;* and *Uncle Abe and David.* Heard in featured roles were Kate McComb, John Thomas, Jean McCoy,

Agnes Young, Katherine Raht, Elsie Mae Gordon, and Sarah Fussell. William Ford Manley was the show's original writer and director and was the major reason for its success. Mobil gas, Krispy crackers, and Procter and Gamble products sponsored the series.

SO YOU WANT TO LEAD A BAND?

1946–1947	ABC	Thurs.	10 PM
1947–1949	ABC	Mon.	9:30 PM
1949–1950	CBS	Sun.	(*)

"Swinging" Sammy KAYE had a much-listened-to musical quiz program called *So You Want to Lead a Band.* Members of the studio audience were invited to try to lead Kaye's band. As the band followed whatever lead the amateur conductors indicated, the results could sometimes be surprisingly effective, but most of the time they were hilarious. Of course, such popular songs—which Kaye had made famous—as "Harbor Lights" and "There Will Never Be Another You" were played regularly. John Cleary was the program's director, and the show was written by Bill Mogle and Marian Stearn.

SONGS BY MORTON DOWNEY (AKA MORTON DOWNEY'S STUDIO PARTY; COKE CLUB)

1930–1931	CBS	Tues., Wed., Fri., Sat.	7 PM
1931–1932	CBS	Mon.–Sat.	7:45 PM
1932–1933	NBC Blue	Wed.	9:30 PM
1933–1934	CBS	Thurs.	8 PM
1934–1935	NBC Blue	Sun.	4:30 PM
1935–1936	NBC Blue	Fri.	8:15 PM
1936–1943	(Local stations only)		
1943–1944	NBC Blue	Mon.–Fri.	3 PM
1944–1947	Mutual	Mon.–Fri.	12:15 PM
1947–1948	(Local stations only)		
1948–1950	NBC	Tues., Thurs., Sat.	11:15 PM
1950–1951	CBS	Sat.	10:30 AM

Singer Morton DOWNEY had a long and distinguished career on radio spanning twenty-one years. On his various 15-minute and half-hour shows, Downey sang popular as well as classical and semiclassical song favorites and specialized in such Irish-tenor standards as "Londonderry Air," "The Rose of Tralee," and "When Irish Eyes Are Smiling." Downey's announcers were David Ross and Harry Burge. Paul WHITEMAN and Ray Sinatra's orchestras were featured on the show for many years. Downey's network sponsors were Camel cigarettes, Woodbury soap, and Coca-Cola soft drink.

SONGS BY SINATRA

See FRANK SINATRA SHOW, THE.

SOSNICK, HARRY (1906–   )

Music director Harry Sosnick, born in Chicago, Illinois, was one of the bandleaders who led the orchestra on YOUR HIT PARADE. A radio musician as early as 1924, he also led the orchestra on *The AL PEARCE SHOW, The Swift Revue, Woodbury's Hollywood Playhouse,* BEAT THE BAND, *The DANNY KAYE SHOW,* HOBBY LOBBY, and *The RALEIGH ROOM.* One of the music industry's most reliable and competent music directors, Sosnick continued to be active on television as both an arranger and a conductor well into the 1980s.

SOTHERN, ANN (HARRIETTE LAKE: 1909–   )

Actress Ann Sothern, born in Lake Valley City, North Dakota, has had a long and memorable career in motion pictures, television, and radio. A frequent guest star on such radio programs as *The LUX RADIO THEATER* and *The SCREEN GUILD PLAYERS* in the 1930s and 1940s, Sothern starred in a radio series for more than eight years, based on her popular *Maisie* films. These films were produced by MGM and featured the actress as a tough chorus girl named Maisie Revere who had a talent for stumbling upon trouble. Considered one of Hollywood's finest comediennes, the actress appeared in such films as *Kid Millions* (1935), *Lady Be Good* (1941), *Panama Hattie* (1942), *A Letter to Three Wives* (1949), *Sylvia* (1965), and *The Whales of*

Ann Sothern (CBS)

August (1987). Sothern was also the star of two very successful, long-running television situation-comedy series, "Private Secretary" (1954) and "The Ann Sothern Show" (1958), which were consistently rated among the top-ten shows on the air during the 1950s and 1960s.

SOULE, OLAN (1910–1994)

Few actors played as wide a variety of roles on as many radio programs as Olan Soule (pronounced soo-LAY). The actor, who was born in La Harpe, Illinois, is perhaps best remembered as Barbara LUDDY's long time costar on FIRST NIGHTER, on which he played every conceivable type of leading role from suave man-about-town to down-and-out vagabond. In addition to his *First Nighter* appearances, Soule was also prominently featured as both a leading man and as a character actor on AMOS AND ANDY, BACHELOR'S CHILDREN, *The COUPLE NEXT DOOR,* JUNIOR NURSE CORPS, *A TALE OF TODAY,* IT CAN BE DONE, MARY NOBLE BACKSTAGE WIFE, CAPTAIN MIDNIGHT, CHANDU THE MAGICIAN, JACK ARMSTRONG, *All-American Boy,* LITTLE ORPHAN ANNIE, MIDSTREAM, CURTAIN TIME, *Trouble with Marriage, The ROMANCE OF HELEN TRENT,* TODAY'S CHILDREN, LET GEORGE DO IT, and DRAGNET. Soule also was a successful character actor in films, playing featured roles in *North by Northwest* (1959), *Days of Wine and Roses* (1962), and *The Towering Inferno* (1974), among others. His TV credits include "The Andy Griffith Show" (1960) playing the choir director, "The Twilight Zone" (1959), "Dallas" (1975), "Fantasy Island" (1979), and "Love Boat" (1979). Frequently heard as the cartoon voice of characters in both feature-length animated films and TV cartoon series "Fantastic Planet" (1973), "The Night Before Christmas" (1968), and "Challenge of the Super Friends" (1978), Soule continued working as an actor until shortly before his death.

SOUND EFFECTS

The illusion of action and activity that people heard on radio would not have been possible without sound effects. Even though sound technicians were vital to the success of a program, they were rarely mentioned in a program's credits. Their sound-effects tables in the studio, however, were full of such paraphernalia as coconut shells and rubber cups to simulate the sound of horses' hooves; large sheets of tin to shake vehemently when thunder was required or to strike with a hammer when the sound of lightning was needed; pieces of cellophane to crinkle to approximate the sound of frying bacon or a forest fire; a blown-up basketball bladder filled with BB shots to shake to simulate the sound of falling rain or even an explosion. The tables also contained real telephones, doorbells, house and car doors, and, on the floor, a staircase to help create the sound of someone climbing up stairs. By using this equipment, sound effects technicians could make listeners believe that what they were hearing was actually happening. Miser Jack BENNY's chained and padlocked vault in the basement of his home as heard on The JACK BENNY SHOW; FIBBER MCGEE AND MOLLY's celebrated hall closet that was crowded with objects that spilled out—usually on top of Fibber every time he opened the door—as well as the gunfire, skidding tires, and fisticuffs heard on GANGBUSTERS— all of these provoked laughter and excitement only because of the creative genius of the sound-effects technicians. Many of the sound men and women, as well as the shows they worked on, are listed below:

Jack Amerine (INNER SANCTUM MYSTERIES, MR. CHAMELEON, MR. KEEN, *Tracer of Lost Persons*), Jack Anderson (The BRIGHTER DAY, LIGHT OF THE WORLD), Al April (OFFICIAL DETECTIVE), Barney Beck (many shows and Bedside Network), Al Binnie (MR. AND MRS. NORTH), Bill Brinkmeyer (The ALDRICH FAMILY), Gus Bayz (AMOS AND ANDY, MELODY RANCH, SUSPENSE), Ed Blainey (The FAT MAN, The FBI IN PEACE AND WAR, GANGBUSTERS, HOP HARRIGAN), Bill Brown (BIG SISTER, The BRIGHTER DAY), Joe Cabibbo (various programs), Floyd Caton (The ABBOTT AND COSTELLO SHOW), Clark Casey (The ADVENTURES OF PHILIP MARLOWE, DR. CHRISTIAN, MY FAVORITE HUSBAND, PURSUIT, The RED SKELTON SHOW), Fred Cole (MR. PRESIDENT, the penguin in the Kool cigarette commercials), Wes Conant (MA PERKINS, PORTIA FACES LIFE, THEATER GUILD ON THE AIR), Al Cooney (QUICK AS A FLASH), Arthur Cooper (The ETERNAL LIGHT), Parker Cornell (BLONDIE, The BOB HOPE SHOW), Manny Cramer (various programs), Lloyd J. Creekmore (TRUTH OR CONSEQUENCES), Keene Crockett (DEATH VALLEY DAYS), Ralph Cummings (The GUIDING LIGHT, HOUSE PARTY), Al De Caprio (*County Fair),* Jerry DeCarlo (many shows), Jack Dick (The CISCO KID, LIFE WITH LUIGI, STARS OVER HOLLYWOOD), Zale Dillon (various programs), Jim Dwan (LET'S PRETEND, AUNT JENNY, The SECOND MRS. BURTON), Ray Erlenborn (AL PEARCE AND HIS GANG, The JOE PENNER SHOW, The JACK BENNY SHOW, SUSPENSE, BURNS AND ALLEN, *Gateway to Hollywood, The* RED SKELTON SHOW), Harry Essman (The HALLMARK PLAYHOUSE, LUM AND ABNER), Edward Fenton, (The MARCH OF TIME), Ronald Fitzgerald (The MARCH OF TIME), James Flynn (various programs), Harold Forry (AUNT JENNY), Mort Frazer (RED RYDER, THIS IS YOUR FBI), Arthur Fulton (QUEEN FOR A DAY), Henry Gautier (LET'S PRETEND), Jim Goode (MARTIN KANE, PRIVATE EYE, TRUE DETECTIVE MYSTERIES), Bill Gould (ESCAPE, OUR MISS BROOKS), Bob Grapperhouse (FITCH BANDWAGON), Charles Grenier (MYSTERY THEATER), Elliott Grey (various programs), Walter Gustafson (various programs), Tom Hanley (GUNSMOKE, STRAIGHT ARROW), Chet Hill (MARY NOBLE, BACKSTAGE WIFE, COLGATE SPORTS NEWSREEL), William B. Hoffman (MARK TRAIL, The ADVENTURES OF SHERLOCK HOLMES), Al Hogan (The FBI IN PEACE AND WAR, MR. AND MRS. NORTH), Bob Holmes (A DATE WITH JUDY), Tommy Horan (MA PERKINS), Agnew Horine (ARCHIE ANDREWS, DIMENSION X, *The* FRED ALLEN SHOW, STELLA DALLAS), Sam Hubbard (*The* CHESTERFIELD SUPPER CLUB), Harold Johnson, Jr. (various programs), Herb Johnson (*Og, Son of Fire*), Jack Keane (*House of Mystery,* MARTIN KANE, PRIVATE EYE, SUPERMAN), Ray Kelly (various programs), Ray Kemper (GUNSMOKE, STRAIGHT ARROW), Wayne Kenworthy (DRAGNET), Fred Knoepfke (various programs), Ray Kremer (DON WINSLOW OF THE NAVY, GANGBUSTERS), Tiny Lamb (*The* RED SKELTON SHOW), Dave Light (AMOS AND ANDY, MELODY RANCH, LUM AND ABNER, SUSPENSE), Vic Livoti (BEULAH), Frank Loughrane (LORENZO JONES, *The* RIGHT TO HAPPINESS), Ed Ludes (AMOS AND ANDY), Jim Lynch (The GOLDBERGS, *The Joe DiMaggio Show,* PERRY MASON, *The* ROMANCE OF HELEN TRENT), Ross Martindale (FRONT PAGE FARRELL, PEPPER YOUNG'S FAMILY, THIS IS NORA DRAKE, YOUNG WIDDER BROWN), Jerry McCarthy (CASEY, CRIME PHOTOGRAPHER, GANGBUSTERS, MR. AND MRS. NORTH), William McClintock (THEATER GUILD ON THE AIR), John McCloskey (HILLTOP HOUSE, OUR GAL SUNDAY), Jerry McGee (CAVALCADE OF AMERICA, RADIO CITY PLAYHOUSE), Max Miller (JUST PLAIN BILL), Sam Monroe (DIMENSION X), Jimmy Murphy (*The* JACK BENNY SHOW, MY FRIEND IRMA), Ross Murray (SUSPENSE), Harry Nelson (various programs), Ora Nichols (GANGBUSTERS, LET'S PRETEND, *The* MARCH OF TIME), George O'Donnell (LET'S PRETEND, YOUNG DR. MALONE), Hamilton O'Hara (*The* GUIDING LIGHT, HILLTOP HOUSE, WENDY WARREN, YOUNG DR. MALONE), Walter Otto (YOUNG DR. MALONE), Kjell Pederson (various programs), Adrian Penner (*The* FALCON, NICK CARTER, MASTER DETECTIVE, QUICK AS A FLASH), Walter Pierson (LET'S PRETEND; Head of the CBS sound-effects department), Frank Pittman (AMOS AND ANDY, FIBBER MCGEE AND MOLLY), John Powers (BIG TOWN, MR. DISTRICT ATTORNEY, RADIO CITY PLAYHOUSE), Bob Prescott (DEATH VALLEY DAYS, GANGBUSTERS, *The* MARCH OF TIME, TRUTH OR CONSEQUENCES), Hal Reid (*The* THIN MAN), Virgil Reime (*The* JACK BENNY SHOW, THIS IS YOUR FBI), Jim Rinaldi (ARMSTRONG THEATER OF TODAY), Jack Robinson (*The* AMAZING MR. MALONE, *The* RED SKELTON SHOW), Vincent Rocca (MA PERKINS), Jim Rogan (LET'S PRETEND, GANGBUSTERS, GRAND CENTRAL STATION, HIT THE JACKPOT, YOU ARE THERE), Terry Ross (ETHEL AND ALBERT, *The* GREATEST STORY EVER TOLD), Vic Rubi (various programs), Max Russell (FRANK MERRIWELL), Harry Saz (various programs), Al Scott (*The* BIG STORY, CAVALCADE OF AMERICA), Manny Segal (FRONT PAGE FARRELL, LORENZO JONES, *The* RIGHT TO HAPPINESS, *The* ROAD OF LIFE), Mario Silitti (NICK CARTER, MASTER DETECTIVE,), Jack Sixsmith (SUSPENSE), Ted Slade (various programs), Norm Smith (RED RYDER), Walter Snow (*The* BOB HOPE SHOW), Art Sorrence (*Case Book of Gregory Hood*), Art Strand (CASEY, CRIME PHOTOGRAPHER, GIVE AND TAKE, LET'S PRETEND), Fritz Street (various programs), Jerry Sullivan (ROSEMARY, THIS IS NORA DRAKE, WINNER TAKE ALL), Berne Surrey (PURSUIT, *The* WHISTLER), Cliff Thorsness (*The* ADVENTURES OF PHILIP MARLOWE, *The* EDDIE CANTOR SHOW, ESCAPE), Bud Tollefson (DRAGNET), Bob Turnbull (RED RYDER), Gene Twombly (MELODY RANCH, *The* HALLMARK PLAYHOUSE, *The* JACK BENNY SHOW, *The* WHISTLER), Max Uhlig (various programs), Bill Verdier (CAVALCADE OF AMERICA), Clem Waters (various programs), Louie Wehr (*Og, Son of Fire*), Byron Winget (*The* FBI IN PEACE AND WAR, GANGBUSTERS, WE, THE PEOPLE), Jack Wormser (various programs), Art Zachs (LIFE CAN BE BEAUTIFUL, WE LOVE AND LEARN). [**Note:** Unfortunately, time and space do not permit inclusion of many of the hundreds of men and women sound-effects artists who contributed their talents to the countless number of radio programs that have been heard over the past seventy years.]

SPACE PATROL

1950–1951	ABC	Mon., Fri.	5:30 PM
1951–1954	ABC	Sat.	7:30 PM & 10 AM
1954–1955	ABC	Sat.	10:30 AM

This 15-minute and then half-hour ABC network show was one of several children's science fiction–adventure serials heard on radio. *Space Patrol* was similar to *Flash Gordon* and BUCK ROGERS IN THE 25TH CENTURY in that it was set in a future century and centered around travel through the universe in a spacecraft. Space traveler Buzz Corey was played by Ed Kemmer. Heard in supporting roles were Robert DRYDEN, Joe DeSantis, Bob READICK, and others. Ralston cereal and Nestle's chocolate sponsored the series.

SPEAKS, MARGARET (1905–1977)

Singer Margaret Speaks, who was born in Columbus, Ohio, was one of the most popular vocalists on radio in the 1930s. The niece of songwriter Oleg Speaks, she frequently guest-starred on most classical and semiclassical music programs. The soprano made her radio debut in 1927, becoming a regular on *The* VOICE OF FIRESTONE, one of the longest running programs in radio history. She was also a popular concert performer, and her personal appearances around the coun-

try, after her radio days, attracted thousands of faithful fans who fondly remembered her broadcasts.

SPEED GIBSON OF THE INTERNATIONAL SECRET POLICE

1937–1938 (Syndicated series. Various stations and times)

This 15-minute weekday radio series was a favorite of young listeners the single season it was aired, but the series failed to attract enough local sponsorship to warrant its continuation. The series starred John GIBSON in the title role and featured Howard McNear, Hanley STAFFORD, Jack Mathers, and Elliott LEWIS. Announcers on the series included Ron Rawson and Franklyn McCormack. The director and writers of this series were not credited.

SPELLING BEE

| 1937–1938 | NBC Blue | Sat. | 8:30 PM |
| 1938–1940 | NBC Red | Sun. | 5:30 PM |

Contestants won prizes by spelling words correctly; the top prize was $50. *Spelling Bee* appealed to listeners who enjoyed pitting their spelling skills against those of the show's contestants. Paul Wing was the series' host and moderator. The half-hour program was sponsored by Energine vitamin supplement.

SPIER, WILLIAM (1906–1973)

Considered by many to be one of radio's best directors, William Spier, born in New York City, became best known for his contributions to the program that was "well calculated to keep you in . . . *Suspense*." When he was 19 years old, Spier went to work for *Musical Drama* magazine in New York City, edited by Deems Taylor. He became the magazine's chief critic before resigning one year later to work on various radio projects for the B.B.D.&O. advertising agency. Leaving the agency in 1941 to join CBS radio on the West Coast, he produced and directed programs such as *The Atwater Kent Hour*, *The General Motors Family Hour*, *The* MARCH OF TIME (for 400 performances), SUSPENSE, *The* ADVENTURES OF SAM SPADE, DETECTIVE, and *The* PHILIP MORRIS PLAYHOUSE.

SPIKE JONES AND HIS CITY SLICKERS SHOW, THE (AKA SPOTLIGHT REVUE)

1945	NBC	Sun.	8 PM
1945–1947	(Off the air)		
1947–1949	CBS	Fri.	10:30 PM
1949	CBS	Sun.	6:30 PM

Madcap musician Spike JONES and his City Slickers band were one of the most popular orchestras in America throughout the 1940s. Jones led his musicians in hilarious spoofs of popular and semiclassical songs, but added the zany sounds of people burping, cars crashing, bazooka's, pops, snaps, and crackles to the tunes he played. This musical satirist's band, heard on a half-hour weekly program, featured Dorothy Shay, "the Park Avenue hillbilly," a sophisticated, urbane-sounding singer who sang country-western songs, as vocalist. Other featured performers were musician-comedian Ish Kabibble, whose real name was Myrvyn Bogue. Bogue wore outrageous bangs that almost covered his eyes and usually had a rather dumb, dazed look on his face and a flat midwestern accent. Characters such as Doodles Weaver, Horatio G. Birdbath, Sir Frederick Gas, George Rock, and Dick and Freddy Morgan were also heard regularly. Jones's announcers were Mike Wallace and Michael Roy. His sponsors at different times were Chase and Sanborn coffee and Coca-Cola.

SPITALNY, PHIL (1890–1970)

Orchestra leader Phil Spitalny was born in Eastern Europe. He worked as a music conductor for several years before he gained recognition as the founder of an orchestra entirely composed of women. The idea "caught on" with the public, and in 1929, the group began to broadcast its concerts. A half-hour radio program, The HOUR OF CHARM, resulted. Spitalny eventually married one of the show's most popular performers, Evelyn Kaye KLEIN, famous as "Evelyn and Her Magic Violin." When The Hour of Charm left the airwaves after fourteen years, Spitalny and his orchestra continued appearing in concerts around the world.

SPONSORS

Reportedly, the first commercial message heard over the airwaves was delivered on WEAF in New York in 1922 by a long-forgotten local real-estate developer who was selling properties in Manhattan. Prior to 1922, all attempts to use radio for commercial purposes was discouraged. One trade journal even said that they were convinced that "any attempt to make the radio an advertising medium would prove positively offensive to a great number of people." The real-estate company, not wanting to offend anyone, merely announced its name and never made a sales pitch. That one simple announcement, however, opened up the floodgates. Other companies began to have their names "mentioned" on the radio and within eight years, commercial radio was a well-established reality. Currently, sponsors buy radio and TV advertising time by the minute, whereas in the 1930s, 1940s, and 1950s one sponsor usually paid for an entire half-hour or hour show. The names of products manufactured by companies who sponsored these network programs became inextricably linked with the show and star they sponsored. The mere mention of a particular program or radio star, and the sponsor's product immediately came to mind, which is basically what network radio advertising was all about. Just say the name Jack BENNY and listeners immediately thought of Jell-O or Lucky Strike cigarettes. Mention The LUX RADIO THEATER and Lux soap came to mind. Whenever MA PERKINS was mentioned, Oxydol laundry detergent was the first thing that came into people's head. (See individual show listings for a more complete list of a show's sponsors, and the Appendix for a list of sponsors and the major programs they were associated with on radio.)

SPOTLIGHT BANDS (AKA THE VICTORY PARADE OF SPOTLIGHT BANDS)

1941–1942	Mutual	Mon.–Sat.	10:15 PM
1942–1945	NBC Blue	Mon.–Sat.	9:30 PM
1945–1946	Mutual	Mon., Wed., Fri.	9:30 PM

On the air in 15-minute and half-hour versions, Spotlight Bands used a World War II background, featuring different big-name bands such as Tommy and Jimmy Dorsey's, Glenn Miller's, and Xavier Cugat's. The emphasis was on boosting the morale of both the folks at home and members of the armed forces; the show was broadcast to troops overseas via the ARMED FORCES NETWORK, as well as being heard on commercial stations. It was sponsored by Coca-Cola soft drink.

STAFFORD, HANLEY (1899–1968)

A busy radio actor in Chicago throughout the 1930s, Hanley Stafford was born in England, entered radio in the United States in 1932, and was heard on hundreds of programs playing all sorts of roles on The ENO CRIME CLUB, PALMOLIVE BEAUTY BOX THEATER, SHOWBOAT, The Court of Human Relations, Woodbury's Hollywood PLayhouse, BIG TOWN, Thrills, Good News, and others. It is, however, as "Daddy" on Fanny BRICE's BABY SNOOKS program that he is best remembered. Stafford began to play Daddy in the late thirties, replacing actors Frank MORGAN and Alan REED. Stafford's ever-exasperated, slow-boiling acting proved the perfect foil to Brice's spoiled-brat, mischievous Snooks and earned him a permanent place in radio's Hall of Fame. In addition to Baby Snooks, Stafford was also featured on such programs as YOUR HIT PARADE, BLONDIE, and JOHN'S OTHER WIFE.

STAFFORD, JO (JOSEPHINE STAFFORD: 1920–   )

One of America's most popular singers, Jo Stafford was born in Goalinga, California. She made her radio debut on a local station, KHJ in Los Angeles, as a member of the Stafford Sisters vocal trio. Later, Stafford became the lead singer of a successful quartet called the Pied Pipers but eventually left the group to work as a solo artist. She starred on *The Music Shop* radio program with Johnny Mercer in 1944 and was subsequently featured on *The* RAILROAD HOUR, *The* CHESTERFIELD SUPPER CLUB, *The* BOB CROSBY SHOW, CLUB FIFTEEN, and then on her own *Jo Stafford Show*. By the late 1940s and throughout the 1950s, Stafford was one of the music industry's most popular recording artists, and her many gold record hits include "You Belong to Me," "Long Ago and Far Away," "Jambalya," "I'll Be Seeing You," and "Shrimp Boats." She hosted for the Radio Luxembourg network, which broadcasted American pop music to European audiences during World War II. However, Stafford, who was married to orchestra leader–arranger Paul Weston, gradually withdrew from the spotlight, claiming she was "uncomfortable" with television's idea of "being seen, instead of just heard, by so many people." In 1957, Stafford, who has perfect pitch, made a series of recordings spoofing pop songs with her husband. For these recordings—cult classics among record collectors—Stafford used the name Darlene Edwards and portrayed a relentlessly off-key singer. Weston was Darlene's equally inept piano-playing accompanist and husband, Jonathan. The Westons continued to make Darlene and Jonathan Edwards albums well into the 1970s, and a "Greatest Hits of Darlene and Jonathan Edward" CD was released in 1987.

STAGE DOOR CANTEEN

1942–1943	CBS	Thurs.	9:30 PM
1943–1945	CBS	Fri.	10:30 PM

In the early years of World War II, a group of prominent Broadway actors opened a club where armed services personnel could spend their off-duty hours on leave in New York City rubbing elbows and sharing a dance or a "cup of Java" with stars. Servicemen were admitted into the Stage Door Canteen free, and entertainers—both famous and aspiring—acted as hosts and hostesses, dancing with the servicemen and women, serving them free refreshments, and talking with them. In 1942, actress Helen MENKEN, an established radio performer who was active on the stage in New York, proposed the idea that a similar club should be broadcast to homes all over America so that the families of servicemen and women would feel "more in touch" with their loved ones. The idea was enthusiastically accepted by CBS network officials, and a half-hour *Stage Door Canteen* program was presented each week; the studio used for the show was decorated to look like the original canteen. Celebrities such as radio personalities FIBBER MCGEE AND

MOLLY, singer Jeanette MacDonald, film star Merle Oberon, and politician Wendell Wilkie, to name a few, were guest stars. Bert LYTELL was the program's official host, and Raymond PAIGE led the show's orchestra. The show was written by Frank Wilson and had numerous volunteer directors. It was sustained by CBS.

STAMP CLUB, THE (AKA IVORY STAMP CLUB; CAPTAIN TIM'S ADVENTURES)

1933–1934	NBC Blue	Mon., Wed., Fri.	6:30 PM
1934–1935	NBC Blue	Mon., Wed., Fri.	5:45 PM
1935–1936	NBC Red	Wed., Fri.	5:45 PM
1936–1937	NBC Blue	Tues., Thurs., Sat.	6:15 PM
1937–1938	NBC Blue	Mon.	5:45 PM
1938–1939	NBC Red	Mon., Wed., Fri.	6:30 PM
1939–1940	NBC Red	Mon., Wed., Fri.	6:15 PM
1940–1941	NBC Red	Mon., Wed., Fri.	6:30 PM

Devoted entirely to a hobby, *The Stamp Club* featured "Captain" Tim Healy as host. Information about the latest stamps issued by the U.S. Postal Department, interviews with stamp collectors, and lists of sought-after valuable stamps were given on this program. Ivory soap flakes and soap and Kellogg's cereal were the show's sponsors at various times.

STANG, ARNOLD (1923–   )

Actor Arnold Stang was born in Chelsea, Massachusetts. A performer with a somewhat nasal, lateral-lisping, and forever-young voice, Stang began his career as a child on *The Horn and Hardart* CHILDREN'S HOUR and *The* GOLDBERGS (as Seymour Fingergood). As a teen, he played Joey Brewster on the situation comedy THAT BREWSTER BOY in the 1940s. Stang became one of radio's best-known voices, however, when he appeared on *The* HENRY MORGAN SHOW and *The* MILTON BERLE SHOW. Stang made occasional guest appearances on various television shows in the 1950s and 1960s and had a cameo role in the film *It's a Mad, Mad, Mad, Mad World* (1963). In the 1970s, the actor was heard on Himan BROWN's CBS MYSTERY THEATER and on the one-hour RADIO PLAYHOUSE programs. As recently as 1994, Stang had a featured role on a "Bill Cosby's Mysteries" episode.

STAR WARS

1981   NPR   (Various stations and times)

In 1981, NATIONAL PUBLIC RADIO presented a thirteen-part, one-hour radio series based on George Lukas's popular science-fiction film *Star Wars*. The series starred actors Mark Hammill and Anthony Daniels, who had appeared in the original film, as Luke Skywalker and See Threepio. Also featured on this series were Brock Peters as Darth Vader, Bernard Behrens as Ben Kenobi, and Perry King as Han Solo. Directed by John Madden and written by Brian Daley, the technically stunning audio effects included realistic stereophonic sound effects and music by the film score's composer, John Williams. The film's sound technician, Tom Voegell, supervised the sound for the radio series. It was the intent of the producers to introduce a whole new generation to radio drama as an art form: the series was produced for an unprecedented $200,000. Unfortunately, this noble experiment did not attract the sizable audience the producers had hoped for, and other promised radio dramas of similar magnitude and an adaptation of *The Empire Strikes Back* were less spectacularly financed. The original *Star Wars* series has been rebroadcast many times since its original presentation on various National Public Radio affiliated stations.

STARK, CHARLES "CHARLIE" (1912–)

Announcer Charles Stark, born in Reading, Pennsylvania, attended the University of Pennsylvania before entering radio in 1927. His deep and commanding voice identified this announcer on such varied programs as CAN YOU TOP THIS, GANGBUSTERS, and daytime drama serials OUR GAL SUNDAY, SCATTERGOOD BAINES, *My Son and I,* STRANGE AS IT SEEMS, and WHEN A GIRL MARRIES. He had a long and distinguished broadcasting career that extended into television as a spot and promotional announcer. Stark retired in the mid-1980s but can still occasionally be heard announcing programs.

STARRING MRS. ROOSEVELT

| 1937 | NBC Blue | Wed. | 7:15 PM |

Although she was often criticized in the press for her around-the-world travels as she championed all sorts of social causes, Eleanor Roosevelt wrote a daily newspaper column and hosted a 15-minute weekly news commentary program on radio in the late 1930s. On her program, Roosevelt—always wearing an evening dress and a shoulder orchid during her broadcasts, even though there was no studio audience in attendance—commented on the news of the day, such as her husband's Works Project Administration and the escalating war in Europe. She additionally interviewed such international celebrities as playwright Sherwood Anderson, novelist Sinclair Lewis, and stage actress Katherine Cornell. Assisted by her personal secretary, Mrs. Milvina Thompson Schneider, whom she always referred to as "Tommy" on her program, Roosevelt donated all of her radio earnings to such charities as the March of Dimes and the War Orphans' Relief Fund.

STARS OVER HOLLYWOOD

1941–1948	CBS	Sat.	12:20 PM
1948–1949	CBS	Sat.	2 PM
1949–1951	CBS	Sat.	11 PM
1951–1954	CBS	Sat.	12:30 PM

This half-hour series, featuring stories written especially for the program as well as adaptations of such famous stories as James Hilton's *Lost Horizon* and Louisa Alcott's *Little Women,* was heard on the CBS network. The plays featured family-oriented material and were usually highly moral in content. Leading Hollywood players such as Joan Crawford, Lizbeth Scott, Dan Duryea, Jan Sterling, Audrey Totter, Hope Emerson, Lionel BARRYMORE, Lynn Bari, Angela Lansbury, Gary MERRILL, Jane Wyman, Arlene Dahl, Dean Stockwell, Barry Sullivan, and John Payne were heard on the series at one time or another. Basil RATHBONE, Alan Hale, Sr., Brenda Marshall, Brenda Joyce, Merle Oberon, Bonita Granville, Anita Louise, Mary Astor, and Ann Rutherford were featured so often that they could almost be called regulars. Radio actors were often heard in supporting roles: Lurene TUTTLE, Janet WALDO, Gale GORDON, Cathy LEWIS, Betty Lou GERSON, Mary Jane CROFT, and Joan BANKS were among them. The series' announcers were Frank Goss, Marvin MILLER, Art Gilmore, and Jim Bannon. Art Gilmore was also one of the program's longtime hosts. Del Castillo was the program's music director. The series was directed by Les Mitchel, Don Clark, and Paul Pierce. *Stars over Hollywood* was sponsored by Dari-Rich dairy products, Armour Star lard, Armour Star foods, Dial soap, Chiffon soap flakes, and Carnation evaporated milk.

STEELE, TED (1918–1985)

Born in Hartford, Connecticut, Ted Steele was an orchestra leader, organist, and program host on radio. Steele led the band on the CHESTERFIELD SUPPER CLUB and *The MGM Screen Test* and played the organ for the SOCIETY GIRL series. He also hosted *Easy Does It* and was hosting the *American Bandstand* program on radio just as rock-and-roll music began to invade the airwaves. Steele made a successful transition from radio to television in the early 1950s and hosted a daytime talk show, "The Ted Steele Show." He was also regularly featured on the NBC television series "Monitor" before he retired in the 1970s.

STELLA DALLAS

1937–1938	NBC Red	Mon.–Fri.	12:30 PM
1938–1941	NBC Red	Mon.–Fri.	4:15 PM
1941–1955	NBC	Mon.–Fri.	4:15 PM

One of radio's most enduring daytime drama series, the 15-minute program was, according to its opening,

The cast of the daytime drama series *Stella Dallas:* (Sitting from left) Vivian Smolen, Anne Elstner, and Jane Houston; (standing from left) Bert Cowan, Helen Claire, and Donald Buka (NBC)

"a continution on the air of the true-life story of mother love and sacrifice, in which Stella Dallas saw her own beloved daughter, Laurel, marry into wealth and society and, realizing the difference in their tastes and worlds, went out of Laurel's life." In reality, Stella only tried to keep out of Laurel's (or "Lolly Baby's") way. Stella, who was a rather common but good-natured woman, was played by actress Anne ELSTNER for the program's entire run on the air. Laurel was played first by actress Joy Hathaway, then for many years by Vivian SMOLEN, and finally for a short while by Anne BURR. Featured on the series were Frederick Tozere as Stephen Dallas, and Julie Benell, Harold Vermilyea, Donald Buka, Nancy Sheridan, Dorothy Sands, Arthur Vinton, Carlton YOUNG, Macdonald CAREY, Spencer Bentley, George Lambert, Michael Fitzmaurice, Frank LOVEJOY, Tom Tully, Mary Jane HIGBY, Mandel KRAMER, Barbara Barton, Helen Claire, Luis VAN ROOTEN, Ara Gerald, Walter KINSELLA, Albert ALEY, Joan Lorring, Hal Studer, Richard Gordon, Kenneth Daigneau, Jane Houston, Grace Valentine, Bill Quinn, Elaine Kent, William J. Smith, Ethel Everett, Peter DONALD, Ed BEGLEY, and Raymond Edward JOHNSON. The program's announcers were Ford BOND,

Howard Claney, Frank Gallop, Jack Costello, Jimmy WALLINGTON, and Roger Krupp. *Stella Dallas* was directed by Richard Leonard, Ernest Ricca, and Norman Sweetser and produced by Frank and Anne HUMMERT. Doris Halman, Helen Walpole, and the Hummerts were the program's writers. Sponsors of this series included Sterling drugs and Phillips Milk of Magnesia antacid, Double Danderine shampoo, Ironized yeast, Diamond salt, and Bayer aspirin pain reliever. The program's theme song was "How Can I Leave Thee?"

STEPMOTHER

| 1938–1940 | CBS | Mon.–Fri. | 10:45 AM |
| 1940–1942 | CBS | Mon.–Fri. | 10:30 AM |

Many years before people in the United States had to deal with a staggering divorce rate and the difficulties of raising other people's children, the 15-minute weekday *Stepmother* series was asking the question, "Can a stepmother successfully raise another woman's children?" Sunda Love, Janet Logan, and Charlotte MANSON played Kay Fairchild, the stepmother; Francis X. Bushman, William Green, Charles Penman, and Willard WATERMAN played her husband, John. John's troubled daughter, Peggy, who always felt that her peers had more material things and love than she did and often had unsavory romances with rather sordid men, was played by Peggy Wall and Barbara Fuller. Also heard on the series in supporting roles were Edith Davis, Arthur HUGHES, Macdonald CAREY, Julie Bonell, Cornelia Osgood, Marvin MILLER, Ethel Owen, Cornelius Peeples, Elmira Roessler, Bess McCammon, Don Gallagher, Ken Christy, Dorothy Gregory, Betty Arnold, June Meredith, Harry Elders, John LARKIN, Robert Guilbert, Forrest Lewis, Betty Hanna, Francis "Dink" Trout, and Karl WEBER. Roger Krupp, Don Hancock, Dan Donaldson, Ford BOND, and Carlton Kadell were the program's announcers. Les Weinrot, Ernest Ricca, Richard Leonard, and Art Glad directed the series, which was written by Roy Maypole, Jr. Sponsors of this program were Colgate tooth powder; Cashmere Bouquet hand lotion, face powder, soap and talcum powder; and Phillips Milk of Magnesia antacid. The show's theme song was Chopin's "Impromptu."

STEREO MORNING

1980s–present   CBC Stereo (FM)   Mon.–Fri.   5 AM

The CANADIAN BROADCASTING CORPORATION's music program *Stereo Morning,* hosted by David Grierson, features the latest as well as vintage recordings of classical music performed by international performers and orchestras. Listeners can also hear such essential early-morning information as general weather and news. Featured on the program is a segment called "the Arts Report," containing reviews of new recordings, plays, and films. Grierson has been hosting the program since April 1991. The executive producer of *Stereo Morning* is Helen Montagna.

STERN, BILL (1907–1971)

Bill Stern's COLGATE SPORTS NEWSREEL and *Bill Stern Show* were among the highest-rated programs on radio for many years. Born in Rochester, New York, Stern has been called one of radio's best sportscasters. He broadcasted many remote "on-the-scene" sports reports during the years he was actively on the air and covered baseball, basketball, football, horse racing, crew racing, tennis, golf, track and field, and any other sporting events he felt would be of interest to his vast listening audience. The last few years his show was on the air, Stern interviewed various celebrities other than sports figures, including Judy GARLAND, Milton BERLE, Margaret Truman, Vice President Albin Barkley, Leon Uris and Kathleen Winsor, as well as sports figures such as Leo Durocher, Joe DiMaggio, and Rocky Graziano. It was, however, Stern's emotionally charged, involved manner of speaking that made him a perfect play-by-play sportscaster. Although he was often accused of being a bit too melodramatic and "show-biz oriented" because of the long pauses and almost frantic response to events that occurred on his program—it is certainly true that he exaggerated certain facts—Bill Stern was nevertheless one of the most important, listened-to (according to newspaper and magazine polls) sportscasters on radio.

STERN, HOWARD (1956–   )

One of radio's most controversial talk-show hosts, Howard Stern, whose syndicated *Howard Stern Show* is heard on several local stations from New York to California, was born in Roosevelt, Long Island. Stern produced puppet shows for parties as a boy and when he was a teen formed a rock band called "The Electric Comic Book." Stern attended Elmira College and entered radio as a disc jockey in 1976 at station WRNW in Briarcliff Manor, New York. Less-than-liberal members of the public are often shocked by Stern and company, and the Federal Communications Commission (FCC) has consistently tried to tone him down by threatening to have him taken off the air. In spite of their objections to the content of his broadcasts, Stern has had consistently high ratings. He moved his show first to WNBC from a local station in Washington, D.C., then, when he was fired by NBC, to WXRK (K-Rock) in New York City, and subsequently into syndication around the country. Stern's often hilarious, somewhat graphic descriptions of various sexual activities and his frequent use of profanity on the show have not detracted from his popularity, and his program has become one of the most talked about, and in some areas, the most listened-to early-morning talk shows on radio. In addition to radio, Stern is also the best-selling author of the book "Private Parts" (1993) and has hosted syndicated and cable-television programs.

STEVENS, JULIE (1918–1984)

Actress Julie Stevens was born in St. Louis, Missouri, and debuted on Broadway in *The Male Animal* in 1939. She became a radio performer in the early 1940s and before long was playing the title roles on *The* ROMANCE OF HELEN TRENT and ABIE'S IRISH ROSE. Stevens was also featured on such programs as ETHEL AND ALBERT, KITTY FOYLE, *The* ROAD OF LIFE, and most of the popular dramatic anthology, mystery, and crime programs on the air. When radio drama was no longer in vogue, Stevens retired from show business after trying television for a while, preferring "the peace and quiet of her New England home to the chaos and endless hours of rehearsal and line memorization" that was such a vital part of daytime television.

STONE, EZRA (EZRA FEINSTONE: 1918–1994)

Born in New Bedford, Massachusetts, actor Ezra Stone adeptly played perennial teenager Henry Aldrich on the long-running ALDRICH FAMILY radio series. The Aldrich family was originally introduced in a hit stage play called *What a Life* (1937); they were first heard on radio on a segment of *The* KATE SMITH program. Stone, star of the Broadway play, re-created Henry Aldrich for radio. The public's reaction to the *Aldrich Family* segment on Kate Smith's program and in particular to Stone's wonderfully comic, typical-teen characterization was overwhelmingly favorable, and in 1939, a weekly radio series called *The Aldrich Family* was on the air. Except for a sabbatical during World War II, when Stone was in the United States Army, the actor played the role for the series' entire run.

During the war, Stone was assigned to the Armed Forces Special Services unit and appeared in numerous Army shows that toured military installations in the United States and abroad. He appeared in the films *Those Were the Days* (1940), *This Is the Army* (1942), and *Miracle on 34th Street* (1947). When *The Aldrich Family* left the airwaves in 1953, Stone wrote, taught, directed stage plays around the country, and was assistant casting director to legendary Broadway director George Abbott. Stone directed television episodes of "The Munsters" (1964), "Lost in Space" (1966), "Julia" (1967), "The Flying Nun" (1967), and

"Petticoat Junction" (1970). He also directed and taught at the American Academy of Dramatic Arts in New York City, which he had attended as a young man. Stone often lectured about radio's golden years at various old-time-radio conventions and was a frequent guest speaker at colleges and universities throughout the country.

STOOPNAGLE AND BUDD (AKA THE GLOOM CHASERS)

1931–1935	CBS	(*)	(*)
1935–1936	CBS	Fri.	10:30 PM
1936–1937	CBS	Sat.	9:30 PM

The zany and unpredictable comedy team of F. Chase Taylor and Wilbur HULICK, better known as Stoopnagle and Budd, were the stars of one of radio's earliest half-hour comedy shows. On this program Budd asked leading questions, which would lead to comic responses, tall tales, and jokes by Stoopnagle. Featured as stooges were actresses Joan BANKS and Alice FROST. Each week, the familiar "Chopsticks" theme and announcers Harry VON ZELL, Louis Dean, or Andre BARUCH told audiences they were about to hear *The Stoopnagle and Budd Show.* One of the show's most popular running gags was a ten-foot pole Stoopnagle claimed to have invented "for people you wouldn't touch with one." Gogo De Luys, Jeanne Lang, Connee BOSWELL, and Donald VOORHEES and his orchestra were also featured on the show during its run. Sponsors included Ivory soap, Pontiac automobiles, Minute tapioca, Camel cigarettes, Schlitz beer, Gulf oil, and Ford automobiles.

STOP ME IF YOU'VE HEARD THIS ONE

1939–1940	NBC Red	Sat.	8:30 PM
1940–1947	(Off the air)		
1947–1948	Mutual	Sat.	9 PM

Joke-telling by such well-known comedians as Harry Hershfield, actor Jay C. Flippen, Henny Youngman, Morey Amsterdam, and Lou Lehr was featured on this half-hour comedy program hosted by Roger Bauer and, at one time, Milton BERLE. Similar to the CAN YOU TOP THIS program, *Stop Me If You've Heard This One* had panelist-comedians finishing jokes sent in by listeners. If the joke was unfamiliar to anyone on the panel, the listener who sent the joke in was awarded a $5 cash prize. The series was directed by Mitch Benson and written by Ray Harvey. The program was heard on the Mutual network. Dan SEYMOUR and Ted Brown were the announcers. Horace HEIDT led the show's orchestra. The series was sponsored by Quaker oats cereal.

STOP THE MUSIC

1948–1952	ABC	Sun.	8 PM
1952–1954	(Off the air)		
1954–1955	CBS	Tues.	8 PM

This half-hour musical quiz program featured songs sung by Kay Armen and Dick Brown. Both sang all of the lyrics of a song except for the title, which contestants were supposed to guess. Listeners whose phone numbers were chosen from cards sent to the show were given the opportunity to identify a song a studio contestant could not name. When callers knew the name of the song, they were then given a chance to identify a mystery melody, which had a $2,000 jackpot prize. Bert PARKS, and later Bill CULLEN, would call out "Stop the music!" when it was time for the contestants to try to identify a song. While it was on the air, the show proved to be so popular with listeners that comedian Fred ALLEN, whose show was scheduled opposite *Stop the Music* on a rival network, offered a $5,000 bond to anyone who was called by *Stop the Music* while listening to *The* FRED ALLEN SHOW. Of course, no one ever claimed the prize. Announcers were Hal Sims and Doug Browning. Harry Salter was *Stop the Music's* orchestra leader, and Mark Goodson was the program's director. Howard Connell was the show's writer. It was sponsored by Old Gold cigarettes, Anacin pain reliever, Smith Brothers cough drops, and Spidel watches.

STORDAHL, AXEL (1913–1963)

Music director–conductor Axel Stordahl, who was born in New York City, was the orchestra leader on the popular YOUR HIT PARADE program for several seasons. Singer Frank SINATRA, who previously appeared on the *Hit Parade* show, left the show when his fame warranted having a program with his name in the title. Sinatra then convinced Stordahl to lead the band on his new FRANK SINATRA SHOW. Stordahl was also the music conductor for many hit recordings.

STORIES BY OLMSTED (AKA DRAMAS BY OLMSTED; WORLD'S GREATEST STORIES; WORLD'S GREATEST SHORT STORIES; STORY FOR TODAY; SLEEP NO MORE)

1930s–1950s	(Various times and days on local NBC and ABC stations)

First-rate storyteller Nelson OLMSTED had many series on the air over the years, but despite the numerous titles they were usually referred to as *Stories by Olmstead.* On his programs, Olmsted read short stories and poems, told anecdotes, and read excerpts from longer works of literature. Olmsted's theme music at one time was "Little Harbor." The program's longtime director was Norman Felton.

STORY OF MARY MARLIN, THE

1935–1936	CBS	Mon.–Fri.	11:15 PM
1936–1937	CBS	Mon.–Fri.	12:15 PM
1937–1938	NBC Blue	Mon.–Fri.	10 AM
	NBC Red	Mon.–Fri.	4:30 PM
1938–1939	NBC Blue	Mon.–Fri.	11 AM
	NBC Red	Mon.–Fri.	4:15 PM
1939–1940	NBC Blue	Mon.–Fri.	11 AM
	NBC Red	Mon.–Fri.	3 PM
1940–1941	NBC Blue	Mon.–Fri.	10:30 AM
	NBC Red	Mon.–Fri.	3 PM
1941–1942	CBS	Mon.–Fri.	11 AM
1942–1943	NBC	Mon.–Fri.	3 PM
1943–1945	CBS	Mon.–Fri.	3 PM
1945–1951	(Off the air)		
1951–1952	ABC	Mon.–Fri.	3:15 PM

The title character on this 15-minute drama series was a U.S. senator from Iowa. Mary succeeded her husband, Joe, as senator when he was thought to be dead. Joe had actually been involved in an accident while away on a trip and developed amnesia. He returned to Mary and the series for a brief time in the early 1940s before wandering off again. Actresses Joan Blaine, Anne SEYMOUR (who acted the role longest), Betty Lou GERSON, Muriel Kirkland, Eloise Kummer, and Linda Carlton played Mary on this series over the years; Robert Griffin played Joe. Also featured on the program in regular supporting roles were Elinor Harriot, Raymond Edward JOHNSON, Gene Morgan, Henry Hunter, Gene Burke, Arthur Jacobson, Louise Fitch, Dora Johnson, Bob Jellison, Cornelius Peeples, Mary Patton, Jane WEBB, baby impersonator Dolores Gillen, Janet Logan, Cliff Soubier, Frank Dane, Eddie Firestone, Jr., Marjorie Hannan, Bess JOHNSON, Carleton Brickert, June Meredith, Judith Lowry, Art Kohl, Loretta Poynton, Betty Caine, Fran CARLON, Rikel Kent, Templeton Fox, Phil Lord, Murray FORBES, Mary Jane HIGBY, Patsy O'Shea, Jess Pugh, Francis X. Bushman, Charme Allen, Isabel RANDOLPH, Rosemary Garbell, Gladys Heen, Frank Pacelli, Bret MORRISON, Bill LIPTON, Arthur PETERSON, Eunice Howard, Fred Sullivan, Harvey Hays, and Rupert La Belle. Truman BRADLEY, Les Griffth, Nelson CASE, John Tillman, Bob Brown, Bill Farren, and Ed Rice were the show's announcers. The program's directors were Basil Loughrane, Don Cope, Nathan Tufts, Kirby Hawkes, and Ed Rice, and the series was created and written by Jane Crusinberry. *Mary Marlin's* familiar theme music was *Clair de Lune* by Debussy. Kleenex tissues, Ivory soap flakes, Ivory Snow soap powder, Ivory soap, and Tender Leaf tea sponsored the program.

STRAIGHT ARROW

1948–1957   (Syndicated series. Various stations and times)

This half-hour and then 15-minute weekday Western-adventure children's series was heard largely in the South and West during the late 1940s and 1950s. *Straight Arrow* originally had a Western variety-show format and each week, broadcasts called *pow-wows*, encouraged young "braves" and "maidens" in the live audience at Hollywood's Hitching Post Theater to follow the heroic adventures of Steve Adams (alias Straight Arrow).

Ben Alexander was the show's host, and he led the children in games, songs, and skits, introducing guest stars from film Westerns such as Johnny Mack Brown (who later made many appearances on the show when it was an adventure drama serial) and Native American actor "Iron Eyes" Cody. Western singers such as Jimmy Wakeley sang and urged the children in the audience and at home to join him in singing "Deep in the Heart of Texas," "Home on the Range," and "You Are My Sunshine."

Actor Howard Culver starred as Steve Adams, a model of "justice, fair play, and all good things." As the mild-mannered owner of the Broken Bow Ranch, he fought outlaws while disguised as a mysterious, heroic Native American named Straight Arrow. Straight Arrow rode a golden palomino horse, Fury, and was an expert with the bow and arrow. The dramatic series was directed by Ted Robertson and written by Sheldon Stark. The program was mainly heard on the Mutual network's affiliated stations.

STRANGE AS IT SEEMS

1937–1939	(Syndicated series. Various stations and times)		
1939–1940	CBS	Thurs.	8:30 PM

Based on a newspaper feature by John Hix, this half-hour series, narrated by Cyril Ambrister, presented unusual stories about ghosts, aliens from other planets, odd hobbies, and visits to exotic places. Heard in 15-minute, 20-minute, and half-hour formats, *Strange As It Seems* featured Hix, Patrick McGeehan, and Gayne Whitman as program hosts at different times. Alois Harvilla was the show's announcer, and Armbrister also directed the program. Ted STEELE was the program's music director. Ex-Lax laxative and Palmolive shave cream sponsored the series.

STRANGE ROMANCE OF EVELYN WINTERS, THE

See EVELYN WINTERS.

STRATTON, CHESTER (1913–1970)

Actor Chester Stratton was born in Paterson, New Jersey, the son of theatrical parents. First heard on radio in 1932, Stratton was a regular on CBS's AMERICAN SCHOOL OF THE AIR, played Mark Scott on AGAINST THE STORM, Tom Ames on AMANDA OF HONEYMOON HILL, Samson on BIG SISTER, and acted many roles on BRIGHT HORIZON and BY KATHLEEN NORRIS. The leading roles of Joe Barton on *Cimarron Tavern*, Jack Winters on *City Desk*, Stan Adamie on *Her Honor, Nancy James,* Hop on HOP HARRIGAN, Josiah on LIGHT OF THE WORLD, Walter on LORENZO JONES, Mickey on *Mickey of the Circus*, Monte Kayden on *The* O'NEILLS, Carter Trent on PAPER YOUNG'S FAMILY, and John Weston on WILDERNESS ROAD were among his credits. He was also heard on FORTY-FIVE MINUTES FROM HOLLYWOOD, JOHNNY PRESENTS, AUNT JENNY'S REAL LIFE STORIES, SMILIN' JACK, SOCIETY GIRL, GANGBUSTERS, *The Woodbury Playhouse,* and many other programs.

STRIKE IT RICH (AKA STRIKE IT LUCKY)

1947–1948	CBS	Sun.	10:30 PM
1948–1950	CBS	Sun.	5:30 PM
1950–1951	CBS	Sun.	5:30 PM
	CBS	Mon.–Fri.	4 PM
1951–1955	NBC	Mon.–Fri.	11 AM
1955–1957	(Off the air)		
1957	CBS	Mon.–Fri.	2:30 PM

Todd Russell and Warren HULL were the hosts of this half-hour weekly audience-participation show. Contestants chosen from the studio audience began the game with a $25 stake and could run their winnings up to $200 by answering a series of general-interest questions correctly. One of the major features on the program was the "Heartline" segment of the show, during which a contestant told a pathetic tale of personal hardship. When a large red heart on the stage lit up (which the studio audience saw) and a phone bell was heard by the radio listening audience, a phone call had been received from a particularly generous listener and the host would inform the contestant and the audience that a manufacturer or an individual listener had offered a cash gift that would help the contestant whose story had moved them to action. Don Baker and Ralph Paul were the show's announcers. Luden's cough drops, Lucky Strike cigarettes, and Fab detergent sponsored the program.

STRIKER, FRAN (1903–1962)

Fran Striker was responsible for having created such classic radio heroes in the 1930s and 1940s as *The* LONE RANGER, *The* GREEN HORNET, and SERGEANT PRESTON OF THE YUKON. Born in Buffalo, New York, Striker became an announcer at a Buffalo radio station in

Program host Warren Hull shares a laugh with a contestant on *Strike It Rich.* (CBS)

1927, where he wrote the *Covered Wagon Days* radio series and began to write *The Lone Ranger* according to his son, Robert, although this has been disputed by others who worked at WXYZ, the station where *The Lone Ranger* originated. A producer at WXYZ, Striker and WXYZ owner George W. TRENDLE were certainly the sparks under the blazing success of these programs.

STUDEBAKER, HUGH (1901–1978)

Hugh Studebaker was a talented announcer and actor whose career on radio spanned a forty-year period. Born in Ridgeville, Indiana, he first performed on radio as a piano player in 1928 but became a radio actor in 1932. He announced Ted Malone's BETWEEN THE BOOKENDS for many years and also played on *Lucky Girl*; Dr. Bob Graham, "the bachelor," on BACHELOR'S CHILDREN; Harry Henderson, Beulah's boss on BEULAH; Ichabod "Ichy" Mudd on CAPTAIN MIDNIGHT; Silly Wilson on FIBBER MCGEE AND MOLLY; Captain Meredith on MIDSTREAM; Fred Minturn on *The* RIGHT TO HAPPINESS; Grandpa Sutter on *The* ROAD OF LIFE; Jim Brewster, THAT BREWSTER BOY'S father; and Dr. Purdy on *The* WOMAN IN WHITE; Studebaker also was regularly featured on such programs as CURTAIN TIME,

SHOW BOAT, *The* ROMANCE OF HELEN TRENT, *The* FIRST NIGHTER, and *The* GUIDING LIGHT.

STUDIO ONE

1947–1949   CBS   Tues.   9:30 PM

This one-hour dramatic anthology series appeared on CBS during its 1947–1948 season. Some of the classic works of literature that were adapted for radio and heard included *Holiday, The Barrots of Wimpole Street, Kitty Foyle, Ah! Wilderness, The Red Badge of Courage, King's Row, Confidential Agent, The Thirty-Nine Steps, The Glass Key, Pride and Prejudice, Dodsworth, A Tree Grows in Brooklyn, Wuthering Heights, The Constant Nymph, Anthony Adverse, Gentle Julia,* and *The Last Tycoon.* A repertory company of radio actor reliables were featured, but midseason, Broadway and Hollywood stars were imported to boost the show's ratings. Produced and directed by Fletcher MARKLE, who also played leading roles on occasion, the superb cast of Markle's repertory company included Everett SLOANE, Miriam WOLFE, Robert DRYDEN, Ivor Francis, Hester Songergaard, Louis Quinn, Hedley Rainnie, Anne BURR, and Mercedes MCCAMBRIDGE. Other actors fre-

quently heard on the series included Gertrude Warner, Ronald LISS, Rosemary RICE, Ruth Gilbert, Elspeth ERIC, Cliff Carpenter, Betty GARDE, Charlotte Holland, Amanda RANDOLPH, Myron MCCORMICK, Leon JANNEY, Cathleen Cordell, Alan Devitt, and Joe DeSantis. For the last half of this series' run, the major stars who played leading roles included John Garfield, Charles Laughton, Gene Kelly, Robert Mitchum, Joan Blondell, Marlene Dietrich, Madeleine Carroll, George Sanders, and Geraldine Fitzgerald. The original music heard on the show was composed and conducted by Alexander Semmler. *Studio One* later became one of television's first major dramatic anthology series.

SULLIVAN, ED (1902–1974)

The ED SULLIVAN SHOW was first heard on CBS radio in 1931, years before Sullivan hosted television's most popular prime-time variety program. Born in Harlem, New York, and raised in Port Chester, New York, Sullivan wrote a column about entertainment for *The New York Graphic* and then for *The New York Daily News.* After hosting live variety shows at the New York Paramount Theater, Sullivan was offered a weekly radio variety show on which he introduced

Members of the repertory cast of *Studio One:* (from left) Hedley Rainnie, Anne Burr, and Everett Sloane; (at far right) producer/director Fletcher Markle (CBS)

soon-to-be-famous entertainers such as Jack BENNY and Jack PEARL, as well as celebrities Irving Berlin, George M. Cohan, and Flo Ziegfeld. In the late 1940s, Sullivan turned his attention toward television; his weekly Sunday-evening variety show, "The Toast of the Town" (later called "The Ed Sullivan Show"), became one of television's longest-running variety shows.

SUNDAY MORNING

1976–present   CBC   Sun.   9:11 AM

Sunday Morning is heard around the world via short-wave and over NPR in the United States. Featuring reports from all continents including Antarctica, the program is hosted by Mary Lou Finlay. The stories presented range from confrontations between Mohawk Indians and the Canadian Army to battles between Iraqui and United Nations forces in the Persian Gulf during the 1991 Middle East war to discussions about what is considered "politically correct." Discussions, interviews, soundscapes, commentaries, music, and satire are all heard on the program. Michael Finlay is the show's executive producer.

SUPERMAN, THE ADVENTURES OF
See ADVENTURES OF SUPERMAN, THE.

SUSPENSE

1942–1943	CBS	Tues.	9:30 PM
1943–1947	CBS	Thurs.	8 PM
1947–1951	CBS	Thurs.	9 PM
1951–1954	CBS	Mon.	8 PM
1954–1955	CBS	Tues.	8 PM
1955–1956	CBS	Tues.	8:30 PM
1956–1958	CBS	Sun.	4:30 PM
1958–1960	CBS	Sun.	5:30 PM
1960–1961	(Off the air)		
1961–1962	CBS	Sun.	6:35 PM

For more than twenty years, the *Suspense* program, which called itself "radio's outstanding theater of thrills," presented half-hour mystery plays that were "well calculated to keep you in Suspense." The original radio plays included Lucille FLETCHER's classic thriller, "Sorry, Wrong Number," which starred actress Agnes MOOREHEAD and was repeated on the series annually for many years. "The Hitchhiker," an incredible story also by Fletcher, starred Orson WELLES and made this series one of radio's most critically and publicly acclaimed mystery programs. Initially, Charles Vanda produced and directed, but it was William SPIER who actually steered the show toward its greatest success. In the late 1940s, Spier began to concentrate on writing and producing television programs; William N. ROBSON, Norman Macdonnell,

Burt Lancaster on *Suspense* (CBS)

Elliott LEWIS, and Anton M. Leader subsequently directed the show. Major motion-picture stars vied to appear on the program because the format gave them the opportunity to play parts that were usually totally different from anything they played on the screen. A stock company of regular supporting actors, including Cathy LEWIS, Jeanette NOLAN, Hans CONREID, Joseph KEARNS, Elliott LEWIS, Lurene TUTTLE, Mary Jane CROFT, Bill JOHNSTONE, William CONRAD, Lillian Buyeff, Paul Frees, and Irene Tedrow, made frequent appearances over the years. The show's host for several years was a character called "The Man in Black," played first by actor Joseph KEARNS and then by Ted Osborne. Some of the excellent writers who wrote scripts for this show, in addition to Fletcher, included Robert Arthur, Morton Fine, Sam Pierce, John Dickson Carr, David Friedkin, Peter Fernandez, and Milton Geiger. In the 1950s a change in the kind of stories presented to those based on actual events that dealt with patriotic, pro-American themes reflected the anticommunist, McCarthy-influenced sentiments of the time. The program's announcers included Truman BRADLEY, Bob Stevenson, Harlow WILCOX, Larry Thor, and Stu Metz. Roma wines, Autolite spark plugs, Philip Morris cigarettes, Marlboro cigarettes, and Kellogg's All-Bran cereal sponsored the series.

See APPENDIX D.

SWAYZE, JOHN CAMERON (1906–1995)

Well known to television viewers in the 1950s and 1960s as the spokesman for the supposedly indestructible Timex watch, John Cameron Swayze, who was born in Wichita, Kansas, was an NBC newscaster for many years. Although Swayze began his career as a cub reporter on the *Kansas City Journal Post,* he originally wanted to be an actor and studied drama in New York City before he returned to Kansas City, attended the University of Kansas, and accepted a job as a news-bulletin reporter on a small Kansas City radio station. In 1941, Swayze became a full-time radio announcer, and in 1947 he was asked to return to New York City and join NBC's news staff, where he remained for many years.

SWENSON, KARL (1908–1978)

A versatile actor whose radio acting career spanned forty years, Karl Swenson was born in Brooklyn, New York. He entered radio in 1935 and became a leading man on such daytime serial drama series as OUR GAL SUNDAY, on which he played Lord Henry Brinthrope; LORENZO JONES as Lorenzo; LINDA'S FIRST LOVE as Danny; and PORTIA FACES LIFE as Elbert Gallo. Swenson also starred on prime-time programs: *Joe Palooka* in the title role, MR. CHAMELEON as Detective Chamelon, and INNER SANCTUM MYSTERIES, *Spy Secrets,*

GRAND CENTRAL STATION, *There Was a Woman, The* MIGHTY SHOW, AUNT JENNY'S REAL LIFE STORIES, *The* COURT OF MISSING HEIRS, *The* MARCH OF TIME, *The* FORD THEATER, and THIS IS YOUR FBI. Swenson was one of the few performers who managed to make a successful transition from radio to television in the early 1950s. The actor costarred on the television version of "Portia Faces Life," with Fran CARLON as Portia; he also played numerous supporting roles on many TV series—notably as a regular on "The Little House on the Prairie"—as well as in films.

SWINGING ON A STAR

| 1990–present | CBC | Sat. | 11:45 AM Stereo |
| | | | 4:08 PM Radio |

Every Saturday, Murray McLauchlan presides over an informal studio session with fellow Canadian singers and songwriters and a small studio audience on the CANADIAN BROADCASTING CORPORATION network. *Swinging on a Star's* coffee-house atmosphere presents musical styles ranging from pop to folk and from country to rock. Featured regularly on the show are Kit Johnson playing bass and Danny Greenspan playing the guitar. McLauchlan plays guitar and piano. The series executive producer is John Dalton.

TAKE IT OR LEAVE IT
See $64 QUESTION.

TALE OF TODAY, A (AKA THE PRINCESS PAT PLAYERS)

1933–1934	NBC Blue	Sun.	4:30 PM
1934–1936	NBC Blue	Mon.	9:30 PM
1936–1939	NBC Blue	Sun.	6:30 PM

When it debuted on the air, *A Tale of Today* was a 10-minute segment on *The Princess Pat Players* program. Because of its popularity, NBC decided to turn it into a once-a-week regularly scheduled half-hour program. *A Tale of Today* was a soap opera that told "the interesting story of the Houston family, filled with poignant drama and typical American appeal," according to its opening. Joan Blaine, Betty Caine, and Luise Barclay played the leading role of Joan Houston Allen. Playing supporting roles were Isabel RANDOLPH and then Ethel Owen as an overbearing society woman named Harriet Brooks, Laurette FILLBRANDT as Dot Houston, Frank Pacelli as Billy Houston, and Harriette WIDMER, Harvey Hays, Bob Jellison, Willard Farnum, Ed Prentiss, Raymond Edward JOHNSON, Sunda Love, and Mercedes MCCAMBRIDGE. Verne Smith was the show's announcer. Howard Keegan directed the series, which was written by Betty Manderville. The show's theme song was Meyerbeer's "Coronation March."

TALES OF FATIMA

| 1948–1949 | CBS | Sat. | 9:30 PM |

Motion-picture actor Basil RATHBONE, perhaps best known as SHERLOCK HOLMES in films and on radio, was the host-narrator of this weekly half-hour mystery-anthology series. The series presented weird and supernatural stories of murder and mayhem. Typical stories involved ghosts or people rising from their graves in such tales as "Return from the Dead" and "The Death Search." Michael Fitzmaurice was the show's announcer. Its sponsor was Fatima cigarettes.

TALLEY, MARION
See MARION TALLEY SHOW, THE.

TARPLIN, MAURICE (1911–1975)
Actor Maurice TARPLIN was born in Boston, Massachusetts, and became well known for playing The Traveler on The MYSTERIOUS TRAVELER series. His calm-if-sinister-sounding voice narrated each week's segment. Telling mystery and crime stories, Tarplin narrated such episodes as "Queen of the Cats," "They Who Sleep," and "The Good Die Young." Tarplin played Inspector Faraday on The BOSTON BLACKIE detective series and was a regular performer on MYRT AND MARGE, GANGBUSTERS, EASY ACES, The MAGIC KEY, STRANGE AS IT SEEMS, The MARCH OF TIME, VALIANT LADY, WHEN A GIRL MARRIES, HOBBY LOBBY, The KATE SMITH HOUR, and SKY BLAZERS. In the early 1960s, he served as a voice-over performer for commercials and dubbed foreign films into English.

TARZAN

1932–1936	(Syndicated series. Various stations and times)		
1936–1952	(Off the air)		
1952–1953	CBS	Sat.	10 AM

Novelist Edgar Rice Burroughs's (1875–1950) best-selling novel *Tarzan of the Apes* (1914) became a 15-

minute series in the early 1930s. The show told of a boy who was raised by gorillas and became a "lord of the jungle." Burroughs's daughter Jane played Tarzan's girlfriend, Jane, on this series, and her husband. James Pierce played Tarzan. The series opened with, "From the heart of the jungle comes a savage cry for victory. This is Tarzan, Lord of the Jungle! From the core of dark Africa, land of enchantment, mystery, and violence, comes one of the most colorful figures of all time."

For this recorded series, equipment was sent to various zoos around the country to tape authentic-sounding jungle background noises such as birds, lions, monkeys, and elephants. The scripts were submitted to Burroughs for final approval, and he often spent hours rewriting the material. Twelve years after the first *Tarzan* series was canceled, another *Tarzan* program surfaced but remained on the air for just one season.

TAYLOR, DEEMS (1895–1966)

Considered one of America's foremost music authorities, radio commentator and critic Deems Taylor was born in New York City and attended New York University. In 1927, he became the editor of *Musical America* magazine after working for various newspapers as a reporter and columnist. Taylor was asked to host a radio program of concerts by the NBC Symphony in the late 1920s and thereafter was a featured music commentator on programs such as *The* KRAFT MUSIC HALL, *The* PRUDENTIAL FAMILY HOUR, *The* METROPOLITAN OPERA BROADCASTS, CHESTERFIELD PRESENTS, and *Music of America.* He also had a weekly series of his own, *Deems Taylor Commentaries,* in which he talked about the contemporary music scene and interviewed various guests from the world of classical music.

TAYLOR, MARY LEE

See MARY LEE TAYLOR SHOW, *The.*

TELEPHONE HOUR, THE

See BELL TELEPHONE HOUR, *The.*

TEMPLETON, ALEC

See ALEC TEMPLETON SHOW, *The.*

TENNESSEE JED

1945–1947   ABC   Mon.–Fri.   (*)

"There he goes, Tennessee! Get him! [A gunshot is heard.] Got 'em . . . D-e-e-ea-a-a-d center!" the Western adventure series *Tennessee Jed* began each broadcast. This 15-minute series, produced for younger listeners, featured John Thomas and then Don

MACLAUGHLIN as "Tennessee Jed" Sloan, a rancher of the Wild West who tracked down outlaws. Humphrey Davis played Sheriff Jackson; Jim Boles, the sheriff's deputy; Juano Hernandez, Jed's Indian Chief friend; and Raymond Edward JOHNSON played Masters, the Gambler. Court Benson was the show's narrator and also played numerous supporting roles, as did John McGovern and George Petrie. The series was produced by Paul DuFour and directed by Bill Hamilton. It was written by Ashley Buck, Howard Carraway, and Tom Taggert. The show's original theme song was written by Elton Britt. The sponsor is unknown.

TERRY AND THE PIRATES

1937–1939	NBC Red	Mon.–Fri.	5:15 PM
1939–1943	(Off the air)		
1943–1945	NBC Blue	Mon.–Fri.	5 PM
1945–1947	ABC	Mon.–Fri.	5 PM
1947–1948	ABC	Mon.–Fri.	5:15 PM

Milton Caniff's popular comic-strip hero, Terry Lee, became the main character of a fifteen-minute children's adventure series in the late 1930s. The exotic South China Sea was the setting for this show about a U.S.-born airplane pilot named Terry and his fellow pilots and friends, Patrick Ryan, Flip Corkin, and Burma, as well as their arch-enemy, the notorious Dragon Lady. The major characters were transported intact from the comic strip by Milton Caniff to radio. Jackie KELK, Cliff Carpenter, and Owen Jordan played Terry, a young pilot for hire; Clayton "Bud" COLLYER, Larry Alexander, Warner Anderson, and Bob Giffin played Terry's mature friend and fellow pilot, Ryan; Ted DeCorsia played Flip Corkin; and Frances Chaney was their assistant, Burma. Agnes MOOREHEAD, Adelaide Klein, and Marion Sweet took turns playing the wonderfully wicked Dragon Lady. Also heard on the series in regular supporting roles were Cliff Norton, Peter DONALD, John GIBSON, Cameron Andrews, John Moore, Charles CANTOR, William Podmore, and Mandel KRAMER. Douglas Browning was the program's announcer on the earliest version of the series. The program was directed at various times by Wylie Adams, Marty Andrews, and Cyril Ambrister, and written by Al Barker. Sponsors included Dari Rich dairy products, Quaker Sparkies cereal, and Quaker Puffed Wheat and Puffed Rice cereals.

TETLEY, WALTER (1915–1975)

When he was in his teens, Walter Tetley, who was born in New York City, was featured on the popular CHILDREN'S HOUR–COAST TO COAST ON A BUS program. This led to his being cast on LET'S PRETEND. Born with a birth defect, Tetley never fully matured, physically or vocally, which enabled him to continue to play juvenile roles on various radio shows well into his adult years. Perhaps best known as Leroy, Throckmorton P. Gildersleeve's wisecracking nephew on *The* GREAT GILDERSLEEVE, Tetley specialized in similar tough-kid parts and was heard on most of the major comedy programs and dramatic anthologies of the 1940s and 1950s originating in Hollywood. The actor also played Julius Abbruzio, the brash grocery boy on *The* FITCH BANDWAGON when that show starred Phil HARRIS and Alice FAYE.

TEX AND JINX SHOW, THE
See FALKENBERG, "JINX."

TEXACO STAR THEATER, THE

1938–1939	CBS	Wed.	8 PM
1939–1940	CBS	Wed.	9 PM
1940–1941	CBS	Wed.	9 PM
1941–1944	CBS	Sun.	9:30 PM
1944–1945	CBS	Sun.	9:30 PM
1945–1946	CBS	Fri.	8 PM

The Texaco Star Theater had several formats during the years it was on the air. When first aired, the hour-long program was a weekly variety show and starred such comics as Fred ALLEN, Ed WYNN ("The Texaco Fire Chief"), tenor James MELTON, vocalist Diane Courney, and Al GOODMAN and his orchestra. In 1940, Ken MURRAY became the program's weekly host, and the series devoted half of its time to variety entertainment from Hollywood and the other half to a complete drama broadcast from New York City. In addition to Murray, Kenny BAKER, Frances LANGFORD, Irene Noblette (RYAN), Tim Ryan, Jane FROMAN, Adolph Menjou, John Barrymore, and David Brockman's orchestra were prominently featured at different times. The occasional dramatic sketches featured such radio actors as Cecil Secrest, Jack MacBryde, William "Bill" Quinn, Milton Herman, Jack Arthur, Betty Worth, Aileen Pringle, Audrey Christie, Joe E. BROWN, Lee Tracy, and Frances Fuller in adaptations of such plays as *The Milky Way* and *The Front Page*. James "Jimmy" WALLINGTON in Hollywood and John Reed KING and Larry Elliott in New York were *The Texaco Star Theater's* announcers. Original music for the show was written by Lehman Engel. For many years, the show was written by Ed James, Paul Conlon, Bob Philips, and Frank Phares.

See also WYNN, Ed; ED WYNN SHOW.

TEXACO TOWN
See EDDIE CANTOR SHOW, THE.

THAT BREWSTER BOY

1940–1942	NBC Blue	Mon.	9:30 PM
1942	CBS	Wed.	7:30 PM
1942–1945	CBS	Fri.	9:30 PM

The half-hour situation-comedy series *That Brewster Boy* was similar to *The* ALDRICH FAMILY in that it centered around a typical American teenage boy and the loving endurance of his parents as he became involved in various problems with girls, at school, and with his friends. The show featured Eddie Firestone, Jr., as Joey Brewster when the series first went on the air. Firestone was replaced by Arnold STANG, and subsequently Stang was replaced by Dick York. Hugh STUDEBAKER played Joey's father, Jim, and Constance Crowder played his mother, Jane. Also heard on the series were Ruth Perrott, Jane WEBB, Patricia Dunlap, Billy Idelson, Bob Jellison, Louise Fitch, Bob BAILEY, Jerry Spellman, Dick Van Patten, and Marilyn Erskine. Marvin MILLER was the program's announcer. The series was directed by Owen Vinson and written by Louis Scofield.

See also THOSE WEBSTERS.

THEATER GUILD ON THE AIR, THE (AKA UNITED STATES STEEL HOUR; THEATER GUILD DRAMAS)

1945–1947	ABC	Sun.	10 PM
1947–1949	ABC	Sun.	9:30 PM
1949–1954	NBC	Sun.	8:30 PM

This hour-long dramatic anthology series was originally hosted by Broadway producer-director Lawrence Langer, one of the founding members of The Theater Guild, an organization that produced Broadway plays and encouraged the development of theater in the United States. When Langer left the program, actor Roger Pryor and then Elliott Reid hosted the series. *Theater Guild on the Air* offered adaptations of celebrated plays and novels by some of the world's most respected authors. The show was considered one of the best drama shows on the air by critics and the public alike. Major stars of theater, motion pictures, and radio appeared on the weekly shows. The program's longtime sponsor was United States Steel. Norman BROKENSHIRE announced the series, and George Hicks was the U.S. Steel spokesman.

See APPENDIX D.

THEME SONGS
Most of the programs on the air have a theme song identified with them. Many are classic works by such composers as Brahms, Debussy, Tchaikovsky, and Chopin, or they are favorite popular and semiclassical songs. These themes become so familiar to radio-show listeners that even when heard in other contexts such as at concerts or music shows, listeners immediately think of the program they are used to hearing it on. *The* LONE RANGER's theme music, for example, from the overture to *William Tell* by Rossini, is probably the

most recognizable piece of music in North America mainly because of its long-term association with that Western-adventure serial. (See individual show listings for the names of show theme songs.)

THIN MAN, THE ADVENTURES OF THE

See ADVENTURES OF THE THIN MAN, THE.

THIS DAY IS OURS

1938–1939	CBS	Mon.–Fri.	1:45 PM
1939–1940	CBS	Mon.–Fri.	1:30 PM
1940	NBC	Mon.–Fri.	10:15 PM

The long-suffering heroine of this 15-minute drama series was a character named Eleanor MacDonald, played by Joan BANKS and then Templeton Fox. The number of tear-rending events that Eleanor and her friends and family experienced on this series was staggering, considering it was only on the air for two years: Eleanor's child was kidnapped; she lost her memory, suffered the death of a beloved parent, nursed her husband back to health after a serious accident, helped a friend find a dangerous killer, and became involved in the problems of everyone she came in contact with. Also heard in regular supporting roles were Jay JOSTYN, Spencer Bentley, Elaine Kent, Tess Sheehan, Patricia Dunlap, Alan Devitt, Julian Noa, House JAMESON, Agnes MOOREHEAD, Effie Palmer, Frank LOVEJOY, and Leslie Bingham. Chick Vincent was the series' director. It was written by Carl Bixby and Don Becker. Mel ALLEN was the show's announcer. Crisco shortening sponsored the program. The theme song for *This Day Is Ours* was "Love for Today."

THIS IS NORA DRAKE

1947–1949	NBC	Mon.–Fri.	11 AM
1949–1956	CBS	Mon.–Fri.	2:30 PM
1956–1959	CBS	Mon.–Fri.	1 PM

This 15-minute series centered around Nora Drake and her husband, family, and friends. It took place in a small Midwestern town where Nora underwent domestic, social, and child-raising problems that seemed of interest to most American housewives of the period. Charlotte Holland was the first actress to play Nora, followed by Joan Tompkins and Mary Jane HIGBY. Joseph Conway, Everett SLOANE, and Ralph Bell played her husband, Arthur. Also heard in regular supporting roles were Alan Hewitt, Elspeth ERIC, Robert READICK, Les DAMON, Leon JANNEY, Lesley Woods, Irene Hubbard, Joan Alexander, Mercedes MCCAMBRIDGE, Roger DeKoven, Joan Lorring, Grant Richards, and Arnold Robertson. Ken ROBERTS and Bill CULLEN were the program's announcers. The series was directed by Art Hanna, Dee Engelbach, and Charles Irving, and written by Milton Lewis. Sponsors

included Toni home permanent, Toni creme shampoo, Airwick room deodorizer, Nylast nasal spray, Bristol Myers tobacco company, and Chesterfield cigarettes.

THIS IS YOUR FBI

1945–1946	NBC Blue	Fri.	8:30 PM
1946–1953	ABC	Fri.	8:30 PM

Often confused with another popular radio series about the FBI, *The FBI in Peace and War*, the half-hour *This Is Your FBI* was equally successful and enjoyed a healthy eight-year tenure on the airwaves. Its stories were taken from actual cases investigated by the Federal Bureau of Investigation, and this series, unlike *The FBI in Peace and War*, received the endorsement of FBI Director J. Edgar Hoover, who appeared on the program's first broadcast. The major character on this weekly crime-adventure program was FBI Agent Jim Taylor, who was played by Stacy Harris. The first narrator for the show was Frank LOVEJOY. Also heard regularly were Karl SWENSON, Joan BANKS, Mandel KRAMER, Geoffrey Bryant, Elspeth ERIC, Helen Lewis, Santos ORTEGA, and James Van Dyke. Milton CROSS, Carl Frank, and Larry Keating were the program's announcers. The series was produced and directed by Jerry Devine. Jerry D. Lewis wrote its scripts. The show's sponsor was the Equitable Life Insurance Company.

THIS IS YOUR LIFE

1948–1949	NBC	Tues.	8 PM
1949–1950	NBC	Wed.	8 PM

Ralph EDWARDS was the host of this radio show that debuted in the late 1940s and became a popular television series in the mid-1950s. Edwards surprised guest celebrities by informing them that their life story was about to be featured for that evening. Edwards would then bring out various people who had played important parts in the celebrity's life and career. Some of the prominent people who were honored on the show were Dr. Lee DEFOREST, Lillian Roth, Buster Keaton, and Clara Bow. Whoever was being honored had usually been tricked into believing that he or she was going to be giving a speech on behalf of some worthy cause or, if brought to the studio first, that he or she was going to introduce another guest celebrity on the program. John Holbrook was the show's announcer. The series was directed by Axel GRUENBERG and written by Jerry Devine. It was sponsored by Philip Morris cigarettes.

THIS LIFE IS MINE

1943–1945	CBS	Mon.–Fri.	9:45 AM

This Life Is Mine was a 15-minute drama series about a kind-hearted and loving young married woman named Ellen Channing, played by actress Betty WIN-KLER, and her somewhat stuffy, conservative husband David, played by Henry B. Neely. The couple's different points of view often put them in conflict, especially when it came to the manner in which they dealt with their children. Playing supporting roles on the series were Paul McGrath, Tony Barrett, and Ruth McDevitt. Tony Marvin and Vincent Pelletier were the series' announcers. Marx Loeb directed the program, which was written by Addy Richton and Lynn Stone. General Mills products sponsored the series.

THOMAS, LOWELL (1892–1981)

One of radio's most famous news commentators, Lowell Thomas, whose broadcasting career spanned a fifty-year period, was born in Woodington, Ohio, but grew up in Colorado. Thomas obtained several college and university degrees from the University of Colorado, New York University, and Columbia University, and is said to have been "one of the best educated newsmen in the business." When he was nineteen years old, Thomas became a reporter for the New York *Daily News* as he worked his way through college. He wrote a book in the late 1920s about writer D. H. Lawrence's wartime experiences in the Middle East fighting the Arabs, which he had personally witnessed. He first covered the story for the *Daily News* in the 1920s, and it brought him worldwide

Bill Thompson (NBC)

notoriety. Debuting on radio in 1930, Thomas commented on the daily news well into the late 1970s and hosted the *Lowell Thomas Remembers* series for NATIONAL PUBLIC RADIO during the last few years of his life.

THOMPSON, WILLIAM "BILL" (1913–1971)

Bill Thompson, who was born in Terre Haute, Indiana, is perhaps best remembered for playing the meek-mannered, henpecked husband Wallace Wimple on the FIBBER MCGEE AND MOLLY program, but his ability to play a wide variety of unusual characters allowed him a long and lucrative career as a radio and cartoon-character voice-over actor. In addition to playing Wimple, Thompson was also heard as Horatio K. Boomer, Vodka, Nick Depopolous, and Uncle Dennis on *Fibber McGee and Molly* and was a regular on *The* BREAKFAST CLUB, *The Saturday Night Jamboree, The Hoofingham Show,* and many others. Thompson worked for the Walt Disney Studios and supplied voices for various cartoon characters in such feature films as *Lady and the Tramp, Peter Pan, Alice in Wonderland,* and the Donald Duck features.

THOSE WE LOVE

1938–1939	NBC Blue	Mon.	8:30 PM
1939–1940	NBC Red	Thurs.	8:30 PM
1940–1941	CBS	Mon.	8 PM
1941–1942	(Off the air)		
1942	NBC Red	Wed.	9 PM

Lowell Thomas (NBC)

Donald Woods and Nan Grey on *Those We Love* (NBC)

1942–1943	(Off the air)		
1943	NBC	Sun.	7 PM
1943–1945	CBS	Sun.	2 PM

Originally a summer-replacement program in 1937, large numbers of people wrote to CBS demanding that *Those We Love* remain on the air when the summer came to an end. They had become thoroughly caught up in the weekly, continuing story of the Marshall family and the romantic Dr. Leslie Foster, and they wanted to hear more.

This series' stories centered around widower John Marshall's difficulties in dealing with his young-adult offspring. Marshall, a good-natured but often distracted patriarch, was played by Hugh Sothern, then Oscar O'Shea, and finally Francis X. Bushman; Marshall's children were Kathy, played by Nan GREY, and Kathy's twin brother Kit, played by Richard Cromwell and then by Bill Henry. Actor Donald WOODS played Dr. Leslie Foster, Kathy's suitor. Woods was a major reason for the show's continuing popularity, especially among female listeners: seeing Woods' picture in the fan magazines proved that he was as attractive as his voice, a rarity in the radio business. Other characters on the series were Aunt Emily Mayfield, played by Alma Kruger; Amy Foster, played by child actress Priscilla Lyon and then Ann Todd; and Elaine Dascomb, played by Jean Rogers and then Helen

Wood. Also heard in regular supporting roles were Bob Cummings, Lou Merrill, Virginia Sale, Anne Stone, Richard Cromwell, Lurene TUTTLE, Mary Gordon, and Gale GORDON. Dick Joy was the program's announcer, and Calvin "Cal" Kuhl directed the series. *Those We Love* was written by Ruth Adams Knight and Agnes Ridgway. Sponsors included Ponds face cream, Royal Gelatine puddings, Teel shampoo, Sal Hapatica antacid, Sanka instant coffee, and Grape Nuts cereal.

THOSE WEBSTERS

| | 1953–1954 | Mutual | Sun. | 6 PM |

For three years before he replaced Hal Peary on *The Great Gildersleeve*, actor Willard WATERMAN played the patriarch of this half-hour situation comedy, *Those Websters*. The show had replaced a program called THAT BREWSTER BOY, and was similar in format and featured many of that earlier series' cast members. The situations enacted on this show revolved around a middle-class, Midwestern family and the typical problems the parents had trying to raise their teenage children. Constance Crowder played Mother Webster on the series to Waterman's "Dad" Webster. Arthur Young and Gil Stratton, Jr., played Billy Webster, and Joan Alt and Jane WEBB played his sister, Belinda. Jerry Spellman was heard as Jeep. Charles Irving was the show's announcer. Frank Worth was the program's music director. The series was produced and directed by Joe Ainsley and Les Weinrot and written by Albert G. Miller, Priscilla Kent, and Doris and Frank Hursley.

TINA AND TED

| 1944–1945 | CBS | Mon.–Fri. | 3:15 AM |
| 1945–1946 | CBS | Mon.–Fri. | 2:45 PM |

This 15-minute drama series starred Peggy Beckmark and James Gardner as Tina and Ted, a newlywed couple who had numerous monetary and adjustment problems. Sometime during the second season, they were replaced by Angel Casey and George Watson. George Cicas and Gladys Heen were featured on the program as Ted's in-laws, Mr. and Mrs. Hutchinson. Harry Holcomb was the show's director. It was written by Peggy Backmark. *Tina and Ted* was sponsored by Old Dutch cleanser and Delrich dairy products.

TO HAVE AND TO HOLD

See RADIO PLAYHOUSE.

TODAY'S CHILDREN

| 1933–1936 | NBC Blue | Mon.–Fri. | 10:30 AM |
| 1936–1938 | NBC Red | Mon.–Fri. | 10:30 AM |

1938–1943	(Off the air)		
1943–1946	NBC	Mon.–Fri.	2:15 PM
1946–1948	NBC	Mon.–Fri.	2 PM
1948–1950	NBC	Mon.–Fri.	2:30 PM

When the 15-minute drama series *Today's Children* first went on the air, it was the story of a German immigrant family, the Schultzes, and the problems they encountered when they settled in their new homeland, the United States of America. Their language, customs, and appearance made them stand out in their new home, and they desperately tried to fit in. As World War II approached and everything "German" became suspicious to many Americans, the program was taken off the air for a while. When it returned to the airwaves, it had changed its central characters to an Irish immigrant family, but it retained its memorable opening: "With our hopes and dreams, laughter and tears shall be the builders of a brighter world tomorrow!" Murray FORBES and Virginia PAYNE played the German couple, the Schultzes, and Patricia Dunlap played their daughter, Bertha, in the first version of the show. Irna PHILLIPS played Mother Moran when the Irish-family format took over. In time, an American family, the Carters, gradually began to dominate the story line on the program. They were played by Helen Kane, Forrest Lewis, and Judith Lowry. Also heard on the series in supporting casts over the years were Ethel Owen, Olan SOULE, Milton Herman, Willard Farnum, Clarence Hartell, Josephine Gilbert, Jack Edward, Jr., Frank Pacelli, Sunda Love, Lucy Gilman, Michael Romano, Willard WATERMAN, Gale Page, Betty Lou GERSON, Fred Sullivan, Bob BAILEY, Ed Prentiss, Laurette FILLBRANDT, Nanette Sargent, Fran CARLON, and Marvin MILLER. The series was produced by Carl Wester and directed by Axel Gruenberg, George Fogle, and Bob Dwan. Irna PHILLIPS was the program's principal writer. The show's theme music was "Aphrodite." Sponsors included Pillsbury's Best flour, Bisquick biscuit mix, Wheaties cereal, Kix cereal, and Betty Crocker cake mixes and soups.

TOM MIX

1933–1935	NBC Red	Mon., Wed., Fri.	5:15 PM
1935–1936	NBC Blue	Mon.–Fri.	5:35 PM
1936–1937	NBC Red	Mon.–Fri.	5:15 PM
1937–1942	NBC Blue	Mon.–Fri.	5:45 PM
1942–1944	(Off the air)		
1944–1949	Mutual	Mon.–Fri.	5:45 PM
1949–1950	Mutual	Mon.–Fri.	4:15 PM

Tom Mix was a popular cowboy star. Although Tom Mix himself was never actually heard on this 15-minute radio show, his fictitious T-M Bar Ranch in Dobie Township, his wonder horse Tony, and his friends the Old Wrangler, Jimmy, Jane, Amos Q. Snood, Sheriff Mike Shaw, Wash, Calamity, and Lee

Loo the Chinese cook were kept intact from his movies.

The episodes usually had Tom tracking down outlaws, fighting cattle rustlers, and settling feuds between neighboring ranchers. Ralston cereal was the program's longtime sponsor, and many premiums such as badges, decoding rings, certificates, pamphlets, and photographs were sent to children who mailed in a Ralston cereal box top and "one thin" dime. Artells Dickson, Russell Thorson, Jack Holden, and Curley Bradley played Tom Mix; Percy Hemus played the Old Wrangler; Andy Donnelly, George Gobel, and Hugh Rowlands played Jimmy; Winifred Toomey and Jane WEBB played Jane; Sidney Ellstrom played Elmer; Leo Curley, Hal PEARY, and Willard WATERMAN played Sheriff Mike Shaw; Bob Jellison played Calamity; and Bruno Wick played Lee Loo. Also heard playing supporting roles regularly were Cornelius Peeples, Harvey Hays, Vance McCune, Templeton Fox, Gertrude Warner, Forrest Lewis, Carl Kroenke, Phil Lord, DeWitt McBride, and Patricia Dunlap. Announcers on the program included Don Gordon, Lynn Brandt, Les Griffith, and Franklyn Ferguson. The series was produced by Al Chance and directed by Charles Chaggett and Clarence L. Menser. It was written by George Lowther, Roland Martini, and Charles Tazewell. The theme song, which was sung to the tune of "When It's Round-Up Time in Texas" (aka "When the Bloom Is on the Sage"), was familiar to young listeners, who memorized every word of the following lyrics:

> Shredded Ralston for your breakfast
> Start your day off shinin' bright!
> Gives you lots of cowboy energy
> With the flavor that's just right.
> It's delicious and nutritious
> Bite-size and ready to eat.
> Take a tip from Tom
> Go and tell your Mom
> Shredded Ralston can't be beat!

TOMMY RIGGS AND BETTY LOU SHOW, THE

1938–1939	NBC Red	Sat.	8:30 PM
1939–1940	NBC Red	Mon.	8 PM
1940–1942	(Off the air)		
1942	CBS	Tues.	9 PM
1942–1943	NBC	Fri.	7:30 PM
1943–1951	(Off the air)		
1951–1952	CBS	Mon.–Fri.	9:45 PM

Although he did not have an actual dummy like Charlie McCarthy, ventriloquist Tommy RIGGS used his voice to create a radio character named Betty Lou to entertain radio listeners. For several seasons, his show was almost as successful as Edgar BERGEN's. On the *Tommy Riggs and Betty Lou Show*, Betty Lou was Rigg's sassy but sweet niece. Betty Lou was a little, bright, and precocious girl who was a bit too wise for her age. The show was knit together by a series of loose sketches and songs in which Betty questioned everything and made cute remarks. In addition to Riggs, Wally Mayer was heard as Betty Lou's boyfriend Wilbur, and Verna FELTON played the overbearing Mrs. McIntyre. Vocalists Anita Kurt, Eileen Woods, Jimmy Cash, and Bea Wain were featured on the program at various times. Don WILSON, Paul Masterson, Dan SEYMOUR, Jack Mather, and Bill GOODWIN announced the show. The series was written by Sam Perrin, Jack Douglas, and George Balzer. Sponsors included Quaker Oats cereal and Swan soap.

TONY WONS SCRAPBOOK

1930–1931	CBS	Sun.	10 PM
1931–1932	CBS	Mon., Sat.	9:30 PM
1932–1933	CBS	Mon.–Sat.	9 AM
1933–1934	CBS	Mon.–Fri.	11:30 AM
1934–1935	NBC Blue	Mon.–Fri.	11:15 AM
1935–1937	(Off the air)		
1937–1938	CBS	Mon., Wed., Fri.	10:15 AM
1938–1940	(Off the air)		
1940–1941	NBC Red	Sun.	11:25 AM
1941–1942	NBC Red	Sun.	4:15 PM

Tony Wons was a radio star who read inspirational poetry and occasionally offered some of his own homespun philosophy to his audiences. He explained how important love, kindness, and religion are in people's lives. Wons' gentle, intimate-sounding delivery made him a great favorite with female listeners. His announcer for many years was Lewis Rowen. Wons' theme song was "Traumerei." Sponsors included International Silver and Johnson's wax.

TOWN CRIER, THE (AKA RADIO'S TOWN CRIER)

1930–1933	CBS	Mon.–Fri.	7:15 PM
1933–1934	CBS	Wed., Fri.	10:30 PM
1934–1937	CBS	Sun.	7 PM
1937–1938	CBS	Sun.	7:30 PM

Acerbic newspaper columnist, critic, and bon vivant, Alexander WOOLLCOTT—the inspiration for the character of Sheridan Whiteside in Moss Hart and George S. Kaufman's comedy play (1939) and film (1941) *The Man Who Came to Dinner*—was the host of this popular radio series in the 1930s. Woollcott interviewed show-business, political, literary, science, and various other celebrities such as Groucho MARX, Edna Ferber, Lillian Hellman, Bette Davis, Katherine Cornell, and Ernest Hemingway. He was known for his caustic wit, somewhat self-centered attitude, and opinionated commentaries about books or performances he had read or seen. In spite of this, he was very entertaining to listeners, who tuned in to hear his comments regularly. *The Town Crier* was sponsored by Gruen

watches, Cream of Wheat cereal, and Granger tobacco, among other products.

TOWN HALL TONIGHT

See FRED ALLEN SHOW, THE.

TOWN MEETING OF THE AIR, THE (AKA AMERICA'S TOWN MEETING)

1935–1944	NBC Blue	Thurs.	9:30 PM
1944–1945	NBC Blue	Thurs.	8:30 PM
1945–1950	ABC	Tues., Thurs.	8:30 PM
1950–1954	ABC	Tues.	9 PM
1954–1956	ABC	Sun.	8 PM

George V. Denney was the moderator of this long-running, hour-long panel-discussion program that centered around politics. Various prominent politicians and business and labor leaders such as John Foster Dulles, Henry Ford, and John L. Lewis were weekly guests. The series was unusual in that networks aired the program during prime-time hours, while programs of similar type were usually relegated to early Sunday-morning time slots, when the number of potential listeners was usually minimal.

TRACY, ARTHUR (1903–   )

Singer Arthur Tracy was born in Philadelphia, Pennsylvania. Known only as "the Street Singer" to radio listeners when his show, MUSIC THAT SATISFIES, was

Arthur Tracy (CBS)

first aired in 1931, Tracy's identity was kept a secret by CBS, the station that produced the show, to intrigue listeners and to add to his appeal. The ploy worked: thousands of listeners wrote to CBS demanding to know the name of the singer who sang so effectively as he accompanied himself on his accordion. After five months of obscurity, the Street Singer's identity was revealed, and Arthur Tracy instantly became a "big name" radio star. When his affiliation with CBS was terminated, Tracy took his theme song, "Marta," his voice, and his accordion to the Mutual network, where he remained until 1935; he then left the United States for England, where he enjoyed a five-year film and music-hall career. Tracy returned to the United States in 1940 and briefly resumed his broadcasting career on WOR, a New York Mutual station, using a 15-minute format. In 1942, Tracy again moved his show to NBC, where he remained for several seasons until he retired in the late 1940s to manage his considerable real-estate and business holdings. At the height of his career, Tracy starred in the film *The Big Broadcast of 1932.*

TRADE AND MARK

1926–1927	NBC Red	Wed.	10 PM
1927–1928	NBC Red	Thurs.	10 PM
1928–1929	NBC Blue	Wed.	9 PM
1929–1930	NBC Blue	Thurs.	9 PM
1930–1931	NBC Blue	Wed.	7:45 PM
1931–1932	NBC Blue	Fri.	8 PM
	CBS	Sat.	9:30 PM
1932–1933	CBS	Fri.	8 PM
	NBC Red	Sun.	7:45 PM
1933–1934	CBS	Sat.	8:45 PM

Smith Brothers cough drops sponsored a half-hour and then 15-minute music and comedy program that featured fictional characters named "Trade" Smith and "Mark" Smith. They were based on the "founders" of the company, the two bearded gentlemen pictured on the cough-drop box. The program featured Billy Hillpot, Scrappy Lambert, and Nat Shilkret's orchestra as well as guest stars such as Morton DOWNEY, Ruth ETTING, and the BOSWELL SISTERS.

TREMAYNE, LES (1913–)

Actor Les Tremayne was born in London, England, attended Northwestern University, Columbia, and U. C. L. A., and began his acting career on radio in Chicago. He was the leading man on *The* FIRST NIGHTER, on which he played every conceivable type of role from man-about-town to down-and-out hobo, and was featured on such programs as *The* ADVENTURES OF THE THIN MAN (as detective Nick Charles), ONE MAN'S FAMILY, ABBOTT MYSTERIES (as Mr. Abbott), BETTY AND BOB (as Bob), *The* BOB CROSBY SHOW (as host), *The* FALCON (as the Falcon, Mike Waring), and

The CHICAGO THEATER OF THE AIR, JOYCE JORDAN, GIRL INTERN, *The* ROMANCE OF HELEN TRENT, *The* SECOND MRS. BURTON, WENDY WARREN, *The* WOMAN IN WHITE, *The Night Court* and JACK ARMSTRONG, *All-American Boy.* A familiar face to moviegoers, Tremayne was featured in such films as *The Blue Veil* (1951), *Susan Slept Here* (1954), and *A Man Called Peter* (1955). The actor made a successful transition from radio to television in the 1950s and was seen on many television series, including "Mission Impossible" (1962), "Perry Mason" (1957), "Peter Gunn" (1958), "One Man's Family" (1950), and "One Life to Live" (1987). He continues to be active in films and on television.

TRENDLE, GEORGE W. (1885–1972)

One of the owners of radio station WXYZ in Detroit, George W. Trendle was a major force behind bringing hit programs such as *The* LONE RANGER and *The* GREEN HORNET to radio. Trendle was born in Detroit, Michigan, began his career working for theater owner John Krunsky, and eventually made his way in Krunsky's company to become a partner. In the 1920s, Trendle convinced Krunsky that the company should invest in radio; they bought the local station. Trendle then hired Fran STRIKER, an artist-writer from Buffalo, New York, who wrote the *Covered Wagon Days* radio series and several *Lone Ranger* scripts, which were first developed for WXYZ. In the 1930s Trendle, along with three other station owners, formed a cooperative of stations that was to become the MUTUAL BROADCASTING SYSTEM.

TRENT, SYBIL (Sybil Elaine: 1926–)

When she was two-and-a-half years old, Sybil Trent, born in Brooklyn, New York, made her professional acting debut: she appeared in a one-reel silent-film short starring comedian Fatty Arbuckle. As a child performer, Trent subsequently appeared in *Earl Carroll's Vanities of 1930* and had a featured role in the musical comedy *Jumbo* (1935) on Broadway. On radio, Sybil's own local show was called *Baby Sybil Elaine and Her Kiddie Revue* on WHN in the early 1930s. She joined the regular cast of child actors on CBS's anthology series LET'S PRETEND in 1935 and was heard on that program until it went off the air in 1954. Trent literally grew up while acting on *Let's Pretend* and graduated from playing children's roles to playing leading ladies on the program. Her articulate, attractive-sounding ingenue voice enabled her to play countless princesses and queens, damsels in distress, and kind mothers and good fairies. The actress was also featured on many other radio programs throughout the late 1930s, 1940s, and 1950s, most notably Nila MACK's *The March of Games* and daytime serials WE LOVE AND LEARN, STELLA DALLAS, and FRONT PAGE FARRELL, and on such evening shows as GANGBUSTERS,

The MARCH OF TIME, and FAMOUS JURY TRIALS. Trent retired from acting in the early 1960s, but remained active in show business as a casting director. She joined the Young and Rubicam advertising agency in 1973 and cast numerous commercials for that company until 1993, when she retired.

TROUT, ROBERT (1908–   )

CBS's "Iron Man of Radio," Robert Trout, earned the title when he broadcasted the 1952 Democratic Convention for 15 hours straight without a script. Born in Wake County, North Carolina, Trout debuted on radio in the early 1930s and, along with Edward R. MURROW, was regularly heard bringing on-the-spot news coverage from the war zones of Europe during World War II. Later, Trout became a popular announcer and program host for CBS and, in addition to broadcasting the nightly news at 7 and 11 PM, he was also heard on such programs as *The* AMERICAN SCHOOL OF THE AIR, *Columbia Presents Corwin, President Roosevelt's* FIRESIDE CHATS, PROFESSOR QUIZ, and *Who Said That?* Trout's face became as familiar to TV viewers as his voice had been to radio listeners as he continued reporting the news on TV well into the 1960s for the CBS network.

TRUE CONFESSIONS

1941–1958   NBC   Mon.–Fri.   (*)

Actress Bess JOHNSON hosted this series of serialized 15-minute adaptations of stories from *True Confessions* magazine. As the program's title implies, the segments were usually somewhat sensational and were directed toward women in the listening audience. Examples of plot lines included complicated love affairs, children born out of wedlock, and marriage. Created and written by Bill Sweets, the program was produced by Roy WINSOR and directed by Ernest Ricca. Heard on the program regularly were Ned WEVER, Charlotte MANSON, Janice Gilbert, Richard WIDMARK, Alfred Ryder, Lucille WALL, and others. *True Confessions* magazine sponsored the program.

TRUE DETECTIVE MYSTERIES

1929–1930	CBS	Thurs.	9:30 PM
1930–1936	(Off the air)		
1936–1937	Mutual	Tues.	9:30 PM
1937–1938	(Off the air)		
1938–1939	Mutual	Tues.	10 PM
1939–1944	(Off the air)		
1944–1945	Mutual	Sun.	1:30 PM
1945–1948	Mutual	Sun.	4:30 PM
1948–1949	Mutual	Sun.	4 PM
1949–1955	Mutual	Sun.	5:30 PM
1955–1956	Mutual	Mon.	8 PM

John Shuttleworth, editor of *True Detective* magazine, narrated the *True Detective Mysteries* program when it

first went on the air. Dick Keith and John Griggs took over the job in the 1940s. Its talented company of New York–based radio actors included John Thomas, Robert DRYDEN, Ted DeCorsia, Joe DeSantis, Gertrude Warner, Elspeth ERIC, Alice REINHEART, and Ralph Bell. The stories were all previously published in *True Detective* magazine and usually pertained to various public law-enforcement agents as well as to private detectives. Announcers on the show included Dan McCullock, Hugh James, and Frank Dunne. Murray Burnett was the series' director and writer. Sponsors included O'Henry candy bar, Baby Ruth candy bar, Viceroy cigarettes, Bi-So-Dol antacid, Curtiss Miracle Aid, Ex-Lax laxative, and the Advertising Council of America.

TRUE OR FALSE

1936–1939	Mutual	Mon., Tues.	10 PM
1939–1943	NBC Blue	Mon.	8:30 PM
1943–1948	(Off the air)		
1948–1949	Mutual	Sat., Thurs.	5:30 PM
			8:30 PM
1950–1951	Mutual	Sat.	5 PM
1951–1953		(Off the air)	
1953	Mutual	Sat.	8:30 PM
1954–1956	Mutual	Sat.	8 PM

Dr. Harry Hagen, Eddie Sunn, and Bill Slater hosted this half-hour quiz program on which contestants chosen from their studio audience could win up to $500 by answering a series of true-or-false questions correctly about a variety of subjects, from history to the entertainment arts. Glenn Riggs and Bill Spargrove were the program's announcers. Jeanne Harrison produced and directed the series. Sponsors included Williams shave cream, Serutan laxative, and Anahist nasal decongestant.

TRUTH OR CONSEQUENCES

1940–1942	NBC Red	Sat.	8 PM
1942–1950	NBC	Sat.	8:30 PM
1950–1951	CBS	Tues.	9:30 PM
1951–1952	NBC	Tues.	9 PM
		Thurs.	9:30 PM
1952–1954	NBC	Thurs.	9 PM
1954–1955	NBC	Wed.	9:30 PM
1955–1956	NBC	Wed.	8 PM

Originally a half-hour radio program, *Truth or Consequences* later became a successful television show. The audience-participation format was hosted on radio by Ralph EDWARDS, Jack Bailey, and Bob Barker and was a variation of an old parlor game in which a player had to pay a consequence if he or she didn't "tell the truth" by answering a question. The contestants had to answer questions such as: "How many men does it take to plant a tree?" If the answer was designated "wrong," Bob Prescott, the sound-effects man, would sound a buzzer called "Beulah," and the contestant usually had to perform some outrageous stunt in front of the studio audience. This included sliding through hoops on a greasy floor, walking and singing like a chicken, or telling a bad joke. One of the most popular promotional gimmicks the show used was a "Mystery Celebrity." Listeners had to try to identify various celebrities given names like "Miss Hush," "Mr. Hush" or "The Walking Man." Mr. Hush, for example, was finally identified after many weeks as former boxing champion Jack Demsey; Miss Hush proved to be silent-screen star Clara Bow; and the Walking Man was comedian Jack BENNY. Clayton "Bud COLLYER, Mel ALLEN, Jay Stewart, Milton CROSS, Ed HERLIHY, Harlow WILCOX, Jay Stewart, Verne Smith, Ken ROBERTS, and Ken CARPENTER were the series' announcers. The program was directed by John Guedel, Gilbert Ralaton, Al Parchall, and Ed Bailey. The show's theme songs were "Merrily We Roll Along" and "Hail, Hail, the Gang's All Here." Sponsors included Ivory soap, Duz detergent, Drene shampoo, Philip Morris cigarettes, Pabst Blue Ribbon beer, and Pet milk.

TUCKER, ORRIN (1911–)

Well-known successful orchestra leader Orrin Tucker was born in St. Louis, Missouri. One of the music conductors on the YOUR HIT PARADE program, Tucker formed his first band while he was a student attending Northwestern University. While his band was playing at the Spanish Gardens in Naperville during Chicago's Century of Progress Exposition, orchestra leader and singer Gus Edwards heard the group and was especially impressed with Tucker's expert musicianship. He offered Tucker a job in a nine-piece band he had formed to perform a long engagement in New Orleans. Later, while performing in Chicago's Beachwater Beach Hotel, Tucker, who had again formed his own band, began to perform on remote-band broadcasts on late-night radio.

TURNER, GRANT (1912–)

Known as "the Voice of the GRAND OLE OPRY," announcer Grant Turner was born in Abilene, Texas, and began to work at Nashville's WSM in 1944 on D-Day. Previously, he had worked at various radio stations throughout the South. The master of ceremonies of *The Grand Ole Opry*, George D. Hay, asked Turner to assist him and Turner's easygoing, personable manner of speaking gave a warm, folksy atmosphere to the show. His commercials for such products as Martha White flour, Rudy's Farm-Fresh Country Sausage, Little Debbie Snack cakes, Cracker Barrel Country Stores, and Goo Goo candy clusters made Turner practically as famous as the *Grand Ole Opry's* singers and comedians themselves.

TUTTLE, LURENE (1907–1986)

Actress Lurene Tuttle's remarkable career on radio included playing every conceivable type of part because she was equally adept at comic or serious roles. Born in Pleasant Lake, Indiana, Tuttle was the daughter of a minstrel named C. U. Tuttle and was heard on many radio programs both as a leading lady and as a supporting player. Her best-remembered role was as Effie Perrine, the gushingly innocent and sweet-voiced secretary on *The* ADVENTURES OF SAM SPADE, DETECTIVE. She also played Junior's Mommy and Daisy June on *The* RED SKELTON SHOW; Harriet's mother on *The* ADVENTURES OF OZZIE AND HARRIET; Marjorie, Gildersleeve's niece on *The* GREAT GILDERSLEEVE; Dolly Snaffle on DUFFY'S TAVERN; and nurse Judy Price on DR. CHRISTIAN. Tuttle was also heard on hundreds of SUSPENSE programs and played leading and supporting roles on *The* LUX RADIO THEATER, HOLLYWOOD STAR TIME, *The* COLUMBIA WORKSHOP, *The* FAMILY THEATER, SCREEN GUILD PLAYERS, GLAMOUR MANOR, *The Unexpected*, ONE MAN'S FAMILY, *Box 13*, *The* ADVENTURES OF MAISIE, and NIGHTBEAT. Tuttle was also featured in such films as *Pycho* (1960), and on television in the "Life with Father" (1953) series. She was also one of the most active film and television cartoon–voice-over actresses and was featured in "The NBC Comics" (1950–1956), "Nutcracker Fantasy"

Lurene Tuttle (CBS)

(1979), "Thanksgiving in the Land of Oz" (1980), and "These Are the Days" (1974–1976).

TWENTY QUESTIONS

1946–1954   Mutual   Sat.   8 PM

Most radio quiz programs were on the air for relatively short periods of time compared to other shows because the public seemed to lose interest in most of them after one or two seasons. The half-hour *Twenty Questions* program was an exception and remained on the air for eight years. Hosted by Bill Slater, and then by Jay Jackson, this program featured panelists Fred Van Deventer, Florence Rinard (who was Mrs. Van Deventer), Bobby and Nancy Van Deventer (their children), Herb Polesi, and Bobby McGuire. On the show, they attempted to identify a given subject, either a person or an object, by asking twenty questions after being told if it was "animal, vegetable, or mineral." Also heard on this series at various times were Jack Irish, Bruce Elliott, and Frank Waldecker as "the Mystery Voice" and Charlotte MANSON as "the Ronson Girl." To play, listeners submitted twenty questions on a particular subject to the show and hoped to stump the panel with their questions and thus win up to $75 in merchandise. The show's producers picked the twenty questions that they believed to be most interesting. The only stipulation in writing them was that all twenty had to be on the same subject. Frank Waldecker was the program's announcer. The series was directed by Gary Stevens and Del Crosby. Sponsors included Ronson cigarette lighters and Wildroot Cream-Oil hair groomer.

TWENTY THOUSAND YEARS IN SING SING

1933	NBC Blue	Sun.	9 PM
1933–1936	NBC Blue	Wed.	9 PM & 9:30 PM
1936–1937	NBC Blue	Mon.	9 PM
1937–1938	NBC Blue	Mon.	10 PM
1938–1939	NBC Blue	Fri.	8 PM

One of radio's most talked-about programs as far as vintage radio-show collectors and enthusiasts are concerned is the *Twenty-Thousand Years in Sing Sing* crime-story series. The half-hour program was extremely popular throughout the 1930s and was the inspiration for such shows as GANGBUSTERS, *The* FBI IN PEACE AND WAR, and THIS IS YOUR FBI. When this series first went on the air, Lewis E. Lawes, an actual prison warden, played himself on the series and narrated the weekly stories about people who were incarcerated and their reasons for having led a life of crime. Later in the series' run, Warden Lewes was played by actor Guy Sorel. Mr. Stark, who interviewed the warden before each story began, was played by Joseph Bell. Kelvin Keech was the program's announcer. Bell and Arnold Michaelis directed the program.

TWO FOR THE MONEY

1952–1953	NBC	Mon.–Fri.	5:45 PM
1953–1954	(Off the air)		
1954–1955	NBC	Mon.–Fri.	3:45 PM
1955–1956	NBC	Mon.–Fri.	10:30 AM

A very successful 15-minute quiz show on radio was *Two for the Money*. It starred comedian Herb Shriner and then Sam Levenson as host. Two contestants competed with each other by trying to be the first to answer a question, such as "Who was the third president of the United States? or "What is the name of the film actress who was known as the 'It' girl?" The contestant who answered more questions correctly won money and prizes. The program was sponsored by Ex-Lax laxatives and Old Gold cigarettes.

TWO ON A CLUE

1944–1946   CBS   Mon.–Fri.   2:45 PM

Similar to MR. AND MRS. NORTH and *The* ADVENTURES OF THE THIN MAN, *Two on a Clue*—unlike those programs, which aired at night for a half-hour each week—was a five-day-a-week daytime mystery-adventure series. Ned WEVER and Louise Fitch played Jeff and Debby Spencer, a husband-and-wife team who solved various murders, thefts, and con-artist schemes. Also heard regularly were Kate McComb as Mrs. Grover, Ronald LISS as Mickey, John GIBSON as Sergeant Cornelius Trumbull, Althena Lorde as "the Midget," and Jim Boles as the Professor. The series was written and directed by Harry Ingram. Sponsors included La France bleach and Satina flour.

U

UNCLE DON

1929–1939	(Local, New York program)		
1939–1940	Mutual	Mon., Wed., Fri.	5:30 PM
1940–1949	(Local, New York program)		

Uncle Don undoubtedly became radio's best-known children's show host due to an incident that, in all probability, never actually occurred. Rumor had it that Uncle Don, or Don CARNEY (born Howard Rice), didn't realize his microphone was still on at the end of his show when he said, "Well, I guess that will hold the little bastards for a while." Even though people swore they heard that broadcast, there is apparently no truth to the story. Carney was certainly never fired from the show as was claimed, nor was the program permanently, or even temporarily, canceled.

Howard Rice as "Uncle Don" Carney (NBC)

The story was, it seems, the invention of a Baltimore radio disc jockey who simply wanted to fill air time one day—the show wasn't even aired in Maryland and was only a network series for one year. The hour and then half-hour show contained stories, songs, birthday messages, and other features that were of interest to kids; commercial messages also abounded because the show's popularity made it especially appealing to advertisers. Some characters who were in Uncle Don's stories were Susan Beduszen and Willipus Wallipus, a typical American boy and girl; and the Meanwells, Slackerminds, Talkabouts, Stuckups, and Cryterions, who were all bad little kids who had terrible habits. Special features of his show were "The Uncle Don Healthy Child Contests," which had kids sending in lists of good deeds they had done for others, and "Uncle Don's Talent Quests," which conducted auditions for children who could sing, play an instrument, or read a story; they would perform on the air. Carney was the first performer to actually check out advertisers before he aired a company's commercial; even so, at one point he was accused of accepting kickbacks for mentioning certain products on the air even though it was not considered illegal at the time. *Uncle Don's* theme song was "Hello, Little Friends, Hello." Donald B. Brent directed Uncle's Don's network series.

See CARNEY, DON.

UNCLE EZRA'S RADIO STATION (AKA STATION E-Z-R-A)

1935–1936	NBC Red	Mon., Wed., Fri.	7:45 PM
1936–1939	NBC Red	Mon., Wed., Fri.	7:15 PM
1939–1940	(Off the Air)		
1940–1941	NBC Red	Sat.	10 PM

The character of Uncle Ezra was first heard on radio's NATIONAL BARN DANCE program and proved to be so popular with listeners that he was given his own show, *Uncle Ezra's Radio Station,* in the mid-1930s. On the series, Uncle Ezra owned a small, rural radio station that gave various local yokels a chance to be heard over the airwaves by their neighbors. Pat Barrett starred as Uncle Ezra, Nora Cunneen played Cecelia, and Fran ALLISON played Aunt Fanny—all comic residents and busybodies of the town. Also featured on the series were Cornelius Peeples and William J. Smith. The program was sponsored by Alka Seltzer antacid and Camel cigarettes.

UNCLE JIM'S QUESTION BEE

1936–1940	NBC Blue	Sat.	7:30 PM
1940–1941	NBC Blue	Tues.	8:30 PM

This half-hour quiz program originally starred Jim McWilliams as host and then featured Bill Slater playing a character named "Uncle Jim." The series asked a panel of contestants a series of questions that required quick responses, such as "How many U. S. presidents have there been?" The contestant who "buzzed in" first and gave a correct answer won points; the person with the most points at the end of the show won the match and the prizes. Joseph Bell was the program's announcer. Preston H. Pumphney and Henry Souvine directed the series. Sponsors of the show included Spry shortening, Rinso cleanser, and Lifebuoy soap.

UNCLE WALTER'S DOG HOUSE

1939–1940	NBC Red	Tues.	10:30 PM
1940–1942	NBC Red	Fri.	9:30 PM

This program, originating in Chicago, was a 30-minute comedy series that featured Tom Wallace as a character named Uncle Walter, a kindly old veterinarian who loved animals. On the show, he chatted with friends and neighbors but somehow always managed to get into trouble by asking, for example, how a lady's "dear old grandmother" was, not realizing the grandmother had been dead for ten years. The show also featured Charles Penman as Mr. Wiggins, Kathryn Card as Mrs. Wiggins, Beryl Vaughn as Beryl, Betty Arnold as Mrs. Damp, and Gladys Heen in various roles. The series announcer was Charles Lyon. The program was directed by Watson Humphrey and was sponsored by B&W's Walter Raleigh pipe tobacco. The show's theme song was "The Prisoner's Song."

UNDER ARREST

1946–1948	Mutual	Sun.	5:30 PM (Summer)
1948–1954	Mutual		(Syndicated series. Various stations and times)

This half-hour syndicated series, mainly heard on selected Mutual network stations, was a mystery-crime program starring Craig McDonnell and then Joe DeSantis as Captain Drake, a police-department homicide detective. The show also featured Betty GARDE, John LARKIN, Bryna Raeburn, Patsy Campbell, Les DAMON, Vicki VOLA, and Kermit Murdock. Created and produced by Wynn Wright, the program was directed by Martin Magner.

UNITED STATES STEEL HOUR

See THEATER GUILD OF THE AIR.

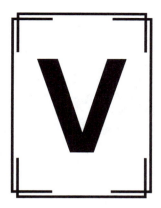

VERA VAGUE

See ALLEN, BARBARA J.

VAIL, MYRTLE (1888–1978)

Actress-writer Myrtle VAIL, who was born in Joliet, Illinois, was well known to daytime serial fans as the heroine Myrt, on MYRT AND MARGE, about two girls waiting for their big breaks as New York actresses. An actress who had toured on the Orpheum and Keith vaudeville circuits with husband George Demerel and daughter Donna, Vail created the radio series that made her a star and played Myrt on the program for the entire eleven years the show was aired. Vail's daughter, Donna Demerel Fick, played Marge until her untimely death in 1941. Vail gave many later-to-be famous actors such as Joseph Cotten, Cliff ARQUETTE, Jackson BECK, Alan REED, Robert Walker, Ed BEGLEY, and Olan SOULE their first major important radio acting jobs on *Myrt and Marge.*

VALENTINE, LEW (1912–1940)

Best known as Dr. I.Q on a much-listened-to radio program of that name, Lew Valentine was born in San Benita, Texas. Educated at Texas University, Valentine's first radio appearances were as a young singer and announcer on various local stations in Texas as early as 1929. He hosted the DR. I. Q. network program from 1939 until 1950 and answered difficult questions asked by people in the studio audience, such as "How do metal airplanes leave the ground?" The questions always required a substantive answer, not a simple "yes" or "no." He was also featured as the chief investigator on GANGBUSTERS for several seasons.

VALIANT LADY

1938–1939	CBS	Mon.–Fri.	1:45 PM
1939–1941	NBC Red	Mon.–Fri.	2:30 PM
1941–1946	CBS	Mon.–Fri.	10 AM
1946–1951	(Off the air)		
1951–1952	ABC	Mon.–Fri.	4 PM

The opening of this 15-minute weekday series began: "*Valiant Lady* . . . the dramatic story of Joan Scott as she struggles to help her unstable husband keep his feet on the ground upon the pathway to success." The part of Joan Hargrave-Scott, the valiant lady of the title, was initially played by actress Joan Blaine and then by Joan BANKS and Florence FREEMAN. Her husband was played by James MEIGHAN. Richard Gordon, William "Bill" JOHNSTONE, and Gene Leonard played Joan's father, Jim. Also heard in regular roles were Alan REED, Barbara Lee, Joseph "Joe" Latham, Elaine Kent, Kate McComb, Craig McDonnell, Milton Herman, Martin Blaine, Cathleen Cordell, Jerry Macy, Rickel Kent, William Shelley, Parker FENNELLY, Raymond Edward JOHNSON, Judith Lowry, Dwight WEIST, Adelaide Klein, Maurice TARPLIN, Sidney Slon, Kingsley Colton, Jack GRIMES, Ethel Owen, Luis VAN ROOTEN, Charme Allen, Jackie KELK, Lawson Zerbe, Elspeth ERIC, Ned WEVER, Joan Lazer, Frank LOVEJOY, and Bartlett Robinson. Art Millet and Dwight WEIST were the show's announcers. The series was directed by Roy Lockwood, Ernest Ricca, Lloyd Griffin, and Rikel Kent. Its writers included Addy Richton, Lynne Stone, Lawrence Klee, and Howard Teichmann. The program's familiar theme song was "Estrelita." Wheaties cereal, Gold Medal flour, Bisquick biscuit mix, and Cheerios cereal sponsored the program.

VALLEE, RUDY (HUBERT PRIOR VALLEE: (1902–1986)

Singer Rudy Vallee was America's first pop-singing radio idol. In the 1920s, he was billed as "the Vagabond Lover" and became a supper-club sensation with his renditions of "The Wiffenpoof Song," "My Time Is Your Time," and "Blue Moon," which he usually sang through a megaphone during the early days of his career. Vallee established himself as the nation's first romantic Jazz Age "crooner," even though he had a somewhat nasal-sounding voice.

Born in Island Pond, Vermont, Vallee grew up in Westbrook, Maine. At fifteen, Vallee joined the Navy, only to be sent home a few days after signing his enlistment papers because he was underage. In 1920, Vallee, an educated musician, joined the Strand Orchestra, playing saxophone in various New England locales. He worked his way through Yale University and then the University of Maine, playing with various college bands. Upon graduation, he entered show business on a full-time basis leading a group of musicians, The Yale Collegians. In 1928, they played at the Heigh-Ho Club in New York City and were so well

Rudy Vallee (NBC)

received that several radio engagements followed. Vallee soon starred on The FLEISCHMANN HOUR, the highest-rated radio program in the 1930s, which introduced performers such as Kate SMITH, Fred ALLEN, and Jack BENNY. The RUDY VALLEE SHOW naturally followed, along with leading and supporting roles in films: The Vagabond (1929), The Palm Beach Story (1942), The Bachelor and the Bobby Soxer (1947), I Remember Mama (1948), The Beautiful Blonde from Bashful Bend (1949), and Gentleman Marry Brunettes (1956). He also starred on Broadway in the musical comedy How to Succeed in Business Without Really Trying (1961) as well as in the film (1967).

VAN HARVEY, ART (ARTHUR H. VAN BERSHOOT: 1883–1957)

Although he is best known for playing the lovable-if-somewhat-cantankerous Vic on the popular VIC AND SADE domestic-comedy series, actor Art Van Harvey was one of the earliest performers to act on radio. Although he was on such programs as SILVER EAGLE and WELCOME VALLEY in the early 1930s, he became so identified with the role of Vic on VIC AND SADE that the listening audience had trouble accepting him in any other part.

VAN ROOTEN, LUIS (1906–1973)

One of movie and radio's most versatile character actors, Luis Van Rooten, was born in Mexico City, Mexico, and educated at the University of Pennsylvania. A small, rather unassuming-looking man, Van Rooten's unusual vocal abilities allowed him to sound effectively like a young hero or an old man. He played Denny, Drummond's British butler-assistant on The ADVENTURES OF BULLDOG DRUMMOND, the mysterious, foreign-born Mr. Astrakham on PRETTY KITTY KELLY, the kindly Dr. Ramey on STELLA DALLAS, and John Perry, the leading man on JOHN'S OTHER WIFE. He also made regular appearances on The CAVALCADE OF AMERICA, The ABBOTT MYSTERIES, and I LOVE A MYSTERY. Van Rooten appeared in the films The Unholy Wife and The Sea Chase (1957).

VAN STEEDEN, PETER (1904–1990)

Born in Amsterdam, Holland, musician Peter Van Steeden immigrated to the United States with his family when he was a boy. He formed a band while attending New York University and eventually became the music conductor for programs such as BREAK THE BANK, The FRED ALLEN SHOW, The JACK PEARL SHOW, For Men Only, What's My Name, The Vitalis Program, MCGARRY AND HIS MOUSE, MR. DISTRICT ATTORNEY, and STOOPNAGLE AND BUDD. Van Steeden was known for his musical arrangements as well as his conducting, and after his departure from radio variety shows in the late 1950s, he remained active in the music industry as a conductor and arranger for numerous recording companies.

VASS FAMILY, THE (EMILY: 1922– , FRANK: 1914– , LOUISA: 1919– , SALLY: 1912– , AND VIRGINIA: 1915–)

The Vass Family from Greenville, North Carolina, was a successful singing group that made its radio debut performing locally before going on to New York and appearing on *The* BEN BERNIE SHOW, *The* PAUL WHITEMAN SHOW, *The* NATIONAL BARN DANCE, and *Sensations in Swing.* Singing the popular and semi-classical songs of the time such as "Tea for Two" and "By the Light of the Silvery Moon," the Vass Family specialized in four-part harmony. They disappeared from the spotlight and retreated into private life in the late 1930s.

VAUGHN DE LEATH SHOW, THE

1922–1931	(Various stations and times)		
1931–1932	CBS	Tues., Thurs.	6:15 PM
1932–1933	CBS	Tues., Thurs.	6:30 PM
1933–1935	NBC Red	Tues.	7:45 PM
	NBC Red	Wed.	2:30 PM
1935–1936	NBC Blue	Mon.–Sat.	10 AM
1936–1937	NBC Blue	Mon.–Fri.	1:30 PM
1937–1938	(Off the air)		
1938–1939	NBC Blue	Sat.	11 AM
1939	Mutual	Mon., Wed., Fri.	1:45 PM

Vaughn de Leath is said to have been the first woman to become a major singing star on radio in the 1920s, and it has even been said that she was the first woman to sing over the airwaves, although this has never been substantiated. De Leath's rich contralto voice was particularly suited to blues songs such as "Blue Indigo" and "I've Got a Right to Sing the Blues." She was heard on local programs in New York City as early as 1921 and starred on her own network radio show in 1931. Her programs were usually 15 minutes long. The singer's longtime sponsor was Lydia Pinkham beauty products.

VIC AND SADE

1932–1933	NBC Blue	Mon.–Sat.	9:30 AM
1933–1934	NBC Blue	Mon.–Sat.	1:30 PM
1934–1936	NBC Red	Mon.–Fri.	3 PM
1936–1937	NBC Blue	Mon.–Fri.	10 AM
	NBC Red	Mon.–Fri.	3:30 PM
1937–1938	NBC Red	Mon.–Fri.	11:30 AM
	NBC Blue	Mon.–Fri.	3:30 PM
1938–1940	NBC Red	Mon.–Fri.	4:30 PM
1940–1941	NBC Red	Mon.–Fri.	3:45 PM
1941–1944	NBC	Mon.–Fri.	11:15 AM
	CBS	Mon.–Fri.	1:30 PM

"And now, folks, get ready to smile again with radio's home folks, Vic and Sade, written by Paul Rhymer,"

(From left) Billy Idelson, Bernadine Flynn, and Art Van Harvey on *Vic and Sade* (NBC)

the announcer stated at the beginning of each 15-minute *Vic and Sade* radio program. For ten years in the 1930s, *Vic and Sade* was one of the most popular domestic comedy shows on radio.

A typical American married couple, Vic and Sade Gook were played by Art VAN HARVEY and Bernadine FLYNN. They lived "in a little house halfway up the next block" in Cooper, Illinois, "40 miles from Peoria." The Gooks' son, Rush, was played by Billy Idelson, Johnny Coons, and Sid Koss; Uncle Fletcher, by Clarence Hartzell; and zany friends and neighbors like Dottie Brainfeeble were played by Ruth Perrott; Chuck Brainfeeble by Carl Kroenke; a nephew named Russell by David Whitehouse and L. J. Gertner; and the city water inspector by Johnny Coons. Other characters, talked about but never heard on the show, had such unforgetable names as Lottie Sterienzi (Vic's secretary), Jake Gumpox (the garbage man), Smelly Clark, Ruthie Stembottom (Sade's friend who attended wash-rag sales at Yamelton's Department Store), Ishigan Fishigan of Sishigan, Michigan (who always called Vic long distance), and Robert and Slobbert Hink (identical twins who occasionally sent Vic and Sade postcards from unusual places).

Few listeners could forget that Vic worked at Plant No. 14 of the Consolidated Kitchenware Company, that Uncle Fletcher always hung out at the Bright Kentucky Hotel to watch the trains go by, or the occasional end-of-the-show credit, "Sade's gowns by Yamelson's Department Store, Illinois." Charles Irving, Vincent Pelletier, Clarence Hartzell, Ralph EDWARDS, Bob Brown, Ed HERLIHY, Glenn Riggs, Roger Krupp, Mel ALLEN, and Ed Roberts were the show's announcers.

Vic and Sade was created and written by Paul Rhymer and directed by Clarence Menser, Earl Ebi, Ted MacMurray, Charles Rinehart, and Roy Winsor.

"Oh, You Beautiful Doll," "Shine on Harvest Moon," and "Chanson Bohemienne" were the show's theme songs. The program was sponsored by Richard Hudnut shampoo, Fraser automobiles, Ironized yeast, Crisco shortening, Ivory soap flakes and soap, and Dash detergent.

VICKS OPEN HOUSE

1934–1935	NBC Blue	Tues.	9 PM
1935–1936	NBC Red	Mon.	9:30 PM
1936–1937	CBS	Sun.	8 PM
1937–1938	CBS	Sun.	7 PM

Popular motion-picture and concert singing stars Jeanette MacDonald, Grace Moore, William Swan, and Nadine Connor were the various hosts of this half-hour weekly music-variety program at different times, which featured opera and semiclassical music by Rudolf Friml and Victor Herbert, and classic popular songs such as "Sweetheart" and "Indian Love Call." Featured on the show regularly was the Joseph Pasternack orchestra. The show was sponsored by Vicks vaporub and Vicks Va-Tro-Nol decongestent.

VICTOR BORGE SHOW, THE

1943	NBC Blue	Mon.–Fri.	7 PM
1943–1945	(Off the air)		
1945	NBC	Tues.	9:30 PM
1945–1946	(Off the air)		
1946–1947	NBC	Mon.	9:30 PM
1947–1951	(Off the air)		
1951	ABC	Mon.–Fri.	5:55 PM
	Mutual	Mon., Wed., Fri.	5:55 PM

Danish pianist-homorist Victor Borge had several 15-minute and half-hour variety programs on the air in the late 1940s to the early 1950s. These shows featured Borge's humorous piano playing and commentaries. The Pat Friday Singers and the Henry Russell Chorus also appeared on some of Borge's shows. Billy Mills and Benny GOODMAN led the show's orchestras. Harlow WILCOX, Ken ROBERTS, and John Reed KING were the program's announcers. Johnson's wax and Sacony Cacuum oil company (Mobilgas) sponsored Borge's programs.

VICTOR LINDLAHR SHOW, THE

See LINDLAHR, VICTOR.

VILLAGE STORE

See SEALTEST VILLAGE STORE.

VOICE OF FIRESTONE, THE

1928–1931	NBC Red	Mon.	8 PM
1931–1942	NBC Red	Mon.	8:30 PM
1942–1955	NBC	Mon.	8:30 PM
1955–1956	ABC	Mon.	8:30 PM

On the air continuously for over more than twenty years, the half-hour *Voice of Firestone* presented classical and semiclassical music, featuring the orchestras of Howard BARLOW, William Daly, Alfred Wallenstein, and Hugo Marini and guest artists such as sopranos Margaret Speaks, Lily Pons, Gladys Swarthout, Patrice Munsel, Rose Bampton, and Eleanor Steber; contralto Vaughn DE LEATH; tenors Richard Crooks, Lauritz Melchoir, John Charles Thomas, and Richard Crooks; baritones Lawrence Tibbett, Igor Gorin, and Nelson EDDY.

In 1936, the FCC announced that it was going to ban "all person-to-person messages by performers on shows." Because *Voice of Firestone* star baritone John Charles Thomas ended all of his broadcasts saying, "Goodnight, Mother," he announced that if he were forced to relinquish his usual message to his mother, "it [would] be either 'Goodnight, Mother' or 'Goodbye, broadcasting.'" Thomas's popularity was such that no one ever demanded that he drop his filial farewell.

The show's long-term announcer was Hugh James; Gene Hamilton also announced the show at one time. Edwin L. Dunham was the program's longtime writer and director. *The Voice of Firestone* was sponsored for many years by the Firestone Tire and Rubber Company. The show's theme songs were "In My Garden" and "If I Could Tell You," the latter written by Firestone's daughter Idabelle.

VOLA, VICKI (1916–1985)

Actress Vicki Vola was born in Denver, Colorado, and began her acting career in regional theater productions when she was sixteen years old. She debuted on radio in 1932. Although Vola was best known as Miss Miller, the faithful secretary-assistant on MR. DISTRICT ATTORNEY, the actress was heard as Kitty Marshall on MARY NOBLE, BACKSTAGE WIFE, the title role on *Brenda Curtis*, the female lead on *Foreign Assignment*, Elaine on OUR GAL SUNDAY, and Faith Richards on THE ROAD OF LIFE. She acted regularly on BUCK ROGERS IN THE 25TH CENTURY, *The* FIRST NIGHTER, *The* MAN I MARRIED, MY TRUE STORY, VALIANT LADY, VIC AND SADE, AUNT JENNY'S REAL LIFE STORIES, *The* LUX RADIO THEATER, DEATH VALLEY DAYS, CALLING ALL CARS, and JUNGLE JIM. In the 1970s, Vola was heard on Himan BROWN's CBS MYSTERY THEATER and on television had a featured role on "Search for Tomorrow" (1959–1960).

VON ZELL, HARRY (1906–1981)

Very few radio announcers actually became full-fledged stars, but Indianapolis, Indiana-born Harry Von Zell, known for his jovial, somewhat knowing laugh, did just that. When he debuted on radio as an announcer in the early 1930s, Von Zell proved himself to be a first-rate actor as well as product spokesman and began to play featured roles on the shows he announced: BURNS AND ALLEN, *The* BEN BERNIE SHOW, *The Old Gold Hour with* PAUL WHITEMAN, *The* ALDRICH FAMILY, *"Whispering"* JACK SMITH, *The* AMAZING MR. SMITH, *Chicken Every Sunday, The* WILL ROGERS SHOW, *The* MARCH OF TIME, *Quizzers Baseball,* STOOPNAGLE AND BUDD, *The* EDDIE CANTOR SHOW, *The* FRED ALLEN SHOW, *The* PHIL BAKER SHOW, and the *Meet the Missus* quiz show, which he hosted.

One of Von Zell's most memorable assignments was adding commentary to broadcasts made by Admiral Richard E. Byrd while Byrd was on his celebrated expedition to the South Pole in 1930. Von Zell was also responsible for one of radio's most famous bloopers when he introduced the then President of the United States, Herbert Hoover, as "Hoobert Heever." The announcer also tirelessly donated time to appear on the wartime COMMAND PERFORMANCE series, heard by members of the military stationed all around the world during World War II.

VOORHEES, DONALD (1904–1989)

The talented music conductor who led NBC's BELL TELEPHONE HOUR orchestra for more than thirty years, Donald Voorhees was born in Allentown, Pennsylvania. The musician began to study violin when he was five years old, and by the time he was seventeen, Voorhees was leading the Allentown, Pennsylvania, symphony. Soon after, he conducted the orchestra for *Brevities of 1920,* a Broadway musical comedy starring comedian Eddie Cantor. Voorhees made his radio debut in 1920 and thereafter became music director for SHOW BOAT, *Texaco Fire Chief, Ford Summer Hour,* and CAVALCADE OF AMERICA. The "Maestro," as he was called by fellow musicians, made a successful transition from radio to television in the early 1950s as music director for NBC television until 1968, when he retired from show business.

VOX POP (AKA SIDEWALK INTERVIEWS)

1935	NBC	Sun.	7:30 PM
1935–1936	NBC	Sun.	2:30 PM
1936–1938	NBC	Tues.	9 PM
1938–1939	NBC	Sat.	9 PM
1939–1941	CBS	Thurs.	7:30 PM
1941–1946	CBS	Mon.	8 PM
1946–1947	CBS	Tues.	9 PM
1947–1948	ABC	Wed.	8:30 PM

Parks Johnson, Jerry Belcher, Wally Butterworth, and Warren HULL hosted this half-hour interview-quiz program written by Roger Brackett. Dick Joy, Butterworth, and Roger Krupp were the program's announcers. The series was directed by Roger Brackett, Nathan Tufts, Herb Moss, and John Bates. Penn Tobacco Company, Fleischmann's yeast, Lipton tea, American Express, and Kentucky Club tobacco sponsored the show.

WALDO, JANET (c. 1928–   )

An actress who retained a perpetually young-sounding voice, Janet Waldo starred on several popular radio programs in the 1950s. Born in Los Angeles, California, she played teenage Corliss Archer on MEET CORLISS ARCHER and major roles on The EDDIE BRACKEN SHOW, The ADVENTURES OF OZZIE AND HARRIET, and ONE MAN'S FAMILY. The actress, in addition to radio performances, was and still is one of the most sought-after cartoon-character voice-over performers. Waldo was the voice of Josie in "Josie and the Pussycats" (1970–1972) on television, Rebecca Boone in "Daniel Boone" (1981), and Alice in the Disney film classic *Alice in Wonderland* (1951); she also had major vocal roles on television cartoon specials "Miss Switch to the Rescue" (1982), "The Secret World of Oz" (1983), and "The Jetsons" (1963–1984).

WALL, LUCILLE (1899–1986)

Well known as Portia Manning on the long-running daytime radio series PORTIA FACES LIFE, actress Lucille Wall was born in Chicago, Illinois. She entered radio in 1927 as a regular performer on *The Collier Hour* program and played major roles on the Chicago-based *The* FIRST NIGHTER and *A* TALE OF TODAY. Wall was Lorenzo Jones's wife, Belle, on LORENZO JONES and Isabel Andrews on PRETTY KITTY KELLY and performed frequently on TRUE CONFESSIONS and YOUR FAMILY AND MINE. The actress played Nurse March on television's "General Hospital" from 1963 until 1982.

WALLINGTON, JAMES "JIMMY" (1907–1972)

Announcer James "Jimmy" Wallington was born in Rochester, New York, began his show-business career as a singer on radio, and then became a staff an-

nouncer for NBC. Wallington announced The ALAN YOUNG SHOW, The BIG SHOW, BURNS AND ALLEN, DUFFY'S TAVERN, The EDDIE CANTOR SHOW, The FRED ALLEN SHOW, The GIBSON FAMILY, The JACK KIRKWOOD SHOW, The ORIGINAL AMATEUR HOUR, The MYSTERIOUS TRAVELER, The RUDY VALLEE SHOW, STELLA DALLAS, The TEXACO STAR THEATER, The Philco Hall of Fame, BLIND

Lucille Wall in *Portia Faces Life* (CBS)

288

DATE, *The Doctor Fights, This Is My Best,* and *Sincerely, Kenny Baker.* Wallington was a voice-over television commercial announcer and introduced various TV programs for NBC-TV.

WALTER WINCHELL SHOW, THE (AKA THE JURGENS JOURNAL)

1931–1932	CBS	Tues.	8:45 PM
1932–1947	NBC Blue	(Days and times varied)	
1949–1955	ABC	(Days and times varied)	
1955–1957	Mutual	Mon.–Fri.	6 PM

"Good evening, Mr. and Mrs. North and South America and all the ships at sea. Let's go to press!" gossip-show host Walter WINCHELL said at the beginning of his 15-minute program. Winchell catered to the public's insatiable appetite for the sordid details of famous people's private and professional lives. His "tips to celebrities," telling them how he thought they should or should not have behaved in certain situations, was one of the program's features. Winchell's announcers over the years included Ben GRAUER and Richard "Dick" Stark. For many years, the show was sponsored by Jurgens lotion and during that time was called *The Jurgens Journal.* Lucky Strike cigarettes and Richard Hudnut shampoo also sponsored the series at different times; when Lucky Strike was the sponsor, the show was called *The Lucky Strike Magic Carpet.*

WARING, FRED (1900–1984)

While an undergraduate at the University of Pennsylvania, Fred Waring from Tyrone, Pennsylvania, formed a glee club that became well known enough to warrant professional bookings around the state. After graduation, he continued to play his banjo and lead his band and chorus. The group eventually evolved into Fred Waring and the Pennsylvanians. Following vaudeville appearances for a number of years and in 1928, Waring accepted an engagement at Les Ambassadeurs in Paris to play in an "All-American" revue. The group received unanimous critical acclaim in Europe and starred in the Broadway musical comedy *Hello Yourself.* In 1929, Fred Waring and the Pennsylvanians performed in the motion picture *Syncopation* and after touring the country playing concert dates debuted on radio. *The FRED WARING AND HIS PENNSYLVANIANS SHOW* became a favorite semiclassical music program. Later, the group was featured on the CHESTERFIELD TIME program and, after their radio days ended, toured the country playing concerts until shortly before his death. The Pennsylvanians can still be seen on occasion led by Waring's daughter.

WATERMAN, WILLARD (1914–1995)

Willard Waterman is best remembered by the public as Throckmorton P. Gildersleeve on *The GREAT GILDERSLEEVE* radio and TV programs. Born in Madison, Wisconsin, Waterman began his show-business career on radio in Chicago. From 1936 until 1946, Waterman, one of radio's busiest actors, was heard on as many as forty shows a week. Among the shows he was featured on were *The LUX RADIO THEATER, Lonely Women, The CHICAGO THEATER OF THE AIR, GIRL ALONE, The GUIDING LIGHT, The HALLS OF IVY, Harold Teen, The ROAD OF LIFE, STEPMOTHER, TOM MIX, The WHISTLER, THOSE WEBSTERS,* and *The FIRST NIGHTER.* He eventually acted on stage and screen in major supporting roles [*Auntie Mame* (1958)] and had regular roles on television in "Dennis, the Menace" (1955), "The Real McCoys" (1957), and "I Love Lucy" (1951–1957). Waterman has been featured on TV commercials, most notably for such products as Alka Seltzer antacid, A-1 steak sauce, and Kellogg's cereals.

WE LOVE AND LEARN (AKA AS THE TWIG IS BENT AND THE STORY OF RUBY VALENTINE)

1942–1944	CBS	Mon.–Fri.	2:30 PM
	NBC	Mon.–Fri.	5:15 PM
1948–1950	NBC	Mon.–Fri.	11:15 AM
1950–1956	NBC	Mon.–Fri.	11 AM

The 15-minute weekday drama series *We Love and Learn* had several settings and formats while it was on the air. In the original production, actor Frank LOVEJOY starred as Bill Peters, and Joan BANKS and then Betty Worth played his love interest, Andrea Reynolds. The series concerned the problems of being young and married during World War II. Sybil TRENT played a newly married young woman named Thelma, and Cliff Carpenter played her husband, Jim. Character actress Charme Allen portrayed Mrs. Carleton, and also heard on this early version in regular supporting roles were Grace Keddy, Juano Hernandez, Horace Braham, Sarah Burton, William Podmore, Norman Rose, Don MCLAUGHLIN, Jose Ferrer, Robert DRYDEN, Ann Thomas, Lesley Woods, Ethel Everett, and Barbara Weeks. Fielden Farrington was the show's announcer.

In 1955, after being off the air for several seasons, the series returned with the show's setting changed from a dress shop to a Harlem beauty parlor, and the cast became African American. The name of the show was changed to *The Story of Ruby Valentine.* African-American actors Juanita Hall, Viola Dean, Earl Hyman, and Ruby Dee joined Hernandez, still playing the role he played on the original show. The new series was written by Don Becker. Carl Eastman was one of the show's many directors. Post Raisin Bran cereal sponsored the earlier version of the series.

WE, THE ABBOTTS

| 1940–1941 | CBS | Mon.–Fri. | 4:15 PM |
| 1941–1942 | NBC Red | Mon.–Fri. | 5:30 PM |

This 15-minute daytime drama series was about the everyday problems of a family called the Abbotts. John McIntire played the patriarch, John Abbott, and Betty GARDE and then Ethel Everett played his wife, Emily. The Abbott children—Linda, Barbara, and Jack—were played by Betty Jane Tyler, Audrey Egan, and Cliff Carpenter. Adelaide Klein played the Abbotses' maid, Hilda; and Bess Flynn played John's mother-in-law. The show's announcers were Ted Phearson and Nelson CASE. The series was written by Bess Flynn. It was sponsored by Nucoa margarine and Hellman's mayonnaise.

WE, THE PEOPLE

1936–1937	NBC Blue	Sun.	5 PM
1937–1938	CBS	Thurs.	7:30 PM
1938–1941	CBS	Tues.	9 PM
1941–1943	CBS	Sun.	7:30 PM
1943–1947	CBS	Sun.	10:30 PM
1947–1949	CBS	Tues.	9 PM
1949–1950	NBC	Fri.	8:30 PM
1950–1951	NBC	Thurs.	9:30 PM

First heard on NBC's Blue network, then on CBS, and finally on NBC once again, the half-hour *We, The People* series presented human-interest stories of courage and ingenuity that were written to inspire listeners to lead better, more productive lives. Originally a short segment on *The* RUDY VALLEE SHOW, the feature was popular enough for network officials to make it a half-hour weekly series. Initially, actor Burgess MEREDITH was the show's host, but news commentator Gabriel HEATTER, Broadway star and producer Eddie Dowling, Milo Boulton, Dwight WEIST, and Danny SEYMOUR also hosted the program at various times. *We, The People*'s orchestra was conducted by Oscar Bradley. The series was produced by Phillips H. LORD and directed by David Levy, Lindsay MacHarrie, and James Sheldon. The writers for the series included Arthur Henley, Richard Dana, Ruth Barth, Ted Adams, Paul Gardner, Paul Adams, Leonard Safir, and Laurence Hammond. Harry VON ZELL was the show's announcer in the late 1930s and early 1940s. The series' theme music was from Brahm's First Symphony. Sponsors included Calumet baking powder, Grape Nuts cereal, Huskies dog food, Minute tapioca, Sanka instant coffee, and Gulf oil.

WEBB, JACK (1920–1982)

Actor-director Jack Webb played police detective Joe Friday on the radio and TV versions of the DRAGNET series. He was probably best remembered for calmly stating "Just the facts, ma'am" when questioning someone in an investigation. Webb, who was born in Santa Monica, California, played several roles similar to his Sgt. Friday on other radio adventure-crime series, such as *Jeff Regan, Detective,* PAT NOVAK FOR HIRE, *Pier 23,* and *One out of Seven.* He was also frequently featured on the *Escape* series and appeared in such films as *The Men* (1950), *You're in the Navy Now* (1952), *Dragnet* (1954), *Pete Kelly's Blues* (1955), *The D.J.* (1957), and *The Last Time I Saw Archie* (1962), the last three of which he also produced and directed.

WEBB, JANE (c1918–   )

Born near Chicago, Illinois, actress Jane Webb began her radio acting career in that city while still in her teens. During the 1930s, 1940s, and 1950s, Webb was prominently featured on shows such as AUNT MARY, MEET THE MEEKS, *The* GUIDING LIGHT, THAT BREWSTER BOY, THOSE WEBSTERS, and *The* BARTON FAMILY. She is probably best known, however, for supplying the voice of Sabrina the Witch for hundreds of "Archie" television cartoons throughout the 1970s. The actress was also an animated-film voice-over in "The Hardy Boys" (1969–1971), *Aesop's Fables* (1971), "My Favorite Martian" (1973–1975), "Lassie Rescue Rangers" (1973–1975), "The New Adventures of Gilligan" (1974–1977), and *Oliver Twist* (1980). Webb was a frequent television commercial spokeswoman as well.

WEBER, KARL (1916–1990)

After he graduated from the University of Iowa, Karl Weber of Columbus Junction, Indiana, stopped over in Chicago on his way to New York—he hoped to become a Broadway actor. That "stopover" lasted six years, at which point Weber, upon a friend's urging, auditioned for and won a radio role, remained in Chicago, and was heard on hundreds of subsequent programs. Weber's radio acting credits include *The Strange Romance of* EVELYN WINTERS, LORENZO JONES, *The* BARTON FAMILY, *Avalon Time, Inside Story,* DON WINSLOW OF THE NAVY, ARNOLD GRIMM'S DAUGHTER, GIRL ALONE, HELPMATE, LONE JOURNEY, *Nona from Nowhere, The* ROMANCE OF HELEN TRENT, *The* SECOND MRS. BURTON, STEPMOTHER, WHEN A GIRL MARRIES, *The* WOMAN IN WHITE, and *Dr. Six Gun,* usually playing lead roles. Eventually, Weber managed to appear in several Broadway plays, but he continued radio acting in New York. On television, Weber was featured on "Search for Tomorrow" (1955–1956) and "Kitty Foyle" (1958).

WEEKEND EDITION

| 1985–present | NPR | Sat., Sun. | 9 AM |

Because of the success of its two-hour (three in some areas) weekday MORNING EDITION news-magazine program, NATIONAL PUBLIC RADIO launched a two-hour Saturday-Sunday *Weekend Edition* in 1985. Highlighted by interviews with well-known actors (Mel Gibson and Glen Close), composers (Andrew Lloyd Webber, Morton Gould, and, shortly before he died, Leonard Bernstein), and writers (Eudora Welty and Judith Krantz), the program presents news features and remote broadcasts from war-torn and famine-ridden areas of the world. Special features, such as the weekly puzzle, asks a selected member of the listening audience to solve, via the phone, a series of difficult puzzle questions. NPR's Susan Stamberg, who originally hosted the program, continues to offer special-interest features as well as occasional hosting, but currently Scott Simon hosts on Saturdays, and Lianne Hansen on Sundays. Other NPR news-department commentators and reporters include Cokie Roberts and Nina Tottenberg.

WEEMS, TED (1901–1963)

Born in Baltimore, Maryland, musician Ted Weems led the orchestra on such popular radio programs as BEAT THE BAND, FIBBER MCGEE AND MOLLY, and *The JACK BENNY SHOW*. During the 1930s and 1940s, he was one of America's favorite remote-broadcast bandleaders, had many hit recordings, and frequently guest-starred on radio's most popular music-variety programs, such as *The FLEISCHMANN HOUR*, *The TEXACO STAR THEATER*, and *The KRAFT MUSIC HALL*.

WEIST, DWIGHT (1910–1991)

Actor-announcer Dwight Weist was born in California and raised in Scranton, Pennsylvania. Deciding to pursue a show-business career and working for a brief period as a stage actor, Weist entered radio as a page boy and then as a staff announcer at NBC. He acted on several shows, was the first MR. DISTRICT ATTORNEY, and played both the Lamont Cranston-Shadow role and Commissioner Weston on *The SHADOW*. The roles of Adolf Hitler and Franklin D. Roosevelt on the MARCH OF TIME series, as well as major parts on *The CAVALCADE OF AMERICA*, BUCK ROGERS IN THE 25TH CENTURY, *The SECOND MRS. BURTON*, ANDY HARDY, BY KATHLEEN NORRIS, *The THEATER GUILD ON THE AIR*, and VALIANT LADY are among Weist's credits. As an announcer, Weist introduced and was the product spokesman on *The ALDRICH FAMILY* and BIG TOWN and the announcer for the "Search for Tomorrow" television series for many years. In recent years, Weist ran a school to teach actors how to perform in TV commercials, the Weist–Barron School in New York City. This multitalented performer appeared in Woody Allen's film *Radio Days* (1986) and was the narrator-storyteller in the film *The Name of the Rose* (1989).

WELCOME TRAVELERS (AKA IT CAN BE DONE)

1947–1948	ABC	Mon.–Fri.	4 PM
1948–1949	ABC	Mon.–Fri.	12 PM
1949–1954	NBC	Mon.–Fri.	10 AM

This 15-minute program presented spontaneous interviews of interesting, unusual, and sometimes famous people passing through the busy Chicago train and bus terminals. Interviewees were given a $50 savings bond and merchandise worth up to $100 for their time and stories. They could win additional prizes by answering questions phoned in by listeners about their hometowns while the show was on the air. This was accomplished by the use of portable phones set up within the train and bus terminals. Tommy Bartlett hosted the show, and Jim AMECHE was the program's announcer. Sponsors included Spic and Span floor cleaner, Prell shampoo, Drene shampoo, Lava soap, Joy detergent, and Ivory soap.

WELLES, ORSON (1915–1985)

If the formidable talents of actor-producer-director Orson Welles had given the world nothing more than the classic motion picture *Citizen Kane* (1941), his place in the show-business Hall of Fame would have been guaranteed, but he additionally had a significant career in radio. Born in Kenosha, Wisconsin, Welles exhibited unusual talent as an artist, actor, and writer when he was a schoolboy attending the Todd School in Woodstock, Wisconsin. At sixteen, he left Wisconsin and went to Europe, where he debuted professionally as an actor at the famous Gate Theater in Dublin. At twenty, Welles returned to the United States and with John Houseman founded the Mercury Theater in New York City, where he produced and starred in a series of productions, including *Macbeth* and *Julius Caesar*.

Welles began to act on radio concurrently "in order to pay the bills," as he put it. He played Lamont Cranston, aka *The SHADOW*, for two seasons and because of his successful stage productions was invited to produce a weekly, hour-long dramatic anthology series for radio, *The MERCURY THEATER OF THE AIR*. Adaptations of literature such as *Treasure Island*, *Les Miserables*, and *Dracula* were very successful, but Welles created a national sensation when he presented a radio-news-format adaptation of H. G. Wells's *The War of the Worlds*. Millions of listeners were convinced that the United States was actually being invaded by alien Martians.

Because of the monumental publicity generated by this broadcast, Welles was offered a contract by RKO Studios to produce, direct, and star in a film; the result was his motion-picture masterpiece, *Citizen Kane*. In the years that followed, Welles worked on and in several other films, including *The Magnificent Ambersons* (1942), *Jane Eyre* (1943), *Tomorrow Is Forever* (1945), *The Stranger* (1946), *Othello* (1951), *Moby Dick* (1956), *Compulsion* (1958), and *A Man for All Seasons* (1967); none of them ever achieved the recognition of his *Mercury Theater* and *Citizen Kane* successes. Welles continued on radio throughout the 1940s and 1950s, hosting and starring in the syndicated BLACK MUSEUM mystery-crime series, performing regularly on SUSPENSE, *America's Hour,* and *The* CAVALCADE OF AMERICA, and contributing to *The* COLUMBIA WORKSHOP series, which he had helped develop for CBS. He also starred in a syndicated radio series called *The* LIVES OF HARRY LIME, based on a character he played in the film *The Third Man* (1949). Harry Lime was the film's villain, albeit a lovable one, but Welles made him the hero of the radio show. During the last several years of his life, Welles continued directing and acting in films and on television spots and became a television-commercial spokesman for a wine company.

WENDY WARREN (AKA WENDY WARREN AND THE NEWS)

1947–1958   CBS   Mon.–Fri.   12 PM

Wendy Warren was a radio newswoman on this dramatic series, which presented 5 minutes of real news reported by actual newsman Douglas EDWARDS. The show followed with 10 minutes of daytime drama revolving around the off-microphone life of Wendy. Actress Florence FREEMAN played Wendy, and the regular cast included Les TREMAYNE, Peter Capell, Rod Hendrickson, Horace Braham, Lamont Johnson, Vera Allen, Anne BURR, Tess Sheehan, John RABY, Hugh James, and Meg Wylie. The program was directed by Don Wallace, Tom McDermott, Hoyt Allen, and Allan Fristoe and written by Frank Provo and John Picard. *Wendy Warren*'s announcer was Bill Flood. Sponsors included Maxwell House coffee, Instant Maxwell House coffee, Gaines dog food, Baker's coconut, Proctor and Gamble products, and Post's sugar crisp cereal.

WEVER, NED (1899–1984)

The radio voice of superhero detectives like Dick Tracy and Bulldog Drummond belonged to actor Ned Wever, who had a long and distinguished career as a leading man. Wever, in addition to starring on *The* ADVENTURES OF DICK TRACY and *The* ADVENTURES OF BULLDOG DRUMMOND, was heard as Alan Bishop on BETTY AND BOB, Jerry Miller on BIG SISTER, Peter Carver on LORA LAWTON, Jeff Spencer on TWO ON A CLUE, Colin Kirby on VALIANT LADY, Dr. Anthony Loring on YOUNG WIDDER BROWN, and numerous roles on the

TRUE CONFESSIONS series. Wever retired from show business shortly after radio dramas began to disappear from the airwaves in the late 1950s–early 1960s.

WHAT'S MY NAME?

1938–1939	Mutual	Fri.	8 PM
1939–1940	NBC Red	Sat.	7 PM
1940–1941	(Off the air)		
1941	NBC Red	Sun.	8:30 PM

Years before "What's My Line" became a popular game-panel show on television, radio had a similar half-hour show called *What's My Name?* Arlene FRANCIS, longtime panelist on "What's My Line," hosted this radio program. Her cohosts at different times were Wilbur "Budd" HULICK, Ward Wilson, and Carl Frank. Peter VAN STEEDEN and Harry SALTER conducted the orchestra. Contestants tried to guess the identity of a famous person's voice as they asked the hidden guest a series of questions. Guests included Jack BENNY, FIBBER MCGEE AND MOLLY, and Milton BERLE. The show was produced by Edward Byron. Ben Larsen directed the series. Harry VON ZELL and Ralph EDWARDS were the show's announcers. Sponsors included Philip Morris cigarettes, Sal Hapatica antacid, Oxydol detergent, and Fleischmann's yeast.

WHEN A GIRL MARRIES

1939–1941	CBS	Mon.–Fri.	12:15 PM
1941–1951	NBC	Mon.–Fri.	5 PM
1951–1953	ABC	Mon.–Fri.	11:15 AM
1953–1955	ABC	Mon.–Fri.	10:45 AM
1955–1957	ABC	Mon.–Fri.	10:30 AM

"*When A Girl Marries,* the tender, human story of young married love, is dedicated to everyone who has ever been in love," this program's opening stated. Perennial newlyweds Joan and Harry Davis, the leading characters on this 15-minute series, faced the usual problems of young married couples—financial adjustments, child rearing, and various involvements with their friends and relatives. Noel Mills first played Joan, followed by Mary Jane HIGBY, who remained until the series left the air. Harry was played by John RABY, Robert Haag, Whitfield Connor, and Lyle Sudrow. Also heard in regular supporting roles were Georgia Burke as Lillie the maid, child impersonator Dolores Gillen as the Davises' son Sammy, and Eunice Howard, John Kane, Joseph "Joe" Latham, Michael Fitzmaurice, Richard KOLLMAR, Staats COTSWORTH, Karl WEBER, Paul MCGRATH, Ed JEROME, Irene Winston, child impersonator Madeleine Pierce as Little Rudy Cameron, Joan Tetzel, Jone Allison, Toni Darnay, Bill Quinn, Marion Barney, Gertrude Warner, Ethel Owen, Helene Dumas, Maurice TARPLIN, King Calder, Peter Capell, Jack Arthur, Ethel Wilson, Anne

Francis, Rosemary RICE, Jeanette Dowling, Audrey Egan, and Anne BURR. Directors included Kenneth MACGREGOR, Maurice Lowell, Theodora Yates, Tom McDermott, Oliver Barbour, Olga Druce, Charles Fisher, Art Richards, Scott Farnworth, Warren Somerville, and Tom Baxter. The series was written by Elaine CARRINGTON and LeRoy Bailey. The show's theme was Drigo's "Serenade." The program's many announcers included Frank Gallop, Dennis King, George Anderson, Don Gardner, Charles STARK, Richard "Dick" Stark, Hugh James, and Wendell NILES. Sponsors included the Prudential Life Insurance Company, Calumet flour, Swans Down cake flour, Maxwell House coffee, Sure-jell gelatin, La France bleach, Baker's coconut, Carnation evaporated milk, Friskies dog food, Durkee's flavor enhancer, Air-wick room deodorant, and Nylast nasal spray.

WHISPER MAN, THE

1945–1946   Mutual   Sat.   9:30 PM, 11:30 AM, 8 PM

Actor Karl SWENSON and then Joseph CURTIN starred as soft-spoken narrator Max Chandler, called "the Whisper Man." A spin-off of such series as The MYSTERIOUS TRAVELER, The Whisper Man featured tales of crime that were solved by running characters on the series. Also featured were Fran CARLON as Chandler's girlfriend and partner in crime solving. The series, heard on the Mutual network, was produced by Dan SEYMOUR and directed by Anton Leader.

WHISPERING STREETS

1952–1953	ABC	Mon.–Fri.	10:30 AM
1953–1955	ABC	Mon.–Fri.	10:25 AM
1955–1957	ABC	Mon.–Fri.	10:45 AM
1957–1958	CBS	Mon.–Fri.	11:05 AM
1958–1960	CBS	Mon.–Fri.	1 PM

Celebrated motion-picture actress Bette Davis was the hostess of this 15-minute weekday drama series starring Anne SEYMOUR as Hope Winslow, a young woman trying to balance her social and business life and find happiness in a troubled world. Gertrude Warner and Cathy LEWIS were featured. George Walsh and Dan Cumberly announced the series, which was sponsored by General Mills flour and Toni home permanent. Davis's contribution to the program was prerecorded.

WHISTLER, THE

1942–1943	CBS	Sun.	8 PM
1943–1944	CBS	Sat.	8 PM
1944–1947	CBS	Mon.	8 PM
1947–1948	CBS	Wed.	8 PM
1948–1955	CBS	Sun.	9:30 PM

"I am the Whistler, and I know many things for I walk by night. I know many strange tales hidden in the hearts of men and women who have stepped into the shadows. Yes, I know the nameless terrors of which they dare not speak!" this crime anthology series began. A particular favorite of mystery-show fans, the Whistler even narrated—as he did on radio—several films, such as The Whistler, The Power of the Whistler, The Mysterious Intruder, and Return of the Whistler in the 1930s and 1940s.

Over the years, Bill Forman, Marvin MILLER, who also announced, and Everett Clark played the Whistler. Regularly heard were William CONRAD, Joan BANKS, Frank LOVEJOY, and Betty Lou GERSON. The show's theme music, an ascending series of wailing notes followed by the soulful whistling of the title character, was extremely difficult for most whistlers to master. The only person who was consistently able to whistle the two-octave theme music was Dorothy Roberts, who performed on the program for most of the years the series was on the air. The Whistler was directed by Sherman Marks and Sterling Tracy. Signal oil and the Household Finance Company were the longtime sponsors.

WHITEMAN, PAUL (1890–1967)

Orchestra leader Paul Whiteman was born in Denver, Colorado, where his father was Supervisor of Music for the Denver public schools. Paul learned to play the viola while in school. When World War I erupted, Whiteman enlisted in the Navy and directed a 40-piece Navy orchestra. It was while in the Navy that Whiteman began to experiment with popular music using syncopated rhythms, a major component of African-American music, though the music did not sound African. He called his new sound swing.

After the war, Whiteman went to Atlantic City, where he formed an orchestra that performed at the Ambassador Hotel. The RCA Victor Talking Machine Company asked Whiteman to make recordings of his innovative music for their company. His very first recording, "Whispering," sold more than 2 million copies, an unprecedented number for that time, and Whiteman became a national celebrity. He appeared in concerts around the country, most notably introducing George Gershwin's Rhapsody in Blue at Carnegie Hall in New York City. In addition to guest-starring on music-variety programs, Whiteman had several radio shows of his own and was a regular performer on the BURNS AND ALLEN program, The KRAFT MUSIC HALL as that program's first host, The Old Gold–Paul Whiteman Hour and The Philco Radio Hall of Fame, and many others that usually bore the title The PAUL WHITEMAN SHOW. Also featured in several films, most notably King of Jazz, in the early

1930s, Whiteman became a radio disc jockey for the American Broadcasting Company in 1947 and had a five-day-a-week show.

WICKER, IREENE (1902–1988)

For forty-five years, from 1930 until 1975, Quincy, Illinois-born singer-actress Ireene Wicker was one of radio's most successful children's show hostesses. Wicker was educated at the University of Florida and the University of Illinois and originally planned to be a teacher. Instead, she began a career in radio, working at WGN in Chicago in 1931, singing and reading stories to children on *The* SINGING LADY. The program was picked up by the NBC Blue network after only six months on local radio, and Wicker became known to young radio listeners as "the Singing Lady." Wicker's children's show was aired on network radio for more than twenty years before it became a local show on WNYC in New York City. Wicker was a star of the *Deadline Dramas* series, on which listeners submitted twenty-word situations that served as the basis for improvised stories acted out by Wicker, Joan BANKS, Frank LOVEJOY, Bob White, and others. She was also featured on JUDY AND JANE, PAINTED DREAMS, and TODAY'S CHILDREN. In the mid-1950s, Wicker won an Emmy award for her Golden Records recordings for children.

WIDMARK, RICHARD (1914–   )

Before his Hollywood career, Richard Widmark was a busy radio actor. Born in Sunrise, Minnesota, he attended Lake Forest College in Illinois and then taught speech and drama for two years before pursuing a career as a professional actor. His early successes included radio programs such as JOYCE JORDAN, GIRL INTERN, TRUE CONFESSIONS, BIG SISTER, GANGBUSTERS, *Home of the Brave*, MYSTERY THEATER, and INNER SANCTUM MYSTERIES. Widmark played the leading roles of Farrell on FRONT PAGE FARRELL and Albert on ETHEL AND ALBERT costarring Peg Lynch. His first film, *Kiss of Death* (1948), in which he played a cold-blooded psychopathic killer, was nothing less than a sensation and led to his being cast in subsequent films as a leading man. Widmark's films include *Panic in the Streets* (1950), *Pickup on South Street* (1950), *The Cobweb* (1955), *The Alamo* (1960), *Judgment at Nuremberg* (1961), *Murder on the Orient Express* (1974), and *Who Dares, Wins* (1982). He continues to be seen occasionally in films and television specials.

WIDMER, HARRIETTE KNOX (1893–1964)

Actress Harriette Widmer was born in Water Valley, Mississippi, and debuted on radio in 1930. The actress, a Caucasian, specialized in playing African-American

Harriette Widmer (NBC)

roles throughout the 1930s and 1940s, including the formidable Madame Queen on AMOS AND ANDY, the title role on AUNT JEMIMA, Mattie Blake on *The* CARTERS OF ELM STREET, Peggy on *Lonely Women,* and Beulah on *A* TALE OF TODAY. In addition, Widmer played character parts on AUNT JENNY'S REAL LIFE STORIES, BETTY AND BOB, *The* FIRST NIGHTER, FIBBER MCGEE AND MOLLY, and *The* COUPLE NEXT DOOR, and on dramatic anthologies such as *The* LUX RADIO THEATER and SCREEN GUILD PLAYERS throughout the 1930s, 1940s, and 1950s.

WILCOX, HARLOW (1900–1960)

Announcer Harlow Wilcox was born in Omaha, Nebraska, while his father and mother were appearing as musicians with the Ringling Brothers-Barnum and Bailey Circus. After attending college, Wilcox became an NBC staff announcer before becoming closely identified with the FIBBER MCGEE AND MOLLY program, which he announced for more than twenty years, and where he extolled the virtues of its longtime sponsor, Johnson's wax. Wilcox also announced BLONDIE, SUSPENSE, *The Old Gold*–DON AMECHE SHOW, ATTORNEY AT LAW, MYRT AND MARGE, *The* MAXWELL HOUSE COFFEE SHOW, AMOS AND ANDY, BABY SNOOKS, MYSTERY THEATER, *The* BEN BERNIE SHOW, TRUTH OR CONSEQUENCES, *The Frank Morgan Show,* FATHER KNOWS BEST, and *The* MAYOR OF THE TOWN.

WILD BILL HICKOK

1951–1952	Mutual	Sun.		7 PM & 4:30 PM
1952–1955	Mutual	Mon., Wed., Fri.	5:30 PM
1955–1956	Mutual	Sun.		5:30 PM

Because of the success of television's "Wild Bill Hickok" series in the early 1950s, the title character was given a half-hour radio series as well. Hickok tracked down outlaws, apprehended bank robbers, and played a heroic "lone ranger" character on the show. Television series stars Guy Madison and Andy Devine starred as Hickok, one of the West's most famous real-life characters, and his fictional sidekick, Jingles. Ken CARPENTER was the series' announcer. The director and writers of the radio series were uncredited. The series was sponsored by General Mills products.

WILLIAMS, FLORENCE (1910–   )

Actress Florence Williams was born in St. Louis, Missouri, and studied to become a professional pianist. Then, in her teens, she decided to become an actress. Williams played Sally Farrell on FRONT PAGE FARRELL the ever-patient, ever-loving wife Anna Cameron on the *Barry Cameron* series, and similar roles on *The* LIGHT OF THE WORLD and ROSES AND DRUMS. In addition to radio, Williams is active on stage: She played Alexandra in the New York production of Lillian Hellman's *The Little Foxes,* Alice in *You Can't Take It with You,* and other roles on Broadway and in regional theaters. In recent years, Williams has been featured in such plays as *The Belle of Amherst,* and *The Madwoman of Chaillot* in regional theaters mainly in New England.

WILLIE PIPER

| 1946–1947 | ABC | Wed. | 8:30 PM |
| 1947–1948 | ABC | Thurs. | 8:30 PM |

This half-hour situation-comedy series told of a young married couple, the Pipers, who lived in a small American town and experienced domestic problems such as financial setbacks, in-law friction, and the difficulties of child rearing. The young husband, Willie Piper, was played by Dick Nelson, and his wife, Martha, was played by Jean Gillespie. Stewart McIntosh played Willie's boss, Mr. Bissell. The *Willie Piper* program's announcer was Jack McCarthy. The series was sponsored by General Electric.

WILLSON, MEREDITH (1902–1984)

Before he became world-famous as the composer of Broadway musicals *The Music Man* and *The Unsinkable Molly Brown,* Iowa-born Meredith Willson was a music conductor on radio, probably best remembered as the cohost and orchestra leader on NBC's BIG SHOW, starring the irrepressible, deep-voiced actress Tallulah BANKHEAD. He always greeted the star with "Good evening, Miss Bankhead, sir." Willson was also music conductor for CAREFREE CARNIVAL, *Good News,* and MAXWELL HOUSE COFFEE TIME.

WILSON, DON (1901–1982)

Well known as Jack BENNY's announcer and comedic foil for more than forty years on *The* JACK BENNY SHOW, Lincoln, Nebraska–born Don Wilson also served as announcer on *The* TOMMY RIGGS AND BETTY LOU SHOW, and *The* KRAFT MUSIC HALL, as well as on numerous COMMAND PERFORMANCE broadcasts during World War II. Wilson, a regular on Benny's television series, was seen in *The Big Broadcast of 1944,* a stage production that toured the United States in the 1960s, as well as on other theatrical offerings.

WILSON, MARIE (Katherine Elizabeth White: 1916–1972)

Actress-comedienne Marie Wilson was born in Anaheim, California, and at age fifteen took a bus from Anaheim to Hollywood determined to become a film actress. She entered a beauty contest there, won it, and was named "Miss Pacific Fleet." As luck would have it, this led to a contract for her to appear in films and she was featured in movies—usually playing "dumb blondes"—such as in *Satan Meets a Lady* (1936), *Boy Meets Girl* (1940), and *Mr. Hobbs Takes a Vacation* (1962). In 1947, she became the star of the MY FRIEND IRMA situation-comedy radio series. On this show, Wilson played the naive, somewhat dim-witted but-always-lovable Irma Peterson. The actress also provided the voice for the cartoon character Penny on the series "Where's Huddles," and also starred on the TV as well as film versions of her hit radio series, *My Friend Irma.*

WINCHELL, WALTER (1898–1972)

Radio gossip–commentator Walter Winchell was born in New York City. As a young newspaperman in the 1920s, Winchell wrote a show-business-celebrity column for *The Vaudeville News,* reporting the more sensational items concerning celebrated people. This attracted considerable attention and led to his being asked to write a column for the prestigious *New York Daily Mirror* in 1925. Shortly thereafter, his writing was syndicated in newspapers throughout the United States, and Winchell became a national celebrity. In 1932 the columnist's fame increased when he was asked to host a celebrity gossip show on radio, and by the 1940s, Winchell was the highest paid gossip columnist in the world. His staccato vocal delivery on the air and the "Dit-dit-dit" of a teletype machine in between his "items" became his audio trademarks. In addition to his show-business and newspaper activities, Winchell also founded the Damon Runyon Fund for Cancer Research and became that organization's tireless champion.

See also WALTER WINCHELL SHOW, *The*.

WINKLER, BETTY (1915–   )

A three-time winner of *Radio-Mirror* magazine's reader's poll as "Best Actress on the Air," Betty Winkler was said to have had the "sweetest, most feminine voice on radio." For many years, Winkler, who was born in Berwick, Pennsylvania, and who studied acting at the Cleveland Playhouse, was an NBC staff actress in Chicago. She starred or was featured on GRAND HOTEL, *The* FIRST NIGHTER, FIBBER MCGEE AND MOLLY, LIGHTS OUT, WELCOME VALLEY, *The Frank Black Show,* and *Jamboree.* The actress was also heard on such dramatic anthologies as *The* CHICAGO THEATER OF THE AIR and CURTAIN TIME and played leading roles opposite Tyrone Power, Franchot Tone, Errol Flynn, and other celebrated actors on the KNICKER-BOCKER PLAYHOUSE series. Miss Winkler's credits also included Patricia Rogers on GIRL ALONE, Rosemary on ROSEMARY, Joyce on JOYCE JORDAN, M.D., and Rose Murphy on ABIE'S IRISH ROSE, as well as regular appearances on INNER SANCTUM MYSTERIES, THIS LIFE IS MINE, *A Thousand and One Wives,* BETTY AND BOB, and *The* O'NEILLS. In recent years, Miss Winkler has lectured at The New School of Social Research, where she taught courses in self-awareness. She is the author *Sensing: Letting Yourself Live.*

WINNER TAKE ALL

1946–1947	CBS	Mon.–Fri.	3:30 PM
1947–1948	CBS	Mon.–Fri.	4:30 PM
1948–1949	CBS	Mon.–Fri.	4:30 PM
		Sat.	9 PM

Bill CULLEN, Clayton "Bud" COLLYER, and Ward Wilson hosted this 15-minute quiz program, which was aired in the mid-1940s. Listeners whose phone numbers were selected by the show's producer from postcards mailed in to the show were given the opportunity to answer general-facts questions and win up to $1,000 in cash and merchandise. The series was directed by Frank Dodge, Mark Goodson, and Bill Todman (Goodson and Todman later produced many successful television quiz and panel shows). The show's announcers were Bern Bennett, Ward Wilson, and Bill Cullen. Lever brothers sponsored the program.

WINSOR, ROY (1912–1987)

Producer-director-writer Roy Winsor is credited with being one of the first people in broadcasting to produce a network daytime serial drama on radio. Born in Chicago, Illinois, Winsor graduated from Harvard University. He wrote mystery novels for a while and then directed the long-running MA PERKINS program on radio for twenty-seven years. Winsor also produced *Sky King, The* GOLDBERGS, KITTY KEENE, TRUE CONFESSIONS, and *Sergeant Square.* In the early 1960s, Winsor developed a serial daytime drama for television called "Search for Tomorrow," which became a longtime favorite of daytime television viewers. He also created "Faraway Hill," "These Are My Children," "Love of Life," and "Hawkins Falls" for daytime television. Winsor served as executive producer of such evening TV shows as "I Love Lucy," "My Little Margie" and "Have Gun, Will Travel."

WITCH'S TALE, THE

1934–1935	Mutual	Mon.	9 PM
1935–1936	Mutual	Tues.	10 PM
1936–1937	Mutual	Fri.	10 PM

When listeners tuned in to *The Witch's Tale* they heard the sound of howling wind, followed by a tower-clock bell tolling ominously in the distance. "*The Witch's Tale,*" the announcer said softly: "The fascination for the eerie . . . weird; blood-chilling tales told by Old Nancy of Salem, and Satan, the wise black cat. They're waiting, waiting for you now," he continued. The eccentric master of many mystery programs, Alonzo Dean COLE, was the creator, chief writer, and director of this series of scary tales. It featured a witch narrating each week's story, usually concerning ghosts, murdering psychopaths, or characters being trapped in supposedly inescapable situations. Nancy was initially played by Adelaide Fitz-Allen, then by teenage actress Miriam WOLFE, and finally by veteran character actress Martha Wentworth. Also heard regularly were Mark Smith, Marie Flynn, Jackson BECK and Don MACLAUGHLIN. In addition to Cole, Roger Bower directed the series. The show's theme music was "Orgie and the Spirits" by Leginski.

WOLFE, MIRIAM (1922–   )

Versatile character actress Miriam Wolfe was born in Brooklyn, New York, and made her professional acting debut reciting poems and reading stories on WGBS in New York when she was four years old. In her early teens, Wolfe played the ancient witch-narrator Old Nancy on Alonzo Dean COLE'S WITCH'S TALE succeeding the late Adelaide Fitz-Allen; Wolfe played this part for five years. The actress joined Nila MACK's

Miriam Wolfe (CBS)

repertory acting company on LET'S PRETEND in 1933, remaining until well into her adult years and playing wicked and wise queens, good and bad spirits, kind and cruel mothers and stepmothers, and countless spooky witches. Wolfe was heard regularly on Fletcher Markle's STUDIO ONE and FORD THEATER, as well as on *The* AMERICAN SCHOOL OF THE AIR, *Mystery Hall*, CASEY CRIME PHOTOGRAPHER, SUSPENSE, and a host of soap operas. On POPEYE THE SAILOR, she played both Olive Oyle and the Sea Hag for several seasons. In the 1950s, the actress became a regular on *The Raeburn and Finch Comedy Hour* and was featured in the U.S. Army production of *So Proudly We Hail* starring film and stage actor Lee Tracy. In 1952, as a regular on the dramatic anthology STUDIO ONE TV, Wolfe played the Virgin Mary in his production of the medieval passion play, "The Nativity." In the late 1950s, Wolfe moved to Canada and became active as a performer, writer, and director with the CANADIAN BROADCASTING CORPORATION. She created and starred on a CBC children's series, *Miss Switch*, playing all the roles on that show, and was also featured on many CBC commercials, comedy hours, and dramas, as well as making appearances on Canadian televi-

sion. In recent years, Miriam Wolfe has mainly concentrated on writing and teaching, having developed her own method of using theater techniques to assuage personality disorders. Her book *The Sounds of English* is currently being used by medical students at the University of Toronto to perfect their speech projection and communication skills.

WOMAN FROM NOWHERE

See IRENE RICH DRAMAS.

WOMAN IN MY HOUSE

1951–1952	NBC	Mon.–Fri.	1:45 PM
1952–1954	NBC	Mon.–Fri.	4:45 PM
1954–1955	NBC	Mon.–Fri.	5 PM
1955–1956	NBC	Mon.–Fri.	4:45 PM
1956–1957	NBC	Mon.–Fri.	2:30 PM
1957–1959	NBC	Mon.–Fri.	3:30 PM

This 15-minute drama series originated on the West Coast and starred Forrest Lewis as James Carter, Janet Scott as his wife, Jessie, Les TREMAYNE as James's brother Jeff, and Peggy Webber, Anne Whitfield, and Shirley MITCHELL as Jeff's wife, Sandy. Alice REINHEART was also heard as the trouble-making vamp Virginia Carter; Bill Idelson as Clay Carter; and Jeff Silver as Peter Carter. The series focused on the problems of two very different brothers—one a successful businessman and the other an impractical, often unemployed dreamer. Charles Lyon was the show's announcer. Sponsors included Sweetheart soap, Blu White, Alka Seltzer antacid, One-A-Day vitamins, Tabsin pain reliever, Listerine antiseptic, and Quaker and Mother's oats cereals.

WOMAN IN WHITE, THE

1938–1940	NBC Red	Mon.–Fri.	10:45 AM
1940–1942	CBS	Mon.–Fri.	1:15 PM
1942–1944	(Off the air)		
1944–1946	NBC	Mon.–Fri.	2:30 PM
1946–1948	NBC	Mon.–Fri.	2:15 PM

The plot of *The Woman in White* centered around a kind-hearted, caring nurse named Karen Adams Harding, who worked in a big city hospital. The difficulty of trying to balance a busy professional life and take care of her family at home was the focus of the story. Luise Barclay, Betty Ruth Smith, Betty Lou GERSON, and Peggy Knudsen played Karen. Willard Farnum and Harry Elders played Karen's husband, John. Also heard in regular supporting roles were Irene Winston, Phil Lord, Louise Fitch, Henrietta Tedro, David GOTHARD, Marvin MILLER, Frank Behrens, Kathryn Card, Leo Curley, Toni Gilman, Constance Crowder, Maurice Copeland, Gail Henshaw, Karl WEBER, Sarajane Wells, Lesley Woods, Barbara LUDDY,

Ian Keith, Les DAMON, Jeanne Juvelier, Eddie Firestone, Jr., Virginia Clark, Herb Nelson, Janet Logan, Les TREMAYNE, and Beverly Taylor. Louis Roen was the show's announcer. The program was directed by Al Urich, H. K. Painter, Carl Wester, Howard Keegan, Robin Black, and Owen Vinson and written by Irna PHILLIPS for many years. Pillsbury flour, Oxydol detergent, Camay soap, and Betty Crocker sponsored the series. The show's theme song was "Interlude" by Lucas.

WOMAN OF AMERICA, A

| 1943–1944 | NBC | Mon.–Fri. | 10:45 PM |
| 1944–1945 | NBC | Mon.–Fri. | 3 PM |

This 15-minute drama series was originally set in the Old West but changed locales and centuries midway through the program's run to a modern big-city newspaper office because the show's producers believed that more people would be interested in a modern, city drama than in one set in the past. The series' heroine, Prudence Dane was first played by Anne SEYMOUR and then when the story became modern by Florence FREEMAN. James Monks was the wagonmaster in the original version; Jackson Beck, Larry Robinson, Nancy Douglas, Louise Larabee, Helene Dumas, Bartlett "Bart" Robinson, Forrest Lewis, and Fran CARLON, were also regularly heard. *A Woman of America* was produced by Don Cope and written by Della West Decker and Doria Folliot. The program's announcer was Frank Gallop. Ivory Snow sponsored the series.

WOMAN OF COURAGE, A

| 1940–1942 | CBS | Mon.–Fri. | 10:45 AM |

A Woman of Courage told of a wife and mother who knew that "if you believe you can win, nothing in life will defeat you . . . and that what is right . . . will be!" The 15-minute program concerned a middle-class family living in a Midwestern state during the pre–World War II Depression years. Selena Royle and then Alice FROST played Martha Jackson, and Albert Hecht played her husband, Jim. Joan Tetzel, Larry Robinson, and Tess Sheehan played their children. In supporting roles were Enid Markey, Carl Eastman, Bill Quinn, Horace Braham, and Doro Merande. John Allen Wolfe announced the series. Maurice Lowell and Theodora Yates directed the program. The show's sponsors were Octagon soap and Crystal White soap. "Look for the Silver Lining" was the program's theme song.

WONS, TONY (1891–1965)

Actor-poet-philosopher Tony Wons had a pleasant, romantic voice that made him particularly favored

Tony Wons (NBC)

among female listeners in the 1930s and 1940s. Offering his sentimental poetry readings and homespun philosophically romantic homilies, Wons starred on TONY WONS SCRAPBOOK for CBS and then hosted *The House by the Side of the Road.* As he read his poems or spoke softly to his listeners, Wons was accompanied on the organ by Ann Leaf.

WOODS, DONALD (1904–   )

Donald Woods was a handsome Hollywood leading man who appeared in such films as *Anna Kerenina* (1935), *Forgotten Girls* (1940), *Love, Honor, and Oh, Baby* (1941), *I Was a Prisoner on Devil's Island* (1941), *Watch on the Rhine* (1943), *Wonder Man* (1945), *Barbary Pirate* (1949), *Undercover Agent* (1954), and *Thirteen Ghosts* (1960). Woods, who was born in Brandon, Manitoba, Canada, had an attractive-sounding baritone voice and he was a major reason THOSE WE LOVE became so popular. Woods played the role of Dr. Leslie Foster. In addition to *Those We Love,* Woods was also featured on *The* ADVENTURES OF MAISIE, starring film star Ann Sothern. On television, Woods was seen on the "Hotel Cosmopolitan" series.

WOOLLCOTT, ALEXANDER (1887–1943)

Acid-tongued critic-columnist and social commentator Alexander Woollcott was born in Phalanx, New

Jersey, and attended Hamilton College. He was the model for cantakerous Sheridan Whiteside, the major character in the hit stage play and film *The Man Who Came to Dinner*. Woollcott had a radio show in the 1930s, *The* TOWN CRIER. Prior to that, he was drama critic for *The New York Times* from 1914 until 1922, for *The World* from 1925 until 1928, and finally for *The New York Herald* in 1932. On his radio program, Woollcott gave reports about the comings-and-goings of his numerous celebrity friends, read stories to his listeners, and interviewed various guests, including stage actress Katherine Cornell, comedian Groucho Marx, and movie legend Jimmy Durante. Because his newspaper column was read by millions, Woollcott wielded enormous power in the entertainment industry, as well as in social and political circles. His personal and idiosyncratic criticisms and caustic comments, often a mixture of sentiment and acrimony, could either "make-or-break" a play, film, or celebrity.

WRITERS AND COMPANY

1990–present   CBC   Sun.   1:05 PM

On this CANADIAN BROADCASTING CORPORATION program, hostess Eleanor Wachtel gives in-depth information about writers and writing. She also interviews playwrights, poets, and novelists and reads selections from their works. Established authors Victoria Glendenning, J. M. Cortez, Amy Tan, Stephen Jay Gould, John Sayles, Angela Carter, Mordecai Rickles, Amos Oz, Peter Ackroyd, and Fay Walden have appeared on this program, as have newcomers to the literary world. The series is produced by Sandra Rabinovitch for CBC.

WYNN, ED (ISAIAH EDWIN LEOPOLD: 1887–1966)

Called "the Perfect Fool" when he appeared on the stage because of his zany costumes, comic lisp, and slapstick humor, comedian Ed Wynn became one of radio's earliest stars. When he came to radio, in fact, he was already one of vaudeville's and Broadway's major stars. Because of this, his earliest broadcasts were readings of entire Broadway shows. Heard on various radio programs, he is perhaps best remembered as the Texaco fire chief on the TEXACO STAR THEATER variety-show series. There, Wynn began to innovate with comic "sound," utilizing kazoos, cymbol crashes, and snaps and pops that were later used routinely throughout the medium. He was also the first radio comedian to realize the effectiveness of broadcasting his show in front of a live studio audience, thereby taking full advantage of the sound of

Milton Berle and Ed "the Perfect Fool" Wynn (NBC)

an audience's laughter to enhance listener enjoyment of a comedy show at home. At one time in the early 1930s, Wynn was so popular that he formed his own radio network, WNEW (the *EW* standing for *Ed Wynn*), in New York City. Although he purchased several other small stations around the country, the company failed because it could not compete with the existing network giants, NBC and CBS. When television replaced radio, Wynn returned to acting and enjoyed success as a serious actor on dramatic anthology shows such as "Studio One," "Playhouse 90," and "Kraft TV Theater." It is in films, however, that Wynn really regained the fame he had previously known in radio. During the late 1950s and throughout the 1960s, he appeared in such films as *Marjorie Morningstar* (1958), *The Diary of Anne Frank* (1959), *The Absent-Minded Professor* (1960), and *The Greatest Story Ever Told* (1965), and he became one of Hollywood's most sought-after character actors.

See also ED WYNN SHOW, *The*.

WYNN, KEENAN (1916–1986)

The son of actor-comedian Ed Wynn, Keenan Wynn, like his father, Ed, had a successful acting career on radio and television, as well as in films. Wynn was born in New York City and attended St. John's University. In his teens, he first performed on radio, featured on such programs as *The* AMAZING MR. SMITH (as Gregory Mr. Smith), *The* GOLDBERGS, and *The* SHADOW. Wynn also had a busy motion-picture career and was seen in *See Here Private Hargrove* (1944), *Kiss Me, Kate* (1953), *The Man in the Grey Flannel Suit* (1956), *A Hole in the Head* (1959), *Dr. Strangelove* (1964), and *The War Wagon* (1967). He was also a regular performer on television dramatic anthologies "Playhouse 90," "Studio One," "The Hallmark Hall of Fame," and "The Kraft Theater."

X MINUS ONE
See DIMENSION X.

YARBOROUGH, BARTON (1912–1951)

Actor Barton Yarborough, born in Goldthwaite, Texas, had one of radio's most distinctive voices, although it was somewhat lethargic-sounding and hesitant. Yarborough played Clifford Barbour, Claudia's twin, on ONE MAN'S FAMILY and "Doc" Long on the adventure-detective program I LOVE A MYSTERY. The actor was also heard on *The* JACK BENNY SHOW, HOLLYWOOD STAR TIME, BLUE RIBBON TOWN, *The* SILVER THEATER, *The* LUX RADIO THEATER, and most notably on DRAGNET, playing Joe Friday's original sidekick-partner, Sergeant Ben Romero. During his career in show business, Yarborough was also very active in the theater and appeared in more than 200 plays in various regional theaters.

YOU ARE THERE (AKA CBS IS THERE)

1947–1949	CBS	Sun.	2:30 PM
1949–1950	ABC	Wed.	9:20 PM

Taking its lead from Orson Welles's MERCURY THEATER OF THE AIR's "War of the Worlds" broadcast—which used an "on-the-spot" news-report style to make listeners feel as if what they were hearing was actually taking place—CBS developed a series of half-hour radio plays featuring actual news reporters and commentators. The show dramatized such historical happenings as *the Pilgrims landing on Plymouth Rock, the Signing of the Magna Carta, the destruction of Pompeii and the eruption of Mount Vesuvius, the Salem Witch Trials,* and so on. The series was created by Goodman Ace and directed by Robert Lewis Shayon. CBS newsmen Don Hollenbeck, Walter CRONKITE, Douglas EDWARDS, and John DALY, familiar announcers such as Ken ROBERTS, and actors such as Guy Sorel, Martin

GABEL, Joan Alexander, and Robert DRYDEN made people feel as if they were indeed hearing live coverage of important historical events. Also heard on the series at various times were newsmen Quincy Howe and Robert TROUT, as well as actors Ted Osbourne, Ronald LISS, Jack GRIMES, Court Benson, Bill LIPTON, John GIBSON, Reese Taylor, Leon JANNEY, Joseph Bell, Ralph Camarge, Guy Repp, Joe De Santis, Clayton "Bud" COLLYER, Santos ORTEGA, Joe JULIAN, Bob Hastings, Mason ADAMS, Raymond Edward JOHNSON, Luis VAN ROOTEN, Staats COTSWORTH, Wendell Holmes, Mandel KRAMER, and John LARKIN. The scripts were written by Irve Tunick, Michael Sklar, and Joseph Liss, and the sound effects were supervised by Jim Rogen. Stu Metz and Art Hannes announced the series, which was sustained by CBS.

YOU BET YOUR LIFE

1948–1949	ABC	Mon.	8 PM
1949–1950	ABC	Wed.	9:30 PM
1950–1951	CBS	Wed.	9 PM
1951–1956	NBC	Wed.	9 PM
1956–1959	NBC	Mon.	8:05 PM

Before becoming a popular television game show, *You Bet Your Life* was a half-hour radio program. The radio series, like the television show, starred movie and stage comedian Groucho MARX as its host. Marx interviewed contestants and then asked them relatively simple questions, such as "How many people does it take to play a singles tennis match?" The prequestion interviews were always hilarious and filled with Marx's droll, *double entendre* quips, such as, "Is that a dress you're wearing, or have I just walked into the ladies' locker room?" If, during the interviews, the contestants mentioned "the secret woid" which the audience had been given at the beginning of the show, a toy duck wearing this word around its neck would fall down in front of the contestant (as it did on television) and the contestant would win a special cash prize. Marx's longtime announcer and foil on the program was George Fennman. Jack Slattery also served as announcer on the show for a short time. The series featured Billy May and his Orchestra, which played various musical bridges as well as the show's theme song, "Hooray for Captain Spaulding." John Guedel, Harfield Weedin, and Bob Dwan produced and directed the series. Sponsors included Elgin American watches, De Soto-Plymouth automobiles, White Rain shampoo, Prom home permanent, Tame Creme Rinse, Toni home permanent, and Pabst Blue Ribbon beer.

YOUNG, CARLTON (1906–1971)

Actor Carlton Young was born in Westfield, New York, studied drama at Carnegie Tech, and was first heard on radio in 1935. He became one of that medium's most active leading men, starring in the title roles on The COUNT OF MONTE CRISTO, The ADVENTURES OF ELLERY QUEEN, and FRONT PAGE FARRELL; he also played Dr. Owen Craig on CAROL KENNEDY'S RO-MANCE, Dr. Robby Clark on HILLTOP HOUSE, Winfield Craig on LIFE BEGINS AT EIGHTY, Bill Jenkins on OUR GAL SUNDAY, Kirk Roder on PORTIA FACES LIFE, Bill Cummings on SECOND HUSBAND, Bryn's brother on SOCIETY GIRL, Dick Grosvenor on STELLA DALLAS, and Bill Mears on TROUBLE HOUSE.

YOUNG DR. MALONE

1939–1940	NBC Blue	Mon.–Fri.	2 PM
1940–1944	CBS	Mon.–Fri.	2 PM
1944–1945	CBS	Mon.–Fri.	2:30 PM
1945–1952	CBS	Mon.–Fri.	1:30 PM
1952–1953	NBC	Mon.–Fri.	9:30 AM
	CBS	Mon.–Fri.	1:30 PM
1953–1960	CBS	Mon.–Fri.	1:30 PM

Young Dr. Malone was both a radio and a television drama series. For a time, it was simulcast on radio and television for 15 minutes each weekday. Jerry Malone was a young doctor who worked at "The Three Oaks Medical Center." With his ever-patient, ever-loving wife, Ann, at his side, Dr. Malone faced professional and personal problems that ranged from having to deal with a patient's death to helping a friend through a difficult financial crisis. Heard on the radio series were Alan BUNCE, Carl Frank, Charles Irving, and Sandy Becker as Jerry Malone, and Elizabeth Reller and Barbara Weeks as Ann. Also heard playing regular supporting roles were Richard Coogan, Franc (pronounced "France") Hale, Eunice How-

ard, Billy Redfield, Joy Terry, Tess Sheehan, Ethel Everett, Bartlett "Bart" Robinson, Evelyn Varden, William Podmore, William J. Smith, Tony Barrett, Robert Haag, Nancy Coleman, Isabel Elsom, Tommy Hughes, Jean COLBERT, James Van Dyk, Helene Dumas, Amanda RANDOLPH, Elspeth ERIC, Ian Martin, Ray Hedge, Paul MCGRATH, Ethel Wilson, Joan Alexander, Gertrude Warner, Berry Kroeger, Jone Allison, Les DAMON, Rosemary RICE, Vera Allen, Joan Lazer, and Bill LIPTON. Young Dr. Malone was produced by Basil Loughrane, Dave Lesan, and Minerva Ellis and directed by Walter Gorman, Cyril Ambrister, Maurice Lowell, Lindsey MacHarrie, Stanley Davis, Fred Weihe, Theodroa Yates, and Ira Ashley. Ron Rawson and Ted Pearson were the program's announcers. Sponsors included Post Toasties cereal, Huskies dog food, Crisco shortening, Campana skin cream, Scott paper, Drene shampoo, Joy dishwashing liquid, Sta-Puf fabric softener, Dr. Caldwell's Senna Laxative, and 4-Way cold tablets.

YOUNG WIDDER BROWN

1938–1939	NBC Red	Mon.–Fri.	11:30 AM
1939–1942	NBC Red	Mon.–Fri.	4:45 PM
1942–1951	NBC	Mon.–Fri.	4:45 PM
1951–1955	NBC	Mon.–Fri.	4:30 PM
1955–1956	NBC	Mon.–Fri.	4:15 PM

"Young Widder Brown is the story of the age-old conflict between a mother's duty and a woman's heart," began this 15-minute series. Then the theme music "In the Gloaming" and later "Wonderful One" swelled dramatically. The story centered around Ellen Brown, a young widow who ran a tea room and later a gift shop in the local hospital, where her "significant other" worked as a doctor. The problems she had trying to start a new life and career were the focus of the program. Florence FREEMAN played Ellen the entire time the program was on the air, and Ned Wever played her boyfriend, Dr. Anthony Loring. Also heard on the series were Marilyn Erskine as Jane Brown, Ellen's daughter; and Tommy Donnelly as Mark, her son. Agnes Young, James "Jimmy" McCallion, Alice Yourman, Clayton "Bud" COLLYER, Jack McBryde, Florence Malone, Robert Haag, Helen Shields, Louis Hall, Irene Hubbard, Toni Gilman, Kay Strozzi, House JAMESON, Frank LOVEJOY, Joan Tompkins, Ethel Intropidi, Joy Hathaway, Arline Blackburn, and Althena Lorde were featured in the supporting cast. The series was produced by Frank and Anne HUMMERT, directed by Martha Atwell, Ed Slattery, and Richard Leonard, and written for many years by Elizabeth Todd and David Davidson. George Ansbro was the program's announcer. The series was sponsored by Sealtest dairy products, Sterling drugs, Phillips Milk of Magnesia antacid, Energine vitamin supplement, Bayer aspirin, Haley M-O antacid, Double Danderine shampoo, Prom home permanent, and White Rain shampoo.

YOUR FAMILY AND MINE

1938–1939	NBC Red	Mon.–Fri.	5:30 PM
1939–1940	CBS	Mon.–Fri.	2:30 PM

Produced by Henry Souvine and directed by Larry Hammond and Harry McGee, the 15-minute drama *Your Family and Mine* starred Raymond Edward JOHNSON as Woody Marshall and Templeton Fox as Claudia Foster. Also featured were Joan Tompkins, William "Bill" ADAMS, Lucille WALL, and Bill LIPTON as members of the Wilbur Family, and Francesca Lenni, Joy Terry, and Maurice Wells as the Putnam family. Also heard on the series regularly were Carl Frank, Jack "Jackie" Jordan, Arthur Maitland, Parker FENNELLY, Peter DONALD, Ruth Yorke, Frank LOVEJOY, Morris Carnovsky, Bill Quinn, and George COULOURIS. Ford BOND and Irene Hubbard were the program's announcers. Clyde North wrote many of the show's scripts. The series was sponsored by Sealtest dairy products.

YOUR HIT PARADE

1935–1936	NBC	Sat.	8 PM
1936–1937	NBC Red	Wed.	10 PM
	CBS	Sat.	10 PM
1937–1938	CBS	Sat.	10 PM
1938–1947	CBS	Sat.	9 PM
1947–1951	NBC	Sat.	9 PM
1951–1952	NBC	Sat.	8 PM
1952–1953	NBC	Fri.	8 PM
1953–1955	(Off the air)		
1955–1956	CBS	Sat.	10:30 PM

The half-hour weekly *Your Hit Parade* program presented the top ten, best-selling song hits of the week, as well as occasional hits from the past, sung by some of the most famous singers of the day: Buddy CLARK, Frank SINATRA, Joan EDWARDS, Georgia Gibbs, Bea Wain, Lawrence Tibbett, Eileen Wilson, Bonnie BAKER, Dinah SHORE, Andy Russell, Doris Day, Lanny ROSS, Kay Thompson, Marie Greene, Beryl Davis, Georgia Gibbs, Jeff Clark, Eileen Farrell, and others starred on the program. The *Your Hit Parade* orchestra was led by Al GOODMAN, Freddie Rich, Lennie Hayton, Johnny Green, Richard Himber, Ray Sinatra, Axel STORDAHL,

Orrin TUCKER, Harry SOSNICK, Raymond Scott, Peter VAN STEEDEN, Leo Reisman, Mark Warnow, and Carl Hoff. Also featured as frequent guests were Fred Astaire, organist Ethel Smith, the Lyn Murray Singers, and the Ken Lane Chorus. In 1938, film comedian W. C. Fields was the program's weekly star, and during that time more comedy than music was presented. Appearing with Fields in various sketches were Hanley STAFFORD, Walter TETLEY, and Elvia ALLMAN. Andre BARUCH was the show's longest-lasting announcer and was actually the host of the show for ten years. Also announcing were Martin Block, Del SHARBUTT, Kenny DELMAR, and Basil Ruysdael. The series was directed for most of its years by Lee Strahorn. The show's theme songs were "This Is Your Lucky Day" and "Happy Days Are Here Again." The program was sponsored by Lucky Strike and Herbert Tareyton cigarettes. "Your Hit Parade" became one of television's most successful music programs as early as the late 1940s and remained on the air for many years.

YOURS TRULY, JOHNNY DOLLAR

1949–1950	CBS	Fri.	10:30 PM
1950–1951	CBS	Tues.	9:30 PM
1951–1952	CBS	Wed.	9 PM
1952–1954	CBS	Tues.	9 PM
1954–1956	CBS	Mon.–Fri.	8:15 PM
1956–1957	CBS	Sun.	5 PM
1957–1960	CBS	Sun.	5:05 PM
1960–1962	CBS	Sun.	6:10 PM

No fewer than six actors played Johnny Dollar, a private eye who tracked down people's missing relatives and solved murders and other crimes. Charles Russell was the first Johnny Dollar, an "insurance investigator with the action-packed expense account." Russell was followed by Edmond O'Brien, John Lund, Bob BAILEY, Bob READICK, and finally Mandel KRAMER. The series always ended with Dollar itemizing his expenses and then signing off his report to his client with "Yours Truly, Johnny Dollar." Jack Johnstone produced and directed the series, which was also directed by Jaime Del Valle. Announcers on the program included Charles Lyon, Roy Rowen, and Art Hannes. Sponsoring the series were Wrigley's gum, 7-Up soft drink, No-Doz stimulant, Sinclair oil, Marlboro and Philip Morris Commanders, Kent, and Newport cigarettes, and Mentholatum Deep Heating cream.

ZIEGFELD FOLLIES OF THE AIR

1932	CBS	Sun.	10:30 PM
1936	CBS	Sat.	8 PM

Although it is known that there were several attempts to bring Broadway's successful stage extravaganza *The Ziegfeld Follies* to radio, the last and perhaps most successful radio version of the show was sponsored by Palmolive and was heard on Saturday evenings beginning in 1936. It featured Al GOODMAN's Orchestra and occasional dramatic sketches as well. John Paul KING was the show's announcer. Many of the performers who had gained popularity in Florenz Ziegfeld's celebrated stage shows were featured. The earlier shows featured Fanny BRICE, Will ROGERS, Billie BURKE (Ziegfeld's wife), Jack PEARL, Eddie CANTOR, Marilyn Miller, and other Follies stars. Theater personality Eddie Dowling hosted the series. Palmolive soap and Chrysler automobiles sponsored it.

Appendix A
Chronology of Radio Events in the United States

1864   James C. Maxwell predicted the existence of electromagnetic waves that travel at the speed of light.

1880s   Henreich Hertz proved Maxwell's theory.

1895   Guglielmo Marconi became the first person to send radio communication signals through the air.

1906   Reginald A. Fessanden broadcasted voice via radio waves.

1909   Passengers on the SS *Republic* were saved in the first sea rescue using radio.

1918   Edward Armstrong developed the superheterodyne circuit.

1919   Woodrow Wilson became the first U.S. president to give a radio broadcast from a ship during World War I to troops on other vessels.

1919   The Radio Corporation of America was founded.

1920   Stations WWJ of Detroit and KDKA of Pittsburgh made the first regular commercial broadcasts.

1920   Westinghouse-owned radio station KDKA began regularly scheduled broadcasts.

1921   RCA broadcasted a sporting event for the first time.

1922   William S. Paley bought several small, local radio stations.

1923   The *A&P Gypsies* program began broadcasts.

1925   The first broadcast of *The Grand Ole Opry* program was heard.

1926   RCA set up the National Broadcasting Company specifically to conduct the company's radio activities. Father Coughlin delivered his first radio broadcast.

1927   The Columbia Broadcasting System was formed by William S. Paley.

1928   The first *Amos and Andy* radio program was presented.

1929   *The Goldbergs* series went on the air.

1931   *The American Album of Familiar Music's* program was heard for the first time. Singer Bing Crosby's first radio broadcast was heard. *Lum and Abner* went on the air.

1932   Comedians Jack Benny and Fred Allen made their debuts on shows of their own. Radio's longest-running family drama serial, *One Man's Family,* made its debut on NBC.

1933   *The Breakfast Club* went on the air. *Jack Armstrong, All American Boy* children's adventure serial was first heard. The first *Lone Ranger* program was presented.

1934   The Mutual Broadcasting System was formed. Bob Hope first broadcasted on the NBC Blue network. The long-running *Kraft Music Hall* variety program went on the air. The first production of the *Let's Pretend* children's program was heard. The first *Shadow* broadcast was transmitted.

1935   The first broadcast of the *Fibber McGee and Molly* program was presented.

1936   Edgar Bergen and Charlie McCarthy appeared on *The Chase and Sanborn Hour* for the first time. The *Gangbusters* (called *G-Men*) program went on the air. Singer Kate Smith was heard on national radio for the first time on *The A&P Bandwagon* program. The first broadcast of *The Lux Radio Theater* was heard.

1937   Herb Morrison reported the *Hindenberg* disaster "live," as it was happening on radio.

1938   Edward R. Murrow began broadcasting nightly news from London during the Nazi bombing raids on that city. The daytime serial drama series *The Guiding Light,* which can still be seen on television, was first heard on radio. The famous "Martian invasion" broadcast, "The War of the Worlds," was presented on *The Mercury Theater on the Air* series.

1939   Bill Stern's long-running *Colgate Sports Newsreel's* show made its radio debut. The first broadcast of Carlton E. Morse's *I Love a Mystery* series was heard.

1941   The Federal Communications Commission authorized FM experimentation.

1943   The beginning of what became the American Broadcasting Company was formed as NBC was forced by the FCC to sell one of its two networks.

1945   Mayor Fiorello LaGuardia read the Sunday comics ("the funny papers") to children during a newspaper strike in New York City.

1947   Scientists at Bell Telephone Laboratories developed the transistor.

1953   Paramount Theaters merged with the American Broadcasting Company.

1960   John F. Kennedy and Richard Nixon held the first radio and TV debates between two presidential candidates.

1961   Soviet space officials held radio talks with cosmonaut Yuri Gagarin from Earth to space.

1969   Radio signals were picked up on Earth coming from the astronauts who landed on the moon for the first time.

1970   National Public Radio was founded.

1974   CBS and Himan Brown placed *The CBS Mystery Theater* in syndication.

1978   *The Larry King Show* was first aired in syndication in various cities around the country.

1982   AM radio stations in the United States began to broadcast in stereo.

1986   General Electric acquired RCA and its NBC radio and TV networks. *The Howard Stern Show* was first simulcast in New York and Philadelphia, and his syndicated program schedule began.

1988   *The Rush Limbaugh Show,* a nationally syndicated program, was launched.

1994   The Disney Company and Time/Warner Corporation began negotiations to acquire either CBS or NBC.

Appendix B
Chronology of Radio Events in Canada

1901 Marconi's transatlantic wireless signal was sent from Cornwall, England, to Newfoundland, Canada.

1913 The Canadian Radio Telegraph Act included "radiotelephony transmission" of voice in its legislative rules and regulations.

1919 The first broadcasting license was issued in Canada to Marconi station XWA in Montreal.

1924 Canadian National radio began to open stations of its own and to lease others.

1927 The first regularly scheduled network service in Canada, linking CN stations in Montreal and Ottawa, was established.

1930 The Canadian Radio League was organized.

1932 The first Parliamentary Committee of Broadcasting was formed.
The Canadian Radio Broadcasting Act was passed, providing for establishment of the Canadian Radio Broadcasting Commission.

1936 The Canadian Broadcasting Corporation (CBC) was established and took over CRBC (Canadian Railroad Broadcasting) facilities.

1939 A declaration of war was broadcast to the public, and Canada entered World War II.

1941 The formal CBC News Service formally began.

1942 The first experimental national school broadcasts were presented.

1944 A second English-language network, the Dominion Network, was established.
The Stage dramatic anthology series was first heard.

1945 The CBC International Service officially began.

1949 The first episode of *Wednesday Night on CBC* was heard.

1952 The Canadian television service began.

1955 A Royal Commission of Broadcasting was appointed.

1967 The Canadian Centennial Year. Some 1500 hours of special programming on CBC radio and television were offered to the Canadian public.

1968 All-night music and news programming on CBC radio began.

1970 The French Regional Production Centre opened in Moncton.

1974 CBC discontinued the use of radio commercials.

1975 CBC mono radio was available to 99 percent of the population.

1983 French and English marketing were consolidated as CBC Enterprises/Les Entreprises Radio-Canada.

1984 CBC was host broadcaster for a twelve-day papal visit.

1986 CBC's 50th-anniversary events included the issue of commemorative postage stamp.

Appendix C
Radio Show Sponsors

Companies that sponsored radio programs during radio's golden years often had their products become inextricably identified with a particular show. Below is a list of well-known products and the shows from the 1920s until the late 1950s, when individually sponsored national network shows virtually disappeared from the airwaves.

Alka Seltzer: *Lum & Abner, National Barn Dance, Quiz Kids*
American Assoc. of Railroads: *Railroad Hour*
American Dairy Association: *Bob Hope Show*
American Meat: *Life of Riley*
Anacin: *Easy Aces, Ellery Queen, Front Page Farrell*
Atlantic oil: *Bob Hope Show*
Autolite: *Suspense*
Bayer aspirin: *Big Town*
Blatz beer: *Duffy's Tavern*
Blue coal: *Shadow*
Bond bread: *Lone Ranger*
Bristol & Myers: *Mr. District Attorney*
Bromoseltzer: *Ellery Queen, Sherlock Holmes*
Budweiser beer: *Bill Stern's Sports Newsreel*
Buster Brown shoes: *Buster Brown Gang*
Camay soap: *Pepper Young's Family*
Camel cigarettes: *Abbott & Costello Show, Blondie, Bob Hope Show, Eddie Cantor Show*
Campana Balm: *First Nighter*
Campbell's soups: *Burns & Allen, Grand Central Station, Mercury Theater (Campbell Playhouse)*
Canada Dry: *Jack Benny Show*
Carter's Little Liver Pills: *Inner Sanctum Mysteries*
Chase & Sanborn coffee: *Chase & Sanborn Hour (Edgar Bergen & Charlie McCarthy Show), Eddie Cantor Show, Original Amateur Hour*
Chesterfield cigarettes: *Bing Crosby Show, Burns & Allen, Dragnet, Gunsmoke, Jack Benny Show, Martin & Lewis Show*
Chevrolet automobiles: *Bob Hope Show, Gangbusters, Jack Benny Show*
Coca-Cola *Pause That Refreshes, Coke Time*
Cocomalt: *Buck Rogers*
Colgate toothpaste: *Our Miss Brooks, Bill Stern's Sports Newsreel*
Cream of Wheat: *Buck Rogers, Grand Central Station, Let's Pretend*
Cue magazine: *Gangbusters*
Dari-Rich: *Terry & the Pirates*
DeSoto-Plymouth automobiles: *You Bet Your Life* (Groucho Marx)
Dodge automobiles: *Roy Rogers Show*
Dr. Lyon's toothpaste: *Backstage Wife*
Duz detergent: *Goldbergs, Truth or Consequences*
Elgin-American: *You Bet Your Life*

Emerson electronics: *Bob Hope Show*
Eversharp: *Henry Morgan Show*
Fatima cigarettes: *Dragnet, Tales of Fatima*
Firestone Tire and Rubber Co.: *Voice of Firestone*
Fitch shampoo: *Fitch Bandwagon (Phil Harris & Alice Faye Show)*
Fleischmann's yeast: *I Love a Mystery, Rudy Vallee Show*
Ford automobiles: *Fred Allen Show, Lum & Abner*
Frigidaire: *Lum & Abner*
General Electric: *Bing Crosby Show*
General Foods: *Aldrich Family, Bob Hope Show, Buck Rogers, Gangbusters, Hopalong Cassidy, Lone Ranger, Roy Rogers Show, Tarzan, Those We Love*
General Mills: *Green Hornet, Jack Armstrong*
George Washington coffee: *Sherlock Holmes*
Goodyear Tire and Rubber Co.: *Greatest Story Ever Told, Roy Rogers Show*
Grape Nuts Flakes: *Burns & Allen, Jack Benny Show*
Gruen watches: *Walter Winchell's Journal*
Gulf oil: *Counterspy*
H. O. Oats: *Bobby Benson*
Heinz foods: *Ozzie & Harriet*
Hinds' foods: *Burns & Allen*
Horlick's malted milk: *Lum & Abner*
Hormel foods: *Burns & Allen*
Household Finance: *Sherlock Holmes*
International Silver: *Ozzie & Harriet*
Ipana toothpaste: *Duffy's Tavern*
Ironized yeast: *Big Town, Lights Out*
Jad salts: *Easy Aces*
Jell-O: *Jack Benny Show*
Jergen's lotion: *Walter Winchell's Journal*
Johnson wax: *Fibber McGee & Molly*
Kaiser-Fraser automobiles: *Walter Winchell's Journal*
Kellogg's cereals: *Buck Rogers, Mark Trail, Superman Tom Corbett, Space Cadet, Tom Mix*
Kentucky Winner tobacco: *One Man's Family*
Kolynos toothpaste: *Front Page Farrell, Just Plain Bill*
Kraft cheese: *Bing Crosby Show, Bobby Benson, Great Gildersleeve, Kraft Music Hall*
Lady Esther face cream: *Mercury Theater, Screen Guild Players*
Langerdorf bread: *Red Ryder*
Lava soap: *FBI in Peace & War*
Lavoris mouthwash: *Easy Aces*

Lifebuoy soap: *Big Town*
Liggett & Meyers cigarettes: *Gunsmoke*
Linit: *Fred Allen Show*
Lipton tea: *Arthur Godfrey's Talent Scouts, Arthur Godfrey Time, Inner Sanctum Mysteries*
Listerine mouthwash: *Grand Central Station*
Lucky Strike cigarettes: *Jack Benny Show, Your Hit Parade*
Lux soap: *Lux Radio Theater*
Mail Pouch: *Counterspy*
Maltex cereal: *Uncle Don Show*
Mars candy: *Dr. I. Q., People Are Funny*
Maxwell House coffee: *Baby Snooks Show, Burns & Allen*
Nabisco: *Straight Arrow*
Nestles: *Space Patrol*
Norge refrigerators: *Red Skelton Show*
Old Gold cigarettes: *Original Amateur Hour*
Orange Crush: *Green Hornet*
Ovaltine: *Captain Midnight, Little Orphan Annie*
Oxydol detergent: *Goldbergs, Ma Perkins*
Pabst Blue Ribbon beer: *Danny Kaye Show, Eddie Cantor Show, Life of Riley, Mercury Theater*
Palmolive: *Gangbusters*
Pebico toothpaste: *Eddie Cantor Show*
Pepsi Cola: *Counterspy*
Pepsodent toothpaste: *Bob Hope Show*
Pet milk: *Truth or Consequences*
Peter Pan peanut butter: *Sky King*
Petrie wines: *Sherlock Holmes*
Philco: *Bing Crosby Show*
Philip Morris cigarettes: *Candid Microphone, Truth or Consequences*
Phillips Milk of Magnesia: *National Barn Dance*
Pillsbury flour: *Grand Central Station*
Ponds cold cream: *Those We Love*
Post cereals: *Baby Snooks Show*
Postum: *Lum & Abner*
Prell shampoo: *Life of Riley*
Prince Albert cigars: *Grand Ole Opry*
Proctor and Gamble: *Beulah, I Love a Mystery, Lorenzo Jones, Right to Happiness, Road of Life, Vic & Sade*
Quaker Oats: *Challenge of the Yukon, Lum & Abner, Roy Rogers Show, Terry & the Pirates*
Raleigh cigarettes: *People Are Funny, Raleigh Room (Hildegarde), Red Skelton Show*
Ralston cereals: *Tom Mix, Space Patrol*
Remington: *March of Time*

Rexall drugs: *Amos & Andy, Phil Harris & Alice Faye Show*
Richard Hudnut: *Walter Winchell's Journal*
Richfield oil: *Escape*
Rinso cleanser: *Amos & Andy, Big Town, Grand Central Station*
Robert Burns cigars: *Burns & Allen*
Roma wines: *Suspense*
Royal gelatin: *Those We Love*
Sal Hepatica: *Eddie Cantor Show*
Sanka coffee: *Baby Snooks Show*
Schick razors: *Duffy's Tavern*
Sealtest dairy: *Rudy Vallee Show*
Selmer Co.: *Sherlock Holmes*
Shutter candy: *Counterspy*
Signal oil: *Whistler*
Silvercup bread: *Lone Ranger*
Skelly oil: *Captain Midnight*
Sloan's liniment: *Gangbusters*
Snow Drift: *One Man's Family*
Spud: *Ed Wynn Show*
Standard Brands: *One Man's Family, Rudy Vallee Show*
Sterling drugs: *Stella Dallas, Young Widder Brown*
Super Suds detergent: *Blondie*
Swan soap: *Burns & Allen*
Swift foods: *Archie Andrews*
Teel soap: *Those We Love*
Tenderleaf tea: *Fred Allen Show*
Texaco oil: *Ed Wynn Show (Texaco Star Theater), Eddie Cantor Show, Fred Allen Show*
Tide laundry detergent: *Red Skelton Show*
Time magazine: *March of Time*
Toni home permanent: *Arthur Godfrey's Talent Scouts, Grand Central Station, Our Miss Brooks, People Are Funny*
Trimont clothing: *Sherlock Holmes*
Tums: *Beulah, Bulldog Drummond*
United States Steel: *U. S. Steel Hour*, aka *Theater Guild on the Air*
United States War Dept.: *Command Performance*
Waterman's pens: *Gangbusters*
Wesson oil: *One Man's Family*
White Owl cigars: *Burns & Allen*
Wildroot Cream Oil: *FBI in Peace & War, Sam Spade*
Wings cigarettes: *People Are Funny*
Woodbury soap: *Bing Crosby Show*
Wrigley's gum: *FBI in Peace & War, Gene Autry's Melody Ranch, March of Time, Yours Truly, Johnny Dollar*

Appendix D
Additional Radio Personalities

The names, occupations, and birth and death dates of people who were active in radio but for whom space did not allow a more detailed biographical entry in the body of this encyclopedia are listed below. The book's Index also lists these personalities' names and the page numbers of the shows on which they were heard.

Approximated birth dates follow the letter *c* (circa). An asterisk replaces an unknown birthdate. The letter *d* following a person's birth date means that he/she has most certainly died, but that a specific death date could not be confirmed.

Abbott, Gregory Anncr. (1900–1981)
Abel, Walter Actor (1899–1987)
Adams, Franklin P. Panelist (1881–d.   )
Adrian, Iris Actress (1913–1994)
Albertson, Mabel Actress (1901–1982)
Aldan, Daisy Actress (1923–   )
Alexander, Ben Actor-Host (1911–1969)
Alexander, Joan Actress (c. 1920–   )
Allen, Charme Actress (1909–1980)
Allen, Steve Host (1921–   )
Allen, Vera Actress (c. 1908–d.   )
Allenby, Peggy Actress (c. 1915–d.   )
Allison, Jone Actress (c. 1920–   )
Allman, Lee Actress (1908–1989)
Ames, Leon Actor (1903–1993)
Amsterdam, Morey Actor (1912–   )
Anderson, Marjorie Actress (c. 1916–1946)
Andrews, Clark Director (1909–1985)
Andrews, Robert Hardy Writer (1903–1976)
Ansbro, George Anncr. (1915–   )
Arnal, Curtis Actor (1910–d.   )
Arnold, Eddy Country-Western Singer (1918–   )
Ashley, Ira Director (1910–1985)
Ascot, Rita Actress (1907–1988)
Atkins, Chet Country-Western Singer (1924–   )
Averback, Hy Producer-Director (1925–   )
Babbitt, Harry Singer (1913–   )
Bacall, Lauren Actress (1924–   )
Baclanova, Olga Actress (1899–1974)
Backus, Georgia Actress (1901–1983)
Bailey, Mildred Singer (1903–1951)
Bailey, Ruth Actress (1905–1989)
Baker, Belle Singer (1897–1957)
Baker, Gene Anncr. (1910–1981)
Baldwin, Bill Anncr. (1917–1982)
Ballew, Smith Bandleader (1902–1984)
Barclay, Luise Actress (c. 1910–d.   )
Barker, Brad Animal Imitator (1895–1951)

Barnes, Paul Actor (1919–1983)
Barney, Marion Actress (1883–d.   )
Barrett, Pat (Uncle Ezra) Actor (1887–1957)
Barrie, Wendy Actress-Hostess (1912–1978)
Bartell, Harry Actor (1913–   )
Barton, Frank Anncr. (1909–1995)
Bauer, Charita Actress (1923–1985)
Beals, Richard Actor (1927–   )
Becker, Sandy Actor-Anncr. (1903–1965)
Behrens, Frank Actor (1919–1986)
Bell, Joseph Director (1912–1987)
Bell, Ralph Actor (c. 1920–   )
Bell, Shirley Actress (1921–   )
Benson, Court (Courtenay E) Actor (1915–1995)
Bentley, Spencer Actor (1908–d.   )
Berkovici, B. S. Newsman (1897–d.   )
Berner, Sara Actress (* –1969)
Berwin, Bernice Actress (c 1910–   )
Bivens, William "Bill" Anncr. (1916–1984)
Bixby, Carl Writer-Actor-Producer (1895–1978)
Blackburn, Arline Actress (1914–   )
Blaine, Joan Actress (1914–d.   )
Bleyer, Archie Musician-Conductor (1910–1989)
Block, Vivian Actress (1922–   )
Boardman, True Writer-Actor-Producer (1909–d.   )
Bogue, Mervyn "Ish Kabibble" Musician-Actor (1908–1994)
Borge, Victor Musician-comedian (1909–   )
Boyd, William (Hopalong Cassidy) Actor (1985–1972)
Bracken, Eddie Actor (1920–   )
Briggs, Donald Actor (1911–1986)
Brown, Bob Anncr. (1904–1980)
Brown, Joe E. Actor (1893–1973)
Bruce, Edwin Actor (1936–   )
Bruce, Nigel Actor (1895–1954)
Brusiloff, Nat Conductor (1904–1951)
Bryant, Geoffrey Actor (1906–d.   )
Buck, Charles Anncr. (1901–1992)

Burke, Billie Actress (1885–1970)
Burrows, Abe Writer-Actor (1911–1985)
Bushman, Francis X. Actor (1883–1966)
Buttram, Pat Actor (1915–1994)
Byron, Ward Director-Producer (1906–   )
Cadman, Dr. S. Parkes Religious Broadcaster (1864–
   1936)
Campbell, Flora Actress (1911–1978)
Campbell, Kay Actress (1905–1985)
Capell, Peter Actor (1907–1986)
Carroll, Gene Actor (1889–1972)
Carroll, Carroll Writer (1902–1990)
Carroll, Madeleine Actress (1907–1987)
Case, Nelson Anncr. (1910–1976)
Chase, Ilka Actress (1906–1978)
Choate, Helen Actress (1911–d.   )
Claire, Helen Actress (1906–1974)
Cline, Patsy Country-Western Singer (1931–1962)
Cobb, Irvin Actor (1877–1944)
Coleman, Nancy Actress (1917–   )
Collins, Ted Producer-Host (1901–1964)
Colton, Kingsley Actor (1924–   )
Conte, John Actor-Anncr. (1915–   )
Conway, Tom Actor (1904–1967)
Cook, Phil Singer (1890–1958)
Cope, Daniel "Dan" Director (1907–d.   )
Copeland, Maurice Actor (1911–1985)
Costello, Jack Anncr. (1908–   )
Cotten, Joseph Actor (1905–1994)
Cowl, Jane Actress (1890–1950)
Crawford, Jess Organist (1896–1962)
Crosby, Lou Anncr. (1914–1984)
Cugat, Xavier Musician-Conductor (1900–1990)
Culver, Howard Actor (1918–1984)
Dane, Frank Actor (1903–d.   )
Darnay, Toni Actress (1922–1983)
D'Aquino, Iva "Tokyo Rose" (1916–   )
DeCorsia, Ted Actor (1904–1973)
Dehner, John Actor (1916–1992)
DeKoven, Roger Actor (1907–1988)
DelValle, Jaime Musician-Conductor (1910–1981)
Denker, Henry Writer (1912–   )
Denning, Richard Actor (1916–   )
DeSantis, Joseph "Joe" Actor (1909–1989)
Desmond, Connie Sportscaster (1908–1982)
Devine, Andy Actor (1906–1977)
Dietrich, Marlene Actress (1901–1991)
Dobkin, Larry Actor (1919–   )
Donlevy, Brian Actor (1901–1972)
Douglas, Hugh Anncr. (1915–1993)
Douglas, Nancy Actress (1913–   )
Dragon, Carmen Musician-Conductor (1915–1984)
Drees, Jack Sportscaster (1917–1988)
Dumas, Helene Actress (1910–1989)
Dupree, Henry Actor (1907–1980)

Durocher, Leo Host (1906–1991)
Elders, Harry Actor (1908–1993)
Ellis, Georgia Actress (1920–1988)
Engelbach, Dee Producer-Director (1910–1983)
Enright, Dan Host-Anncr. (1918–1992)
Evans, Dale Actress-singer (1912–   )
Everett, Ethel Actress (1891–d.   )
Farrington, Fielden Anncr. (1909–d.   )
Fenneman, George Anncr. (1919–   )
Ferguson, Elsie Actress (1885–1968)
Fiedler, Arthur Musician-Conductor (1893–1979)
Fields, Gracie Actress (1898–1979)
Fifield, Georgia Actress (1901–1985)
Fio Rito, Ted Bandleader (1900–1971)
Firestone, Edward "Eddie" Actor (1920–   )
Fitch, Louise Actress (c. 1915–   )
Fitzmaurice, Michael Actor (c. 1908–d.   )
Flynn, Charles Actor (1920–   )
Fontaine, Frank Actor (1920–1978)
Fox, Templeton Actress (1913–   )
Francis, Ivor Actor (1918–1986)
Fredericks, Carlton Host (1911–1987)
Frees, Paul Actor (1920–1986)
Fridell, Vivian Actress (1912–d.   )
Fuller, Barbara Actress (1918–   )
Furness, Betty Actress (1916–1994)
Fussell, Sara Actress (1917–1978)
Garber, Jan Conductor (1895–1977)
Gargan, William Actor (1906–1979)
George, Earl Actor (1912–   )
Gibbons, Floyd News commentator (1887–1939)
Gilbert, Janice Actress (1923–   )
Gilbert, Jody Actress (* –1979)
Gilbert, Ruth Actress (1922–1993)
Gillars, Mildred "Axis Sally" (1901–1988)
Gilman, Page Actor (1918–   )
Gilman, Lucy Actress (1925–   )
Gilmore, Arthur "Art" Anncr. (1912–   )
Gordon, Joyce Actress (c. 1926–   )
Gordon, Richard Actor (1882–d   )
Gould, Mitzi Actress (1915–   )
Grayson, Mitchell Director (1913–1979)
Green, John "Johnny Musician-Conductor (1907–1989)
Greenstreet, Sydney Actor (1879–1954)
Haenschen, Gustav Musician (1890–1980)
Haines, Larry Actor (1917–   )
Hale, Alan Actor (1892–1950)
Hamilton, Margaret Actress (1903–1985)
Hanna, Arthur "Art" Director (1906–1981)
Hannan, Majorie Actress (1916–   )
Haymes, Dick Singer (1919–1980)
Heen, Gladys Actress (c. 1908–d.   )
Heflin, Van Actor (1910–1971)
Henshaw, Gail Actress (1912–   )
Hernandez, Juano Actor (1898–1970)

Hicks, George Anncr. (1905–d.   )
Hitz, Elsie Actress (c. 1910–d.   )
Holloway, Jean Writer (1917–1989)
Holloway, Sterling Actor (1905–1992)
Homeier, George Vincent "Skip" Actor (1929–   )
Hookey, Robert "Bobby" Singer-Host (c. 1930–   )
Hopper, Edna Wallace Beauty Expert (1864–1954)
Houston, Jane Actress (1891–1979)
Howard, Eunice Actress (c. 1915–   )
Howell, Wayne Anncr. (1921–1993)
Huston, Walter Actor (1884–1950)
Idelson, William "Billy" Actor (1920–   )
Irving, Charles Actor-Anncr. (1915–1981)
Ives, Burl "The Waxfaring Stranger" Singer (1910–1995)
James, Hugh Anncr.-Host (1915–   )
Janis, Elsie Actress (1889–1956)
Janiss, Vivi Actress (* –1988)
Jellison, Robert "Bob" Actor (1908–d.   )
Johnson, Dora Actress (c. 1918–   )
Johnstone, William Actor (c. 1910–   )
Jones, Louis Marshall "Grandpa" Singer-Actor (1913–   )
Jones, Virginia "Ginger" Actress (c. 1920–   )
Josefsberg, Milton Writer (1911–1987)
Joslyn, Allyn Actor (1902–1981)
Joy, Richard "Dick" Anncr. (1915–   )
Juster, Evelyn "Evie" Actress (* –1988)
Kadell, Carlton Actor (1905–1975)
Kane, John Actor (1910–   )
Karloff, Boris Actor (1887–1969)
Keane, Teri Actress (c. 1925–   )
Keith, Ian Actor (1899–1960)
Kelly, Nancy Actress (1921–1995)
Kent, Elaine Actress (1920–   )
Kibbee, Lois Actress (1922–1993)
King, Frank "Pee Wee" Country-Western Singer (1914–   )
King, Jean "The Lonesome Girl" Singer (1917–1993)
Kingston, Lenore Actress (1916–   )
Kirby, Durwood Anncr. (1912–   )
Kleeb, Helen Actress (1914–   )
Klein, Adelaide Actress (c. 1890–d.   )
Kohl, Arthur "Art" Actor (1898–d.   )
Knight, Victor Actor (1909–1984)
Kroenke, Carl Actor (1895–d.   )
Kruger, Alma Actress (1872–1960)
Kruschen, Jack Actor (1922–   )
Kuhl, Cal Director (1907–1973)
Larsen, Bobbie Actor (1933–   )
Latham, Joseph Actor (1890–1970)
Lawrence, Charlotte Actress (1921–1993)
Leader, Anton M. Director (1914–1988)
Lee, Barbara Actress (1912–   )
Lee, Madaline Actress (* –1974)

Lee, Peggy Singer (1920–   )
LeGrand, Richard Actor (1882–c. 1954)
Leonard, Sheldon Actor (1907–   )
Levant, Oscar Musician-Wit (1906–1972)
Leslie, Philip "Phil" (1909–1988)
Lewis, Forrest Actor (1899–d.   )
Lillie, Bea Comedienne (1894–   )
Livingstone, Charles Director (1903–1986)
Lloyd, Rita Actress (1930–   )
Lopez, Vincent Bandleader (1894–1975)
Lorde, Althena Actress (1916–1973)
Lowell, Dorothy Actress (1917–1946)
Lowry, Judith Actress (1890–1976)
Lucas, Nick Singer (1897–1982)
Lund, John Actor (1911–1992)
Luther, Frank Singer-Anncr. (1900–1980)
Lyman, Abe Bandleader (1897–1957)
Lynch, Christopher Singer (1921–1994)
Mack, Gilbert "Gil" Actor (1912–   )
Mack, Helen Actress-Producer-Director (1914–1986)
Mack, Ted Host (1904–1976)
MacLeish, Archibald Writer (1893–1982)
MacRae, Gordon Singer (1921–1986)
Maher, Wally Actor (1908–d.   )
Manning, Knox Announcer (1904–1980)
Manson, Charlotte Actress (c. 1920–   )
Markey, Enid Actress (1890–1981)
Martin, Frank Anncr. (1915–1995)
Martin, Freddy Bandleader (1907–1983)
Marvin, Johnny Singer (1897–1944)
Marvin, Tony Anncr. (1912–   )
Massey, Curt Singer (1910–1991)
Maxwell, Elsa Hostess (1883–1963)
McCallion, James "Jimmy" Actor (1919–1991)
McCarthy, Jack Actor (* –1977)
McComb, Kate Actress (1878–d.   )
McNear, Howard Actor (1905–1969)
McNellis, Maggie Hostess (1918–1989)
McPherson, Aimee Semple Evangelist (1890–1944)
McQueen, Thelma "Butterfly" Actress (1911–   )
Meiser, Edith Writer (1898–1993)
Merkel, Una Actress (1904–1986)
Miller, Glenn Musician-Conductor (1911–1944)
Mix, Tom Actor (1880–1940)
Monroe, Vaughn Musician-Singer (1912–1973)
Monks, James Actor (1913–1994)
Morgan, Dennis Singer-Actor (1910–1994)
Morgan, Helen Singer (1900–1941)
Morgan, Jane Actress (1880–1972)
Munson, Ona Actress (1906–1955)
Murphy, George Actor-Host (1904–1992)
Nash, Clarence Actor (1905–1985)
Nebel, John "Long John" Host (1912–1978)
Nelson, Herbert Actor (1914–1994)
Nesbitt, John Narrator (1910–1960)

Niesen, Gertrude Singer (1918–1975)
Novello, Jay Actor (1904–1982)
Novis, Donald Singer (1906–1966)
Oakie, Jack Actor (1904–1978)
Ocko, Daniel Actor (1913–1991)
O'Connell, Helen Singer (1920–1993)
Olsen and Johnson Comedians Olsen, Ole (1892–1963), John, Chick (1891–1962)
Olson, Johnny Anncr.-Host (1910–1976)
Ormont, David Actor-Anncr. (1915–1994)
Owen, Ethel Actress (c. 1890–d.   )
Pantages, Lloyd Gossip Show Host (1908–   )
Page, Gale Actress (1911–1983)
Peeples, Cornelius Actor (1920–d.   )
Peerce, Jan Singer (1904–   )
Pelletier, Vincent Anncr. (1908–1994)
Perrin, Vic Actor (1916–1989)
Persons, Fern Actress (c. 1916–   )
Petrie, George Actor (1908–d.   )
Petrie, Howard Anncr. (1907–1968)
Peyton, Father Patrick Host (1909–1992)
Pierce, Madeleine Actress (1901–1973)
Pickford, Mary Actress (1893–1979)
Pitts, ZaSu Actress (1898–1963)
Platt, Robert Writer (1919–1993)
Poynton, Loretta Actress (1914–   )
Prentiss, Ed Actor (1909–1992)
Presnell, Robert Director (1915–1986)
Pryor, Roger Actor (1901–1974)
Quinn, Bill Actor (1912–   )
Raby, John Actor (* –1975)
Ralston, Esther Actress (1902–1994)
Randall, Tony Actor (1920–   )
Rawson, Ron Announcer (1918–1994)
Reeves, Jim Country-Western Singer (1924–1964)
Reisman, Leo Musician-Conductor (1897–1961)
Rich, Freddie Musician-Conductor (1898–1956)
Richman, Harry Singer-Host (1895–1992)
Ritter, Thelma Actress (1905–1969)
Ritter, Woodward Maurice "Tex" Country-Western Singer (1905–1974)
Robbins, Martin "Marty" Country-Western Singer (1925–1982)
Robertson, Bartlett Actor (1913–1986)
Robinson, Larry Actor (c. 1930–   )
Rogers, Will Actor (1879–1935)
Rose, Harry Comedian (1892–1962)
Rothafel, S. L. "Roxy" Host-Bandleader (1882–1936)
Roy, Cecil Actress (1901–1995)
Royle, Selena Actress (1905–1983)
Rubin, Jack Actor-Host (1898–1952)
Rubinoff, David Violinist (1895–1986)
Ruffner, Edmund "Tiny" Anncr.-Producer (1900–1983)
Russell, Ruth Actress (1914–   )

Ryan, Quin Sportscaster (1899–1978)
Sangster, Margaret Writer (1891–1981)
Sanville, Richard Director (1909–1971)
Sargent, Anne Actress (c. 1925–   )
Schnabel, Stefan Actor (1912–1983)
Seaton, George Actor (1911–1979)
Seeley, Blossom Singer (1892–1974)
Selby, Sarah Actress (1906–1980)
Semmler, Alexander Musician (1901–1972)
Shay, Dorothy Singer (1921–1978)
Sheehan, Tess Actress (1888–d.   )
Shirer, William Newscaster (1904–1993)
Shields, Helen Actress (* –1963)
Shirley, Thomas "Tom" Anncr.-Actor (1905–d.   )
Shockley, Marion Actress (c. 1922–   )
Skilkret, Nathaniel Conductor (1895–1982)
Sloane, Robert Actor-Producer-Director (1912–1955)
Slon, Sidney Actor-Writer (1912–1995)
Smart, J. Scott Actor (1903–1960)
Smith, Sidney Actor (1910–1978)
Smith, William J. Actor (1907–1992)
Snow, Hank Country-Western Singer (1914–   )
Soubier, Clifford "Cliff" Actor (1891–d.   )
Stander, Lionel Actor (1908–1994)
Stehli, Edgar Actor (1884–1972)
Stevenson, Margot Actress (c1918–   )
Stevens, K. T. Actress (1920–1994)
Stewart, Paul Actor (1915–1986)
Storm, Gale Actress (1921–   )
Sudrow, Lyle Actor (c. 1918–d.   )
Sullivan, Barry Actor (1913–1994)
Sullivan, Fred Actor (1880–d.   )
Summers, Hope Actress (1901–1978)
Svihus, Richard Actor (1932–   )
Swarthout, Gladys Singer (1904–1969)
Sweet, Marion Actress (1916–1978)
Sweet, William Writer (1896–1968)
Tedrow, Irene Actress (1908–1995)
Tetzel, Joan Actress (1921–1977)
Thomas, Ann Actress (1914–1989)
Thomas, John Charles Singer (1889–1960)
Thorson, Russell Actor (1907–1982)
Tibbett, Lawrence Singer (1896–1960)
Tilton, Martha Singer (1916–   )
Tinney, Cal Actor (1908–   )
Tompkins, Joan Actress (c. 1920–   )
Toscanini, Arturo Conductor (1907–1957)
Tovrov, Orin Writer (1919–1980)
Treacher, Arthur Actor (1894–1975)
Trotter, John Scott Musician (1907–1975)
Tubb, Ernest Country-Western Singer (1914–1984)
Tyler, Betty Jane Actress (1928–1984)
VanDyk, James Actor (1894–1951)
VanPatten, Dick Actor (1928–   )
Walliser, Blair Producer-Director (1908–d.   )

Walter, Wilmer Actor (1884–1941)
Warner, Gertrude Actress (* –1986)
Webber, Peggy Actress (1925–   )
Wells, Sarajane Actress (1914–1987)
Wentworth, Martha Actress (* –1974)
Whiting, Margaret Singer (1924–   )
Williams, Hiram King "Hank" Country-Western Singer (1923–1953)
Wilson, Ethel Actress (1892–1980)
Wilson, Kathleen Actress (1912–   )
Winstanley, Ernie Actor (1920–1992)
Winninger, Charles Actor (1884–1969)

Wolfe, Winifred Actress (1924–   )
Woods, Lesley Actress (c. 1920–   )
Woolly, Monty Actor (1888–1963)
Wragge, Betty Actress (1917–   )
Wright, Ben Actor (1915–1989)
York, Dick Actor (1928–1992)
Yorke, Ruth Actress (c. 1910–d.   )
Young, Alan Actor (1919–   )
Young, Robert Actor (1907–   )
Zerbe, Lawson Actor (1915–d.   )
Zuckert, Bill Actor (c. 1916–   )

Appendix E
Vintage Radio Show Clubs, Conventions, Museums, Newsletters, and Organizations

Abbott and Costello Quarterly (newsletter)
(Abbott and Costello Fan Club)
Box 1084
Toluca Lake, CA 91610

Air Check (newsletter)
(Radio Enthusiasts of Puget Sound)
W. Michael Sprague
11732 N.E. 148th Place
Kirland, WA 98034

Airwaves (newsletter)
(Yesterday USA)
Bill Bragg
1001 Plymouth Rock
Richardson, TX 75081

Al Jolson Society
(Jolson Journal [newsletter])
Jay Brockson
933 Fifth Avenue
Prospect Park, PA 19076

Buffalo Old Time Radio Club
Jerry Collins
56 Christian Ct.
Lancaster, NY 14086

Chattanooga Airwaves (newsletter)
(Chattanooga Old Time Radio Club)
Box Axley
4940 Bal Harbor Dr.
Chattanooga, TN 37416

Cincinnati Old Time Radio Club
Robert Newman
11509 Islandale Dr.
Forest Park, OH 45240

Cincinnati's Old Time Radio Nostalgia Convention
Bob Burchett
Box 6176
Cincinnati, OH 45206

Cinnamon Bear Brigade
10419 N.E. Knott
Portland, OR 97220

Collectrix (newsletter)
389 New York Avenue
Huntington, NY 11743

Columbia Radio Club
John Wrisley
1 Myrtle Court
Columbia, SC 29205

Daily Sentinel (newsletter)
Robert Brunet
21 West 74th Street
New York, NY 10028

Eddie Cantor Appreciation Society (newsletter)
Shelia Riddle
Box 312
Mount Gray, WV 25637

Friends of Kate Smith/God Bless America Foundation
122 Main Street
Lake Placid, NY 12946

Friends of Old Time Radio
Hello Again (newsletter)
Jay Hickerson
Box 4321
Hamden, CT 06514

Golden Radio Buffs of Maryland
On The Air (newsletter)
Owen Pomeroy
3613 Chestnut Drive
Baltimore, MD 21211
or
Gene Leetner
7506 Iroquois Road
Baltimore, MD 21219

Houston Old Time Radio Club
Raleigh Barker
6206 Bankside Drive
Houston, TX 77096

Illinois Old Time Radio Show Society
10 South 540 County Line Road
Hinsdale, IL 60521

Indiana Recording Club
Tape Squeal (newsletter)
William Davis
1729 East 77th
Indianapolis, IN 46240

Jack Benny Fan Club
Jack Benny Times (newsletter)
3561 Somerset Avenue
Castro Valley, CA 94546

JFL, Inc.
P.O. Box 23276
Portland, OR 97281

Laugh (newsletter)
Peter Tarchell
40 Bambra Road
Caulfield, Victoria, Australia 3161

Lum and Abner Society
Tim Holles
Route 3, Box 110
Dora, AL 35062

Manhattan Radio Club
Suzanne Siegel
405 East 63rd Street
New York, NY 10021

Metropolitan Washington Old Time Radio Club
James Burnette
6704 Bidensee Lane
Manassas, VA 22110

Mid-Atlantic Antique Radio Club
Joe Koesler
249 Spring Gap South
Laurel, MD 20724

Milwaukee Area Radio Enthusiasts
Kim Pabst
4442 North 77th Street
Milwaukee, WI 53218

Modern Radio Drama (newsletter)
J. Coleman
Box 12631
Berkeley, CA 94701

Movie-Entertainment Book Club
15 Oakland Avenue
Harrison, NY 10528

Museum of Television and Radio
25 West 52nd Street
New York, NY 10019

National Broadcaster's Hall of Fame
Anaheim Stadium Hall of Fame Office Complex
Anaheim, CA 92806

National Broadcasters Hall of Fame and Museum
Berkeley Corteret Hotel
Ocean Avenue
Asbury Park, NJ 07712

National Museum of Communication
6305 North O'Connor Road
Suite 123
Irving, TX 75039-3510

National Old Time Radio
Steven Hiss
Route 1, Box 253
Alacha, FL 32615

North American Radio Archives
NARA News (newsletter)
Box 11962
Reno, NV 89510
or
Ron Staley
14144 Burbank Boulevard #4
Van Nuys, CA 91401

Nostalgia Digest (newsletter)
Chuck Shader
Box 421
Morton Grove, IL 60053

Old Time Radio Club
(Illustrated Press & Memories [newsletter])
100 Harvey Drive
Lancaster, NY 14086

Old Time Radio Digest (newsletter)
Royal Promotions
4114 Montgomery Road
Cincinnati, OH 45212

Old Time Radio Gazette (newsletter)
(Tom Miller)
2004 East 6th Street
Superior, WI 54880

O.R.C.A.
Old Time Radio Show Collector's Association of England
North American Branch
Tom Monroe
2055 Elmwood Avenue
Lakewood, OH 44107

Past Times (newsletter)
J. Young and R. Skretvedt
7308 Fillmore Drive
Buena Park, CA 90620

Radio Classics Live Program
Massasoit Community College
Brockton, MA 02401

Radio Collectors of America
RCA Newsletter
Bob Jennings
984 Main Street
Worcester, MA 02132

or
Mel Simons
635 Wild Street
W. Roxbury, MA 02132

Radio Enthusiasts of Puget Sound
Air Check (newsletter)
W. Michael Sprague
11732 N.E. 148th Place
Kirkland, WA 98034

Radio Forum (newsletter)
Edgar Cole & Bob Burnham
Box 3508
Lakeland, FL 23802

Radio Recall
(Metropolitan Washington Old Time Radio Club)
James Burnette
67-4 Bodensee Lane
Manassas, VA 22211

Radio Historical Association of Colorado
(Return With Us Now [newsletter])
Box 1908
Engelwood, CO 80150
or
John Adams
2811 So. Valentia Street
Denver, CO 90231

RLL On the Air (newsletter)
Radio Listener's Lyceum
Robert Newman
11509 Islandale Drive
Forest Park, OH 45240

Reminisce (newsletter)
Ray Reiman
5400 S. 60th Street
Glendale, WI 53129

Revival of Creative Radio
Wavelengths (newsletter)
Tim Coco
Box 1585
Haverkill, MA 01831

Sparks (newsletter)
Michael Packer
Box 3540
Grand Rapids, MI 49501

S.P.E.R.D.V.A.C.
SPERDVAC Radiogram (newsletter)
Society to Preserve and Encourage Radio Drama, Variety
and Comedy
P.O. Box 7177
Van Nuys, CA 91409

Straight Arrow Pow Wow
Bill Harper
301 East Buena Vista Avenue
North Augusta, GA 29841

Texas Broadcasting Museum
1703 Market Street
Dallas, TX 75202

Thrilling Days of Yesteryear (newsletter)
Carol and John Rayburn
7222 West Stanford Avenue
Littleton, OH 80123

Tune In (newsletter)
Rob Innes
1844 E. Longmeadow
Trenton, MI 48183

Vic and Sade Society
Barbara Schwarz
7232 N. Keystone Avenue
Lincolnwood, IL 60646

WRHU-FM 88.7
126 Hofstra University
Hempstead, NY 11550-1090

Yesterday USA
Airwaves (newsletter)
Bill Bragg
2001 Plymouth Rock
Richardson, TX 75081

Appendix F
Stations That Feature Vintage Radio Shows
(as of May 1995)

(Check with the station listed below that is in your area for the days and times vintage radio programs are broadcast because they often change.)

STATION	FREQUENCY	CITY
WADS-AM	690	Ansonia, CT
WJBL-AM	590	Austin, TX
WBLV-AM	1540	Bellevue, WA
WBCS-FM	91.3	Bellevue, WA
KBOL-AM	1490	Boulder, CO
WICC-AM	600	Bridgeport, CT
WCWP-FM	88.1	Brookville, NY
WEBR-AM	970	Buffalo, NY
CHQR-AM	770	Calgary, Canada
WAIT-AM	850	Chicago, IL
WBBM-AM	780	Chicago, IL
WNIB-FM	97.1	Chicago, IL
WVXU-FM	91.7	Claremont, CA
KSPC-FM	88.7	Claremont, CA
WTAW-AM	1150	College Station, TX
WCLI-AM	1450	Corning, NY
KNUS-AM	710	Denver, CO
WHO-AM	1040	Des Moines, IA
WCAR-AM	1090	Detroit, MI
KARP-AM	930	Douglas, AZ
CHED-AM	630	Edmonton, Canada
WDOE-AM	1410	Dunkirk, NY
WJKL-FM	94.3	Elgin, IL
WXFM-FM	105.9	Elmwood Pk, IL
KENU-AM	1330	Enunclaw, WA
WSWI-AM	820	Evansville, IN
KSER-FM	90.7	Everett, WA
WAJD-AM	1390	Gainesville, FL
WUFT-FM	89.1	Gainesville, FL
WWSC-AM	1450	Glen Falls, NY
CHMD-AM	900	Hamilton, Canada
WPOP-AM	1410	Hartford, CT
WRCQ-AM	910	Hartford, CT
WWCC-AM	1590	Honesdale, PA
KTRH-AM	740	Houston, TX
WJFF-FM	90.5	Jeffersonville, NY
KCMO-AM	810	Kansas City, MO
WBZW-AM	1040	Knoxville, TN

STATION	FREQUENCY	CITY
CKNW-AM	980	Ladysmith, Canada
KRWG-FM	90.7	Las Cruces, NM
KANU-FM	92.5	Lawrence, KS
KNX-AM	1070	Los Angeles, CA
KPCC-FM	98.3	Los Angeles, CA
WCAP-AM	980	Lowell, MA
WJUL-FM	91.5	Lowell, MA
KKSU-AM	580	Manhattan, KS
KLBB-AM	1400	Minneapolis, MN
WNQM-AM	1300	Nashville, TN
WBSM-AM	1420	New Bedford, MA
WTIX-AM	690	New Orleans, LA
WODT-AM	1280	New Orleans, LA
CFMI-FM	101.1	New West, BC
KCSN-FM	88.5	Northridge, CA
WBAI-FM	99.5	New York, NY
WFUV-FM	90.7	New York, NY
WQEW-AM	1560	New York, NY
CFMI-FM	101.1	New West, Canada
KCSN-FM	88.5	Northridge, CA
CHWO-AM	1250	Oakville, Canada
CFRA-AM	580	Ottawa, Canada
KPCC-FM	89.3	Pasadena, CA
WCBU-FM	89.9	Peoria, IL
WDUV-FM	90.5	Pittsburgh, PA
WTKN-AM	970	Pittsburgh, PA
WEDO-AM	810	Pittsburgh, PA
KSPC-FM	88.7	Pomona, CA
KBOO-FM	90.7	Portland, OR
KZUU-FM	90.7	Pullman, WA
WINY-AM	1350	Putnam, CT
KWEB-AM	1270	Rochester, MN
KSJN-AM	1330	Rochester, MN
WHAM-AM	1180	Rochester, NY
WPRS-FM	88.3	Rockland, MA
KLBB-AM	1400	St. Paul, MN
KSL-AM	1160	Salt Lake City, UT

STATION	FREQUENCY	CITY	STATION	FREQUENCY	CITY
KLAF-AM	1230	Salt Lk. Cty, UT	KLBB-AM	1400	St. Paul, MN
KALW-FM	91.7	San Fran., CA	WRVO-FM	89.9	Syracuse, NY
KIRO-AM	710	Seattle, WA	CFRB-AM	1010	Toronto, Canada
KSER-FM	90.7	Seattle, WA	CHUM.FM	104.5	Toronto, Canada
KWYS-AM	1230	Seattle, WA	CKNW-AM	980	Vancouver, Canada
KVI-AM	570	Seattle, WA			
KUOW-FM	94.9	Seattle, WA	CFMS-FM	96.5	Victoria, Canada
KCOZ-FM	100	Shreveport, LA	WCRB-FM	102.5	Waltham, MA
KXLY-AM	920	Spokane, WA	WAMU-FM	88.5	Washington, DC
CHRE-FM	105.7	St. Catherine	WKFI-AM	1090	Wilmington, OH
KFEQ-AM	680	St. Joseph, MO	KFH-AM	1330	Wichita, KS

Appendix G
Logs of Long-running Dramatic Anthology Shows

Lux Radio Theater Dates, Shows, and Stars in parentheses

1934: 10/14 "Seventh Heaven" (Miriam Hopkins), 10/21 "What Every Woman Knows" (Helen Hayes), 10/28 "The Barker" (Walter Huston), 11/4 "Sailin' Through" (Jane Cowl), 11/18 "The Nervous Wreck" (June Walker), 11/18 "Rebound" (Ruth Chatterton), 11/25 "Mrs. Dane's Defense" (Ethel Barrymore), 12/2 "Let Us Be Gay" (Tallulah Bankhead), 12/9 "Berkley Square" (Leslie Howard), 12/16 "Turn to the Right" (James Cagney), 12/23 "The Goose Hangs High" (Walter Connolly), 12/30 "Daddy Long Legs" (John Boles).

1935: 1/6 "The Green Goddess" (Claude Rains), 1/13 "Counselor at Law" (Paul Muni), 1/20 "The Late Christopher Bean" (Walter Connolly), 1/27 "The Bad Man" (Walter Huston), 2/3 "Peg O' My Heart" (Margaret Sullavan), 2/10 "The First Year" (Lila Lee), 2/17 "The Old Soak" (Wallace Beery), 2/24 "Nothing But the Truth" (Frank Morgan), 3/3 "Lillac Time" (Jane Cowl), 3/10 "Holiday" (Claudette Colbert), 3/17 "Her Master's Voice" (Roland Young), 3/24 "Secrets" (Irene Dunne), 3/31 "The Romantic Age" (Leslie Howard), 4/7 "The Prince Chap" (Gary Cooper), 4/14 "The Broken Wing" (Lupe Velez), 4/21 "Little Women" (Lillian Gish, Dorothy Gish), 4/28 "Ada Beats the Drum" (Mary Boland), 5/5 "Adam and Eva" (Cary Grant), 5/12 "The Bishop Misbehaves" (Walter Connolly, Jane Wyatt), 5/19 "The Lion and the Mouse" (Ruth Chatterton), 5/26 "Michael and Mary" (Elissa Landi), 6/2 "The Vinegar Tree" (Billie Burke), 6/9 "Candlelight" (Robert Montgomery), 6/16 "The Patsy" (Loretta Young), 6/23 "Polly with a Past" (Ina Claire), 6/30 "Elmer the Great" (Joe E. Brown), 7/29 "Bunty Pulls the Strings" (Helen Hayes), 8/5 "Lightnin'" (Wallace Beery), 8/12 "Man in Possession" (Robert Montgomery), 8/19 "Ladies of the Jury" (Mary Boland), 8/26 "The Church Mouse" (Otto Kruger, Ruth Gordon), 9/2 "Whistling in the Dark" (Charles Ruggles), 9/9 "Petticoat Influence" (Ruth Chatterton), 9/16 "Leah Kleschna" (Conrad Nagel, Judith Anderson), 9/23 "Mary, Mary Quite Contrary" (Ethel Barrymore), 9/30 "Alias Jimmy Valentine" (Richard Barthelmess), 10/7 "The Wren" (Helen Chandler), 10/14 "Within the Law" (Joan Crawford), 10/21 "Merely Mary Ann" (Joan Bennett), 10/28 "Dulcy" (ZaSu Pitts), 11/4 "The Milky Way" (Charles Butterworth), 11/11 "His Misleading Lady" (Clark Gable), 11/18 "Sherlock Holmes" (William Gillette), 11/25 "Way Down East" (Lillian Gish, Dorothy Gish), 12/2 "The Swan" (Elissa Landi), 12/9 "The Showoff" (Joe E. Brown), 12/16 "The Truth" (Grace George), 12/23 "Applesauce" (Jack Oakie), 12/30 "The Queen's Husband" (Frank Morgan).

1936: 1/6 "The Third Degree" (Sylvia Sidney), 1/13 "The Boss" (Edward G. Robinson), 1/20 "A Prince There Was" (Ricardo Cortez), 1/27 "Grumpy" (John Barrymore), 2/3 "Green Grow the Lilacs" (John Boles), 2/10 "The Bride the Sun Shines On" (Douglas Fairbanks, Jr.), 2/17 "The Old Soak" (Wallace Beery), 2/24 "Peter Pan" (Freddie Bartholomew), 3/2 "Alias the Deacon" (Victor Moore), 3/9 "Girl of the Golden West" (Eva LeGallienne), 3/16 "The Last of Mrs. Cheyney" (Miriam Hopkins), 3/23 "The Song and Dance Man" (George M. Cohan), 3/30 "Bought and Paid For" (Bette Davis), 4/6 "Lickin'" (Ann Sothern), 4/13 "Shore Leave" (Lee Tracy), 4/20 "Harmony Lane" (Lawrence Tibbett), 4/27 "Undercover" (Richard Barthelmess), 5/4 "The Music Master" (Jean Hersholt), 5/11 "Bittersweet" (Irene Dunne), 5/18 "Get-Well Quick Wallingford" (George M. Cohan), 5/25 "East Is West" (Fay Bainter), 6/1 "The Legionaire and the Lady" (Marlene Dietrich, Clark Gable), 6/6 "The Voice of Bugle Ann" (Lionel Barrymore), 6/8 "The Thin Man" (William Powell, Myrna Loy), 6/13 "The Brat" (Joel McCrea, Marion Davies), 6/15 "Burlesque" (Al Jolson, Ruby Keeler), 6/19 "Irene" (Jeanette MacDonald), 6/20 "The Barker" (Claudette Colbert, Walter Huston), 6/22 "The Dark Angel" (Merle Oberon, Herbert Marshall), 7/27 "Chained" (Joan Crawford, Franchot Tone), 8/3 "Main Street" (Barbara Stanwyck, Fred MacMurray), 8/10 "The Jazz Singer" (Al Jolson), 8/17 "The Vagabond King" (John Boles, Evelyn Venable), 8/24 "One Sunday Afernoon" (Jack Oakie, Helen Twelvetrees), 8/21 "Cheating Cheaters" (George Raft), 9/7 "Is Zat So?" (James Cagney), 9/14 "Quality Street" (Brian Aherne, Ruth Chatterton), 9/21 "Trilby" (Grace Moore, Peter Lorre), 9/28 "The Plutocrat" (Wallace Beery), 10/5 "Elmer the Great" (Joe. E. Brown, Lou Gehrig), 10/12 "The Curtain Rises" (Ginger Rogers), 10/19 "Captain Applejack" (Frank Morgan, Maureen O'Sullivan), 10/26 "Saturday's Children" (Robert Taylor, Olivia deHavilland), 11/2 "The Virginian" (Gary Cooper), 11/9 "Alias Jimmy Valentine" (Pat O'Brien), 11/16 "Conversation Piece" (Lily Pons, Adolph Menjou), 11/23 "The Story of Louis Pasteur" (Paul Muni), 11/30 "Polly of the Circus" (Loretta Young), 12/7 "The Grand Duchess and the Waiter" (Robert Montgomery, Elissa Landi), 12/14 "Madame Sans-Gene" (Jean Harlow, Robert Taylor), 12/21 "The Golddiggers" (Dick Powell, Joan Blondell), 12/28 "Cavalcade" (Herbert Marshall, Madeleine Carroll).

1937: 1/4 "Men in White" (Spencer Tracy, Frances Farmer), 1/11 "The Gilded Lily" (Claudette Colbert, Fred MacMurray), 1/18 "The Criminal Code" (Edward G. Robinson), 1/25 "Tonight or Never" (Jeanette MacDonald), 2/1 "Mr. Deeds Goes to Town" (Gary Cooper, Barbara Stanwyck), 2/8 "Graystark" (Gene Raymond), 2/15 "Brewster's Millions" (Jack Benny, Mary Livingstone), 2/22 "Captain Blood" (Errol Flynn, Olivia deHavilland), 3/1 "Cappy Ricks" (Charles Winninger), 3/8 "Madame Butterfly" (Cary Grant, Grace Moore), 3/15 "Desire" (Marlene Dietrich), 3/22 "Death Takes a Holiday" (Fredric March, Florence Eldridge), 3/29 "Dulcy" (George Burns, Gracie Allen), 4/5 "A Farewell to Arms" (Clark Gable), 4/12 "Dodsworth" (Walter Huston, Fay Bainter), 4/19 "Alibi Ike" (Joe E. Brown), 4/26 "Magnificent Obsession" (Robert Taylor, Irene Dunne), 5/3 "Hands Across the Table" (Claudette Colbert, Joel McCrea), 5/10 "Mary of Scotland" (Joan Crawford), 5/17 "Another Language" (Bette Davis), 5/24 "Under Two Flags" (Herbert Marshall, Olivia deHavilland), 5/31 "The Plainsman" (Fredric March, Jean Arthur), 6/7 "British Agent" (Errol Flynn), 6/14 "Madame X" (James Stewart), 6/21 "Monsieur Beaucaire" (Leslie Howard), 6/28 "The Front Page" (Walter Winchell), 7/5 "Beau Brummel" (Robert Montgomery), 9/13 "A Star Is Born" (Robert Montgomery), 9/20 "The Outsider" (Fredric March, Florence Eldridge), 9/27 "Cimarron" (Clark Gable), 10/4 "Dodsworth" (Walter Huston), 10/11 "Stella Dallas" (Barbara Stanwyck) 10/18 "Up Pops the Devil" (Fred MacMurray), 10/25 "Arrowsmith" (Spencer Tracy), 11/1 "A Free Soul" (Ginger Rogers), 11/8 "She Loves Me Not" (Bing Crosby, Joan Blondell), 11/15 "Come and Get It" (Edward Arnold), 11/22 "The Petrified Forest" (Herbert Marshall), 11/29 "Peg O' My Heart" (Brian Aherne, Marion Davies), 12/6 "These Three" (Barbara Stanwyck, Errol Flynn), 12/13 "The Thirty-Nine Steps" (Robert Montgomery, Ida Lupino), 12/20 "The Song of Songs" (Marlene Dietrich, Douglas Fairbanks, Jr.), 12/27 "Beloved Enemy" (Madeleine Carroll).

1938: 1/3 "Alice Adams" (Claudette Colbert, Fred MacMurray), 1/10 "Enter Madame" (Grace Moore, Basil Rathbone), 1/17 "Disrali" (George Arliss), 1/24 "Clarence" (Bob Burns, Gail Patrick), 1/31 "Green Light" (Olivia deHavilland, Errol Flynn), 2/7 "Anna Christie" (Joan Crawford, Spencer Tracy), 2/14 "Brief Moment" (Ginger Rogers, Douglas Fairbanks, Jr.), 2/21 "Romance" (Madeleine Carroll, Herbert Marshall), 2/28 "Forsaking All Others" (Bette Davis, Joel McCrea), 3/7 "Poppy" (W. C. Fields, John Payne), 3/14 "The Boss" (Edward Arnold, Fay Wray), 3/21 "The Man Who Played God" (George Arliss), 3/28 "Naughty Marietta" (Lawrence Tibbett), 4/4 "Dark Victory" (Barbara Stanwyck, Melvyn Douglas), 4/11 "Mary Burns, Fugitive" (Miriam Hopkins, Henry Fonda), 4/18 "Mad About Music" (Deanna Durbin), 4/25 "Dangerous" (Madeleine Carroll, Don Ameche), 5/2 "The Prisoner of Shark Island" (Gary Cooper, Fay Wray), 5/9 "My Man Godfrey" (William Powell, Carole Lombard, Gail Patrick), 5/16 "The Girl from Tenth Avenue" (Loretta Young, George Brent), 5/23 "The Letter" (Merle Oberon, Walter Huston), 5/30 "I Met My Love Again" (Joan Bennett, Henry Fonda) 6/6 "A Doll's House" (Joan Crawford, Basil Rathbone), 6/13 "Theodora Goes Wild" (Cary Grant, Irene Dunne), 6/20 "Manslaughter" (Fredric March, Florence Eldridge), 6/27 "Jane Eyre" (Helen Hayes, Robert Montgomery), 7/4 "I Found Stella Parish" (Herbert Marshall, George Brent), 9/12 "Spawn of the North" (Dorothy Lamour, George Raft, Fred MacMurray), 9/19 "Morning Glory" (Barbara Stanwyck, Ralph Bellamy), 9/26 "Seven Keys to Baldpate" (Jack Benny, Mary Livingstone) 10/3 "Another Dawn" (Madeleine Carroll, Franchot Tone), 10/10 "Viva Villa" (Wallace Beery), 10/17 "Seventh Heaven" (Jean Arthur, Don Ameche), 10/24 "Babbitt" (Edward Arnold, Fay Bainter), 10/31 "That Certain Woman" (Carole Lombard, Basil Rathbone), 11/7 "Next Time We Love" (Margaret Sullavan, Joel McCrea), 11/14 "The Buccaneer" (Clark Gable), 11/21 "Confession" (Miriam Hopkins, Richard Greene), 11/28 "Interference" (Herbert Marshall, Leslie Howard), 12/5 "The Princess Comes Across" (Fred MacMurray, Madeleine Carroll), 12/12 "The Scarlet Pimpernel" (Leslie Howard, Olivia deHavilland), 12/19 "Kid Galahad" (Wayne Morris, Edward G. Robinson), 12/26 "Snow White and the Seven Dwarfs."

1939: 1/2 "The Perfect Specimen" (Errol Flynn, Joan Blondell), 1/9 "Meyerling" (William Powell, Janet Gaynor), 1/16 "Front Page Woman" (Paulette Goddard, Fred MacMurray), 1/23 "Cardinal Richelieu" (George Arliss), 1/30 "The Arkansas Traveler" (Bob Burns), 2/6 "The Count of Monte Cristo" (Robert Montgomery), 2/13 "The Return of Peter Grimm" (Lionel Barrymore), 2/20 "Stage Door" (Ginger Rogers, Rosalind Russell), 2/27 "Ceiling Zero" (James Cagney), 3/6 "One-way Passage" (William Powell,

Kay Francis, William Gargan), 3/13 "So Big" (Barbara Stanwyck), 3/20 "It Happened One Night" (Clark Gable, Claudette Colbert), 3/27 "A Man's Castle" (Loretta Young, Spencer Tracy), 4/3 "Silver Dollar" (Edward Arnold), 4/10 "The Lives of the Bengal Lancers" (Errol Flynn), 4/17 "Bullets or Ballots" (Edward G. Robinson, Humphrey Bogart, Mary Astor), 4/24 "Broadway Bill" (Robert Taylor), 5/1 "Lady for a Day" (May Robson), 5/8 "The Life of Emile Zola" (Paul Muni), 5/15 "Tovarich" (William Powell, Miriam Hopkins), 5/22 "Angels with Dirty Faces" (James Cagney, Pat O'Brien), 5/29 "Only Angels Have Wings" (Cary Grant, Jean Arthur), 6/5 "The Prisoner of Zenda" (Ronald Colman), 6/12 "White Banners" (Fay Bainter, Jackie Cooper), 6/19 "The Ex Mrs. Bradford" (William Powell, Claudette Colbert), 6/26 "Mrs. Moonlight" (Janet Gaynor, George Brent), 7/3 "Bordertown" (Don Ameche, Joan Bennett, Claire Trevor), 7/10 "Ruggles of Red Gap" (Charles Laughton), 9/11 "The Awful Truth" (Cary Grant, Claudette Colbert), 9/18 "Wuthering Heights" (Barbara Stanwyck, Ida Lupino), 9/25 "She Married Her Boss" (Ginger Rogers), 10/2 "You Can't Take It With You" (Edward Arnold), 10/9 "The Sisters" (Irene Dunne, David Niven), 10/16 "If I Were King" (Douglas Fairbanks, Jr.), 10/23 "Invitation to Happiness" (Fred MacMurray, Madeleine Carroll) 10/30 "The Old Maid" (Loretta Young, Miriam Hopkins), 11/6 "Only Yesterday" (Barbara Stanwyck, George Brent), 11/13 "The Champ" (Wallace Beery), 11/20 "Goodbye, Mr. Chips" (Lawrence Olivier), 11/27 "Pygmalian" (Jean Arthur, Brian Aherne), 12/4 "A Man to Remember" (Bob Burns, Anita Louise), 12/11 "In Name Only" (Carole Lombard, Cary Grant), 12/18 "Four Daughters" (The Lane Sisters), 12/25 "Pinocchio" (John Garfield, Cliff Edwards).

1940: 1/1 "Sorrell and Son" (Herbert Marshall), 1/8 "Dark Victory" (Bette Davis, Spencer Tracy, Lurene Tuttle), 1/15 "Sing You Sinners" (Bing Crosby), 1/22 "Bachelor Mother" (Ginger Rogers, Fredric March) 1/29 "Intermezzo" (Ingrid Bergman, Herbert Marshall), 2/5 "The Young at Heart" (Don Ameche, Ida Lupino), 2/12 "The Sidwalks of London (Charles Laughton, Elsa Lanchester), 2/19 "Made for Each Other" (Carole Lombard, Fred MacMurray), 2/26 "Swing High, Swing Low" (Rudy Vallee), 3/4 "Trade Winds" (Joan Bennett, Errol Flynn, Mary Astor) 3/11, "My Son, My Son" (Brian Aherne, Madeleine Carroll) 3/18 "The Rains Came" (George Brent, Kay Francis), 3/25 "Remember the Night" (Fred MacMurray, Barbara Stanwyck), 4/1 "Love Affair" (Irene Dunne, William Powell), 4/8 "Mama Loves Papa" (Jim and Marion Jordan), 4/15 "The Underpup" (Gloria Jean, Robert Cummings, Nan Grey) 4/22 "Abe Lincoln in

Illinois" (Raymond Massey, Fay Bainter), 4/29 "Smilin' Through" (Robert Taylor, Barbara Stanwyck), 5/6 "Our Town" (William Holden, Martha Scott, Frank Craven), 5/13 "True Confession" (Loretta Young, Fred MacMurray), 5/20 "Midnight" (Don Ameche, Claudette Colbert), 5/27 "Vigil in the Night" (Olivia deHavilland), 6/3 "Alexander's Ragtime Band" (Alice Faye, Ray Milland) 6/10 "Till We Meet Again" (Merle Oberon, Pat O'Brien), 6/17 "After the Thin Man" (William Powell, Myrna Loy), 6/24 "Show Boat" (Irene Dunne, Charles Winninger), 7/1 "Alias the Deacon" (Bob Burns), 7/8 "To the Ladies" (Helen Hayes), 9/9 "Manhattan Melodrama" (William Powell, Myrna Loy, Don Ameche), 9/16 "Love Is News" (Bob Hope, Madeleine Carroll), 9/23 "The Westerner" (Gary Cooper, Walter Brennan), 9/30 "His Girl Friday" (Claudette Colbert, Fred MacMurray) 10/7 "Wings of the Navy" (George Brent, Olivia deHavilland), 10/14 "The Littlest Rebel" (Shirley Temple), 10/21 "Lillian Russell" (Alice Faye, Victor Mature), 10/28 "Strike Up the Band" (Mickey Rooney, Judy Garland), 11/4 "Wuthering Heights" (Ida Lupino, Basil Rathbone), 11/11 "Nothing Sacred" (Douglas Fairbanks, Jr., Joan Bennett), 11/18 "The Rage of Manhattan" (Tyrone Power, Anabella), 11/25 "Jezebel" (Loretta Young), 12/2 "Knute Rockne" (Pat O'Brien, Ronald Reagan), 12/9 "My Favorite Wife" (Lawrence Olivier, Rosalind Russell), 12/16 "Fifth Avenue Girl" (Ginger Rogers), 12/23 "Young Tom Edison" (Mickey Rooney), 12/30 "A Little Bit of Heaven" (Gloria Jean).

1941: 1/6 "Vivacious Lady" (Alice Faye, Don Ameche), 1/13 "Libel" (Ronald Colman), 1/20 "The Cowboy and the Lady" (Gene Autry), 1/27 "Captain January" (Shirley Temple), 2/3 "Rebecca" (Ronald Colman, Ida Lupino), 2/10 "The Moon's Our Home" (James Stewart, Carole Lombard), 2/17 "Johnny Apollo" (Burgess Meredith, Dorothy Lamour), 2/24 "The Whole Town's Talking" (Jim and Marion Jordan), 3/3 "My Bill" (Kay Francis), 3/10 "The Awful Truth" (Bob Hope, Constance Bennett), 3/17 "Cheers for Miss Bishop" (Martha Scott, William Gargan), 3/24 "Flight Command" (Robert Taylor, Walter Pidgeon, Ruth Hussey), 3/31 "Stablemates" (Mickey Rooney, Wallace Beery), 4/7 "Stand-in" (Warner Baxter, Joan Bennett), 4/14 "Dust Be My Destiny" (John Garfield, Claire Trevor), 4/21 "The Letter" (Bette Davis), 4/28 "Wife, Husband, and Friend" (George Brent, Priscilla Lane), 5/5 "Kitty Foyle" (Ginger Rogers, Dennis Morgan), 5/12 "Craig's Wife" (Rosalind Russell), 5/19 "Model Wife" (Dick Powell, Joan Blondell), 5/26 "Virginia City" (Errol Flynn, Martha Scott), 6/2 "They Drive by Night" (George Raft, Lana Turner, Lucille Ball) 6/9 "Mr. and Mrs. Smith" (Bob

Hope), 6/16 "The Lady from Cheyenne" (Loretta Young), 6/23 "The Shop Around the Corner" (Claudette Colbert, Don Ameche), 6/30 "I Love You Again" (Cary Grant, Myrna Loy), 7/7 "Algiers" (Charles Boyer, Hedy Lamarr), 9/8 "Tom, Dick, and Harry" (Ginger Rogers, George Murphy), 9/15 "Lost Horizon" (Ronald Colman), 9/22 "Lydia" (Merle Oberon, Edna May Oliver), 9/29 "Third Finger, Left Hand" (Martha Scott), 10/6 "Unfinished Business" (Irene Dunne, Don Ameche), 10/13 "Buck Privates" (Bud Abbott, Lou Costello), 10/20 "Blood and Sand" (Tyrone Power, Anabella), 10/27 "Her First Beau" (Jackie Cooper, Jane Withers), 11/3 "Hired Wife" (William Powell, Myrna Loy), 11/10 "Hold Back the Dawn" (Charles Boyer, Paulette Goddard, Susan Hayward), 11/17 "Merton of the Movies" (Mickey Rooney, Judy Garland), 11/24 "Maisie Was a Lady" (Ann Sothern, Lew Ayres), 12/1 "A Man's Castle" (Spencer Tracy, Ingrid Bergman), 12/8 "The Doctor Takes a Wife" (Melvyn Douglas), 12/15 "All This and Heaven Too" (Bette Davis, Charles Boyer), 12/22 "Remember the Night" (Fred MacMurray, Jean Arthur), 12/29 "The Bride Came C.O.D." (Bob Hope, Hedy Lamarr).

1942: 1/5 "Smilin' Through" (Jeanette MacDonald), 1/12 "A Tale of Two Cities" (Ronald Colman), 1/19 "The Devil and Miss Jones" (Lionel Barrymore, Lana Turner), 1/26 "Here Comes Mr. Jordan" (Cary Grant, Evelyn Keyes), 2/2 "Skylark" (Claudette Colbert, Ray Milland), 2/9 "City for Conquest" (Alice Faye), 2/16 "Blossoms in the Dust" (Greer Garson, Walter Pidgeon), 2/23 "Appointment for Love" (Myrna Loy, Charles Boyer), 3/2 "The Great Lie" (Loretta Young, Mary Astor), 3/9 "The Lady Eve" (Barbara Stanwyck, Ray Milland), 3/16 "Manpower" (Marlene Dietrich, Edward G. Robinson, George Raft), 3/23 "Strawberry Blonde" (Rita Hayworth, Don Ameche), 3/30 "I Wanted Wings" (Veronica Lake, Ray Milland, William Holden), 4/6 "The Flying 69th" (Pat O'Brien), 4/13 "Northwest Mounted Police" (Gary Cooper, Paulette Goddard), 4/20 "One Foot in Heaven" (Fredric March, Martha Scott), 4/27 "Penny Serenade" (Robert Taylor, Barbara Stanwyck), 5/4 "Suspicion" (Joan Fontaine, Brian Aherne), 5/11 "The Last of Mrs. Cheyney" (Walter Pidgeon, Norma Shearer), 5/18 "A Man to Remember" (Lionel Barrymore), 5/25 "Test Pilot" (Robert Taylor, Rita Hayworth), 6/1 "Ball of Fire" (Barbara Stanwyck, Fred MacMurray) 6/8 "Arise My Love" (Loretta Young, Ray Milland), 6/15 "You Belong to Me" (Merle Oberon, George Brent), 6/22 "Bedtime Story" (Loretta Young, Don Ameche), 6/29 "The Champ" (Wallace Beery), 7/6 "Love Affair" (Charles Boyer, Irene Dunne), 7/13 "H. M. Pulham, Esq." (Hedy Lamarr, Robert Young), 7/20 "The Philadelphia Story" (Katharine Hepburn, Cary Grant),

9/14 "This Above All" (Tyrone Power, Barbara Stanwyck), 9/21 "How Green Was My Valley" (Roddy MacDowall, Maureen O'Hara, Walter Pidgeon), 9/28 "The Magnificent Dope" (Don Ameche, Henry Fonda, Lynn Bari), 10/5 "Love Crazy" (William Powell, Hedy Lamarr), 10/12 "Morning Glory" (Judy Garland, John Payne), 10/19 "My Favorite Blonde" (Bob Hope), 10/26 "Wake Island" (Brian Donlevy, Broderick Crawford), 11/2 "A Woman's Face" (Ida Lupino), 11/9 "Sullivan's Travels" (Veronica Lake), 11/16 "To Mary with Love" (Irene Dunne, Ray Milland), 11/23 "The Gay Sisters" (Barbara Stanwyck, Robert Young), 11/30 "Broadway" (George Raft, Janet Blair), 12/7 "The War Against Mrs. Hadley" (Fay Bainter, Van Johnson), 12/14 "Algiers" (Charles Boyer, Loretta Young), 12/21 "The Pied Piper" (Frank Morgan, Roddy MacDowell, Anne Baxter), 12/28 "A Star Is Born" (Judy Garland, Walter Pidgeon).

1943: 1/4 "The Bugle Sounds" (Wallace Beery), 1/11 "She Knew the Answers" (Joan Bennett, Eve Arden), 1/18 "My Gal Sal" (Mary Martin, Dick Powell), 1/25 "This Gun for Hire" (Alan Ladd, Joan Blondell, Laird Cregar), 2/1 "Showoff" (Harold Peary, Una Merkel), 2/8 "The Maltese Falcon" (Edward G. Robinson, Laird Cregar), 2/15 "Are Husbands Necessary" (George Burns, Gracie Allen), 2/22 "This Is the Army" (All Army Cast), 3/1 "The Lady Is Willing" (Kay Francis), 3/8 "Reap the Wild Wind" (Paulette Goddard, Ray Milland), 3/15 "Libel" (Ronald Colman), 3/22 "Each Dawn I Die" (George Raft, Franchot Tone, Lynn Bari), 3/29 "Crossroads" (Lana Turner), 4/5 "The Road to Morocco" (Bing Crosby, Bob Hope, Ginny Simms), 4/12 "Once Upon a Honeymoon" (Claudette Colbert, Laird Cregar), 4/19 "A Night to Remember" (Ann Sothern, Robert Young), 4/26 "The Lady Has Plans" (William Powell, Rita Hayworth), 5/3 "The Navy Comes Through" (Pat O'Brien, Ruth Hussey), 5/10 "Now Voyager" (Ida Lupino, Paul Henreid), 5/17 "The Talk of the Town" (Ronald Colman, Cary Grant, Jean Arthur), 5/14 "Hitler's Children" (Bonita Granville, Otto Kruger), 5/31 "The Major and the Minor" (Ginger Rogers, Ray Milland), 6/7 "My Friend Flicka" (Roddy MacDowell), 6/14 "The Philadelphia Story" (Robert Taylor, Loretta Young), 6/21 "In Which We Serve" (Ronald Colman), 6/28 "The Great Man's Lady" (Barbara Stanwyck, Joseph Cotten), 7/5 "My Sister Eileen" (Rosalind Russell, Janet Blair), 7/12 "Air Force" (George Raft), 9/13 "The Phantom of the Opera" (Nelson Eddy, Susanna Foster, Basil Rathbone), 9/20 "Flight for Freedom" (Rosalind Russell), 9/27 "Ladies in Retirement" (Ida Lupino), 10/4 "The Pride of the Yankees" (Gary Cooper), 10/11 "Heaven Can Wait" (Don Ameche, Maureen O'Hara), 10/18 "Mr. Lucky" (Cary Grant, Laraine Day), 10/25

"Slightly Dangerous" (Lana Turner, Victor Mature), 11/1 "So Proudly We Hail" (Veronica Lake, Claudette Colbert, Paulette Goddard), 11/8 "Salute to the Marines" (Wallace Beery), 11/15 "Hello, Frisco, Hello" (Alice Faye, Robert Young), 11/22 "China" (Alan Ladd, Loretta Young, William Bendix), 11/29 "The Navy Comes Through" (Pat O'Brien, Ruth Warrick), 12/6 "Mrs. Miniver" (Greer Garson, Walter Pidgeon), 12/13 "Five Graves to Cairo" (Franchot Tone, Anne Baxter), 12/20 "Dixie" (Bing Crosby, Dorothy Lamour), 12/27 "Kathleen" (Shirley Temple).

1944: 1/3 "Shadow of a Doubt" (William Powell, Teresa Wright), 1/10 "The Constant Nymph" (Charles Boyer, Alexis Smith), 1/17 "War Loan Drive" (Most of Hollywood's major stars appeared on this program, which was produced in order to support the war-bond sales effort), 1/24 "Casablanca" (Alan Ladd, Hedy Lamarr), 1/31 "Random Harvest" (Greer Garson, Ronald Colman), 2/7 "His Butler's Sister" (Deanna Durbin, Pat O'Brien), 2/14 "The Fallen Sparrow" (Robert Young, Maureen O'Hara), 2/21 "Wake Up and Live" (Frank Sinatra, Bob Crosby, Marilyn Maxwell), 2/28 "Guadalcanal Diary" (Preston Foster, Lloyd Nolan, William Bendix), 3/6 "The Letter" (Bette Davis, Herbert Marshall, Vincent Price), 3/13 "In Old Oklahoma" (Roy Rogers), 3/20 "The Hard Way" (Miriam Hopkins, Franchot Tone, Ann Baxter), 3/27 "The Phantom Lady" (Ella Raines, Brian Aherne), 4/3 "Destroyer" (Edward G. Robinson, Dennis O'Keefe), 4/10 "The Happy Land" (Don Ameche, Frances Dee), 4/17 "Coney Island" (Dorothy Lamour, Alan Ladd), 4/24 "This Land Is Mine" (Charles Laughton, Maureen O'Sullivan), 5/1 "Appointment for Love" (Paul Lukas, Olivia deHavilland), 5/8 "Penny Serenade" (Irene Dunne, Joseph Cotten), 5/15 "Action in the North Atlantic" (George Raft, Raymond Massey), 5/22 "Springtime in the Rockies" (Betty Grable, Carmen Miranda, Dick Powell), 5/29 "Old Acquaintance" (Alexis Smith, Miriam Hopkins), 6/5 "Jane Eyre" (Orson Welles, Loretta Young), 6/12 "Naughty Marietta" (Jeanette MacDonald, Nelson Eddy), 6/19 "Lost Angel" (Margaret O'Brien, James Craig), 6/26 "Christmas in July" (Dick Powell, Linda Darnell), 7/3 "It Happened Tomorrow" (Don Ameche, Anne Baxter) 9/4 "Maytime" (Jeanette MacDonald, Nelson Eddy), 9/11 "Break of Hearts" (Orson Welles, Rita Hayworth), 9/18 "Suspicion" (William Powell, Olivia deHavilland), 9/25 "Lucky Partners" (Lucille Ball, Don Ameche), 10/2 "Home in Indiana" (Walter Brennan, Charlotte Greenwood), 10/9 "In Old Chicago" (Dorothy Lamour, Robert Young, John Hodiak), 10/16 "Seventh Heaven" (Van Johnson, Jennifer Jones, Jean Hersholt), 10/23 "The Story of Dr. Wassel" (Gary Cooper), 10/30 "Standing Room Only" (Paulette God-dard, Fred MacMurray), 11/6 "The Pied Piper" (Frank Morgan, Margaret O'Brien, Signe Hasso), 11/13 "Magnificent Obsession" (Claudette Colbert, Don Ameche), 11/20 "It Started with Eve" (Charles Laughton, Dick Powell), 11/27 "Dark Waters" (Merle Oberon), 12/4 "The Unguarded Hour" (Robert Montgomery, Laraine Day), 12/11 "Casanova Brown" (Gary Cooper, Joan Bennett), 12/18 "Berkley Square" (Ronald Colman, Maureen O'Sullivan), 12/25 "The Vagabond King" (Dennis Morgan, Kathryn Grayson, J. Carroll Naish).

1945: 1/1 "Bride by Mistake" (Laraine Day, John Hodiak), 1/8 "I Never Left Home" (Bob Hope, Frances Langford, Jerry Colonna), 1/15 "The Master Race" (George Coulouris, Nancy Gates), 1/22 "Tender Comrade" (Olivia deHavilland), 1/29 "Lady in the Dark" (Ginger Rogers, Ray Milland), 2/5 "Laura" (Gene Tierney, Dana Andrews), 2/12 "For Whom the Bell Tolls" (Gary Cooper, Ingrid Bergman), 2/19 "Sunday Dinner for a Soldier" (Anne Baxter, John Hodiak), 2/26 "Bedtime Story" (Cary Grant, Greer Garson), 3/5 "Disputed Passage" (Alan Ladd), 3/12 "The Devil and Miss Jones" (Frank Morgan, Linda Darnell), 3/19 "Grissley's Millions" (Pat O'Brien, Lynn Bari), 3/26 "A Tale of Two Cities" (Orson Welles, Rosemary DeCamp), 4/2 "Swanee River" (Al Jolson, Dennis Morgan, Frances Gifford), 4/9 "The Suspect" (Charles Laughton, Ella Raines, Rosalind Ivan), 4/16 "Only Yesterday" (Ida Lupino, Robert Young), 4/23 "The Petrified Forest" (Ronald Colman, Susan Hayward), 4/30 "Moontide" (Humphrey Bogart), 5/7 "Sing You Sinners" (Bing Crosby, Joan Caulfield), 5/14 "Alexander Graham Bell" (Don Ameche), 5/21 "And Now Tomorrow" (Loretta Young, Alan Ladd), 5/28 "Kentucky" (Laraine Day, Walter Brennan, Tom Drake), 6/4 "Intermezzo" (Ingrid Bergman, Joseph Cotten), 6/11 "Murder, My Sweet" (Dick Powell, Claire Trevor), 6/18 "The Canterville Ghost" (Charles Laughton, Margaret O'Brien), 6/25 "The Woman in the Window" (Edward G. Robinson, Joan Bennett), 8/27 "Practically Yours" (Claudette Colbert, Ray Milland), 9/3 "The Enchanted Cottage" (Dorothy McGuire, Robert Young), 9/10 "Experiment Perilous" (Paul Henreid), 9/17 "Christmas Holiday" (Loretta Young, William Holden), 9/24 "It's a Date" (Diana Lynn, Brian Aherne), 10/1 "Mr. Skeffington" (Bette Davis, Paul Henreid), 10/8 "Roughly Speaking" (Rosalind Russell, Jack Carson), 10/15 "A Medal for Benny" (Dorothy Lamour, J. Carroll Naish), 10/22 "Lost Angel" (Margaret O'Brien, George Murphy), 10/29 "The Affairs of Susan" (Joan Fontaine), 11/5 "Destry Rides Again" (James Stewart, Joan Blondell), 11/12 "Guest in the House" (Robert Young), 11/19 "Keys of the Kingdom" (Ronald Colman), 11/26 "Salty O'-

Rourke" (Alan Ladd, Marjorie Reynolds), 12/3 "Blood on the Sun" (James Cagney), 12/10 "Guest Wife" (Olivia deHavilland, Don Ameche), 12/17 "Made for Each Other" (James Stewart, Marsha Hunt), 12/24 "I'll Be Seeing You" (Joseph Cotten, Dorothy Mc-Guire), 12/31 "Pride of the Marines" (John Garfield, Eleanor Parker).

1946: 1/7 "You Came Along" (Van Johnson, Lizabeth Scott), 1/14 "Valley of Decision" (Greer Garson, Gregory Peck), 1/21 "Johnny Eager" (Robert Taylor, Susan Peters, Van Heflin), 1/28 "The Clock" (Judy Garland, John Hodiak), 2/4 "This Love Of Ours" (Rita Hayworth, Charles Coburn), 2/11 "Now Voyager" (Bette Davis, Gregory Peck), 2/18 "Captain January" (Margaret O'Brien, Lionel Barrymore), 2/25 "Thunderhead, Son of Flicka" (Roddy MacDowell), 3/4 "The Amazing Mrs. Holiday" (Gene Tierney, Walter Brennan), 3/11 "Presenting Lily Mars" (June Allyson, Van Heflin), 3/18 "A Tale of Two Cities" (Ronald Colman, Heather Angel), 3/25 "Wonder Man" (Danny Kaye, Virginia Mayo), 4/1 "Barnacle Bill" (Wallace Beery, Majorie Main), 4/8 "Honky Tonk" (Lana Turner, John Hodiak), 4/15 "Whistle Stop" (Alan Ladd, Evelyn Keyes), 4/22 "Love Letters" (Loretta Young, Joseph Cotten), 4/29 "Gaslight" (Ingrid Bergman, Charles Boyer), 5/6 "Tomorrow Is Forever" (Claudette Colbert, Van Heflin), 5/13 "Pardon My Past" (Fred MacMurray, Marguerite Chapman), 5/20 "Deadline at Dawn" (Joan Blondell, Paul Lukas), 5/27 "Music for Millions" (Margaret O'Brien, Jose Iturbi, Jimmy Durante), 6/3 "None But the Lonely Heart" (Ethel Barrymore, Brian Aherne), 6/10 "And Now Tomorrow" (Olivia deHavilland, John Lund), 6/17 "Fallen Angel" (Linda Darnell, Maureen O'Hara, Mark Stevens), 6/24 "State Fair" (Jeanne Crain, Dick Haymes, Vivian Blaine), 8/26 "Without Reservations" (Claudette Colbert, Robert Cummings), 9/2 "Our Vines Have Tender Grapes" (Margaret O'Brien, Frances Gifford), 9/9 "The Barretts of Wimpole Street" (Loretta Young, Brian Aherne), 9/16 "Madame Curie" (Greer Garson, Walter Pidgeon), 9/23 "Sentimental Journey" (John Payne, Lynn Bari), 9/30 "Coney Island" (Betty Grable, Victor Mature, Barry Sullivan), 10/7 "Dragonwyck" (Gene Tierney, Vincent Price), 10/14 "To Have and Have Not" (Humphrey Bogart, Lauren Bacall), 10/21 "Miss Susie Slagle's" (Joan Caulfield, William Holden, Billy DeWolfe), 10/28 "From This Day Forward" (Joan Fontaine, Mark Stevens), 11/4 "I've Always Loved You" (Joseph Cotten), 11/11 "Gallant Journey" (Glenn Ford, Janet Blair), 11/18 "O.S.S." (Alan Ladd, Veronica Lake), 11/25 "Mrs. Parkington" (Greer Garson, Walter Pidgeon), 12/2 "Meet Me in St. Louis" (Judy Garland, Margaret O'Brien, Tom Drake), 12/9 "Together Again" (Irene Dunne, Walter Pidgeon), 12/16 "Killer Kates" (Jack Benny, Gail Patrick, James Gleason) 12/23 "Do You Love Me?" (Dick Haymes, Maureen O'Hara), 12/30 "Crackup" (Pat O'Brien, Lynn Bari).

1947: 1/6 "Till the End Of Time" (Laraine Day, Robert Mitchum), 1/13 "The Green Years" (Charles Coburn, Tom Drake), 1/20 "Anna and the King of Siam" (Irene Dunne, Rex Harrison), 1/27 "Cluny Brown" (Olivia deHavilland, Charles Boyer), 2/3 "National Velvet" (Elizabeth Taylor, Mickey Rooney, Donald Crisp), 2/10 "Frenchman's Creek" (Joan Fontaine, David Niven), 2/17 "Devotion" (Jane Wyman, Ida Lupino, Vincent Price), 2/24 "Kitty" (Paulette Goddard), 3/3 "Somewhere in the Night" (John Hodiak, Lynn Bari), 3/10 "It's a Wonderful Life" (James Stewart, Donna Reed, Victor Moore), 3/17 "Leave Her to Heaven" (Gene Tierney, Cornel Wilde), 3/24 "Smoky" (Joel McCrea, Constance Moore), 3/31 "How Green Was My Valley" (Donald Crisp, David Niven, Maureen O'Sullivan), 4/7 "Alexander's Ragtime Band" (Al Jolson, Dinah Shore, Tyrone Power), 4/14 "Monsieur Beaucaire" (Bob Hope), 4/21 "My Reputation" (Barbara Stanwyck, George Brent), 4/28 "My Darling Clementine" (Henry Fonda, Richard Conte), 5/5 "The Egg and I" (Claudette Colbert, Fred MacMurray), 5/12 "Johnny O'Clock" (Dick Powell, Lee J. Cobb, Marguerite Chapman), 5/19 "It Happened on Fifth Avenue" (Victor Moore, Charles Ruggles, Gale Storm), 5/26 "Vacation from Marriage" (Deborah Kerr, Van Heflin), 6/2 "The Jazz Singer" (Al Jolson, Gail Patrick), 6/9 "The Animal Kingdom" (Jane Wyman, Dennis Morgan), 6/16 "The Other Love" (Barbara Stanwyck, George Brent), 6/23 "Cynthia" (Elizabeth Taylor, Mary Astor), 4/23 "A Stolen Life" (Bette Davis, Glenn Ford), 9/1 "Three Wise Fools" (Margaret O'Brien, Lionel Barrymore), 9/8 "Margie" (Jeanne Crain, Glenn Langan), 9/15 "The Seventh Veil" (Ida Lupino, Joseph Cotten), 9/22 "Two Years Before the Mast" (Alan Ladd, Wanda Hendrix, MacDonald Carey), 9/29 "The Web" (Vincent Price, Ella Raines), 10/6 "Undercurrent" (Katharine Hepburn, Robert Taylor), 10/13 "Great Expectations" (Robert Cummings, Ann Blyth), 10/20 "13 Rue Madeleine" (Robert Montgomery, Lloyd Nolan), 10/27 "Stairway to Heaven" (Ray Milland, Lloyd Nolan), 11/3 "Singapore" (Fred MacMurray, Ava Gardner), 11/10 "Dark Corner" (Lucille Ball, Mark Stevens), 11/17 "Nobody Lives Forever" (Jane Wyman, Ronald Reagan), 11/24 "Saratoga Trunk" (Ida Lupino, Zachary Scott), 12/1 "The Ghost and Mrs. Muir" (Madeleine Carroll, Charles Boyer), 12/8 "Ride the Pick Horse" (Robert Montgomery), 12/15 "Magic Town" (James Stewart, Jane Wyman), 12/22 "Miracle on 34th Street" (Maureen O'Hara, Edmund Gwenn, John Payne), 12/29

"Anchors Aweigh" (Frank Sinatra, Gene Kelly, Kathryn Grayson).

1948: 1/5 "The Farmer's Daughter" (Loretta Young, Joseph Cotten), 1/12 "The Kiss of Death" (Richard Widmark, Victor Mature, Coleen Grey), 1/19 "The Yearling" (Gregory Peck, Jane Wyman, Claude Jarman, Jr.), 1/26 "Notorious" (Ingrid Bergman, Joseph Cotten), 2/2 "Mother Wore Tights" (Betty Grable, Dan Dailey), 2/9 "Lady in the Lake" (Robert Montgomery, Audrey Totter), 2/16 "The Jolson Story" (Al Jolson, Evelyn Keyes), 2/23 "T-Men" (Dennis O'Keefe, Gail Patrick), 3/1 "Bad Bascomb" (Wallace Beery, Margaret O'Brien), 3/8 "Spellbound" (Joseph Cotten, Valli), 3/15 "Irish Eyes Are Smiling" (Dick Haymes), 3/22 "A Woman's Vengeance" (Charles Boyer, Ann Blyth), 3/29 "I Love You Again" (William Powell, Ann Sothern), 4/5 "Daisy Kenyon" (Ida Lupino, Dana Andrews), 4/12 "Perfect Marriage" (Ray Milland, Lizabeth Scott), 4/19 "Random Harvest" (Ronald Colman, Greer Garson), 4/26 "Dear Ruth" (Joan Caulfield, William Holden), 5/3 "Cloak and Dagger" (Ronald Reagan, Lilli Palmer), 5/10 "Intrigue" (George Raft, June Havoc, Jeff Chandler), 5/17 "Homestretch" (Maureen O'Hara, Cornel Wilde), 5/24 "I Walk Alone" (Burt Lancaster, Lizabeth Scott), 5/31 "Miracle of the Bells" (Fred MacMurray, Frank Sinatra, Valli), 6/7 "Relentless" (Robert Young, Claire Trevor), 6/14 "Jane Eyre" (Ingrid Bergman, Robert Montgomery), 6/28 "You Were Meant for Me" (Dan Dailey, Donna Reed), 8/30 "I Remember Mama" (Irene Dunne), 9/6 "Mr. Peabody and the Mermaid" (William Powell), 9/13 "Another Part of the Forest" (Walter Huston, Vincent Price, Ann Blyth), 9/20 "Gentlemen's Agreement" (Gregory Peck, Anne Baxter), 9/27 "Tap Roots" (Van Heflin, Susan Hayward), 10/4 "Stallion Road" (Ronald Reagan, Alexis Smith, Zachary Scott), 10/11 "Larceny" (John Payne, Joan Caulfield), 10/18 "Razor's Edge" (Ida Lupino, Mark Stevens), 10/25 "Secret Heart" (Walter Pidgeon, Deborah Kerr), 11/8 "Pitfall" (Dick Powell, Jane Wyatt, Lizabeth Scott), 11/15 "Body and Soul" (John Garfield, Jane Wyman), 11/22 "The Big Clock" (Ray Milland, Maureen O'Sullivan), 11/19 "Brief Encounter" (Greer Garson, Van Heflin), 12/6 "The Foxes of Harrow" (Maureen O'Hara, John Hodiak), 12/13 "The Seventh Veil" (Ingrid Bergman, Robert Montgomery), 12/20 "Miracle on 34th Street" (Maureen O'Hara, John Payne, Edmund Gwenn), 12/27 "Luck of the Irish" (Anne Baxter, Dana Andrews).

1949: 1/3 "The Mating of Millie" (Glenn Ford), 1/10 "The Velvet Touch" (Rosalind Russell, Sydney Greenstreet), 1/17 "You Gotta Stay Happy" (James Stewart, Joan Fontaine), 1/24 "High Barbaree" (Van Johnson), 1/31 "Street with No Name" (Richard Widmark, Lloyd Nolan), 2/7 "Captain from Castile" (Cornel Wilde, Jean Peters), 2/14 "Sitting Pretty" (Clifton Webb, Robert Young), 2/21 "The Unafraid" (Burt Lancaster, Joan Fontaine), 2/28 "Apartment for Peggy" (Jeanne Crain, William Holden), 3/7 "Red River" (John Wayne, Joanne Dru), 3/14 "What a Woman" (Rosalind Russell, Robert Cummings), 3/21 "That Wonderful Urge" (Don Ameche, Gene Tierney), 3/28 "The Accused" (Loretta Young, Robert Cummings), 4/4 "Family Honeymoon" (Claudette Colbert, Fred MacMurray), 4/11 "The Song of Bernadette" (Anne Baxter, Charles Bickford), 4/18 "The Treasure of the Sierra Madre" (Humphrey Bogart, Walter Huston, Lauren Bacall), 4/25 "When My Baby Smiles at Me" (Betty Grable, Dan Dailey), 5/2 "Miss Tatlock's Millions" (John Lund, Wanda Hendrix), 5/9 "The Paradine Case" (Joseph Cotten, Valli), 5/16 "April Showers" (Jack Carson, Dorothy Lamour), 5/23 "To the Ends of the Earth" (Dick Powell, Signe Hasso), 5/30 "Anna and the King of Siam" (Irene Dunne, James Mason), 6/6 "Mildred Pierce" (Rosalind Russell, Zachary Scott), 6/13 "The Bachelor and the Bobby Soxer" (Cary Grant, Shirley Temple), 6/20 "Merton of the Movies" (Mickey Rooney, Arlene Dahl), 6/27 "Every Girl Should Be Married" (Cary Grant, Betsy Drake), 8/29 "June Bride" (Bette Davis, James Stewart), 9/5 "Saigon" (John Lund, Lizabeth Scott), 9/12 "Deep Waters" (Dana Andrews, Donna Reed), 9/19 "Green Dolphin Street" (Lana Turner, Peter Lawford, Van Heflin), 9/26 "Emperor Waltz" (Bing Crosby, Ann Blyth), 10/3 "It Happens Every Spring" (Ray Milland), 10/10 "Mr. Blandings Builds His Dream House" (Cary Grant, Irene Dunne), 10/17 "Mother Was a Freshman" (Loretta Young, Van Johnson), 10/24 "Scudda Hoo, Scudda Hay" (June Haver, Lon McCallister), 10/31 "Portrait of Jennie" (Joseph Cotten, Anne Baxter), 11/7 "High Wall" (Van Heflin, Janet Leigh), 11/14 "Mother Wore Tights" (Betty Grable), 11/21 "Sorrowful Jones" (Bob Hope, Lucille Ball), 11/28 "Key Largo" (Edward G. Robinson, Claire Trevor, Edmund O'Brien), 12/5 "Dear Ruth" (William Holden, Joan Caulfield), 12/12 "Street with No Name" (Mark Stevens, Stephen McNally), 12/19 "The Bishop's Wife" (Tyrone Power, David Niven), 12/26 "My Dream Is Yours" (Jack Carson).

1950: 1/2 "To Each His Own" (Olivia deHavilland, John Lund), 1/9 "Sorry, Wrong Number" (Barbara Stanwyck, Burt Lancaster), 1/16 "Mr. Belvedere Goes to College" (Clifton Webb), 1/23 "I'll Be Yours" (William Bendix, Ann Blyth, Robert Cummings), 1/30 "California" (Ray Milland, Lizabeth Scott), 2/6 "Red Hot, and Blue" (Betty Hutton, John Lund), 2/13 "The Stratton Story" (James Stewart, June Allyson), 2/20 "A Letter to Three Wives" (Paul Douglas, Linda Darnell),

2/27 "Easy to Wed" (Van Johnson, Esther Williams), 3/6 "Slattery's Hurricane" (Maureen O'Hara, Veronica Lake), 3/13 "Little Women" (June Allyson, Margaret O'Brien, Peter Lawford), 3/20 "Father Was a Fullback" (Paul Douglas, Maureen O'Hara), 3/27 "The Man Who Came to Dinner" (Clifton Webb, Lucille Ball), 4/3 "Come to the Stable" (Loretta Young, Hugh Marlowe), 4/10 "The Snake Pit" (Olivia deHavilland, Leo Genn), 4/17 "Every Girl Should Be Married" (Cary Grant, Betsy Drake), 4/24 "Mrs. Mike" (Dick Powell, Gene Tierney), 5/1 "All My Sons" (Burt Lancaster, Edward Arnold), 5/8 "The Life of Riley" (William Bendix), 5/15 "The Lady Takes a Sailor" (Jane Wyman, Dennis Morgan), 5/22 "Jolson Sings Again" (Al Jolson, Barbara Hale), 5/29 "Night Song" (Dana Andrews, Joan Fontaine), 6/5 "Bride for Sale" (Robert Young, Claudette Colbert), 6/12 "The Corn Is Green" (Olivia deHavilland, Richard Basehart), 6/19 "John Loves Mary" (Ronald Reagan, Patricia Neal), 6/26 "The Bride Goes Wild" (June Allyson, Van Johnson), 8/28 "My Foolish Heart" (Susan Hayward, Dana Andrews), 9/4 "One Sunday Afternoon" (Dennis Morgan, Patricia Neal, Ruth Roman), 9/11 "The Heiress" (Olivia deHavilland, Louis Calhern), 9/18 "Pinky" (Ethel Barrymore, Jeanne Crain), 9/25 "Good Sam" (Ann Sheridan, Joel McCrea), 10/2 "Flamingo Road" (Jane Wyman), 10/9 "Love That Brute" (Paul Douglas, Jean Peters), 10/16 "House of Strangers" (Anne Baxter, Richard Conte), 10/23 "A Woman of Distinction" (Cary Grant, Rosalind Russell), 10/20 "Double Indemnity" (Barbara Stanwyck, Fred MacMurray), 11/6 "Rebecca" (Lawrence Olivier, Vivien Leigh), 11/13 "Wabash Avenue" (Betty Grable, Victor Mature), 11/20 "Pretty Baby" (Betsy Drake, Dennis Morgan), 11/27 "You're My Everything" (Anne Baxter, Phil Harris), 12/4 "Apartment for Peggy" (Jeanne Crain), 12/11 "BF's Daughter" (Barbara Stanwyck, Stewart Granger), 12/18 "Holiday Affair" (Laraine Day, Robert Mitchum), 12/25 "The Wizard of Oz" (Judy Garland).

1951: 1/1 "The Barkleys of Broadway" (Ginger Rogers, George Murphy), 1/8 "Once More My Darling" (Ann Blyth, Van Heflin), 1/15 "The Farmer's Daughter" (Loretta Young, Joseph Cotten), 1/22 "Broken Arrow" (Burt Lancaster, Debra Paget, Jeff Chandler), 1/29 "Treasure Island" (James Mason, Bobby Driscoll), 2/5 "Louisa" (Ronald Reagan, Ruth Hussey), 2/12 "Battleground" (Van Johnson, John Hodiak, George Murphy), 2/19 "Dear Wife" (William Holden, Joan Caulfield), 2/26 "When Johnny Comes Marching Home" (James Stewart, Joanne Dru), 3/15 "Panic in the Streets" (Richard Widmark, Paul Douglas), 3/12 "She Wore a Yellow Ribbon" (John Wayne, Mel Ferrer), 3/19 "The Red Danube" (Walter Pidgeon, Peter

Lawford, Janet Leigh), 3/26 "Seventh Heaven" (Janet Gaynor, Charles Farrell), 4/2 "Where the Sidewalk Ends" (Anne Baxter, Dana Andrews), 4/9 "The Third Man" (Joseph Cotten, Evelyn Keyes), 4/16 "Oh, You Beautiful Doll" (Joan Caulfield, Bob Crosby, George Jessel), 4/23 "Family Honeymoon" (Claudette Colbert, Fred MacMurray), 4/30 "Down to the Sea in Ships" (Lionel Barrymore, Richard Widmark), 5/7 "Cheaper by the Dozen" (Clifton Webb), 5/14 "Brief Encounter" (Olivia deHavilland, Richard Basehart), 5/21 "Love Letters" (Loretta Young, William Holden), 5/28 "Bright Leaf" (Gregory Peck, Virginia Mayo), 6/4 "A Ticket to Tomahawk" (Anne Baxter, Dan Dailey), 6/11 "Our Very Own" (Farley Granger, Diana Lynn), 6/18 "Edward My Son" (Walter Pidgeon, Deborah Kerr), 6/25 "The Reformer and the Redhead" (Dick Powell, June Allyson), 8/27 "The Mudlark" (Irene Dunne, Sir Cedrick Hardwicke), 9/3 "Payment on Demand" (Bette Davis, Barry Sullivan), 9/10 "Fancy Pants" (Bob Hope, Lucille Ball), 9/17 "Sunset Boulevard" (Gloria Swanson, William Holden), 9/24 "Movietime, USA"—50th Anniversary of Movies—(All Star Cast), 10/1 "All About Eve" (Bette Davis, Gary Merrill, Anne Baxter), 10/8 "Borderline" (Claire Trevor, Fred MacMurray), 10/15 "Mister 880" (Edmund Gwenn, Dana Andrews), 10/22 "Margie" (Jeanne Crain, High Marlowe), 10/29 "I'd Climb The Highest Mountain" (Susan Hayward, William Lundigan), 11/5 "That Forsythe Woman" (Greer Garson, Walter Pidgeon), 11/12 "Winchester 73" (James Stewart), 11/19 "Samson and Delilah" (Hedy Lamarr, Victor Mature), 11/26 "To Please a Lady" (Donna Reed, Adolph Menjou, John Hodiak), 12/3 "Strangers on a Train" (Frank Lovejoy, Ray Milland, Ruth Roman), 12/10 "The Lemon Drop Kid" (Bob Hope, Marilyn Maxwell), 12/17 "The Men" (William Holden, Teresa Wright), 12/24 "Alice in Wonderland" (Kathryn Beaumont, Jerry Colonna, Ed Wynn), 12/31 "Bird of Paradise" (Louis Jourdan, Debra Paget, Jeff Chandler).

1952: 1/7 "Duchess of Idaho" (Van Johnson, Esther Williams), 1/14 "Goodbye My Fancy" (Barbara Stanwyck, Robert Young), 1/21 "Captain Horatio Hornblower" (Gregory Peck, Virginia Mayo), 1/28 "Branded" (Burt Lancaster, Mona Freeman), 2/4 "Showboat" (Ava Gardner, Kathryn Grayson, Howard Keel), 2/18 "Kim" (Errol Flynn, Dean Stockwell), 2/25 "My Blue Heaven" (Betty Grable, Dan Dailey), 3/3 "Young Man with a Horn" (Kirk Douglas, Jo Stafford), 3/10 "Follow the Sun" (Anne Baxter, Burgess Meredith, Gary Merrill), 3/17 "Top O' the Morning" (Barry Fitzgerald, Ann Blyth), 3/24 "Come to the Stable" (Loretta Young), 3/31 "I Can Get It for You Wholesale" (Susan Hayward, Dan Dailey), 4/7 "Union Station" (William Holden, Nancy Olsen), 4/14

"Royal Wedding" (Jane Powell, George Murphy), 4/21 "Crisis" (Robert Taylor), 4/28 "No Highway in the Sky" (James Stewart, Marlene Dietrich), 5/5 "On Moonlight Bay" (Gordon MacRae, Jane Wyman), 5/12 "Riding High" (Rhonda Fleming, Fred MacMurray), 5/19 "The Magnificent Yankee" (Ann Harding, Louis Calhern), 5/26 "Room for One More" (Cary Grant, Phyllis Thaxter, 9/8 "Two Weeks with Love" (Jane Powell, Debbie Reynolds, Ricardo Montalban), 9/15 "Here Comes the Groom" (Jane Wyman, Fred MacMurray), 9/22 "I'll Never Forget You" (Tyrone Power, Debra Paget), 9/29 "Adam and Evelyn" (Jean Simmons, Stewart Granger), 10/6 "The Model and the Marriage Broker" (Jeanne Crain, Thelma Ritter), 10/13 "Five Fingers" (James Mason), 10/20 "My Six Convicts" (Dana Andrews), 10/27 "My Son John" (John Lund, Fay Bainter, Dean Jagger), 11/3 "Viva Zapata" (Charlton Heston, Jean Peters), 11/10 "Grounds for Marriage" (Van Johnson, Kathryn Grayson), 11/17 "Submarine Command" (William Holden, Alexis Smith), 11/24 "The Blue Veil" (Jane Wyman), 12/1 "King Solomon's Mines" (Deborah Kerr, Stewart Granger), 12/8 "Strictly Dishonorable" (Janet Leigh, Fernando Lamas), 12/15 "The African Queen" (Humphrey Bogart, Greer Garson), 12/22 "Les Miserables" (Ronald Colman, Debra Paget, Robert Newton), 12/29 "Westward the Women" (Robert Taylor).

1953: 1/5 "Phone Call From A Stranger" (Shelley Winters, Gary Merrill), 1/12 "The Will Rogers Story" (Will Rogers, Jr., Jane Wyman), 1/19 "Appointment with Danger" (William Holden, Colleen Gray), 1/26 "September Affair" (Joseph Cotten, Joan Fontaine), 2/2 "Captain Carey, USA" (Charlton Heston, Wanda Hendrix), 2/9 "With a Song in My Heart" (Susan Hayward, David Wayne, Thelma Ritter), 2/16 "Lady in the Dark" (Judy Garland, John Lund), 2/23 "You're My Everything" (Jeanne Crain, Dan Dailey), 3/2 "Close to My Heart" (Ray Milland), 3/9 "The People Against O'Hara" (Walter Pidgeon, Janet Leigh), 3/16 "This Woman Is Dangerous" (Virginia Mayo, Dennis Morgan), 5/23 "Fourteen Hours" (Paul Douglas), 3/30 "Miracle of Our Lady of Fatima" (J. Carroll Naish), 4/6 "Angels in the Outfield" (Janet Leigh, George Murphy), 4/13 "Just for You" (Jane Wyman, Dick Haymes), 4/20 "Deadline, USA" (Dan Dailey, Debra Paget), 4/27 "Somebody Loves Me" (Betty Hutton, David Wayne), 5/4 "Wait Till the Sun Shines, Nellie" (Jean Peters, Phyllis Thaxter, Les Tremayne), 5/11 "The Bishop's Wife" (Cary Grant), 5/18 "The Girl in White" (June Allyson), 5/25 "Lure of the Wilderness" (Jean Peters, Jeffrey Hunter), 6/1 "High Tor" (William Holden), 6/8 "China Run" (Virginia Mayo), 6/15 "The Lady and the Tumbler" (Fred MacMurray), 6/22 "The Fall of Maggie Phillips" (Dor-

othy McGuire), 6/29 "One More Spring" (Jeanne Crain), 7/6 "Cynara" (Joseph Cotten), 7/13 "Physician in Spite of Himself" (Robert Young), 7/20 "The Birds" (Herbert Marshall), 7/27 "One Foot in Heaven" (Dana Andrews), 8/3 "Romance to a Degree" (Joseph Cotten), 8/10 "Leave Her to Heaven" (Joan Fontaine), 8/17 "Edward My Son" (Walter Pidgeon), 8/24 "The Affairs of Susan" (Anne Baxter), 8/31 "Our Last September" (Claire Trevor), 9/7 "My Cousin Rachel" (Olivia deHavilland), 9/14 "The Steel Trap" (Joseph Cotten), 9/21 "I Confess" (Cary Grant, Phyllis Thaxter), 9/28 "The President's Lady" (Charlton Heston, Joan Fontaine), 10/5 "Our Very Own" (Terry Moore, Joan Evans), 10/12 "Breaking the Sound Barrier" (Robert Newton), 10/19 "Taxi" (Dan Dailey), 10/2 "Skirts Ahoy" (Esther Williams, Barry Sullivan), 11/ "Because of You" (June Allyson, Jeff Chandler), 11/ "Thunder on the Hill" (Claudette Colbert), 11/16 "I Grows on Trees" (Ginger Rogers), 11/23 "The Browning Version" (Ronald Colman, Bonita Hume), 11/3 "Undercurrent" (Joan Fontaine, Mel Ferrer), 12/ "Man on a Tightrope" (Edward G. Robinson), 12/1 "Million Dollar Mermaid" (Esther Williams, Walter Pidgeon), 12/21 "Peter Pan" (Kathryn Beaumont, Bobby Driscoll, John Carradine), 12/28 "June Bride" (Irene Dunne, Fred MacMurray).

1954: 1/4 "The Day the Earth Stood Still" (Michael Rennie, Jean Peters), 1/11 "Has Anybody Seen My Gal?" (Piper Laurie, Rock Hudson), 1/18 "The Winslow Boy" (Ray Milland, Brian Aherne, Dorothy McGuire), 1/25 "People Will Talk" (Jeanne Crain, Cary Grant, Joseph Cotten), 2/1 "Laura" (Gene Tierney), 2/8 "The Third Man" (Ray Milland, Ruth Roman), 2/15 "Trouble Along the Way" (June Haver, Jack Carson), 2/22 "September Affair" (Dana Andrews, Eleanor Parker), 3/1 "Mississippi Gambler" (Tyrone Power), 3/8 "The Glass Menagerie" (Jane Wyman, Fay Bainter, Frank Lovejoy), 3/15 "Jeopardy" (Barbara Stanwyck, Barry Sullivan), 3/22 "Carbine Williams" (Ronald Reagan, Jean Hagen, Wendell Corey), 3/2 "A Blueprint for Murder" (Dan Dailey, Dorothy McGuire), 4/5 "Welcome Stranger" (Cary Grant, Barry Fitzgerald), 4/12 "Strangers on a Train" (Dana Andrews, Robert Cummings, Virginia Mayo), 4/1 "The Star" (Ida Lupino, Edmund O'Brien), 4/26 "Detective Story" (Kirk Douglas, Eleanor Parker), 5/ "Going My Way" (Barry Fitzgerald, Eleanor Parker), 5/10 "Holy Matrimony" (Charles Laughton, Fay Bainter), 5/17 "The Corn Is Green" (Claudette Colbert, Cameron Mitchell), 5/24 "The Model and the Marriage Broker" (Jeanne Crain, Thelma Ritter), 5/3 "What a Woman" (Rosalind Russell, Robert Cummings), 6/7 "The Naked Jungle" (Charlton Heston, Donna Reed), 6/14 "Mildred Pierce" (Claire Trevor,

Zachary Scott), 6/21 "Pickup on South Street" (Thelma Ritter, Terry Moore), 6/28 "Goodbye My Fancy" (Rosalind Russell, Robert Young), 9/14 "Wuthering Heights" (Merle Oberon, Cameron Mitchell), 9/21 "So Big" (Ida Lupino, Robert Stack), 9/28 "How Green Was My Valley" (Michael Rennie, Donna Reed, Donald Crisp), 10/5 "The Turning Point" (Fred MacMurray, Joanne Dru), 10/12 "Great Expectations" (Rock Hudson, Barbara Rush), 10/19 "David and Bathsheba" (Arlene Dahl, Michael Rennie), 10/26 "The Song of Bernadette" (Ann Blyth, Charles Bickford), 11/2 "The Big Trees" (Van Heflin, Nancy Gates), 11/9 "My Man Godfrey" (Jeff Chandler, Julia Adams), 11/16 "Mother Didn't Tell Me" (Dorothy McGuire, Frank Lovejoy), 11/23 "All About Eve" (Ann Blyth, Ida Lupino), 11/30 "The Blue Gardenia" (Dana Andrews), 12/7 "Battleground" (Van Johnson, George Murphy), 12/14 "Legend of the Incas" (Charlton Heston), 12/21 "Miracle on 34th Street" (Edmund Gwenn), 12/28 "The Iron Mistress" (Virginia Mayo, John Lund).

1955: 1/4 "Mother Wore Tights" (Dan Dailey, Mitzi Gaynor), 1/11 "Island in the Sky" (Dick Powell), 1/18 "The Awful Truth" (Cary Grant, Irene Dunne), 1/25 "Sangaree" (Arlene Dahl), 2/1 "Five Fingers" (James Mason, Pamela Mason), 2/8 "War of the Worlds" (Dana Andrews), 2/15 "Treasure of the Sierra Madre" (Edmund O'Brien, Walter Brennan), 2/22 "Shane" (Alan Ladd, Van Heflin), 3/1 "The Bishop's Wife" (Cary Grant, Phyllis Thaxter), 3/8 "The Walls of Jericho" (Cornel Wilde), 3/15 "Gentlemen's Agreement" (Ray Milland, Dorothy McGuire), 3/22 "Rawhide" (Jeffrey Hunter, Donna Reed), 3/29 "Trouble Along the Way" (Van Johnson, Joanne Dru), 4/5 "Come Fill the Cup" (Van Heflin, Mona Freeman), 4/12 "Stairway To Heaven" (David Niven, Barbara Rush), 4/19 "Forever Female" (Ginger Rogers), 4/26 "The Story of Alexander Graham Bell" (Robert Cummings), 5/3 "Elephant Walk" (Joan Fontaine), 5/10 "Together Again" (Maureen O'Hara), 5/17 "Little Boy Lost" (Dick Powell), 5/24 "Now Voyager" (Dorothy McGuire), 5/31 "Rope of Sand" (Barry Sullivan), 6/7 *last show of the series* "Edward My Son" (Walter Pidgeon).

Mercury Theater on the Air and **Campbell Playhouse** Dates, Shows and Stars (in parentheses)
1938: "Dracula" (7/11), "Treasure Island" (7/18, "A Tale of Two Cities" (7/25), "The Thirty-Nine Steps" (8/1), "Three Short Stories" (8/8), "Abraham Lincoln" (8/15), "Affairs of Antole" (8/22), "The Count of Monte Cristo" (8/29), "The Man Who Was Thursday" (9/5), "Julius Caesar" (9/11), "Jane Eyre" (9/18), "Sherlock Holmes" (9/25), "Oliver Twist" (10/2), "Hell on Ice" (10/9), "Seventeen" (10/16), "Around

the World in 80 Days" (10/23), "War of the Worlds" (10/30), "Heart of Darkness" (11/6), "Bishop Muder Case" (11/13), "Pickwick Papers" (11/20), "Clarence" (11/27), "Bridge of San Luis Ray" (12/4), "Rebecca" (Margaret Sullavan 12/9), "Call It a Day" (12/16), "A Christmas Carol" (12/23), "A Farewell to Arms" (Katharine Hepburn 12/30).

1939: "Counselor at Law" (Gertrude Berg 1/6), "Mutiny on the Bounty" (1/13), "Chican Wagon Family" (Burgess Meredith 1/20), "I Lost My Girlish Laughter" (Ilka Chase 1/27), "Arrowsmith" (Helen Hayes 2/3), "Green Goddess" (Madeline Carroll 2/10), "Burlesque" (Sam Levene 2/17), "State Fair" (Burgess Meredith 2/24), "Royal Regiment" (Mary Astor 3/3), "The Glass Key" (3/10), "Beau Geste" (Lawrence Olivier 3/17), "Twentieth Century" (Joan Blondell, Sam Levene 3/24), "Show Boat" (Margaret Sullavan, Helen Morgan, Edna Ferber 3/31), "Les Misarbles" (Walter Huston 4/7), "The Patriot" (Anna May Wong 4/14), "Private Lives" (Gertrude Lawrence 4/21), "Black Daniel" (Joan Bennett 4/28), "Ordeal" (5/5), "Our Town" (5/12), "The Bad Man" (Ida Lupino 5/19), "American Cavalcade" (Cornelia Otis Skinner 5/26), "Victoria Regina" (Helen Hayes 6/2), "Peter Ibbetson" (Helen Hayes 9/10), "Ah Wilderness" (9/17), "What Every Woman Knows" (Helen Hayes 9/24), "The Count of Monte Cristo" (10/1), "Algiers" (Paulette Goddard 10/8), "Escape" (Wendy Barrie 10/15), "Liliom" (Helen Hayes 10/22), "The Magnificent Ambersons" (Walter Huston 10/29), "Hurricane" (Mary Astor 11/5), "The Murder of Roger Ackroyd" (Edna May Olivier 11/12), "The Garden of Allah" (Claudette Colbert 11/19), "Huckleberry Finn" (11/26), "Lost Horizon" (Ronald Colman 12/3), "Vanessa" (Helen Hayes 12/10), "There's a Woman" (Merle Oberon 12/17), "A Christmas Carol (Lionel Barrymore" 12/24).

1940: "Becky Sharp" (Helen Hayes 1/7), "Theodora Goes Wild" (Loretta Young 1/14), "The Citadel" (Geraldine Fitzgerald 1/21), "It Happened One Night" (Miriam Hopkins 1/28), "Broome Stages" (Helen Hayes 2/4), "Mr. Deeds Goes to Town" (Gertrude Lawrence 2/11), "Dinner At Eight" (Hedda Hopper, Lucille Ball 2/18), "Only Angels Have Wings" (Joan Blondell 2/25), "Rabble in Arms" (Frances Dee 3/3), "Criag's Wife" (Fay Bainter 3/10)—*last show of series.*

MGM Musical Comedy Theater Dates, Shows, and Stars (in parentheses)
1952: 1/2 "Holiday in Mexico" (Walter Pidgeon, Jane Powell) 1/9 "No Leave, No Love" (Barry Sullivan, Keenan Wynn, Monica Lewis), 1/25 "It Happened in Brooklyn" (Russel Nype, Mimi Benzell), 1/23 "Cuban Love Song" (Alfred Drake, Olga San

Juan), 1/30 "Born to Dance" (Vera-Ellen, Georgia El-lis, Johnny Johnston), 2/6 "Going Hollywood" (De-nise Darcel, Andy Russell, Mary McCarty), 2/13 "Honolulu" (Robert Alda, Carole Bruce), 2/20 "Yo-landa and the Thief" (Boris Karloff, Lisa Kirk), 2/27 "Ship Ahoy" (Bert Lahr, Martha Wright, Jackie Coo-per), 3/5 "Lady Be Good" (Arlene Dahl, Phyllis Kirk, Lex Barker), 3/12 "Babes on Broadway" (Mickey Rooney, Kitty Kallen), 3/19 "On an Island with You" (Edward E. Horton, Polly Bergen, Earl Wrightson), 3/26 "Two Sisters from Boston" (Lauritz Melchoir, Jules Munshin), 4/2 "The Kissing Bandit" (John Conte, Olga San Juan), 4/9 "Two Girls on Broadway" (Joan Blondell, Dick Foran, Rosemary Clooney), 4/16 "Born to Sing" (Connie Haines, Russell Nype), 4/25 "Three Daring Daughters" (Gladys Swarthout, Basil Rathbone, Edith Fellows), 4/30 "The Barkleys of Broadway" (Alfred Drake, Yvonne deCarlo), 5/7 "Luxury Liner" (Patrice Munsel, Igor Gorin, Audrey Totter), 5/14 "For Me and My Gal" (Johnnie Des-mond, Peggy Lee), 5/21 "Neptune's Daughter" (Fran Warren, Carl Revazza, Jules Munshin), 5/28 "Fiesta" (Aldo Ray, Nannette Fabray), 6/4 "Two Girls and a Sailor" (Howard Keel, Monica Lewis, Patsy Kelly), 6/11 "Summer Holiday" (Kitty Kallen, Annette War-ren, Carlton Carpenter), 6/18 "Everybody Sing" (John Raitt, Eileen Barton), 6/25 "Hullabaloo" (Ar-lene Dahl, Arnold Stang, Ray Middleton). "Hullaba-loo" was the last show of the season. After a summer hiatus, the show resumed with one new program: 10/1 "Dancing Co-Ed" with Gloria deHaven, Johnny Johnston, Patsy Kelly. From 10/1/52 until 11/19, the **MGM Musical Comedy Theater of the Air** repeated the first twelve programs in this series, which had been recorded when originally presented.

MGM Theater of the Air Dates, Shows, and Stars (in parentheses)
1949: 10/14 "Vacation from Marriage" (Deborah Kerr), 10/21 "Johnny Eager" (Van Heflin), 10/28 "The Canterville Ghost" (Charles Laughton), 11/4 "The Shopworn Angel" (Margaret Sullavan), 11/11 "Married Bachelor" (Burgess Meredith), 11/18 "Cita-del" (Fredric March, Florence Eldridge), 11/25 "A Stranger in Town" (Edward Arnold), 12/1 "The Prize Fighter and the Lady" (John Garfield), 12/9 "Anna Karenina" (Marlene Dietrich), 12/16 "The Youngest Profession" (Margaret O'Brien), 12/23 "H. M. Pul-ham, Esq." (Brian Aherne), 12/30 "Hideout" (Cornel Wilde).

1950: 1/6 "Three Loves Has Nancy" (Ann Sothern), 1/13 "Crossroads" (Rex Harrison), 1/20 "Slightly Dangerous" (Celeste Holm), 1/27 "Riptide" (Made-leine Carroll), 2/3 "Stablemates" (Mickey Rooney),

2/10 "Third Finger, Left Hand" (Melvyn Douglas Arlene Francis), 2/17 "Queen Christina" (Basil Rath bone, Lilli Palmer), 2/24 "Come Live with Me" (Pete Lawford), 3/3 "Undercurrent" (Robert Taylor), 3/1 "Dramatic School" (Luise Rainer, Martin Gabel), 3/2 "Fast Company" (Nina Foch, George Murphy), 3/3 "Reckless" (June Havoc), 4/7 "Three Hearts for Julia (Jane Wyatt), 4/14 "The Big House" (Pat O'Brien 4/21 "Feminine Tough" (Marsha Hunt, Louise Allbrit ton), 4/28 "Unholy Partners" (George Raft), 5/ "They Met in Bombay" (Herbert Marshall), 5/1 "Chained" (Ava Gardner), 5/19 "A Tale of Tw Cities" (Maurice Evans), 5/26 "His Brother's Wife (Franchot Tone), 6/2 "Joe Smith, American" (Ronal Reagan, 6/9 "Young Ideas" (Peggy Ann Garner, Mir iam Hopkins), 6/16 "Camille" (Marlene Dietrich 6/23 "Escape" (William Holden, Brenda Marshall 7/7 "The Duke Steps Out" (Jack Carson), 7/14 "Step ping Out" (Lee Bowman), 7/21 "My Dear Miss Ald rich" (Donna Reed), 7/28 "Public Hero Number One (William Eythe, Nina Foch), 8/4 "A Letter for Evie (Hume Cronyn, Marsha Hunt), 8/11 "Stambou Quest" (Angela Lansbury), 8/18 "Vanishing Virgin ian" (Edward Arnold), 8/25 "See Here, Private Har grove" (Eddie Albert), 9/1 "William Tell" (Raymon Massey), 9/15 "Guilty Hands" (Gene and June Lock hart), 9/22 "Billy the Kid" (Zachary Scott), 9/29 "Var ity Fair" (Jessica Tandy), 10/6 "I Take This Woman (Ralph Bellamy), 10/13 "Love Crazy" (Arlene Fran cis), 10/27 "Thunder Afoot" (Brian Donlevy), 11/ "Hold That Kiss" (Ruth Hussey), 11/10 "A Yank a Oxford" (Dane Clark), 11/17 "The Count of Mont Cristo" (Jose Ferrer), 11/24 "Our Blushing Brides (Jane Wyatt), 12/1 "Kid Gloves Killer" (Willian Holden), 12/8 "Dance, Fool, Dance" (Barbara Star wyck), 12/15 "The Man in the Iron Mask" (Bria Aherne), 12/22 "The Sailor Takes a Wife" (Bonit Granville, Tom Drake), 12/29 "A Woman of the Year (Madeleine Carroll).

1951: 1/5 "Red Dust" (Veronica Lake), 1/12 "Faith ful to My Fashion" (Ann Rutherford), 1/19 "Apach Trail" (William Lundigan), 1/26 "Mill on the Floss (Sarah Churchill), 2/2 "High Wall" (John Payne), 2/ "Too Hot to Handle" (Anita Louise, Mel Ferrer), 2/1 "Easy to Wed" (Van Johnson), 2/23 "The Spy" (Corne Wilde), 3/2 "A Stranger's Return" (Charles Coburn 3/9 "I Love You Again" (Lee Bowman, Coleen Gray 3/16 "Hold Your Man" (Patricia Neal, Jeffrey Lynn 3/23 "Lady of the Tropics" (John Ireland, Sign Hasso), 3/30 "Manhattan Melodrama" (John Hodiak Janis Paige), 4/6 "Life Is a Headache" (Joan Bennett 4/13 "Wife vs. Secretary" (Laraine Day), 4/20 "W Who Are Young" (Richard Conte). From 5/1/195 until 12/20/52, recorded broadcasts were repeated i the exact order in which they were originally heard (10/14/49–4/20/51).

Screen Director's Playhouse Dates, Shows, Stars (in parentheses) and Directors
1949: 7/1 "Mr Blandings Builds His Dream House" (Cary Grant) Director: H. C. Potter, 7/8 "The Big Clock" (Maureen O'Sullivan, Ray Milland) Director: John Farrow, 7/15 "Yellow Sky" (Gregory Peck) Director: William Wellman, 7/22 "Casbah" (Tony Martin, Marta Toren) Director: John Berry, 7/29 "Saigon" (Alan Ladd) Director: Leslie Fenton, 8/5 "Fort Apache" (John Wayne, Ward Bond) Director: John Ford, 8/12 "Jezebel" (Bette Davis) Director: William Wyler, 8/19 "Love Crazy" (William Powell) Director: Jack Conway, 8/26 "Appointment for Love" (Charles Boyer, Gale Storm) Director: William Seiter, 9/2 "Apartment for Peggy" (Jeanne Crain) Director: George Seaton, 9/8 "Whispering Smith" (Alan Ladd) Director: Francis Searle, 9/23 "Don't Trust Your Husband" (Fred MacMurray) Director: Lloyd Bacon, 9/30 "Pride of the Yankees" (Gary Cooper) Director: Sam Wood, 3/3 "The Senator Was Indiscreet" (William Powell) Director: George S. Kaufman, 3/10 "Criss Cross" (Burt Lancaster) Director: Robert Siodmak, 2/17 "Pitfall" (Dick Powell, Jane Wyatt) Director: Andre de Toth, 3/24 "Love Letters" (Joseph Cotten) Director: William Dieterle, 3/31 "Remember the Night" (Barbara Stanwyck) Director: Mitchell Leisen, 11/11 "Body and Soul" (John Garfield) Director: Robert Rossen, 11/18 "The Uninvited" (Ray Milland) Director: Lewis Allen, 11/25 "The Spiral Staircase" (Dorothy McGuire) Director: Robert Siodmak, 12/2 "All My Sons" (Edward G. Robinson, Jeff Chandler) Director: Irving Reis, 12/9 "Call Northside 777" (James Stewart) Director: Henry Hathaway, 12/16 "The Affairs of Susan" (Joan Fontaine) Director: William Seiter, 12/23 "Miracle on 34th Street" (Edmund Gwenn) Director: George Seaton, 12/30 "One Way Passage" (William Powell) Director: Tay Garnett.

1950: 1/6 "Magic Town" (James Stewart) Director: William Wellman, 1/13 "Tomorrow Is Forever" (Claudette Colbert) Director: Irving Pichel, 1/20 "Mr. Lucky" (Cary Grant) Director: H. C. Potter, 1/27 "It Had to Be You" (Joan Fontaine) Director: Don Hartman, 2/3 "The Sea Wolf" (Edward G. Robinson) Director: Michael Curtiz, 2/10 "This Thing Called Love" (Rosalind Russell) Director: Alex Hall, 2/17 "It's in the Bag" (Fred Allen) Director: Richard Wallace, 2/24 "Incendiary Blonde" (Betty Hutton) Director: George Marshall, 3/3 "Paleface" (Bob Hope, Jane Russell) Director: Norman McLeod, 3/10 "Portrait of Jennie" (Joseph Cotten) Director: William Dieterle, 3/17 "Champion" (Kirk Douglas) Director: Mark Robson, 3/24 "Chicago Deadline" (Alan Ladd) Director: Lewis Allen, 3/31 "Dark Mirror" (Olivia deHavilland) Director: Robert Siodmak, 4/7 "Fighting O'Flynn" (Douglas Fairbanks, Jr.) Director: Arthur Pierson, 4/14 "It Happens Every Spring" (Ray Milland) Director: Lloyd Bacon, 4/21 "A Kiss in the Dark" (Jane Wyman) Director: Delmer Davis, 4/26 "Rope of Sand" (Burt Lancaster) Director: William Dieterle, 5/5 "When My Baby Smiles at Me" (Betty Grable) Director: Walter Lang, 5/12 "Ruth Minds the Baby" (Broderick Crawford), 5/19 "Miss Grant Takes Richmond" (Lucille Ball) Director: Lloyd Bacon, 5/26 "Flamingo Road" (Joan Crawford) Director: Michalel Curtiz, 6/2 "She Wouldn't Say Yes" (Rosalind Russell) Director: Alex Hall, 6/9 "Mr. Blandings Builds His Dream House" (Cary Grant) Director: H. C. Potter, 6/16 "A Star Is Born" (Fredric March) Director: William Wellman, 6/23 "The Strange Love of Martha Ivers" (Barbara Stanwyck) Director: Lewis Milestone, 6/30 "Cinderella" (Verna Felton, I. Woods) Director: Walt Disney, 11/9 "Shadow of a Doubt" (Joseph Cotten) Director: Alfred Hitchcock, 11/16 "Lifeboat" (Tallulah Bankhead) Director: Alfred Hitchcock, 11/23 "Cluny Brown" (Dorothy McGuire, Charles Boyer) Director: Ernst Lubitsch, 11/30 "Mrs. Mike" (Evelyn Keyes, Joseph Cotten) Director: Lewis King, 12/7 "My Favorite Wife" (Cary Grant, Irene Dunne) Director: Garson Kanin, 12/14 "The Lady Gambles" (Barbara Stanwyck) Director: Michael Gordon, 12/21 "Miracle on 34th Street" (Edmund Gwenn) Director: George Seaton, 12/28 "Alias Nick Beal" (Ray Milland) Director: John Farrow.

1951: 1/4 "Prince of Foxes" (Douglas Fairbanks, Jr.) Director: Henry King, 1/11 "Ivy" (Joan Fontaine) Director: Sam Wood, 1/18 "The Big Lift" (Edmund O'Brien, Paul Douglas) Director: George Seaton, 1/25 "Spellbound" (Mercedes McCambridge, Joseph Cotten) Director: Alfred Hitchcock, 2/1 "Take a Letter, Darling" (Rosalind Russell, Alan Ladd, Bob Hope) Director: Mitchell Leisen, 2/8 "Lucky Jordan" (Alan Ladd) Director: Frank Tuttle, 2/15 "Dark Victory" (Tallulah Bankhead, Edmund O'Brien) Director: Edmund Goulding, 2/22 "No Minor Vices" (Louis Jourdan, Dana Andrews) Director: Lewis Milestone, 3/1 Unannounced, 3/8 Unannounced, 3/15 "The File on Thelma Jordan" (Barbara Stanwyck, Wendell Corey) Director: Robert Siodmak, 3/22 "The Great Lover" (Bob Hope, Rhonda Fleming) Director: Alex Hall, 3/29 "Next Time We Love" (James Stewart, Eleanor Parker) Director: Edward Griffith, 4/5 "The Damned Don't Cry" (Joan Crawford) Director: Vincent Sherman, 4/12 "Hired Wife" (Rosalind Russell) Director: William Seiter, 4/19 "Humoresque" (Tallulah Bankhead) Director: Jean Negulesco, 4/26 "Jackpot" (James Stewart) Director: Walter Lang, 5/3 "Captain from Castile" (Douglas Fairbanks, Jr.) Director: Henry King, 5/10 "No Time for Love" (Claudette Colbert) Director: Mitchell Leisen, 5/17 "Rogue's Regiment" (Dick Powell) Director: Robert Florey, 5/24 "Back Street" (Mercedes McCambridge, Charles Boyer) Director: Robert Stevenson, 5/31 "Beyond Glory" (Alan Ladd) Director: John Farrow, 6/7 "The Gunfighter" (Gregory Peck) Director: Henry King, 6/14 "Dead on Arrival" (Edmund O'Brien) Director: Rudolph Mate, 6/21 (Unannounced), 6/28 "The Lady Takes a Chance" (Joan Caulfield, John Lund) Director: William Seiter, 7/5 "Only Yesterday" (Mercedes McCambridge, Jeff Chandler) Director: John M. Stahl, 7/12 "The Fugitive" (Henry Fonda) Director: John Ford, 7/19 "Remember the Night" (William Holden) Director: Mitchell Leisen, 7/26 "Stairway to Heaven" (Robert Cummings) Director: Michael Powell, 8/1 "Caged" (Eleanor Parker) Director: John Cromwell, 8/9 "The Ghost and Mrs. Muir" (Charles Boyer, Jane Wyatt Director: Joseph L. Mankiewicz, 8/16 (Unannounced), 8/23 "Mother Is a Freshman" (Loretta Young, William Lundigan) Director: Lloyd Bacon, 8/30 Unrecorded—last show of series.

Screen Guild Players Dates, Show, and Stars (in parentheses)
1939: 9/24 Variety Show (Cary Grant, Mickey Rooney, Judy Garland, Ann Sothern), 10/1 "Imperfect Lady" (Clark Gable, Ginger Rogers), 10/8 Variety Show (Gary Cooper, Bob Hope, Marlene Dietrich, Connie Boswell), 10/15 Variety Show (Ronald Colman, Joan Crawford), 10/22 Variety Show (Burns and Allen, James Cagney, Gloria Jean), 10/29 "We Were Dancing" (Adolph Menjoe, Robert Montgomery, Hedda Hopper), 11/5 "Going My Way" (James Stewart, Loretta Young, Edward Arnold), 11/12 "The Beachcomber" (Charles Laughton, Jean Hersholt, Elsa Lanchester), 11/19 Variety Show (Fred Allen, Robert Benchley), 11/26 "The Enchanted Cottage" (Helen Hayes, Fredric March), 12/3 "Accent on Youth" (Gertrude Lawrence, Herbert Marshall), 12/10 "Mr. Capricorn Goes to Sea" (Bing Crosby, Andy Devine, Jean Parker), 12/17 "Smilin' Through" (Norma Shearer, Basil Rathbone, Leslie Howard), 12/24 "The Blue Bird" (Shirley Temple, Nelson Eddy), 12/31 Variety Show (Eddie Cantor, Gene Autry, Little Josephine).

1940: 1/7 "Petrified Forest" (Joan Bennett, Tyrone Power, Humphrey Bogart), 1/14 "This Lonely Heart" (Bette Davis), 1/21 "Firebrand" (Douglas Fairbanks, Jr., Paulette Goddard, Frank Morgan), 1/28 "Private Worlds" (Claudette Colbert, Charles Boyer), 2/4 "I Met Him in Paris" (Ann Sothern, Melvyn Douglas,

Robert Young), 2/11 "Single Passage" (Myrna Loy, William Powell), 2/18 "Dynamite" (James Cagney, Olivia deHavilland), 2/25 "Blind Alley" (Edward G. Robinson, Isabel Jewell), 3/3 "Winter in Paris" (Maureen O'Sullivan, Don Ameche), 3/10 "Slightly with Accent" (Bette Davis, William Powell), 3/17 "The Awful Truth" (Carole Lombard, Robert Young), 3/24 "Morning Glory" (Miriam Hopkins, Adolph Menjou), 3/31 "Allergic to Love" (Barbara Stanwyck), 4/7 "Vivacious Lady" (Ginger Rogers, Fred MacMurray), 4/14 "Elmer the Great" (Bob Hope, Ann Sheridan), 4/21 "Ninotchka" (Rosalind Russell, Spencer Tracy), 9/29 "The Shop Around the Corner" (Margaret Sullavan, James Stewart), 10/6 "Red Dust" (Clark Gable, Ann Sothern), 10/13 "Private Lives" (Vivien Leigh, Lawrence Olivier), 10/20 Variety Show (Basil Rathbone, Jack Benny, Claudette Colbert, Edward Arnold, 10/27 "Jezebel" (Jean Arthur, Walter Pidgeon), 11/3 "The Great Man Votes" (John Barrymore), 11/10 "History Is Made at Night" (Charles Boyer), 11/17 "A Star Is Born" (Loretta Young, Burgess Meredith), 11/24 "Allergic to Ladies" (Errol Flynn), 12/1 "Desire" (Marlene Dietrich, Fred MacMurray), 12/8 "Torrid Zone" (James Cagney, Joan Bennett), 12/15 "Seventh Heaven" (Tyrone Power, Annabella), 12/22 "The Juggler of Notre Dame" (Ronald Colman, Nelson Eddy), 12/29 "Drink a Glass of Sassafras" (Fay Bainter).

1941: 1/5 "Love Affair" (Madeleine Carroll, Melvyn Douglas), 1/12 "Waterloo Bridge" (Brian Aherne, Joan Fontaine), 1/19 "Magnificent Obsession" (Myrna Loy, Don Ameche), 1/26 "If She Could Only Cook" (Alice Faye, Herbert Marshall, Humphrey Bogart), 2/2 "Destry Rides Again" (Henry Fonda, Paulette Goddard), 2/9 "No Time for Comedy" (Norma Shearer, Franchot Tone), 2/16 "Brother Orchid" (Pat O'Brien, Carol Landis), 2/23 "Altar Bound" (Bing Crosby, Bob Hope, Betty Grable), 3/2 "Jane Eyre" (Bette Davis, Brian Aherne), 3/9 Variety Show: Gary Cooper, Edward Arnold, Joan Bennett, Frances Langford, Fibber McGee and Molly), 3/16 "My Love Came Back" (Olivia deHavilland, Robert Young), 3/23 "My Favorite Wife" (Irene Dunne, Robert Montgomery), 3/30 "His Girl Friday" (Rosalind Russell, Cary Grant), 4/6 "Lucky Partners" (Ginger Rogers, William Powell), 4/13 "True Confessions" (Carole Lombard, Fred MacMurray), 4/20 "Hired Wife" (Melvyn Douglas, Joan Blondell, Mary Pickford), 9/28 "Meet John Doe" (Gary Cooper, Barbara Stanwyck), 10/5 "Strawberry Blonde" (James Cagney, Olivia deHavilland), 10/12 "Alice Adams" (Deanna Durbin), 10/19 "Nothing Sacred" (Barbara Stanwyck, Robert Taylor), 10/26 "Goodbye, Mr. Chips" (Basil Rathbone, Greer Garson), 11/2 "Amazing Dr. Clitterhouse" (Edward G.

Robinson, Humphrey Bogart, Marsha Hunt), 11/9 "Babes in Arms" (Mickey Rooney, Judy Garland), 1/16 "Penny Serenade" (Cary Grant, Irene Dunne), 1/23 "If She Could Only Cook" (Adolph Menjou, Humphrey Bogart), 11/29 "The Perfect Specimen" (Melvyn Douglas, Betty Grable), 12/7 "Between Americans" (Orson Welles), 12/14 "My Life with Car- line" (William Powell, Ann Sothern), 12/21 "The Juggler of Our Lady" (Nelson Eddy, Ronald Colman), 12/28 "Long Engagement" (Madeleine Carroll, George Murphy).

1942: 1/4 "High Sierra" (Humphrey Bogart, Claire Trevor), 1/11 "Love Affair" (Myrna Loy, Herbert Mar- shall), 1/18 "Sgt. York" (Gary Cooper), 1/25 "Torrid Zone" (George Raft, Betty Grable), 2/1 "Bachelor Mother" (Henry Fonda, Laraine Day), 2/8 "Mr. and Mrs. Smith" (Errol Flynn, Lana Turner), 2/15 "Liber- ty's a Lady" (Loretta Young), 2/22 "Love Is News" (Kay Kyser, Betty Grable, James Gleason), 3/1 "Mid- night" (Joan Bennett, Robert Young), 3/8 "Too Many Husbands" (Bing Crosby, Bob Hope, Hedy Lamarr), 3/15 "Come and Get It" (Edward Arnold, Walter Brennan, Laraine Day), 3/22 "How Green Was My Valley" (Walter Pidgeon, Roddy MacDowell), 3/29 "Parent by Proxy" (Jack Benny), 4/5 "Philadelphia Story" (Greer Garson, Henry Fonda, Fred MacMur- ray), 4/12 "Tight Shoes" (Red Skelton, Lucille Ball), 4/19 "A Woman's Face" (Bette Davis).

For Lady Esther Face Cream: 9/19 "Yankee Doodle Dandy" (James Cagney, Rita Hayworth, Betty Grable), 10/26 "A Yank in the RAF" (Tyrone Power, Betty Grable), 11/2 "My Favorite Wife" (Barbara Stanwyck, Robert Taylor), 11/9 "Take a Letter, Darling" (Rosa- lind Russell, Cary Grant), 11/16 "Goodbye, Mr. Chips" (Merle Oberon, Basil Rathbone), 11/23 "Bache- lor Mother" (Fred MacMurray, Ann Sothern), 11/30 "Ball of Fire" (Paulette Goddard, Kay Kyser), 12/7 "Mrs. Miniver" (Greer Garson, Walter Pidgeon), 12/14 "Mr. and Mrs. Smith" (Joan Bennett, Robert Young), 12/21 "The Juggler of Our Lady" (Nelson Eddy, Ronald Colman), 12/28 "The Male Animal" (Olivia deHavilland, Joel McCrea).

1943: 1/4 "Suspicion" (Basil Rathbone, Joan Fon- taine, Nigel Bruce), 1/11 "Holiday Inn" (Bing Crosby, Fred Astaire, Dinah Shore), 1/18 "To Be Or Not to Be" (William Powell), 1/25 "Across the Pacific" (Mary Astor, Humphrey Bogart), 2/1 "Dodsworth" (Bette Davis, Walter Huston), 2/8 "Hold Back the Dawn" (Charles Boyer, Susan Hayward), 2/15 "They Got Me Covered" (Bob Hope, Dorothy Lamour), 2/22 "Louisiana Purchase" (Annabella, Victor Moore, Wil- liam Gaxton), 3/1 "This Above All" (Virginia Bruce, Herbert Marshall), 3/8 "Stand By for Action" (Chester

Morris, Charles Laughton, Brian Donlevy), 3/15 "The Palm Beach Story" (Claudette Colbert, Rudy Vallee, Randolph Scott), 3/22 "For Me and My Gal" (Judy Garland, George Murphy, Gene Kelly), 3/19 "This Thing Called Love" (Alice Faye, Robert Young), 4/5 "A Journey for Margaret" (Margaret O'Brien, Robert Young), 4/12 "Pittsburgh" (Marlene Dietrich, John Wayne), 4/19 "Woman of the Year" (Katharine Hep- burn, Spencer Tracy), 4/20 "Casablanca" (Humphrey Bogart, Ingrid Bergman, Paul Henreid), 5/3 "Nothing But the Truth" (Humphrey Bogart, Lucille Ball), 5/10 "Johnny Eager" (John Garfield, Carole Landis), 5/17 "Whistling in Dixie" (Red Skelton, Claire Trevor, Vir- ginia Grey), 5/24 "Shadow of a Doubt" (Deanna Dur- bin, Joseph Cotten), 5/31 "Rebecca" (Joan Fontaine, Brian Aherne), 6/7 "Devil and Miss Jones" (Laraine Day, George Murphy), 6/14 "Love Is News" (Jack Benny, Ann Sheridan), 6/21 "Back Street" (Charles Boyer, Martha Scott), 6/28 "Remember the Day" (Lo- retta Young, Franchot Tone), 7/5 "Tennessee John- son" (Gary Cooper, Ruth Hussey, Lionel Barrymore), 7/12 "Human Comedy" (Mickey Rooney, Frank Mor- gan), 7/19 "Men in White" (Jean Hersholt), 7/26 "Once Upon a Honeymoon" (Linda Darnell), 8/2 "Come Live with Me" (Hedy Lamarr), 8/9 "Spitfire" (Basil Rathbone), 8/16 "The Pied Piper" (Monty Wool- ley, Roddy McDowall), 8/23 "Skylark" (Ginger Rog- ers), 8/30 "The Moon Is Down" (Sir Cedric Hardwicke, Lewis Stone), 9/6 "Major and the Minor" (Ruth Warrick), 9/13 "Birth of the Blues" (Bing Crosby, Ginny Simms, Johnny Mercer), 9/20 "The Maltese Falcon" (Humphrey Bogart, Sydney Greenstreet, Mary Astor), 9/27 "Thank Your Lucky Stars" (Eddie Cantor, Dinah Shore), 10/4 "Hi Diddle Diddle" (Martha Scott, Dennis O'Keefe, Mary Boland), 10/11 "Love Affair" (Herbert Marshall, Virginia Bruce), 10/18 "My Sister Eileen" (Rosalind Russell, Brian Aherne, Janet Blair), 10/25 "Edge of Darkness" (John Garfield, Maureen O'Hara), 11/1 "You Belong to Me" (Mary Astor, Don Ameche), 11/8 "George Washington Slept Here" (Carol Landis, Jack Carson), 11/15 "Design for Scandal" (Olivia deHavilland, Wal- ter Pidgeon), 11/22 "Immortal Sergeant" (Maureen O'Sullivan, Franchot Tone), 11/29 No Title (Irene Dunne), 12/6 "Only Yesterday" (Loretta Young, Jo- seph Cotten), 12/13 "Holy Matrimony" (Fay Bainter, Frank Morgan), 12/20 "The Youngest Profession" (Virginia Weidler, Jean Porter, Edward Arnold), 12/27 "Let's Face It" (Bob Hope, Jane Wyman).

1944: 1/3 "The North Star" (Walter Huston, Anne Baxter, Farley Granger), 1/10 "Watch on the Rhine" (Bette Davis, Paul Lukas), 1/17 "I Love You Again" (William Powell, Paulette Goddard, 1/24 "Iron Major"

(Pat O'Brien, Ruth Warrick), 1/31 "Lucky Jordan" (Alan Ladd, Marjorie Main, Helen Walker), 2/7 "True to Life" (Dick Powell, Joan Leslie), 2/14 "Gentleman Jim" (Errol Flynn, Alexis Smith, Ward Bond), 2/21 "Design for Scandal" (Carol Landis, Robert Young), 2/28 "Three Men on a Horse" (Charles Laughton, Ann Sothern), 3/6 "The Gay Divorcee" (Frank Sinatra), 3/13 "The Tuttles of Tahiti" (Charles Laughton, Elsa Lanchester), 3/20 "The Constant Nymph" (Charles Boyer, Maureen O'Sullivan, Alexis Smith), 3/27 Variety Show (Jack Benny, Basil Rathbone, Barbara Stanwyck, Jean Hersholt), 4/3 "Hello, Frisco, Hello" (Ginny Simms, Dick Powell, Jack Oakie), 4/10 "A Farewell to Arms" (Joan Fontaine, Gary Cooper), 4/17 "High Sierra" (Humphrey Bogart, Ida Lupino), 4/24 "Snow White and the Seven Dwarfs" (Edgar Bergen and Charlie McCarthy, Jane Powell), 5/1 "A Night to Remember" (Lucille Ball, Brian Donlevy), 5/8 "Dark Angel" (Merle Oberon, Ronald Colman), 5/15 "Priorities on Parade" (Bob Crosby), 5/22 "Up in Mable's Room" (Dennis O'Keefe, Marjorie Reynolds), 5/29 "Congo Maisie" (Ann Sothern, John Hodiak), 6/5 "Amazing Dr. Clitterhouse" (Edward G. Robinson, Claire Trevor, Lloyd Nolan), 6/19 "No Time for Love" (Claudette Colbert, Fred MacMurray), 7/3 "My Son, My Son" (Herbert Marshall, Freddie Bartholomew), 7/10 "The Informer" (Charles Bickford), 7/17 "Make Your Own Bed" (Jack Carson, Jane Wyman), 7/24 "Night Must Fall" (James Cagney, Rosemary DeCamp), 7/31 "The Good Fairy" (Deanna Durbin), 8/7 "Alias the Deacon" (Charles Winninger), 8/14 "Nervous Wreck" (Edward E. Horton, Mary Astor), 8/21 "The Ghost Goes West" (Basil Rathbone), 8/28 "The Uninvited" (Ray Milland, Ruth Hussey), 9/4 "Too Many Husbands" (Frank Sinatra), 9/11 "Phantom Lady" (Ralph Bellamy, Louise Allbritton), 9/18 "The Oxbow Incident" (Edward Arnold), 9/25 "It Happened Tomorrow" (Dick Powell, Linda Darnell), 10/2 "Shopworn Angel" (Laraine Day, Adolph Menjou), 10/9 "A Girl, A Guy, and A Dog" (Lucille Ball), 10/16 "Mad About Music" (Herbert Marshall), 10/23 "Ninotchka" (Robert Young, Signe Hasso), 10/30 "Anna Karinina" (Ingrid Bergman, Gregory Peck), 11/13 "Holiday" (Loretta Young, Joseph Cotten), 11/20 "Once Upon a Honeymoon" (Lana Turner, John Hodiak), 11/27 "You Belong to Me" (Paulette Goddard, Lee Bowman), 12/4 "China Seas" (Clark Gable, Lucille Ball), 12/11 "San Diego, I Love You" (Jon Hall), 12/18 "Age of Innocence" (Merle Oberon, John Payne), 12/25 "Pinocchio" (Fannie Brice, Hanley Stafford).

1945:   1/1 "Mr. and Mrs. North" (Joan Blondell, Preston Foster), 1/8 "Going My Way" (Bing Crosby, Barry Fitzgerald), 1/15 "Three Is a Family" (Charles Ruggles, Fay Bainter), 1/22 "Love Before Breakfast" (Virginia Bruce, Brian Donlevy), 1/29 "No Time for Comedy" (Jack Carson, Alexis Smith), 2/5 "Joan of the Ozarks" (Judy Canova, Joe E. Brown), 2/12 "Belle of the Yukon" (Gail Patrick, Randolph Scott, Bob Burns), 2/19 "Take a Letter, Darling" (Don Ameche, Linda Darnell), 2/26 "The Shop Around the Corner" (Van Johnson, Phyllis Thaxter), 3/5 "Double Indemnity" (Barbara Stanwyck, Fred MacMurray), 3/12 "So This Is Washington" (Edward Arnold, Lum and Abner), 3/19 "Next Time We Love" (Joan Fontaine, Robert Cummings), 3/26 "The Princess and the Pirate" (Bob Hope, Virginia Bruce), 4/2 "This Gun for Hire" (Alan Ladd, Veronica Lake), 4/9 "Abroad with Two Yanks" (William Bendix, Dennis O'Keefe), 4/16 "The Mask of Demetrius" (Sydney Greenstreet, Peter Lorre, Zachary Scott), 4/23 "Flesh and Fantasy" (Charles Boyer, Ella Raines), 4/30 "Ramona" (Loretta Young, Joseph Cotten), 5/7 "Heaven Can Wait" (Susan Hayward, Walter Pidgeon), 5/14 "First Love" (Shirley Temple, Peter Lawford), 5/21 "Desert Song" (Dennis Morgan), 5/28 "Joy of Living" (Louise Allbritton, Robert Young), 6/4 "Heavenly Body" (Ann Sothern, William Powell), 6/11 "Parson from Panamint" (Charles Ruggles), 6/18 "Alibi Ike" (Jack Carson), 6/25 "New Wine" (Ilona Massey, Paul Henreid), 7/2 "Standing Room Only" (Ray Milland, Marguerite Chapman), 7/9 "Romance" (Gregory Peck), 7/16 "Flesh and Fantasy" (Edward G. Robinson, Vincent Price), 7/23 "Smilin' Through" (Laraine Day, Van Heflin), 7/30 "Voice of Bugle Anne" (Lionel Barrymore), 8/6 "The Little Foxes" (Bette Davis, Otto Kruger), 8/13 "Gildersleeve's Bad Day" (Hal Peary), 8/20 "Laura" (Gene Tierney, Dana Andrews, Clifton Webb), 8/27 "The Great McGinty" (Brian Donlevy, Akim Tamiroff), 9/3 "Flesh and Fantasy" (John Hodiak, Claire Trevor), 9/10 "Private Worlds" (Claudette Colbert, Herbert Marshall), 9/17 "The Valiant" (Dorothy McGuire, Humphrey Bogart), 9/24 "Kiss the Boys Goodbye" (Dinah Shore, Sonny Tufts), 10/1 "Those Endearing Young Charms" (Virginia Bruce, Robert Young), 10/8 "My Life with Caroline" (Mary Astor, Brian Aherne), 10/15 "Model Wife" (Martha O'Driscoll, Robert Paige), 10/22 "If You Could Only Cook" (Linda Darnell, Dennis O'Keefe), 10/29 "You Only Live Once" (Sylvia Sidney, Henry Fonda), 11/5 "Hail the Conquering Hero" (Eddie Bracken, Donna Reed), 11/12 "My Favorite Wife" (Greer Garson, Richard Ney), 11/19 "Paris Underground" (Constance Bennett, Gary Cooper), 11/26 "Biography of a Bachelor Girl" (Louise Allbritton), 12/3 "Vivacious Lady" (James Stewart, Janet Blair), 12/10 "Along Came Jones" (Gary Cooper), 12/17 "Ruggles of Red Gap

(Charles Laughton, Charles Ruggles), 12/24 "Pinocchio" (Fannie Brice, Hanley Stafford), 12/31 "From Pillar to Post" (Ida Lupino, John Payne).

1946: 1/7 "Lost Weekend" (Ray Milland, Jane Wyman), 1/14 "History Is Made at Night" (Virginia Bruce, Paul Lukas), 1/21 "Suspicion" (Cary Grant), 1/28 "Brother Rat" (Wayne Morris, Ronald Reagan), 2/4 "My Client Curley" (Robert Montgomery, Ted Donaldson), 2/11 "Don Juan Quilligan" (William Bendix, Phil Silvers), 2/18 "Over Twenty-one" (Irene Dunne, Alexander Knox), 2/25 "Wuthering Heights" (Merle Oberon, Cornel Wilde), 3/4 "Getting Gertie's Garter" (Dennis O'Keefe), 3/11 "When Irish Eyes Are Smiling" (June Haver, Dick Haymes), 3/18 "Love Is News" (Bob Hope, Linda Darnell, James Gleason), 3/25 "Sweethearts" (Nelson Eddy, Jeanette MacDonald), 4/1 "On Borrowed Time" (Lionel Barrymore, Agnes Moorehead), 4/8 "Barbary Coast" (Claire Trevor, Brian Donlevy), 4/15 "Her First Beau" (Lon McAllister, Elizabeth Taylor), 4/22 "Perfect Speciman" (Betty Grable, Jack Carson), 4/29 "The Cowboy and the Lady" (Olivia deHavilland, Gregory Peck), 5/6 "Bachelor Mother" (Ginger Rogers, Francis X. Bushman, David Niven), 5/13 "Talk of the Town" (Ronald Colman, Virginia Bruce), 5/20 "Guest Wife" (Claudette Colbert, Fred MacMurray), 5/27 "Firebrand" (Douglas Fairbanks, Jr., Virginia Field), 6/3 "Lightnin'" (Barbara Britton, Florence Bates), 6/10 "House on 92nd Street" (Signe Hasso, Lloyd Nolan), 6/17 "Marriage Is a Private Affair" (Lana Turner, John Hodiak), 6/24 "Barbary Coast" (Charles Bickford, Mary Astor), 7/1 "Come Live with Me" (Henry Fonda, Ilona Massey), 7/8 "The Great O'Malley" (William Bendix, Anita Louise), 7/15 "Naughty Marietta" (Allan Jones, Irene Manning), 7/22 "The Glass Key" (Alan Ladd), 7/22 "Naughty Marietta" (Repeat Broadcast), 8/5 "Christmas in Connecticut" (Ronald Reagan, Jane Wyman), 8/12 "The Devil and Miss Jones" (Van Johnson, Donna Reed), 8/19 "Hired Wife" (Lucille Ball, Brian Aherne), 8/26 "The Bells of St. Mary's" (Bing Crosby, Ingrid Bergman), 9/2 "Weekend for Three" (Lynn Bari), 9/9 "Waterloo Bridge" (Barbara Stanwyck, Robert Taylor), 9/16 "Arrowsmith" (Gregory Peck, Barbara Britton, Jean Hersholt), 9/23 "Susan and God" (Bette Davis, Walter Pidgeon), 9/30 "Junior Miss" (Peggy Ann Gardner, Allyn Joslyn), 10/7 "The Old Lady Shows Her Medals" (Ethel and Lionel Barrymore), 10/21 "Michael and Mary" (Ann Todd, Herbert Marshall), 10/28 "Adorable" (Shirley Temple, Charles Coburn, Peter Lawford), 11/4 "Experiment Perilous" (Ruth Hussey, George Brent), 11/11 "The First Years" (Ozzie Nelson, Harriet Hilliard), 11/18 "Blind Alley" (Edward G. Robinson, Isabel Jewell,

Broderick Crawford), 11/25 "Arsenic and Old Lace" (Boris Karloff, Eddie Albert), 12/2 "Love Letters" (Loretta Young, Rex Harrison), 12/9 "The Last of Mrs. Cheyney" (Joan Fontaine), 12/16 "This Love of Ours" (Merle Oberon, Joseph Cotten), 12/23 "Snow White and the Seven Dwarfs" (Edgar Bergen and Charlie McCarthy), 12/30 "Pinocchio" (Fannie Brice, Hanley Stafford).

1947: 1/6 "The Yearling" (Gregory Peck, Jane Wyman, Claude Jarmon, Jr.), 1/13 "Parents by Proxy" (Paulette Goddard, Jack Benny), 1/20 "Dragonwyck" (Theresa Wright, Vincent Price), 1/27 "Swell Guy" (Joseph Cotten, Ann Blyth), 2/3 "Gaslight" (Charles Boyer, Susan Hayward), 2/10 "Heavenly Days" (Fibber McGee and Molly), 2/17 "You Belong to Me" (Don Ameche, Carole Landis), 2/24 "Stork Club" (Betty Hutton), 3/3 "Kitty Foyle" (Olivia deHavilland, Henry Fonda), 3/10 "A Tree Grows in Brooklyn" (Anne Baxter, Peggy Ann Garner), 3/17 "Philadelphia Story" (Katharine Hepburn, James Stewart, Cary Grant), 3/24 "The Moon Is Our Home" (Fred MacMurray, Virginia Bruce), 3/31 "Brewster's Millions" (Dennis O'Keefe, Eddie Anderson), 4/7 "Christmas in July" (Eddie Bracken), 4/14 "Bluebeard's Eighth Wife" (Claudette Colbert, Fred MacMurray), 4/21 "Too Many Husbands" (Bob Hope, Frank Sinatra, Lucille Ball), 4/28 "Stork Bites Man" (Jackie Cooper, Anita Louise), 5/5 "Pardon My Past" (John Hodiak, Marguerite Chapman), 5/12 "Brief Encounter" (Herbert Marshall, Lili Palmer), 5/19 "The Best Years of Our Lives" (Dana Andrews, Virginia Mayo, Donna Reed), 5/26 "Johnny Apollo" (Tyrone Power, Dorothy Lamour, Lloyd Nolan), 6/2 "Saturday's Children" (John Garfield, Jane Wyman), 6/9 "Outward Bound" (David Niven), 6/16 "The Postman Always Rings Twice" (Lana Turner, John Garfield), 6/23 "Rose Marie" (Jeanette MacDonald, Nelson Eddy), 10/6 "The Bells of St. Mary's" (Bing Crosby, Ingrid Bergman), 10/13 "My Favorite Brunette" (Bob Hope, Dorothy Lamour), 10/20 "Elizabeth, the Queen" (Bette Davis, Brian Aherne), 10/27 "The Shocking Miss Pilgrim" (Betty Grable, Tony Martin), 11/3 "The Secret Life of Walter Mitty" (Danny Kaye, Virginia Mayo), 11/10 "Boomerang" (Dana Andrews, Jane Wyatt, Richard Widmark), 11/17 "Secret Heart" (Walter Pidgeon, Claudette Colbert), 11/24 "The Best Years of Our Lives" (Fredric March, Myrna Loy), 12/1 "The Trouble with Women" (Ray Milland, Betty Hutton), 12/8 "Moss Rose" (Victor Mature, Ida Lupino, Ethel Barrymore), 12/15 "Sweethearts" (Nelson Eddy, Jeanette MacDonald), 12/22 "Pinocchio" (Fannie Brice, Hanley Stafford), 12/29 "It's a Wonderful Life" (James Stewart, Donna Reed, Victor Moore).

1948: 1/5 "The Fugitive" (Gregory Peck, J. Carroll Naish), 1/12 "Fury" (Lizabeth Scott, Wendell Corey, Mary Astor), 1/19 "Ivy" (Joan Fontaine), 1/26 "Brief Encounter" (Irene Dunne, Herbert Marshall), 2/2 "The Dark Mirror" (Loretta Young, Lew Ayers), 2/9 "Johnny Come Lately" (James Cagney, Agnes Moorehead), 2/16 "Easy to Wed" (Esther Williams, Van Johnson), 2/23 "The Foxes of Harrow" (Rex Harrison, Maureen O'Hara), 3/1 "The Bishop's Wife" (Cary Grant, Loretta Young, David Niven), 3/8 "The Late George Apley" (Ronald Colman, Peggy Cummings), 3/15 "Suddenly It's Spring" (Fred MacMurray, Paulette Goddard), 3/22 "Cheyenne" (Dennis Morgan, Jane Wyman), 3/29 "You Belong to Me" (Linda Darnell, Robert Young), 4/5 "One Way Passage" (Barbara Stanwyck, Robert Taylor), 4/12 "The Great Man Votes" (Edward G. Robison), 4/19 "Sleep, My Love" (Claudette Colbert, Melvyn Douglas, Ronald Reagan), 4/26 "It Had to Be You" (Lucille Ball, Cornel Wilde), 5/3 "Next Time We Meet" (Margaret Sullavan, Joseph Cotten), 5/10 "The Bachelor and the Bobby Soxer" (Cary Grant, Shirley Temple, Myrna Loy), 5/17 "The Valiant" (Gregory Peck, Jeanne Crain, Edward Arnold), 5/24 "Casbah" (Tony Martin, Peter Lorre), 5/31 "Hold Back the Dawn" (Charles Boyer, Ida Lupino), 6/7 "Snow White and the Seven Dwarfs" (Margaret O'Brien, Jimmy Durante), 6/14 "Love Affair" (Greer Garson, Walter Pidgeon), 6/21 "Shadow of a Doubt" (Joseph Cotten), 6/28 "Up in Central Park" (Dick Haymes, Deanna Durbin, Vincent Price), 10/7 "Calling Northside 777" (James Stewart), 10/14 "Welcome, Stranger" (Bing Crosby, Barry Fitzgerald), 10/21 "The Babe Ruth Story" (William Bendix, Lurene Tuttle), 10/28 "Kiss of Death" (Victor Mature, Richard Widmark), 11/4 "Take a Letter, Darling" (Fred MacMurray, Rosalind Russell), 11/11 "All My Sons" (Edward G. Robinson, Burt Lancaster), 11/18 "Rebecca" (Loretta Young, John Lund, Agnes Moorehead), 11/25 "13 Rue Madeleine" (Humphrey Bogart, Leon Ames), 12/2 "Night Song" (Merle Oberon, Hoagy Carmichael), 12/9 "Michael and Mary" (Ronald Colman, Claudette Colbert), 12/16 "Where There's Life" (Bob Hope, Signe Hasso), 12/23 "Snow White and the Seven Dwarfs" (Edgar Bergen and Charlie McCarthy), 12/30 "Pinocchio" (Fannie Brice, Hanley Stafford).

1949: 1/6 "Notorious" (Ingrid Bergman, John Hodiak), 1/13 "So Evil, My Love" (Ray Milland, Deborah Kerr), 1/20 "Fuller Brush Man" (Red Skelton, Janet Blair), 1/27 "Walls of Jericho" (Cornel Wilde, Claire Trevor), 2/3 "The Big Punch" (Wayne Morris), 2/10 "Fury at Furnace Creek" (Victor Mature, Barbara Britton), 2/17 "Deep Waters" (Dana Andrews, Jean Peters), 2/24 "One Way Passage" (Jane Wyman, Lew Ayres), 3/3 "Command Decision" (Clark Gable, Walter Pidgeon, John Hodiak, Van Johnson), 3/10 "A Letter from an Unknown Woman" (Joan Fontaine, Louis Jourdan), 3/17 "Dark Victory" (Joan Crawford, Robert Young), 3/24 "Enchantment" (David Niven, Theresa Wright), 4/7 "Good Sam" (Gary Cooper, Ginger Rogers), 4/14 "Fighting O'Flynn" (Douglas Fairbanks, Jr.), 4/21 "The Blue Dahlia" (Veronica Lake, Alan Ladd), 4/28 "Bachelor Mother" (Lucille Ball, Joseph Cotten, Charles Coburn), 5/5 "Undercurrent" (Barbara Stanwyck, Robert Taylor), 5/12 "Temptation Harbor" (Herbert Marshall, Signe Hasso), 5/19 "The Bride Goes Wild" (June Allyson, Van Johnson), 5/26 "Flesh and Fantasy" (Kirk Douglas, Ava Gardner), 6/2 "Road House" (Ida Lupino, Richard Widmark, Lloyd Nolan), 6/9 "One Sunday Afternoon" (Dennis Morgan, June Haver), 6/16 "Together Again" (Irene Dunne, Walter Pidgeon), 6/23 "Stairway to Heaven" (David Niven, Herbert Marshall), 6/30 "The Old Lady Shows Her Medals" (James Cagney, Ethel and John Barrymore), 10/6 "Homecoming" (Lana Turner, Clark Gable), 10/13 "Champion" (Kirk Douglas, Marilyn Maxwell), 10/20 "Paleface" (Bob Hope, Jane Russell), 10/27 "A Kiss in the Dark" (David Niven, Jane Wyman), 11/3 "A Letter to Three Wives" (Linda Darnell, Paul Douglas), 11/10 "The Bribe" (Joseph Cotten, Ava Gardner), 11/17 "Street with No Name" (Richard Widmark, Lloyd Nolan), 11/24 "Suspicion" (Joan Fontaine, Cary Grant, Nigel Bruce), 12/1 "Command Decision" (Clark Gable, Walter Pidgeon, John Hodiak), 12/8 "Alias Nick Beal" (Ray Milland), 12/15 "Family Honeymoon" (Claudette Colbert, Fred MacMurray), 12/22 "Little Women" (June Allyson, Peter Lawford), 12/29 "It's a Wonderful Life" (James Stewart).

1950: 1/5 "You're My Everything" (Dan Dailey, Anne Baxter), 1/12 "The Ox Bow Incident" (Edward Arnold), 1/19 "You Belong to Me" (Lucille Ball, Don Ameche), 1/26 "I Love You Again" (William Powell, Ruth Hussey), 2/2 "John Loves Mary" (Ronald Reagan, Patricia Neal), 2/9 "Calcutta" (Alan Ladd, Gail Russell), 2/16 "Double Indemnity" (Barbara Stanwyck, Robert Taylor), 2/23 "Laura" (Gene Tierney, Dana Andrews, Clifton Webb), 3/2 "Everybody Does It" (Paul Douglas, Linda Darnell), 3/9 "A Foreign Affair" (Joan Fontaine, John Lund), 3/16 "What a Woman" (Rosalind Russell, Joseph Cotten), 3/23 "The Sun Comes Up" (Jeanette MacDonald), 3/30 "Adventure in Baltimore" (Shirley Temple, Preston Foster), 4/6 "It Started with Eve" (Charles Laughton, Diana Lynn), 4/20 "The Cowboy and the Lady" (Ginger Rogers, Macdonald Carey), 4/27 "The Shocking Miss Pilgrim" (Betty Grable, Macdonald Carey), 5/4 "Hold Back the Dawn" (Olivia deHavilland, Charles Boyer),

/11 "Mad About Music" (George Brent, Alan Mow-ay), 5/18 "The Maltese Falcon" (Humphrey Bogart, auren Bacall), 5/25 "Seventh Veil" (Ida Lupino, eorge Sanders), 6/1 "The Dark Corner" (Herbert arshall, John Hodiak), 6/8 "My Son, My Son" (Her-rt Marshall, Angela Lansbury), 6/15 "The Mating Millie" (Robert Cummings, Barbara Hale), 6/29 ou're My Everything" (Dan Dailey, Anne Baxter), 7 "Twelve O'Clock High" (Gregory Peck, Ward nd), 9/14 "Ninotchka" (Joan Fontaine, William owell), 9/21 "Secret Fury" (Claudette Colbert, Robert an), 9/28 "The Captive" (Theresa Wright, Lew yres), 10/5 "Champagne for Caesar" (Ronald Col-an, Vincent Price), 10/12 "Any Number Can Play" roderick Crawford, Alexis Smith), 10/19 "The In-rmer" (Paul Douglas), 10/26 "Mother Didn't Tell e" (Dorothy McGuire), 11/2 "Tell It to the Judge" osalind Russell, Robert Cummings), 11/9 "Dark irror" (Bette Davis, Dana Andrews, Gene Tierney), /16 "Father Was a Fullback" (Fred MacMurray, nda Darnell), 11/23 "Romance of Rosy Ridge" (Janet igh, Van Johnson), 11/30 "Woman in Hiding" oward Duff, Ida Lupino), 12/7 "Tom, Dick, and rry" (Ginger Rogers, Dennis O'Keefe, George Mur-y), 12/14 "The Seventh Veil" (Anne Baxter, Van flin), 12/21 "Come to the Stable" (Loretta Young, th Warrick, Hugh Marlowe), 12/28 "Snow White d the Seven Dwarfs" (Edgar Bergen and Charlie Carthy) and Pinocchio (Fannie Brice, Hanley fford).

51: 1/4 "Paleface" (Bob Hope, Jane Russell), 1/11 rief Encounter" (Deborah Kerr, Stewart Granger), 18 "Birth of the Blues" (Bing Crosby, Dinah Shore, l Harris), 1/25 "House of Strangers" (Edward G. binson, June Havoc, Victor Mature), 2/1 "Free for l" (Ann Blyth, Donald O'Connor), 2/8 "The Post-n Always Rings Twice" (Lana Turner, John Ho-k), 2/15 "June Bride" (Jane Wyman, Frank vejoy), 2/22 "Miss Grant Takes Richmond" (Eve den, William Holden), 3/1 "The Guilt of Janet nes" (Joseph Cotten, Mercedes McCambridge), 3/8 l About Eve" (Bette Davis, Anne Baxter, George nders), 3/15 "It's a Wonderful Life" (James Stewart, nna Reed, Victor Moore), 3/22 "Easter Parade" dy Garland, Fred Astaire), 3/29 "Kiss of Death" ctor Mature, Richard Widmark), 4/5 "No Time for medy" (Eve Arden, Ronald Reagan), 4/12 "Twelve Clock High" (Gregory Peck, Hugh Marlowe, Ward nd), 4/19 "Mr. 880" (Edmund Gwenn, Dorothy Guire, Burt Lancaster), 4/26 "The Trouble with men" (Lucille Ball, John Lund), 5/3 "Together ain" (Irene Dunne, Charles Boyer), 5/10 "The Se-t Heart" (Joan Crawford), 5/17 "Valley of Deci-

sion" (Greer Garson, Barry Sullivan), 5/24 "Michael and Mary" (Helen Hayes, Walter Pidgeon), 5/31 *last show of series* "Apartment for Peggy" (Diana Lynn, William Lundigan, Edmund Gwenn).

Suspense Motion Picture Stars and Year Heard on Show
1942: Charles Ruggles, James Cagney, Richard Widmark, Orson Welles

1943: Peter Lorre, Bela Lugosi, Sydney Greenstreet, Mary Astor, Geraldine Fitzgerald, Susan Hayward, Nancy Coleman, Agnes Moorehead, Paul Lukas, Charles Laughton, Margo, Maureen O'Hara, Laird Cregar, Robert Young, Lillian Gish, Virginia Bruce, Vincent Price.

1944: Alan Ladd, Lucille Ball, Dane Clark, Joseph Cotten, Sonny Tufts, Katina Paxinou, Orson Welles, Ed Gardner, Gene Kelly, Eddie Bracken, Vincent Price, Thomas Mitchell, Geraldine Fitzgerald, Keenan Wynn, Paul Muni, Herbert Marshall, Peter Lorre, Maureen O'Sullivan, Agnes Moorehead, Charles Laughton, Fredric March, Olivia deHavilland, Joseph Cotten, Nancy Kelly, Virginia Bruce, Lena Horne, Robert Cummings, Cary Grant, Robert Montgomery.

1945: Keenan Wynn, Nancy Kelly, Boris Karloff, Frank Sinatra, Joseph Cotten, Edward G. Robinson, Humphrey Bogart, Lloyd Nolan, Dane Clark, William Bendix, Lana Turner, John Garfield, Ronald Colman, John Payne, Clifton Webb, J. Carroll Naish, George Coulouris, Bonita Granville, Joan Lorring, Peter Lorre, Myrna Loy, Joseph Cotten, Agnes Moorehead, George Murphy, Henry Fonda, Lucille Ball, Lee J. Cobb, Zachary Scott, Robert Taylor, Marsha Hunt.

1946: Paul Henreid, Joseph Cotten, Dame May Whitty, Fay Bainter, James Stewart, Richard Greene, Cary Grant, Gregory Peck, Brian Donlevy, Agnes Moorehead, Vincent Price, Keenan Wynn, Nancy Kelly, Jackie Cooper, Claire Trevor, Alan Hale, Robert Young, Hume Cronyn, Elliott Reid, Sheldon Leonard, Henry Daniell, Joan Lorring, Rita Hayworth, John Lund, Susan Hayward, Jack Carson, Judy Garland, Chester Morris, Robert Taylor, Susan Peters, Lilli Palmer.

1947: Mark Stevens, Dan Duryea, Roddy MacDo-wall, Van Heflin, Glenn Ford, Agnes Moorehead, Anne Baxter, Eddie Bracken, Howard DaSilva, Claude Rains, Phil Silvers, Kirk Douglas, Richard Conte, Ava Gardner, Robert Mitchum, Angela Lansbury, June Havoc, Eva La Gallienne, Gloria Swanson, Vincent Price, Lynn Bari, Jerome Cowan, Walter Abel, Donald O'Connor, John Lund, Edmund O'Brien, Michael O'Shea, Claire Trevor, Kirk Douglas, Richard Ney, Marsha Hunt, Dennis O'Keefe, June Havoc, Henry Morgan, Howard Duff, Jose Ferrer, Jackie Cooper, Dan Duryea, Boris Karloff, Harriet Nelson.

1948: Robert Montgomery, James Cagney, Robert Ryan, Sam Jeffe, Helen Walker, Cary Grant, Ida Lupino, Douglas Fairbanks, Jr., Agnes Moorehead, Charles Laughton, Ann Sothern, Martha Scott, Van Heflin, Madeleine Carroll, Burt Lancaster, Gregory Peck, Robert Young, Edward G. Robinson, Ray Milland, Lucille Ball, William Powell, John Garfield, Margaret O'Brien, Vincent Price, Rosalind Russell, William Bendix.

1949: Gene Kelly, Danny Kaye, Dana Andrews, Jim Jordan, Jane Wyman, James Mason, Joan Fontaine, Gregory Peck, Pat O'Brien, Edward G. Robinson, Ronald Colman, Edmund Gwenn, Betty Grable, Mickey Rooney, Bob Hope, James Stewart, Joan Crawford, John Lund, Agnes Moorehead, Ralph Edwards, Joseph Cotten, Dorothy McGuire, Van Johnson, Edward Arnold, Bette Davis, Victor Mature, Red Skelton, Lucille Ball, Burt Lancaster, Mickey Rooney, Eddie Cantor, Ida Lupino.

1950: Danny Kaye, Robert Taylor, William Powell, Ozzie Nelson, Rosalind Russell, Kirk Douglas, Marlene Dietrich, Dick Powell, Loretta Young, James Mason, Ronald Reagan, Alan Ladd, Joseph Cotten, Van Johnson, Dan Dailey, Ray Milland, Agnes Moorehead, Joan Bennett, John Lund, Claire Trevor, Dennis O'Keefe, Edward G. Robinson, Charles Boyer, Broderick Crawford, Jack Carson, Pat O'Brien, Dana Andrews, Miriam Hopkins, Milton Berle, Barbara Stanwyck, Richard Widmark, William Holden, Cary Grant, Ozzie Nelson, Alan Ladd, Dennis Day, Cornel Wilde.

1951: Mickey Rooney, Ginger Rogers, Eve Arden, Ezio Pinza, Paul Douglas, Fred MacMurray, Agnes Moorehead, Jim Jordan, Marian Jordan, Ronald Colman, Van Johnson, Joan Crawford, Jack Benny, Lucille Ball, James Stewart, Anne Baxter, Charles Boyer, Rosalind Russell, Phil Harris, Jeff Chandler, Dick Powell, Richard Widmark, James Mason, William Holden, Charles Laughton, Tony Curtis, Jeanne Crain, Herbert Marshall, Cornel Wilde, Ray Milland, Joseph Cotten, John Hodiak, John Lund, Frank Lovejoy, Victor Mature, Greer Garson.

1952: Jeff Chandler, Agnes Moorehead, Richard Basehart, Joseph Cotten, J. Carroll Naish, James Mason, Linda Darnell, Frank Lovejoy, Robert Young, Deborah Kerr, Dan Duryea, Dinah Shore, Macdonald Carey, Fred MacMurray, George Murphy, Jack Benny, Agnes Moorehead, Charles Laughton, Charles Boyer, Cedric

Hardwicke, Richard Widmark, Anne Baxter, Cor[n]el Wilde, Paul Douglas, John Hodiak, Lloyd Nolan.

1953: Herbert Marshall, Jack Benny, Richard Wid[m]ark, William Powell, Victor Mature, Rosema[ry] Clooney, Agnes Moorehead, Joseph Cotten, Van Joh[n]son, Fred MacMurray, Frank Lovejoy, Dick Haym[es] Ronald Colman, Jeff Chandler, Broderick Crawfo[rd] Edmund O'Brien, Peter Lawford, Cornel Wilde, Gr[eer] Garson, James Mason.

1954: Frank Lovejoy, Dana Andrews, Jack Ben[ny] Ethel Merman, Jeff Chandler, William Holden, H[er]bert Marshall, William Powell, Victor Mature, Tyro[ne] Power, David Niven, Charles Boyer, Char[les] Laughton, Robert Wagner, Peter Lawford.
*From mid-1954 until *Suspense* left the air on Septe[m]ber 30, 1962, radio actors and only occasional "[big] name" stars played the leading roles on *Suspense*.

Theater Guild on the Air Dates, Play and Auth[or] and Stars (in parentheses)
1945: Sept. 9 "Wings Over Europe" by Robert Ni[ch]ols (Burgess Meredith), Sept. 16 "Jacobowsky and t[he] Colonel" by Franz Werfel and S. N. Behman (Lo[uis] Calhern, Annabella), Sept. 23 "The Guardsman" [by] Ferenc Molnar (Alfred Lunt, Lynn Fontanne), Oct[. 7] "Ah, Wilderness" by Eugene O'Neill (Walter Husto[n], Oct. 14 "Mr. Pim Passes By" by A. A. Milne (Arle[ne] Francis, Leo G. Carroll), Oct. 21 "Sing Out, Sw[eet] Land" by Walter Kerr (Burl Ives, Arthur Godfr[ey] Josh White), Oct. 28 "At Mrs. Beam's" by C. K. Mun[ro] (Paulette Goddard, Burgess Meredith), Nov. 4 "Sto[p] Over Patsy" by James Bridle (Martha Scott, Ali[ne] MacMahon, Richard Widmark), Nov. 11 "Empe[ror] Jones" and "Where the Cross Is Made" by Euge[ne] O'Neill (Canada Lee, Boris Karloff), Nov. 18 "Pri[de] and Prejudice" by Jane Austen (Joan Fontaine), N[ov.] 25 "Mornings At Seven" by Paul Osborn (Stu Erw[in] Shirley Booth, Aline MacMahon), Dec. 2 "Elizab[eth] The Queen" by Maxwell Anderson (Alfred Lunt, Ly[nn] Fontanne), Dec. 9 "Ned McCobb's Daughter" by Si[d]ney Howard (Alfred Lunt, Shirley Booth), Dec. [16] "The Royal Family" by Edna Ferber and George [S.] Kaufman (Frederic March, Estelle Winwood), D[ec.] 23 "Little Women" by Louisa May Alcott (Kathari[ne] Hepburn, Oscar Homolka), Dec. 30 "Knickerbock[er] Holiday" by Maxwell Anderson (Walter Huston).

1946: Jan. 6 "Three Men on a Horse" by John Ce[cil] Holm and George Abbott (Stu Erwin, Shirley Boo[th] Sam Levene), Jan. 13 "The Silver Cord" by Sidn[ey] Howard (Ralph Bellamy, Ruth Hussey, Estelle Wi[n]wood), Jan. 20 "Yellow Jack" by Sidney Howard a[nd] Paul de Kruif (Walter Abel, Alan Baxter, Luther A[d]ler), Jan. 27 "The Front Page" by Ben Hecht a[nd]

Charles MacArthur (Melvyn Douglas, Michael O'Shea), Feb. 3 "The Second Man" by S. N. Behman (Alfred Lunt, Peggy Conklin, Jessie Royce Landis), Feb. 10 "Prologue to Glory" by E. P. Conkle (Zachary Scott, Ed Begley, Susan Douglas), Feb. 17 "On Borrowed Time" by Paul Osborn (Walter Huston), Feb. 24 "Dead End" by Sidney Kingsley (Richard Conte, Alan Baxter, Joan Tetzel), March 3 "The Show Off" by George Kelly (Alfred Lunt), March 10 "The Barker" by Kenyon Nicholson (Pat O'Brien), March 17 "The Mask of Kings" by Maxwell Anderson (Ray Milland, Sir Cedric Hardwicke), March 24 "I Remember Mama" by John van Druten (Mady Christians, Oscar Homolka), March 31 "Strange Interlude—Part One" by Eugene O'Neill (Lynn Fontanne, Walter Abel), April 7 "Strange Interlude—Part Two" by Eugene O'Neill (Lynn Fontanne, Walter Abel), April 14 "Seven Keys to Baldpate" by George M. Cohan (Walter Pidgeon, Martha Scott), April 21 "The Green Pastures" by Marc Connelly (Juano Hernandez, Richard Huey, Hall Johnson Choir), April 28 "Mary of Scotland" by Maxwell Anderson (Helen Hayes, Helen Menken), May 5 "Mary, Mary Quite Contrary" by St. John Ervine (Gertrude Lawrence), May 12 "Payment Deferred" by Jeffrey Dell (Charles Laughton, Elsa Lanchester), May 19 "They Knew What They Wanted" by Sidney Howard (John Garfield, June Havoc, Leo Carillo), May 26 "Boy Meets Girl" by Bella and Sam Spewak (Gene Kelly), June 2 "Call It a Day" by Dodie Smith (Alfred Lunt, Lynn Fontanne), Sept. 8 "Angel Street" by Patrick Hamilton (Helen Hayes, Victor Jory, Leo G. Carroll), Sept. 15 "You Can't Take It with You" by George S. Kaufman and Moss Hart (Josephine Hull, Kenny Delmar), Sept. 22 "Graig's Wife" by George Kelly (Fredric March, Florence Eldridge), Sept 29 "Our Town" by Thornton Wilder (Thorton Wilder, Dorothy McGuire), Oct. 6 "Dodsworth" by Sinclair Lewis (Walter Huston, Jessie Royce Landis), Oct. 13 "Berkeley Square" by John Balderson (Rex Harrison), Oct. 20 "The Green Goddess" by William Archer (Ronald Colman, Anita Louise, Walter Abel), Oct. 27 "Accent on Youth" by Samson Raphaelson (Basil Rathbone, Jane Wyatt), Nov. 3 "The Last of Mrs. Cheyney" by Frederick Lonsdale (Gertrude Lawrence), Nov. 10 "Kind Lady" by Edward Chodorov (Lillian Gish, John Loder), Nov. 17 "The Man Who Came to Dinner" by George S. Kaufman and Moss Hart (Fred Allen, Sam Levene), Nov. 24 "Burlesque" by George M. Waters and Arthur Hopkins (Bert Lahr, June Havoc), Dec. 1 "A Bill of Divorcement" by Clemence Dane (James Mason), Dec. 8 "Golden Boy" by Clifford Odets (Dana Andrews, June Havoc, Sam Levene), Dec. 15 "The Old Maid" by Zoe Akins (Judith Anderson, Helen Menken), Dec. 22 "Papa Is All" by Patterson Greene (Oscar Homolka, Aline MacMahon,

Peggy Conklin), Dec. 29 "Broadway" by Philip Dunning and George Abbott (James Dunn, Shirley Booth).

1947: Jan. 5 "The Great Adventure" by Arnold Bennett (Alfred Lunt, Lynn Fontanne), Jan. 12 "The Male Animal" by James Thurber and Elliott Nugent (Elliott Nugent, Peggy Conklin, Paul Douglas), Jan. 19 "A Doll's House" by Henrik Ibsen (Dorothy McGuire, Basil Rathbone), Jan. 26 "Men in White" by Sidney Kingsley (Burgess Meredith, Marsha Hunt), Feb. 2 "The Farmer Takes a Wife" by Frank Elser and Marc Connelly (William Holden, Claire Trevor, Kenny Delmar), Feb. 9 "Abe Lincoln In Illinois" by Robert E. Sherwood (Raymond Massey, Helen Menken, Alan Baxter), Feb. 16 "The Time of Your Life" by William Saroyan (Dane Clark, Mary Anderson, John Lund), Feb. 23 "Blithe Spirit" by Noel Coward (Clifton Webb, Peggy Wood), March 2 "What Every Woman Knows" by James M. Barrie (Helen Hayes), March 9 "No Time For Comedy" by S. N. Behman (Fredric March, Florence Eldridge), March 16 "Gold" by Eugene O'Neill (Raymond Massey, Angela Lansbury), March 23 "The First Year" by Frank Craven (Gene Tierney, Betty Garde, Parker Fennelly), March 30 "Ladies In Retirement" by Edward Perry and Reginald Denham (Fay Bainter, Estelle Winwood, Mildred Dunnock), April 6 "Still Life" by Noel Coward (Ingrid Bergman, Sam Wanamaker, Peggy Wood), April 13 "The Importance of Being Ernest" by Oscar Wilde (John Gielgud, Margaret Rutherford), April 20 "The Age of Innocence" by Margaret Ayet Barnes (Gene Tierney, Arthur Kennedy), April 27 "Escape" by John Galsworthy (George Sanders), May 4 "The Animal Kingdom" by Philip Barry (Fred Astaire, Wendy Barrie), May 11 "Macbeth" by William Shakespeare (Maurice Evans, Judith Anderson), May 18 "Uncle Harry" by Thomas Job (Paul Henreid, Geraldine Fitzgerald), May 25 "Ethan Frome" by Edith Wharton (Raymond Massey, Pauline Lord, Mary Anderson), June 1 "Three Men on a Horse" by John Cecil Holm and George Abbott (Sam Levene, Shirley Booth, David Wayne), June 8 "A Church Mouse" by Ladislaus Fodor (Basil Rathbone, Pamela Brown), June 15 "Clarence" by Booth Tarkington (Robert Walker), June 22 "Old Acquaintance" by John Van Druten (Ilka Chase, Dorothy Gish, Roger Pryor), June 29 "Alice Sit-by-the-Fire" by James M. Barrie (Helen Hayes), Sept. 7 "One Sunday Afternoon" by James Hagan (James Stewart), Sept. 14 "Kiss and Tell" by F. Hugh Herbert (Elizabeth Taylor, Dick Van Patten), Sept. 21 "Guest in the House" by Hagar Wilde and Dale Eunson (Mary Anderson, Walter Abel, Wendy Barrie), Sept. 28 "Saturday's Children" by Maxwell Anderson (John Garfield), Oct. 5 "The Admirable Crichton" by James M. Barrie (Basil Rathbone, June Duprez), Oct. 12 "Cyrano de Bergerac" by

Edmond Rostand (Fredric March, Florence Eldridge), Oct. 19 "Lady in the Dark" by Moss Hart (Gertrude Lawrence), Oct. 26 "Apple of his Eye" by Kenyon Nicholson and Charles Robinson (Walter Huston), Nov. 2 "The Petrified Forest" by Robert E. Sherwood (Robert Montgomery, Peggy Conklin), Nov. 9 "Victoria Regina" by Laurence Housman (Helen Hayes), Nov. 16 "The Shining Hour" by Keith Winter (Joan Fontaine), Nov. 23 "The Straw" by Eugene O'Neill (Robert Mitchum, Mary Anderson), Nov. 30 "Old English" by John Galsworthy (Charles Laughton), Dec. 7 "The Wisdom Tooth" by Marc Connelly (Gene Kelly), Dec. 14 "The Corn Is Green" by Emlyn Williams (Helen Hayes), Dec. 21 "Little Women" by Louisa May Alcott (Katharine Hepburn, Paul Lukas), Dec. 28 "Her Master's Voice" by Clare Kummer (Alfred Drake, Arlene Francis, Betty Garde).

1948: Jan. 4 "The Little Foxes" by Lillian Hellman (Agnes Moorehead, Thomas Mitchell, Zachary Scott), Jan. 11 "Holiday" by Philip Barry (Margaret Sullavan, Kent Smith), Jan. 18 "Three-Cornered Moon" by Gertrude Tonkonogy (Joan Caulfield, Eddie Albert), Jan. 25 "Is Zat So" by James Gleason and Richard Taber (Pat O'Brien, Arlene Francis), Feb. 1 "Missouri Legend" by E. B. Ginty (Raymond Massey, Alfred Drake, Mary Anderson), Feb. 8 "Romeo and Juliet" by William Shakespeare (Dorothy McGuire, Maurice Evans, Florence Reed) Feb. 15 "Dark Victory" by George Brewer, Jr. and Bertram Bloch (Madeleine Carroll, Walter Abel), Feb. 22 "The Far-Off Hills" by Lennox Robinson (Jessica Tandy, Hume Cronyn, Mildred Natwick), Feb. 29 "The Barretts of Wimpole Street" by Rudolf Besier (Madeleine Carroll, Brian Aherne), March 7 "Anna Christie" by Eugene O'Neill (Dorothy McGuire, Burgess Meredith, Oscar Homolka), March 14 "She Loves Me Not" by Howard Lindsay (Eddie Albert, Judy Holliday, Paul Douglas), March 21 "Grand Hotel" by Vicki Baum (Marlene Dietrich, Ray Milland), March 28 "Remember the Day" by Philo Higley and Philip Dunning (Deborah Kerr, John Conte), April 4 "The Philadelphia Story" by Philip Barry (James Stewart, John Conte, Joan Tetzel), April 11 "Libel" by Edward Wooll (Michael Redgrave, Walter Hampden, June Duprez), April 18 "Anna Karenina" by Leo Tolstoy (Ingrid Bergman), April 25 "Laburnam Grove" by J. B. Priestley (Charles Laughton), May 2 "Rebecca" by Daphne du Maurier (Michael Redgrave, Flora Robson, June Duprez), May 9 "The White-Headed Boy" by Lennox Robinson (Sara Allgood, Kenny Delmar), May 16 "Daisy Mayme" by George Kelly (Ethel Merman, Dean Jagger), May 23 "Wednesday's Child" by Leopold Atlas (Ona Munson, Walter Abel, Arlene Francis), May 30 "Reflected

Glory" by George Kelly (Irene Dunn, Audrey Ch[...]tie), Sept. 12 "A Bell for Adano" by Paul Osb[...] (Robert Montgomery), Sept. 19 "For Love or Mon[...] by F. Hugh Herbert (Joan Caulfield, John Lod[...] Sept. 26 "That's Gratitude" by Frank Craven (Ja[...] Stewart), Oct. 3 "The Letter" by W. Somer[...] Maugham (Marlene Dietrich, Walter Pidgeon), [...] 10 "Music in the Air" by Jerome Kern and Os[...] Hammerstein, II (Mary Martin, Peter Lawford), [...] 17 "Laura" by Laura Caspary and George Sklar (B[...] Lancaster, June Duprez, George Coulouris), Oct. [...] "The Wind and the Rain" by Merton Hodge (Cele[...] Holm, John Dall, Otto Kruger), Oct. 31 "Morning St[...] by Sylvia Regan (Fay Bainter, Kenny Delmar, K[...] Malden), Nov. 7 "The Criminal Code" by Mar[...] Flavin (Pat O'Brien, Joan Chandler), Nov. 14 "Vall[...] Forge" by Maxwell Anderson (Claude Rains, Ju[...] Duprez, George Coulouris), Nov. 21 "The Winsl[...] Boy" by Terence Rattigan (Frank Allenby, Alan Wel[...] Valerie White), Nov. 28 "The Two Mrs. Carrolls [...] Martin Vale (Lilli Palmer, Macdonald Carey, Ed[...] Albert), Dec. 5 "Lovers and Friends' by Dodie Sm[...] (Walter Pidgeon, Madeleine Carroll), Dec. 12 "Spri[...] Again" by Isabel Leighton and Bertram Bloch (Mor[...] Woolley, Elizabeth Patterson), Dec. 19 "Miss Lu[...] Bett" by Zona Gale (Jean Arthur), Dec. 26 "Rip V[...] Winkle" by Washington Irving (Fred Allen).

1949: Jan. 2 "The Game of Love and Death" [...] Romain Rolland (Katharine Hepburn, Paul Henre[...] Claude Rains), Jan. 9 "O Mistress Mine" by Teren[...] Rattigan (Alfred Lunt, Lynn Fontanne), Jan. 16 "T[...] Late George Apley" by John P. Marquand and Geor[...] S. Kaufman (Robert Morley, William Eythe, Ire[...] Rich), Jan. 23 "Journey's End" by R. C. Sherriff (R[...] Harrison), Jan. 30 "The Late Christopher Bean" [...] Sidney Howard (Irene Dunne, Thomas Mitchell), Fe[...] 6 "Beyond the Horizon" by Eugene O'Neill (Jo[...] Lund, Richard Widmark, Beatrice Pearson), Feb. [...] "Ah, Wilderness" by Eugene O'Neill (Walter Hustor[...] Feb. 20 "Mary of Scotland" by Maxwell Anders[...] (Deborah Kerr, Martita Hunt), Feb. 27 "Payment D[...] ferred" by C. S. Forester (Charles Laughton, Jessi[...] Tandy, Elsa Lanchester), March 6 "Interference" [...] Roland Pertwee and Harold Deardon (Raymond Ma[...] sey, Zachary Scott, June Duprez), March 13 "T[...] Gioconda Smile" by Aldous Huxley (Charles Boyer[...] March 20 "Yesterday's Magic" by Emlyn Willia[...] (Jean Arthur, Robert Morley), March 27 "June Moo[...] by Ring Lardner and George S. Kaufman (June Havo[...] Eddie Albert, Kenny Delmar), April 3 "Camille" b[...] Alexandre Dumas (Joan Fontaine, Louis Jourdan[...] April 10 "The Taming of the Shrew" by Willia[...] Shakespeare (Burgess Meredith, Joyce Redman), Apr[...]

17 "Summer and Smoke" by Tennessee Williams (Dorothy McGuire, Todd Andrews), April 24 "Alien Corn" by Sidney Howard (Bette Davis, Kirk Douglas), May 1 "The Skin Game" by John Galsworthy (Charles Laughton, Sir Cedric Hardwicke, Martita Hunt), May 8 "Of Mice and Men" by John Steinbeck (Burgess Meredith, June Havoc, George Matthews), May 15 "Ladies and Gentlemen" by Charles MacArthur (Van Heflin, Ida Lupino), May 22 "Flare Path" by Terence Rattigan (Deborah Kerr, Peter Lawford, Ian Hunter), May 29 "The Perfect Alibi" by A. A. Milne (Boris Karloff, Joan Lorring), June 5 "John Loves Mary" by Norman Krasna (Robert Cummings, Ann Blyth), Sept. 11 "Dream Girl" by Elmer Rice (John Lund, Betty Field), Sept. 18 "Libel" by Edward Wooll (Rex Harrison, June Duprez), Sept. 25 "The Gentle People" by Irwin Shaw (Dan Duryea, Sam Levene, Kenny Delmar), Oct. 2 "Counsellor-At-Law" by Elmer Rice (James Cagney), Oct. 9 "Burlesque" by George M. Watters and Arthur Hopkins (Bert Lahr, Ann Sothern), Oct. 16 "Coquette" by George Abbott and Ann Preston (Dorothy McGuire, Cornel Wilde), Oct. 23 "The Thunderbolt" by Arthur Wing Pinero (Van Heflin, Celeste Holm), Oct. 30 "Justice" by John Galsworthy (Robert Donat, Jessica Tandy, Hunme Cronyn), Nov. 6 "The Traitor" by Herman Wouk (Tyrone Power, William Eythe, Nina Foch), Nov. 13 "Still Life" by Noel Coward (Helen Hayes, David Niven), Nov. 20 "The Great Adventure" by Arnold Bennett (Alfred Lunt, Lynn Fontanne), Nov. 27 "The Enchanted Cottage" by Arthur Wing Pinero (Ray Milland), Dec. 4 "The Amazing Dr. Clitterhouse" by Barre Lyndon (Madeleine Carroll, Basil Rathbone), Dec. 11 "Street Scene" by Elmer Rice (Richard Conte, Diana Lynn, Shirley Booth), Dec. 18 "The Browning Version" by Terence Rattigan (Maurice Evans, Edna Best), Dec. 25 "The Passing of the Third Floor Back" by Jerome L. Jerome (Paulette Goddard, Sir Cedric Hardwicke).

1950: Jan. 1 "While the Sun Shines" by Terence Rattigan (Peter Lawford), Jan. 8 "The Scarlet Pimpernel" by Baroness Orczy and Montague Barstow (Rex Harrison, Lilli Palmer, Francis L. Sullivan), Jan. 15 "Another Language" by Rose Franklin (Helen Hayes, Richard Basehart, Walter Abel), Jan. 22 "The Willow and I" by John Patrick (Jane Wyman, Beatrice Pearson, Mel Ferrer), Jan. 29 "Dulcy" by George S. Kaufman and Marc Connelly (Celeste Holm, Franchot Tone, Lee Bowman), Feb. 5 "Autumn Crocus" by C. L. Anthony (Dorothy McGuire, Charles Boyer), Feb. 12 "Goodbye Again" by Allan Scott and George Haight (Ezio Pinza, Madeleine Carroll, Linda Darnell), Feb. 19 "The Druid Circle" by John van Druten (Charles Laughton, Burgess Meredith), Feb. 26 "Heaven Can Wait" by Harry Segall (Kirk Douglas, Walter Huston), March 5 "Lady in the Dark" by Moss Hart (Gertrude Lawrence, Macdonald Carey, Hume Cronyn), March 12 "Our Town" by Thorton Wilder (Elizabeth Taylor, Walter Huston), March 19 "There's Always Juliet" by John van Druten (Teresa Wright, Richard Widmark), March 26 "The Milky Way" by Lunn Root and Harry Clark (Danny Kaye, Shirley Booth), April 2 "All That Money Can Buy" by Stephen Vincent Benet (Cornel Wilde, Walter Huston, Martha Scott), April 9 "Seventh Heaven" by Austin Strong (Joan Fontaine, Robert Cummings), April 16 "Great Expectations" by Charles Dickens (Joan Fontaine, Richard Todd, Francis L. Sullivan), April 23 "National Velvet" by Enid Bagnold (Peggy Ann Garner, Mickey Rooney), April 30 "Double Door" by Elizabeth McFadden (Douglas Fairbanks, Jr., Geraldine Fitzgerald), May 7 "Petticoat Fever" by Mark Reed (Gertrude Lawrence, Walter Pidgeon, Arthur Treacher), May 14 "The Trial of Mary Dugan" by Bayard Veiler (Paulette Goddard, Pat O'Brien, Tom Drake), May 21 "Page Miss Glory" by Philip Dunning and Joseph Shrank (Betty Hutton, Ronald Reagan, Jack Carson), May 28 "Minick" by George S. Kaufman and Edna Ferber (Lee Bowman, Sterling Holloway, Arlene Francis), June 4 "Call It a Day" by Dodie Smith (Gertrude Lawrence, Franchot Tone), Sept. 10 "Edward, My Son" by Robert Morley and Noel Langley (Rosalind Russell, Charles Laughton), Sept. 17 "The Barker" by Kenyon Nicholson (Ginger Rogers, Paul Douglas), Sept. 24 "There Shall Be No Night" by Robert E. Sherwood (Alfred Lunt, Lynn Fontanne), Oct. 1 "Brigadoon" by Alan Jay Lerner and Frederick Lowe (Dennis Morgan, Patrice Munsel), Oct. 8 "Blow Ye Winds" by Valentine Davis (William Holden, Celeste Holm) Oct. 15 "I Know Where I'm Going" by Michael Powell and Emeric Pressberger (David Niven, Geraldine Fitzgerald), Oct. 22 "A Farewell to Arms" by Ernest Hemingway (Joan Fontaine, Humphrey Bogart), Oct. 29 "Michael and Mary" by A. A. Milne (Joan Fontaine, Herbert Marshall), Nov. 5 "Alice Adams" by Booth Tarkington (Judy Garland, Thomas Mitchell), Nov. 12 "The Boysey Inheritance" by Harley Granville-Barker (Douglas Fairbanks, Jr., Angela Lansbury), Nov. 19 "Dr. Jekyll and Mr. Hyde" by Robert Louis Stevenson (Fredric March, Barbara Bel Geddes), Nov. 26 "Theatre" by Guy Bolton and Somerset Maugham (Gloria Swanson, Melvyn Douglas), Dec. 3 "Carousel" by Richard Rodgers and Oscar Hammerstein II (Cornel Wilde, Patrice Munsel), Dec. 10 "Lottie Dundass" by Enid Bagnold (Dorothy McGuire, Jessica Tandy), Dec. 17 "Boomerang" by Richard Murphy (Kirk Douglas), Dec. 24 "David Copperfield" by Charles Dickens (Boris Karloff, Flora Robson, Cyril Ritchard), Dec. 31

"State Fair" by Phil Strong (Van Heflin, Gene Lockhart).

1951: Jan. 7 "The Third Man" by Graham Greene (Joseph Cotten, Signe Hasso), Jan. 14 "Trilby" by George du Maurier (Teresa Wright, Rex Harrison), Jan. 21 "The Fortune Hunter" by Winchell Smith (John Lund, Jeanne Crain), Jan. 28 "The Morning Glory" by Zoe Akins (Anne Baxter, John Hodiak), Feb. 4 "Come Back, Little Sheba" by William Inge (Gary Cooper, Shirley Booth), Feb. 11 "Within the Law" by Bayard Veiller (Ginger Rogers, Lee Tracy), Feb. 18 "Promise" by Henry Bernstein (Gloria Swanson, Hume Cronyn, Margaret Phillips), Feb. 25 "Father of the Bride" by Edward Streeter (Spencer Tracy, Joan Bennett, Elizabeth Taylor), March 4 "Hamlet" by William Shakespeare (John Gielgud, Dorothy McGuire, Pamela Brown), March 11 "The Hasty Heart" by John Patrick (John Lund, Jane Wyatt, Richard Greene), March 18 "Jeannie" by Aimee Stuart (Barry Sullivan, Margaret Phillips, Signe Hasso), March 25 "A Tale of Two Cities" by Charles Dickens (Douglas Fairbanks, Jr.), April 1 "The Fallen Idol" by Graham Greene (Walter Pidgeon, Signe Hasso, Jack Hawkins), April 8 "This Side of Paradise" by F. Scott Fitzgerald (Richard Widmark, Nina Foch), April 15 "Light Up the Sky" by Moss Hart (Joan Bennett, Sam Levene, Thelma Ritter), April 22 "The First Year" by Frank Craven (Richard Widmark, Kathryn Grayson), April 29 "Man in Possession" by H. M. Harwood (Rex Harrison, Lilli Palmer), May 6 "Candida" by George Bernard Shaw (Katherine Cornell, Alfred Ryder), May 13 "Craig's Wife" by George Kelly (Rosalind Russell, Melvyn Douglas), May 20 "Ethan Frome" by Edith Wharton (Shirley Booth, Raymond Massey, Margaret Phillips), May 27 "Elmer the Great" by Ring Lardner (Paul Douglas), June 3 "Biography" by S. N. Behman (Rosalind Russell, Burgess Meredith), Sept. 9 "The Heiress" by Henry James (Betty Field, Cornel Wilde, Basil Rathbone), Sept. 16 "The Glass Menagerie" by Tennessee Williams (Helen Hayes, Montgomery Clift), Sept. 23 "This Woman Business" by Benn W. Levy (David Niven, Margaret Phillips, Nigel Bruce), Sept. 30 "Main Street" by Sinclair Lewis (Joseph Cotten, Joan Fontaine), Oct. 7 "Casanova Brown" by Nunnally Johnson (Dan Dailey, Diana Lynn, Kenny Delmar), Oct. 14 "The Major and the Minor" by Edward Carpenter (Ray Milland, Joan Fontaine), Oct. 21 "Pygmalion" by George Bernard Shaw (Alfred Lunt, Lynn Fontanne), Oct. 28 "Skylark" by Samson Raphaelson (Rosalind Russell, Macdonald Carey), Nov. 4 "A Foreign Affair" by George Fox and George Tilton (Marlene Dietrich, Richard Widmark), Nov. 11 "Age of Innocence" by Margaret Ayer Barnes (Claudette Colbert, Macdonald Carey), Nov. 18 "Twentieth Century" by Ben Hecht and Charles MacArthur (Claudette Colbert, Gregory Ratoff), Nov. 25 "Allegro" by Richard Rodgers and Oscar Hammerstein II (Jane Powell, John Lund, Kenny Delmar), Dec. 2 "Good Housekeeping" by William McCleery (Rosalind Russell, Walter Abel), Dec. 9 "The Lost Weekend" by Charles Jackson (William Holden, Brenda Marshall), Dec. 16 "Arrowsmith" by Sinclair Lewis (Tyrone Power, Loretta Young), Dec. 23 "The Beloved Vagabond" by William J. Locke (Rex Harrison, Beatrice Pearson), Dec. 30 "Goodbye, Mr Chips" by James Hilton (Alan Webb, Margaret Phillips).

1952: Jan. 6 "I Know My Love" by S. N. Behman (Alfred Lunt, Lynn Fontanne), Jan. 13 "Look to the Mountain" by LeGrand Cannon, Jr. (Dorothy McGuire, John Ireland), Jan. 20 Daisy Mayme" by George Kelly (Betty Hutton), Jan. 27 "The Thief" by Henry Bernstein (Dorothy McGuire, David Niven, Roddy McDowell), Feb. 3 "The Old Lady Shows Her Medals" by Alfred Lunt (Lynn Fontanne), Feb. 10 "The Traitor" by Herman Wouk (Humphrey Bogart, Lauren Bacall), Feb. 17 "The Meanest Man in the World" by Augustin MacHugh (James Stewart, Josephine Hull, Coleen Gray), Feb. 24 "Oliver Twist" by Charles Dickens (Basil Rathbone, Boris Karloff, Leueen McGrath), March 2 "Portrait in Black" by Ivan Goff and Ben Roberts (Barbara Stanwyck, Richard Widmark), March 9 "The Search" by Richard Schweizer and David Wechsler (Montgomery Clift, Fay Bainter), March 16 "Love from a Stranger" by Agatha Christie (Ray Milland, Edna Best), March 23 "Second Threshold" by Philip Barry (Fredric March, Dorothy McGuire), March 30 "An Ideal Husband" by Oscar Wilde (Rex Harrison, Lilli Palmer), April 6 "The Silver Whistle" by Robert E. McEnroe (James Stewart, Diana Lynn), April 13 "Florence Nightingale" by Cecil Woodham-Smith (Katherine Cornell, Brian Aherne), April 20 "The Truth About Blayds" by A. A. Milne (Madeleine Carroll), April 27 "The Sea Wolf" by Jack London (Burgess Meredith, Boris Karloff, Margaret Phillips), May 4 "Dear Brutus" by James M. Barrie (David Niven, Angela Lansbury, Madeleine Carroll), May 11 "Prologue To Glory" by E. P. Conkle (John Lund, Wanda Hendrix), May 18 "Over 21" by Ruth Gordon (Van Heflin, Ruth Gordon), May 25 "The Bishop Misbehaves" by Frederick Jackson (Charles Laughton, Josephine Hull, Vanessa Brown), June "Remember the Day" by Philo Higley and Philip Dunning (Helen Hayes, Macdonald Carey), Sept. "The Wisteria Trees" by Joshua Logan (Helen Hayes, Joseph Cotten), Sept. 21 "George Washington Slept Here" by George S. Kaufman and Moss Mart (Van Heflin, Ann Rutherford, Kenny Delmar), Sept. 28 "Elmer the Great" by Ring Lardner (Eddie Bracken

Wanda Hendrix), Oct. 5 "Morning Star" by Sylvia Regan (Gertrude Berg, Sylvia Sidney), Oct. 12 "Tommy" by Howard Lindsay and Bertrand Robinson (Wanda Hendrix, Wally Cox, Kenny Delmar), Oct. 19 "The Sea Gull" by Anton Chekhov (John Lund, Viveca Lindfors), Oct. 26 "Hobson's Choice" by Harold Brighouse (Madeleine Carroll, Burgess Meredith, Melville Cooper), Nov. 2 "Lo and Behold" by John Patrick (Ann Blyth, Basil Rathbone, Jeffrey Lynn), Nov. 9 "Magnificent Obsession" by Lloyd Douglas (Rosalind Russell, Mel Ferrer), Nov. 16 "All About Eve" by Mary Orr (Tallulah Bankhead), Nov. 23 "The Winslow Boy" by Terence Rattigan (Basil Rathbone, Alan Webb, Margaret Phillips), Nov 30 "Liliom" by Ferenc Molnar (Richard Widmark, Karl Malden, Geraldine Page), Dec. 7 "The Damask Cheek" by John van Druten (Rosalind Russell, Kevin McCarthy), Dec. 14 "The House of Mirth" by Edith Wharton (Joan Fontaine, Franchot Tone), Dec. 21 "The Pickwick Papers" by Charles Dickens (Alan Webb, Cyril Ritchard, Melville Cooper), Dec. 28 "The Unguarded Hour" by Bernard Merivale (Michael Redgrave, Nina Foch).

1953: Jan. 4 "State Fair" by Phil Strong (Van Johnson, Nancy Olson), Jan. 11 "Jane" by S. N. Behman (Michael Redgrave, Edna Best), Jan. 18 "Trial by Forgery" by Bernard C. Schoenfeld (Joseph Cotten, Anne Baxter), Jan. 25 "The Scarlet Letter" by Nathaniel Hawthorne (Dorothy McGuire, Sir Cedric Hardwicke), Feb. 1 "Reflected Glory" by George Kelly (Bette Davis, Macdonald Carey), Feb. 8 "Man and Superman" by George Bernard Shaw (Maurice Evans, Deborah Kerr), Feb. 15 "Cass Timberlane" by Sinclair Lewis (Fredric March, Nina Foch), Feb. 22 "The Show-Off" by George Kelly (Paul Douglas, Jan Sterling), March 1 "O'Halloran's Luck" by Stephen Vincent Benet (James Stewart, John Lund, Gloria De Haven), March 8 "Vanity Fair" by William Makepeace Thackery (Joan Fontaine), March 15 "A Square Peg" by Lewis Beach (Thomas Mitchell, Thelma Ritter, Jane Wyatt), March 22 "The Old Maid" by Zoe Akins (Betty Field, Nina Foch), March 29 "The Brass Ring" by Irving Elman (Melvyn Douglas, Gloria De Haven), April 5 "Great Expectations" by Charles Dickens (Boris Karloff, Melville Cooper, Margaret Phillips), April 12 "The Glass Menagerie" by Tennessee Williams (Shirley Booth), April 19 "The Petrified Forest" by Robert E. Sherwood (Tyrone Power), April 26 "1984" by George Orwell (Richard Widmark), May 3 "Quiet Wedding" by Esther McCracken (Diana Lynn, John Dall, Jessie Royce Landis) May 10 "Black Chiffon" by Lesley Storm (Judith Anderson, Burgess Meredith), May 17 "The Importance of Being Ernest" by Oscar Wilde (Rex Harrison, Lilli Palmer), May 24 "Kate Fennigate" by Booth Tarkington (Wendell Corey Martha Scott), May 31 "The Grand Tour" by Elmer Rice (Jean Arthur), June 7 "Julius Caesar" by William Shakespeare (Maurice Evans, Basil Rathbone)—last show of the series.

Selected Bibliography

llen, Fred. *Much Ado About Me.* Boston: Little, Brown and Company, 1956.

llen, Fred. *Treadmill to Oblivion.* Boston: Little, Brown and Company, 1954.

nderson, Arthur. *Let's Pretend: A History of Radio's Best-Loved Children's Show.* North Carolina: McFarland and Company, 1994.

ndrews, Bart, and Julliard, Ahrgus. *Holy Mackeral, The Amos and Andy Story.* New York: E. P. Dalton, 1986.

rcher, Gleason L. *History of Radio.* New York: American Historical Society, 1938.

arabas, Gabriel, and Barabas, SuzAnne. *Gunsmoke: A Complete History.* North Carolina. McFarland and Company, 1990.

arnouw, Erik. *A Tower in Babel.* New York: Oxford University Press, 1966.

oemer, Marilyn Lawrence. *The Children's Hour: Radio Programs for Children.* New Jersey: The Scarecrow Press, 1989.

uxton, Frank, and Owen, Bill. *The Big Broadcast; 1920–1950.* New York: Viking Press, 1972.

ampbell, Robert. *The Golden Years of Broadcasting.* New York: Scribners. 1976.

arroll, Carroll. *None of Your Business.* New York: Cowles Book Company, 1970.

hernow, Barbara A., and Vallasi, George A., eds. *Columbia Encyclopedia Fifth Edition.* New York: Columbia University Press, 1993.

rosby, John. *Out of the Blue.* New York: Simon and Schuster, 1952.

uthbert, Margaret, ed. *Adventures in Radio.* New York: Howell, Siskin, 1945.

onaldson, Charles E. *Radio Stars: Brief Biographical Sketches of More Than One Hundred Best Known Actors, Musicians, Commentators and Other Stars of Radio Programs.* Washington, D.C.: Newspaper Information Service, Inc., 1942.

unning, Charles. *Tune in Yesterday.* Englewood Cliff, N.J.: Prentice-Hall Inc., 1976.

aver, Jack, and Stanley, Dave. *There's Laughter in the Air.* New York, 1945.

owdy, Curt. *Cowboy at the Mike.* New York: Doubleday and Company, 1966.

ross, Ben. *I Looked and I Listened.* New York: Arlington House, 1954.

alliwell, Leslie. *The Filmgoers Companion.* New York: Hill and Wang, 1967.

armon, Jim. *The Great Radio Comedians.* New York: Doubleday and Company, 1970.

armon, Jim. *The Great Radio Heroes.* New York: Doubleday and Company, 1967.

ickerson, Jay. *The Ultimate History of Network Programming and Guide to All Circulating Shows.* Hamden, Ct.: Presto Print 11, 1992.

ickerson, Jay. *What You Always Wanted to Know About Circulating Old Time Radio Shows (But Could Never Find Out).* Hamden, Ct.: Hello Again, 1990.

Higby, Mary Jane. *Tune in Tomorrow.* New York: Ace Publishing, 1968.

Illustrated Press, The (Newsletter). New York: Old Time Radio Club of Buffalo, New York, 1975–Present.

Kittnos, John M., and Sterling, Christopher H. *Stay Tuned: A Concise History of American Broadcasting.* Belmont, Ca.: 1975.

Lamparski, Richard. *Whatever Became Of . . .* series. Crown, New York: 1967–1989.

Langguth, A. J., ed. *Norman Corwin's Letters.* California: Barricade, 1994.

Lenburg, Jeff. *The Encyclopedia of Animated Cartoons.* New York: Facts on File, Inc., 1991.

Lloyd, Anne and Fuller, Graham, eds. *Illustrated Who's Who of the Cinema, The.* New York: Portland House, 1983.

Maltin, Leonard, ed. *TV Movies.* New York: New American Library, 1983–1984.

McBride, Mary Margaret. *Out of the Air.* New York: Doubleday and Company, 1960.

McCambridge, Mercedes. *The Quality of Mercy.* New York: New York Times Books, 1981.

Michael, Paul. *The American Movies Reference Book: The Sound Era.* New Jersey: Prentice-Hall, Inc., 1970.

Morse, Carlton E. *The One Man's Family Album.* Woodside, Ca.: Seven Stones Press, 1988.

Osgood, Dick. *W.Y.X.I.E Wonderland.* Ohio: Bowling Green University Press, 1981.

Schemering, Christopher. *The Soap Opera Encyclopedia (TV)* New York: Ballantine Books, 1987.

Schwartz, Jon D., and Reinehr, Robert C. *Handbook of Old-Time Radio: A Comprehensive Guide to Golden Age Radio Listening and Collecting.* New York: Scarecrow, 1993.

Sennett, Ted, ed. *Old Time Radio Book.* New York: Pyramid Publications, 1986.

Settel, Irving. *A Pictorial History of Radio.* New York: Grosset and Dunlap, 1967.

Shulman, Arthur, and Yourman, Roger. *The Golden Age of Television (How Sweet It Was).* New York: Bonanza Books, 1979.

Skretvedt, Randy, and Young, Jordan R. *The Nostalgia Entertainment Sourcebook; The Complete Guide of Classic Movies, Vintage Music, Old Time Radio and Theatre.* Beverly Hills Ca.: Moonstone Press, 1991.

Slate, Sam J., and Cook, Joe. *It Sounds Impossible.* New York: Macmillan Company, 1953.

Slide, Anthony. *Great Radio Personalities, In Historic Photographs.* Vestal, New York: The Vestal Press, Ltd., 1988.

Smith, Ronald L. *Who's Who in Comedy; Comedians, Comics and Clowns from Vaudeville to Today's Stand-Ups.* New York: Facts on File, Inc., 1992.

Stedman, Raymond William. *The Serials.* Norman, Okla.: The University of Oklahoma Press, 1971.

Stumpf, Charles, and Price, Tom. *Heavenly Days, The Story*

of Fibber McGee and Molly. Waynesville, N.C.: The World of Yesterday, 1987.

Summers, Harrison B. *A Thirty Year History of Programs Carried on National Radio in the United States.* Columbus, Oh: Ohio University Press, 1958.

Woodfin, June. *Of Mikes and Men.* New York: Doubleday and Company, 1961.

Wylie, Max. *Radio Writing.* New York: Rinehart and Company, 1939.

INDEX

This subject index is designed to be used in conjunction with the A-to-Z entries. The main A-to-Z entries are indicated by **boldface** page references. *Italicized* page references indicate illustrations.